TWELFTH EDITION

THE STRUCTURE OF AMERICAN INDUSTRY

James W. Brock

Moeckel Professor of Economics
Miami University (Ohio)

PEARSON

Prentice
Hall

Upper Saddle River, New Jersey 07458

Library of Congress Cataloging-in-Publication Data

The structure of American industry/[edited by] James Brock.—12th ed.
   p. cm.
 Includes bibliographical references and index.
 ISBN 0-13-230230-6
 1. Industries—United States. I. Brock, James W.
 HC106.S85 2008
 338.60973—dc22

                                        2008000234

AVP/Executive Editor: Chris Rogers
Editor-in-Chief: Eric Svendsen
Product Development Manager: Ashley Santora
Editorial Project Manager: Mary Kate Murray
Editorial Assistant: Vanessa Bain
Senior Marketing Manager: Jodi Bassett
Associate Director, Production Editorial: Judy Leale
Production Project Manager: Kerri Tomasso
Permissions Coordinator: Charles Morris
Senior Operations Supervisor: Arnold Vila
Operations Specialist: Michelle Klein
Cover Design: Bruce Kenselaar
Cover Illustration/Photo: Boris Lyubner/Illustration Works/Getty Images, Inc.
Composition/Full-Service Project Management: Ann Courtney, GGS Book Services
Printer/Binder: STP/RRD/Harrisonburg
Typeface: 10/12 Times Ten

Credits and acknowledgments borrowed from other sources and reproduced, with permission, in this textbook appear on appropriate page within text.

Pearson Education LTD. London
Pearson Education Singapore, Pte. Ltd
Pearson Education, Canada, Ltd
Pearson Education–Japan

Pearson Education Australia PTY, Limited
Pearson Education North Asia Ltd
Pearson Educación de Mexico, S.A. de C.V.
Pearson Education Malaysia, Pte. Ltd.

This book is not for sale or distribution in the U.S.A. or Canada.

10 9 8 7 6 5 4 3 2 1
ISBN-13: 978-0-13-230230-2
ISBN-10:   0-13-230230-6

For prodesse quam conspici
and those who sustain it

Contents

Preface   **00**

About the Authors   **00**

CHAPTER 1   **The Agriculture Industry**   **1**
Bruce W. Marion and James M. MacDonald

CHAPTER 2   **The Petroleum Industry**   **30**
Stephen Martin

CHAPTER 3   **The Electricity Industry**   **58**
Alan R. Schriber and James W. Brock

CHAPTER 4   **The Cigarette Industry**   **99**
George A. Hay

CHAPTER 5   **The Beer Industry**   **128**
Kenneth G. Elzinga

CHAPTER 6   **The Automobile Industry**   **155**
James W. Brock

CHAPTER 7   **The Music Recording Industry**   **183**
Peter J. Alexander

CHAPTER 8   **The Telecommunications Industry**   **205**
James McConnaughey

CHAPTER 9   **The Airline Industry**   **235**
William G. Shepherd and James W. Brock

CHAPTER 10   **The Banking Industry**   **265**
Steven J. Pilloff

CHAPTER 11   **The Health Care Industry**   **294**
John Goddeeris

CHAPTER 12   **The Public Accounting Industry**   **330**
Philip G. Cottell, Jr.

CHAPTER 13   **The College Sports Industry**   **360**
John L. Fizel and Randall W. Bennett

CHAPTER 14   **Public Policy in A Free Enterprise Economy**   **389**
James W. Brock

Name Index   **00**

Subject Index   **00**

Preface

Each day our lives intersect the major industries that comprise the American economy—from the agriculture that provides our food and the petroleum refineries that produce our gasoline, to the banks through which we conduct our finances, the telecommunications and electricity we depend on, the beer that we (of legal age) imbibe, the acrid second-hand cigarette smoke we sometimes inhale, and the college sports that thrill us.

Individual industries also raise vexing public policy challenges that are front-burner issues: accounting and financial fraud that bilk billions from investors; the surging cost of health care; geopolitical events in the Middle East and elsewhere that trigger spikes at home in gasoline prices; the fares we pay (and disrobement we endure) to travel by air; concerns about fuel consumption, national security, and global warming in an automotive age; the consequences of genetically modified crops and the fate of the family farm; brownouts and blackouts in the provision of electricity; and scandals in college sports.

These issues, in turn, raise a host of economic questions. How are these individual industries organized and structured? What is their history? Who are the major producers and providers, and what share of their market do they represent? What is the nature of competition in these fields and how effectively does it govern economic decision making? How do these industries perform in terms of efficiency, innovation, and the allocation of resources? What are the major public policy issues they raise, and what are the economic consequences of the various options available for addressing them?

These questions spark lively interest but, unfortunately, economic treatments of them are typically focused on theoretical expositions, so that an understanding of the industries themselves is haphazard and disjointed, with a glimpse of an aspect of one field here and a side glance at an aspect of another there, but with no coherent comprehension of an individual industry in its entirety.

Twelve editions of this book have been published in an effort to redress this imbalance by treating each selected industry in a comprehensive way as an organic whole. Each edition has put the individual industry front and center in painting a panoramic portrait. Methodologically, the collection is as much an exercise in induction—reasoning from the specific to the general—as it is a deductive process of deriving conclusions from abstract assumptions. The approach, as Walton Hamilton put it in his classic *Price and Price Policies*, "is that of every day, of experience, of finding out"—of proceeding "by way of sample and type, of incident and detail"—stemming from the premise that "as a temptation to human curiosity industry can have few rivals."

This latest edition once more offers a kaleidoscopic collection of individual industry studies that, it is hoped, readers will find attractive for analyzing and understanding major industries and issues in the American economy. Each chapter, written by an expert in the field, continues to offer a live laboratory for clinical examination and comparative analysis, as well as for evaluating public policies and options. As such, the collection continues to serve as a supplement, if not a necessary antidote, to the economist's penchant for the abstractions of theoretical model-building.

The editor is appreciative for the contributors' conscientious cooperation in engagingly addressing their fields; for the editing and production efforts of Ann Courtney at GGS Book Services, Ann McKelvie, Kerri Tomasso, project editor at Prentice Hall; for the generosity of his chair, George Davis. in providing release time to prepare the book; and for the opportunity to sustain Professor Walter Adams's book into its second half-century, hopefully infused with some of his infectious spirit of intellectual adventure and industrial inquiry that generated earlier editions of the book.

James W. Brock
Oxford, Ohio

About the Authors

Peter J. Alexander is a senior economist at the Federal Communications Commission whose research explores the economics of media, bargaining theory, and technological change. He has served on the faculty at Ohio Wesleyan University, and has published on a variety of topics in industrial economics.

Randall W. Bennett is Professor of Economics at Gonzaga University, Spokane, Washington, where he has published numerous articles on the economics of sports and served as a consultant on antitrust issues.

James W. Brock is Moeckel Professor of Economics at Miami University, Oxford, Ohio, where he teaches courses in industrial organization, public policy and American industry, and publishes books and articles in these areas.

Philip G. Cottell, Jr. is Professor of Accountancy at Miami University, Oxford, Ohio, where he publishes and teaches in the areas of financial accounting, pensions and retirement, and accounting pedagogy, as well as indulging his passion for the carp. He has received numerous awards in recognition of his outstanding classroom teaching.

Kenneth G. Elzinga is Robert C. Taylor Professor of Economics at the University of Virginia. He has served as Special Economic Advisor to the Justice Department's Antitrust Division, published extensively on economic issues of antitrust policy, and been an expert witness in a number of antitrust cases, including three that have reached the Supreme Court.

John L. Fizel is Professor of Economics and Director of the Online MBA (iMBA) program at Pennslyvania State University. He has published numerous articles and books on the economics of professional and collegiate sports, and has served as a consultant on antitrust and sports-related issues.

John Goddeeris is Professor of Economics and Associate Dean in the College of Social Science at Michigan State University. He has published widely on the economics of health care, has served as an expert consultant for the state of Michigan on issues of public finance and access to health care, and has been a visiting scholar at the Congressional Budget Office.

George A. Hay is Edward Cornell Professor of Law and Professor of Economics at Cornell University and a special consultant to Charles River Associates. He was formerly Director of Economic Policy for the Justice Department's Antitrust Division, writes regularly on antitrust law and policy, and has been an expert witness in numerous antitrust cases.

James M. MacDonald is Chief of the Agricultural Structure and Productivity Branch of the Economic Research Service of the U.S. Department of Agriculture, where he received the USDA Secretary's Honor Award. He has published widely on the economics of agriculture and the food system.

Bruce W. Marion is Professor Emeritus of Agricultural and Applied Economics, University of Wisconsin-Madison. He has published numerous books and articles on the organization and competitive performance of industries in the U.S. food system, testified before various congressional committees, and received several awards from the American Association of Agricultural Economics. He also puts economic theory into practice on his farm in southwestern Wisconsin.

Stephen Martin is Professor of Economics at the Krannert School of Management of Purdue University, where he also is Chair of the Economics Policy Committee. He has been on the faculties of the University of Amsterdam, the University of Copenhagen, and the European University Institute, as well as having served as co–Managing Editor of the International Journal of Industrial Organization.

James McConnaughey is Senior Economist at the National Telecommunications and Information Administration, in the Office of Policy Analysis and Development, where he analyzes issues in telecommuncations competition, regulatory reform, and universal service and Internet access.

Steven J. Pilloff is Assistant Professor of Economics at Hood College in Frederick, Maryland. He formerly served as Economist in the Division of Research and Statistics of the Board of Governors of the Federal Reserve System, and has published numerous articles on the economics of bank mergers and other aspects of banking.

Alan R. Schriber is serving his second term as Chairman of the Public Utilities Commission of Ohio, where he oversees state regulation of electic power, natural gas, telecommuncations, and transportation. He also serves on the National Association of Regulatory Utility Commissioners (NARUC) Electricity Committee and the National Governors Association Electricity Task Force, and was a member of the United States–Canada Power Outage Task Force appointed to investigate the August 2003 electrical blackout.

William G. Shepherd is Professor Emeritus of Economics at the University of Massachusetts. He was Special Economic Assistant to the chief of the Antitrust Division at the Department of Justice and edited the Review of Industrial Organization for many years. He has served as an economic expert in numerous antitrust and regulatory cases and has published widely in the industrial organization field.

TWELFTH EDITION

THE STRUCTURE OF
AMERICAN INDUSTRY

The Agriculture Industry

BRUCE W. MARION AND JAMES M. MACDONALD[*]

As the supplier of most of the food we eat, agriculture is clearly a vital part of the U.S. economy. However, its importance extends well beyond this simple fact. In nations where farm productivity is low, most of the population is needed to grow food; few can be spared for education, production of investment goods, or other activities required for economic growth. Indeed, one of the factors that correlates most closely with rising per capita income is the declining fraction of the labor force that is engaged in agriculture. In the poorest nations of the world, 50 to 80 percent of the population lives on farms, compared with less than 5 percent in Western Europe, and 2 percent in the U.S.

In short, economic development in general depends on the performance of farmers, and this performance, in turn, depends on how agriculture is organized, its market structure, and the research and education institutions that develop and promote technological change. In the United States, land grant universities and the Federal government have played a role that is unique internationally; they have been a primary source of research and education that has encouraged productivity improvements in U.S. agriculture.

As business enterprises, the ownership and management of farms distinguish them from firms in the other industries described in this book. Most farms are owned and operated by a family, and many farm businesses that are not family owned are instead owned and operated by a few owner-operators who know each other well. Only a small number are owned or operated by large publicly held corporations. That is, farm businesses tend to be small, with decisions made by one or a few people. Farms typically operate as price-takers, with little control over the prices they receive for their products or the prices they pay for inputs. While farm businesses may operate in competitive markets, they also frequently face buyers who can exercise some monopsony power, or input providers who can exercise some monopoly power over prices. Because those prices can fluctuate sharply, and because farm production can be powerfully affected by weather and disease, these businesses can face substantial financial risks.

Farms are usually family-owned small businesses, but that doesn't mean farming is economically stagnant—productivity growth in U.S. agriculture has exceeded that in

---

[*]Dr. MacDonald's views in this chapter are his own, and not those of the U.S. Department of Agriculture.

the rest of the economy for many years. But it does mean that many business decisions on farms are inextricably linked to family decisions. Family members may mix work on the farm with off-farm employment, and families may choose to reinvest farm profits in the farm business or in off-farm opportunities. Farm business expansion decisions are often tied to household structure, specifically the ages of family members and the interest of succeeding generations in the farm business. And because farms are closely linked to individual farm families, business risks are also household financial risks, and the links between business risks and family ownership drive many farm business strategies. Those links also drive farmers' participation in the political process, and government policies have important impacts on the economics of agriculture.

We have organized the chapter to illustrate several important concepts in industrial organization. Our foremost concern is to help readers understand the forces driving competition in agriculture. Compared to the other industries in this book, agriculture is unique; its structure and competitive behavior are best characterized by the theory of pure competition.

▪▪▪ I. Structure

Agriculture comprises many commodities, many of which have distinct markets and marketing channels. Competition in agriculture is strongly influenced by the characteristics of individual commodity production and marketing. For example, while oranges, beef, milk and lettuce are all food and can keep us from starving if we are stranded on a desert island, they are produced on farms that compete only indirectly, and have very different production cycles and marketing channels.

Farmers and Risk

Farming is a risky enterprise for several reasons. Operators must make substantial capital commitments in land, structures, and equipment before production commences. They then commit their labor and bear the direct expenses associated with crop or livestock production well before realizing any revenues from the sale of farm products. None of these commitments can be easily adjusted in the very short run, once crops have been planted, and as a result short-run market supply curves for many farm products are very *inelastic*, as depicted in Figure 1-1. Moreover, the farm production that results from a given investment of capital, operator labor, and materials can vary substantially because of unexpected changes in weather or disease. Hence, market supply curves can also shift unexpectedly, as between S_0 and S_1 in Figure 1-1.

Market demands for most farm commodities are quite inelastic with respect to price, as depicted in Figure 1-1, because food is a necessity and because people can only eat so much. In addition, most commodities have few good substitutes, and they constitute small shares of the total costs of the processed products to which they are converted. With inelastic supply and demand curves, unexpected supply or demand shocks can lead to sharp price fluctuations—the essence of the price risk that farmers face in addition to yield or production risks.

Figure 1-2 provides an example of price risks in agriculture, showing annual average corn prices received by Iowa farmers over the period from 1970 through 2006. Prices show hardly any trend, but sharp fluctuations through time. While the mean price was

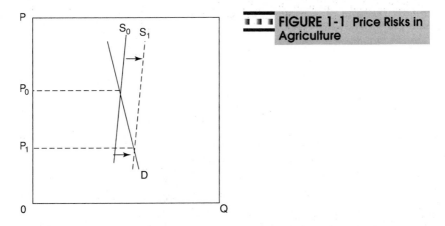

▪ ▪ ▪ **FIGURE 1-1 Price Risks in Agriculture**

$2.23 a bushel, annual prices ranged from a low of $1.04 to a high of $3.20. The mean annual change in price was 40 cents a bushel, or 18 percent of the mean price.

Figure 1-3 demonstrates yield risks, tracing annual corn yields in Hardin County, Iowa, from 1970 to 2006. There has been a strong upward trend in corn yields in the U.S.; Hardin County was no exception, with an average annual increase of 1.96 bushels per year driving the trend expectation from 96 bushels an acre in 1970 to 167 in 2006.

▪ ▪ ▪ **FIGURE 1-2 Annual Corn Prices Received by Iowa Farmers, 1970–2006**

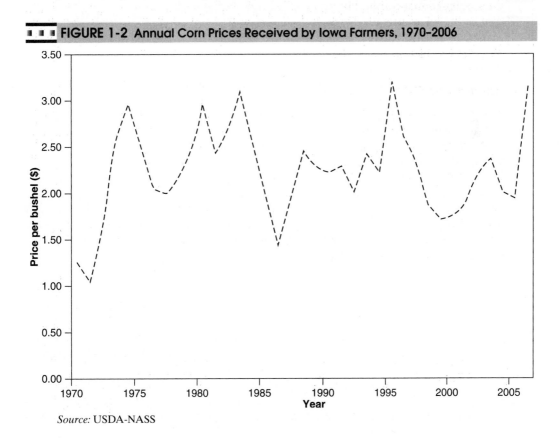

Source: USDA-NASS

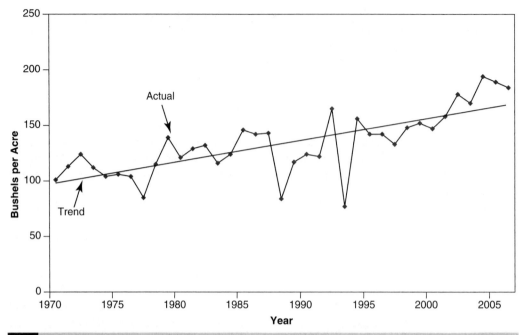

▪ ▪ ▪ **FIGURE 1-3** Corn Yields in Hardin County, Iowa, 1970–2006

Source: USDA-NASS

However the increase isn't smooth, as weather events (such as droughts or hurricanes, or unusually good growing weather) can cause large variations around the trends—resulting in the yield risks referred to above. For example, in 1993, the actual corn yield in Hardin County was 77 bushels per acre, 46 percent below the trend yield of 141 bushels; by contrast, the actual yield in the previous year, 165 bushels, was 19 percent above the trend yield of 139. Such wide swings, which are quite common in many crops and many locations, can lead to large year-to-year swings in total production and revenues.[1]

While short-run supply curves for agricultural commodities tend to be inelastic, easy entry into (or exit from) most commodities makes for elastic long-run supply curves. Moreover, rapid productivity growth has also shifted long-run supply curves out to the right. On the demand side, domestic demand growth for agricultural commodities has been limited by low rates of domestic population growth and by low income elasticities of demand for most commodities. These long-run supply and demand developments carry two important implications. First, real prices for agricultural commodities have fallen steadily, creating significant further income risks for those farmers who fail to adopt successful new cost reducing technologies. Second, foreign markets are extremely important in agriculture.

About 20 percent of U.S. agricultural production is exported, while agriculture accounts for 10 percent of all U.S. exports. Exports are particularly important for field

---

[1]If a wide production area were to realize a fall in yields, it would likely have an opposite effect on prices (thus limiting the effects on revenues); but locally-based yield shocks will be largely divorced from price movements, which are determined in national or world markets.

crops—nearly half of wheat production and three-quarters of cotton production is exported. Exports account directly for about 20 percent of corn production and 30 percent of soybean production. The U.S. also exports about 10 to 15 percent of the poultry, beef and pork produced here, which is fed on corn and soybean diets. While agricultural exports exceed imports, the gap has been closing in recent years, and agricultural imports now account for about 18 percent of total domestic supplies of agricultural products. Imports include some tropical products that aren't grown here, such as coffee, bananas, or cocoa; but important competing products include cheese, flowers, sugar, vegetables, and red meats.

Global trade creates expanded sales opportunities for U.S. farmers, but it also creates risks. Fluctuating exchange rates, as well as macroeconomic developments in other countries, can lead to sharp changes in import and export volumes. Agriculture is at the center of some of the most contentious disputes in international trade negotiations, including controversies over subsidies given to farmers in industrialized countries, restrictions on agricultural imports in many countries, and disputes over food safety. Farmers seek to limit risk, and many of the government policies and organizational designs in agriculture reflect attempts by farmers to manage or eliminate the risks they face.

Trends in Farm Structure

Figure 1-4 summarizes several key long-run trends in U.S. farm structure. The number of farms, which peaked at about 6.8 million in 1935, declined quite sharply over the next 40 years to 2.3 million farms in 1974. The rate of decline has slowed considerably since then, with 2.1 million farms recorded in the 2002 Census of Agriculture.

▪ ▪ ▪ **FIGURE 1-4** Trends in Farms, Farmland and Farm Productivity

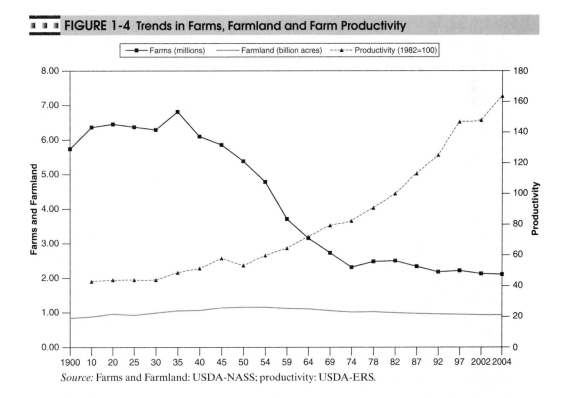

Source: Farms and Farmland: USDA-NASS; productivity: USDA-ERS.

In contrast to changes in farm numbers, the total amount of land in farms fell slowly, from a peak of 1.16 billion acres in 1950 to 938 million acres in 2002. Finally, agricultural productivity growth accelerated after the Second World War. The U.S. Department of Agriculture (USDA) productivity series, which measures the growth in farm output relative to the growth in all inputs (land, labor, and capital, as well as intermediate inputs such as chemicals, energy and seeds), grew by 206 percent between 1950 and 2004, a growth rate of 2.1 percent per year.

Figure 1-4 suggests that farm sizes stabilized after the mid-1970s, but that apparent stability is a bit misleading, because many places were counted as farms in 2002 that would not have been counted in the 1970s. The government defines a farm as any place that sold (or normally could have sold) $1,000 worth of agricultural commodities in a year. The definition is not adjusted for inflation, or changes in how farm commodities are defined.

Table 1-1 provides a closer look at the distribution of farm sizes, using data from a large annual survey of farm operators. There were about 2.1 million farms in each of the three years shown in the table. But over half had less than $10,000 in sales, and most of those were closer to $1,000 than to $10,000 (one could realize $10,000 by selling either 12 beef cattle, the milk from 5 dairy cows, 25 acres of corn, or 3 acres of vegetables). Very small farms account for a growing share of all farms but a small and declining share of farm production. Their growth reflects the preference of many people for a rural lifestyle.

Once we account for very small farms, Table 1-1 shows a continuing sharp restructuring of agriculture toward larger operations. Small, commercially oriented family farms—with sales between $10,000 and $250,000—hold declining shares of farm numbers and production while production shifts to very large family farms and nonfamily

TABLE 1-1 Recent Trends in U.S. Farm Structure

Item	1989	1995	2003
Number of farms	2,148,740	2,068,000	2,121,107
		Percent of farms	
Family farms			
Less than $10,000 in sales	49.5	48.4	57.2
$10,000-$249,999 in sales	43.4	44.2	34.0
$250,000-$499,999 in sales	4.1	3.6	4.0
$500,000 or more in sales	1.8	2.2	3.1
Non-family farms	1.2	1.5	1.7
		Percent of the value of farm production	
Family farms			
Less than $10,000 in sales	2.1	2.0	1.6
$10,000-$249,999 in sales	40.2	35.6	25.5
$250,000-$499,999 in sales	19.9	14.9	14.4
$500,000 or more in sales	31.6	33.1	44.7
Non-family farms	6.2	14.5	13.7

Source: USDA, Economic Research Service, 1989 and 1995 Farm Costs and Returns Survey and 2003 Agricultural Resource Management Survey, Phase III. Sales classes are in 2003 dollars, using the Producer Price Index for Farm Products.

farms. In 2003, there were about 66,000 family farms with at least $500,000 in sales, and they accounted for 45 percent of all farm production; adjusting for inflation, there were far fewer (39,000) such farms 14 years before in 1989, and they held about 32 percent of all production.

Family farms include proprietorships, partnerships, and family corporations—those in which people related by blood or marriage hold at least half the stock. Table 1-1 also shows a sharp shift to nonfamily operations after 1989, up to about 14 percent of farm production. Some of that shift reflects production by large and diversified public corporations, particularly in hog production and cattle feedlots, but much of it reflects shifts of production to closely held corporations owned and operated by a few unrelated individuals.

The shift to larger farms occurs in almost all commodity specialties. Table 1-2 shows how the typical enterprise size has changed for selected commodities between 1987 and 2002. In this case, "typical" denotes a median size, at which half of all production occurs

TABLE 1-2 Changes in Enterprise Size, by Commodity, 1987–2002.

Commodity	*1987*	*2002*
	Typical Acres Harvested[a]	
Field crops:		
Corn	200	450
Soybeans	243	480
Wheat	404	784
Cotton	450	920
Vegetables:		
Asparagus	160	236
Lettuce	949	2,225
Potatoes	350	810
Sweet corn	100	222
Tomatoes	400	700
Tree Crops:		
Apples	83	129
Almonds	203	361
Oranges	450	1,015
	Typical Annual Sales[b]	
Poultry/Livestock		
Broilers	300,000	520,000
Hogs	1,200	23,400
Fattened cattle	17,532	34,494
	Typical Herd Size[c]	
Dairy Cows	80	275

[a] Median of acres harvested, by farm size. Half of all harvested acres of a commodity were on farms harvesting more than the typical amount, and half were on farms harvesting less.

[b] Median of head sold, by farm size. Half of the sales of a given species were from farms with more than the typical sales, and half were on farms selling less

[c] Median of herd size, by farm size. Half of all dairy cows were on farms with herds larger than the typical size, and half were on farms with smaller herds.

Source: Authors' calculations, based on unpublished data from the U.S. Census of Agriculture.

on larger farms, and half on smaller. For example, half of all corn production (first row) occurred on farms that harvested at least 200 acres of corn in 1987, and half occurred on operations with fewer acres of corn (an acre, which is 4,840 square yards, is slightly smaller than a football field, which measures 5,333 square yards). By 2002, the median corn farm harvested 450 acres, more than twice that of the 1987 farm. Other crops show similar changes, with most medians roughly doubling in the 15-year period. In this case, increases in enterprise size reflect increases in the size of the whole farm, and also reflect increased specialization as farms devote more of their acreage to their primary commodity enterprise.

Livestock and poultry production shows similar trends, although we measure median enterprise size on a different basis—the number of head sold for broiler, hog, and fed cattle operations, and the herd size for dairy farms.[2] Here we also see dramatic changes. In 1987, farms with less than 80 dairy cows accounted for half of the national dairy cow herd; by 2002, that midpoint farm size had more than tripled to 275 cows. The hog sector showed an even bigger shift: In 2002, the typical hog enterprise was 20 times larger than typical 1987 enterprise.

Table 1-3 provides farm financial information, sorted according to size classes, and suggests a reason for structural change. Larger farms are more profitable, on average.

TABLE 1-3 Business Financial Performance and Household Incomes, by Farm Size

Item	Family Farms, by Sales Class ($000)				Nonfamily farms
	<10	*10–250*	*250–500*	*500+*	
	Farm business performance				
Operating profit margin[a]	−98.0	−13.3	10.5	18.0	23.3
% of farms in category:					
Showing loss	42.7	33.1	18.2	16.7	28.5
Showing margin>10%	21.6	30.3	50.6	60.1	57.2
	Farm Household Income ($)				
Mean household income	60,841	64,340	105,862	221,800	
(median)	(45,351)	(48,528)	(83,244)	(118,982)	
Farm earnings	−4,405	8,280	64,376	175,198	
Off-farm income	65,246	56,060	41,486	46,602	
Earned[b]	50,276	40,914	30,056	32,384	
Unearned[b]	14,970	15,146	11,430	14,218	

[a] Operating profit margin = 100% × (net farm income + interest − charge for unpaid operators' labor and management)/gross farm income.

[b] Earned income: wages and salary, and off-farm self employment income. Unearned income includes interest and dividends, benefits from Social Security and other public programs, alimony, annuities, net income from estates or trusts, private pensions, regular contributions from people living outside the household, net rental income from nonfarm properties, and royalties from mineral leases.

Source: USDA Economic Research Service, data derived from 2003 Agricultural Resource Management Survey.

---

[2]Broilers are young chickens sold for meat—the chicken you see in supermarkets and fast-food restaurants, sometimes called fryers. Fed cattle are cattle that are fed a ration of corn in large commercial feedlots prior to marketing, as distinct from cattle that are grazed only on pastures or rangeland.

Mean operating profit margins range from -98 percent in the smallest size class to 18.5 percent among farms in the largest size class. (Operating profits are calculated by subtracting cash expenses and the opportunity cost of the operator's time from gross income, and very small "hobby" farms will have expenses but little gross income). Hence, many very small farms show negative net farm income. Moreover, while substantial shares of farms in each size class show profit margins that exceed 10 percent, higher fractions of the larger farms do than smaller farms. If small farms report low profits or, in many cases losses, how do their owner-operators support themselves? The lower panel of Table 1-3 explains the sources of income to farm households. Mean annual household income varies from just over $60,000 for operators of the smallest farms to well over $200,000 for operators of the largest farms. By comparison, mean household income across *all* U.S. households was $59,100 in 2003 (median income was $43,300). Farm operators are not, on average, a low-income group.

Operators of the smallest farms lose money from farming, on average, but their losses are more than offset by substantial off-farm incomes. Among operators of small commercial farms ($10,000 to $250,000 in sales), farm income supplements their far more substantial earnings from off-farm employment. Many of these households operate small part-time grain or cattle businesses on the farm. Operators of larger farms make substantial household incomes from farming and they also frequently generate income from off-farm employment; a household member may have a salaried job, or may operate another business.

What the Averages Hide

The previous discussion indicates the national trends in farm size and profitability. Substantial technological economies are driving increases in farm size. But we would be remiss if we did not also note two other important elements of farm structure. First, although farms are becoming larger, even large farms are usually still fairly small businesses. Second, note the wide range of financial performance among farm businesses in Table 1-3, which suggests that many small farms remain financially viable. While a third of small commercial farms showed a loss, nearly a third showed substantial operating profit margins of at least 10 percent. Moreover, one in six of the largest family farms recorded a loss from farming in 2003, even while many others record substantial profits. Indeed, one can combine the data in tables 1 and 3 to realize that the vast majority of farms with operating profit margins of at least 10 percent were small.

The variation in financial performance provides one indicator of risks in farming, stemming from local weather conditions, natural disasters, and commodity price shocks. This variation also provides an indicator of real disparities in farm operator skills and sustained performance. Profitable small farms can be found in almost all commodities, including fruit and vegetable operations, livestock and poultry producers, part-time field crop producers, and specialty crop operations (e.g., maple syrup and ginseng). Some have found niche markets in small and focused products and services not being supplied by mainstream providers. Farmers can access niche markets through the way products are marketed—for example, through local farmers' markets, internet retailing, or direct sales to restaurants. They can also develop specific varieties of products, such as heirloom tomatoes, Boer goats raised for meat, rapini and other cooking greens, tofu-variety soybeans, or kiwifruit. Niche markets also exist for products distinguished by the cultural practices used in production, such as free-range chicken, organic vegetables, or milk from pasture-grazed cows. Some producers combine all three features—marketing, product varieties, and cultural practices.

Organic farming covers an important set of niche markets. Organic crops are produced without most conventional pesticides or synthetic fertilizers, with producers relying instead on cultural and biological pest, disease and weed management, and fertilizers from animal manure. Organic meat, poultry, egg, and dairy operations use organic feed and eschew the use of antibiotics or growth-promoting hormones. Consumer demand for organic products is growing sharply, leading to significant price premiums and good financial opportunities for producers. In turn, farmers and acreage are shifting to organic production; certified organic cropland acreage grew by 45 percent, while pasture and rangeland acreage more than doubled between 2000 and 2005. Organic production is still, however, a small part of U.S. agriculture, accounting for just 0.5 percent of all U.S. cropland, and the same share of pastureland.[3]

Small farms are often more important in niche markets than they are in conventional commodity production, particularly in the early stages of these markets. If these markets grow in size, larger farms often become more involved. For example, large farms are increasingly important in organic farming, which appears to have some scale economies. Because entry is generally easy, niche markets tend to attract entrants looking for higher returns, often eroding any supra-competitive profits that early entrants may have garnered.

Commodity Markets

Although farms are getting larger, farmers are still price-takers in almost all agricultural commodity markets—that is, there are many sellers, and no individual seller is large enough to affect price. The same cannot be said for the buying side—the elevators, processors, packers, and retailers who purchase agricultural commodities. While quite a few competitive markets remain in which farmers can sell to many buyers, there are a growing number of agricultural markets with very few buyers in which monopsony power is a real issue. Monopsony power can arise from several sources:

- **High nationwide concentration.**   Some commodity processing industries have become highly concentrated, due in some cases to scale economies in production, in some cases to the influence of advertising and product differentiation, and often because of mergers among large producers. For example, the four largest packers of fed cattle slaughtered 80 percent of the U.S. total in 2005, up from 36 percent in 1980. Nationwide concentration measures have also increased sharply in hog packing, poultry processing, fluid milk processing, grain and oilseed processing industries and many of the food manufacturing industries, such as beer, that produce consumer products.[4]

---

[3]Organic production has made significant inroads in fruit and vegetable sectors, accounting for 6 percent of carrot acreage, 4 percent of lettuce, and 3 percent of apples. One percent of dairy cows are certified organic. Moreover, since organic products command significant price premiums, the organic share of the value of production in each of these sectors is 1.5 to 3 times higher than the share of physical acreage.
[4]For 96 comparable food manufacturing/processing industries, the percent of shipments accounted for by the four leading firms increased from 49 percent in 1967 to 61 percent in 1992. Unfortunately, comparable figures for more recent years are not available except for selected industries. See Rogers, Richard T., "Structural Change in U.S. Food Manufacturing, 1958-1997," *Agribusiness*, 17 (2001): 3-32.

- **Transport costs.**   Many commodity markets are effectively local or regional, rather than national, because of high commodity transportation costs. For example, fed cattle are usually shipped less than 100 miles to a packing plant. Leading national firms may not be active in every local market—for example, Smithfield buys most of the hogs produced in the Southeast, but has not been active in the Oklahoma/Kansas market. In such markets, even if there are 5 to 6 buyers nationwide, a farmer may only have only 1 or 2 in the relevant local market.

- **Product perishability.**   Although grains and oilseeds can be stored by farmers while they search for a better price, livestock lose value when they are fed beyond their optimal weights. Many fresh fruits and vegetables spoil quickly and milk must be marketed at least every other day. Perishable products limit the options for farmers to seek better prices.

- **Specialty varieties.**   Farmers are increasingly being asked to produce specific varieties of commodities. For example, New York City's 2006 ban on transfat in its restaurants led to a surge in demand for low-linolenic soybeans, which when processed provide transfat-free soybean oil. Both Monsanto and Pioneer/Dupont developed low-linolenic soybean varieties quite recently. The challenge facing the industry is to get farmers to plant the new varieties and use soybean crushing plants to process them; that is, to create a new parallel channel for transfat-free soybean oil. An older example concerns potatoes. Round white potatoes are used in making potato chips, while russet potatoes are preferred for making frozen potatoes. The two channels have distinct sets of concentrated buyers and compete only indirectly. Direct consumer demands also lead to varietal and cultural specialties, such as organic foods, free-range chickens and turkeys, and hormone-free milk and pork. In these cases, the relatively small size of the markets means that farmers may have only a few buyers.

- **Asymmetric information.**   Economic theory suggests that competitive markets require large numbers of informed buyers and sellers. Many agricultural commodity buyers make hundreds of transactions every day, while farmers selling commodities may make only a few transactions in a year. As a result, buyers may be better informed about market alternatives, and may use this knowledge to develop some local monopsony power.

Although commodity markets often exhibit high buyer concentration, farmers rarely face a pure monopsony—that is, a single buyer. They have some choices and they may expand their range of options if they can store or ship their products. Farmers also have a wider range of options before they commit to production of a particular commodity. But the potential exercise of monopsony power has an important impact on farmer decisions, and strongly affects the design of marketing institutions. The following discussion examines several such institutions.

Vertical Linkages: Contracts

A growing percentage of farmers now rely on formal contracts with processors or first handlers. Production and marketing contracts covered 39 percent of the value of U.S. agricultural production in 2004, up from 28 percent in 1991 and only 12 percent in 1969.

The use of contracts varies widely by commodity (Figure 1-5). They are used heavily by producers of broilers, eggs, sugar beets, hogs, milk, some fruits, and processed

**Percent
of Production**

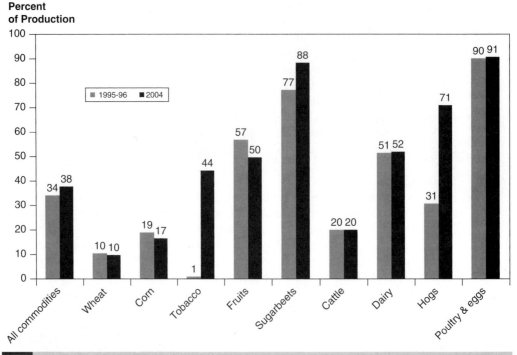

▪▪▪▪ **FIGURE 1-5** Share of Production Under Contract, Selected Commodities, 1994–95
and 2004

Source: USDA-NASS; USDA-ERS.

vegetables. Those producers typically face just a few buyers, and perishability and high commodity transport costs limit their options. By contrast, contracts receive little use by producers of food and feed grains and soybeans, because these commodities are storable, can be more easily transported for long distances, and have more buyers. By negotiating over contract terms before a production cycle is completed, or in many cases before it has even begun, farmers can avoid the harshest element of monopsony, when the product is harvested and there is only one nearby buyer.

Farmers use marketing contracts to identify a buyer, set a delivery schedule and establish a method for determining price before a commodity is harvested. Prices may be set at the time the contract is written, or they may be tied to a national or regional reference price for the commodity. The pricing method frequently includes a schedule of premiums and discounts tied to product characteristics, such as leanness in hogs or oil content in corn. Farmers can use marketing contracts to limit price risks, ensure a market outlet, and obtain higher returns for superior product quality, while buyers can assure themselves of timely supplies of products with desired characteristics. Transactions costs are reduced compared to negotiated spot transactions.

Farmers may also enter into production contracts, which are widely used in livestock and poultry industries. Farmers with production contracts provide a service — usually a single stage of the production of a commodity; in most cases, they do not take ownership or market the commodity. For example, in the broiler industry, farmers receive young chicks from an integrator, such as Tyson Foods or Perdue Farms, who also provide feed, veterinary supplies, transportation services, and production guidelines and advice. The integrator usually owns hatcheries, feed mills, and processing plants. The farmer provides housing, utilities, and labor, and in 6 to 8 weeks the chicks grow to market weights, at which time the integrator picks them up and takes them to slaughtering/processing plants.

Production contracts are spreading widely in many commodities. Dairy farmers often contract with a specialized operation to raise the dairy farmers' calves to be replacement milk cows. Some owners of beef cattle contract with feedlots to raise animals to market weight and to market them to meat packers. In horticulture, integrators provide young seedlings to farmers who grow them to market size, whereupon the integrators market the mature plants to large retail chains. Seed companies contract with farmers to grow crops that will be harvested for seeds.

Farmers with production contracts typically receive a fee for their services, rather than a price that varies with market prices for the commodity. For example, broiler growers usually receive 4 to 6 cents per pound for their birds. While the fees paid usually vary with the grower performance regarding feed efficiency and bird mortality, production contracts typically remove almost all the price risk that independent growers would face, as well as those yield risks, usually due to weather, that they face in common with other growers.

One function of contracts is to shift the risk of price fluctuations. However, other mechanisms may also exist; for example, corn, soybean, wheat, and many commodities have active futures markets which can be used to shift price risk.[5] An additional purpose of contracts is to improve coordination of the quality and timing of production so it meets the preferences of the buyer. Contracting of hogs has increased largely to ensure that farmers produce the lean hogs desired by processors and consumers. In the case of grains and soybeans, federal grades enable most users to obtain the quality desired.

Contracts are also a means of shifting decision control and can be instrumental in developing a tightly coordinated, efficient vertical system, as in the broiler industry. In broilers, integrators such as Tyson, Pilgrim Pride and Gold Kist (a cooperative), own the hatcheries, feed plants, and broiler processing plants and contract with growers to feed out the chicks provided by the integrator. This tightly coordinated complex has an excellent record for technological advances and increased efficiency. At the time of World War II, chicken was a luxury eaten on special occasions and grown in many small farm flocks. Today, chicken is one of our least expensive meats and is produced by growers under contract with one of about 40 integrators. The nominal price of broilers has remained virtually the same over the last 50 years: Live weight price per pound was 36 cents in 1948 versus 39.3 cents in 2001 (Figure 1-6). Broiler production has soared from 1.1 billion pounds live weight in 1945 to 42.4 billion pounds in 2001.

---

[5]Futures contracts allow farmers to lock in prices at harvest time before they even plant the crop, if they choose. For example, the December 2007 corn contract on the Chicago Board of Trade was $4.05 per bushel in mid-March when this chapter was being written. Corn belt farmers might elect to sell short a December corn contract with the intent of either delivering on that contract (rarely done) or offsetting the transaction by buying back a contract when the corn is harvested. In either case they have assured themselves of the $4.05 selling price but forsake any higher prices.

Cents per pound

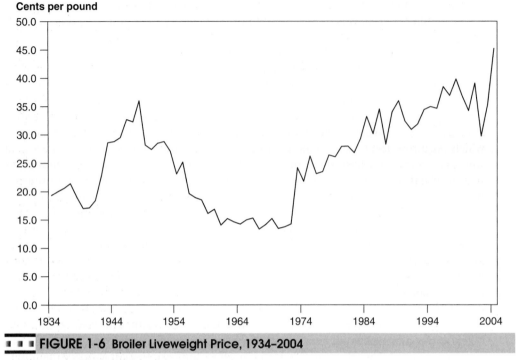

▪▪▪ **FIGURE 1-6** Broiler Liveweight Price, 1934–2004

Source: USDA-NASS.

The farmers who grow-out broilers for Tyson, Pilgrim Pride and others are sometimes characterized as indentured servants with very little management discretion. This is perhaps true, but farmers accepted this arrangement roughly 50 years ago as a trade-off for the transfer of price risk. At that time growers usually had several firms to contract with in their area. This is no longer the case. The largest four broiler processors now account for 55 percent of the nation's broilers; the largest 10 account for 74 percent. The increased concentration of broiler integrators has resulted in a decline in the number operating in local markets. Many broiler growers have only 1 or 2 integrators contracting in their area. Little negotiation of contract terms is possible.

▪▪▪ II. Conduct

Because the "market price" for individual commodities plays such a central role in providing market signals and determining how returns are allocated, there is considerable interest in maintaining open and competitive markets (usually spot markets), whether prices are determined via auction, private treaty, administered pricing or formula pricing. Since the early 1900s, the U.S. Department of Agriculture (USDA) price reporters have provided daily, weekly, and monthly market reports for many commodities and locations, as a way to quickly disseminate accurate price and quantity information to aid in the smooth working of spot markets.

Indeed, users of marketing contracts often use a spot market price index to set their own base prices. However, as farmers and their customers have shifted toward contracts (whose terms are not typically detailed in market reports), spot market volumes often decline and become less representative of the overall market. In some cases, spot markets that have been used as national reference markets have become so "thin" that they become problematic as a basis for national prices.

One example of the "thin market" problem has occurred in markets for beef cattle. As fed cattle shifted to contract transactions during the late 1990s, many daily market reports became uninformative, as they had no spot market or contract transactions to report. With ebbing confidence in market reports, even more transactions shifted to contracts. In response, Congress passed the Mandatory Livestock Reporting Act, which required disclosure of sale terms for transactions in the hog, cattle, lamb, and wholesale meat industries. Once the new reporting system began offering comprehensive information, substantial volumes of fed cattle shifted back to spot markets, and price movements across local markets became more tightly linked to one another.

The U.S. cheese industry provides another example of the thin markets problem. For decades, prices on the National Cheese Exchange (NCE) in Green Bay, Wisconsin were used as the national reference price for bulk cheddar cheese. A handful of buyers and sellers met for 30 minutes every Friday morning to exchange carloads of 500-pound barrels or 40-pound blocks of cheddar cheese. Some weeks, no carloads were traded; other weeks, several carloads were exchanged. Although the volume sold on the NCE generally represented less than 1 percent of the cheese manufactured in the U.S., the NCE price was used to formula-price over 90 percent of all bulk cheese sold throughout the country.

The leverage represented by this situation was too tempting for some of the major cheese companies to resist. Kraft, the dominant seller of cheese in the U.S. (with about 40 percent of the retail market), manufactured one-third of its cheese and purchased the remaining two-thirds from other manufacturers. All the cheese it purchased was priced based upon the NCE. Although Kraft was the largest *buyer* of bulk cheese in the U.S., it accounted for 74 percent of the *sales* on the NCE during the 6 years studied. Following its acquisition by Phillip Morris in 1988, Kraft was pressured to increase its margins in cheese. By selling a few carloads periodically on the NCE, Kraft was able to depress the price on which all its purchases were based while maintaining or increasing the selling prices for its branded finished cheeses, thereby increasing its margins. After a Wisconsin study[6] identified that market manipulation had occurred, the NCE market was closed and replaced with a spot cheese market on the Chicago Mercantile Exchange. While this shift did not totally solve the thinness of this market, it appears to have been a step in the right direction.

The cheese industry also illustrates the influence of government programs on price levels and volatility. For decades, farm milk prices in the U.S. have been supported by federal government purchases of bulk cheddar cheese through the Commodity Credit Corporation (CCC) at politically set price levels (Figure 1-7). Because the price support level was generally higher than the market clearing price during 1980 to 1988, the CCC purchased large quantities of cheese. Market supply and demand forces were muted in their influence; prices were essentially administered by the government.

---

[6]Mueller, Willard F., Bruce W. Marion, Maqbool H. Sial and F. E. Geithman. Cheese Pricing: A Study of the Cheese National Exchange. Department of Agricultural and Applied Economics, University of Wisconsin-Madison, March 1996.

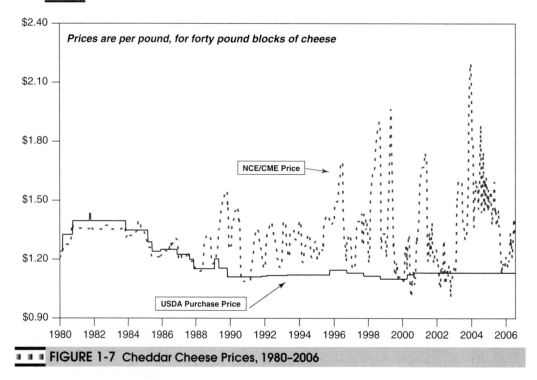

Prices are per pound, for forty pound blocks of cheese

NCE/CME Price

USDA Purchase Price

▪ ▪ ▪ ▪ **FIGURE 1-7** Cheddar Cheese Prices, 1980–2006

However, as Figure 1-7 indicates, support levels dropped sufficiently during the 1980s so that market forces (including the trading on the NCE) took on a greater role in price discovery. Since 1988, cheese prices have been much more volatile as they respond to supply and demand forces. While market determined prices are preferred on most grounds, they may also increase the incentives for market manipulation.

Market Power Dilemma of Farmers

In nearly all agricultural commodities, individual farmers are price takers. Farm numbers in all commodities are large. Individual farmers account for a tiny share of the commodity produced. Even if they go out of production completely or double their output, they will have no influence on market price. This is one of the big frustrations of farming. The fertilizer, seed, feed, diesel and equipment suppliers that provide inputs to farmers generally set the price they charge based upon what the products cost them and market conditions. For farmers, prices are determined by an impersonal market that may or may not allow them a profit. With no control over the price of their output, they are helpless if price volatility results in handsome profits some years and substantial losses in others. Their main control is over their cost of production.

Farmers are also disadvantaged in that they buy from and sell to firms with substantial and growing market power. Farm input industries such as farm machinery, seed, petroleum and pesticide manufacturing are relatively concentrated with a few dominant firms. And, as has been noted, the industries processing farm commodities are also relatively concentrated and increasingly dominated by a few extremely large firms. Indeed, while there are roughly 16,000 food processing/manufacturing companies, the *largest 20* accounted for over 50 percent of the value added in 1995 and did 75 percent of the media advertising. These are truly mammoth companies.

In an effort to gain some degree of pricing power, farmers have often organized cooperatives or sought government protection from the vagaries of the market. But here also, it has been difficult for farmers to develop enduring market power for one central reason: there are few if any barriers to entry into farming.[7] In farming as in other industries, even monopolists have very limited ability to enjoy monopoly rents if entry is easy.

However, this is not to say that farmer cooperatives have no influence on the balance of power in the food and fiber system. Both economic theory and empirical evidence indicate that open membership cooperatives can negate market power imperfections and benefit both farmers and consumers. Thus, cooperatives play an important role in the food and fiber economy. However, while cooperatives can be effective in countering the market power farmers face in input or output markets, they have difficulty achieving enduring market power.

Because individual farmers generally have no control over the price of their output, the Capper-Volstead Act of 1922 granted farmers the right to jointly market their agricultural commodities through cooperatives without violating section 1 of the Sherman Act (which prohibits combinations or conspiracies that restrain trade). In 2002, approximately 1,560 agricultural marketing cooperatives in the U.S. marketed $70 billion of agricultural commodities.[8] Most of these cooperatives are "first handlers" or assemblers of farm output and provide little added value. Cooperative grain elevators, for example, buy corn, soybeans, wheat and other grains from local farmers and ship carloads or barge loads to companies processing grain or oilseed into human food (e.g. flour, cooking oil, breakfast cereal), animal feed, or for export.

This means that most cooperatives are in the commodity business and are unable to differentiate their products, which leads to little, if any, market power. Number 2 yellow corn and Grade A milk are the same whether sold by a cooperative or an investor-owned company. Thus, while cooperatives have provided access to market for their farmer members and have often provided important alternative outlets to proprietary firms, they have generally not achieved enduring market power.

Possible exceptions have been cooperatives that further process their members' output and develop branded products. Land O' Lakes butter, Welch's grape products, Sun-Maid dried fruits, Sunkist oranges, Florida Natural citrus juices, Blue Diamond nuts and Ocean Spray cranberry products are examples. Once again, the presence or absence of entry barriers strongly influences the degree of market power achieved. Most cooperatives have open membership; that is, they will accept any farmer who wants to join. With open membership, if a cooperative is able to achieve a premium price for its products and therefore pay its farmers a premium price, other farmers are

---

[7]While the capital requirements necessary to enter some farming activities may be substantial (on the order of several million dollars), there is no shortage of potential entrants who can raise the necessary capital, either from investors or lenders. Moreover, because the enterprise size necessary to realize available scale economies is rarely large enough to materially affect prices, agricultural markets rarely display scale-related entry barriers.

[8]There were also 1,200 farm input cooperatives that had sales of $25 billion. (See Farmer Cooperative Statistics, 2002, USDA, Service Report 62, June 2004).

quick to join, increase the quantity the cooperative has to sell, and thereby drive down its selling price.[9]

The Ocean Spray Cooperative illustrates the dilemma faced by many cooperatives. Ocean Spray emerged in the late 1950s as the dominant cranberry marketing cooperative. By the 1970s, it was marketing 90 percent of all cranberries produced. During the 1970s and 1980s, Ocean Spray aggressively developed several new products and was often identified as a highly successful, market-oriented cooperative. Its sales grew from $87 million in 1972 to $736 million in 1987.[10]

The explosion of the blended juice market during the late 1970s, 1980s, and early 1990s resulted in demand for cranberries outrunning supply, even though supply also grew rapidly. As Figure 1-8 shows, grower prices jumped from the $10 to $20 range during the 1950s, 1960s and early 1970s to over $40 per barrel during the 1980s and 1990s. During the latter period, a serious market disequilibrium was building. Growers responded to high prices by planting new bogs, mostly with hybrid varieties that yielded 2 or 3 times the older varieties. Cranberry beds cost $25,000 to $40,000 per acre to establish but, once established, bear fruit for 100 years or more. Thus, though cranberry prices crashed in 1998 and 1999, production fell very little. Because the cost of

▪ ▪ ▪ **FIGURE 1-8** U.S. Cranberry Production and Grower Prices, 1934–2005

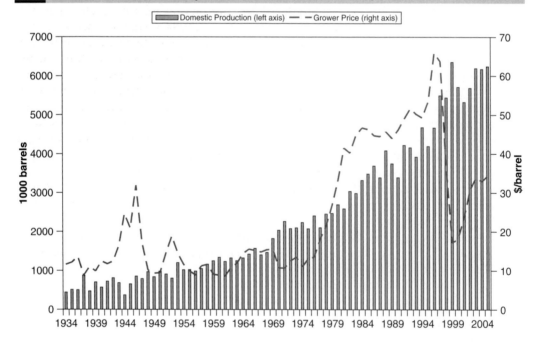

[9]National Grape Grower's Cooperative, which owns the Welch's brand and processing facilities, is an exception. The cooperative has closed membership and restricts the quantity of grapes it will accept from its members. National Grape/Welch's has thus achieved control over the supply it markets and has successfully maintained a premium price for its Welch's products and in its pay price to farmers.
[10]Jesse, Edward V. and Richard T. Rogers, The Cranberry Industry and Ocean Spray Cooperative, Food System Research Group Mono. 19, University of Wisconsin-Madison, Jan. 2006.

planting the beds was a sunk cost, there was no economic incentive to abandon bogs. Without control over the quantity produced by its members or nonmembers, Ocean Spray had no ability to temper the growth in production so that it was in line with the growth in demand. As the production from new bogs came on stream, grower prices plummeted from $64 per barrel in 1997 to $17 in 1999.

Because entry into cranberry processing is relatively easy, new firms entered to compete with Ocean Spray during the 1980s and 1990s. Most of these supplied the generic juice market and eroded some of Ocean Spray's influence over the national cranberry market. With the assistance of the Cranberry Marketing Order, Ocean Spray and the industry are gradually recovering. Perhaps if Ocean Spray had closed membership, been content to ignore the rapidly growing blended juice market (which was largely generic) and focused on those products in which its brand commanded a premium, it might have been able to protect its brand and its members to some extent during the market collapse.

III. Performance

The most striking feature of agriculture's performance is its high rate of productivity growth over a long period. Table 1-4 provides some examples, comparing trends in average yields for several major commodities. Just before World War I, U.S. farmers produced 26 bushels of corn per acre of land planted to corn. From 2001 to 2005, corn yields averaged 143 bushels per acre. In the early period, milk production per cow averaged 3,840 pounds, but by 2006 it reached nearly 20,000 pounds of milk per cow!

Yields are a "single-factor" measure of productivity growth, and they powerfully demonstrate how we can produce food for a much larger population with little change in land devoted to farming. While such measures are quite useful, they can also be misleading because some of the increase in yields is accomplished through more intensive use of other inputs, such as capital equipment, fertilizers, herbicides and pesticides. More accurate measures of productivity growth, called total factor measures, account for the use of all inputs when measuring productivity. The USDA has developed such measures for the post–World War II period.

Figure 1-4 tracks USDA's productivity series. Between 1950 and 2004, total factor productivity growth in U.S. agriculture averaged 2.1 percent per year, and the growth

TABLE 1-4 Yields in U.S. Agriculture, 1910–2005

Crop	Measure	1910–1914	1945–1949	1965–1969	1982–1986	2001–2005
Corn	bu/acre	26.0	36.1	48.7	109.3	143.4
Wheat	bu/acre	14.4	16.9	25.9	37.1	40.8
Potatoes	cwt/acre	59.8	117.8	205.2	283.9	373.6
Sugar Beets	tons/acre	10.6	13.6	17.4	20.4	21.8
Cotton	lbs/acre	201.0	273.0	505.0	581.0	747.4
Soybeans	bu/acre	n.a.	19.6	24.2	30.7	39.4
Milk	lbs/cow	3,840	4,990	8,260	12,730	18,810

Yields are averaged across 5-year periods to smooth weather-related annual fluctuations.
Source: U.S. Department of Agriculture, National Agricultural Statistics Service.

was remarkably persistent. In contrast, multifactor productivity in the private nonfarm business sector grew by 1.15 percent per year over the same time period, according to the U.S. Bureau of Labor Statistics. Superior productivity performance shows up in price trends: farm product prices increased by only 15 percent between 1980 and 2005, while overall consumer prices rose by 122 percent.[11]

Technological change is the driving force in agriculture's productivity growth. New knowledge, embodied in innovations adopted widely across agriculture, fall into several broad areas:

- **Equipment.** Over time, a series of innovations allowed mechanical power to replace human and animal power; larger, faster and more reliable machines are now used in all phases of farm production. In recent years, farm equipment has incorporated advances in electronics and information technology to better monitor production processes and to better target applications of fertilizers and other agricultural chemicals. Global positioning systems, for example, allow farmers to monitor the yields within large fields and precisely target production practices (e.g., fertilizer application) accordingly.
- **Agricultural chemicals.** Early innovations led to the development of commercial fertilizers to replace or augment animal manure and pesticides, herbicides, and fungicides to control pests, weeds and diseases. More recent innovations have led to improvements in nearly all types of chemicals and in targeting of applications.
- **Genetics, including seed and plant development and livestock breeding.** Plant breeding research has led to higher yielding varieties with improved survival traits for local weather, pest, and disease conditions. Over the same period, improvements in livestock and poultry genetics have led to substantial and continuing increases in meat and milk yields per animal and per unit of feed.

New seed varieties increasingly rely on genetic modification, in which a gene from one organism is transferred to another organism, with the gene becoming a permanent part of the recipient organism's genome. Such genetically modified organisms (GMOs) are now widely used for three major field crops grown in the U.S: nearly 90 percent of soybean acreage, 65 percent of cotton acreage, and 40 percent of corn acreage are planted to varieties that are either herbicide tolerant or pest resistant. Farmers adopt genetically modified varieties because they are either more effective or less costly than alternatives and also reduce the amount of chemicals applied to land. Although the most commonly used GMOs in the U.S. possess "input traits" that reduce production costs, other GMOs contain "product traits" that appeal to consumers, such as rice with vitamin A, canola high in antioxidants, or fruits that ripen slowly.

GMOs are controversial, generating both environmental and food safety concerns. Consumer acceptance also varies. Some GMO crops sold in the United States are not approved for sale in Europe. In addition, the European Union requires labeling of all foods made with GMO ingredients, while the U.S only requires labeling if the foods are rendered "substantially different" by the GMOs. The differing treatments reflect noticeable differences in consumer acceptance of GMOs between Europe and the U. S. This has become an important issue in trade negotiations. It is difficult to judge the

---

[11]According to the Producer Price Index for Farm Products, and the Consumer Price Index for all urban consumers.

extent to which government opposition to genetically modified products may also be based on desires to protect their domestic producers. With viable markets for non-GMO crops in Europe, procedures for maintaining the integrity of non-GMO crops in the U.S. have become important.

Innovation underlies agricultural productivity growth, but farmers rarely develop the innovations themselves. Instead most have been developed by researchers in the nonprofit sector, including universities, government labs, and foundations, or by input suppliers, such as seed, chemical, or equipment companies. As a result, productivity growth in agriculture depends on the incentives and opportunities for research and development of innovations in related sectors, and on the speed and effectiveness with which innovations are adopted by farmers.

Farmers have strong incentives to adopt new technologies. Since individual farmers are price takers, the main way they can improve income is by reducing their costs of production and/or increasing production. Thus, they have quickly adopted new cost-reducing or output-increasing technologies. Early adopters of a technology derive only temporary benefits; cost-reducing technology results in an increased total supply of the product affected, driving down the prices and profits of early adopters and forcing late adopters to use the new technology merely to stay in business. This phenomenon is known as the technological treadmill. Because of this, the farm sector has been very progressive, and the benefits of productivity increases have largely been passed on to consumers of farm products.

Several institutional innovations have contributed to speedier adoption and diffusion of innovations among farmers. For example, the agricultural extension system, jointly financed by federal, state and county governments and administered through the land grant universities, employs a network of subject specialists and local agents to provide advice and spread new information to farmers. Private suppliers also provide information, and can more directly spread innovations through the integrated systems of production contracts used in poultry, hog, and vegetable production. Innovations in credit, beginning in the 1930s, also eased the adoption of innovations since that time.

Some have argued that, by reducing price risks, commodity programs led to more rapid adoption of innovations and faster productivity growth. Specifically, improved productivity growth in agriculture began in the 1930s, and accelerated in the next decade. Further, the timing is no coincidence, and the commodity programs also introduced in the 1930s, led to wider adoption of new technologies by reducing the financial risks facing farmers.

This argument is important because it points to long-run cumulating gains: if commodity programs actually caused productivity to grow by, for example, 1 percent more per year for many years, the gains from lower costs could substantially outweigh the static efficiency losses associated with distorted price signals. However, other factors likely accounted for the acceleration seen in Figure 1-4. In particular, public and private investments in science and in research and development had been accelerating in the years prior to the productivity take-off and continued to expand for many years thereafter. Extension programs and financial innovations, which directly assist adoption, were also expanded during the 1930s and thereafter. Because other factors can explain innovation and diffusion, the argument that commodity programs sped adoption is not widely accepted.

The productivity measure shown earlier in Figure 1-4 does not account for the environmental stresses created by modern agriculture. Crop production entails the application of substantial quantities of chemical inputs to the land. Chemical fertilizers, herbicides and pesticides can contaminate groundwater supplies and degrade nearby streams and rivers; via transport along those rivers, they can impose substantial environmental damages on ocean bays and coasts. They also can create potentially serious health risks for farm operators and workers.

Modern industrialized livestock and poultry operations, which concentrate large numbers of hogs, chickens, turkeys, dairy cows or beef cattle into confined feeding operations, create another potentially serious hazard because they also concentrate animal manure and poultry litter. Odors from the wastes impose substantial air quality "costs" on neighbors. Animal wastes can be spread as fertilizer on nearby fields, but when spread in heavy concentrations can contribute to water pollution. Some treatment alternatives mitigate water pollution concerns but create air pollution. Storage facilities can fail, creating catastrophic events in particular river systems.

In economic analysis, we can view the pollution caused by agricultural activities as a negative externality, resulting when farm activities impose uncompensated costs on others, and causing a failure of the price system to fully reflect all costs. Economists often propose solutions to externalities through adjustments to the price system, that is, by taxing processes that generate diseconomies or subsidizing actions that ameliorate the externalities. Federal conservation programs frequently aim to subsidize ameliorating actions in agriculture, while other federal and state policies aim at directly regulating the offending conduct. For example, in many states "industrial livestock farms" must have manure disposal plans approved by state and county agencies before they are permitted to build, must maintain buffer strips along streams and are not allowed to spread manure during periods when the ground is frozen. Some agricultural chemicals, such as DDT, have been banned; others are restricted as to their use.

Competition generates unremitting pressure to extract greater output from available resources and passes these productivity gains on to consumers in the form of lower prices and higher standards of living. However, in doing so, the market operates without regard for the fate or the feelings of the people involved. Modern agriculture has not only forced many family farmers out of business but also impacted the economic viability of local communities. Very large farms often bypass local merchants, buy needed supplies directly from manufacturers and market their output to more distant buyers. Thus, the decline of small family farms has also led to a decline in many rural communities.

A performance assessment of U.S. agriculture and the U.S. food system depends upon the criteria used. If the goal is a food production and delivery system that emphasizes efficiency, low prices and generally acceptable and safe food products, the U.S. system would score well. If the goal is a system that emphasizes very high product quality, genetic diversity, environmental benefits and rural communities, the U.S. system would score less well. The industrial model that has been adopted in the U.S. to achieve high productivity and generally low food prices is a model of efficiency through uniformity. Attributes such as taste, impact on the environment, health and safety of food, treatment of animals, and impact on small farmers and rural communities receive less attention than many people feel is warranted. This is one of the weaknesses of competitive markets; attributes that are not easily expressed in market prices can receive too little attention by either producers or customers.[12]

▬▬▬ IV. Public Policy

The Federal government supports agricultural research and the diffusion of research findings to farmers; produces and disseminates information designed to improve the operation of agricultural markets; and subsidizes crop insurance and credit programs aimed at farmers. The government provides substantial indirect support to dairy and sugar farmers through programs that restrict imports and remove production from domestic markets in order to raise the prices they receive. But the majority of taxpayer support to farmers is now provided through payments made directly to farmers in three major categories: conservation payments, ad hoc and emergency payments, and commodity programs. In the last decade such payments ranged from $7 billion (in 1996) to over $24 billion (in 2005) (Table 1-5). Conservation payments amounted to $2.8 billion in 2005, with $1.8 billion of that spent to take erodible land out of production under the Conservation Reserve Program (CRP). The CRP was first included in the 1985 farm bill and currently removes 37 million acres (an area slightly larger than the state of Iowa) from agricultural production under 10 to 15 year contracts that require the land to be placed in grass, trees, or other soil conserving practices. It is a very popular program with environmentalists and sportsmen. Under CRP, enrolled landowners receive annual payments comparable to market rent in their area. Since

TABLE 1-5   Direct Federal Government Payments to Farmers, 2003-2006

Program Type	2003	2004	2005	2006
		—Millions of dollars—		
Commodity Programs	11,486	10,060	18,405	13,951
Direct Payments	6,704	5,242	5,199	5,250
Counter-cyclical Payments	2,301	1,122	4,074	4,185
LDPs & Marketing Loan Gains	774	2,990	5,407	2,060
Other Commodity Payments	1,707	706	3,725	2,456
Conservation Programs	2,167	2,320	2,767	2,900
Ad Hoc & Emergency Programs	3,142	583	3,168	1,338
Total: All Direct Payments	16,795	12,963	24,340	18,196

Source: USDA Economic Research Service, at www.ers.usda.gov/Briefing/FarmPolicy/

---

[12]Several organizations are trying to develop procedures that allow consumers to choose food produced by farms that fairly and humanely treat their workers and livestock, avoid genetically modified crops and livestock, reduce the use of pesticides and hormones, conserve soil and water resources, and provide a reasonable return to family farms. For example, the Association of Family Farms hopes to provide a seal of certification on products produced under such standards. Many local and regional organizations have similar goals of allowing consumers to choose a type of food production and marketing system different from the dominant system. Whether these efforts will have a more widespread impact, as has the organic movement, remains to be seen. European countries place much more emphasis on knowing the type of farm that produces various food products.

the CRP reduces the total acres planted to agricultural production in the U.S., it tends to bolster commodity prices.

The CRP is part of an expanding set of policy tools aimed at agriculture's effects on the environment. Under another policy initiative, the Environmental Quality Incentives Program (EQIP), USDA spent $995 million in 2005 to provide technical assistance, cost-sharing, and incentive payments to farmers to undertake various practices on the farm aimed at promoting environmental quality. Since 1985, the government has also sought to leverage the money spent under commodity programs by requiring those who wish to receive commodity payments to meet minimal levels of environmental compliance. For example, farms in unglaciated southwestern Wisconsin must have a conservation plan and adhere to the plan to participate in corn, soybean, dairy or other federal programs. The compliance mechanisms are very important environmental policy tools because most federal government payments to farmers (75 percent in 2005) are made under commodity programs. Most farmers want to be eligible to participate in commodity programs and also recognize that sound conservation practices are in their long-run interests.

Commodity programs have been at the center of farm policy debates since the 1930s and are major issues in agricultural trade negotiations. Supporters argue that agriculture is subject to significant risks that can deter farmers from investing in productivity-enhancing technologies, and that government programs can and should limit such risks. They also argue that such risks are particularly important for field crops, the focus of most commodity program expenditures.

Critics assert that the programs do not improve productivity, but rather shift income from taxpayers to relatively high-income households, and exacerbate environmental damages. More broadly, critics argue that U.S. commodity programs, as well as those used in other industrialized countries, lead to increased production and lower market prices. In turn, reduced world prices for such widely traded commodities harm producers elsewhere, especially in low-income countries.[13]

U.S. commodity programs are primarily directed at land that has traditionally been planted to barley, corn, oats, peanuts, rice, sorghum, soybeans, upland cotton, or wheat. Today's programs feature three tools: direct payments, countercyclical payments, and marketing loans.[14]

Direct payments are fixed annual payments provided to operators of land that has historically been enrolled in a commodity program (known as base acres). The amount received per acre depends on past yields from the land and a payment rate per bushel that is set in legislation and varies by commodity.

Countercyclical payments are provided when market prices fall below a target price. Target prices are set in legislation and vary by commodity. Payments are made on

---

[13]This is the essence of arguments brought against U.S. agricultural policies by Brazil in World Trade Organization (WTO) proceedings. The U.S. accounts for 40 percent of world cotton exports; Brazil, which is also a major producer and exporter of cotton, argues that elements of U.S. commodity programs harm Brazilian producers by driving down world prices, and has sought relief under the WTO's dispute resolution process.

[14]Congress sets farm policies and the tools of commodity programs in legislation known as the Farm Bill, which is revised every 4 to 7 years. Commodity loans have been a tool of agricultural policy since the 1930s, although their use has varied over time. Direct and countercyclical payments have been introduced more recently. Other tools, such as acreage controls and marketing quotas that raise market prices for commodities, were widely used in the past.

the same base as direct payments (base acreage and past average yields), and vary with the gap between the target price and the market price of a commodity.

Marketing loans constitute the third major tool. Producers of designated commodities can receive a postharvest loan, equal to a commodity-specific loan rate per unit of production, with the production pledged as collateral. Repayment can be made at the loan rate (plus interest), or at an alternative loan repayment rate that essentially allows producers to pay back the loan at the commodity's market price, which can be below the loan rate. For example, the loan rate for corn was $1.95 a bushel in 2006; after harvest, the farmer could borrow $1.95 on each bushel, and if the price fell to $1.75, repay the loan at that ($1.75) rate, thus realizing a gain of 20 cents a bushel. Such payments increase as market prices fall and, unlike the other tools, payments are based on current production.

Effect of Commodity Payments on Farm Revenues

Figure 1-9 illustrates the effects of commodity payments on farm revenues, using corn production as an example. If an acre yields 140 bushels of corn, the line a-b-c-d shows that market revenue per acre will vary from $210 to $420 as price rises from $1.50 to $3.00 per bushel.[15]

▪▪▪ **FIGURE 1-9** Impact of Commodity Programs on Revenue—Corn as an Example

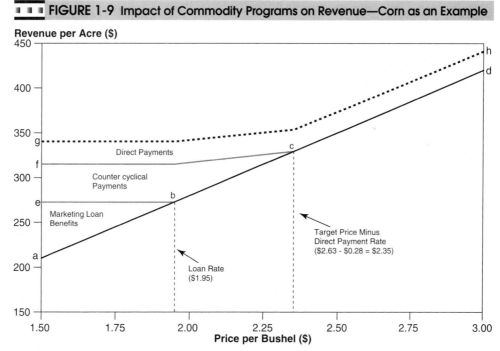

Note: *The figure represents an acre that yields 140 bushels of corn, with three key parameters that determine commodity payments: it's classed as corn base acreage, it has a direct payment yield of 102.4 bushels, and a counter cyclical payment yield of 114.4 bushels.*

---

[15]This analysis is derived from work by economists Paul Westcott, Edwin Young and Michael Price, as illustrated in their report *The 2002 Farm Act: Provisions and Implications for Commodity Markets* (USDA Economic Research Service, Agriculture Information Bulletin No. AIB778, November, 2002).

Marketing loans provide benefits whenever the market price falls below $1.95 (assuming the 2006 loan rate); the program sets an effective price floor for farmers and shifts the revenue curve to the line e-b-c-d. Countercyclical payments are made when the market price falls below $2.35 per bushel (the target price of $2.63 minus the direct payment of $0.28), and the size of countercyclical payments increases as the price falls from $2.35 to $1.95. When combined with marketing loan payments, countercyclical payments shift the revenue curve to the line f-c-d. Finally, direct payments amount to 28 cents per bushel and do not vary with market prices. The three programs combine to shift the relationship between revenue and market price to the dashed line g-h.

Revenues with the programs (line g-h) are clearly less sensitive to variations in market prices than are market revenues alone (line a-b-c-d). Because payments per acre vary sharply and inversely with market prices, payments can change considerably from year to year. When commodity prices are low, payments can constitute a large share of total revenues from affected commodities.

The dramatic recent developments in corn markets illustrate the interplay between market forces and government programs. In November, 2005, the average price paid for corn at local elevators in Illinois stood at $1.75 a bushel. At that price, a farmer producing 140 bushels per acre could expect to receive revenues of $368.20 on each base acre of corn—$245 from market prices and $123.20 from government payments. But booming demand for ethanol, a fuel which can be blended with gasoline, has led to substantially increased demand for corn, a primary source of ethanol. Corn prices at Illinois local elevators rose to $3.53 by December, 2006. The 102 percent increase in market price would eliminate government payments from marketing loans and countercyclical programs. Hence, expected revenues on base acres would increase by just 45 percent, to $533.40 per acre ($494.20 from prices and $39.20 from direct payments).

Do Commodity Programs Affect Production and Market Prices?

This is a key issue in program evaluation, and the answer varies. To understand why, we look more closely at program design.

Direct payments depend on the acreage enrolled, the payment rate, and historic yields. Because the level of production in any particular year has no effect on direct payments for that year, farmers have no short-run incentive to produce more. In fact, direct payments are made as long as the land is held in an agricultural use, even if the crop is not produced.[16] From a longer-run perspective, the direct payment program may encourage farmers to maintain their base acreage because they expect future payments to be updated based on their actual plantings. In this sense, the program may result in more acres being planted to corn, wheat and other program commodities than would occur without the program.

Like direct payments, countercyclical payments are made on historic yields of base acreage from cropland and are not tied to changes in current production. Therefore, since the payments do not affect the marginal revenue that the farmer can expect to

---

[16]"Agricultural uses" include grazing, and idling the land. As a result, landowners who do not farm can continue to receive payments. Recipients may not, however, convert their land to fruit or vegetable production. This restriction provides an indirect benefit to fruit and vegetable producers by limiting production of those commodities.

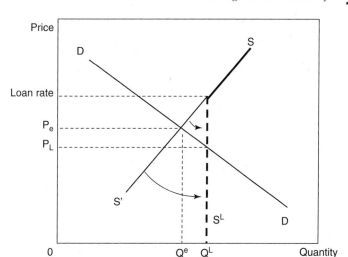

▪ ▪ ▪ **FIGURE 1-10** Effects of a Marketing Loan Program

receive from a crop, economic theory suggests they would not cause production to increase. However, farmers are also responsive to their risk exposure. Countercyclical payments do reduce the price-related revenue risk if a base crop is planted and therefore may encourage increased production of crops covered by the countercyclical program.

Marketing loans clearly can affect production and commodity prices. Figure 1-10 describes how this works, using standard demand and supply curves, with equilibrium price, Pe, and Quantity, Qe. Under the terms of the program, the loan rate sets the minimum the farmer will receive. As a result, the supply curve effectively rotates at the loan rate, from SS' to SS^L, making the supply curve perfectly inelastic at any market price below the loan rate.[17] As a result, quantity produced increases to Q^L, and the market price falls to P^L.

Marketing loans take effect when prices are relatively low and essentially prevent farmers from being subject to prices below the loan rate. Because of this, marketing loans can encourage production that is larger than would be forthcoming without the program, and can thereby reduce market prices and increase price variability. We can use standard tools of economic analysis to evaluate how large the quantity and price effects are likely to be.

Note that the effect of the program on production (the shift of quantity from Q^e to Q^L) depends on the wedge between the loan rate and the equilibrium price and on the price elasticity of supply. For example, if the loan rate is 10 percent above the equilibrium price, and the price elasticity of supply is 0.2, then the effect of the program will be to raise production by 2 percent; larger price elasticities will give larger production effects.

---

[17]If the loan rate sets the effective minimum price to farmers, in theory they will respond by producing the quantity consistent with the loan rate, no matter how far market prices fall; hence quantity supplied will be unresponsive to market prices below the loan rate.

Given the increased supply, market prices will have to fall enough to equate quantity demanded with production, a change given by the reciprocal of the price elasticity of demand. Thus, if the price elasticity of demand was -0.5, and production increased by 2 percent, market price would have to fall by 4 percent (2*(1/-0.5)) to induce enough additional demand to equate quantity supplied and quantity demanded. The more inelastic the demand, the larger the price decline needed to equate supply and demand.

One additional complication appears in the analysis. Marketing loans are made to domestic (U.S.) producers, and hence directly affect only U.S. supply. But most of the commodities covered by the marketing loan program are traded in global export markets; the relevant demand is therefore world demand. Thus the effect of a change in U.S. production on world prices can be approximated by including the U.S. share of global exports in the analysis, such that the effect on prices will be equal to the product of the U.S. quantity change, the U.S. export share, and the reciprocal of the world demand elasticity.

The supply elasticity is a key factor in evaluating the impact of U.S. commodity programs. Those who argue that the programs have strong impacts on world prices, reducing them by 8 to 15 percent (depending on the commodity), also argue that supply is responsive to price, with elasticities around 1.0. In contrast, those who argue that the effects are considerably smaller believe that supply elasticities are much lower, in the range of 0.2 to 0.4.[18]

Who Benefits from Farm Payments?

Commodity payments are limited to producers of certain commodities, primarily field crops. As crop production shifted to larger farms, payments followed, flowing to larger farms and higher-income operators. By 2003, USDA data show that most (50.1 percent) commodity program payments flowed to farms whose operators earned at least $75,770 in annual household income, and more than one quarter of payments flowed to farms whose operators earned at least $160,142.

However, payments do not add dollar-for-dollar to farmer household incomes, because payments also raise farm expenses, primarily by raising land rents. About half of all U.S. cropland is rented, and large operations usually rent more. Farm payments raise the value of an acre of cropland, and competition among farmers for land will drive up the rents paid to landlords for the land. Moreover, if payments lead to increased production and reduced feed prices, then some of the benefits will be passed through to livestock producers. As a result, the constituency in favor of commodity programs includes landowners, farmers who are direct recipients of payments, and other farmers who realize higher revenues or lower input prices because of the programs. Because farmers and landowners reap substantial benefits from the programs, they have strong incentives to support them actively through political action.

---

[18]The supply elasticity for all supported commodities will be considerably lower than that for any single commodity, such as corn, because corn production can be expanded by shifting land from other field crops. Thus changes in support for one commodity will have larger production and price effects on that commodity if support for other commodities is unchanged.

CONCLUSION

U.S. agriculture is not without its limitations. However, from an efficiency, productivity and cost standpoint, it has had remarkable performance over the last century. The rapid and enduring growth in productivity and the passing on of most of the benefits to American consumers reflects the combination of an atomistic farm structure constantly hungry for productivity improvements; the generators of technological change in land grant universities, federal government, and private industry; and the lack of any long-term market power in farming. Agricultural industries behave very much like purely competitive industries are expected to behave and, in the U.S., have benefited from the engines of technological change in the public sector that have been essential partners with U.S. farmers.

SUGGESTIONS FOR FURTHER READING

Publications

Gardner, Bruce L. *American Agriculture in the Twentieth Century*. Cambridge: Harvard University Press. 2002.

Marion, Bruce W. and NC 117 Committee, *The Organization and Performance of the U.S. Food System*, Lexington, MA: Lexington Books. 1986.

Winston, Mark L. *Travels in the Genetically Modified Zone*. Cambridge: Harvard University Press. 2002.

Web sites

U.S. Department of Agriculture. Economic Research Service. *Briefing Rooms*. http://www.ers.usda.gov/Briefing/

CHAPTER 2

The Petroleum Industry

STEPHEN MARTIN

A company's most valuable asset is its customers.
–Business school saying.

Just as fossilized footprints mark the passage of a great dinosaur long after the dinosaur itself is gone, so the record of fluctuations in the price of crude oil marks passages in the world oil market. The tracks of major political events can be seen in Figure 2-1: the Arab-Israeli War of October 1973, the fall of the Shah of Iran in January 1979, Iranian counteroffensives in January 1981 during the Iran-Iraq War, the First and Second Gulf Wars, and Hurricane Katrina. Economic changes, which for the most part are less dramatic but have longer-lasting effects, also underlie the movements depicted in Figure 2-1.[1] Some of these economic changes are:

- the shift in ownership and control over Mideast crude-oil reserves from vertically integrated, Western-based international oil companies ("the majors") to national oil companies;
- the development by the majors of new oil supplies, outside OPEC control;
- the diffusion of energy-conserving practices on the demand side of the market and of high-technology production techniques on the supply side of the market;
- the vertical integration of national companies forward into refining and distribution; and
- the return of international majors to nationalized oil provinces.

The market for crude oil is a world market, and one that is rich in lessons for students of industrial economics. It illustrates the ease with which firms may engage in limited collusion, and the difficulty with which they engage in complete collusion. It illustrates the endogeneity of market structure and the importance of vertical market structure for horizontal market performance. It also illustrates governments' lack of understanding of and lack of faith in market processes.

---

[1]The source for the nominal price data upon which Figure 2-1 is based is the U.S. Department of Energy, Energy Information Administration, http://tonto.eia.doe.gov/dnav/pet/pet_pri_imc1_k_m.htm.

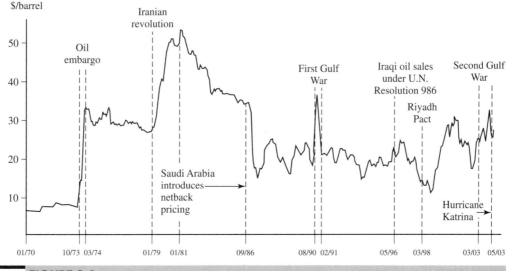

FIGURE 2-1 Real Price per Barrel of Crude Oil, January 1970–December 2006 (2006 Dollars).

We will examine the economic and political forces that have determined the performance of the world oil market and the U.S. oil submarket. Some of the questions we address are: What industry characteristics have allowed the exercise of market power, and by whom? What industry characteristics limit the exercise of market power? What has been the role of the major oil companies in the market, and what has been the role of smaller, independent companies? How have government policies affected the market? What does industrial economics suggest concerning likely future market performance?

▪▪▪ I. Structure And Structural Change

The petroleum industry is made up of four vertically related stages: production, refining, marketing, and transportation. Production involves the location and extraction of oil and natural gas from underground reservoirs; these may be so close to the surface that their oil seeps up through the ground, or they may require extensive drilling from platforms located miles offshore. The refinery segment manufactures finished products ranging from petroleum coke to motor gasoline and jet fuel. Wholesale and retail marketers distribute these products to consumers. Connecting these three vertical levels is a specialized transportation industry, including pipelines, tankers, barges and trucks, that moves crude oil from fields to refineries and finished product from refineries to marketers.

In principle, these four vertically related segments might be supplied by independent firms, and at some times and in some places this has been the case. But throughout the history of the industry, the tendency has been for firms to integrate vertically and operate all along the line from production to distribution. These vertical links have been and continue to be critical in determining industry structure-performance relationships.

TABLE 2-1 Ownership Shares in Middle East Joint Ventures, 1970

	Aramco	*Kuwait Oil Company*	*Iranian Consortium*	*Iraq Petroleum Company*
Exxon	30		7	11.875
Texaco	30		7	
Gulf		50	7	
Chevron	30		7	
Mobil	10		7	11.875
Royal Dutch/Shell			14	23.75
British Petroleum		50	40	23.75
CFP (Total)			6	23.75
Others			5	5

▪▪▪▪▪▪▪▪▪

Source: Schneider, Steven A. The Oil Price Revolution, p. 40, © 1983 The John Hopkins University Press. Reprinted with permission of The Johns Hopkins University Press.

Domination By The International Majors

During the decade or so immediately following World War II, the world oil market was dominated by the seven vertically integrated major oil companies. The Seven Sisters were actually eight,[2] including the French firm Compagnie Française des Pétroles (CFP, later Total). Five of these firms were based in the United States, and three of these five (Exxon, Mobil, and Chevron) were survivors of the landmark 1911 antitrust decision that dismantled the Standard Oil Trust.[3] The other two were British Petroleum (BP) and Royal Dutch/Shell. BP was half-owned by the British government. CFP was 25 percent owned by the French government, and effectively a public firm. Both are early examples of the continuing government belief that "oil [is] too important to be left to the oil companies."[4]

Together, these eight firms controlled 100 percent of 1950 production of crude oil outside North America and the Communist bloc. Twenty years later, their combined share remained slightly above 80 percent.

The basis for this control was the system of joint ventures—partial horizontal integration—under which the vertically integrated majors divided ownership of the operating companies that exploited Middle East oilfields, the richest in the world (see Table 2-1).

This interconnecting network of joint ventures developed with the support of the home governments of the international majors, each concerned, for reasons of national security, to ensure the access of domestically based firms to crude petroleum reserves. Thus, the U.S. Department of State induced American firms to take part in the 1928 "Red Line Agreement," which formalized control of the Iraq Petroleum Company.

[2]Such is the power of alliteration.

[3]In a certain sense, they were second-generation survivors, each being a combination of Standard Oil survivor firms. Exxon combined Standard Oil of New Jersey and the Anglo-American Oil Company; Mobil, for part of its life known as Socony-Vacuum, combined Standard Oil of New York and Vacuum Oil Company; and Chevron combined Standard Oil of California and Standard Oil of Kentucky.

[4]Anthony Sampson, *The Seven Sisters* (Bantam Books, 1976), 68.

The French government set up Compagnie Française des Pétroles to exploit its share of the Iraq concession.

The British government was similarly involved in the 1934 agreement that divided the Kuwait operating company between Gulf and BP. The U.S. government was instrumental in the 1948 reorganization of the Arabian-American Oil Company (Aramco) as a joint venture of Exxon, Texaco, Chevron, and Mobil to produce Saudi Arabian crude oil. The Iranian consortium—which delivered Persian oilfields into the hands of the seven majors, CFP, and a handful of American independents—was established after a CIA-backed coup returned the Shah of Iran to power in August 1953 (reversing the nationalization of Iranian oil by the Mossadegh government). The fact that such a joint venture involving five American firms was contrary to U.S. antitrust law was set aside, at the urging of the Department of State, for reasons of national security.

The ongoing contacts required for the management of these joint ventures resulted in a sharing of information and a commonality of interest that is inconsistent with the kind of independent decision-making that is characteristic of competition in a market economy:

> [T]he international companies' vertical integration was complemented in practice by a degree of informal but effective horizontal integration. Their joint ownership of operating companies in the Middle East, and their voting rights under the complex operating agreements through which they controlled exploration, development and offtake there, gave them a unique degree of knowledge of each others' opportunities to increase crude offtake, and some leverage to influence each others' opportunities.[5]

The Mideast joint ventures were operated under restrictions that had the effect of ensuring output limitations. For example, partners in the Iraq Petroleum Company were obliged to file their requirements for crude oil five years in advance. Each partner thus gained definite information about the plans of every other partner. A firm that filed requirements for expanded output would telegraph its plans to rivals, exposing itself to immediate retaliation.[6]

With the international majors joined by an extensive network of horizontal and vertical linkages, the world oil market operated as a small-numbers oligopoly in which rivalry manifested itself in development of reserves, in marketing efforts, and in the development of brand names but not, in general, in price competition. The prosperity of the international majors depended on secure access to crude oil deposits. But with concessions to produce from such deposits in many parts of the world, solid political support from their home country governments, and control over channels of distribution

---

[5]J. E. Hartshorn, *Oil Trade: Politics and Prospects* (Cambridge: Cambridge University Press, 1993), 117. The economic and political tensions among the international cartel partners are described in Walter Adams and James W. Brock, "Retarding the development of Iraq's oil resources: an episode in oleaginous diplomacy, 1927–1939," *Journal of Economic Issues* (March 1993): 69–93.

[6]M. A. Adelman, *The World Petroleum Market* (Baltimore: Johns Hopkins, 1972), 84–87. Stigler's theory of oligopoly explains why joint ventures affect market performance: The more rapidly is cheating likely to be detected, and therefore subject to retaliation, the less likely is cheating to occur. George J. Stigler, "A Theory of Oligopoly," *Journal of Political Economy* 72, no. 1, (February 1964): 44–61; reprinted in George J. Stigler, *The Organization of Industry* (Homewood, IL: Richard D. Irwin, Inc. 1968), 39–63.

to final consumers, the majors were relatively immune to pressure by the governments of the less developed countries where the highest-quality deposits were located.

The same firms dominated supply on the world market and the U.S. submarket, but government regulations kept the two separate. From the 1930s until the 1950s, controls on oil production by state governments (importantly, the Texas Railroad Commission) held crude oil prices in the United States at artificially high levels.[7] These prices proved attractive to foreign suppliers, and by 1948 the United States became a net importer of refined oil products. Three congressional investigations of the matter in 1950 revealed to the oil companies a congressional preference for low imports. When domestic oil producers raised the price of U.S. crude oil in June 1950, the U.S. coal industry, with the support of the petroleum industry, sponsored a bill to place import quotas on petroleum. The Eisenhower Administration set up "voluntary" import-restraint programs in 1954 and 1958, and when these proved ineffective, imposed mandatory quotas in 1959.

These formal and informal restrictions on the flow of oil into the United States meant higher prices for U.S. consumers, perhaps by as much as $3 billion to $4 billion a year.[8] At a time when the price of crude oil on the Eastern seaboard was about $3.75 a barrel, a cabinet task force estimated that the elimination of oil-import quotas would reduce the price of crude oil by $1.30 a barrel.[9]

Although the quotas had been justified on national security grounds, the effect of high U.S. prices in an artificially isolated market was to encourage the extraction of relatively high-cost U.S. crude oil, accelerating the depletion of U.S. reserves and conserving lower-cost reserves elsewhere in the world. It became clear, in 1973, that U.S. national security would have been better served if the pattern of extraction had been reversed.

Rise of Independent Oil Companies

One of the most important lessons of modern industrial economics is that market structure is itself the product of economic forces. The world oil market provides more than one example. Within limits, the Seven Sisters could hold the price of crude oil at artificially high levels. But they could not control entry. Their domination of the world oil market set in motion a process of entry by new firms in search of profit. This process occupied the period from the mid-1950s through 1973, and triggered a transition from a market dominated by the international majors to a market dominated by the governments of producing countries.

The first step in the transition was the 1954 Iranian consortium, when the U.S. government insisted that the majors make room for nine independents. Having gained a toehold in the Middle East, the independents sought to expand their roles. Just as the majors had once been able to play host nation against host nation by shifting production

---

[7]Decades later, OPEC was to use the Texas Railroad Commission as a model; see Robert Mabro "OPEC behavior 1960–1998," *Journal of Energy Literature* 4, no. 1 (June 1998): 8.
[8]S. A. Schneider, *The Oil Price Revolution* (Baltimore: Johns Hopkins, 1983), 46.
[9]U.S. Congress. Senate. Subcommittee on Antitrust and Monopoly, Committee on the Judiciary. The Petroleum Industry: Part 4, The Cabinet Task Force on Oil Import Control (Washington, D.C.: U.S. Government Printing Office, March 1970).

from country to country to resist pressure to expand output, so host nations gained the option of playing independent companies against major companies.

In 1956, Libya granted concessions to 17 firms. Independents subsequently accounted for half of Libyan output, and in due course products refined from this oil found their way to European markets.[10]

The activities of Enrico Mattei, head of the Italian national firm Ente Nazionale Idrocarburi (ENI), had far-reaching consequences. He sought access to oil supplies in Iran and elsewhere, and ultimately found it in the Soviet Union. After 1959, products refined from Russian oil joined the flow of independent oil onto world markets.

The increased flow of oil from these various independent sources created an excess supply at prevailing prices, despite rapidly expanding demand. The result was downward pressure on prices, which the international majors could not resist. But the governments of the oil producing nations collected taxes based on a "posted price" for oil, a paper price that was largely divorced from transactions prices. From the companies' point of view, the posted-price system worked well as long as transaction prices were level or rising. Falling transaction prices combined with unchanging posted prices meant that an increasing share of profit went to host countries in the form of taxes that were levied based on the posted price.

In August 1960, Exxon reduced its posted prices for oil. The remaining major firms followed suit. This reduction in the posted prices for oil was no more than a reflection of reductions in transaction prices. The reduction in transaction prices was the natural result of a more rapid expansion in supply than in demand. The more rapid expansion in supply than in demand was, in turn, a result of the actions of the host countries, which had granted independents access to crude supplies as a way of breaking the grip of the Seven Sisters on the world oil market.

The reduction in posted prices was, therefore, an inevitable consequence of the actions of host countries. But it appeared to them as a unilateral reduction in their own tax revenues, imposed by international corporations. The reaction came at a September 1960 meeting of Saudi Arabia, Iran, Iraq, Kuwait, and Venezuela, when it was agreed to establish the Organization of Petroleum Exporting Countries—OPEC.

The 13 years that followed the formation of OPEC saw a long dance between the two loosely coordinated oligopolies, one of the international majors and one of producing countries. At the start of this dance, the balance of power lay with the companies; at the end, it lay with the countries.

Although OPEC member states were beneficiaries of this shift in power, they did not initiate it. The international companies had a long history of effective cooperation, and they were better at it than the producing countries. By negotiating on a country-by-country basis, the major companies were able to prevent the countries from combining their bargaining power. OPEC was able to prevent further declines in the posted price, but it was not able to reverse the reductions in the posted price that had prompted OPEC's formation.

The catalyst for change was the interaction of independent companies and the revolutionary government of a relatively new oil province, Libya. Colonel Muamer Qadaffi's government took power in September 1969, and soon set about renegotiating

---

[10]Sampson, *Seven Sisters*, 174–175.

the terms of Libyan oil concessions. As we have already remarked, independent oil firms had major roles in exploiting these concessions, and the independents were in a much weaker bargaining position, vis-à-vis the host countries, than the majors. Any one of the integrated majors, faced with an unattractive proposal from a producing country, could credibly threaten to reduce output in that country and turn to supplies elsewhere around the world. Independent companies had no such alternative.

In August 1970, Occidental Petroleum Company agreed to Libyan demands for higher prices and higher taxes. This example inspired other oil producing nations. In February 1971, oil companies agreed in Tehran to the higher price demanded by the Shah of Iran. The major oil companies revised the terms of their arrangement with Libya in April 1971.[11]

The oil producing countries had demonstrated their ability to control the terms upon which oil was lifted from their territories. But it was the major companies that owned the operating companies, through their joint ventures (see Table 2-1). This too was to change.

Again it was the radical states, rather than OPEC, that led the way. Algeria nationalized 51 percent of French ownership in Algerian reserves in February 1971; Libya nationalized British Petroleum's interests in November 1971; Iraq nationalized the Iraqi Petroleum Company in June 1972. Long negotiations between Saudi Arabia and Aramco followed. Aramco agreed to yield an initial 25 percent of its Saudi Arabian concession to Saudi Arabia.[12]

In the absence of intervening political developments, the transfer of control of the world market from the international majors to the producing countries would likely have continued at a gradual pace. The producing countries would have slowly replaced the international majors, with little change in market performance. In such an alternative reality, the Western "man in the street" would have remained blissfully unfamiliar with the nature of the world oil market. Events unfolded rather differently.

OPEC

The 1970s opened with the demand for oil increasing throughout the industrial world. Figure 2-2 shows the steady growth of the U.S. oil demand through the 1960s and early 1970s. Similar growth took place in Europe and Japan. In 1973, with simultaneous booms in North America, Europe, and Japan, world demand for energy—and oil—was at an all time high.

At the same time, supply and the control of supply were increasingly concentrated in the low-cost Middle East. In 1970, proved reserves[13] of crude oil in the Middle East were 333,506 million barrels, versus 67,431 million barrels of proved reserves in the Western Hemisphere and 54,680 million barrels in Africa.

---

[11]Ibid., 253–272.

[12]Ibid., 278–282. On the eventual end of this process, see Youssef M. Ibrahim, "A U.S. era closes at Aramco," *International Herald Tribune* (April 6, 1989): 13.

[13]The American Petroleum Institute definition of proved reserves is: Proved reserves of crude oil are the estimated quantities of all liquids statistically defined as crude oil, which geological and engineering data demonstrate with reasonable certainty to be recoverable in future years from known reservoirs under existing economic and operating conditions.

■ ■ ■ FIGURE 2-2 U.S. Demand for Refined Petroleum Products, 1970–2006.

Source: American Petroleum Institute (2007, Section VII, Table 2).

The location and development of crude oil reserves is a time-consuming process, particularly when oil fields are located offshore or in other hostile climates. Thus, the 1970s opened with a relatively small short-run supply of crude oil available from fringe, non-OPEC suppliers. These fringe suppliers faced substantially higher costs—development and operating costs—than Middle East producers (Table 2-2).

TABLE 2-2 Oil and Gas Production, Finding And Development Costs ($ per barrel of oil equivalent)	
	$/barrel
Saudi Arabia	≤2
Indonesia	6
Nigeria	7
Venezuela	7
Gulf of Mexico	10
North Sea	11
Russia	14

Source: The Economist 6 March 1999, p. 23

This kind of market is illustrated in stylized fashion in Figure 2-3(a). Here fringe supply q_1^F, taken to be constant,[14] is small relative to market size; the residual demand curve left for the cartel, the part of the demand curve to the left of the dashed vertical line at q_1^F, comprises the bulk of the market. In such a market, a dominant firm or perfectly colluding cartel would maximize profit by selecting an output that equates marginal revenue along the residual demand curve—the market demand curve after subtracting fringe output—to marginal cost. In Figure 2-3(a), the corresponding cartel output is q_1^c, which would sell at price P_1. Because fringe supply is small and demand inelastic, p_1 is much above cartel marginal cost MC_c.

Since the economic interests of the OPEC member nations diverge in fundamental ways, OPEC was (and is) far from being able to act as a monopolist or a perfectly colluding cartel. It was a political rather than an economic event that triggered coordinated OPEC action and allowed it to take advantage of a demand—supply relationship of the kind depicted in Figure 2-3(a). In reaction to Western support for Israel during the Egypt-Israeli War of October 1973, Arab nations imposed production cutbacks and an embargo of crude oil supplies to the West.

The international oil companies were based in the West, and they had long benefited from the political support of their home governments, governments that sought to protect their perceived national security interest in a safe supply of oil. But the international

▪ ▪ ▪ **FIGURE 2-3** **Fringe Supply and Cartel Output**

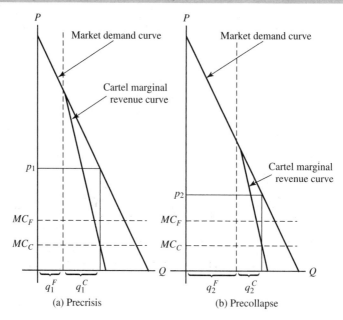

(a) Precrisis

(b) Precollapse

---

[14]It is an exaggeration to draw fringe supply as completely inelastic with respect to price (a vertical line), but only a modest one. Most of oilfield development cost is fixed and sunk, so that price would have to fall very low before fringe firms would reduce output. Given the constraints of location and development, even if price rises very high, it is not possible to expand output much in the short run. Thus the fringe supply curve will be nearly vertical.

majors administered the embargo of Western nations according to OPEC directives, going so far as to provide Saudi Arabia with information on the shipment of refined oil products to U.S. military bases around the world.[15]

As the producing countries cut back the supply of crude oil to the international majors, the international majors cut back supplies to independent companies. With their survival threatened, the independents turned to the market for oil that was not tied up by long-term contracts—the relatively narrow spot market. Independents bid up the spot-market price of oil, and official OPEC prices soon followed. The immediate result was the 1973 rise in official prices shown in Figure 2-1.

From this price increase flowed longer-run changes. OPEC revenue from the sale of oil rose from $13.7 billion in 1972 to $87.2 billion in 1974. Real U.S. gross national product, which grew 5.2 percent in 1973, fell 0.5 percent in 1973 and 1.3 percent in 1974.

Aside from the accelerated shift in control of production to the producing nations, remarkably few structural changes occurred during the period following the first price increase. U.S. demand for oil fell slightly in 1974 and 1975, but then rose to new heights by 1978 (Figure 2-2). The share of imports in the U.S. market, and specifically imports from OPEC, peaked in 1977 but remained higher than in 1973 (Figure 2-4). The pattern of consumption and supply was much the same in other industrialized countries.

▪ ▪ ▪ **FIGURE 2-4 Import and OPEC Shares of U.S. Crude Oil Supplies, 1947–2005 and 1960–2005, respectively.**

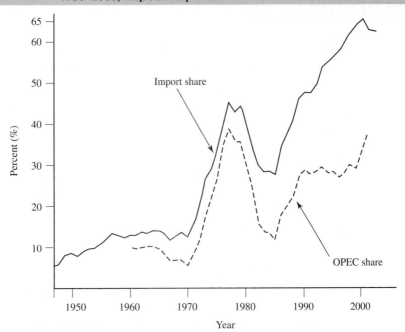

Source: American Petroleum Institute, Basic Petroleum Fact Book, 2007, Section IX, Table 2; Section X, Table 1; Section XIV, Table 4.

---

[15]Louis Turner, *Oil Companies in the International System* (London: Allen & Unwin, 1983), 136.

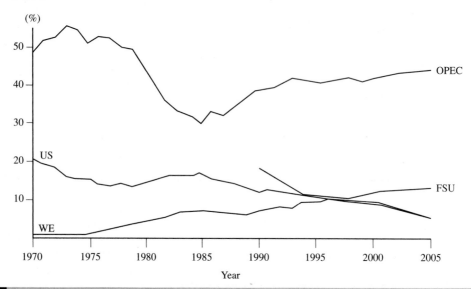

▪ ▪ ▪ ▪ **FIGURE 2-5 Shares of World Crude Petroleum Production, 1970–2005.**

Note: *Former Soviet Union (FSU), OPEC, United States (US), Western Europe (WE).*

Source: American Petroleum Institute, *Basic Petroleum Fact Book,* 2007, Section 4, Table 1, Section 14, Table 2.

As shown in Figure 2-5, OPEC's share of world crude-oil production fell only about 5 percent over the period 1973 to 1979. World production of crude oil grew throughout this period, but OPEC's production was essentially level: 30,989 thousand barrels per day in 1973, and 30,911 thousand barrels per day in 1979.

Because of the length of time needed to develop new petroleum reserves and to install energy-saving residential and industrial equipment, the underlying market conditions that greeted the fall of the Shah of Iran in January 1979 were essentially the same as those at the time of the Arab-Israeli War of 1973: peak demand, concentration of supply in the Middle East, and absence of spare capacity in the West.

The impact of the course of events on the market was also similar. Supply was disrupted. Independent refiners had their crude supplies cut off. Desperate for crude oil, they turned to the spot market, and the price of oil, shown in Figure 2-1, shot up.

Cultivation of Crude Oil Supplies Outside OPEC

The response to the second oil-price shock, on both the demand side and the supply side of the market, was different from the response to the first oil-price shock. As shown in Figure 2-6, energy use in relation to gross domestic product in the European Union, Japan, and the United States rose over the decade preceding the first oil shock. Energy use declined in the United States and Japan from the first oil shock, and was essentially level in the European Union over the period between the first and second oil price shocks. Since then the intensity of energy use has declined in all three regions, slightly in Japan and the European Union, more so in the United States. Energy use in

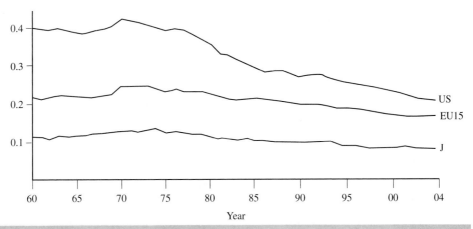

▪ ▪ ▪ ▪ **FIGURE 2-6** Total Primary Energy Supply (in millions of tons of oil equivalent) per Billion Dollars of Gross Domestic Product (measured in 2000 U.S. dollars), 1960–2004.

Note: European Union (EU15), Japan (J), United States (U. S.).
Source: International Energy Agency, *Energy Balances of OECD Countries*, digital database.

relation to gross domestic product in the European Union and Japan is consistently lower than in the United States.

These changes illustrate the long response time required to realize changes in the demand for energy resources. There was a long-term shift to greater efficiency in energy use, partly due to the higher real price of energy and partly to increasing concern about the impact of energy consumption on the environment. Demand for energy, and oil, was lower in the 1980s (Figure 2-2) than it would have been without the oil shocks of the 1970s.

There is a corresponding effect on the supply side of the market, described in Table 2-3.[16] U.S. crude oil production peaked in 1970 and has since followed a downward trend. This trend will continue, mitigated by new technology[17] but not by the discovery or exploitation of new reservoirs. Long isolated from the world market by protective quotas, the United States has been thoroughly explored. But output from Western Europe increased sharply over this period, as the North Sea oilfields of Britain and Norway came into production. North Sea oil output reached a plateau in the mid-1990s, and will decline (although technological progress continues to extend its potential beyond original expectations). The North Sea will remain an important source of natural gas.[18]

---

[16]In the "demand" column of Table 2-3, the figure given for Western Europe refers to Europe, which includes the Czech Republic, Hungary, Poland, Romania, and Slovakia. The figure given for the F.S.U. refers to the former U.S.S.R. and Eastern Europe. The figure given for Asia refers to Austral-Asia.

[17]The importance of technological advance in petroleum extraction should not be underestimated. An often prescient geologist, Eckel (*Coal Iron and War*, New York, 1920, 127) predicted in 1920 that the U.S. supply of oil would be exhausted by 1930 or 1935. See more recently Jad Mouawad, "Oil Innovations Pump New Life into Old Wells," *New York Times*, 5 March 2007, internet edition.

[18]See Steve Martin (no relation to the author of this chapter), "North Sea Oil Statistics," *Journal of Energy Literature* 3, no. 2, (December 1997): 32–48.

TABLE 2-3 World Crude Production by Area, 1974, 1985, 2005, and Estimated Demand for Refined Products, by Area

	1974		1990		2005		Demand: 2005	
	million barrels	*%*	*million barrels*	*%*	*million barrels*	*%*	*million barrels*	*%*
United States	3,203	15.6	2,685	12.4	1,890	7.1	7,592.8	25.8
Canada	617	3.0	567	2.6	865	3.2	818.0	2.8
Western Europe	142	0.7	1,314	6.1	1,845	6.9	6,430.2	21.8
Latin America	1,789	8.7	2,487	11.5	3,926	14.7	1,743.2	5.9
Asia	816	4.0	2,262	10.4	2,686	10.0	8,744.3	29.7
Eastern Europe	3,995	19.5	NA		67	0.3	—	
Former Soviet Union			3,960	18.3	4,043	15.1	1,004.8	3.4
Africa	1,990	9.7	2,174	10.0	3,234	12.1	1,008.5	3.4
Middle East	7,987	38.9	5,997	27.7	8,222	30.7	2,094.7	7.1
Total	20,538		21,664		26,777		29,436.6	

Source: American Petroleum Institute, Basic Petroleum Fact Book, 2007, Section 4, Table 1, Section 7, Table 1.

Output in Latin America rose over this period, and this trend is likely to continue. Venezuela, although a charter member of OPEC, continues to expand its oil reserves. It markets a coal-water mixture that is a good substitute for fuel oil, but exempt from OPEC output quotas. In addition, Venezuela has aggressively acquired networks of refineries and service stations, to ensure outlets for its oil. Other Latin American countries, including Peru and Columbia, continue to expand their oil industries; Mexico has increasingly cooperated with international oil companies to exploit its oil deposits.

Crude oil output from the Third World, including China and less-developed countries (LDCs) in Africa, will increase. This reflects a convergence of interest between LDCs and the international majors. Nationalizations by OPEC member states cut the international majors off from the Mideast oilfields that were for generations the foundation of their dominant market positions. They will search anywhere outside OPEC's sphere of influence for new reserves, which they can feed into their existing refining and marketing networks. They will do so as long as the new reserves can be developed for a cost at or below the spot market price for oil.

At the same time, LDCs know from bitter experience that their development efforts suffer from dependency on foreign sources of oil. For political reasons, LDCs will encourage the development of local oil supplies even if the cost seems likely to exceed the spot market price of oil. Their national security (and often the lives of their leaders) depends on it.

The same applies to the world's newest group of less developed countries, the former members of the Soviet Union. Crude oil output from these countries declined during a transitory period, as the foundations of market economies were laid. While that process is not yet complete, for these countries petroleum deposits represent a valuable source of foreign exchange, and will be exploited accordingly. Major oil companies are gingerly establishing ties in this part of the world, despite the uncertain political and legal environments.[19]

The international majors will, therefore, be welcome in the new oil provinces around the world. The supply of oil from less developed countries will increase, and to some extent this increase will result from political rather than economic considerations.

Along with the substantial increases in crude oil production outside OPEC in the 1980s came the reduction in Middle East output shown in Figure 2-5. By mid-1985, OPEC found itself in the kind of market illustrated in Figure 2-3(b). Fringe supply, after a decade of development efforts, was large in relation to the market. Demand, after a decade of conservation efforts, had grown much less rapidly than expected. The residual part of the market left for OPEC was substantially reduced, compared with the kind of situation of Figure 2-3(a). In such circumstances, the best OPEC could do would be to set a price p_2, much lower than p_1, and market a substantially smaller quantity q_1^C (see the second set of columns in Table 2-3).

Just as the international majors' long domination of the world oil market created an incentive for the entry and expansion of independent oil firms, so OPEC's somewhat briefer period of control created an incentive for the development of new oil provinces. The entry of independent firms undercut the resource base of the international majors, which reacted by seeking new supplies of oil. The entry of new oil-producing countries undercut the power base of OPEC member states, and they reacted by seeking secure outlets for their oil. The result has been a renewed trend to vertical integration, by OPEC member states and by oil companies, with horizontal concentration reduced at all levels of the industry.

The North Sea Oil Markets

Perhaps the most ironic consequence of OPEC's assertion of control over the world crude market is the development of active spot and futures markets for Brent crude blend, which has made the price of North Sea crude a bellwether for the industry and ratified OPEC's inability to do more than move along a shifting residual demand curve.

Sovereignty over North Sea oil deposits lies primarily with Britain and Norway. A large number of international oil companies exploit the North Sea oil fields through a complex web of joint ventures.[20] Concentration of production is high, although declining. Output is dominated by Exxon and Shell, whose combined market share was near 70 percent for much of the 1980s, and remained over 50 percent in 1993.[21]

North Sea oilfields benefit from a location near the major consuming centers of Europe and from a product with desirable physical properties as far as refining is concerned. North Sea oil is a good substitute for U.S. and OPEC products. For these reasons, and because the North Sea came "on line" at a time when international oil companies were scampering to acquire access to oil outside OPEC influence, the spot market for North Sea oil assumed a central place in the interlocking world network of

---

[19]See, for example, Greg Walters, "BP bid for Rosneft Stake Spurs Questions in Russia," *Wall Street Journal*, 24 March 2007, p.A3.

[20]Exxon and Shell, for example, are equal partners in all their North Sea assets.

[21]Paul Horsnell and Robert Mabro, *Oil Markets and Prices* (Oxford: Oxford University Press, 1993), 25–28.

oil markets. The economic importance of the North Sea market is far greater than its share of world oil output (never more than 6 percent). The prices of many other transactions are tied to those on the North Sea market. In times of real or perceived shortage, surges of demand on the North Sea futures market (the market for oil to be delivered one, two, or more months in the future) can drive prices up very rapidly, and often down again just as rapidly (examine Figure 2-1 for the time around the Iraqi invasion of Kuwait, which precipitated the First Gulf War).[22] The role of the price of Brent blend as a marker price for the world petroleum industry confirms OPEC's long-run inability to control the world oil market. But the picture is not entirely rosy: the spot and futures markets for North Sea oil are subject to speculative binges, and price fluctuations on these markets often have little to do with the fundamentals of supply and demand.

Consolidation and Integration

On balance, changes on the supply side of the world market for crude oil bode well for long-run market performance. Major oil companies are merging and restructuring their activities to reduce costs. State-owned oil firms, the product of the nationalizations of the 1970s, are integrating forward from production into refining and distribution, competing with the international majors at all vertical levels. An increasing number of countries that nationalized their oil industries at the dawn of the OPEC era are allowing the international majors to return, on carefully controlled terms, to develop new reserves. In a fundamental sense, the structure of the world oil market is returning to what it was before the rise of OPEC, but with a larger number of players.

August 1998 saw the merger of BP and Amoco (a Standard Oil survivor company). Amoco was short of reserves of crude oil, and the merger would permit the combined firm to scrap outmoded refineries and reduce costs. Six months later, BP Amoco proposed to take over Atlantic Richfield, another Standard Oil survivor and a company pressed by low oil prices and the high cost of extracting oil from the North Slope of Alaska.

In December 1998, Exxon and Mobil, the two largest Standard Oil survivor companies, proposed to merge. Once again, low oil prices and the value of secure access to reserves lay behind the merger. The Exxon-Mobil merger was approved by both the European Commission's Directorate General for Competition, the competition law enforcement arm of the European Union, and by the U.S. Federal Trade Commission (FTC). To obtain FTC approval, Exxon and Mobil agreed to sell off a refinery and nearly 5,000 retail gas stations, to avoid substantially increasing seller concentration in regional or local markets.

The BP Amoco–Atlantic Richfield merger was approved by the European Union. After initial hesitation (on the grounds that the merger would create too great a concentration of sales of Alaskan crude oil and worsen performance in the West Coast market for supply of crude oil to refiners), the U.S. Federal Trade Commission

---

[22]See Steven Butler, "Oil Traders Devise Strategies for the Twenty-First Century," *Financial Times*, May 25, 1990; and Horsnell and Mabro, *Oil Markets and Prices*.

approved the merger in April 2000, although the FTC required a number of divestitures before giving its approval.

Also in December 1998, the French firm Total (formerly the eighth of the seven sisters, Compagnie Française des Pétroles) acquired the Belgian firm Petrofina. In October 1999, TotalFina proposed to take over the French firm Elf Aquitaine, a combination which would ensure European representation among the major private oil firms. The European Commission approved the merger in February 2000, requiring the companies to sell off certain assets, including a number of retail outlets.

The pattern of mergers continued into the new century. October 2001 saw the combination of Chevron and Texaco to create what would be the third-largest U.S. oil and gas producer, Chevron-Texaco. In August 2003, Phillips Petroleum and Conoco merged to become ConocoPhillips.

This wave of consolidation among private firms accompanies, and in a certain sense is a consequence of, the diversification of national oil companies out of production and into refining and distribution. Such companies include Saudi Aramco, Venezuela's PDV, Brazil's Petrobras, and Norway's Statoil.[23]

Through a subsidiary of the Kuwait Petroleum Corporation, Kuwait owns two European refineries with a capacity of 135,000 barrels per day, together with 4,800 retail gasoline stations in seven different European countries. Kuwait has acquired a 22 percent ownership of British Petroleum, much to British government concern, and has sought refining assets in Japan.

Venezuela has employed joint ventures to acquire partial interests in refineries in West Germany, Sweden, Belgium, and acquired Citgo's refining and distribution operations in the United States.

Other OPEC members also integrated forward into the U.S. market. In November 1988, Saudi Arabia acquired half-ownership of Texaco, Inc.'s U.S. refining and distribution network. The three refineries involved had a capacity of 615,000 barrels per day; the distribution network included 11,450 retail gasoline stations. With this investment, the largest source of crude oil in the world moved to secure a market for its product. It also acquires an interest in maintaining profitability at the refining and distribution levels of the market, as well as the crude level.

The motives for this forward integration are partly political and partly economic. A move forward into refining is a way of broadening the local industrial base while taking advantage of existing assets and skills. At the same time, a refinery associated with a national oil company of an oil-producing state has an almost insuperable advantage when compared with an independent refiner. The real cost of crude oil to the integrated refiner is the cost of crude production (regardless of the transfer price from the crude division to the refinery division). But the cost of crude oil to an independent, nonintegrated refiner is the much higher market price for crude oil. Refining and distribution networks associated with producing nations will always be able to undersell independents. When there is a surplus of crude oil, it will be profitable to do so.

Geographically, statistics for the U.S. refining market are reported by Petroleum Administration for Defense Districts (PADDs), of which there are five (East Coast,

---

[23]The merger of Statoil with SDFI (the State's Direct Financial Interest) was proposed by Statoil management to strengthen Statoil on the way to privatization.

Midwest, Gulf Coast, Rocky Mountain, and West Coast).[24] According the U.S. Government Accountability Office (GAO),[25] the wave of oil industry mergers in the 1990s increased market concentration in regional U.S. refining markets. Their figures suggest (Table 2-4[26]) that in 1990, PADDs were as concentrated as markets supplied by between 9 and 19 equally-sized firms. By 2000, they were as concentrated as markets supplied by between 5 and 14 firms.

The GAO analyzed the impact of eight late 1990s mergers on the wholesale gasoline distribution margin. Six of the eight mergers were estimated to increase the wholesale margin by about 2 cents a gallon; the other two caused price decreases of about 1 cent a gallon. The GAO also acknowledged that[27] "Higher wholesale gasoline prices were also a result of other factors: high refinery capacity utilization rate; low gasoline inventories, which typically occur in the summer driving months; and supply disruptions, which occurred in the Midwest and on the West Coast."

The firms that supply regional U.S. refining and distribution markets are typically vertically integrated from production through retail distribution. As one would expect, regional concentration is less at the retail than at the wholesale level (compare Table 2-4

TABLE 2-4 U.S. Refining: Herfindahl Index (H) and Inverse Herfindahl Index (1/H), 1990 and 2000, by PADD

PADD	1990		2000	
	H	*1/H*	*H*	*1/H*
East Coast	0.1136	8.8	0.1819	5.5
Midwest	0.0699	14.3	0.0980	10.2
Gulf Coast	0.0534	18.7	0.0704	14.2
Rocky Mountain	0.1029	9.7	0.1124	8.9
West Coast	0.0937	10.7	0.1267	7.9

Source: U.S. Government Accountability Office, "Mergers and Other Factors that Affect the U.S. Refining Industry," Statement of Jim Wells, Director, Natural Resources and Environment Before the Subcommittee on Energy and Air Quality, Committee on Energy and Commerce, U.S. House of Representatives, 15 July 2004.

---

[24]For a breakdown of states by PADD, see the U.S. Energy Information Administration web page http://tonto.eia.doe.gov/oog/info/gdu/padddiesel.html.

[25]U.S. Government Accountability Office, "Mergers and Other Factors that Affect the U.S. Refining Industry," Statement of Jim Wells, Director, Natural Resources and Environment Before the Subcommittee on Energy and Air Quality, Committee on Energy and Commerce, U.S. House of Representatives, 15 July 2004.

[26]The Herfindahl index is the sum of squares of the market shares (measured here between zero and one) of firms supplying a market. The inverse of the Herfindahl index is the number of equally-sized firms that would generate a given value of the Herfindahl index, and is a "numbers equivalent" measure of seller concentration. See M. A. Adelman, "Comment on the 'H' Concentration Measure as a Numbers Equivalent," *Review of Economics and Statistics,* 51 (February 1969): 99–101.

[27]Ibid., 5.

TABLE 2-5 Four-(CR4) and Eight-(CR8) Firm Retail Concentration Ratios, 2006, by PADD.

PADD	CR4	CR8
East Coast	45.66	68.66
Midwest	52.28	73.76
Gulf Coast	51.38	76.87
Rocky Mountain	42.89	68.93
West Coast	60.84	89.51

Source: Energy Information Administration EIA-782C Prime Supplier Sales.

and Table 2-5).[28] But the suppliers meet in many markets, and those contacts likely impact refining and distribution market performance as much as market concentration at the refining level. In any case, fluctuations in the retail price of gasoline are largely, although not entirely, determined by fluctuations in the price of crude oil (Figure 2-7).

The firms created by the merger wave of the late 1990s are large in an absolute sense but small in proportion to the size of the market. A combined Mobil and Exxon, the largest of the lot, would supply about four percent of world crude production. Taking the rivalry of state-owned firms into account, the mergers among private firms seem unlikely to worsen performance on the world oil market.

FIGURE 2-7 Price Indices, Retail Gasoline, and Crude Oil, August 1990 = 100, August 1990–December 2006.

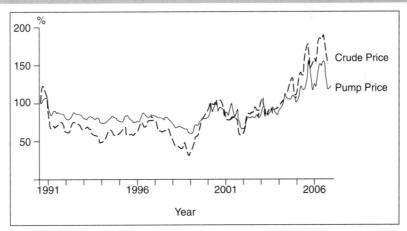

Source: American Petroleum Institute, Basic Petroleum Data Book, various issues, and U.S. Department of Energy internet database.

---

[28]It should be kept in mind that retail geographic markets are local rather than state or PADD. Seller concentration on the supply side of local retail markets will generally be higher than the PADD figures reported in Table 2-5.

An encouraging structural change is the return of the international majors to oil provinces that were nationalized in the early 1970s. Several OPEC governments have confronted the harsh reality that the development of new reserves—their source of future oil revenues—is risky and expensive. For many such governments, the economic profits collected in the 1980s are gone, spent on wars, welfare and development efforts, and the option to work with the international majors has become more attractive than once it was. When the international majors are in place, the discretion of national governments to restrict output will be reduced.[29]

▪ ▪ ▪ II. Conduct

It is sometimes asserted that the price increases of 1973 and 1979 to 1982 were no more than the working of competitive forces. In this view, favored in particular by oil producing nations, a price of oil at or near extraction cost fails to take into account the scarcity that current consumption imposes on future generations. A price substantially above marginal extraction cost, in this view, is a good thing, because it encourages conservation and spreads consumption of a finite resource over a long time period.

This argument might explain the price increases observed in 1973 and 1979 to 1982. It cannot explain the price decline from a real price[30] of more than $53 per barrel in January 1981 to under $14.50 per barrel in July 1986 (and to $10 per barrel at the end of 1998). Oil is, after all, as much a finite resource as it ever was, and if future scarcity would produce a high price in 1982 it would, seemingly, produce a still higher price moving into the 21st century. Statistical tests do not support the argument that OPEC pricing is competitive.[31]

Some analysts have suggested that the world oil industry is driven by a single dominant firm: Saudi Arabia. According to the figures in Table 2-6, Saudi Arabia holds about 20.4 percent of world proven reserves. It is widely believed that Saudi Arabia substantially understates its reserve holdings. This quantitative description does not capture the fact that Saudi crude is by far the least expensive in the world, with an estimated extraction cost less than $1 a barrel.

These reserve holdings mean that Saudi Arabia will be a factor on the world oil market so long as there is a world market for oil. If Saudi Arabia were to act as a wealth-maximizing dominant firm, it would restrict output and raise price above the cost of production. It would then gradually give up market share, as other producers expanded output to take advantage of the opportunity for profit created by the price increase.[32]

A variation on this theme suggests that although no single OPEC member has sufficient control of reserves to exercise control over price, OPEC, as a group, is able to

---

[29]The Iranian constitution prohibits granting concessions to foreign firms. Iran has therefore offered so-called "buyback agreements" to foreign firms. Under such an arrangement, foreign firms develop an oilfield for a fixed compensation, over a specified period, that is paid by Iranian receipts from the sale of oil. If the price of oil drops, Iran must sell more oil to pay the foreign developer.

[30]Measured in 2002 U.S. dollars.

[31]James M. Griffen, "OPEC Behavior: A Test of Alternative Hypotheses," *American Economic Review* 75, Number 5 (December 1985): 954–963.

[32]Darius Gaskins, "Dynamic Limit Pricing: Optimal Limit Pricing Under Threat of Entry," *Journal of Economic Theory* 3 (September 1971): 306–322.

TABLE 2-6 Estimated Proven Reserves Of Crude Oil, 2003 (billion barrels);	
Saudi Arabia	264.3
Canada	178.8
Iran	132.5
Iraq	115.0
Kuwait	101.5
United Arab Emirates	97.8
Venezuela	79.7
Former Soviet Union	77.8
Libya	39.1
Nigeria	35.9
United States	21.4
China	18.3
Qatar	15.2
Mexico	12.9
Algeria	11.4
Brazil	11.2
Norway	7.7
India	5.8
Oman	5.5
Angola	5.4
Total World	1,292.5

Source: American Petroleum Institute Basis Petroleum Fact Book, 2007, Section 2, Table 4.

act as a collusive price leader. The predicted market performance is much the same as under the dominant-firm model. OPEC's share of the market should decline over time as independent producers respond to the incentive created by a price above the cost of production.

Figures 2-1 and 2-5 suggest that the dominant-firm and dominant-group models had a certain degree of explanatory power for perhaps 12 or 15 years after the 1973 oil shock. OPEC's share of world crude-oil production fell very slowly from 1973 to 1979. As already noted, this is a reflection of the long lead times in discovery and development of oil reserves. OPEC's market share fell sharply in the 1980s, bottoming out at 30 percent of the world market in 1985. It has leveled off at around 40 percent moving into the 21st century, as OPEC has taken back market share at the expense of a lower price.

Cartel Dynamics

What the dominant-firm and dominant-group analyses do not capture is the oligopolistic interactions that flavor OPEC behavior. When price is raised above the cost of production, individual OPEC member-nations (not just independent producers) have an incentive to increase their own output. The problem of OPEC, like any cartel, is to achieve agreement on a course of action (raising price to some level) and then to secure adherence to the agreement. As is the case with any group, differences make for disagreements. OPEC has been plagued by differences in the urgency with which its members wish to turn their asset in the ground—crude oil reserves—into disposable income.

Countries such as Saudi Arabia, Kuwait, and the United Arab Emirates have small populations, high GNPs per capita, and ruling elites that are well served by modernization at a slow pace. Their massive oil reserves ensure they will earn oil revenue for the foreseeable future.

Other OPEC members, such as Indonesia, Nigeria, and Algeria, have larger populations, smaller GNPs per capita, and substantially smaller oil reserves. Their best hope for economic development is through the maximization of short-run oil revenues. Political pressures reinforce this economic incentive. More than once, governments of OPEC nations have been overturned because of mismanagement of the oil sector, and the ousted leaders often do not survive to collect retirement benefits.

By 1985, OPEC's market share had fallen to 30 percent, mostly on the strength of output cutbacks by Saudi Arabia, which enjoyed an OPEC quota of 4.353 million barrels per day but was estimated to be producing only 2.5 million barrels a day in September 1985. OPEC's official price remained at $28 a barrel, but the spot-market price for oil was no more than half that.

At this point, Saudi Arabia introduced a system of "netback pricing," under which the price paid for Saudi crude oil was determined by the market prices of the products refined from the crude. The immediate effect of the netback pricing system was to eliminate risk for the purchaser of Saudi crude: if the price of refined products should fall, the price of crude would fall proportionately. The consequence was a sharp increase in the demand for Saudi oil, output of which reached six million barrels a day by July 1986.

Other OPEC members soon adopted their own netback pricing schemes, and oil prices fell as low as $6 a barrel. By August 1986, OPEC members, with the exception of Iraq, which held out for a quota equal to that of Iran, reaffirmed their support for the quota schedule that they were all violating. A series of ineffective agreements followed, and crude prices stayed at levels which, while yielding OPEC members handsome profits, remained below the levels of the early 1980s.

Iraq's August 1990 occupation of Kuwait led to a brief spike in the price of oil (Figure 2-1), but otherwise caused hardly a ripple in the supply of oil to world markets. Supplies from Iraq and Kuwait were abruptly cut to zero, but Saudi Arabia increased output from 5.4 million barrels a day in August 1990 to 8.2 million barrels a day in November 1990, maintaining overall supply at a comfortable level. It was to insist on keeping output at this level for most of the rest of the 1990s.

Judging by its actions, Saudi Arabia perceives its own self-interest to be served by stable oil markets and prices that do not give too much encouragement to conservation efforts or the search for alternative fuels. At the time of the Iraqi invasion of Kuwait, Saudi Arabia was able to act in its own self interest and expand output because it had excess capacity that allowed it to do so. Other OPEC members with significant petroleum reserves were not slow to draw the conclusion that bargaining power within OPEC is related to production capacity. In the immediate aftermath of the First Gulf War, Kuwait (naturally enough), Abu Dhabi, and Iran all set in motion substantial investment programs aimed at increasing crude capacity. Not to be out-done, Saudi Arabia initiated an expansion of capacity to more than 10 million barrels a day.

OPEC's pattern of ineffective collusion continued after Iraq was driven from Kuwait in February 1991. Ecuador and Gabon (both small producers) withdrew as OPEC members.[33] Amid bickering over how members would adjust (reduce) their own output as Kuwaiti oilfields returned to production and as Iraq began limited oil sales under U.N. supervision to raise funds for humanitarian needs, OPEC found its residual part of the market increasingly small.

In November 1997, OPEC oil ministers agreed to raise quota output by 1.5 million barrels a day (m b/d), to 27.5m b/d. A portion of this increase simply acknowledged reality — actual output was reported to be 27.0m b/d — but the decision was also based on a predicted increase in demand going into the Northern hemisphere winter. By expanding output, OPEC could supply the expected increase in demand rather than letting it go to suppliers outside the organization.

But the Northern hemisphere winter of 1997 to 1998 was mild, a severe economic slowdown in Asia reduced energy demand in that part of the world, a large stock of crude oil was held in inventory. All three factors meant that crude oil prices fell sharply, and Saudi Arabia reached outside OPEC in pursuit of its long-term goals.

In March 1998, OPEC members Saudi Arabia and Venezuela agreed with non-member Mexico to reduce output by 1.5m b/d, some 2 percent of world production. Additional output reductions were later pledged by other OPEC members and non-members (in particular, Norway), and producers came closer than in the past to meeting their commitments. The price of crude oil tripled in a little more than a year (from about $9.40 a barrel in December 1998 to peaks over $30 a barrel early in 2000). Jawboning by governments of consuming countries was ineffective in per-suading OPEC member states to increase output, but in March 2000 the govern-ments of moderate OPEC countries seemed ready to implement such increases in the pursuit of their own perceived self-interest in avoiding disruptions in world economic activity.

The Second Gulf War had no more fundamental impact on the world oil market than had the first. Indeed, during this period, continuing unrest in Venezuela unsettled the oil market as much as the situation in the Gulf of Arabia. Prices fluctuated during this period — down in anticipation of increased Iraqi oil supplies, up when the pro-longed nature of U.S. intervention became apparent.

Part of the upward trend in prices shown in Figure 2-1 is transitory, a consequence of continuing unrest in the Middle East. Part of it is a consequence of expanding world demand for energy. Asian demand for refined petroleum products, 13.5 percent of world demand in 1970, was 29.7 percent of world demand in 2005 (Table 2-3). The price of crude oil is not trending upward because OPEC is cutting back the supply of crude oil. The price of crude oil is rising because the world demand for energy is increasing.

---

[33]In March, 2007, Ecuador's oil minister explained that it would rejoin OPEC because of the "numerous benefits such as controlling the price of oil" (Oil & Gas Journal, 5 March 2007, p. 5). Wishing will not make it so.

OPEC has at most taken advantage of the opportunities thrown its way by the market; it has not controlled the market. OPEC decided to reduce its output by 1.2m b/d in November 2006, and by a further 500,000 b/d in February 2007. The February 2007 output ceiling for OPEC members, excluding Iraq, was 25.8m b/d. The U.S. Energy Information Administration estimated that the February 2007 output of OPEC members, excluding Iraq, was 26.5m b/d. It will be business as usual for OPEC in the 21st century, and for OPEC, "business as usual" means agreements that are more honored in the breach than the observance.

▪ ▪ ▪ III. Public Policy

U.S. Antitrust

The oil industry lies at the foundation of U.S. antitrust policy. It was hostility toward the Standard Oil Trust, widely believed to have acquired control of the post-Civil War U.S. market by means of strategic anticompetitive behavior, that prompted passage of the Sherman Antitrust Act of 1890.[34] Antitrust has been the traditional approach to the preservation of competition in the United States and, as we have noted, in 1911 the Supreme Court upheld a finding that the Standard Oil Company had violated the Sherman Antitrust Act while acquiring a dominant position in the refining, marketing, and transportation of petroleum. The Court imposed a structural remedy, ordering the parent holding company to divest itself of controlling stock interests in 33 subsidiaries.[35] This first case was also the last successful major case involving the U.S. oil industry.

To be sure, the oil industry has from time to time attracted the attention of antitrust authorities. In 1940, a case so broad that it became known as the "Mother Hubbard" case was filed.[36] Twenty-two major oil companies, 344 subsidiary and secondary companies, and the American Petroleum Institute were charged, in a Justice Department civil suit, with violating both the Sherman and Clayton Acts. The case was postponed because of the onset of World War II, and thereafter languished until it was dismissed in 1951 at the request of the Justice Department. ·

Throughout the postwar period, antitrust action against U.S. oil firms was suspended on grounds of national security. In the closing days of the Truman Administration, the government accused the five U.S.-based international majors (along with British Petroleum and Royal Dutch Shell, which were beyond the jurisdiction of U.S. authorities) of seeking to restrain and monopolize crude oil and refined petroleum products, in violation of the Sherman Antitrust Act. But the State Department urged that the oil companies receive antitrust immunity for their cooperation in setting up the 1954

---

[34]Before the development of the automobile, oil was a source of light rather than a fuel. See George R. Gibson "A Lampful of Oil," *Harper's New Monthly Magazine* 72, no. 428 (January 1886): 235–257. (which can be downloaded from URL http://cdl.library.cornell.edu/cgi-bin/moa/moa-cgi?notisid=ABK4014-0072-26).

[35]See Bruce Bringhurst, *Antitrust and the Oil Monopoly* (Westport, Connecticut: Greenwood Press, 1979).

[36]*U.S. v. American Petroleum Institute et al.*, Civil No. 8524 (D.D.C., October 1940).

Iranian consortium, and this immunity weakened the cartel case, which dragged on for years. The cases against Exxon, Texaco, and Gulf were eventually settled by consent decrees, and charges against Mobil and Socal were dismissed. The last parts of the case were dropped by the Justice Department in 1968.[37]

Much of the vitality of American antitrust law derives from the possibility of private enforcement. A private antitrust suit filed in 1978 by the International Association of Machinists and Aerospace Workers (IAM) sought to apply U.S. antitrust law to OPEC. OPEC declined to appear when the case was heard, and the Department of Justice refused to submit the amicus curiae brief requested by the District Court. The District Court declined to hear the case on technical grounds, among others that the IAM did not have "standing" to sue OPEC since IAM was not a direct purchaser from OPEC. IAM appealed this dismissal to the Circuit Court of Appeals, which upheld the lower court refusal to hear the case on the ground that the case would interfere with U.S. foreign relations. Once again, conditions of national security short-circuited the application of the antitrust laws.[38]

More recently, as indicated earlier, the American antitrust agencies allowed a number of major mergers over the 1998 to 2001 period among large U.S. oil firms—Exxon's merger with Mobil; BP's acquisition of Amoco and ARCO; and mergers between Chevron and Texaco, and between Conoco and Phillips—after requiring the merging firms to divest various portions of their production, refining, distribution and retailing facilities.

Government Policy Responses to OPEC

The fact that the oil crisis of 1973 was repeated just six years later is testimony that Western governments generally were unable to develop adequate energy policies the first time around. The founding of the International Energy Agency (IEA) in November 1974 suggests government recognition of the importance of cooperation among consuming countries. However, France refused to join the IEA, apparently preferring bilateral government-to-government negotiations with oil-producing nations. Such government-to-government negotiations became common during the tight crude markets of 1978 to 1980, when security of supply was a matter of concern. Since that time, as more and more oil became available on spot markets, sales with government involvement have declined.

Three interrelated aspects of the continuing debate over proper government policy toward the petroleum industry merit discussion. All reflect a failure to understand the way markets work.

---

[37]B.I. Kaufman, "Oil and Antitrust: The Oil Cartel Case and the Cold War," *Business History Review* 51, no. 37 (Spring 1977); Sampson, *Seven Sisters*, pp. 150–159.

[38]See Irvin M. Grossack, "OPEC and the Antitrust Laws," *Journal of Economic Issues* 20, no. 3 (September 1986): 725–741. U.S. antitrust laws are effects-based: if actions restrain trade on U.S. markets, those actions are covered by the antitrust laws no matter where they take place. The same is true of the competition policy of the European Union. While the governments that are members of OPEC might enjoy sovereign immunity for their actions, the same cannot be said for the legally independent companies through which OPEC decisions are implemented.

The International Energy Agency.

Twenty-one Western nations are members of the IEA.[39] They are pledged to share oil supplies if it is determined that a shortage of oil has occurred or is likely to occur. "Shortage" is defined in terms of a physical interruption in supply, and it seems clear that the focus of the IEA is embargoes imposed for political reasons. Price increases, however, have been an important aspect of past oil shocks, and the assessment of market conditions in terms of physical supplies rather than prices reflects a failure to appreciate the role of prices in a market economy. It would be desirable to alter IEA procedures to facilitate a response to a sharp price increase as well as to a sharp supply decrease.

The Strategic Petroleum Reserve.

In 1975, Congress established a Strategic Petroleum Reserve (SPR) as insurance against future interruptions in foreign supplies. Targets, set in later detailed plans, were for 500 million barrels in storage by 1980 and a billion barrels by 1985. 545 million barrels were actually stored in salt caverns around the Gulf of Mexico by March 1988. Modest sales from the SPR were made during the First Gulf War, and supplies were added in the run-up to the Second Gulf War, bringing the total to just under 600 million barrels. But the U.S. government declined to release supplies from the SPR in the face of price increases in the months before the Second Gulf War (it did use the SPR in the immediate aftermath of Hurricane Katrina). Although it seems likely that the knowledge that the SPR exists has a calming effect on world oil markets, it would be desirable to let price spikes trigger the release of strategic reserves.

Low Price or Energy Independence?

The debate on U.S. policy toward the petroleum industry has long been bedeviled by a failure to come to grips with the limitations imposed by the way markets work. Figure 2-8 shows a stylized demand curve for the world oil market. U.S. policymakers have long recognized the negative impact of a high oil price on economic activity. Supply shocks mean short-run bursts of inflation. A high oil price raises the cost of all energy-intensive activity, by consumers and by industry. Economic growth is slowed, and the U.S. trade balance —because the high price applies to a good for which the U.S. is a net importer—is made worse. One might think, therefore, that low oil prices would be welcomed by U.S. policymakers. But solicitude for the domestic oil industry has led successive U.S. administrations to defend a position that would have the U.S. at a point like Y in Figure 2-8: a low price for oil, but we don't buy much of it, at least not from foreign suppliers.

What is striking is that OPEC member nations suffer from a symmetric failure to come to grips with the way markets work. In the long run, a monopolist or complete cartel can be anywhere that it wants to be on the demand curve. The constraint imposed by the market is that price and quantity are inversely related: a high price means a low quantity demanded, a low price means a high quantity demanded. It is

---

[39]See Douglas R. Bohi and Michael A. Toman, "Oil Supply Disruptions and the Role of the International Energy Agency," *The Energy Journal* 7, no. 2 (April 1986): 37–50; David R. Henderson, "The IEA Oil-Sharing Plan: Who Shares With Whom?," *The Energy Journal* 8, no. 4 (October 1987): 23–31; and George Horwich and David Leo Weimer, editors, *Responding to International Oil Crises.* (Washington, D.C.: American Enterprise Institute for Public Policy Research, 1988).

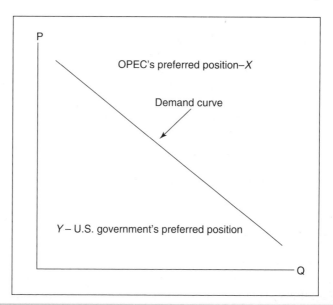

▮ ▮ ▮ **FIGURE 2-8** Wishful Thinking at Home and Abroad.

clear from endless public statements that OPEC oil ministers want very much to be at a point like X in Figure 2-8. They want to charge a high price for oil and sell a great deal of oil, and over the long run the market will not let them.

National Security: The Short Run

The current consumption of U.S. oil always increases future dependence on foreign oil, barrel for barrel. The only way to avoid this is permanent tariffs or quotas that artificially raise the price of oil in the United States and distort input/consumption choices in less efficient and productive ways. It is not in the national security interest of the United States to be protected from foreign oil that is cheaper than domestic oil.

The specter is raised of unending Middle East reserves and vulnerability to a cutoff of oil supplies from a politically unstable region of the world. The best supply-side response to this possibility is to diversify sources of supply away from politically unstable regions, and this diversification is increasingly feasible as new oil provinces open up around the world. The expansion of oil reserves outside OPEC implies that U.S. security interests lie in an open world market.

There is no long-run U.S. security interest in avoiding the current consumption of cheap foreign oil. There is a short-run U.S. security interest in neutralizing run-ups of oil price due to sporadic supply interruptions, and that is a problem that can be addressed, in the event, through proper use of the Strategic Petroleum Reserve.

National Security: The Long-Run

Energy security does not consist only in diversified sources of oil supply around the world. It also consists in alternatives to conventional oil and natural gas: shale oil, coal gasification, solar power, nuclear fusion, and others. Experience shows that this sort of research cannot be left entirely to market forces. The costs of commercial-scale plants are far higher, and the development times far longer, than commercial enterprises can support. If government investment in a Strategic Petroleum Reserve to maintain short-run energy security is appropriate, then government support for the long-term (20-or 50-year) research needed to ensure long-run energy security is also appropriate.

On the demand side, energy security lies in conservation and in the efficient use of energy. Yet Figure 2-2 shows that U.S. demand for oil has climbed above the previous peak, between the oil shock of 1973 and the oil shock of 1979. Figure 2-6 suggests that there is still progress to be made in bringing U.S. energy efficiency to the levels of other industrialized counties.

CONCLUSION ▪ ▪ ▪ ▪ ▪ ▪ ▪

The oil price increases of 1973, 1979, and 1981 reduced the level of world demand for energy below what it otherwise would have been. A decade of moderate prices in the 1990s dulled incentives for the efficient use of energy, and U.S. (more generally, developed country) demand for oil, the primary source of energy, has risen to levels that should evoke concern.

Against this unfavorable evolution on the demand side of the market can be set some favorable developments on the supply side of the market. A critical change in market structure is the expanded number of players. For generations, the world oil market was dominated by the Seven Sisters, the vertically integrated majors. For something more than a decade, the world oil market was dominated by OPEC member states. For the foreseeable future, events on the world oil market will reflect the actions of the OPEC member states (integrating forward toward the final consumer), the international majors (integrating backward through the development of OPEC and non-OPEC reserves), new supplying nations, and independent oil companies. These various firms and nation-firms will collude when they can and compete when they must. The increased number of suppliers reduces the likelihood of successful exercise of control over price.

Nonetheless, when the growth of demand and a reduction in independent supply presents the opportunity to extract monopoly profits, OPEC or (more likely) a group of high-reserve oil producers who are able perceive a common set of interests, OPEC members or not, it will be taken. Periodically, supply will be cut back and oil prices will rise. At this writing, the world oil market is more like Figure 2-3(a) than Figure 2-3(b). There will be future oil price shocks. But OPEC does not control the price of crude oil. OPEC's situation is much like that of a surfer riding a wave: a skillful surfer can ride at the top of a wave, and a clumsy surfer can wipe out. But the surfer does not move the ocean, the ocean moves the surfer.

Governments can—if they will—mitigate the effects of oil shocks. The policy to do so will use the market price as a trigger to release and share strategic reserves over the short-run and will promote the development of alternative sources of supply and efficient use of energy over the long run. Policies that fail to use the information provided by the market in the short-run, and that rely on the market alone to develop new technology over the long run, will exacerbate future oil shocks.

SUGGESTIONS FOR FURTHER READING ▰▰▰▰▰▰▰

Publications

Adelman, M. A. 1993. *The Economics of Petroleum Supply*. Cambridge, MA: MIT Press.

The Genie Out of the Bottle. 1995. Cambridge, MA: MIT Press.

Blair, John M. 1976. *The Control of Oil*. New York: Random House.

Boué, Juan Carlos Venezuela. 1993 *The Political Economy of Oil*. Oxford: Oxford University Press.

Chernow, Ron Titan. 1998. *The Life of John D. Rockefeller, Sr*. New York: Random House.

Eckel, Edwin C. 1920. *Coal Iron and War*. New York: Henry Holt and Company.

Hartshorn, J. E. 1993. *Oil Trade: Politics and Prospects*. Cambridge: Cambridge University Press.

Harvie, Christopher. 1995. *Fool's Gold: the Story of North Sea Oil*. London: Penguin Books.

Heal, Geoffrey and Chichilnisky, Graciela. 1991. *Oil and the International Economy*. Oxford: Claredon Press.

Horsnell, Paul and Mabro, Robert. 1993. *Oil Markets and Prices*. Oxford: Oxford University Press.

Moss, Diana L. "Competition in U.S. Petroleum Refining and Marketing: Part I — Industry Trends," American Antitrust Institute Working Paper 07-02, January 2007 (http://www.antitrustinstitute.org./Archives/oil_1.ashx).

"Competition in U.S. Petroleum Refining and Marketing: Part II — Review of The Economic Literature," American Antitrust Institute Working Paper 07-03, January 2007 (http://www.antitrustinstitute.org./Archives/oil_2.ashx).

Sampson, Anthony. 1976. *The Seven Sisters*. New York: Bantam Books.

Schneider, Steven A. 1983. *The Oil Price Revolution*. Baltimore: The Johns Hopkins University Press.

Tarbell, Ida M. 1904. *The History of The Standard Oil Company*. McClure, Phillips and Co. (http://www.history.rochester.edu/fuels/tarbell/MAIN.HTM).

Turner, Louis. 1983. *Oil Companies in the International System*, 3rd edition. London: George Allen & Unwin.

U.S. Congress. Senate. Subcommittee on Monopoly. 1952. The International Petroleum Cartel: Staff Report to the Federal Trade Commission. 82d Cong., 2d sess.

Yergin, Daniel. 1991. *The Prize*. New York: Simon & Schuster.

Web sites

American Petroleum Institute: http://www.api.org/

International Energy Agency: http://www.iea.org/

OPEC: http://www.opec.org/

Oxford Institute for Energy Studies: http://www.oxfordenergy.org/

Texas Railroad Commission: http://www.rrc.state.tx.us/

U.S. Department of Energy: http://www.doe.gov/

Energy Information Administration links page: http://www.eia.doe.gov/links.html#petroleum

CHAPTER 3

The Electricity Industry

ALAN R. SCHRIBER* AND JAMES W. BROCK

Communism, Lenin said, is Soviet government plus electrification of the country. We leave cosmological definitions of political ideology for others, but it is hard to imagine a necessity of life more important yet more taken for granted than electricity. Without giving it a thought we flip a switch and the lights come on; our homes and offices are cooled in the summer, our ovens bake, and our computers navigate the web. Behind the wall sockets and light switches, however, thousands of tons of fuel are consumed each day in boilers generating steam at temperatures as high as 2,000 degrees to spin the turbines that create electric current. Electricity flows from the generating plant and is transmitted along wires that carry hundreds of thousands of volts of power across regions to local areas all across the country, where voltages are dropped down and the electricity reaches millions of homes and businesses. When the lights flicker and the power abruptly goes out, however, our dependence on this industry is palpable. Then we glimpse how vital electricity is, how much the nation's economic health and welfare depend on it, and how this renders even more important the clash of conflicting economic conceptions and regulatory policies that are convulsing the field.

I. History

Although interest in electricity can be traced to the ancient Greeks, and while Ben Franklin flew his kite in a thunderstorm to study its properties and Joseph Priestly warned the English aristocracy to tremble before it, the age of commercial electricity in the U.S. commenced on September 4, 1882, when Thomas Edison opened his Pearl Street electric station in New York City. Edison's station generated 560 kilowatts of power for 59 customers who paid a price of 24 cents per kilowatt hour.[1] Fourteen years later, in 1896, George Westinghouse demonstrated the superiority of alternating current

---

* The views in this chapter are not those of the Public Utility Commission of Ohio nor are they endorsed by it.
[1] For a concise history of the field, see U.S. Energy Information Administration, "The Changing Structure of the Electric Power Industry 2000" (Washington, D.C., October 2000), appendix A. See also Charles F. Phillips, Jr., *The Economics of Regulation*, rev. ed. (Homewood, IL: Richard D. Irwin, Inc, 1969), Chapter 15.

(AC) over Edison's direct current (DC) system in enabling larger generating stations to be built farther from the final point of consumption, thereby greatly expanding the ability to serve more consumers by transmitting power over greater distances (in this case, the twenty miles from Westinghouse's hydroelectric plant at Niagara Falls to his customers in Buffalo, New York).[2] By the turn of the 20th century, more than 3,000 electric organizations had been launched in the U.S., with municipally owned operations providing the bulk of power for street lighting and trolley service, and privately owned firms supplying electricity for other urban uses.[3] The development of electric motors and their incorporation into manufacturing processes and home appliances greatly boosted demand.

The provision of electricity soon came to be predicated on the foundational conception that would prevail for sixty years—that a central plant for generating electricity, transmission of power along lines from the generating plant, and the local distribution of that electricity to final customers constituted an all-encompassing natural monopoly, wherein a single vertically integrated organization controlling all three stages as a monopoly would function most economically. Larger, more productive generating plants were developed, and smaller electric firms merged to take advantage of the economies of large-scale vertical integration. The belief that the naturally monopolistic nature of the endeavor precluded competition, coupled with the growing importance of the service, led states to regulate the field in order to obtain the efficiencies of monopoly while preventing its abuse. Wisconsin, Georgia, and New York led the way, establishing state regulation of electric power in 1907; by 1914, 45 states had enacted legislation to regulate the field. Electric utilities would now operate within the geographic boundaries of franchise areas mandated by state regulatory commissions, with the traditional public utility obligation imposed on them to serve the public at just prices and on fair terms. The federal government's role in the industry stemmed from its ownership of most of the nation's hydroelectric resources: the Federal Power Commission was created in 1920 to regulate the construction and operation of hydroelectric plants on the nation's waterways.

The industry grew 12 percent per year over the next 30 years, with the number of electric organizations peaking at nearly 7,000 in the early 1920s. The number of municipal electric companies and their share of power generation declined, however, and although federal power systems continued to grow, privately owned utilities came to dominate the field, eventually accounting for more than 90 percent of electric power. Prices fell by a third, while the proportion of American homes served by electricity grew from 8 percent to nearly 70 percent (80 percent in urban areas).

Electricity had moved from curiosity, to luxury, to necessity of daily life. Rural areas lagged behind badly, however, with only 11 percent of farm dwellings supplied with electric power in 1932, spurring demands by rural interests for government aid in obtaining access to this miracle of the modern age. Congress and President Roosevelt's New Deal administration responded, building hydroelectric dams (Hoover, Grand Coulee), launching the Tennessee Valley Authority electric project in the southeast and the Bonneville Power Administration in the northwest, and establishing the Rural Electrification

---

[2]Legend has it that Edison sought to discredit Westinghouse's alternating current system in the public's eyes by designing his electric chair to operate on alternating current rather than on his own direct current system.

[3]John E. Kwoka, Jr., *Power Structure: Ownership, Integration, and Competition in the U.S. Electricity Industry* (Boston: Kluwer Academic Publishers, 1996): 5.

Administration to support the formation of rural electric cooperatives—all of which triggered years of ideological combat between advocates of publicly produced power for the people versus champions of laissez-faire who feared socialism on the march.

An abrupt new development transformed the field in the 1920s, however, when scores of electric companies began to merge together to form much larger holding companies. The pace of consolidation among electric companies accelerated to 200 to 300 mergers and acquisitions per year.[4] Soon these holding companies began to merge with each other, creating "super" holding companies—holding companies of holding companies—which further concentrated control of the field. By the late-1920s, 16 of these giants together accounted for three-quarters of the nation's electric power; three of them (United Corporation, Electric Bond and Share, and the sprawling Insull empire) together controlled 45 percent of the field.[5] While these vast empires initially may have benefited from some economies of scale, their primary attraction seemed to be the lucrative opportunities they afforded their creators for profiteering by pyramiding ownership and leveraging control, watering stock shares, artificially inflating asset values, and selling services to their operating subsidiaries at high prices—all beyond the reach of state regulatory commissions because they were operated on an interstate basis.[6]

When financial abuses and the 1929 failure of the nation's capital markets combined to cause the collapse of these massive holding companies, a flurry of government investigations and reports[7] culminated in the Public Utility Holding Company Act of 1935. The Act gave the Securities and Exchange Commission (SEC) extensive regulatory power over electric firms, including their capital structures, financial operations, accounting practices, and transactions among their subsidiary operating divisions. The Act's "death sentence" clause, dubbed "the most stringent corrective measure ever applied to American business,"[8] directed the SEC to break up these huge empires into separate, individual electric systems, with each system limited to serving a prescribed geographic area, and with each to engage only in the operations considered necessary for the well-ordered functioning of a utility. The SEC implemented its trust-busting mandate over the ensuing years, directing the divestiture of more than 900 electric utilities from holding company control.[9] (By 1958, the number of electric holding companies had dropped to 18 compared to 216 twenty years earlier.[10]) The Public Utility Holding Company Act also expanded the role of the Federal Power Commission by empowering it to regulate the transmission of electricity across state lines, as well as assigning it responsibility for encouraging the formation of pooling arrangements to promote coordination and reliability of electric power across more regions of the country.

---

[4]Dennis Ray, Rodney Stevenson, Roger Schiffman, and Howard Thompson, "Electric Utility Mergers and Regulatory Policy," National Regulatory Research Institute, June 1992, p. 4.
[5]Phillips, 553–54.
[6]Ibid., 554–60.
[7]See Federal Trade Commission, *Control of Power Companies*, Senate Doc. 213, 69th Cong., 2d sess., 1927, and idem, Utility Corporations, Senate Doc. 92, 70th Cong., 1st sess., 1935. See also James C. Bonbright and Gardiner C. Means, The Holding Company (New York: McGraw-Hill Book Co., 1932).
[8]Clair Wilcox, *Public Policies Toward Business*, 3rd ed. (Homewood, IL: Richard D. Irwin, Inc., 1966): 366.
[9]Phillips, 563.
[10]Jack Casazza and Frank Delea, *Understanding Electric Power Systems* (Hoboken, NJ: John Wiley & Sons, 2003): 139.

The decades of the 1940s and 1950s, in retrospect, constituted a golden age in the field. Demand soared during the war years and increased steadily thereafter. Ever-larger generating plants and technological improvements in transmission and distribution, including gains in the distances over which power could be moved, fostered declining costs and prices, while company profits (and government regulatory commissions) were stable and healthy. The peaceful development of atomic power offered the allure of electricity "too cheap to meter" and after the government opened the field to private enterprise in 1954, scores of nuclear power plants were put on utility company drawing boards. Generated electricity grew at average rates of 7.5 to 8.5 percent per year, productivity in power generation increased by 35 percent, and residential prices (adjusted for inflation) continued to drift downward.[11]

Alas, this happy bonhomie began to crumble in the 1960s. The great Northeast power blackout of 1965 raised alarm about the reliability and vulnerability of an industry that had become critical to the nation's wellbeing. Energy crises in the 1970s caused the industry's costs, prices and profits to gyrate unpredictably. The environmental movement called the nation's attention to millions of tons of pollutants spewed into the air by the industry's generating plants, and the Clean Air Acts of 1970 and 1977 ordered utilities to control and reduce their emissions. Dramatic events at Pennsylvania's Three Mile Island nuclear power plant in 1979, together with construction costs for nuclear power plants that were spiraling out of control, underscored the physical and financial hazards of atomic energy and brought the expansion of this once-promising technology to a halt. Conservation, not growth, became the new categorical imperative, with the Public Utility Regulatory Policies Act of 1978 (PURPA) ordering utilities to connect their systems to outside sources of electricity (such as electricity "co-generated" by industrial firms), and to purchase power from them as a way to contain electric plant construction costs and better utilize the nation's energy resources. Electricity prices, instead of declining, now began to rise.[12]

By the mid-1980s, these developments coalesced to call into question the bedrock foundation on which the industry had been built over the preceding decades: that electric power is a naturally monopolistic endeavor most efficiently conducted by centrally controlled, vertically integrated monopolies operating under the direct oversight of government regulation. Support began to grow for radically reorganizing the field in ways it was hoped would promote competition and efficiency and contain costs and prices, while reducing regulation and monopoly. The Energy Policy Act of 1992 called for a new class of electric power producers, exempt wholesale generators (EWGs), that would specialize in building unregulated plants to generate electricity for sale in competitive wholesale markets. The transmission systems required to make this wholesale market work and move the power—transmission systems built, owned and operated by vertically integrated utility monopolies—were to be pried open and made available on nondiscriminatory terms to nonintegrated producers on the generation side, and to local utilities and consumers on the distribution side. Power, it was believed, would be competitively priced, while reliability of service would be protected. Major regulatory

---

[11]See "Changing Structure of the Electric Power Industry 2000," 114, and Paul L. Joskow, "Productivity Growth and Technical Change in the Generation of Electricity," *Energy Journal* 8, (1987): 17–18.
[12]U.S. General Accounting Office, "Lessons Learned from Electricity Restructuring," Washington, D.C., December 2002, 17–18.

steps toward these goals were launched by the Federal Energy Regulatory Commission (the successor to the Federal Power Commission, now subsumed within the Department of Energy) in 1996 and 1999. States with the country's highest electricity prices (Massachusetts, Rhode Island, New Hampshire and Pennsylvania in the Northeast, California in the West) also embraced this new policy: By 2001, two dozen of them had embarked on restructuring programs to promote competition in electricity generation (while retaining regulation of the distribution and transmission of it).[13]

The glow of this brave new world was severely tarnished, however, by developments at the turn of the new century: The electric power debacle in California in 2000 and 2001 featured soaring prices, rolling blackouts, and major utility company bankruptcies; the scandalous collapse of the Enron Corporation, one of the brashest advocates of this new power paradigm; persistent concerns about monopolistic manipulation of newly created electricity markets; and a spate of what seemed to be a disconcerting number of major blackouts and power disruptions. States intending to implement the new competitive paradigm began to put their plans on hold; some states that earlier had chosen the restructuring route began having serious doubts about the wisdom of their choice. Even a bastion of private enterprise like the Cato Institute seemed to some to lose faith in the free-market adventure, pining for a return to the "good old days."[14] Recrimination, finger-pointing, and charges and countercharges—inflamed by turf wars between state and federal regulatory agencies—became conspicuous features of the electric power landscape at the dawn of its second century.

▪▪▪ II. Structure

Today electricity is a $300 billion industry supplying 4 billion megawatt-hours of power to 136 million customers. As Table 3-1 indicates, the industry has grown at a healthy pace in recent years, spurred by the electricity required to power the desktop computer revolution, the internet, servers and the explosion of electronic commerce.

TABLE 3-1 U.S. Electric Power Industry, 1990–2005.

	1990	*2000*	*2005*
Electricity Generated (million megawatt hours)	3,038	3,802	4,055
Retail Revenues (billion)	$ 178.2	$ 233.3	$ 298.0
Customers (million)	110.6	127.6	136.4

Source: U.S. Energy Information Administration, State Electricity Profiles 2005, Washington, D.C., March 6, 2007, tables 5 and 8, and U.S. Census Bureau, *Statistical Abstract of the United States: 2007* (Washington, D.C., 2006): 585.

[13]Paul L. Joskow, "Markets for Power in the United States: An Interim Assessment," *Energy Journal*, 2006; and Electric Energy Market Competition Task Force, "Report to Congress on Competition in Wholesale and Retail Markets for Electric Energy," Washington, D.C., April 5, 2007.
[14]Peter Van Doren and Jerry Taylor, "Rethinking Electricity Restructuring," Cato Institute Policy Analysis, November 30, 2004.

Vertical Industry Structure and the Nature of Electricity

The industry remains very much defined by its vertical three-stage structure. At the initial stage, electricity is generated in plants where shafts attached to turbines are spun between magnetized coils to create current. There are some 17,000 of these generating plants across the country. Once generated, electricity leaves the plant at levels of 100,000 to as high as 765,000 volts, and enters the transmission stage of 160,000 miles of high-voltage lines (where 4 to 7 percent of the power dissipates). Electricity terminates at its destination, substations, where the voltage is stepped down by passing it through transformers. It then enters the final stage of local distribution comprising another maze of poles, wires and transformers where, after the voltage is further dropped down, it reaches homes and businesses.

It has been said that electricity is not a commodity, but a phenomenon, and its unique physical characteristics are crucial to the functioning of the industry. Perhaps the most important characteristic is that electricity cannot be stored. As a result, and because electric current flows at the speed of light, the generation, transmission, distribution and consumption of electric power all transpire simultaneously. In the United States, electricity is primarily generated, transmitted and distributed as a three-phase alternating current oscillating at 60 cycles per second. This means that the industry's three main stages constitute a system, or "grid," of integrally interdependent parts, each of which must operate in balance and strict physical synchronization with the others. A disturbance in one part of the system will quickly impact the other parts: A change in the power being generated by one plant connected to the grid, for example, will affect electricity throughout the system's transmission lines and, thus, affect the system's ability to handle power being generated by other plants. In the case of the Midwest electric blackout of August 2003, the sagging of a transmission line into a tree in northern Ohio triggered, in just seven minutes, the loss of electric power to 50 million people in eight states and Canada. Once electricity is put into this grid of interdependent parts, the power generated by one organization cannot be distinguished or segregated from the power generated by another organization, as it all seeks the path of least resistance. Congestion occurs when this flow exceeds the system's physical capacity to handle it: Then the system becomes unstable, unpredictable, and overheats and ceases functioning unless its capacity is increased or demands pulling power through it are cut back. Maintaining stable voltage in the grid is also critical: Low voltage ("brownouts") slows industrial motors, computers and appliances; high voltage destroys them.

The Coordination Function

Clearly the electric power system must be operated in a highly coordinated way. Traditionally, this coordination function was conducted internally by vertically integrated utilities operating their own individual systems of generating plants, transmission lines, and local distribution franchises (Figure 3-1).

Over recent decades, however, the locus of this vital coordination function has changed. Power pooling agreements among utilities developed as early as 1927 as a way for cooperating organizations to economize and rationalize their operations. These pools varied in terms of how tightly or loosely organized they were; one of them, the Northwest Power Pool, was created in 1942 and continues to serve as a forum for promoting cooperation among its members. The Northeast electric blackout of 1965

▪▪▪ **FIGURE 3-1** Coordination of the Electric Industry.

Structure of the Traditional Utility

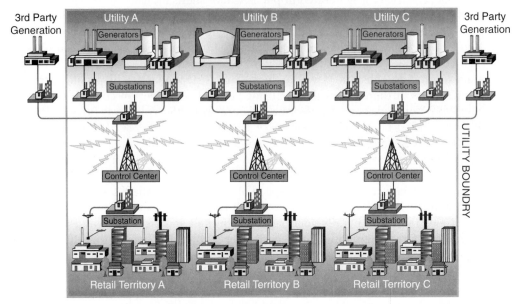

Structure of the Deregulated Electric Supply System

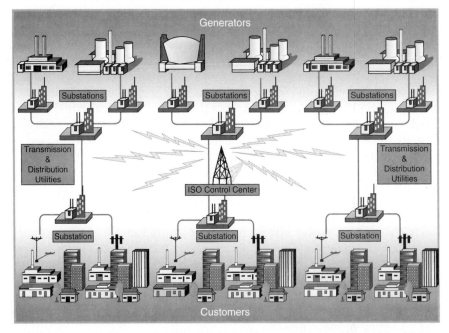

Source: M.W. Warwick, Primer on Electric Utilities, Deregulation, and Restructuring of U.S. Electricity Markets, Department of Energy, Washington, D.C., May 2002, p. 6.5.

spurred the formation of regional councils to better promote reliability by more closely coordinating the operations of utilities across wider regions of the country. Ten of these reliability councils, which operate on the basis of voluntary participation by electricity organizations, were established by the end of the 1960s and subsumed under the auspices of a national umbrella organization (the North American Electric Reliability Council, or NERC). These regional reliability councils, depicted in Figure 3-2, continue to function by developing uniform operating procedures and technical standards, monitoring current and projected power demands and supplies, assessing breakdowns and blackouts, and acting as liaison to local, state, and federal government agencies. Subsumed within these 10 regional reliability councils are 150 subregional control areas for monitoring, controlling and, if necessary, isolating portions of regional electric grids.

Since the 1990s, newer regional operating entities called independent service operators (ISO) and regional transmission organizations (RTO) have emerged within, and been superimposed on all or parts of the areas encompassed by some of these regional reliability councils. Promoted by the Federal Energy Regulatory Commission in its effort to restructure the field, these new entities have been created to conduct the coordination function as the industry has been restructured and markets for wholesale power have been opened up (see Figure 3-1). In the regions where these new entities

▪ ▪ ▪ FIGURE 3-2 U.S. Electric Reliability Councils.

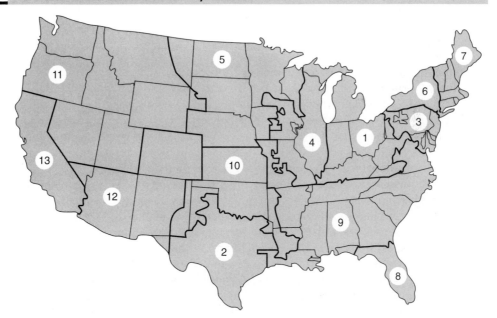

1. East Central Area Reliability Coordination Agreement (ECAR)
2. Electric Reliability Council of Texas (ERCOT)
3. Mid-Atlantic Area Council (MAAC)
4. Mid-America Interconnected Network (MAIN)
5. Mid-Continent Area Power Pool (MAPP)
6. New York (NY)
7. New England (NE)
8. Florida Reliability Coordinating Council (FL)
9. Southeastern Electric Reliability Council (SERC)
10. Southwest Power Pool (SPP)
11. Northwest Power Pool (NWP)
12. Rocky Mountain Power Area, Arizona, New Mexico, and Southern Nevada (RA)
13. California (CA)

Source: Energy Information Administration.

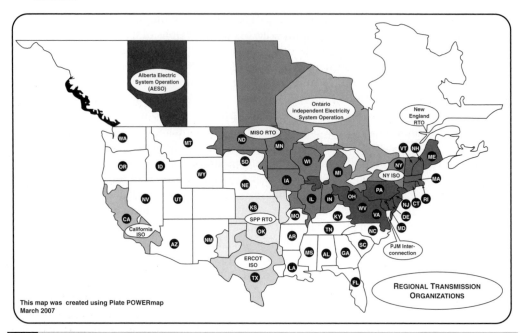

This map was created using Plate POWERmap
March 2007

▮▮▮▮ **FIGURE 3-3** Regional Transmission Organizations and Independent Service Organizations.

Source: Federal Energy Regulatory Commission.

operate, depicted in Figure 3-3, the task of coordinating the various parts of the grid—but not ownership of them—is transferred to what is supposed to be an independent, not-for-profit, third-party operator charged with administering the grid in a fair, open and unbiased way.[15] In these regions, producers and buyers of power contract for supplies of electricity, but it is the ISO or RTO that balances overall supply and demand on the system, directs ("dispatches") the operation of generating plants, and orchestrates transmission in order to balance the load on the grid.

These new regional transmission organizations are extensive: The PJM system, for example, comprises 1,300 generating plants and 450 electric firms in 13 states from Indiana and Ohio to Maryland and New Jersey; directing 165,000 megawatts of electricity through 56,000 miles of transmission lines to 51 million customers, it bills itself as the largest centrally dispatched electric grid in the world. Similarly, the Midwest ISO orchestrates the flow of 100,000 megawatts of electricity in 15 states and Manitoba through 94,000 miles of high-voltage transmission lines.[16] California and Texas are large enough power markets to each have their own ISO; the Texas ISO (ERCOT) coordinates and directs the flow of 77,000 megawatts of power through 37,000 miles of

---

[15]An independent service operator is officially designated an RTO by the Federal Energy Regulatory Commission (FERC) upon demonstrating that it satisfies criteria specified by FERC, including independence of operation, unbiased tariff design and administration, open auctions for power, and equal real-time information ("transparency") for all participants.
[16]Data from these organizations' websites.

transmission lines.[17] Some of these organizations also function as market-makers, providing forward and spot markets for commodity trading of electricity, conducting markets for transmission rights, as well as providing an online stream of continuously updated data concerning electric power prices, availability of transmission capacity, anticipated consumption and production of power, and congestion problems.

Approximately half the nation's electric generating capacity now operates under the direction of these new regional transmission organizations. However, the Southeast, Mountain West and Northwest regions of the country have refrained from adopting them, preferring instead to retain the traditional arrangement of vertically integrated utilities voluntarily participating in reliability councils. In these latter cases, access by generating firms to transmission systems owned by vertically integrated producers is mandatory, but there is no centralized, third-party who operates the grid and coordinates it.

Types of Generating Plants

Conventional power plants generate electricity by spinning a turbine, either by the flow of water (hydropower) or by burning a fuel source to create steam. The shaft of the turbine rotates within magnetic fields, and it is this rotation that generates electric current. The number of various types of plants and their relative importance in terms of overall power production are depicted in Table 3-2, while their economic cost characteristics are shown in Table 3-3. (These cost estimates are greatly affected by changes in the cost of fuel, economic conditions of surplus or shortage in markets for conventional generating turbines, additional costs of waste disposal in the case of nuclear power, and technological developments in the case of alternative sources for generating electricity like wind, solar and biomass.)

TABLE 3-2 Types of U.S. Electric Generating Plants

Fuel Type	Number of Plants	Capacity (000 megawatts)
Coal	1,522	336
Petroleum	3,753	65
Natural Gas	5,467	437
Other Gases	102	2
Nuclear	104	106
Hydroelectric Conventional	3,933	77
Other Renewables	1,671	24
Pumped Storage	150	20
Other	45	1
Total	16,807	1,067

Source: U.S. Energy Information Administration (www.eia.doe.gov/cneaf/electricity/epa/epat2p2.html).

---

[17]Ross Baldick and Jui Niu, "Lessons Learned: The Texas Experience," in James M. Griffin and Steven L. Puller eds., *Electricity Deregulation: Choices and Challenges* (Chicago: University of Chicago Press, 2005): 186.

TABLE 3-3 Estimated Economic Characteristics of New Generating Plants

Plant Type	Plant Size (mW)	Capital Cost ($/kW)	Operating Cost (mills/kWh)
Coal (scrubbed)	600	1,290	4.32
Conventional Gas Combustion Turbine	160	420	3.36
Conventional Hydropower	500	1,500	3.30
Advanced Nuclear	1,350	2,081	0.47
Integrated Coal Gasification (combined cycle)	550	1,491	2.75
Wind	50	1,206	0.00
Biomass	80	1,869	2.96

Note: *Capital costs include contingency factors; estimates for 2006.*
Source: Energy Information Administration, Electricity Market Module, April 2007.

The electric system has a minimum level of demand that is met by plants that run continuously. Such plants, or "baseload" facilities, are usually either nuclear or coal-fired because their fuel costs are relatively low and stable, and their reliability of operation is high.

Because of the lack of inexpensive access to coal, a significant number of electric generating plants in the Northeast are fueled by natural gas or oil. Despite the convenience of seaports for transporting these fuels, the volatility of their prices translates into electric rates in the Northeast that are among the highest in the nation. In recent years, as the wholesale market for electricity has expanded, a number of power plants fired by natural gas have been built; such plants are less costly to construct, but have operating costs that are tied to, and fluctuate with, the price of petroleum. For the most part, gas-fired plants have been used as "peaker" plants that power up during periods of high demand to supplement the output of the baseload generators, and are powered down at other times. An advanced version of gas-fired plants, known as combined-cycle, has been built to have longer duty cycles, that is, better capacity factors. This type of plant is more efficient because it generates electricity twice (first by burning gas, and then once more by using the exhaust to turn another turbine), but it too is tied to the price of natural gas. An important advantage of gas plants is that they are less environmentally damaging than coal and oil-burning plants.

Although no nuclear power plants have been built in the U.S. since the 1970s, 104 continue to operate. While they generally have been reliable and operate close to capacity, they carry a stigma: The fear of an accidental release of lethal radiation. Waste disposal is another issue that has plagued nuclear power: Although as we will see in the following discussion, the Federal Government has been assessing for years waste disposal sites for spent nuclear fuel rods, no such facility is yet operating. As a result, spent fuel rods have been accumulating in pools of water at nuclear generating plants. In addition, few nuclear plants operating in the U.S. are alike. This lack of standardization stymied the construction of these plants because of the long time it took for each one to meet the certification requirements of the Nuclear Regulatory Commission (NRC). Recently, however, interest has been renewed in nuclear power, in part due to the nation's concern with energy independence and national security. Furthermore, air quality standards have become more stringent, rendering nuclear power relatively more attractive on this basis compared to coal. The NRC has precertified uniform nuclear plant designs, and some utilities are expected to begin the licensing process required to build them.

Hydropower generated from water flow represents approximately 9 percent of the nation's generating plant capacity. Electricity generated from renewable energy sources other than water (such as wind turbines, solar panels, geothermal, and the burning of biomass and solid waste) has increased 17 percent since 2000, but still represents only 2 percent of the total amount of electricity generated in the U.S. Electricity generated by wind-powered turbines is growing faster yet, at an annual rate of nearly 30 percent, but still accounts for only 0.4 percent of all electric power generated.[18]

Fuel is the primary variable cost in generating electricity. So far, during the first decade of this new century, the price of natural gas has been highly volatile, due in part to weather-related disruptions as well as to increased demand by industrial manufacturers. Because of the relatively low cost of constructing gas-powered plants, a large number of them were built by nonregulated utilities attempting to sell energy to newly opened wholesale markets. Many of these plants have been rendered uneconomical by escalating gas prices, however, and their owners have suffered financially: Today they sell at deep discounts to their original cost of construction.

Economies of Scale and Natural Monopoly

Conventional electric power-generating plants involve financial investments of large magnitude. Boilers, turbines, generators, and transformers push the cost of conventional plants into the billion-dollar range. A typical pulverized coal burning plant can cost over $2 million per megawatt, with the typical plant size ranging from 600 to 800 megawatts. There are economies of scale in siting as well: The geographic "footprint" of a 1000-megawatt plant requires little more ground area than a plant half that capacity. Economies of scale are greater yet for nuclear plants, owing to the higher design and construction costs required for safety reasons.

There are limits to economies of scale in generation, however. The trend toward building ever bigger, higher pressure coal-burning plants from the 1950s to the early 1970s was subsequently reversed due to the escalating operating problems suffered by the largest of them. Plagued by lower reliability and greater downtimes, the higher operating costs of these biggest plants were compounded by their operators' need to purchase more expensive replacement power from other producers (problems only partly attributable to the advent of generating plant pollution controls).[19] At the same time, technological developments have reduced scale economies for other kinds of generating plants, particularly various types of gas- and oil-powered plants, to the point

[18]Energy Information Administration, Renewable Energy, available at www.eia.doe.gov/neic/infosheets,renewableenergy.html.

[19]Paul L. Joskow and Nancy L. Rose, "The Effects of Technological Change, Experience, and Environmental Regulation on the Construction Cost of Coal-Burning Generating Units," *Rand Journal of Economics* 16 (1985): 4, 23. For an exhaustive survey of empirical studies of economies of scale in the industry, see Francisco Javier Ramos-Real, "Cost Functions and the Electric Utility Industry: A Contribution to the Debate on Deregulation," *Energy Journal* 33 (2005): 69–87.

where plants producing 65 to 400 megawatts of electricity are capable of operating as efficiently as much larger plants.[20]

Transmission, in contrast, entails enormous economies of scale: A single transmission line carrying 300,000 volts operates at lower average cost than do three parallel lines each carrying 100,000 volts. Building new high-voltage lines is also expensive, costing upwards of $500,000 per mile, with upgrades of existing lines to carry higher voltages costing as much as $1 million per mile.[21] Transmission lines are also difficult to build because of resistance by property owners to towers, cables and wires. Rights of eminent domain vary from state to state, further complicating the construction process. In addition, operation of the transmission grid—continuously balancing supplies and demands for electricity across a region encompassing numerous plants, lines, and consumers—is most effectively conducted by a single central operator.[22]

Finally, at the local level, it would be inefficient and costly to have parallel systems of distribution lines, transformers, and poles operated by different companies and clogging the streets and neighborhoods. Local distribution, like long distance transmission, displays the classic hallmarks of a naturally monopolistic technology.

Types of Electric Entities

There are four main types of electric organizations: Publicly owned entities at the federal and local municipal level; cooperatives; private investor-owned utilities (known as "IOUs"); and privately owned "nonutility" firms (Table 3-4).

TABLE 3-4 Types of U.S. Electric Organizations

Type	*Number*	*Customers (000)*	*Generating Capacity (000 megawatts)*
Private Investor-Owned	219	95,226	390
Municipally Owned	2,010	20,048	100
Cooperatives	883	17,021	42
Federal Power Agencies	9	38	72
Power Marketers	158	6,033	na
Non-Utility Power Producers	600	na	446

Note: *Number of non-utility producers is approximate.*

Source: American Public Power Association, 2007–2008 Annual Directory and Statistical Report; Edison Electric Institute, "Key Facts About the Electric Power Industry," www.eei.org; and "North American Electricity Business Structure Changing," *Transmission and Distribution World*, December 6, 2004.

---

[20]"Changing Structure of the Electric Power Industry 2000," 44–45.

[21]Denise Warkentin-Glenn, *Electric Power Industry* (Tulsa, OK: PennWell Corporation, 2006): 167–169.

[22]See Paul L. Joskow, "Restructuring, Competition and Regulatory Reform in the U.S. Electricity Sector," *Journal of Economic Perspectives* 11 (1997): 123, 129. Generating plants and transmission lines are sometimes considered substitutes for one another, because a congested area can be served either by constructing a generator nearby or by running transmission lines to distant power plants already operating.

[23]The following descriptions are taken from Electric Energy Market Competition Task Force, "Report to Congress on Competition in Wholesale and Retail Markets for Electric Energy," April 5, 2007.

Municipally Owned Organizations.

The more than 2,000 municipally owned power systems range from small distribution entities to large operations like the Los Angeles Department of Water and Power.[23] Operating in every state but Hawaii, these systems represent 60 percent of all electric power organizations but serve only 14 percent of retail electric customers and generate only 10 percent of the nation's electricity. About a third of them generate some or all of their own power, with the remainder purchasing electricity generated by others.

Cooperatives.

Electric cooperatives operate in 47 states. Owned by their customers who share any profits, co-ops are predominantly rural in nature, serving an average 6 members per mile of line (compared to 34 per mile of line for investor-owned electric firms). These organizations generate less than 5 percent of the nation's electric power; like municipal systems, much of co-op electricity is purchased from others.

Federal Power Organizations.

Federal power systems include the Tennessee Valley Authority, as well as electric generating facilities operated by the U.S. Army Corps of Engineers, the Bureau of Reclamation, and the Bureau of Indian Affairs. Federal systems are by far the most heavily dependent on hydropower While hydropower accounts for 9 percent of all U.S. electricity output, federal power systems generate nearly 60 percent of their power from this source.[24] Wholesale power from federal facilities is marketed through four federal marketing agencies (Bonneville Power Administration, Western Area Power Administration, Southeastern Power Administration, Southwestern Power Administration), which are charged to cater primarily to cooperatives and other publicly owned organizations.

Investor-Owned Utilities.

It is the private investor-owned firms that are by far the largest entities in the field in terms of proportion of the nation's generating capacity and number of electricity customers, as well as owning approximately 70 percent of the nation's high-voltage transmission lines.[25] The 20 largest of these firms are profiled in Table 3-5.

Over the past decade, with the approval of FERC, most of these entities have reorganized themselves as holding companies, and have engaged in mergers and acquisitions to assemble operations encompassing extensive areas of the country. Duke Energy, for example, is a holding company with the capacity through its generating subsidiary to produce 37,000 megawatts of electricity from 81 plants in North Carolina, South Carolina, Ohio, Indiana, and Kentucky. It owns more than 20,000 miles of high-voltage transmission lines, and another 106,000 miles of local distribution lines; at the local level, it owns subsidiary franchised local utilities servicing 4 million customers across five states.[26] The American Electric Power Company (AEP), another giant, owns as subsidiaries the franchised utilities AEP Ohio, AEP Texas, AEP Appalachian

---

[24] American Public Power Association, "U.S. Electric Utility Industry Statistics," available at www.appanet.org.
[25] Energy Information Administration, "Changing Structure of the Electric Power Industry 2000," 13.
[26] Company website and SEC Form 10-K.

TABLE 3-5 Twenty Largest Investor-Owned Electric Companies, 2006

Company	Stock Market Value (mil)	Annual Revenue (mil)	Generating Capacity (000 mW)
Duke Energy	$ 41,645	$ 15,184	37
Exelon	41,528	15,655	38
Dominion Resources	29,503	16,482	26
Southern Co.	27,383	14,360	41
TXU Corp.	24,882	10,856	18
FPL Group	21,491	15,710	24
FirstEnergy	19,417	11,501	14
Entergy	19,238	10,932	30
American Electric Power	16,772	12,622	36
Public Service Enterprise Group	16,711	12,164	15
PG&E Corp.	16,424	12,539	6
Edison International	14,827	12,622	9
Sempra Energy	14,430	11,761	3
PPL Corp.	13,648	5,886	11
Constellation Energy Group	12,367	19,285	9
Progress Energy	12,319	9,570	23
Consolidated Edison	11,969	12,137	2
Ameren Corp.	11,063	6,880	16
XCEL Energy	9,365	9,840	15
DTE Energy	8,569	4,737	11

Stock market value on December 31, 2006.
Source: Edison Electric Institute, 2006 Financial Review, and company websites.

Power, Indiana Michigan Power, Kentucky Power, Columbus & Southern Power Company, Public Service Company of Oklahoma, and Southwest Electric Power Company (Arkansas, Louisiana and Texas). AEP's generating subsidiary owns 83 generating plants. AEP also owns 39,000 miles of transmission lines, and provides franchised local service to 5 million customers through local distribution systems comprising over 200,000 miles of local lines.[27] Likewise, Dominion Resources has the capacity through its generating subsidiary to produce 26,000 megawatts of electicity from 50 plants in Connecticut, Massachusetts, Rhode Island, Pennsylvania, Ohio, Wisconsin, Illinois, Indiana, Virginia, West Virginia, and North Carolina. Dominion also owns 6,000 miles of high-voltage transmission lines, 54,000 miles of local distribution lines, and supplies 2.3 million customers through its various local utility subsidiaries.[28]

---

[27]Company website.
[28]Company website and SEC Form 10-K.

"Nonutilities."

A major development of recent years has been the emergence of a privately owned "nonutility" segment of the industry, comprising firms not directly engaged in regulated local utility operations. Primarily a response to government restructuring and reorganization policies at the state and federal levels, this category of electric entities includes specialized, non-integrated generating firms ("merchant generators" or "independent power producers"); generating subsidiaries or affiliates of electric utility holding companies; nonintegrated transmission operators; and firms that trade in electric power but own no generation, transmission or distribution facilities ("power marketers").[29]

In generation, nonutilities have come to account for 40 percent of the nation's electric generating capacity, up from an 8 percent share in 1993.[30] Approximately half of this capacity is owned by genuinely independent power producers, with the other half owned by subsidiaries or affiliates of vertically integrated holding companies that also own regulated electric utilities.[31] Examples of genuinely independent generating firms include Calpine, founded in 1984, with the capacity to produce 25,000 megawatts of power from 84 plants in 18 states; Mirant, divested by the Southern Company in 2001, with 18 plants in 6 states; and NRG Energy, founded in 1989, and owning 45 generating plants in 11 states. Generating subsidiaries owned by IOU holding companies include Constellation Energy Generating Group (78 electric power plants), a subsidiary of Constellation Energy, a holding company formed by Baltimore Gas & Electric; Exelon Generation (109 generating plants), a subsidiary of Exelon, a holding company that owns Commonwealth Edison in Illinois and Philadelphia Electric Company (PECO) in Pennsylvania; and FPL Energy, the electric generating subsidiary of FPL Group, a holding company created by Florida Power & Light that operates in 26 states. The extent to which regulated firms have shed generating operations—either to subsidiaries of their own holding companies or to independent outside owners, and have done so either voluntarily or in response to orders by state regulatory commissions—is evidenced by the sharp decline in generating plants directly operated by regulated utilities in various states: Over recent years, these include Illinois (proportion of generating plants in the state directly operated by regulated utilities has dropped from 97 percent to 9 percent); Massachusetts (declined from 87 percent to 9 percent); Pennsylvania (fallen from 92 percent to 12 percent); and Texas (dropped from 88 percent to 41 percent).[32]

At the transmission stage, few genuinely independent transmission companies exist. One of the largest, ITC Holdings, has been created by acquiring transmission systems previously operated by Consumers Energy and Detroit Edison; it currently operates 5,400 miles of transmission lines as an independent "transco" corporation. Another transmission firm, American Transmission Company, has assets of $2 billion and operates 9,000 miles of transmission lines, but is owned by a host of publicly and privately owned electric organizations and utilities. Overall, FERC has found that

---

[29]Electric Energy Market Competition Task Force, 13–14. The Electric Power Supply Association represents the interests of these firms (www.epsa.org).
[30]Electric Energy Market Competition Task Force, 13–14, and American Public Power Association, U.S. Electric Utility Industry Statistics.
[31]Electric Energy Market Competition Task Force, 14.
[32]Electric Energy Market Competition Task Force, 93.

stand-alone transmission companies have assets amounting to only 3 percent of the transmission assets held by investor-owned utilities.[33]

In addition to generating electric power or transmitting it, other nonutility firms are specialized concerns that buy, sell, trade and market electricity, but do not physically generate, transmit or distribute it themselves or through subsidiaries. This segment comprises 152 firms trading 400 million megawatt hours of electricity, and with combined revenues of $20 billion.[34]

Mergers and Acquisitions

Electric power has been the scene of a voracious merger and acquisition movement over the past decade, on a scale unrivaled since the formation of the great electric holding companies 60 years ago (Table 3-6). These mergers were approved by the Federal Energy Regulatory Commission on the ground that they represented combinations of "contiguous" operations and, thus, did not violate the proscriptions of the Public Utility Holding Company Act of 1935 (which was not repealed until 2005).

Examples of major mergers include the $5 billion combination of Ohio Edison and Centerior Energy (comprising the Cleveland Illuminating Company and Toledo Edison) to form FirstEnergy in 1997—a merged firm that redoubled its size in 2001 in a subsequent $5 billion merger with GPU (the holding company for Metropolitan

TABLE 3-6 U.S. Electric Company Mergers, 1993–2006

Year	Number Completed	Number Announced	Number Withdrawn
1993	2	3	1
1994	1	5	0
1995	2	8	4
1996	1	13	3
1997	13	11	3
1998	9	10	0
1999	10	26	2
2000	23	9	1
2001	6	5	4
2002	5	2	3
2003	1	2	1
2004	1	3	1
2005	1	3	0
2006	3	7	2
Total	77	107	25

Source: Edison Electric Institute, 2006 Financial Review, 44.

---

[33]Company websites, and Office of Market Oversight and Investigations, Federal Energy Regulatory Commission, "2004 State of the Markets Report," (Washington, D.C., June 2005).
[34]American Public Power Association, U.S. Electric Utility Industry Statistics.

Edison, Pennsylvania Electric Company, and Jersey Central Power & Light). Commonwealth Edison in Illinois acquired PECO in an $8 billion merger in 2000 to create the Exelon holding company. Other major mergers include the $9.4 billion merger in 2005 of MidAmerican Energy Holdings's operations in Iowa, Illinois, South Dakota and Nebraska, with Pacificorp's operations in Utah, Oregon, Washington, Wyoming, Idaho and California; Ameren's $1 billion merger of Union Electric Company with Central Illinois Public Service Company in 1997, its $885 million acquisition of Central Illinois Light Company in 2003, and its $2.3 billion acquisition of Illinois Power Company in 2004; and Duke Energy's $14.6 billion acquisition of Cinergy and its Ohio, Indiana and Kentucky operations in 2005 (after Cinergy was created nine years before by an $8 billion merger of Cincinnati Gas & Electric with Public Service Company of Indiana).[35]

Combinations of electric firms have played a major role in driving the $380 billion of mergers and acquisitions recorded for all U.S. utility firms (including gas and water) over the 1996 to 2006 period.[36] Sales and transfers of individual generating plants among electric firms have proceeded at an equally feverish pace, with 264 such sales reported over the past three years alone.[37]

One consequence of mergers of this magnitude has been to reduce by a third the number of investor-owned utilities, from 98 in 1995 to 64 by the end of 2006.[38] Another result, as Table 3-4 suggests, has been to greatly expand the absolute size and geographic reach of these merged giants.

Market Concentration

Determining the relative size of the largest firms, or the degree of concentration, in electricity is challenging because the geographic boundaries of markets and, thus, the number of competitors and their relative size, vary across the industry's three main stages. Moreover, when congestion occurs, the geographic scope of markets and the number of viable sources of supply can shrink dramatically.

Local Retail Distribution.

The degree of concentration at the local level of distribution and final consumption is extremely high: A single regulated utility company typically controls all electricity sales in its government-mandated local franchise market. Even when considered at the broader level of an entire state, concentration in local distribution remains very high: The five largest retailers of electricity collectively account for 60 percent or more of total sales in 45 states; for 75 percent or more of sales in 32 states; and for 80 percent or more of retail electricity sales in 20 states.[39] Examples of individual states and the combined

---

[35]Federal Energy Regulatory Commission, "List of Mergers Filed," available at www.ferc.gov/industries/ electric. The American Public Policy Association maintains a list of electric mergers on its website, along with a chronological list of holding company formations in the field, at www.appanet.org.

[36]*Mergers & Acquisitions* magazine, annual almanac issues, and John Kwoka and Michael Pollitt, "Industry Restructuring, Mergers, and Efficiency: Evidence from Electric Power," unpublished manuscript, April 2007.

[37]Energy Information Administration, "Plants Sold and Transferred," available at www.eia.doe.gov/ cneaf/electricity;epm/tablees4.html.

[38]Edison Electric Institute, *2006 Financial Review*, 44.

[39]Energy Information Administration, *State Electricity Profiles 2005*, Washington, D.C., March 7, 2007.

share of the largest five electric retailers operating in them include Alabama and California (78 percent each); Colorado (75 percent); Florida (82 percent); Illinois and Indiana (77 percent each); Iowa (81 percent); New York (62 percent); Ohio (59 percent); Virginia (90 percent); and Oregon (77 percent).[40]

Transmission.

At the transmission stage, ownership of the critically important high-voltage lines that connect generators and producers on one side, with local utilities and consumers on the other, also is highly concentrated. Of the approximately 160,000 miles of high-voltage transmission lines in the U.S., four large electric holding companies—Duke, AEP, Dominion, and Xcel—claim to own a combined 82,000 miles of these lines, or approximately half of the estimated total. A recent estimate by the Census Bureau puts the four largest firms' combined share higher, at 85 percent; the top eight firms' share at 92 percent; and the share of the 20 largest transmission firms at 98 percent.[41]

Most of these transmission lines have been built over many years by vertically integrated utilities to service their own systems of generating plants and retail operations, and these firms continue to own most of them. This raises a host of anticompetitive concerns: They might exploit them to favor their own generating and retail operations at the expense of other competitors. Also, transmission lines can carry only so much electricity before they are overloaded; at these times, vertically integrated firms might move their own power rather than that generated by others. Over the longer run, vertically integrated owners may underinvest in transmission capacity, thereby limiting access to their markets by other generating firms. In areas of the country where regional transmission organizations and independent service organizations have been established, operation of transmission lines has been transferred by the firms that own them to a single, central directing authority, which is regulated by FERC in an effort to provide open, nondiscriminatory access to transmission services. But as we shall see below, complaints in these regions concerning market power and manipulation of access to the grid continue to occur.

Generation.

At the generation stage, concentration is typically high at the state level and, while it is lower within the broader geographic markets in which power is bought and sold, it nonetheless is substantial.

At the state level, the combined share of generation accounted for by the three largest electricity producing firms exceeds 50 percent in 43 states; is greater than 66 percent in 35 states; and exceeds 75 percent in 27 states.[42] Examples include Alabama (top two generating companies with a combined state share of 86 percent); Georgia (largest generator with 86 percent state share); Florida (three largest generators have a combined share of 65 percent); Pennsylvania (four largest with 52 percent combined

---

[40]Energy Information Administration, *State Electricity Profiles 2005*, Washington, D.C., March 7, 2007.
[41]U.S. Census Bureau, "Electric Power Generation, Transmission, and Distribution," *2002 Economic Census*, December 2004.
[42]Calculated on the basis of data contained in Energy Information Administration, Form 906/920 for January–December 2005 (available at www.eia.doe.gov/cneaf/electricity/page/eia906_920.html).

share); Illinois (three largest generators have a 72 percent share); Minnesota (top two generators account for 87 percent share); Missouri (top two generators account for 70 percent share); Colorado (two largest generators account for 68 percent share); Texas (six largest generators account for 45 percent share); and California (top six account for 41 percent share).[43]

Regional generation markets encompass a number of states and generating firms, so concentration at this more expansive level is lower than at the state level, but is substantial nonetheless. Various regional markets and the combined share of generating capacity accounted for by the ten largest generating entities in them include the Midwest ISO (60%), PJM (77%), New England ISO (73%), Southwest Power Pool (73%), ERCOT in Texas (78%), Southeast electric market (72%), Northwest electric market (82%), and New York ISO (81%).[44] Recognizing the existence of generating plants jointly owned by multiple firms in these regions would push these concentration statistics even higher.

As we have seen, there appears to have been a great deal of churning in the generation stage in recent years. These changes may exaggerate the degree of meaningful reorganization, however, because many divestitures of generating plants represent either the transfer of generating plants to newly formed subsidiaries of vertically integrated holding companies, or the transfer of generating plants between vertically integrated utility firms.[45] Another important consideration in assessing concentration in generation stems from the fact that electricity cannot be stored: At times when a grid is congested, the geographic range shrinks from which power can be drawn, the number of viable suppliers drops, and the effective level of concentration of available generation sources rises. In these circumstances, conventional concentration measures may understate the effective degree of "pivotal" market power. In the PJM regional transmission organization, for example, the ten largest firms together account for over 90 percent of the critical margin of generating capacity required to meet peak loads on the system.[46] In other regions, the single largest generating concern may account for 30 percent or more of this critical peaking capacity.[47]

Demand Characteristics

The demand side of the industry is characterized by two important factors. First, consumers do not use electricity on a steady, constant basis, so demand varies considerably through the day, month, and year. Consider the ordinary household: while the youngsters are at school and the parents at work, the residential demand on the electric system is at

---

[43]Calculated on the basis of data contained in Energy Information Administration, Form 906/920, Monthly Time Series File, for January–December 2005 (available at www.eia.doe.gov/cneaf/electricity/page/eia 906_920.html).

[44]Federal Energy Regulatory Commission, "State of the Markets Report: 2004" (Washington, D.C., June 2005).

[45]See Energy Information Administration, "The Changing Structure of the Electric Power Industry 1999: Mergers and Other Corporate Combinations" (Washington, D.C., December 1999): 49–50, and Jun Ishii, "From Investor-Owned Utility to Independent Power Producer," Center for the Study of Energy Markets, University of California, November 2002.

[46]"State of the Markets Report: 2004," 109.

[47]Energy Information Administration, "State of the Markets Report: 2004" (Washington, D.C., January 2004): 24.

TABLE 3-7 Retail Electric Sales by Customer Class, 1995–2005

Customer Class	*1995*	*2000*	*2005*
Residential:			
Megawatt hours	1,043	1,193	1,359
Revenues	$ 87,610	$ 98,209	$ 128,393
Commercial:			
Megawatt hours	862.7	1,055	1,275
Revenues	$ 66,365	$ 78,405	$ 110,522
Industrial:			
Megawatt hours	1,013	1,064	1,019
Revenues	$ 47,175	$ 49,369	$ 58,445

Note: *Megawatt hours and revenues in millions.*

Source: Energy Information Administration (www.eia.doe.gov/cneaf/electricity/epa/epat7).

a minimum. Between five o'clock and bedtime, however, activity in the kitchen and the laundry room, as well as at the computers and the television sets puts an increased demand-load on the system. This variability is greatly magnified by weather: Air conditioning in the summer, particularly in offices and other commercial establishments, can severely strain the electric system.

Second, the sensitivity of consumers to price, or the elasticity of demand, differs significantly among different categories of customers. Residential consumers have virtually no real-time awareness of either the amount of power consumption or the price being paid at the time electricity is being used; residential electric bills reflect the price-quantity relationship of the month before. Consequently, there are few if any contemporaneous price signals to respond to, and residential demand is relatively inelastic. Commercial consumers, such as fast-food restaurants, "big box" stores, and office buildings are similarly characterized: Although the largest of these are attentive to managing their energy bills, they compete in local markets, and any change in the price of electricity for one of them will apply equally to their local rivals as well. Hence, it is difficult to argue that this class of customers is particularly sensitive to price changes. The demand for electricity by industrial consumers is much more elastic, however, because it is a major expense. Moreover, manufacturers compete in national and global markets, where their rivals may pay significantly lower electric prices. Industrial firms also have the option of generating their own power if their operations are substantial. Consequently, the demand of industrial users is much more price-sensitive than that of other customer classes.

Retail sales of electricity to these classes of customers are depicted in Table 3-7 for recent years.

▪▪▪ III. Conduct

The most important aspects of the industry's conduct are pricing at its various stages, and issues of market power and manipulation of electric power markets.

Pricing: Local Distribution

The price of electricity to final consumers at the local distribution level is regulated by state public utility commissions according to traditional principles of "rate-base, rate-of-return" regulation. Hearings are convened periodically, during which the allowable costs and assets of electric companies are assessed, and a "rate structure" of prices is approved to provide the revenues required to cover the firm's expenses and enable it to earn a fair rate of return, or profit, on its assets.

This rate structure includes prices that differ substantially for different customer classes: highest for residential consumers, lowest for industrial users, and typically somewhere in between for commercial users (Table 3-8). These price differences are justified on a variety of grounds. Residential consumers are said to be the most expensive class to serve because they have low "load factors": Peak demand for them occurs just a few hours a day, and is high relative to their average consumption. This raises the cost to serve them because electric firms must maintain sufficient capacity to serve their peak demand, leaving this capacity underutilized the rest of the time. Industrial users, in contrast, have steadier rates of power consumption, and so are considered relatively less expensive to serve. Also, a larger base of industrial consumers may smooth out the system-wide average level of power consumption, thereby reducing the overall cost of providing service for all classes of customers. Lower industrial prices for electricity also can be used by state regulatory commissions to attract or retain industry and the jobs and economic growth that go with it. In any event, the result is that the customer class with the most inelastic demand pays the highest price.

Electricity prices at the local level also vary considerably across the country (Figure 3-4), with prices generally higher in the Northeast and California, and lower in the Midwest and Northwest. In important part, this is due to the differing cost of generating

TABLE 3-8 Average Price and Total Revenue by Customer Class, 1994–2005

	Residential		Commercial		Industrial	
	Average Price	*Revenue*	*Average Price*	*Revenue*	*Average Price*	*Revenue*
1994	8.38	$ 84.6	7.73	$ 63.4	4.77	$ 48.1
1995	8.40	87.6	7.69	66.4	4.66	47.2
1996	8.36	90.5	7.64	67.8	4.60	47.5
1997	8.43	90.7	7.59	70.5	4.53	47.0
1998	8.26	93.4	7.41	72.6	4.48	47.1
1999	8.16	93.5	7.26	72.8	4.43	46.9
2000	8.24	98.2	7.43	78.4	4.64	49.4
2001	8.58	103.2	7.92	85.7	5.05	50.3
2002	8.44	106.8	7.89	87.1	4.88	48.3
2003	8.72	111.2	8.03	96.3	5.11	51.7
2004	8.95	115.6	8.17	100.6	5.25	53.5
2005	9.45	128.4	8.67	110.5	5.73	58.5

Average price in cents per kilowatt hour; revenue in billions.
Source: U.S. Energy Information Administration (www.eia.doe.gov/cneaf/electricity/epa/epat7p4.html).

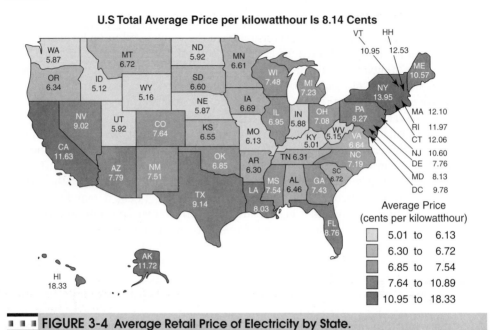

U.S Total Average Price per kilowatthour Is 8.14 Cents

Average Price (cents per kilowatthour)	
	5.01 to 6.13
	6.30 to 6.72
	6.85 to 7.54
	7.64 to 10.89
	10.95 to 18.33

▪▪▪▪ **FIGURE 3-4** Average Retail Price of Electricity by State.

Source: Energy Information Administration, *Electric Power Annual*, November 2006.

power in these different regions—lower-cost coal generation in the Midwest and inexpensive hydropower in the Northwest, versus higher-cost oil and natural gas generation in the Northeast and California.

Sixteen states have undertaken regulatory initiatives to allow electricity customers, including residential consumers, to choose their generation provider, with the local utility acting as monopoly distributor of that power. In these cases, the incumbent utility is designated the "provider of last resort" for users who fail to choose an alternative power supplier, or for consumers whose alternative power supplier might fail. A number of states permit individual residential consumers and communities to pool, or "aggregate," their purchases.

Industrial and commercial consumer classes have been far more responsive in exercising this choice among power suppliers than have residential consumers: The proportion of residential consumers switching to alternative electricity suppliers in prochoice states ranges from 0.0 percent in Illinois and New Jersey, to 1.5 percent in Maryland, and 6 to 9 percent in Massachusetts and New York, with a high of 27 percent in Texas. (Some states, such as Texas, randomly assign residential consumers to various power producers, so high switch rates are not necessarily indicative of voluntary consumer choice.) Supplier switch rates for industrial and commercial consumers are much higher, including 72 percent switching among electricity suppliers by large commercial and industrial users in Illinois, 79 percent in Maryland, and 46 to 65 percent in New Jersey, New York, Massachusetts and Texas.[48] Overall, competitive electric providers account for more than 5 percent of residential power consumption in only four states (Massachusetts,

---

[48]Electric Energy Market Competition Task Force, Appendix D.

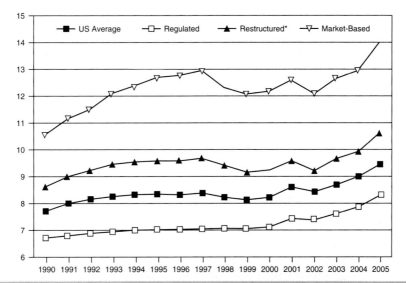

▪▪▪▪ **FIGURE 3-5 Residential Prices for States with Market-Based Prices, Regulated, and Restructured States.**

Source: Kenneth Rose and Karl Meeusen, "2006 Performance Review of Electric Power Markets," Institute of Public Utilities, Michigan State University, August 27, 2006, 3.

Ohio, New York, Texas), while competitive suppliers account for 30 percent or more of the power consumed by large industrial and commercial customers in nine states (with Texas the highest at 86 percent).[49]

Finally, as Figure 3-5 indicates, restructuring at the retail level has not significantly reduced the higher residential prices that impelled states to initiate restructuring in the first place. Moreover, a number of the states that have implemented restructuring policies temporarily lowered residential prices and capped them; as these regulated caps now begin to expire, residential electricity prices have begun to climb at rates of 24 to 72 percent or more.[50]

Pricing: Wholesale Generation

The price of wholesale power at the generation stage is negotiated between buyers and sellers, including between affiliates owned by the same vertically integrated holding company. If the generator has been designated as having "market-based rate authority" by the FERC, the unregulated market price is presumed to be just and reasonable unless shown otherwise, and is not subject to traditional cost-of-service regulation. Obtaining this pricing status requires the generator to demonstrate that it lacks horizontal market power in generation; it lacks vertical market power in transmission; it has not erected barriers to entry to the market; and, in the case of holding companies,

---

[49]Kenneth Rose and Karl Meeusen, "2006 Performance Review of Electric Power Markets," Institute of Public Utilities, Michigan State University, August 27, 2006.
[50]Alexei Barrionuevo, "Generating Anger: Soaring Utility Prices Bring Calls to Re-Examine Regulation," *New York Times* (February 17, 2007) B1.

that relationships among its subsidiary generating, transmission, and local franchise affiliates satisfy a number of regulatory requirements.[51] The firm must file detailed transactions reports with FERC quarterly, and the courts have held that FERC must conscientiously review these filings. Approximately 500 generating firms hold this market-based rate authority. If a generating firm has not received such authority, the wholesale price of its power is regulated by FERC and set on the traditional regulatory basis of cost of service.

The pricing of wholesale power also depends on whether the electricity is bought or sold in a region presided over by an RTO or not. In regions without an RTO, buyer and seller negotiate a price, amount of power, date and time, and then contract with transmission entities to transport the electricity. In regions of the country presided over by an RTO, buyer and seller negotiate a price, amount of power, date and time. When the contracted-for date and time arrive, the generator puts the power into the RTO grid, while the seller withdraws an equal amount of power. The seller receives the price for power prevailing on the grid at the time it is added, and the buyer pays the prevailing price in withdrawing it from the grid. Buyer and seller settle differences between the prevailing price and the price originally contracted for. The market price of power on the RTO grid is continuously adjusted to balance supply with demand, primarily utilizing "one-bid" auctions. This means that the highest price required to attract the last increment of supply to meet the demand is paid to all suppliers, even if they initially had bid less to supply electricity from their plants. Prices in these markets vary substantially through the day, month and year. Should serious congestion conditions arise, "mitigation" procedures are invoked, putting a cap on the maximum allowable price for power.

As Figure 3-6 shows for the western hub of the PJM RTO, prices fluctuated between $40 and $60 for most of the year, but rose dramatically when hot weather and air conditioning use spiked in mid-July and early August.[52] Markets for wholesale power in regions of the country not governed by RTOs are thinner and less extensively used, with power traded more on a traditional, bilateral basis of negotiations between individual buyer and seller, the details of which may or may not be publicly disclosed.

Pricing: Transmission and Congestion

The Federal Electric Regulatory Commission requires that all electric entities operating transmission lines offer access to their lines through an Open Access Transmission Tariff (OATT). There are two main types of transmission tariffs: OATT contracts for "network transmission service" are for putting power into the grid and taking it out. In this case the user pays a monthly fee based on its share of the total amount of power in the system (its "load ratio share"). The user may also be required to make its facilities available as "network resources" and agree to redispatch them when requested by the transmission operator, such as when congestion occurs. The second major type of transmission price, "point-to-point transmission service," covers transmission of power

---

[51]Federal Energy Regulatory Commission, "Market-Based Rates for Wholesale Sales of Electric Energy, Capacity, and Ancillary Services by Public Utilities," 119 FERC ¶61,295 (June 21, 2007).
[52]Electricity futures are traded on the Intercontinental Exchange (ICE), the New York Mercantile Exchange, and the Chicago Board of Trade.

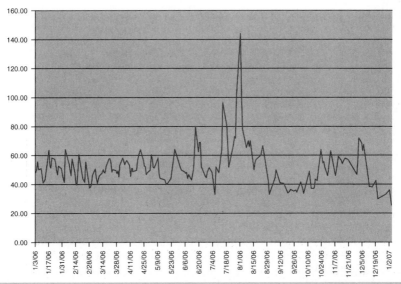

■ ■ ■ **FIGURE 3-6** Wholesale Prices: PJM West.

Source: Energy Information Administration.

between specified locations; in these cases, the user pays a fee based on the amount of the transmission system's capacity used.

Participants in regional transmission organizations pay a transmission access fee plus the additional cost of congestion when it arises. When congestion occurs in the system, the price of electricity at that location rises to reflect what is, in effect, a congestion charge. Users can purchase rights to physically transmit a contracted-for amount of power. Alternatively, a "financial transmission right" may be assigned or bought as a hedge entitling the user to receive a portion of a higher congestion charge should it be imposed.

To address congestion, some regional transmission organizations have developed "locational marginal pricing" (LMP) at the nodes of a grid where substantial amounts of electricity are injected or withdrawn. These location-specific prices add a congestion charge to the cost of the power, so that the market price is higher when a particular node is congested. Other RTOs divide their regions into zones, and adjust prices to reflect the relative extent of congestion between zones. These congestion costs are substantial: In the PJM region, for example, they have ranged between $1.6 and $2.1 billion in recent years; in the Texas ERCOT they have run to $270 million per year.[53]

Instead of using location marginal pricing to bring demand and supply into balance under congestion, some system operators issue "transmission loading relief" (TLR) orders requiring users to reduce their power transfers. In other cases, the central operator may redispatch and redirect electricity among generating plants in order

---

[53]PJM, 2006 State of the Market Report (available at www.pjm.com), and ERCOT News Update, March 31, 2006 (www.ercot.com/news/press_releases/2006).

to relieve congestion at a particular node. When a regional operating system confronts a serious overload, "mitigation" procedures may be invoked either by state regulatory commissions, FERC, or the regional organization operator, capping the maximum price of power in the market.

The revenues produced by these tariffs, fees and charges are substantial: Total annual revenues for all bulk electricity transmission and control in the U.S. amounts to $12.7 billion according to one recent estimate; for the PJM RTO, they totaled $758 million over the 2004 to 2006 period.[54]

Market Power and Market Manipulation

The exercise of market power and the manipulation of new electricity markets are major controversies in the field.

One market power issue stems from the vertically integrated firms that own the bulk of the nation's transmission lines—the backbone on which the functioning of the industry depends—and their ability to manipulate access to their lines in anticompetitive ways. Vertically integrated firms can do this, FERC repeatedly has found, in an almost unlimited variety of ways: offering more advantageous transmission terms to their own generating subsidiary than to the generating plants operated by others; preferentially providing advance notification of the availability of transmission service (or the availability of new services) to their own generating subsidiary before providing it to other generating firms; altering procedures (such as scheduling deadlines) in ways that preference their own generating operations over other generators; failing to make information about transmission capacities available in a timely fashion for others; overly restrictive transmission planning, expansion, and connection policies; prolonging negotiations for transmission service; and selectively targeting the generating plants of others for cutbacks when congestion occurs.[55] Limiting the availability of long-term transmission service contracts also may raise the costs and risks for nonintegrated generating rivals, as may imposing on them a disproportionate share of the cost of expanding the capacity of transmission lines.[56] In areas where no regional transmission organization operates, anticompetitive relationships among the subsidiaries of vertically integrated holding companies can be shrouded in secrecy.[57]

Another major concern is the vulnerability of prices in electric markets to manipulation. The problem stems from a combination of high levels of concentration in generation, particularly for the critically important plants last brought online to meet peak demand,

---

[54]PJM, 2006 Annual Financial Report, and U.S. Census Bureau, "Electric Power Generation, Transmission, and Distribution," 2002 Economic Census, December 2004 (available at http://www.census.gov/epcd/ec97/ industry/E221121.HTM).

[55]See the litany of these complaints discussed at length in Federal Energy Regulatory Commission, Order No. 890, Final Rule, February 16, 2007; Order No. 2003, 104 FERC ¶61,103 (July 24, 2003); and Order No. 2000, 89 FERC ¶61,285 (December 20, 1999). For an earlier Supreme Court decision finding anticompetitive manipulation of transmission lines by a vertically integrated electric firm, see *Otter Tail Power Co. v. United States*, 410 U.S. 366 (1973).

[56]See American Public Power Association, "Restructuring at the Crossroads," (Washington, D.C., December 2004), and Paul L. Joskow and Jean Tirole, "Transmission Rights and Market Power on Electric Power Networks," *RAND Journal of Economics* 31 (2000): 450–487.

[57]See Rebecca Smith, "How Southern Co. Flourishes in Humbled Electricity Industry," Wall Street Journal (June 27, 2003), 1.

and the "one-price" rule governing power auctions: By withholding electricity supplies from auctions, or by submitting artificially inflated demands for power that create the appearance of congestion, generating firms can inflate the equilibrium price required to balance supply and demand, and greatly increase their profits. This was spectacularly the case in the California electric power crisis of 2000 and 2001, where it is estimated that artificially withholding supplies from power auctions—what one court has described as "manipulation on a massive scale"—played a key role in inflating electricity prices by 500 percent and more.[58] Concerns about market manipulation continue to be raised in other regions too, including the Texas ERCOT, where an independent market monitor recently found one of the state's largest electric firms, TXU, to have market power in generation sufficient to manipulate the price of electricity, and to have exercised its power to raise prices by millions of dollars at critically congested times of the year.[59] The fact that a few large power producers continuously interact in these power markets may further enhance their ability to tacitly collude in engaging in such market manipulation.[60]

▪▪▪ IV. Performance

Important aspects of the electric industry's performance are its productivity, technological innovativeness, service reliability, and its impact on the environment.

Productivity and Efficiency

Over the first three decades after World War II, the electric industry performed well in terms of efficiency and productivity gains. Its annual average growth rate in total factor productivity of 2.7 percent over the period from 1947 to 1973 ranked third highest among 45 industries in one study, while its labor productivity growth rate of 4.9 percent over the 1948 to 1979 period was double the rate of labor productivity improvement in American business generally.[61]

However, these and other studies found that the industry's productivity and efficiency performance deteriorated over the latter years of this postwar period: Its total

---

[58]Severin Borenstein, James B. Bushnell, and Frank A. Wolak, "Measuring Market Inefficiencies in California's Restructured Wholesale Electricity Market," *American Economic Review* 92 (2002): 1376–1405; and Paul Joskow and Edward Kahn, "A Quantitative Analysis of Pricing Behavior in California's Wholesale Electricity Market During Summer 2000," *Energy Journal* 23 (2002): 1–35. The court's characterization is contained in *Lockyer v. Coral Power et al., 383 F.3d 1006* (Ninth Cir. 2004).
[59]See David Cay Johnston, "Flaws Seen in Markets for Utilities," *New York Times*, November 21, 2006, p. C1; and Rebecca Smith, "Fight Brews Among Utilities in Illinois," *Wall Street Journal* (March 22, 2007) A9. For an in-depth analysis of market manipulation in the Texas ERCOT, see Potomac Economics, Ltd., "Investigation of the Wholesale Market Activities of TXU from June 1 to September 20, 2005," report to the Public Utility Commission of Texas, March 2007 (available at http://www.puc.state.tx.us/about/reports/2005_TXU_Investigation_IMM_Cover.pdf). Additional concerns have been raised about the ability of firms to manipulate energy prices on the nation's commodities exchanges. See U.S. Senate, Permanent Subcommittee on Investigations, "Excessive Speculation in the Natural Gas Market," Staff Report, June 25, 2007.
[60]Rose and Meeusen, 6–7.
[61]Frank M. Gollop and Dale W. Jorgenson, "U.S. Productivity Growth by Industry: 1947–73," in John W. Kendrick and Beatrice N. Vaccara eds., *New Developments in Productivity Measurement and Analysis* (Chicago: University of Chicago Press, 1980), and John W. Kendrick, *Interindustry Differences in Productivity Growth* (Washington, D.C.: American Enterprise Institute, 1982).

factor productivity fell from nearly 6 percent per year from 1947 to 1953, to −0.4 percent by the 1966 to 1973 period. This deteriorating performance has been attributed to a number of factors, including disruptions induced by gyrating energy prices in the 1970s, and compounded by the advent of environmental regulations and controls. In addition to these, however, the industry's efficiency suffered from ever-larger generating plants whose economies failed to materialize, and which suffered lower reliability rates and higher operating costs.[62] It also suffered from its multi-billion investment in nuclear power plants that cost far more to build and operate than was expected; a number of these plants were either abandoned before they were completed, or were converted to burn conventional fuels, at an aggregate cost of more than $22 billion.[63]

More recently, electric companies have improved their productivity, but not to the high rates the industry achieved in earlier years: Since 1990, the industry's labor productivity has grown at an annual average rate of 2.9 percent, compared to an annual average rate of labor productivity growth for all U.S. manufacturing of 4.1 percent.[64] Interestingly, one study finds that all of the improvement in productivity over the 1975 to 1987 period came from small and medium-sized plants.[65] Another study estimates that generating plants suffer an average cost inefficiency of 13 percent, implying that the industry's costs could be reduced by a large aggregate dollar amount if plants operated more efficiently.[66]

A perennial issue is whether government regulation induces electric firms to inefficiently overinvest in capital plant and equipment. Named for the authors of an article published in 1962,[67] this Averch-Johnson effect posits that inefficient overinvestment occurs because government regulatory commissions allow utilities to earn a profit rate on their assets in excess of the cost to the firms of raising capital funds to invest. The result is to inflate costs and reduce efficiency in electricity, although the magnitude of this effect is a matter of dispute. It may, however, partly explain the industry's insistence on building nuclear plants and ever-bigger conventional power plants, even as their economic disadvantages began to surface.

An important current issue concerns the effect on efficiency stemming from the recent restructuring of the field. One study suggests that labor productivity has risen, and average fuel and nonfuel costs both have declined, in states that have restructured electric power, and that these improvements represent upwards of $5 billion in potential cost savings if greater restructuring were implemented nationwide.[68] Another study, however, finds that deregulation harms efficiency, at least in the transition

---

[62]Paul L. Joskow and Richard Schmalensee, "The Performance of Coal-Burning Electric Generating Units in the United States: 1960–1980," *Journal of Applied Econometrics* 2 (1987): 85–109.

[63]See Walter Adams and James W. Brock, *The Bigness Complex* (New York: Pantheon, 1987), chapter 21.

[64]Bureau of Labor Statistics, "Industry Productivity and Costs, and Major Sector Productivity and Costs Index," available at www.bls.gov/lpc/home.htm#data.

[65]J. Douglass Klein, Shelton Schmidt and Suthathip Yaisawarng, "Productivity Changes in the U.S. Electric Power Industry," in David B. Audretsch and John J. Siegfried eds., *Empirical Studies in Industrial Organization: Essays in Honor of Leonard W. Weiss* (Boston: Kluwer Academic Publishers, 1992): 229.

[66]Andrew N. Kleit and Dek Terrell, "Measuring Potential Efficiency Gains from Deregulation of Electricity Generation: A Bayesian Approach," *Review of Economics and Statistics* 83 (2001): 523–30.

[67]Harvey Averch and Leland L. Johnson, "Behavior of the Firm Under Regulatory Constraint," *American Economic Review* 52 (1962): 1052–1069.

[68]Catherine Wolfram, "The Efficiency of Electricity Generation in the United States after Restructuring," in James M. Griffen and Steven L. Puller eds., *Electricity Deregulation: Choices and Challenges* (Chicago: University of Chicago Press, 2005): 227–255.

period, and that this transition period can be a decade or more owing to the long planning horizon in the field.[69] One disturbing finding is that the recent wave of mergers in the field has undermined efficiency because acquiring firms have relatively poorer efficiency records compared to the firms they acquire. Moreover, the operations of acquired firms suffer efficiency losses following merger, and these losses are not offset by efficiency gains on the part of the acquiring firms' operations.[70]

Technological Innovation

The general record of innovation in the industry is one in which substantial evolutionary gains were made until the 1970s, when the industry's satisfaction with the status quo collided with a fundamentally changed industrial environment.[71] The high productivity gains discussed above for the years prior to the 1970s were the product of sustained, incremental increases in size, steam pressure, and operating temperatures of conventionally fueled generating plants. The advent of nuclear power in the latter-1950s was perceived as affording another step in the industry's conventional march to giantism. Technological advances were made in boiler design, turbine generators, pollution abatement equipment, and automated controls, but the very largest firms did not account for a disproportionate share of them.[72]

The average size of new coal-fired plants steadily grew, from 124 mW in the early 1950s, to 400 mW in the mid-1960s, to nearly 600 mW by the early 1970s.[73] But bigger ceased to be better. The thermal efficiency of the largest plants (the efficiency with which fuel is converted into electricity) began to deteriorate as limits of metallurgy, physics, and complexity were reached: "Whether using nuclear or fossil fuel, these [giant] plants required congeries of redundant systems to ensure safety and good performance. They also needed massive pipes, fittings, and connectors—in general, large components and many more of them than a smaller plant."[74] According to some assessments, the thermal efficiency of coal-burning plants, the industry's generating workhorse, has not significantly improved in 40 years. In its attitude toward technology, according to others, the industry had become "stale and risk-averse."[75] It was slow to recognize that its commercial environment had begun to change fundamentally in the 1970s and 1980s: Uncertainties of fuel costs as well as uncertainty concerning demand growth put a premium on employing smaller, more efficient generating units, such as combined cycle gas turbines,[76] either built by themselves or drawn on as cogeneration

[69]Magali Delmas and Yesim Tokat, "Deregulation, Governance Structures, and Efficiency: The U.S. Electric Utility Sector," *Strategic Management Journal* 26 (2005): 441–460.

[70]John Kwoka and Michael Pollitt, "Industry Restructuring, Mergers, and Efficiency: Evidence from Electric Power," unpublished manuscript, April 2007.

[71]For a comprehensive examination, see Richard F. Hirsh, *Technology and Transformation in the American Electric Utility Industry* (New York: Cambridge University Press, 1989).

[72]Bruce A. Smith, "Technological Innovation in Electric Power Generation: 1950–1970," *Land Economics* 50 (1974): 336–347.

[73]Joskow and Rose, 4.

[74]Hirsh, 96.

[75]Ibid.,142.

[76]See Jorge Islas, "The Gas Turbine: A New Technological Paradigm in Electricity Generation," *Technological Forecasting and Social Change* 60 (1999): 129–148, and Ulrika Claeson Colpier and Deborah Cornland, "The Economics of the Combined Cycle Gas Turbine," *Energy Policy* 30 (2002): 309–316.

plants built and operated by others. Large incumbent electric firms were slow to adjust to these developments, perhaps in part from concern that reorienting themselves in these directions would jeopardize their monopoly dominance of the field.[77]

Electric utilities also grew passive on the technological front over the postwar decades, increasingly relying on electrical equipment manufacturers like General Electric and Westinghouse to do the innovating for them. Having become users of technology rather than makers of it, electric utilities were late to recognize the escalating risks of the ever-larger plants that the manufacturers were selling them. It was not until 1971 that the utilities established a collective research arm, the Electric Power Research Institute (EPRI), and then only to defuse momentum in Congress for creating a government agency to conduct research in the field.[78]

The industry continues to devote a surprisingly small effort to research and development. Research and development spending by all utilities (gas and water as well as electric) totaled $600 million over the 1999 to 2003 period. This represents only 0.08 percent of utility revenues, far below the 3.4 percent rate recorded for all U.S. industries.[79] Put differently, some experts estimate that if the electric power industry devoted just two percent of its revenues to R&D over the next ten years, the resulting amount would exceed the cumulative dollar amount of all R&D in the field over the past thirty years. Instead, the concern today is that the industry's R&D spending is moving in the opposite direction, falling by half in recent years as utilities cut their EPRI dues and their own research programs.[80]

Reliability and Congestion

As befits its status as a necessity, the reliability of electric power is an important dimension of the industry's performance. Reliability, in turn, is directly related to the frequency with which congestion occurs in the grid, a factor that has been of particular concern as restructuring has engulfed the field.

One measure of reliability is the number of major disturbances that occur across the nation's electric power systems. These include uncontrolled losses of power, voltage losses, or other unusual events that impair the reliability of electric service and are reported to the Department of Energy and the North American Electric Reliability Corporation. These statistics have been rising over recent years, from 50 major disturbances in 2001, to 72 in 2005 and 80 in 2006.[81] Another indicator of deteriorating reliability is congestion serious enough to threaten the functioning of an electric system, and requiring the imposition of transmission loading relief (TLR) procedures to stabilize the flow of power. As Figure 3-7 indicates, the number of these TLRs also is increasing over recent years and by a substantial amount.

---

[77]Hirsh, 167.

[78]Ibid., 135.

[79]National Science Foundation, "Company and Other Nonfederal Funds for Industrial R&D as a Percent of Net Sales of Companies that Performed Industrial R&D in the United States," available at www.nsf.gov/statistics/showpub.cfm.

[80]Gregory F. Nemet and Daniel M. Kammen, "U.S. Energy Research and Development: Declining Investment, Increasing Need, and the Feasibility of Expansion," *Energy Policy* 35 (2007): 746–755.

[81]North American Electric Reliability Corporation (available at www.nerc.com/~filez/dawgdisturbancereports.html).

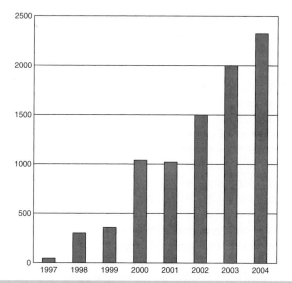

■ ■ ■ **FIGURE 3-7** Number of Transmission Loading Relief Events (Level 2 or higher).

Source: Seth A. Blumsack, Jay Apt, and Lester B. Lave, "Lessons from the Failure of U.S. Electricity Restructuring," *Electricity Journal* 19 (2006): 26.

Given the widespread use of electricity, congestion and disruptions constitute a substantial problem estimated to cost the nation $20 to 100 billion.[82] The August 14, 2003 blackout alone is estimated to have cost the nation $4 to 10 billion. A FERC commissioner estimates that a 5 percent improvement in this area would save an amount of electricity equivalent to that generated by 42 new coal-fired plants.[83]

In a restructured environment, the concern is that reliability is being jeopardized by growth in electric power demand and generation that is outstripping investment in the transmission system required to handle it.[84] Reliability and congestion may suffer from the economic problem of being a public good because "free riders" benefit from reliability whether they pay for it or not—a problem that may be compounded by the incentives of the vertically integrated holding companies that own the transmission lines, and who may be less than enthusiastic about expanding their transmission capacity to enable other generators to better compete with their own generating operations. At the local distribution stage, competition in generation may be shrinking a source of funds that formerly could be drawn on to maintain and enhance the quality of utility distribution systems (an especially important concern given the sensitivity of electronic equipment and computers to slight fluctuations in power). Finally, the regulatory priorities of individual states may militate against promoting reliability by increased investment in

---

[82]Casazza and Delea, 119.
[83]Prepared testimony of Jon Willinghoff, Commissioner, Federal Energy Regulatory Commission, before the U.S. House, Subcommittee on Energy and Air Quality, May 3, 2007.
[84]Federal Energy Regulatory Commission, "Commission Proposes Transmission Pricing Reforms to Increase Power Grid Investment," press release, November 17, 2005.

transmission, when doing so raises consumer prices in one state but benefits power consumers in other states.[85]

Environmental Pollution

According to the Environmental Protection Agency, electric power generation is the dominant industrial source of air emissions in the United States. Fossil fuel–fired generating plants are responsible for producing 67 percent of the nation's sulfur dioxide emissions, 40 percent of carbon dioxide emissions, and 23 percent of nitrogen oxide emissions.[86] In quantities, the industry annually emits 2.5 billion tons of carbon dioxide, 10.3 million tons of sulfur dioxide, and 4 million tons of nitrogen oxides.[87] Table 3-9 shows the average emissions of these major air pollutants by plant fuel type, where it can be seen that natural gas is a relatively less polluting fuel source while coal is the most polluting. The industry's conventional power plants reduced their emissions of sulfur dioxide and nitrogen oxides by 13 and 50 percent, respectively, over the 1995 to 2005 decade; however, emissions of carbon dioxide, the major contributor to global warming, have increased by nearly 20 percent over the same decade.[88]

For nuclear power, the pollution problem is different: The radioactivity of the spent fuel rods that power nuclear generating plants, as well as the plants themselves when they are functioning and once they are removed from service, is toxic for 200,000 years or longer and, thus, somehow must be safely disposed. Over 20,000 tons of spent fuel rods have been accumulating at nuclear plant sites as the industry has looked to the federal government for a permanent disposal site—a challenge that will grow as the oldest plants begin reaching the end of their service lives and must be safely dismantled and disposed of. Two major concerns are whether the government's Yucca Mountain repository in Nevada will be licensed to receive and store radioactive nuclear waste, and

TABLE 3-9 Fossil Fuels Impact on Air Quality

Generator Fuel	*Carbon Dioxide Emissions*	*Sulfur Dioxide Emissions*	*Nitrogen Oxides Emissions*
Coal	2,249 lbs/mWh	13 lbs/mWh	6 lbs/mWh
Oil	1,672 lbs/mWh	12 lbs/mWh	4 lbs/mWh
Natural Gas	1,135 lbs/mWh	0.1 lbs/mWh	1.7 lbs/mWh

Source: Environmental Protection Agency (www.epa.gov/cleanenergy/emissions.htm)

---

[85]For comprehensive examinations of these issues, see Department of Energy, National Transmission Grid Study, Washington, D.C., May 2002, and Eric Hurst, "U.S. Transmission Capacity: Present Status and Future Prospects," study prepared for Edison Electric Institute and U.S. Department of Energy, August 2004. For recent federal regulatory initiatives to address the transmission reliability and congestion problem, see Federal Energy Regulatory Commission, Promoting Transmission Investment through Pricing Reform, Order No. 679, 116 FERC ¶61,057 (July 31, 2006).
[86]www.epa.gov/cleanenergy/emissions.htm.
[87]Energy Information Administration, "Emissions from Energy Consumption for Electricity Production and Useful Thermal Output at Combined Heat-and-Power Plants," available at www.eia.doe/cneaf/electricity/epa/epat5p1.html.
[88]Ibid.

whether the industry has been accumulating sufficient funds to pay the hundreds of millions of dollars that will be required to safely decommission its nuclear power plants.[89]

▪ ▪ ▪ V. Public Policy

Major public policy issues in the industry revolve around the question of whether deregulation and restructuring of electric power is succeeding; environmental pollution policy; and the efficacy of public policies to promote alternative sources of energy for generating electricity.

Regulation and Restructuring

Regulation of electric firms as naturally monopolistic public utilities commenced at the individual state level early in the industry's history. States created (or expanded) regulatory commissions to review electric companies' prices, profits, accounting methods, capital structures, and terms of service in order to compel the firms to operate in accordance with the general regulatory standard of "just and reasonable." In return for this regulatory oversight and control, and to achieve what were considered to be the efficiencies and economies of large scale, utilities were granted monopoly franchises in their service areas. At the federal level, the Federal Power Commission (FPC) was created in 1920 to regulate construction and operation of hydroelectric power projects on domestic waterways. The FPC's powers were expanded in 1935, with passage of the Public Utility Company Act, giving the FPC broad authority over the interstate transmission of electricity. The 1935 act also gave the Securities and Exchange Commission extensive regulatory control over electric utility holding companies and, as we have seen, empowered the SEC to implement a comprehensive break up of electric holding companies. At the federal level as at the state level, the premise was that electricity is a naturally monopolistic field where competition is incapable of functioning adequately, and which thus requires thoroughgoing government regulatory control.[90] Regulation at the federal level was expanded in 1954, when the Atomic Energy Act opened the development of nuclear power to private firms and empowered the Atomic Energy Commission (today the Nuclear Regulatory Commission) to regulate the nuclear generation of electricity.

But beginning in the 1970s, the fundamental premise of natural monopoly began to change in profound and initially unexpected ways. The Public Utility Regulatory Policies Act of 1978 was originally enacted in response to the energy crises of the 1970s, and was aimed at conserving the nation's energy use: It required electric utilities to connect their grids with co-generation facilities (primarily operated by industrial firms in their manufacturing activities) and other outside power producers who met the statutory criteria for operating a "qualifying facility" (QF).

The growth of this new source of power (filings for QFs with the Federal Energy Regulatory Commission (formerly the Federal Power Commission) jumped from

---

[89]For the first concern, see General Accounting Office, Yucca Mountain: "Persistent Quality Assurance Problems Could Delay Repository Licensing and Operation" (Washington, D.C., April 2004). For the second concern, see idem, "NRC Needs More Effective Analysis to Ensure Accumulation of Funds to Decommission Nuclear Power Plants," (Washington, D.C., October 2003).
[90]See Phillips for a useful examination of these developments.

29 applications in 1980 covering 700 megawatts of power, to 979 applications by 1986 covering over 18,000 megawatts of electric power[91]) suggested that generators other than utilities could compete without disrupting the power grid. The Energy Policy Act of 1992 sought to promote this opening up of the electric grid to competition by creating a new category of wholesale generating firms that would be exempt from the burden of much of conventional electric power regulation, and the 1992 Act expanded FERC's authority to order utilities to open their transmission facilities and transmit power generated by others. FERC sought to achieve this by promulgating its Orders 888 and 889 in 1996, and its Order 2000 three years later in 1999. Orders 888 and 889 require that all utilities transmitting electricity across state lines file OATT tariffs to make their transmission facilities available on a nondiscriminatory basis to all qualified buyers and sellers of electric power. Order 889 requires utilities operating interstate transmission facilities to make information concerning transmission capacity and prices available to others through an Open-Access Same-Time Information System (OASIS). With its Order 2000, FERC has sought to reduce the ability of vertically integrated utilities to use their transmission systems in anticompetitive ways by promoting the formation of regional transmission organizations as independent third parties to orchestrate the functioning of electric grids in a fair, nondiscriminatory way.

The Energy Policy Act of 2005 repealed the 1935 Public Utility Holding Company Act and its extensive holding company controls, and replaced it with provisions providing FERC and states access to the accounting and financial records of electric holding companies. The 2005 Act also repealed the mandatory obligation of electric firms to purchase power from co-generator sources, and authorizes the Secretary of Energy to study congestion problems and to designate "National Interest Electric Transmission Corridors" in order to promote expansion of the nation's electric transmission capacity.

At the same time, restructuring efforts were implemented at the state level by two dozen states, which required vertically integrated utilities to unbundle their retail rates into separate prices reflecting the separate costs of generating power, transmitting it, and distributing it at the local franchise level. In addition to mandating that consumers be allowed to choose their generators of electric power, some states also required utilities to divest all or part of their generating operations (California, Connecticut, Maine and New Hampshire) or to assign them to separate subsidiaries. In all, 42 states initiated electricity restructuring studies during the 1990s.

Today, the burning public policy question is whether this restructuring is succeeding and should be sustained, or is failing and should be abandoned.

Supporters of restructuring contend that it is succeeding and that, while it has suffered unexpected setbacks and complications, it is working better than the alternative of an anachronistic status quo. They point to the far-reaching changes that have transpired in the industry: The nation's transmission system has proceeded a long way toward prying open a traditionally monopolized field for greater access by producers and consumers of power. Real-time information about supplies, demand, and prices—a prerequisite for competitive markets—is available to all. More than half of the nation's generating capacity now operates under regional transmission organizations, and over

---

[91]Electric Energy Market Competition Task Force, 21.

40 percent of electric power is generated by unregulated plants. Supporters contend that electricity prices are lower than they would be if the regulated monopoly regime had remained in place, saving consumers $34 billion over recent years.[92] They claim that one major regional transmission organization, PJM, produces annual benefits for consumers exceeding $3 billion while enhancing reliability in its region.[93] Average costs of generation, they say, have fallen, and efficiency has improved, in the states that have most restructured their electricity industries.[94] Freer prices, in turn, are playing a valuable social role in signaling imbalances and attracting additional resources into the field. They attribute the California fiasco of 2000 and 2001 to a fatally flawed program that regulated retail prices and held them fixed but freed wholesale prices to fluctuate and rise—a serious defect compounded by a rise in price of the natural gas that fuels much of the state's generation, and a drought that simultaneously reduced supplies of hydropower from the Northwest and raised electricity demand.[95] Supporters of restructuring concede that problems have arisen, including congestion, a stressed transmission system, and exercises of market power. But, they add, far more serious problems arose in "the good old days" under the vertically integrated arrangement of regulated monopoly, which brought customers "poor performance in terms of too much generation capacity that always cost more than expected, generators that were not available as much as they could be, declining investment in the electric transmission system that would otherwise have broadened customer access to the lowest-cost resources, and a culture that was resistant to new technology."[96] Restructuring, they conclude, will lower prices and costs "if policymakers will support the regulatory and institutional changes needed to allow competitive market forces to work."[97]

The critics, on the other side, charge that the restructuring experiment has failed. "Restructuring" is an illusory sleight of hand because generation, transmission and distribution assets have merely been re-shuffled but remain firmly controlled by the same vertically integrated firms as before. Abandoning the 1935 Public Utility Holding Company Act has invited a reincarnation of the massive holding companies that dominated the field 7 decades ago; their resurgence has enabled them to once again engage in a variety of financial legerdemain between subsidiaries that inflates prices and profits—all beyond the reach of effective regulatory oversight. Competition has failed to materialize at the retail level, particularly for residential users, the most vulnerable group. The consumer savings cited by supporters of restructuring stem from artificial reductions in prices forced on utilities as an interim measure by state regulators; as

---

[92]Cambridge Energy Research Associates, "Beyond the Crossroads: The Future Direction of Power Industry Restructuring," available at www.cera.com.

[93]Center for the Advancement of Energy Markets, "Estimating the Benefits of Restructuring Electricity Markets: An Application to the PJM Region," September 2003, available at www.caem.org.

[94]Catherine Wolfram, "The Efficiency of Electricity Generation in the United States after Restructuring," in Griffin and Puller.

[95]See Charles J. Cicchetti, Jeffrey A. Dubin, and Colin M. Long, *The California Electricity Crisis* (Boston: Kluwer Academic Publishers, 2004).

[96]See the "Open Letter to Policy Makers," May 31, 2007, signed by nine former chairs and commissioners of the Federal Energy Regulatory Commission, available at http://www.energylegalblog.com/files/Former CommissionersLetter53107.pdf.

[97]Paul L. Joskow, "Markets for Power in the United States: An Interim Assessment," *Energy Journal* 27, (2006): 1–36.

these regulated price reductions now begin to expire, consumer prices are skyrocketing. Reliability of service is deteriorating, and the costs of congestion are escalating, as are the billion-dollar costs incurred in administering unwieldy regional transmission organizations.[98] Restructuring caused a catastrophe in California and invites manipulation of markets for electric power elsewhere by financial speculators and tacitly colluding oligopolists. Increased risk has raised the cost of capital for utility companies, caused their stock market values to plunge and, because electricity is highly capital-intensive, is raising the price of power.[99] Electricity, the critics insist, has unique characteristics, and "is a real-time product produced and consumed simultaneously, cannot be stored, is a necessity of modern life, and has no reasonable substitute." Because of this, they say, electric power "is a complex network industry and all parts—generation, transmission and distribution—must work together. This situation necessitates planning to ensure optimum use of individual facilities and the network, as well as associated infrastructure investments."[100] These unique traits, the critics conclude, as well as actual developments in the field, prove that it is foolish to expect any invisible hand to reliably and efficiently provide electricity.

Environmental Policy

As we have seen, the electric power industry is a major source of pollution. This is primarily the case for conventional coal- and oil-fired generating plants, which are major sources of carbon dioxide, sulfur dioxide, and nitrogen oxide emissions, pollutants that are major causes of acid rain and global warming. It also is the case in a different way for nuclear power and the radioactive waste it produces as a byproduct. Pollution, of course, is a classic economic example of a negative externality, where costs are imposed but not taken into account through market transactions, and which thus constitutes a market failure requiring collective action and government intervention.

For conventional coal- and oil-burning plants, government regulation occurs primarily through the Clean Air Act of 1970 and its subsequent amendments, and is jointly implemented by state and federal environmental regulation agencies. The Environmental Protection Agency (EPA) sets ambient air quality standards in terms of the maximum amounts of pollutants permitted during a specified period of time, and states develop and carry out the implementation programs to reduce air pollutants to these federally set levels.

Emissions of carbon dioxide are regulated by technology-based standards that specify the particular pollution control technologies that electric plants must adopt. These requirements vary between regions of the country, depending on whether a region is or is not in conformity with pollution levels specified by the EPA, and depending on whether the generating facility is a new plant or an existing one: New plants in nonconforming ("nonattainment") regions must meet a more stringent standard by incorporating pollution control technologies that achieve the "Lowest Achievable

---

[98]GDS Associates, "Electric Market Reform Initiative Task 2," Report prepared for American Public Power Association, February 5, 2007, available at www.gdsassociates.com.
[99]Seth A. Blumsack, Jay Apt, and Lester B. Lave, "Lessons From the Failure of U.S. Electricity Restructuring," *Electricity Journal* 19 (2006): 15–32.
[100]Testimony of Alan H. Richardson, President, American Public Power Association, before the Senate Committee on Energy and Natural Resources, March 27, 2003.

Emission Rate"; existing plants in nonattainment regions must adopt pollution-control technologies that meet a less stringent standard of "Reasonably Available Control Technology."[101]

Economists have criticized this "command and control" approach of mandating the particular technology that firms must use on the grounds that it is inefficient and ineffective. Forcing all firms to adopt the same technologies, they have argued, prevents firms from individually responding with technologies better economically suited to their own situation. It also inefficiently forces all firms to reduce their emissions to the same levels, rather than focusing reductions in the firms and sources that can achieve them at lowest cost.

In response to this economic criticism, emissions of sulfur dioxide and, more recently, nitrogen oxide are regulated through an alternative, market-oriented "cap and trade" policy: A limit or cap on the quantity of pollutant is set by the EPA, and permits allowing a specified physical quantity of the pollutant to be emitted are issued which firms can buy, sell, or save ("bank") for future years. Firms must hold permits equal to the amount of pollution they emit, or pay a penalty for exceeding the emissions allowed by the permits they possess.[102] Rather than specifying the particular pollution control technology that firms must employ, this approach allows firms to choose: They can reduce their emissions and dispense with the cost of buying and holding permits, or they can purchase permits sufficient to cover their emissions. The objective is to create an economic incentive for individual firms to choose the most efficient, least costly method for reducing their pollution, while ensuring that the combined decisions of all firms result in emissions levels that decline to the overall desired level.[103] This approach can also stimulate innovation by encouraging firms to develop better, less polluting plants, such as coal gasification plants that convert coal to gas and remove the bulk of pollutants from the gas before it is burned.

The expense of complying with these environmental regulations is not trivial: According to the industry's main trade association, the electric power industry spent $21 billion from 2002 to 2005 complying with them.[104] The EPA estimates the cost to electric companies of controlling emissions of sulfur dioxide and nitrogen oxides to be $3 billion each year. But these regulations have worked, although the exact value of their dollar costs and benefits, and the ratio of benefits to costs incurred, are matters of debate. Emissions of sulfur dioxide and nitrogen oxides have fallen 30 to 40 percent compared to 1990 levels, with the EPA estimating that the value of the benefits exceeds the cost by a factor of forty to one.[105] Progress in reducing carbon dioxide is less apparent: Emissions

---

[101]Whether modifications of generating plants represent routine repairs and maintenance, or instead constitute significant plant expansions that must meet stricter pollution standards is a hotly contested issue that recently reached the Supreme Court. See *Environmental Defense v. Duke Energy Corp.*, 127 S. Ct. 1423 (April 2, 2007).

[102]Statistics about the actual functioning of markets for these tradable permits are available from the EPA at www.epa.gov/airmakets/trading.

[103]Some economists contend that directly taxing pollutant would be more efficient and effective than this cap-and-trade approach. See "Doffing the Cap," *The Economist*, June 16, 2007, 86.

[104]Edison Electric Institute, "Key Facts About the Electric Power Industry," available at www.eei.org/industry_issues/industry_overview_and_statistics/nonav_key_facts/index.htm.

[105]Environmental Protection Agency, "Acid Rain Benefits Exceed Expectations," and "Cap and Trade: Acid Rain Program Results," both available at www.epa.gov.

of this greenhouse gas by electric generating plants have increased 20 percent over the past decade, to 2.5 billion tons per year, although the more relevant standard for assessment would compare this actual level to the amount of carbon dioxide that would have occurred in the absence of regulation.

Nuclear power poses the different environmental challenge of safely disposing of spent fuel rods and decommissioned plants whose radioactivity levels are toxic for hundreds of thousands of years. With the Nuclear Waste Policy Act of 1982, the federal government (and taxpayers) assumed responsibility for permanently disposing nuclear wastes in an underground repository, where radioactive materials are to be encapsulated in corrosion-resistant "caskets", buried, and monitored for leaks. In 2002, the Secretary of Energy and President Bush recommended that this disposal site be located at Yucca Mountain, 100 miles northwest of Las Vegas. The cost to complete the facility is currently estimated at $18.5 billion, with the costs to operate it projected at an additional $2 billion per year.[106] To finance this facility, utilities have been paying one-tenth of a cent per kilowatt hour of the power generated from nuclear plants into a nuclear waste fund, which now stands at $19.5 billion. The Department of Energy is expected to file soon with the Nuclear Regulatory Commission the formal request for a license to open and operate the facility. However, the viability of Yucca Mountain has been challenged by a swarm of opponents, including the State of Nevada, as well as other states concerned about the transportation of radioactive wastes through them on its way to this final burial site. Meanwhile, a number of utilities with nuclear plants have sued the government seeking $7 billion in damages for delay in completing and opening the Yucca Mountain facility. In addition to these issues, concerns have been raised about the adequacy of the funds that utilities have been accumulating to pay the costs of decommissioning their nuclear plants, as well as the safety of nuclear plants they have been operating substantially beyond their original service life.[107]

An intriguing question is how the restructuring in which the industry is ensnarled will affect its environmental record.[108] To the extent that restructuring leads to lower prices, higher consumption of electricity and greater utilization of coal-fired generating plants, the pollution problem would be aggravated. Also, under more competitive conditions, electric firms would face greater pressure to keep their costs down and, thus, might be more resistant to complying with environmental regulations. On the other hand, if newer, more efficient and less polluting plants are developed and commercialized, or if utilities emphasize conservation and demand-side management as ways to hold down their costs in a more competitive milieu, then the industry's environmental performance could be improved.[109]

---

[106]Office of Civilian Radioactive Waste Management, Department of Energy, "National High-Level Radioactive Waste Repository: Budget Projection FY 2009-FY 2023," Washington, D.C., March 2007.
[107]See General Accounting Office, "Nuclear Regulation: NRC Needs More Effective Analysis to Ensure Accumulation of Funds to Decommission Nuclear Power Plants," Washington D.C., October 2003, and Matthew L. Wald, "Nuclear Reactors Found to Be Leaking Radioactive Water," *New York Times* (March 17, 2006).
[108]For thorough examination of this question, see Timothy J. Brennan et al, *A Shock to the System: Restructuring America's Electricity Industry* (Washington, D.C.: Resources for the Future, 1996), chapter 7.
[109]For some current efforts along this line, see Rebecca Smith, "New Ways to Monitor Your Energy Use," *Wall Street Journal* (June 19, 2007) D1. Over the past decade, the industry has spent $1 to 2 billion yearly to manage and curb electricity consumption. For doubts about the efficacy of these efforts, see David S. Loughran and Jonathan Kulick, "Demand-Side Management and Energy Efficiency in the United States," *Energy Journal* 25 (2004): 19–43.

Promoting Alternative Energy

A different kind of market imperfection concerns whether the private market is sufficiently capable of promoting the development of alternative fuel sources to advance the national interest in energy independence and energy security. Twenty-two states have enacted "renewable energy portfolio" standards, mandating that specified percentages of electric power be generated from alternative or renewable energy sources by a future date. While these state programs vary, they generally require that 10 to 20 percent of electricity be generated from renewable sources by years ranging from 2015 to 2025.

Supporters claim these mandates will hold electricity prices down by promoting competition among renewable energy sources (wind, solar, geothermal, biomass); by promoting competition between these and conventional fuels such as coal and natural gas; and by shielding consumers from spikes in the cost of fossil fuels burned to generate electricity. They also claim that promoting the development of renewable fuels will enhance the nation's energy security by diversifying it away from petroleum-influenced fuels, and by encouraging capital formation and technological progress in alternative energies. Conventional fuel sources have long benefited from government subsidies, they say, so why not extend the same benefit to alternative and renewable fuels?[110]

Opponents, including the privately owned industry's trade association, criticize these renewable energy mandates. They contend that requiring by government fiat such predetermined percentages of power to be generated from renewable sources will raise electricity prices for consumers by forcing utilities to use more expensive fuel sources, and to do so to a far greater extent than is economically desirable. They say such an approach at the national level would ignore important regional differences among states in terms of the availability of renewable fuels like water, wind and sun. In the case of wind power, they point to the higher costs of building transmission lines to remote parts of the country where wind turbines are most likely to be built. Such policies, they say, also divert desperately needed investment for improving the reliability of conventional power grids.[111]

VI. Conclusion ▪▪▪▪▪▪▪

Electric power over the past century has evolved from outlandish oddity to everyday necessity. Over the same period the paradigmatic economic conception of the industry has changed from one of all-encompassing, vertically integrated monopoly requiring tight government supervision, to one of opportunities to improve economic performance by expanding competition, paring back monopoly, and withdrawing government regulation. A similar transformation is underway in the European Community.[112] In the coming years,

---

[110]See, for example, American Wind Energy Association, "State-Level Renewable Energy Portfolio Standards," available at www.awea.org.

[111]Edison Electric Institute, "A Nationwide 'Renewable Portfolio Standard (RPS) Would Raise Consumers' Electricity Prices and Create Inequities Among States," available at http://www.eei.org/industry_issues/electricity_policy/federal_legislation/EEI_RPS.pdf.

[112]European Commission Directive 2003/54/EC contains the general and operational principles guiding this restructuring process to create a community-wide electric power market, and is available at http://bccm.belspo.be/about/mucl_directive_200054EC.pdf. Annual reports on the progress of this effort are available at http://ec.europa.eu/energy/electricity/benchmarking/index_en.htm. According to these assessments, restructuring of electricity is "complete" in the UK, Sweden, Finland, Norway and Denmark, and "well developed" in Austria and the Netherlands. For more on this topic, see "European Electricity Liberalisation," special edition, *Energy Journal* 26 (2005), and Jean-Michel Galant and Dominique Finon eds., *Competition in European Electricity Markets: A Cross-Country Comparison* (Northampton, MA: Edward Elgar Pub., 2003).

the clash between these antagonistic conceptions will continue to drive developments in the field—deflected in probably unexpected ways by the rivalry between state and federal government policies and priorities that crackles through the field..

SUGGESTIONS FOR FURTHER READING ▮▮▮▮▮▮▮

Publications

Casazza, Jack, and Frank Delea. 2003. *Understanding Electric Power Systems*. Hoboken, NJ: John Wiley & Sons.

Electric Energy Market Competition Task Force. "Report to Congress on Competition in Wholesale and Retail Markets for Electric Energy." Washington, D.C., April 5, 2007, available at http://www.ferc.gov/legal/maj-ord-reg/fed-sta/ene-pol-act/epact-final-rpt.pdf.

Energy Information Administration. "The Changing Structure of the Electric Power Industry, 1970–1991." Washington, D.C., March 1993, available at http://tonto.eia.doe.gov/FTPROOT/electricity/0562.pdf.

_____. "The Changing Structure of the Electric Power Industry 1999: Mergers and Other Corporate Combinations." Washington, D.C., December 1999, available at http://tonto.eia.doe.gov/FTPROOT/electricity/056299.pdf.

Faruqui, Ahmad, and B. Kelly Eakin eds. 2002. *Electricity Pricing in Transition. Boston*: Kluwer Academic Publishers.

Federal Energy Regulatory Commission. Office of Market Oversight and Investigations. *State of the Markets Report*. Washington, D.C., annual.

General Accounting Office. *Electricity Restructuring: Key Challenges Remain*. Washington, D.C., November 2005.

Griffen, James M., and Steven L. Puller eds. 2005. *Electricity Deregulation: Choices and Challenges*. Chicago: University of Chicago Press.

Hertsgaard, Mark. 1983. *Nuclear Inc.* New York: Pantheon.

Hirsh, Richard F. 1989. *Technology and Transformation in the American Electric Utility Industry*. New York: Cambridge University Press.

_____. 1999. *Power Loss: The Origins of Deregulation and Restructuring in the American Electric Utility System*. Cambridge, MA: MIT Press.

Hyman, Leonard S., and Andrew S. Hyman and Robert C. Hyman. 2005. *America's Electric Utilities*, 8th ed. Vienna, VA: Public Utility Reports.

Kleit, Andrew N. ed. 2007. *Electric Choices: Deregulation and the Future of Electric Power*. New York: Rowman & Littlefied.

McCraw, Thomas K. 1971. *TVA and the Power Fight, 1933–1939*. Philadelphia: Lippincott.

Munson, Richard. 2005. *From Edison to Enron*. Westport, CT: Praeger.

Phillips, Charles F., Jr. 1993. *The Regulation of Public Utilities: Theory and Practice*. Arlington, VA: Public Utilities Reports, Inc.

U.S. Congress, House. Committee on Government Reform. Hearing: Ensuring the Reliability of the Nation's Electricity System. 109th Cong., 1st sess., 2005.

U.S. Congress, Senate, Committee on Energy and Natural Resources. Hearings: Electric Power Legislation, parts 1–2, 106th Congress, 1999–2000.

Warkentin-Glenn, Denise. 2006. *Electric Power Industry*, 2nd ed. Tulsa, OK: PennWell Corp.

Web sites

American Public Power Association: www.appanet.org

American Wind Energy Association: www.awea.org

Center for the Study of Energy Markets, University of California: http://repositories.cdlib.org/ucei/csem

Edison Electric Institute: www.eei.org

Energy Information Administration: www.eia.doe/fuelelectric.html

Electric Power Supply Association (independent power generating and marketing firms): www.epsa.org

Federal Energy Regulatory Commission: www.ferc.gov

National Association of Regulatory Commissioners: www.naruc.org

Nuclear Regulatory Commission: www.nrc.gov

Solar Electric Power Association: www.solarelectricpower.org

4

The Cigarette Industry

GEORGE A. HAY[1]

Americans purchase some 19 billion packs of cigarettes annually at a retail expenditure of $82 billion. In inflation-adjusted dollars, this represents a substantial increase over the past 4 decades. Yet this gain is due entirely to higher prices and taxes; aggregate physical consumption of cigarettes has actually plunged by about half over this same period. Of the total dollars spent, approximately $32 billion goes to federal, state, and local governments in taxes and settlement payments. Therefore the actual industry revenues are approximately $50 billion per year, roughly a 20 percent increase since 1967. The industry is clearly important in the United States, not only because of the magnitude of consumer expenditures devoted to the purchase of cigarettes, but also because of its significant contribution to government revenues at the state and federal levels.

The cigarette industry is also a fiercely fought focus of public policy because of the health impacts of smoking. It is estimated that as many as 440,000 people die each year due to smoking-related illnesses, representing almost 20 percent of all deaths in the United States and rendering smoking the single largest preventable cause of death in this country. The nation's health care costs due to smoking, according to some estimates, total $89 billion per year. Despite a steady decline in the number of smokers each year, it is estimated that one-fifth of the adults in the U.S. continue to smoke.

The health consequences of smoking, in turn, make the analysis of the "performance" of the cigarette industry fundamentally different from that of other industries. Issues related to pricing, advertising, and product development in this industry all have complex public policy ramifications that go beyond the normal analysis of consumer benefit applied to other fields. In addition, the tobacco industry has been involved in litigation related to its health effects that is unprecedented in scope and potential financial impact. In 1998, a group of state attorneys general settled a series of lawsuits seeking reimbursement for the costs of treating victims of smoking-related diseases.

---

[1]In some of the earlier editions of this book, the chapter was written by Adam Jaffe. It has been substantially revised since then. Kira German, Cornell Law School 2007, assisted in updating the data for the current version. The author has consulted and served as an expert witness in several antitrust matters involving the cigarette companies.

This settlement, in conjunction with ongoing federal regulation, will have significant consequences for conduct and performance in the industry in the years ahead.

▪▪▪ I. History

The economic significance of the cigarette industry and the widespread prevalence of lung cancer in the population are phenomena of the twentieth century. Prior to 1900, cigars, plug tobacco, and loose-smoking tobacco all enjoyed greater sales than cigarettes. However, the low cost and convenience of cigarettes almost certainly facilitated the spread of the tobacco habit through the population, particularly among women, who had not been major consumers of other tobacco products.

The birth of the modern cigarette industry can be dated to the invention in the 1880s of a practical machine for mass production. Prior to this time, cigarettes were rolled by hand, and commercial cigarettes were produced by relatively small firms. It required skilled workers to roll the cigarettes and significant supervision to oversee the quality of the product. Then, in 1881, James Bonsack obtained a patent for a machine that could produce 12,000 cigarettes per hour, compared to the approximately 3,000 per day that could be rolled by a skilled worker. The patented Bonsack machine was leased to cigarette manufacturers at a price that reduced direct manufacturing costs by about half. Probably more important, the machine produced a standardized output so that many machines could be combined with relatively unskilled operators on a large scale with minimal supervision and quality-control efforts.

Mechanization of production thus removed the barrier to large-scale operation and laid the groundwork for rapid industry growth and industry concentration. In particular, James B. Duke seized the opportunity created by the Bonsack machine, even though his W. Duke Sons & Co. had produced only loose-smoking tobacco prior to 1880. In return for making a large-scale commitment to the new technology, Duke was able to license the machine on favorable terms, giving him a cost advantage over his competitors. He then invested aggressively in manufacturing, and also in advertising and inducements to jobbers and retailers to promote his products. By 1889, Duke was the country's largest manufacturer of cigarettes.

The other firms found it difficult to compete with Duke's cost advantage and aggressive advertising. What ensued resembled the agglomeration that occurred in many manufacturing industries during the closing decades of the nineteenth century. Duke convinced all five major manufacturers of cigarettes to join him in forming the American Tobacco Company in 1890. At the outset, the "Tobacco Trust" controlled approximately 90 percent of U.S. cigarette production.

The trust acted aggressively to preserve its dominant position over the next 20 years. It purchased exclusive rights to the Bonsack machine and accumulated patents on other machines. It was accused of using a variety of tactics to make life difficult for competitors, including attempting to organize strikes among their workers, making exclusive distribution deals with wholesalers and jobbers, and bidding up prices for tobacco leaf in markets where the independents were active. The trust also purchased a number of independents and added their brands to its own. At the same time, in a pattern that has echoes in the modern market, the trust's heavy advertising and promotion succeeded in creating strong brand loyalty to its premier brands. The "Marlboro" of that era was called Sweet Caporal, and it had a market share of approximately

50 percent at the turn of the century. Overall, the trust increased its share of the market to about 95 percent by 1899.

In its two decades of existence, the trust acquired approximately 250 formerly independent firms. Some of these were shut down, but many continued to operate either as members of the trust or as wholly owned subsidiaries. In 1911, however, the Tobacco Trust suffered the fate of its sisters in oil and other industries, and was found by the Supreme Court to have violated the Sherman Antitrust Act. As a result of this decision, it was ordered that the trust be reorganized and broken up. The cigarette business and principal assets were put in the hands of four companies: the American Tobacco Company, R.J. Reynolds Tobacco Company, Liggett & Myers Tobacco Company, and P. Lorillard Company.

World War I facilitated the spread of cigarette smoking among men. During this period, Reynolds introduced the Camel brand, which incorporated a new and supposedly premium blend of tobaccos. Reynolds abandoned the use of coupons that had previously been a major promotional tool and instead advertised Camels as a more expensive smoke that was worth the higher price. This established the concept of premium brands marketed at premium prices—a concept that continues to characterize the industry today. During the interwar period, the industry was dominated by Reynolds, American Tobacco, and Liggett & Myers, all of which had strong brands that were advertised heavily and priced at levels that yielded high profit margins. In addition, cigarette smoking began to spread among women, who were wooed by advertising campaigns like Lucky Strike's "Reach for a Lucky instead of a sweet."

The onset of the Great Depression set the stage for a series of events that eventually landed the descendants of the Tobacco Trust back at the Supreme Court. Despite falling tobacco-leaf prices and falling consumer incomes, the major tobacco companies raised cigarette prices in 1931 to a level that produced retail prices of approximately 14 to 15 cents per pack.

Because of low leaf prices, however, it was possible for new, small firms to produce a premium-quality cigarette that sold at retail for only 10 cents. The size of the pricing gap and the pressure of hard times allowed these 10-cent brands to make significant inroads into the market, capturing almost a quarter of cigarette sales by 1932. (This pattern in which high prices for premium brands create an opportunity for what we now call discount or generic varieties to get established is one we will see repeated subsequently in the 1980s and 1990s.)

The major manufacturers responded to the success of the 10-cent brands. In January 1933, American cut the price of its Lucky Strikes by about 12 percent at wholesale —a cut that was followed by the other premium brands. In February, the price was cut by an additional 10 percent and again matched by the other majors. The majors also pressed distributors to reduce their margins so that the premium brands could sell at retail for 10 cents. The discount brands could not compete at pricing parity, and many of them disappeared.

After a period of intense competition, Reynolds led a price increase in 1934 that brought the price of the premium brands partway back to where it was before. It was later shown that Lucky Strike and Camel had been sold at a loss during the price war.

Despite the aggressive response of the Big Three to the incursion of the 10-cent brands, the former were never able to reclaim the dominant market position they enjoyed at the beginning of the 1930s. In addition to the 10-cent brands, incursions were made by Philip Morris & Co., an independent manufacturer that had never been part of the trust, and Brown & Williamson Tobacco Co., the U.S. subsidiary of the British American Tobacco Co. As a result, the combined share of Reynolds, American, and Liggett & Meyers, which had been 91 percent in 1930, fell to 69 percent by 1939. The advent of Philip Morris and Brown & Williamson in the 1930s represents the last time significant new competitors were established in the field; the "Big Six" of American, Reynolds, Liggett & Meyers, Lorillard, Philip Morris, and Brown & Williamson would collectively dominate the industry through the modern era.

The apparently predatory pricing response of the majors to the growth of the 10-cent brands formed the core of new accusations that the majors had engaged in monopolization and conspiracy in violation of the Sherman Act. The companies were convicted of these charges in 1941 in a decision that eventually was upheld by the Supreme Court. This time though, no structural remedies were imposed on the firms. Instead, they were required to pay fines and were subjected to restrictions on their abilities to communicate and coordinate their actions.

The Cancer Era

The competitive playing field was fundamentally transformed by the emergence in the early 1950s of significant concerns regarding the connection between cigarettes and cancer. Health concerns associated with tobacco and cigarettes were not entirely new; as far back as colonial times (and before), some criticized tobacco as a dirty, dangerous habit, but these concerns had never significantly impinged on the market. This situation changed dramatically in the decade following the end of World War II, however, as the emergence of cigarettes as a mass-produced product, the spread of the smoking habit through the population, and the development of new scientific research techniques led to scientific studies suggesting that cigarette smoking causes lung cancer.

An article in *Reader's Digest* in 1953 summarized this research and sparked widespread discussion and concern about the health consequences of smoking. For the first time, the major tobacco companies perceived these health concerns to be a major threat: The presidents of five of the Big Six companies met for 2 days at a hotel in New York to discuss the situation, the first time since the antitrust conviction of the 1940s that such a meeting had occurred. This meeting was the apparent genesis of an industry agreement on a collective response to the health "problem." With the exception of Liggett & Meyers, the companies joined together to create the Tobacco Industry Research Committee (TIRC), later renamed the Council for Tobacco Research. They published a statement, signed by the company presidents, in major newspapers throughout the United States. The statement was entitled "A Frank Statement to Cigarette Smokers."

In its Frank Statement, the industry disputed the evidence that cigarettes were harmful but nonetheless accepted "an interest in people's health as a basic responsibility, paramount to every other consideration in our business," and promised to fund through the TIRC "research efforts into all phases of tobacco use and health."[2] The

---

[2]*State of Minnesota and Minnesota Blue Cross/Blue Shield v. Philip Morris, Inc. et al. (1998).* Trial Exhibit No. 14145.

statement established a common public industry position on smoking and health that would stand for 40 years. Although the precise expression of this position varied, it amounted to saying that the evidence that smoking was harmful was inconclusive, that more research was necessary, and that the industry was supporting such research in the hope of determining the truth.

Over the ensuing decade, the industry's position that the danger of smoking was unproven became increasingly untenable. In 1964, the U.S. surgeon general issued a report compiled by a special advisory committee he had convened. After reviewing approximately 7,000 published studies, the report concluded that cigarette smoking was a cause of lung cancer and laryngeal cancer in men, a probable cause of cancer in women, and the most important cause of chronic bronchitis. Subsequent surgeon general's reports have confirmed these findings and added other forms of cancer, heart ailments, and emphysema to the list of diseases whose risk and mortality rates are significantly raised by smoking.

The 1964 surgeon general's report marked a watershed. From that time forward, reducing smoking has become a major public policy objective. In fact, no other legal product has ever been the target of such a large and sustained government effort to reduce its consumption. As shown in Figure 4-1, the incidence of smoking in the United States has declined significantly since the 1960s. Of all the people alive today who were ever regular smokers of cigarettes, approximately half have quit smoking. On the other hand, 40 years after the government found and reported that cigarettes kill people, approximately one quarter of adult Americans still smoke cigarettes, and many of them took up the habit after the publication of the surgeon general's 1964 report.

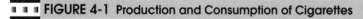

▪ ▪ ▪ FIGURE 4-1 Production and Consumption of Cigarettes

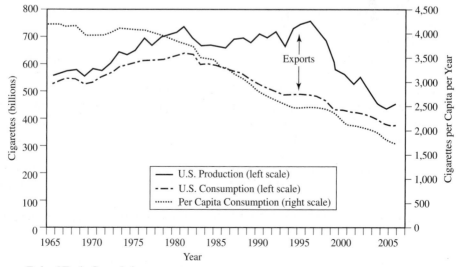

Source: Federal Trade Commission.

▪▪▪ II. Industry Structure

Concentration

As shown in Figure 4-2, the cigarette industry is one of the most concentrated industries in the United States and has been so throughout the postwar period. In 1954, it was the ninth most concentrated manufacturing industry; in 1992, it was the fourth most concentrated, and it is the only industry that was among the 10 most concentrated industries in both these years. In 1996, following the acquisition of American Tobacco by Brown & Williamson, the remaining top 5 firms controlled 99.9 percent of the U.S. market, with the top 4 firms controlling 98 percent. In terms of manufacturing establishments, total U.S. cigarette production in 1997 came from only 13 manufacturing establishments, of which only 10 had 20 or more employees.[3]

In 2004, the Federal Trade Commission (FTC) approved a merger agreement between R.J. Reynolds Tobacco Holdings, Inc. and British American Tobacco to combine the assets and operations of their respective U.S. tobacco businesses (R.J. Reynolds Tobacco Co. and Brown & Williamson Tobacco Corp.). Immediately following the merger the top two firms, Philip Morris and Reynolds American, had a combined market share of 82 percent and the top three firms collectively controlled 90 percent of the

▪▪▪ FIGURE 4-2 Four Firm Concentration Ratio

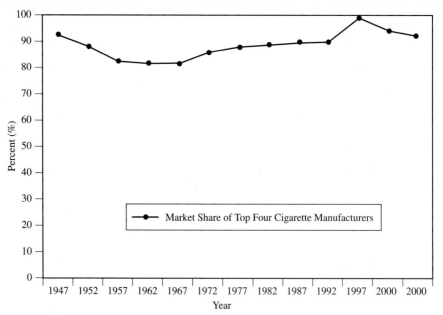

Source: Federal Trade Commission 1997, U.S. Economic Census, and Information Resources Inc., *CDC Fact Sheet 2007.*

---

[3]U.S. Census Bureau, 1997 Economic Census, Cigarette Manufacturing.

market. The FTC, however, rejected antitrust concerns and determined that the merger was unlikely to substantially lessen competition in the U.S. cigarette market.[4]

Barriers to Entry

Contributing to this continuing high concentration is the fact that the industry is characterized by significant barriers to entry. With the possible exception of the discount or generic brands that will be discussed later, no significant entry into the industry has occurred during the postwar period. Several reasons account for this: First, smokers exhibit significant brand loyalty that would have to be overcome by a new entrant. Most smokers have a preferred brand; although a smoker might occasionally purchase another brand, the vast majority of a smoker's purchases will be of the same preferred brand.

In fact, it has been estimated that fewer than 10 percent of smokers change their preferred brands in any given year.[5] This brand loyalty is sustained in part by massive advertising and promotion. Economies of scale in promotion make entry of a major new brand an expensive and risky proposition. In addition, one of the most cost-effective ways of launching a new national advertising campaign was taken away from the cigarette industry in 1970, when the Federal Trade Commission banned advertising of tobacco products on television and radio; the regulatory effects of recent litigation with the states further limit the ability of a new entrant to promote its brand.

Access to distribution channels is another major hurdle for a new entrant. Cigarettes are distributed through thousands of wholesalers and more than a million retail outlets. The major companies have large field-sales staffs that take orders, supervise stocking and point-of-sale displays, and provide a variety of incentives and promotions. A new entrant would have to choose between limited distribution, which would inherently limit brand growth, and a large investment in these distribution activities.

Finally, the fact that industry demand is in a long-run secular decline diminishes entry incentives, even in the face of high current industry profitability. This disincentive is exacerbated by the potential problems of legal liability for health impacts that would have to borne by any new entrant. On the other hand, despite relatively strong brand loyalty, episodes such as the introduction of the 10-cent brands in the 1930s and the recent, albeit limited, growth of the discount segment of the market in the face of large litigation-induced price increases suggest that smokers will switch brands in response to significant price differences. Youth smokers especially are more sensitive to cigarette prices. These situations also indicate that opportunities might exist for new entry.

In fact, despite these daunting obstacles, some new cigarette firms have recently entered the market for the first time in decades. Steady, substantial price boosts by the majors have tempted some small, new producers to enter the field by creating a new, "deeply discounted" category. One of these, Carolina Tobacco Company, began in Beaverton, Oregon, but manufactured its cigarettes at a factory in the former Soviet republic of Latvia. The number of small new producers is estimated to have increased

---

[4]Statement of the Federal Trade Commission, RJ Reynolds Tobacco Holdings, Inc./British American Tobacco p.l.c. File No. 041 0017 (2004).
[5]U.S. Surgeon General, Reducing the Health Consequences of Smoking—25 Years of Progress: A Report of the Surgeon General (Washington, D.C., 1989).

from 5 in 1996 to perhaps 50 by 2002, together accounting for some 8 percent of total sales.[6] How many of these new entrants will survive, however, is an open question, particularly as the majors have made overtures to acquire them.[7]

The passage of the Fair and Equitable Tobacco Reform Act of 2004 (FETRA), which ended more than 60 years of government regulation of tobacco farmers, may have some beneficial impact on the potential for new entry into cigarette production or for the expansion of smaller producers by reducing the cost of the basic raw material. FETRA was enacted as part of the American Jobs Creation Act of 2004 and became effective in 2005 with the ultimate goal of trading tobacco in international markets. Congress enacted the Agricultural Adjustment Act of 1938 to protect farmers from the significant reductions in the price of tobacco. The regulation was administered though quotas and a nonrecourse loans, which created a price support system. Quotas could be bought or leased, creating a large secondary market and inflating the cost of tobacco. Because the quota was set yearly by the government based on past demand, the decrease in consumption of cigarettes beginning in 1997 had led to sharp decreases in the number of quotas awarded.[8] Furthermore, U.S. tobacco growers began to face strong competition from abroad; by 2003 nearly 50 percent of cigarettes sold in the U.S. contained foreign tobacco. As a result, the tobacco industry, together with tobacco farmers, had been lobbying for quota buyouts. Manufacturers that sell or import tobacco products into the U.S. will pay farmers $10 billion, based on the manufacturer's market share, over the next 10 years.

Immediately following the buyout in 2005, tobacco production decreased significantly as nearly half of the tobacco farmers left the industry and prices of the raw materials fell by 20 to 25 percent. However 2005 is projected to be the lowest point and production in 2006 was expected to increase by 13 percent.[9] Cost of production is expected to decline because of the elimination of the transaction cost created by the quota system. Production can now be consolidated to larger farms in the most favorable climate, which can achieve greater economies of scale. Nevertheless, despite this rebound, tobacco production is not expected to return to its prequota buyout levels as the U.S. Department of Agriculture estimates that from 2007 to 2017, cigarette sales will continue to decline 2 to 3 percent annually because of a decrease in the number of smokers.

Individual Market Shares

Figure 4-3 depicts the evolution of the major firms' market shares in the industry. The dominant long-term trend has been the decline of American Tobacco and Liggett & Myers, and the rise of Philip Morris to almost 50 percent of the field by 1997. Indeed, American, the company that bore the name of the fabled trust, disappeared from the corporate scene when it was acquired by Brown & Williamson in 1996.

Figure 4-4 traces these reversals of fate to particular brands. Chesterfield and Lucky Strike accounted for almost 40 percent of the market in 1950 but had shrunk to

---

[6]Diana Moss, "Antitrust Analysis of the Proposed Merger of R.J. Reynolds and British American Tobacco," American Antitrust Institute, March 4, 2004, p. 10.

[7]See, for example, Gordon Fairclough, "Tobacco Titans Bid for 'Organic' Cigarette Maker," *Wall Street Journal* (December 10, 2001) B1.

[8]See *State v. Philip Morris USA Inc.,* No. 2PA05, 2005 N.C. LEXIS 834 (N.C. August 19, 2005).

[9]Thomas C. Capehart, USDA, *Tobacco Situation and Outlook Yearbook (2006),* http://usda.mannlib .cornell.edu/usda/ers/TBS-yearbook//2000s/2007/TBS-yearbook-01-12-2007.pdf

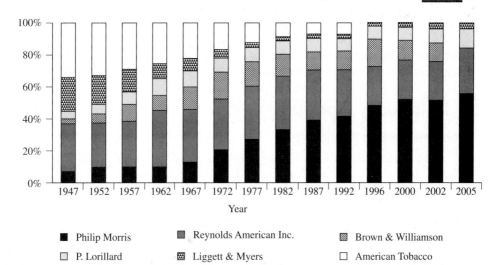

Source: Federal Trade Commission 1997, Grocery Headquarter, 2001, Company 10-Ks.

FIGURE 4-4 Leading Brand Sales

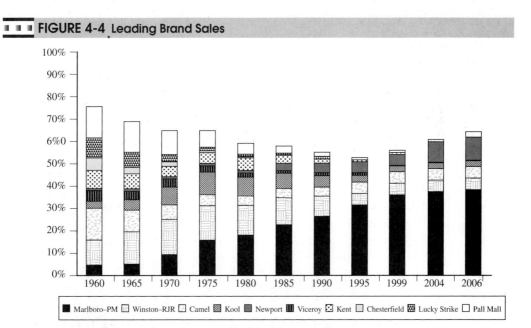

Source: Maxwell Consumer Reports, various years; Company 10-Ks.

Note: *Lucky Strike and Pall Mall brands were acquired by Brown & Williamson in 1996. Philip Morris acquired the Chesterfield brand in 1999 and no longer provides individualized data for Chesterfield which, along with 15 other brands, makes up 1.5% of the market. Reynolds American Inc. does not provide individualized data for its 12 nonsupported brands such as Lucky Strike and Viceroy, which in aggregate make up 9.6% of the market.*

insignificance by 1996. Conversely, Marlboro, today's dominant brand with about 40 percent of all sales, was insignificant in the 1950s. Clearly, the industry has been and remains highly concentrated, but substantial shifts have occurred within the field as the leading firms have jockeyed for position.

▪ ▪ ▪ III. Industry Conduct

Advertising and Promotion

Cigarettes are one of the most heavily advertised and promoted products in the United States. In 2003, cigarette companies spent $15 billion on advertising and promotion. This is an astounding expenditure for a product that does not have complicated performance characteristics or design changes that need to be communicated, and whose purchasers have, for the most part, been purchasing the same brand for years. As shown in Figure 4-5, these expenditures have climbed significantly even as the number of smokers has decreased.

Advertising of cigarettes on television and radio was prohibited in 1970, which led to an initial decline in overall advertising and promotional expenditures. However, beginning in the mid-1970s, promotional expenditures grew rapidly, quickly exceeding what was spent previously on broadcast media. Promotional spending now includes coupons and payments to retailers, distribution of specialty gift items, and sponsorship

▪ ▪ ▪ **FIGURE 4-5** Cigarette Advertising and Promotional Expenditures (inflation adjusted)

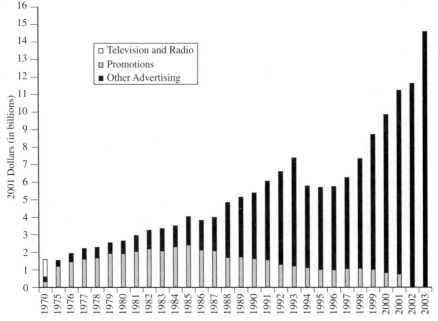

Source: Federal Trade Commission, 2003.

Note: *FTC now breaks down promotional spending into retail price discounts and other promotional expenditures. Retail price discounts represent more than 80% of total promotional expenditures in 2003.*

of public entertainment. The latter has been especially controversial because of its potential impact on children.

An important aspect of the advertising history of the industry is the "Marlboro Man." Prior to 1954, Marlboro was an unimportant brand, and its owner, Philip Morris, was the fourth largest of the six major firms. In the mid-1950s, however, Philip Morris repositioned Marlboro as a "man's" cigarette, modified its tobacco blend to produce a stronger flavor, and changed its packaging from white to the now familiar red-and-white chevron design. At the same time, its advertising began to feature men depicted in tough, action-filled situations. Initially, the nature of these situations varied, but by the mid-1960s, the Marlboro Man was always a cowboy who was photographed in the American West, which was identified as Marlboro Country. The Marlboro Man and Marlboro Country have now been used in ads and packaging in 150 countries; Marlboro has become by far the world's best-selling cigarette and one of the best-known consumer brands of any product around the world.

Advertising and promotion in the field have two general purposes. Defensive advertising and promotion are designed to create or reinforce a smoker's loyalty to his or her preferred brand. Offensive advertising and promotion, on the other hand, are designed to induce a smoker to try a brand other than his or her preferred brand and, having sampled the alternative brand, to switch loyalties to it. Point-of-sale advertising and promotion, such as counter displays that call attention to special offers (e.g., two packs for the price of one), are primarily designed to serve the second purpose (inducing the smoker to sample an alternative brand).

A related dimension of industry conduct is the large and increasing number of varieties of cigarette brands offered for sale: More than 1,294 varieties of cigarettes were offered for sale in 1998, up from fewer than 600 in 1991.[10] This brand proliferation is due primarily to line extensions, as sellers try to maximize the strength of popular brands by offering them in many different versions. The best-selling Marlboro brand, for example, was offered in 29 distinct varieties in 2003.

Pricing

It is clear that pricing in the cigarette industry, despite the high level of market concentration and significant barriers to entry, does not approximate the level that would occur if the firms were engaging in joint-profit maximization (i.e., setting prices at the level that would be chosen by a single cigarette monopolist). Indeed, a monopolist would never choose a price level at which the elasticity of demand is less than 1 (in absolute value); monopoly profits could always be increased by raising the price until the elasticity becomes greater, and there is no question, at least until the recent round of litigation-induced price hikes, that the elasticity of overall industry demand is significantly less than one. It is difficult to estimate what the monopoly price would be, because it requires extrapolation of demand outside of the range of observed prices, but a recent estimate (although it preceded litigation-induced cost and price increases) was that a cigarette monopolist would raise the price to approximately twice the then-current level.[11]

---

[10]See annual reports by the Federal Trade Commission on the tar, nicotine, and carbon monoxide of the smoke of domestic cigarette varieties.

[11]Jeffrey Harris, "American Cigarette Manufacturers' Ability to Pay Damages: Overview of a Rough Calculation," *Tobacco Control* 5 (1996): 292–294.

On the other hand, evidence suggests that cigarette pricing is above competitive levels. The average real wholesale price of cigarettes rose approximately 200 percent between 1980 and 2002, an increase that cannot be attributed to increased input costs. Historically, wholesale cigarette price changes have occurred infrequently, with no apparent relation to costs, and virtually simultaneously and uniformly among the major manufacturers. As the Supreme Court noted as recently as 1993:

> The cigarette industry has long been one of America's most profitable, in part because for many years there was no significant price competition among the rivals. . . . List prices for cigarettes increased in lock-step twice a year, for a number of years, irrespective of the rate of inflation and changes in the cost of production, or shifts in consumer demand.[12]

An important aspect of pricing in the industry is the division of the market into premium, discount, and deep-discount segments. The modern form of this segmentation was instigated by Liggett & Myers, which pioneered low-price generics in 1980. Liggett was once a major force in the field with a market share in excess of 20 percent, but by 1980 Liggett's share barely exceeded 2 percent. At the urging of a distributor, Liggett took an unusual step to revive its prospects—developing a line of generic cigarettes whose principal competitive characteristic was low price. Liggett's generic cigarettes were an immediate success, accounting for 4 percent of industry sales by 1984. Reminiscent of the 10-cent brand episode of the 1930s, the other majors responded by introducing their own discount brands.

In the early 1990's, premium prices increased steadily even as price cuts for deep-discount and discount brands increased the price gap with the premium segment. By 1992, a price gap of approximately 40 cents had emerged between the premium and discount brands, compared to a manufacturing cost difference of only a few cents per pack. As a result, the discount segment had grown to about 40 percent of the overall market, and the market share of Philip Morris's flagship Marlboro brand slipped after climbing steadily for more than 2 decades. This resulted in a major realignment of prices in 1993 on what has come to be called "Marlboro Friday." On that day, Philip Morris cut the price of its premium brands by 40 cents, eliminating the price differential between the premium and discount brands. Explained the firm in its 1993 annual report:

> We believe . . . that had we not responded promptly to this discount challenge mounted by our competition, our share losses in premium brands would have accelerated further, and damage to our premium brand franchises would have become irreversible.

The immediate financial consequences were huge: Philip Morris stock plunged 23 percent in a single day, wiping out $13 billion in shareholder equity. This price move by Philip Morris arrested the rapid growth of the discount and deep-discount segments, and the firm's loss of market share was reversed, as can be seen in Figure 4-6.

After 1993, Philip Morris initiated a series of premium price increases that eventually restored a significant portion of the pre-1993 gap between the discount and

---

[12]Brooke Group, Ltd. v. Brown & Williamson Tobacco Corp., 509 U.S. 209 (1993), at 213.

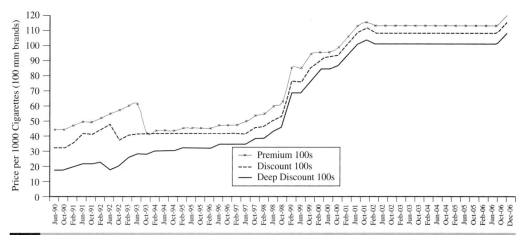

▮ ▮ ▮ **FIGURE 4-6** Wholesale Cigarette Prices (not including taxes)

Source: U.S. Dept. of Agriculture, Economic Research Service, http://www.ers.usda.gov/Briefing/Tobacco/

Note: *Wholesale price revisions had remained unchanged from 2002 until the latest price revision in December of 2006.*

premium brands, thereby paving the way for the continued presence of the discount brands. Today all the majors sell discount brands, although they differ markedly in their dependence on discount sales. Although discount brands account for only about one quarter of industry sales, they do have an important impact on industry pricing. Figure 4-6 shows the pattern of price changes, by segment, over the last decade.

The Battle for Shelf Space

As a result of recent regulations and marketing restrictions, opportunities for the kind of mass advertising and promotion that the cigarette companies historically have used to build overall demand and expand or sustain market share have been substantially foreclosed. This has led to a major shift in the companies' focus toward point-of-sale advertising, especially in convenience stores and gas stations, which account for more than half of all cigarette sales. These are often referred to as "pack outlets," because the majority of purchasers in these outlets purchase by the pack rather than by the carton. (In contrast, in supermarkets and cigarette and tobacco specialty stores, most sales are by the carton.) Pack sales are especially important in the battle for market share because, among smokers of premium or branded discount cigarettes, those who purchase by the pack are most likely to buy a brand other than their usual brand, and thus are the most susceptible to being influenced by the manufacturers' point-of-sale marketing efforts and by the degree of visibility the product enjoys in the retail outlet.

The emphasis on point-of-sale promotion and visibility has manifested itself in manufacturer programs designed to "capture" the most and the best display space in retail outlets. In most convenience stores, the principal display space is on the back wall behind the counter where the cash registers are located. The best space behind the counter is the space above counter height, because this is the most visible to those walking past or waiting in line.

In 1998, Phillip Morris (PM) implemented an aggressive policy of offering retailers enhanced monthly payments and increased opportunities for price discounts in exchange for a commitment to give PM brands a disproportionate amount of the most visible behind-the-counter space, as well as exclusivity or near exclusivity with respect to the placement of signs and other promotional materials throughout the store. R.J. Reynolds and the other majors responded with programs of their own,[13] but PM's dominant market share (and especially the strength of the Marlboro brand) gave it an enormous advantage in dealing with retailers.

Hence, PM's competitors responded in the modern American fashion—by filing a lawsuit against PM, alleging that its marketing programs were akin to "exclusive dealing" (an arrangement where the retailer agrees to carry only a single manufacturer's products) and are illegal under the antitrust laws. After several years of litigation, the suit was dismissed on the grounds that PM's program did not really foreclose rivals' opportunities to compete for the loyalty of retail stores, especially given the short duration of most of PM's retailer contracts. Although it is too early to tell, this competition for the contract is likely to intensify as other opportunities for marketing and promotion of cigarettes continue to be narrowed.

▬▬▬ IV. Industry Performance

Assessing the performance of the cigarette industry requires consideration of multiple and conflicting objectives: First is the usual criteria related to allocative efficiency that prices approximate competitive levels in order to maximize consumer surplus; second is the government's fiscal interest in the tax revenues generated by cigarette sales; and third is the public interest in reducing the negative health consequences of smoking.

Exactly what form these concerns should take is unclear. One view is that adult smokers are aware of the health consequences and choose to smoke because those adverse consequences are more than offset by the benefits they receive from smoking. According to this viewpoint, public policy concern should be limited to adverse health consequences that are not borne by the smokers themselves. These concerns include health care expenditures borne by insurers and other third-party payers, and the health consequences of secondhand smoke.

A broader view is that smokers are addicted to cigarettes and hence incapable of rationally balancing the costs and benefits of the habit. According to this viewpoint, it should be a goal of public policy to prevent such addictions from forming and to help those addicted to break the habit. A potential intermediate view would allow adults to make up their own minds but would judge that children are often incapable of making well-informed choices about their futures; therefore, it should be a policy goal to prevent them from smoking. Because the overwhelming majority of smokers began smoking before they reached age 18, this view would put a primary policy focus on preventing youth from smoking.

These philosophical issues have an important influence on how the performance of this particular industry is assessed. For most industries, the elevation of prices above

---

[13]RJR Tobacco later adopted a similar plan to PM's Retail Leader program and was, in turn, sued by Liggett for violating the Sherman Antitrust Act. The case was voluntarily dismissed.

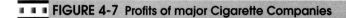

cost is viewed as undesirable. If we believe that smokers are rationally balancing the risks and benefits of smoking, then this view carries over to the cigarette market, perhaps with a modest adjustment allowing some taxation to compensate for the externalities that smokers impose on others. If, however, we believe that public policy should affirmatively discourage smoking, then high cigarette prices are a good thing, not a bad thing, because they reduce cigarette consumption.

Profits

Despite the long-term decline in industry sales, cigarette manufacturing remains one of the most profitable of all businesses. Figure 4-7 depicts the profits of the major companies. Because the profit margins on premium brands are so much greater than the margins on discount brands, participation in the premium segment is the primary determinant of company profitability. Lorillard and Philip Morris, which both have most of their sales in premium brands, have the highest profit rates. Liggett derives only 8.7% percent of its sales from premium brands. The industry's overall profit margin of 24 percent of sales is one of the highest of any field.[14]

FIGURE 4-7 Profits of major Cigarette Companies

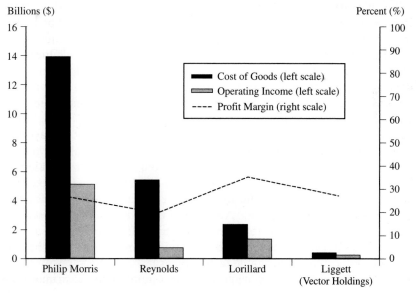

Source: Company 10-Ks, British American Tobacco Annual Review.

---

[14]Economic theory suggests that profitability should be determined on the basis of the rate of return on assets rather than on sales. Census of Manufacturing data indicate that the investment intensity of the industry is not above average, suggesting that the high profit/sales ratio also corresponds to a high rate of return on assets.

Product Development and the Health Issue

As discussed previously, the industry's public response to the rising concern about cigarettes and health in the 1950s was to question incriminating evidence and call for more research. Privately, however, the companies understood the strength of the evidence against their product and recognized that it had profound competitive implications. For example, a Philip Morris scientist wrote in 1958:

> Inasmuch as the evidence is building up that heavy cigarette smoking contributes to lung cancer . . . I'll bet that the first company to produce a cigarette claiming a substantial reduction in tars and nicotine, or an ersatz cigarette whose smoke contains no tobacco tars, and with good smoking flavor, will take the market. Further, if he has the intestinal fortitude to jump on the other side of the fence (provided he has some convincing experimental evidence to back him up) on the issue of tobacco smoking and health, just look what a wealth of ammunition would be at his disposal.[15]

Thus, the companies were publicly denying the significance of the health threat, but internally they understood that consumers' desire for safer products created an opportunity to gain competitive advantage. This situation created a fundamental conflict between the industry's collective interest in minimizing the health threat and firms' individual incentives to profitably exploit consumer demand for safer cigarettes. Documents subsequently obtained in legal proceedings formed the basis of allegations that the industry's collective interest prevailed, and that the producers entered into a collusive agreement to suppress research that might have undermined their public position and led to the development of new competition in responding to consumers' health concerns.[16]

If such a collusive agreement existed, it did not eliminate all efforts by the firms to compete in ways that exploited the health issue. The most important product development attempting to reduce the harmfulness of cigarettes was a device called Premier, test-marketed by Reynolds in 1988. Premier was a new concept in cigarette design; indeed, one could question whether it was really a "cigarette" at all. Instead of burning tobacco, Premier burned a small core of graphite, which heated tobacco extract and a substrate containing nicotine to produce a smoke-like aerosol containing nicotine and tobacco aroma. Reynolds undertook a substantial research program that demonstrated that the "smoke" from Premier showed dramatically reduced biological activity, using essentially all of the scientific tests that were available and indicative of possible adverse human health effects.[17] Although it is clear that Premier was not a safe cigarette, it is also clear that it represented a major effort to develop a product that was likely to be safer than existing products (and to demonstrate that the smoking hazard could be reduced using available technologies.)

Premier failed in the marketplace for a number of reasons: First, the Premier smoking experience was a major departure for the smoker; it was difficult to light and keep lit, and it was generally perceived to have an odd taste. Second, Premier was

---

[15]Minnesota Trial Exhibit No. 11662.
[16]Minnesota Trial Exhibit Nos. 18904 and 18905.
[17]See Minnesota Trial Exhibit No. 12873.

strongly opposed by public health groups, which seemed uninterested in affording smokers an opportunity to use a potentially safer form of tobacco; instead, they argued that the marketing of a product like Premier would undermine antismoking efforts by suggesting that the health hazard could be reduced. At the same time, Reynolds avoided any marketing attempt to utilize the considerable scientific evidence it had amassed regarding the reduced biological activity of Premier, claiming only that Premier offered a "cleaner" smoke.

For innovation in this area, data produced in litigation indicate that the companies' aggregate expenditure on research and development and product development related to the health effects of smoking totaled approximately $3 billion between 1954 and 1996 (about $2.7 billion of this was in the form of company expenditures, and another $0.3 billion came in the form of funding to the Council for Tobacco Research). Although this might seem like a significant expenditure, it is a small fraction of the almost $50 billion that the firms spent on advertising and promotion over the same period, and a tiny portion of the almost $500 billion of industry revenues over those years.

The Development of "Low-Delivery" Products

The primary product response of the manufacturers to consumers' health concerns has been the development of low-tar/low-nicotine (LTLN) cigarettes, although the companies have consistently denied that these products are designed to reduce the health hazards of smoking. Indeed, they apparently have done no research to determine whether these products provide any reduction in negative health effects. Nonetheless, it is clear that the products are designed to take advantage of the demand for products perceived to be safer without having to admit that any cigarette products are unsafe.

The market response to products perceived to be safer has been clear since the 1950s. That decade saw the introduction and rapid growth of a variety of filter-tipped cigarettes. Filtered brands accounted for less than 1 percent of the market in 1952 but had grown to 51 percent by 1959. Viceroy, which received a favorable rating regarding its tar delivery from an article in *Readers' Digest*, and Kent, which advertised the superiority of its "micronite" filter, enjoyed especially rapid growth. Overall, the sales-weighted average tar delivery has fallen from more than 30 milligrams per cigarette to 12 milligrams in 1998; approximately 86 percent of cigarettes sold in 2001 had machine-measured tar yields of 15 milligrams or less.

The trend toward LTLN products was encouraged by public health authorities, who have suggested since the mid-1960s that reduced deliveries would likely reduce the health risks. It is unclear, however, what, if any, health benefit is associated with LTLN products.

Reduced delivery of tar and nicotine on a testing machine does not necessarily translate into reduced human intake, largely because of the phenomenon of "compensation": Because people smoke to get nicotine, they take larger and longer puffs to compensate for a cigarette that delivers less of it. Further, some of the technologies used to reduce deliveries, such as perforating the cigarette paper with tiny holes to draw in additional air, show reduced deliveries on smoking machines but are often ineffective in human smoking. As a result, the health benefit associated with the reduction in machine-measured tar and nicotine yields is probably considerably less than would be implied by the average reduction in yields. Indeed, some experts contend that the compensation phenomenon completely eliminates the potential health benefit of LTLN products.[18]

▮▮▮ V. Public Policy

Antitrust Action

The advent of low-priced generics in the early 1980s led to an important antitrust decision by the U.S. Supreme Court, a decision that has had significant implications extending beyond the cigarette industry. We have seen that the growth of generics came at the expense of the profitable branded cigarettes. Brown & Williamson, with 11 percent of the market overall, was particularly hard hit. Brown & Williamson responded with its own line of value and generic cigarettes and a price war ensued, primarily in the form of rebates at the wholesale level. The price war became so intense that Liggett sued Brown & Williamson under the antitrust laws, claiming that the company was predatorily pricing its discount brands by setting prices below the average variable costs to produce them.

This claim was significant because, in response to a well-known and widely cited article by Harvard Law School professors Phillip Areeda and Donald Turner,[19] many courts had adopted as a test of unlawful predatory pricing whether prices fell below average variable costs. The key concept here is that when a firm's prices do not even cover its incremental costs, the firm loses more money with every additional unit of output sold and would seemingly be better off by substantially restricting its output and perhaps even by shutting its doors and ceasing to produce altogether. If the firm persists in selling at prices that are below incremental costs, the article suggested, the most plausible rationale would be that the firm expects to achieve the power to charge supra-competitive prices and thereby recoup its short-run losses. However, the significance of the so-called Areeda-Turner test is that the plaintiff does not have to prove that prices eventually will go up; the fact that the defendant is pricing below incremental costs is considered sufficient to permit a court to infer that supra-competitive prices are almost certain to follow. (Because incremental costs are difficult to measure, average variable costs are used as a proxy.)

The question presented to the Supreme Court was two-fold. First, could Liggett win simply by showing that Brown & Williamson's prices were below its average variable costs? Second, if evidence of below-cost pricing was not enough standing on its own, what more would Liggett have to prove, and had they done so? On the first question, the Supreme Court ruled that evidence of below-cost pricing was not enough, and it established an additional test.

In addition to proving that prices were below costs, the plaintiff also had to show that there was a reasonable chance that the defendant eventually would be able to

---

[18]See Federal Trade Commission, *Report to Congress for 1997 Pursuant to the Federal Cigarette Labeling and Advertising Act* (1999); National Cancer Institute, Smoking and Tobacco Control Monograph 8: *Changes in Cigarette-Related Disease Risk and Their Implications for Prevention and Control* (1997).
[19]P. Areeda, and D. Turner, "Predatory Pricing and Related Practices under Section 2 of the Sherman Act," 88 *Harvard Law Review* 697 (1975).

raise prices high enough to offset or recoup its short-term losses. Absent a serious threat of recoupment, it did not matter what prices the defendant charged. What made this part of the opinion particularly significant is that the so-called "recoupment test" is now routinely applied in all predatory pricing cases. Unless the plaintiff can make a plausible argument that the defendant eventually will be in a position to charge prices that are sufficiently above the competitive level to offset whatever losses are incurred during the period of predation, the case can be dismissed even before trial and before the plaintiff can introduce potentially inflammatory documentary evidence ("let's kill our competitors!") to a jury.

With respect to the second question, it is understood that in the context of alleged predatory pricing, a firm can achieve the ability to charge supra-competitive prices either by driving most or all of its competitors out of the market, or by intimidating them into competing less aggressively and cooperating with the predator by matching its prices as they are raised above competitive levels. In this case, no one believed that Brown & Williamson on its own, with an 11 percent market share, could ever achieve control of the market. (Several of the other majors eventually joined in the generic price war, but no allegation was made that they had conspired to do so.) Therefore, the only way that the predatory scheme could succeed would be by intimidating Liggett and the other suppliers of generic cigarettes to compete less aggressively in the hope that the major producers could then cooperate in elevating prices above competitive levels and maintaining them there.

Unfortunately for Liggett, the Supreme Court saw no realistic possibility that the generic threat would subside. Even if Liggett were to pull back somewhat, the market had been opened to the possibility of deep-discount or generic cigarettes and there was little likelihood of turning back. Moreover, even if the generic threat were somehow to subside, it would take an unlawful conspiracy among the major producers or a degree of oligopolistic interdependence that the Supreme Court considered implausible to raise prices high enough to recoup the losses that would be incurred during an extended period of below-cost pricing. Hence, the Supreme Court determined that Liggett had not satisfied its burden, and the jury's award of approximately $150 million in damages to Liggett was thrown out.[20] With the wisdom of hindsight, we can see that the Court was right in being skeptical about the demise of the generic segment of the market, although the Court might have been somewhat more cautious in its prediction that growth of the generic segment would prevent significant price increases in the branded cigarette segment.

Interestingly, in permitting the merger of the R.J. Reynolds and Brown & Williamson, the FTC, which had previously challenged other industry mergers, took into account the special characteristics of the cigarette industry. Namely, the FTC considered the high differentiation and strong brand association among cigarette consumers as well as the changing market conditions and uncertainty about future regulation. Significantly, while both R.J. Reynolds and Brown & Williamson produced premium brands, those brands were less popular with consumers under the age of 30 who were essential for future viability. Furthermore, the FTC considered Brown & Williamson's competitive significance to be overstated because it obtained the majority of its revenue from discount rather than premium brands. Because of increased

---

[20]The jury had found that Liggett's actual damages amounted to $49.6 million, but under the U.S. antitrust laws, damages are tripled as a deterrent to unlawful conduct.

competition in the discount sector, Brown & Williamson's market share had declined from 15 percent in 1998 to 10 percent by 2004.

Additionally, the FTC considered the effects of the 1998 Master Settlement Agreement (MSA) between tobacco companies and 46 states. Because this settlement, which is discussed in detail in subsequent sections, imposed higher costs on the large manufacturers which in turn raised the price of cigarettes, many smokers switched from premium to discount brands. The FTC noted that in order to combat the loss of consumers, the top companies stopped raising the price of their premium brands and increased advertisement and promotions spending. These efforts increased competition in the industry from 2002 to 2004. The FTC concluded that the combination of these conditions would make coordination more difficult for cigarette manufacturers compared to other industries. Finally, the FTC determined that price increases from 1997 to 2001 were unilateral as manufacturers followed the price increases set by Philip Morris. Thus there was no evidence of collusion.

Regulation

Concern about the marketing activities of the industry has led to efforts to restrict them to some extent. As early as the 1950s, the FTC became concerned that the companies were making exaggerated and unsubstantiated claims related to the use of filters to reduce tar deliveries. The FTC responded by promulgating a regulation prohibiting cigarette advertising from making health claims unless those claims could be scientifically substantiated, and specifically prohibiting any reference to tar and nicotine. Because none of the companies were doing the kind of research that could have conceivably substantiated claims for reduced health hazards of particular products, this regulation was interpreted as prohibiting all health claims for cigarettes.

By the mid-1960s, however, the public health community came to believe that reductions in tar and nicotine yield probably would reduce health hazards due to cigarette smoking. As a result, the FTC partially reversed itself, allowing the advertising of tar and nicotine yields as determined by a standardized smoking machine. These tar and nicotine ratings were combined with health warnings that were first required in the 1960s and that have been strengthened since then.

Tobacco advertising on radio and television was prohibited in 1970; in 1997, the FTC filed a complaint against Reynolds's "Joe Camel" advertising campaign, claiming it was at least partially targeted at underage smokers.

Although the FTC regulates cigarette advertising, it has no authority to regulate the cigarettes themselves. The Food and Drug Administration (FDA) has authority under its authorizing legislation to regulate the safety of drugs and "drug-delivery devices." In 1996, the FDA determined that cigarettes were drug-delivery devices within the meaning of the law, because they delivered nicotine that causes psychoactive effects and is addictive. The FDA also held that the pharmacological effects of smoking were a feature of cigarette design. It also concluded that the most appropriate way to address the adverse consequences of smoking was to prevent minors from smoking.

Accordingly, it began developing regulations to prevent the sale of cigarettes to minors and to restrict advertising that makes cigarette smoking attractive to young people. The cigarette companies challenged these regulations in federal court. A trial judge upheld the regulations but was overruled by the court of appeals and the Supreme Court in early 2000. In the meantime, enforcement of regulations against cigarette sales to minors have been strengthened, but the FDA's advertising restrictions have been suspended.

Legislation is currently under consideration in Congress to give the FDA authority to impose new restrictions on advertising, make it harder for young people to buy cigarettes, and perhaps to even require companies to remove harmful ingredients from their cigarettes. Remarkably, Philip Morris has supported the effort to get this legislation passed. Aside from possibly insulating the cigarette industry from further government criticism, Philip Morris, as market leader, would have the most interest in preserving the status quo, so its support for the measure has been derided by some groups as the "Marlboro Monopoly Act." Smaller manufacturers worry that direct government regulation of cigarette ingredients and manufacturers could lead to higher costs and raise barriers to entry and expansion; larger manufacturers such as Reynolds and Lorillard seem to believe that additional restrictions on advertising would eliminate their most effective means to gain market share from Philip Morris.[21] Although this legislation had been abandoned in 2004, a new bipartisan committee reintroduced the bill in February of 2007.

Litigation and the Settlement with the States

The cigarette companies have been the target of litigation seeking recovery of smoking-related health costs for more than three decades. Until recently, most of these lawsuits were filed on behalf of individual smokers, and until very recently, all such suits were unsuccessful, because juries often concluded that smokers were aware of the harmful effects of smoking and, therefore, could not blame the manufacturers.[22]

This unsuccessful record led to a new strategy by plaintiffs' attorneys in the early 1990s: A number of lawsuits were filed on behalf of insurers and state Medicaid programs to recover the expenditures these entities had made to treat people with smoking-related diseases. In this way, the issue of smoker responsibility was sidestepped; the smokers might have known that smoking was harmful, but their insurers nonetheless had to bear the costs of treating their illness. The states and insurers argued that the cigarette companies knowingly sold a dangerous product, that they consciously sought to dispel smokers' fears about health risks, that they suppressed information about the addictiveness of smoking, and that they conspired to suppress competition that otherwise would have led to better information about health consequences and the development of potentially safer cigarette products.

---

[21]See Vanessa O'Connell, "Why Philip Morris Decided to Make Friends with the FDA," *Wall Street Journal*, September 25, 2003, p. 1; John Carey, "Tobacco Regulation: It's No Pipe Dream," *Business Week* (January 12, 2004): 45. Andrew Martin, "Trying Again for a Bill to Limit Tobacco Ads," *New York Times* (February 16, 2007) 1.

[22]There is reason to believe that this situation is changing. Perhaps in response to the publicity generated by the settlement with the states, several cases on behalf of individual smokers or groups of smokers have resulted in initial findings of manufacturer liability for smoking-related health costs in the trial courts. In a recent case, *Engle v. R.J. Reynolds Tobacco Co.*, punitive damages of $145 billion were levied against the major tobacco companies. The state Supreme Court later overturned the punitive damage amount, but such success in the trial courts can only spur the filing of more lawsuits.

These lawsuits presented the industry with the risk of enormous potential legal liability, and the cigarette companies chose to seek an out-of-court settlement. A tentative settlement was reached during the summer of 1997.[23] In return for an initial lump-sum payment of approximately $10 billion, annual payments tied to cigarette sales that amounted to hundreds of billions more over 25 years, and restrictions on their advertising and promotional activities, the cigarette companies would have received immunity not only from the ongoing legal cases but from any class-action lawsuits in the future. In addition, they would have received immunity from the antitrust laws for the purpose of collectively implementing the settlement. Because of these immunity provisions, this initial settlement could be implemented only with a law passed by Congress. After extensive debate and hearings during the spring of 1998, Congress attempted to enact a bill that would have implemented higher cigarette taxes and marketing restrictions, but not the broad immunity against future suits provided for in the original settlement agreement. For the latter reason, the tobacco companies opposed the bill and it was defeated.

As the public debate unfolded, the tobacco companies reached settlements to avoid trial verdicts in four individual lawsuits brought by each of the states of Florida, Texas, Mississippi, and Minnesota. An agreement with the remaining states was finally reached in November 1998. The major features of this "global" settlement are as follows:

- Defendants made an initial payment of $2.4 billion to the states, with each company's payment based on its market value.
- Defendants will make annual payments to the states in perpetuity that ramp up to $9 billion per year by 2018. These payments will be adjusted for inflation and changes in cigarette sales.
- Restrictions are imposed on cigarette marketing, including a ban on the use of cartoon characters, restrictions on sponsorship of sporting events and concerts, a ban on outdoor and transit advertising, a ban on nontobacco merchandise bearing tobacco brand names, and limits on the distribution of free samples.
- The states agreed to pass laws imposing similar payment obligations on any cigarette sellers that are not party to the settlement.
- The states waived all rights to sue on behalf of state agencies (but no restrictions are placed on lawsuits filed by others).

This settlement generates significant revenue for the states, some of which is used for smoking prevention and smoking cessation efforts. However, public health groups have become increasingly vocal in criticizing the states for spending ever-larger portions of their tobacco settlement funds for purposes unrelated to tobacco—especially lately when state budgets have been ravaged by recession. By these groups' calculations, only four states currently fund antitobacco programs at the minimum level recommended by the U.S. Centers for Disease Control and Prevention; collectively, the states' spending on such programs has declined by 28 percent in recent years.[24]

---

[23]Liggett & Myers, by far the smallest of the major firms, had reached a separate settlement in 1996, in which it agreed to admit publicly that smoking is harmful and to assist the states in their ongoing suits against the other firms.

[24]Campaign for Tobacco-Free Kids, American Heart Association, American Cancer Society, and American Lung Association, "A Broken Promise to Our Children: The 1998 State Tobacco Settlement Five Years Later," November 2003.

The marketing and promotion restrictions incorporated in the settlement will likely have some beneficial effects. However, the primary market consequence of the settlement is that it has significantly increased the price of cigarettes to consumers. In fact, the overwhelming majority of the monies that will be paid under the settlement will come from higher cigarette prices. By tying the payments to the quantity of cigarettes sold, the settlement, in effect, converts most of the payments into a cigarette excise tax increase. It was expected that cigarette prices would be increased to cover the cost of the settlement payments, and this has in fact occurred. The payments made by each company in the future depend on future sales, not on past sales or any other measure of the harm caused.

In contrast, if the companies had lost any of the lawsuits pending against them, the amounts they would have owed would not have been tied to future cigarette sales, and it is not clear that they could have coordinated the price increases designed to recover from consumers the amounts they would have been required to pay. Indeed, to the extent that existing prices represent the most profitable level that can be sustained given the various firms' market positions and competing interests, one could argue that the assessment of lump-sum penalties unconnected to future market performance would not have affected prices, so all the cost of such a penalty would have been borne by the firms' shareholders.

Settlement-Induced Price Increases

Substantial increases in cigarette prices are a direct result of this settlement. Thus, the end result of litigation with the purported purpose of making the tobacco companies compensate the states and other insurers for increased health costs is that future smokers will compensate the states instead.[25] Figure 4-8 displays the approximate breakdown of the price of an average pack of cigarettes before the settlement and after it is fully implemented, along with scheduled increases in federal cigarette excise taxes. (The estimates in this figure are based on the assumption that the cost of the settlement is passed along to consumers.) Contrary to early estimates, advertising and promotional expenses and legal costs have gone up, resulting in industry profit margins becoming lower.[26]

In response to higher prices, the tobacco industry significantly increased promotional expenditures, which have more than doubled since 1998. A year after signing the agreement, companies increased their advertising expenditures from $6 billion to $8 billion. Yet, despite the increased advertising outlays, cigarette consumption has steadily declined. For example, from 2002 to 2003 advertising increased by 21.5 percent while the total number of cigarettes sold decreased by 5.1 percent. The vast majority of

---

[25]The difference between the settlement payments and state excise taxes is that each state's revenues depend on national cigarette sales, not sales in that particular state. This means that any state that aggressively reduces smoking will not suffer a large revenue reduction as a result; this structure thereby minimizes the awkward incentives that are otherwise created when governments simultaneously try to reduce smoking and collect significant tax revenues from cigarette sales. It is worth noting that the same incentive structure could have been achieved by passing a federal excise tax increase, with the resulting revenues returned to the states.

[26]These are the assumptions used by the FTC in its analysis of the earlier proposed settlement. Federal Trade Commission, *Competition and the Financial Impact of the Proposed Tobacco Industry Settlement*, Washington, D.C., 1997.

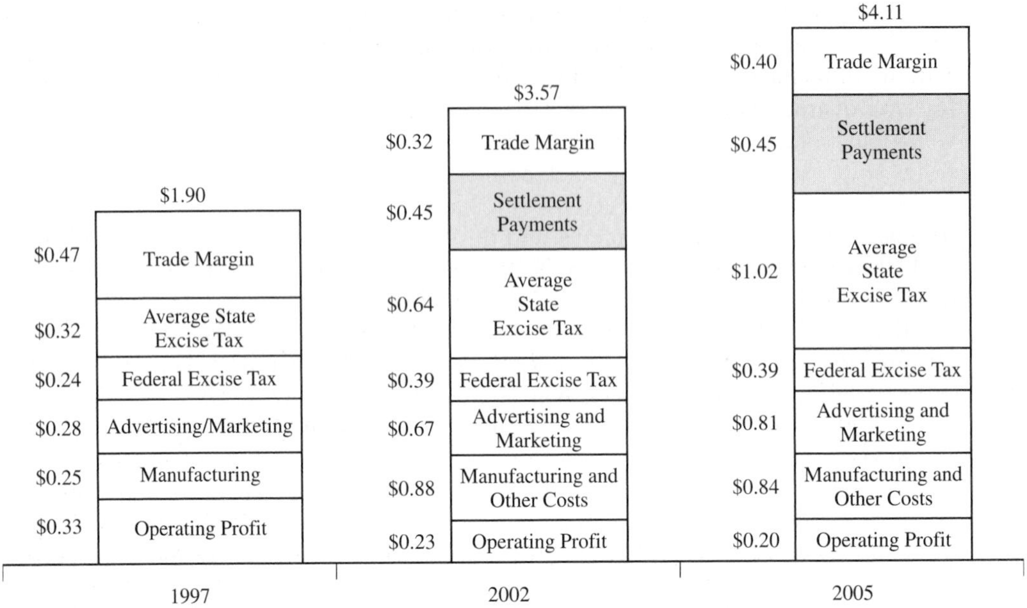

	1997		2002		2005
	$1.90		**$3.57**		**$4.11**
			$0.32 Trade Margin	$0.40	Trade Margin
$0.47	Trade Margin	$0.45	Settlement Payments	$0.45	Settlement Payments
$0.32	Average State Excise Tax	$0.64	Average State Excise Tax	$1.02	Average State Excise Tax
$0.24	Federal Excise Tax	$0.39	Federal Excise Tax	$0.39	Federal Excise Tax
$0.28	Advertising/Marketing	$0.67	Advertising and Marketing	$0.81	Advertising and Marketing
$0.25	Manufacturing	$0.88	Manufacturing and Other Costs	$0.84	Manufacturing and Other Costs
$0.33	Operating Profit	$0.23	Operating Profit	$0.20	Operating Profit

▪ ▪ ▪ ▪ **FIGURE 4-8** Estimated Breakdowns of Retail Cigarette Prices

Source: Federal Trade commission 1997, Company 10-Ks, RJR Tobacco website.

the 2003 advertisement expenditure, approximately $10.8 billion, was attributed to price discounts paid to retailers and wholesalers to reduce the price to consumers. This is a significant increase even in comparison to 2002 as the companies collectively spent $7.87 billion on similar discounts—a number greater than total advertisement spending in 1997.

Interestingly, one potential consequence of large settlement-induced price increases by the traditional manufacturers may be to expose those manufacturers to competition from new entrants or from other firms that either were not defendants in the original lawsuit or that, like Liggett & Myers, signed their own separate settlements with the states (Liggett & Myers signed in 1996). In fact, manufacturers of discount cigarettes have been able to increase their combined market share from 2.5 percent in 1997 to possibly as high as 10 to 15 percent in 2003, with the price increase induced by the settlement acting as a main force driving the recent growth.

The most successful of these new, smaller manufacturers has been Commonwealth with its USA Gold brand. Initially, many of these manufacturers simply opted not to sign the Master Settlement agreement, avoiding the legal cost and allowing them to price their cigarettes much lower. As a result, the settling states enacted new statutory schemes in order to force nonparticipating manufacturers to make payments similar to those of the participating manufacturers (these measures have been subject to legal challenges and are the topic of the next section).

Nevertheless, the U.S. market continues to be a lucrative one as domestic cigarette manufacturers also face competition from international companies. In early 2007, British manufacturer Imperial Tobacco PLC announced plans to buy Commonwealth

Brands for $1.9 billion in order to gain entry into the U.S. discount market, in a deal expected to be completed in 2007. Commonwealth is currently the fourth largest cigarette manufacturer in the U.S. with a 3.7 percent market share; its USA Gold brand ranks third among discount brands.[27]

Challenges to the MSA

Ironically, the MSA has failed to put an end to litigation with the states and instead has prompted a myriad of antitrust and constitutional law challenges by tobacco manufacturers. Since its execution on November 23, 1998, 45 tobacco companies, including the "Original Participating Manufacturers" (OPMs), have joined the MSA.[28] Like the OPMs, "Subsequent Participating Manufacturers" (SPMs) must abide by the settlement restrictions and make payments to the settling states. Under the settlement, OPMs and SPMs are collectively referred to as Participating Manufacturers (PMs). Tobacco companies that have not joined the MSA are referred to as Nonparticipating Manufacturers (NPMs). While the number of small manufacturers varies by region and even by state, it is illustrative to note that 41 SPMs have joined the MSA since its signing, and probably a comparable number have remained NPMs. Individually and collectively, however, their market shares are small. For example, in 2005 the top four manufactures had a 90.4 percent aggregate market share. Most NPMs are small, independent manufacturers, with as few as 100 employees, but several are affiliated with large foreign manufacturers. Notably, KT&G, a South Korean company, sells 100 billion cigarettes worldwide; likewise PT Gudang Garam, an Indonesian manufacturer, sells 60 billion cigarettes worldwide.

For PMs, payments to the states are based on the number of cigarettes sold. Payments are deposited into an escrow account and each settling state then receives a payment equal to its fixed "allocable share." Each OPM makes annual per carton payments up to its share (using 1997 market shares) of the aggregate base amount. In 2006, this amount was $8 billion dollars and will reach a maximum of $9 billion dollars in 2018 and each year thereafter. If the aggregate market share of OPMs declines because of an increase in the market shares of NPMs, the firms may decrease their base amount payments to the states accordingly.

SPMs' payments are calculated in relation to their market share as compared to other SPMs. Those companies that joined within 90 days of the original settlement must pay according to either their 1998 market share or 125 percent of their 1997 market share depending on which value is higher. Furthermore, if the company's share falls below this set value in any given year, the SPM need not make any payments to the states. Manufacturers that joined after the 90-day period do not have a set maximum and pay their portion of the market share.

Both the settling states and PMs were concerned that NPMs would be able to charge lower prices and increase their market share. This would hurt the states by decreasing the settlement payments and undermine the effectiveness of the settlement

---

[27]Richard Craver, British Tobacco Firm Poised to Invade U.S. Market, *Winston-Salem Journal*, February 26, 2007.
[28]Master Settlement Agreement, http://www.naag.org/backpages/naag/tobacco/msa/participating_manu/

agreement. As a result, the settling states agreed to enact complementary legislation to the MSA, requiring a manufacturer to either join the MSA or make payments into an escrow account in order to legally sell cigarettes within the state.[29] The alternate escrow funds would be used to pay future judgments or settlements against the NPM to the state or to parties residing in the state. The funds will be held in escrow for 25 years and are then released back to the NPM. In 2004 the settling states (excluding Missouri) amended their escrow statutes, requiring NPMs to make escrow payments based on units sold within each state rather than the states' allocable shares. The NPM may still be eligible for a refund if it pays more than it would have as an SPM, thus ensuring that all NPMs face a payment scheme similar to that of PMs, whether they sell cigarettes regionally or nationwide. Nevertheless, although NPMs must make the same payments as do PMs, they are not bound by any other MSA restrictions. NPMs have filed numerous suits claiming that the combination of the MSA, escrow statutes, and contraband statutes are anticompetitive and encourage supracompetitive prices. They allege that the state statutes run afoul of Section 1 of the Sherman Antitrust Act by creating a per se illegal output cartel in order to protect the market shares of OPMs, thereby ensuring settlement payments to the states are not reduced. NPMs argue that the statutory scheme in effect exploits the states' regulatory power to enforce the private price setting behavior of the PMs, thus creating a restraint on trade which is preempted by federal antitrust law.

NPMs allege that the states create a disincentive for PMs to engage in price competition because an increase in their relative market share corresponds to an increase in settlement payments. As a result, rather than attempting to compete, PMs have responded by following the price increases of large manufacturers. Because all firms are forced to either abide by the MSA or the escrow statutes, manufacturers are discouraged from engaging in price competition, thereby realizing monopolistic prices. NPMs contend that the MSA and the complementary legislation have led to substantial price and revenue increases above those that would have been necessary to alleviate the cost of the settlement. NPMs have had mixed success with their legal claims. The Second Circuit Court of Appeals has affirmed a lower court decision that their antitrust claims should not be dismissed on summary judgment. Furthermore, the Second Circuit held that it is not clear that state immunity doctrine should apply, because the states failed to articulate a clear rationale for the market share provisions of the escrow statutes and failed to provide for active supervision of the decision to set prices.

Other courts have not been persuaded by the Second Circuit. For example, the Sixth Circuit Court of Appeals has dismissed antitrust claims, holding that the finding of an anticompetitive effect is not enough.[30] Yet another court has held that price setting in this case was unilateral, based on the higher costs faced by manufacturers complying with the MSA and is protected by the state immunity doctrine.[31]

---

[29]Cigarettes sold on Native American reservations are exempt from escrow statutes.
[30]*Tritent Int'l Corp, et al., v. Kentucky*, 467 F.3d 547 (6th Cir. October 30, 2006).
[31]*Int'l Tobacco Partners, LTD., v. Kansas*, No. 05-2319-KHV, 2007 U.S. Dist. LEXIS 9359 (D.C. Kansas Feb. 8, 2007).

Nor has the MSA put an end to health claims by private individuals or the U.S. government. For example, as of February 2007, Philip Morris had a total of 189 individual smoking and health cases, 10 class actions and aggregate claims litigation, 5 health care cost and recovery actions, 20 light/ultra-light class actions, and 2 tobacco price cases still pending against it.[32] The company faces 2,600 cases filed by individual flight attendants. Furthermore, a New York district court has granted a nationwide "lights" class certification, in which it is[33] alleged that the company's marketing of light cigarettes as a safer alternative violated the Racketeer Influenced and Corrupt Organizations Act (RICO).[34]

Less than a year after the 1998 settlement, the U.S. government sued nine tobacco manufacturers to disgorge $289 billion of ill-gotten gains derived by violating and conspiring to violate RICO.[35] The court recently held that the tobacco company defendants:

1. falsely denied that smoking causes cancer and other diseases,
2. denied that nicotine is highly addictive while manipulating levels of nicotine to maintain addiction,
3. marketed light cigarettes as less harmful despite evidence to the contrary,
4. falsely denied that second hand smoke is hazardous,
5. intentionally marketing to attract youth smokers, and
6. suppressed scientific research.

In a lengthy opinion describing numerous instances of tobacco industry misconduct, the district judge concluded that tobacco manufacturers violated RICO.[36]

Since January 1999, courts have decided 45 tobacco litigation cases against the major manufacturers, with 28 of those cases decided in favor of the defendant tobacco manufacturers. The Florida Supreme Court reversed a $145 billion punitive award to a class of smokers because it was "clearly excessive."[37] The U.S. Supreme Court also has upheld the Illinois Supreme Court in reversing a $7.1 billion judgment in favor of 1 million cigarette smokers.[38] Recently, the Supreme Court also vacated a $79.5 million punitive damage award to a smoker's widow, holding that a jury could not base a punitive damage award on harm to other smokers in order to punish the defendant.[39]

---

[32]Company 10-K Filings. The company reports as one case an aggregate of 928 individual claims that will be tried together in West Virginia.

[33]*Schwab v. Philip Morris USA*, Inc., 449 F. Supp. 2d 992 (D.C. NY September 25, 2006).

[34]The Second Circuit Court of Appeals has stayed the trial and is currently reviewing whether class certification is appropriate.

[35]*U.S. v. Phillip Morris*, No. 99-2496 (GK), 2006 U.S. Dist. LEXIS 61412 (D.C. August, 17, 2006). That number was later adjusted to $14 billion.

[36]"In short, Defendants have marketed and sold their lethal product with zeal, with deception, with a single-minded focus on their financial success, and without regard for the human tragedy or social costs that success exacted." *Philip Morris*, 2006 U.S. Dist. LEXIS 61412, *19.

[37]*Engle v. Liggett Group, Inc.*, 945 So. 2d 1246 (Fla. December 21, 2006).

[38]See *Price v. Philip Morris, Inc.*, No. 96236, 2005 Ill. LEXIS 2071 (Ill December 15, 2005) cert denied *Price v. Philip Morris, Inc.*, No. 06-465, 2006 U.S. LEXIS 9046 (November 27, 2006).

[39]See *Philip Morris USA v. Williams,* No. 05-1256, 2007 U.S. LEXIS 1332 (February 20, 2007).

A recent study has called into question the underlying rationale of the entire 1998 settlement. It suggests that significantly lower rates of smoking would lead to only temporary improvements in overall population health because certain individuals would eventually succumb to nonsmoking related disabilities. The authors conclude that while "promoting smoking cessation is . . . worthwhile . . . statements to the effect that 400,000+ persons die annually from smoking [are] somewhat misleading."[40] Furthermore, the authors suggest that smoking-related costs are low for Medicaid and are negative for Medicare and Social Security. Because many individuals who smoke do not survive to receive full benefits, studies that calculate the costs to Medicare and Social Security are overstated because they do not take this mortality factor into account. The authors therefore conclude that "[s]moking imposes a huge social cost, but the governments and taxpayers have not generally been the main victims."[41]

Youth Smoking

Public policy has been particularly concerned about the effects of cigarette marketing and promotion in stimulating youth smoking. The majority of all smokers begin smoking before age 18, despite legal restrictions on the sale of cigarettes to minors. Some public health advocates reason that if youngsters could be prevented from starting to smoke, the overall rate of smoking initiation in the population would be dramatically reduced. In addition to marketing restrictions, some point to the price increases associated with the settlement as an especially significant antiyouth smoking measure. Some studies have suggested that teen smoking is somewhat more price elastic than adult smoking, which is plausible given that young smokers tend to be less addicted, and cigarette expenditures comprise a larger portion of their disposable income.[42] In addition, part of the revenues from the settlement are being used by some states to fund aggressive countermarketing measures designed to discourage teen smoking. Again though, public health groups charge that the states' spending on youth tobacco programs has been declining while tobacco company expenditures on marketing, promotion, and advertising have been rising.[43] For example, after signing the MSA, tobacco companies have increased the list prices for cigarettes; however, they also have significantly increased price promotions, especially for those brands popular with youth smokers, thus decreasing the effective price to consumers. They additionally have increased advertisements in youth oriented magazines and have increased their use of direct marketing promotions.[44] Unfortunately, no one seems to understand why teens start smoking well enough to know how much difference these measures will make.

---

[40]Frank Sloan et al., *The Price of Smoking* (Cambridge, MA: The MIT Press, 2004), 257.

[41]Ibid. 261.

[42]Ibid.

[43]"A Broken Promise to Our Children."

[44]*U.S. v. Phillip Morris,* No. 99-2496 (GK), 2006 U.S. Dist. LEXIS 63478, 247–557.

CONCLUSION

The history of the cigarette industry presents a unique and complex challenge to students of industrial organization. One of the most concentrated of industries, resting behind apparently significant barriers to entry, it has enjoyed persistently high profits but also has engaged in periodic price wars. The firms spend huge amounts—absolutely and relative to sales—on advertising and promotion, supposedly in a largely self-defeating effort to steal each others' customers. The industry charges prices that are clearly above competitive levels, but government desire for tax revenue combined with a belief that high prices will discourage smoking have made higher rather than lower prices the aim of public policy.

An epic legal battle over liability for smoking-related health care costs has strained the legal system and produced a significant increase in tobacco taxation. It also has resulted—perhaps much later than anyone in the industry would have guessed 30 years ago—in the companies' finally admitting publicly what they knew but admitted only privately decades ago: that smoking is a deadly and addictive habit initially undertaken primarily by youngsters and then continued by adults, most of whom would like to quit.

The next phase in the industry's evolution is difficult to predict. The higher prices brought about by the settlement will likely accelerate the decline in smoking somewhat. If the FDA is ultimately given authority by Congress to regulate cigarettes, we could see tighter marketing restrictions, and perhaps even limits on permissible levels of tar, nicotine, and other characteristics and ingredients of cigarettes. Yet the very addiction that makes smoking such a pernicious public policy problem makes it difficult to identify good solutions, even if legal authority is available. It is clear, for example, that there is no political will for another prohibition era. Mandatory reductions in nicotine levels are unlikely to work for addicted smokers and could even be counterproductive as smokers consume more cigarettes to obtain their desired nicotine. The technological potential for cigarette-like products that deliver nicotine without other adverse health effects has never been adequately explored, and it is unclear whether anyone is now pursuing such products. Therefore, it seems likely that the peculiar industrial organization and performance of the cigarette industry will continue to be hotly debated.

SUGGESTIONS FOR FURTHER READING

Publications

Adams, Walter, and James Brock. 1998. *The Tobacco Wars*. Cincinnati: South-Western College Publishing.

Bulow, Jeremy, and Paul Klemperer. 1998. "The Tobacco Deal." Brookings Papers on Economic Activity: Microeconomics. Brookings Institution, pp. 323–394.

Federal Trade Commission. Annual. *Report to Congress, Persuant to Federal Cigarette Labeling and Advertising Act* (yearly).

Kluger, Richard. 1996. *Ashes to Ashes*. New York: Alfred Knopf.

Sloan, Ostermann, Picone, Conover, and Donald H. Taylor. 2004. *The Price of Smoking*. Cambridge, MA: The MIT Press.

Tenant, Richard. 1950. *The American Cigarette Industry*. New Haven, CT: Yale University Press.

CHAPTER 5

The Beer Industry

KENNETH G. ELZINGA

In 1620, as every youngster knows, the Pilgrims landed at Plymouth Rock. Less commonly known is that the Pilgrims had set sail for Virginia, not Massachusetts. What led them to change their destination? The fact of the matter is, they were running out of beer. One voyager recorded the following entry in his diary: "Our victuals are being much spente, especially our beere." We leave to historians the question of how a dwindling beer inventory affected the course of American history. We turn to economics for understanding the structure, conduct and performance of the U.S. beer industry today.[1]

Beer is a potable product with four main ingredients.

1. Malt, a grain (usually barley) that has been allowed to germinate in water and then dried.
2. Flavoring adjuncts, usually hops and corn or rice, which give beer its lightness and provide the starch that the enzymes in the malt convert to sugar.
3. Cultured yeast, which ferments the beverage and feeds on the sugar content of the malt to produce alcohol and carbonic acid.
4. Water, which acts as a solvent for the other ingredients.

Because the process of brewing (or boiling) is intrinsic to making beer, the industry often is called the brewing industry.

All beers are not the same. The white beverage (spiced with a little raspberry syrup) favored in Berlin; the warm, dark-colored drink served by the English publican; and the amber liquid kept at near-freezing temperatures in the cooler of the American convenience store are all beer. Generically, the term *beer* means any beverage brewed from a starch (or farinaceous) grain. Because the grain is made into a malt, another term for beer is *malt liquor*, or *malt beverage*. In this study, the terms *beer, malt liquor,* and *malt beverage* are used interchangeably to include all such products as beer, ale,

---

[1]For a scholarly book-length treatment on the economics of the brewing industry, see Tremblay and Tremblay (2005). There are a number of recent (and readable) books of general interest about this industry. Three of the best are Ogle (2006), Van Munching (1997), and Wells (2004). Important book-length treatments of particular brewing firms include Hernon and Ganey (1991, regarding Anheuser-Busch), Baum (2000, regarding Coors), and Slosberg (1998, regarding Pete's Wicked Ale). An excellent history of British brewing is by Cornell (2003).

light beer, dry beer, ice beer, porter, stout, malt liquor, and flavored malt beverages.[2] The factor common to these beverages, and which differentiates them from other alcoholic and nonalcoholic beverages, is the brewing process of fermentation applied to a basic grain ingredient.

The U.S. market for beer is sizable. Among commercial beverages, beer ranks fourth in per capita consumption behind soft drinks, coffee, and milk. Among alcoholic beverages, beer accounts for close to 85 percent of U.S. consumption (by gallons), well ahead of wine and distilled spirits. However during the period 1995 to 2005, the amount of alcohol consumed in the form of beer declined while the amount consumed as wine and distilled spirits had double-digit growth.

▬▬▬ I. History

In 1625, the first recorded public brewery was established in New Amsterdam (now New York City). Other commercial brewing followed, although in seventeenth-century America considerable brewing was done in homes. Beer was a common beverage among the early settlers in America. All that was needed were a few vats for mashing, cooling, and fermenting. The resulting product would not be recognized (or consumed) as beer today. The process was crude, the end result uncertain. Brewing was referred to as "an art and mystery."

Brewing was encouraged in early America. For example, the General Court of Massachusetts passed an act in 1789 to support the brewing of beer "as an important means of preserving the health of the citizens . . . and of preventing the pernicious effects of spiritous liquors." James Oglethorpe, trustee of the colony of Georgia, was even blunter: "Cheap beer is the only means to keep rum out."

The 1840s and 1850s were pivotal decades in the beer industry. The product beer, as it is generally known today, was introduced in the 1840s with the brewing of lager beer. Before this time, malt beverage consumption in America resembled English tastes—oriented toward ale, porter, and stout. English style ale was brown in color, heavy in the stomach, and viscous to the tongue. Ale also went bad very quickly. Lager beer, on the other hand, was clear, amber in color, and lighter to the taste. It also was lower in alcohol content. Lager beer reflected a German influence on the industry.[3] The influx of German immigrants provided skillful brewers, and eager customers for this type of beer. While German-based beer took longer to brew (it had to "lagern" or rest), it lasted longer (especially if kept cold). At the start of the decade in 1850, the 431 brewers in the United States were producing 750,000 barrels of beer. By the end of that decade, 1,269 brewers produced more than a million barrels of beer—evidence of the bright future expected by many for this industry.

The latter half of the nineteenth century also saw technological advances in production and marketing. Mechanical refrigeration aided both the brewing and the

---

[2]Flavored malt beverages (FMBs) also are known as Ready-to-Drink beverages (RTDs), Flavored Alternative Beverages (FABs), and Malternatives. Recall that the alcohol in beer comes from fermentation, not distilling. Some FMBs derive over 70 percent of their alcohol content from the distilled alcohol that serves as the flavoring agent in the drink. These products, the beer industry maintains, are not true malt beverages and, at least for tax and advertising purposes, should be treated as distilled spirits, not beer.
[3]For an economic comparison of the U.S. and German beer industries, see Adams (2006).

storage of beer. Prior to this, beer production was partly dependent on the amount of ice that could be cut from lakes and rivers in the winter. Cities such as St. Louis, with its underground caves where beer could be kept cool while aging, lost this (truly natural) advantage with the advent of mechanical refrigeration. Pasteurization, a process originally devised to preserve wine and beer (not milk) was adopted during this period. Beer no longer had to be kept cold; it could be shipped into warm climates and stored without refermenting. Once beer was pasteurized, wide-scale bottling and off-premise consumption became viable. In addition, developments in rail and motor transport enabled brewers to sell output beyond their local markets. The twentieth century saw the rise of the national brewer.

The twentieth century also saw beer sales outlawed. The temperance movement, which began by promoting voluntary moderation and abstention from hard liquors, veered toward a goal of compulsory abstention from all alcoholic beverages. The beer industry seemed blissfully ignorant of this. Many brewers thought (or hoped) the temperance movement would ban only liquor.

In 1919, 36 states ratified the Eighteenth Amendment to enact the national prohibition of alcoholic beverages. This led many brewers to close up shop; some produced candy and ice cream. Anheuser-Busch and others built a profitable business selling malt syrup, which was used to make "home brew." Because a firm could not state the ultimate purpose of malt syrup, the product was marketed as an ingredient for making baked goods, such as cookies. Prohibition lasted until April 1933, and brewers reopened rapidly after repeal. By June 1933, 31 brewers were in operation; in another year, the number had risen to 756.

In 1948, the demand for beer in the U.S. began a slow decline, from a 1947 record sale of 87.2 million barrels. During this period, per capita consumption of beer fell from 18.5 gallons in 1947 to 15.0 gallons in 1958. It was not until 1959 that sales surpassed the 1947 total. In the 1960s and 1970s total demand began to grow again at an average rate of better than 3 percent per year. In 1965, for the first time, more than 100 million barrels were sold. The rightward shift in the demand curve for beer was due to the increased number of young people in the United States (the result of the post–World War II baby boom), the lowered age requirements for drinking in many populous states, and the enhanced acceptability of beer among females. Moreover, the number of areas in the United States that were "dry" (i.e., where alcoholic beverages are prohibited) shrank considerably.

In the early 1980s, the market demand for beer stabilized. Demographic patterns reversed themselves as the pool of young people (18 to 34 years of age) declined. Minimum age requirements for the purchase of alcoholic beverages rose to 21 years. Other factors that cut into demand included the pursuit of physical fitness and the increasing concern with alcohol abuse, particularly drunk driving. In some states, laws restraining the use of one-way (nonreturnable) containers also may have reduced consumption.

Two more recent developments favored market growth. From 1998 to 2008, the population in the 21 to 24 age bracket was projected to grow. While this group comprises only 8 percent of the U.S. population, it accounts for about 14 percent of all beer consumption. In addition, recent medical studies claim that moderate alcohol consumption (including beer) reduces the risk of cardiovascular disease. The *Wall Street Journal* polled 800 readers as to whether such studies would affect their drinking habits: 36 percent replied that these findings would lead people to drink a little more, 18 percent thought they would be an excuse for drinking a lot more, while 46 percent indicated that people just don't believe such studies. Notwithstanding these developments, in 1990 beer consumption in the U.S. was 24.3 gallons per capita; by 2005, per capita consumption had fallen to 21.3 gallons. The stagnant market demand for beer stands in contrast with the growing demand for soft drinks, bottled water, wine and distilled spirits.

▬▬ II Structure

The most important components of the structure of the brewing industry are the nature of demand, the size distribution of firms, entry conditions, and product differentiation.

Demand

The demand for beer is a function of personal income, the weather, government regulations on alcohol consumption, the price and quality of beer and that of other substitute beverages, demographics, religion, and health concerns. In the United States, demand varies from state to state. Per capita beer consumption in Utah was only 12.2 gallons in 2005, while Nevada had a per capita consumption of 30.4 gallons (the Nevada figure is biased by beer-quaffing tourists). The highest per capita consumption by natives of a state probably occurs in Wisconsin.

Although economists are not able to measure price elasticity infallibly, statistical estimations indicate the market demand for beer is inelastic—in the range of 0.7 to 0.9. Brand loyalty is not strong enough to make the demand for any particular malt beverage inelastic. Indeed, the demand for individual brands of beer appears to be quite elastic. This places an important limitation on the market power of a brewer's attempt to raise price unilaterally.

Concentration

According to economic theory, consumers facing a monopolist likely will pay higher prices than consumers buying in a competitive market. Consumers buying from an oligopoly will be affected by the nature of competition that takes place among the handful of sellers. For this reason, the size distribution of brewing firms arrayed before consumers is of economic interest. Is the beer industry unconcentrated, with its customers courted by many firms, or highly concentrated, leaving beer drinkers with little choice?

In the first three decades of the post–World War II period, two contrary trends were at work in the industry. The number of major brewers located in the United States declined. But the size of the market area served by existing brewers and the volume of beer supplied by the major brewers increased. Beer drinkers lost some (local and regional) sources of supply but gained access to others that were shipped into their part of the country. And in the 1960s, a new domestic source of supply emerged. The new source is the *craft* or *specialty* segment (the terms will be used interchangeably) of the U.S. beer industry.

Fritz Maytag merits the title of pioneer of craft brewing in the U.S. Heir to the Maytag appliance company, he rescued the Steam Beer Company of San Francisco (whose brand was Anchor) and turned it into a model (indeed inspiration) for numerous craft brewers who were to follow. Maytag recognized that his small operation could never match the cost efficiencies of modern, large-scale brewing facilities. To cover costs, his beer would have to sell at retail prices matching expensive import brands. The task was to make beer that would be worth the candle. Maytag's dogged persistence in learning the craft of brewing and his tenacity in persuading retail accounts to stock his product became an inspiration to legions of craft brewers who followed.

One of these was Jim Koch (pronounced Cook) of Boston Beer Company, who introduced a different business model to the craft segment: the virtual brewery. Koch recognized that existing breweries, many with excess capacity, could brew specialty beers if given the proper recipe and proper brewmaster attention. Using the equipment at the Pittsburg Brewing Company (main brand: Iron City), the Boston Beer Company soon was selling thousands of barrels of Sam Adams beer at prices well above that of Iron City. In 10 years, Koch's firm was the tenth largest seller of beer in the United States, providing evidence of how low are the entry barriers into brewing if a firm has the right business model.[4]

In the 1980s, the entry of dozens of craft brewers increased consumers' choice set of malt beverages even more. Craft brewers include microbrewers and brewpubs. The number of craft brewers went from 1 in 1965 to over 1400 in 2005, achieving a critical mass in 1995 by producing over 1 million barrels of beer. Some craft brewers no longer can claim "micro" status because they now sell lots of beer (current examples are Boston Brewing and Sierra Nevada). In 2005, the craft brewing part of the beer industry comprised almost 1,000 brewpubs (most of which produce fewer than 1,000 barrels of beer annually), 380 microbreweries (producing fewer than 15,000 barrels per year) and over 55 regional specialty brewers (with capacity of over 15,000 barrels).

In recent years, U.S. consumers also have chosen imported beers in increasing numbers. In 2005, imports held over 12.5 percent of the U.S. beer market; craft brewers held 3.5 percent. Thus, while concentration has increased among the largest domestic sellers, craft brewing and imports have caused an explosion in new beer brands that offer consumers different taste signatures and price points.

The Decline in Numbers

In 1935, shortly after repeal, 750 brewing plants were operating in the United States. Between 1960 and 2005, the number of traditional beer companies dropped over 90 percent (although beer sales doubled). Beer analyst Robert S. Weinberg counted 175 "traditional brewers" operating in 1960; by 2005, the number of traditional domestic brewers had fallen to only 21 firms.[5] Few, if any, American industries have undergone a similar structural shakeup. However, the number of specialty breweries increased from zero to 1,346 over the same 45-year time frame. Table 5-1 shows the decline in the number of traditional breweries. It also reveals the explosion in the number of specialty breweries. This table reveals the yin and yang of U.S. brewing in this period: the

---

[4]The second largest craft brewer, Sierra Nevada Brewing Co., has taken a different supply tack. It now owns a sizable brewing capacity of over 600,000 barrels per year.

[5]These are brewing plants of at least 15,000 barrels per year capacity and do not include microbrewers and brewpubs whose capacity falls below a 15,000 barrel annual potential.

TABLE 5-1 U.S. Breweries in Operation 1960–2005

Year	Traditional Breweries	Specialty Breweries	Total Breweries	Beer Wholesalers*
1960	175	0	175	
1965	126	0	126	
1970	82	1	83	
1975	52	1	53	
1980	40	8	48	5,109
1985	34	37	71	
1990	29	269	298	2,975
1995	29	977	1,006	2,967
2000	24	1,471	1,495	2,357
2005	21	1,346	1,367	

Source: Brewing Industry Research Program, The Office of R.S. Weinberg, 2006
Source: Wholesaler count from NBWA

dramatic decline in the number of major brewers in the industry and the dramatic increase in the number of small brewers in the specialty or craft segment of the market.

As the number of once-prominent brewers declined, the largest brewers who survived increased their share of the market. As shown in Table 5-2, in 1947 the top five sellers accounted for only 19 percent of the industry's barrelage; in 2006 their share was 84 percent. In 2005, three firms met almost 80% of domestic demand: Anheuser-Busch (48.5%), Miller (18.3%), and Coors (10.9%). Another way economists summarize the distribution of firm size in a particular market is to compute the Herfindahl

TABLE 5-2 Concentration of Sales by Top Brewers: 1947–2006

Year	Five Largest	HHI
1947	19.0%	140
1954	24.9%	240
1964	39.0%	440
1974	64.0%	1,080
1984	83.9%	1,898
1994	87.3%	2,641
2004	85.2%	2,924
2006	83.9%	2,785

Based on beer volume. The HHI includes only the top five brewers in that year.

Adapted from A. Horowitz and I. Horowitz, "The Beer Industry," *Business Horizons 10* (Fall 1967):14; various issues of *Modern Brewery Age*; Beer Marketer's Insights 2001 Beer Industry Update; and Beer Marketer's Insights 2006 Beer Insights Seminar.

Hirschman Index (HHI): The HHI is each individual seller's market share squared and these numbers are then summed (so a monopolist generates an HHI of 10,000). The rising HHI from 140 (in 1947) to 2,785 (in 2006) shown in Table 5-2 also testifies to the industry's structural transformation.

The Widening of Markets

In the days of hundreds of brewing companies, most consumers faced an actual choice of only a few brewers because most brewers served a small geographic area. Beer is an expensive product to ship, relative to its value, and few brewers could afford to compete in the "home markets" of distant rivals. Thus, at one time, it was meaningful to speak of local, regional, and national brewers. Of these, the local brewer who brewed for a small market, perhaps smaller than a single state and often only a single metropolitan area, was far and away the most common. The regional brewer was multi-state, but usually encompassed no more than two or three states. The national brewers, those selling in all (or almost all) states, were very few and rarely were the largest seller in any particular local area. In addition, it was uncommon for a firm to operate more than one plant.

Today, the terms *local*, *regional* and *national* brewers are antiquated.[6] The geographic territory served by the major brewers from one plant has grown due to the economies of large-scale production and, to some extent, marketing. A second factor extending the reach of national brewers to serve new geographic regions is their propensity to operate more than one plant.

Size of the Market

Determining the degree of market concentration in brewing entails knowing how far the geographic markets for beer extend. If there is one national market, then concentration statistics for the entire nation are relevant. But if brewing, like cement or milk, has regional markets, delineating their boundaries is necessary before the industry's structure can be analyzed.

The federal courts have to solve this problem when deciding antimerger cases in the brewing industry. In an early antitrust case involving the merger of two brewers located in Wisconsin, the Antitrust Division asked an eminent economist at Northwestern University to testify in support of the view that the state of Wisconsin alone was a separate market for beer. The economics professor told the government lawyers such a position was economically untenable. Nevertheless, the lawyers persisted in this view without him and eventually persuaded the Supreme Court that Wisconsin, by itself, is "a distinguishable and economically significant market for the sale of beer."

Although Wisconsin was held to have been a separate market for legal purposes, to single it out as a market in the economic sense is to draw the market boundaries too

---

[6]Robert S. Weinberg bifurcates the contemporary beer market into two broad components: the "core" (the major brands of the large domestic brewers) and the "non-core" (imports and domestic specialty brands). William James Adams splits the industry into two strategic groups: "mass brewers . . . who differentiate their products primarily through advertising on television; and craft brewers, who . . . differentiate their products primarily with raw materials." (Adams 2006, 201)

narrowly (and such a position would not be taken by antitrust authorities today). In 1991, brewers in the state of Wisconsin produced over 17 million barrels of beer; that year, consumers in Wisconsin drank fewer than 5 million barrels of beer. Because beer also is "imported" into Wisconsin from brewers in other states, obviously more than two-thirds of Wisconsin beer is "exported" for sale outside the state. To say that Wisconsin was a separate geographic market would be to overlook the impact of most beer production in that state, not to mention the impact on the supply of beer coming into Wisconsin in competition with beer produced in Wisconsin. In this case, the court erred by singling out Wisconsin as an economically meaningful market. The geographic market for beer is now nationwide.

Reasons for the Decline in the Number of Brewers

In this section, two possible explanations for the decline in the number of major brewers are considered: mergers and economies of scale.

Mergers

A conventional hypothesis for high concentration in a market is a merger-acquisition trend among the industry's firms. At first glance, this seems to be the case in brewing: during the period 1950 to 1983, about 170 horizontal mergers were consummated in the beer industry. But corporate marriages between rival brewers do not explain the increase in concentration by the leading firms, as is evident when one reviews the merger history of the top three brewers.

The first antimerger action in the beer industry was taken by the Antitrust Division in 1958 against the industry's leading firm, Anheuser-Busch, which had purchased the Miami brewery of American Brewing Company. The government successfully argued that this merger would eliminate American Brewing as an independent brewer and end its rivalry with Anheuser-Busch in Florida. The impact of this early antimerger action was profound. Anheuser-Busch had to sell this brewery and refrain from buying any others without court approval for a period of 5 years. As a result, Anheuser-Busch for many years forsook acquiring rival brewers and instead began an extensive program of building large, efficient plants in Florida and at other locations around the United States. It deviated only once from its internal growth policy in 1980 when it acquired the Baldwinsville, New York, brewing plant of the Schlitz Brewing Company.[7] (Only recently has Anheuser-Busch made domestic acquisitions, none with antitrust vulnerability). In June 1994 the company acquired a 25 percent interest in craft brewer Red Hook. In 2006, Anheuser-Busch acquired the Rolling Rock brands (by this time owned by Belgian-based InBev).

Miller Brewing Company, the second largest brewer, also grew primarily by internal expansion. Miller did purchase brewing plants in Texas and California in 1966 but acquired no other breweries until 1987, when it acquired Leinenkugel, a small family-run brewery in Wisconsin. Miller Brewing Company itself was the subject of a conglomerate acquisition by Philip Morris in 1970. From that point, Miller, the number two–ranked firm, had a large corporate parent, unlike Anheuser-Busch, the market leader.

---

[7]Schlitz's sales had declined so much that it did not need the brewery; the plant's capacity was so huge that only an industry leader could absorb its output.

In 1972, just after being acquired by Philip Morris, Miller acquired three brand names from Meister Brau, a defunct Chicago brewing firm. Hardly anyone noticed at the time, but out of this acquisition came the low-calorie or "light beer" phenomenon. The Meister Brau trademarks included one called Lite, a brand of low-calorie beer once marketed locally by Meister Brau to upper-middle-class weight-conscious consumers. The Miller management noticed that Lite had sold fairly well in Anderson, Indiana, a town with many blue-collar workers. In what is now a marketing classic, Miller zeroed in on "real" beer drinkers, claiming that its low-calorie beer allowed them to drink Lite without a filled-up feeling. The upshot of this advertising campaign was remarkable. Lite became the most popular new product in the history of the beer industry.

In 1974, Miller bought the rights to brew and market Lowenbrau, a prominent German beer, in the United States. Miller was never able to develop this brand into an important U.S. product. After this event, mergers played no role at Miller until 1993 when it acquired the marketing rights in the United States for the brands of Molson, a Canadian brewer. In 2001, Miller sold these rights back to Molson which sold them to Coors.

In 1999, Miller, Stroh (then the number four brewer) and Pabst (then number five) consummated a complex acquisition associated with Stroh's exit from the industry. Miller acquired four brands (Henry Weinhard, Mickey's, Hamm's, and Olde English 800) and Pabst acquired all other Stroh brands (including the former Schlitz and Heileman brands[8]). Miller also acquired Pabst's Tumwater, Washington, brewery (which it closed in 2003) and Pabst acquired Stroh's Lehigh Valley, Pennsylvania, brewery.[9] Miller agreed to produce some of Pabst's beer on a contract brewing basis. Most of the remaining Stroh breweries were to be sold as real estate for nonbrewing purposes.[10] Despite the deal's magnitude in terms of brand rearrangement, it resulted in only a small increase in industry concentration and had no antitrust consequences. In 2002, Philip Morris sold Miller to South African Breweries, a London-based firm that is the second largest brewer in the world behind Anheuser-Busch.[11] The venerable Miller Brewing Company is now called SABMiller.

Third-ranked Coors had a long-term policy to brew its Coors brand only in one location: Golden, Colorado. Later, Coors began shipping beer in bulk to Elkton, Virginia, where it is bottled and canned for sale in the East. In 1990, Coors acquired the Memphis brewery of Stroh. There, as in Virginia, the company only *packages* the Coors brand (but brews the company's lower-priced Keystone brand). One reason Coors is a high-cost producer relative to Anheuser-Busch is that its beer travels an average of 1,000 miles; Anheuser-Busch, with its dispersed breweries, ships its beer an average of 200 to 250 miles. In 2002, Coors acquired Carling, Britain's best-selling brand, from Interbrew, marking Coors's first major acquisition outside North America. Continuing

---

[8]These included, in addition to Stroh, Old Milwaukee, Schlitz, Schaefer, Old Style, Schmidt's, Lone Star, Special Export, Schlitz Malt Liquor, and Rainier.

[9]This facility was recently acquired by Guinness-Bass Import Co. (GBIC), the U.S. branch of the British firm Diageo, in part to produce Smirnoff Ice, GBIC's best-selling flavored malt beverage.

[10]Yuengling acquired Stroh's 1.6 million–barrel capacity Tampa brewery and will use it to meet current demand in the Northeast and for geographic expansion in the Southeast. Stroh's Portland, Oregon, brewery (the former Blitz-Weinhard plant) has ceased operations.

[11]SAB markets such brands as Pilsner Urquell and Castle Lager.

this trend, in 2005 Coors merged with Canadian-based brewer Molson to form Molson Coors Brewing Company, whose combined beer sales made it the fifth largest brewer in the world.

Stroh had been a prominent brewer since 1850 and was itself an acquirer until its demise. In 1980, when Stroh was the seventh largest brewer in the country, it acquired the F. M. Schaefer Brewing Company. In 1982, Stroh acquired the Joseph Schlitz Brewing Company, itself in a sales tailspin, but at the time the fourth largest brewer. This acquisition catapulted Stroh to number three in the industry, but also shackled the firm with debt and set the stage for its demise. In 1996, Stroh made another sizable acquisition: the G. Heileman Brewing Company.[12] But its size did not insulate Stroh from market competition. In 1999, then the fourth-ranking firm in the beer industry, Stroh exited the market.

Most recently, in the fall of 2007 Coors and SABMiller announced a proposed joint venture combining their U.S. operations, claiming this consolidation will enable them to exploit sizable cost savings. While Anheuser-Busch would continue to be the largest brewer in the U.S., its lead over a combined Coors-SABMiller would no longer be as large (a 50 percent market share for Anheuser-Busch versus a 30 percent share for a Coors-SABMiller joint venture).

Notwithstanding these sizable corporate marriages, mergers have not made much of an imprint on the structure of the brewing industry and have not resulted in market power for merging partners. The most active merging firms, Stroh and Heileman, eventually failed. Much of the increase in concentration in the past 3 decades has been due to the growth of Anheuser-Busch, Miller and Coors, whose expansion has been largely internal. Indeed, the early enforcement of the antimerger law was partly responsible for the emphasis on internal growth by the leading brewers. Later mergers went largely unchallenged. The antitrust authorities recognized in the mid-1970s that beer mergers they once would have attacked do not merit challenge, even if the merger involved sizable regional sellers.[13] Whether the antitrust authorities will allow the Coors-SABMiller joint venture announced in late 2007 remains to be seen and will turn on how the projected cost savings are evaluated, how broadly the scope of the relevant market is defined, and how much malt beverages are seen to be in head-to-head competition with other alcoholic beverages.

Most of the mergers in the beer industry did not involve firms of significant stature. Generally, they represented the demise of an inefficient firm that salvaged some remainder of its worth by selling out to another brewer. The acquiring brewer gained no market power but might have benefited by securing the barrelage to bring one plant to full capacity or by gaining access to an improved distribution network or new territory. Mergers such as these are not the *cause* of structural change; they are the *effect*, as firms exit or rearrange their assets through the merger route. The trend to concentration in brewing would have occurred even if all mergers had been prohibited. As a consequence, one must look to factors other than mergers to explain the industry's structural shakeup.

---

[12]Heileman had been the industry's fifth-ranking firm, itself the product of over a dozen acquisitions from 1960 on, notably Wiedemann, Associated Brewing, the Blatz brand, Rainier, Carling, and portions of Pabst.
[13]For an analysis of beer mergers and the antimerger law in the U.S., see Elzinga and Swisher (2005).

Economies of Scale

Economies of scale exist if large plants produce at lower unit costs than small ones. Exploiting economies of scale through assembly line production did not begin with Henry Ford and the automobile industry in Detroit. Years earlier, in St. Louis and Milwaukee, brewing companies began to exploit the cost efficiencies of large scale production.

Figure 5-1 is a representation of economies of scale that currently exist in the brewing industry. The figure illustrates the fairly sharp decline in long-run unit costs until a plant size of 4.0 million barrels per year of capacity is reached. Beyond this capacity, costs continue to decline, but less sharply, until a capacity of 10 to 12 million barrels (an enormous brewery) is attained. There are only modest cost economies, if any, that can be exploited in plants with capacity above 10 to 12 million barrels, and production economies may be offset by the high shipping costs necessary to move so much beer to market.

Figure 5-1 also has a single short-run average cost curve above the long-run average cost curve. A long-run cost curve represents the envelope of different-sized plants, each of which uses the latest production techniques. The short-run average cost curve standing by itself better portrays the situation of many breweries that met their demise in the 1960s and 1970s. Not only were these breweries too small to exploit all the economies of scale but their capital equipment was also of such an outmoded vintage that their costs were elevated even more.

Table 5-3 shows one method—the survivor test—used by economists to estimate the extent of economies of scale. As its name implies, the survivor test considers plants that have survived over time to be the optimum size. The number of breweries with a capacity under 2 million barrels has declined steadily (dramatically in some cases), while the number with a capacity of 4 million barrels and above has increased. Because large brewing plants not only survived but grew in number, this is considered, by a

■ ■ ■ FIGURE 5-1 Economies of Scale in Brewing

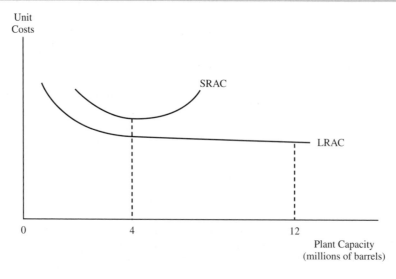

TABLE 5-3 Surviving Breweries by Capacity: 1959–2006

Listed Capacity Barrels (in thousands)	1959	1967	1975	1983	1989	1998	2001	2006
10–100	68	36	10	15	8	77	81	83
101–500	91	44	19	12	7	19	19	19
501–1,000	30	35	13	2	3	1	1	4
1,001–2,000	18	18	13	13	5	4	2	2
2,001–4,000	8	10	12	9	6	7	5	3
4,001+	2	4	15	23	20	20	20	22

Source: Compiled from plant capacity figures listed in the *Modern Brewery Age Blue Book* (various years); Charles W. Parker, (1984), "The Domestic Beer Industry," and industry trade sources. These figures do not include plants listed only on a company consolidated basis (in the case of multiplant firms) or single-plant firms not reporting their capacity, and these figures exclude microbreweries that produce fewer than 10,000 barrels of capacity.

survivor test, to be prima facie evidence of their lower unit costs.[14] One understands better the success of Anheuser-Busch and Miller in recognizing that their 18 plants have an average capacity of slightly over 8.6 million barrels. These are the huge, cost-efficient production units for the U.S. market's leading brands. The only exception to this economies-of-scale thesis is the notable jump in smaller breweries, especially in the 10,000 to 100,000 barrel capacity range. These are primarily the new craft or specialty brewers whose survival does not depend upon scale economies.

Table 5-3 does not reflect the appearance of very small breweries in the craft beer segment—microbrewers or brewpubs (where food is served with on-premise beer consumption). In 2005, there were about 1,300 such firms with sales of 10,000 barrels or less. Some of these are very small indeed, such as Little Apple Brewing Company in Manhattan, Kansas, capable of brewing about 600 barrels per year in 2006. Microbrewers receive much attention in the business press, in part because there had been, until their arrival, so little de novo entry into the beer industry in the post–World War II period. Brewers in the craft segment have their own trade journal, *The New Brewer*, and this segment of the industry is promoted by the Brewers Association.[15]

Some of the economies from larger brewing operations come in the packaging of the plant's output. The bottling lines at the Anheuser-Busch Houston brewery have line speeds of 1,100 bottles per minute. Modern canning lines are even faster: 2,000 cans per minute. It takes a brewery of substantial size to utilize such equipment at capacity. Large plants also save labor costs via the automation of brewing and warehousing and save capital costs, as well. Construction cost per barrel is cut by about one

---

[14]For a sophisticated treatment of cost efficiencies in brewing, see the paper by Joe R. Kerkvliet, William Nebesky, Carol H. Tremblay and Victor J. Tremblay (1998).

[15]This association defines a "craft brewer" by size (under 2 million barrels of production/year); ownership (at least 75% self-owned); and brewing method (percentage of malt and adjuncts). By this taxonomy, former craft brewers and pioneers such as Redhook and Widmer are defined out of the segment.

third for a 4.5-million-barrel-capacity plant relative to a 1.5-million-barrel-capacity plant.[16]

Cost efficiency relates not only to some finite production capacity but also to management's ability to use the capacity efficiently. Shortly after the repeal of prohibition in 1933, new entrants flooded into the brewing industry, all expecting to be met by thirsty customers. However, the demand for beer was unexpectedly low after repeal. From a high of 750 brewers operating in 1935, almost 100 were quickly eliminated in only 5 years. Quite a few of these enterprises had operated before prohibition, but many were under new management. Some were family-owned firms, and heredity had been cruel to the second or third generations, not endowing them with the brewing and/or managerial capabilities of their fathers or grandfathers. Competitive pressures, with no respect for nepotism, eliminated such firms.

A small brewer, producing a quality product and marketing it with minimal transportation costs, can survive in today's industry by finding a special niche for itself. This seems to be the status, by way of examples, of Wisconsin's Stevens Point Brewery; D. G. Yuengling & Son in Pennsylvania (the nation's oldest brewing firm still in business); and the pioneer craft brewer, San Francisco's Steam Beer Company. However, large, capital-intensive plants are necessary to exploit economies of scale and meet mainstream beer tastes. In markets where vigorous competitive pressures exist, firms that do not exploit economies of scale or operate with internal efficiency will not survive. This has been the fate of many brewers; they have exited from the industry because of inefficient plants, poor management, or both. The continued success of higher-cost craft brewers pivots upon their brands' product differentiation sustaining a higher price point.

The Condition of Entry

The ease with which newcomers can enter an industry is an important structural characteristic for ensuring competitive performance. If entry is not blocked, existing firms will be unable to raise prices significantly lest they encourage an outbreak of new competition. On the other hand, if entry is barred, perhaps by a patent or government license, a dominant firm's market position may be insulated.

Entry into the beer industry is not hindered by the traditional barriers of patents and exclusive government grants. Nor are there key inputs whose supply is controlled or limited by existing firms. Likewise, economies of scale are not so important that an efficient entrant would have to supply an enormous share of industry output. However, the sheer expense of entering the beer industry is considerable. The price of constructing a modern 4- to 5-million-barrel brewery is over $250 million. Marketing the new brew also is costly because entrants must introduce their products to consumers already smitten by the advertising of incumbent firms.

Since World War II, no new entrant has cracked the top three sellers of beer in the U.S. beer market. De novo entry has been from imported beer and craft brewers. By 2005, over 28 new entrants (since 1995) in the craft brewing segment were producing at least 15,000 barrels annually. The lack of new entry at the very top is explained by the

---

[16]However, no significant reduction in production costs was detected in a study of multiplant scale economies by F. M. Scherer and others.

relatively low profitability of the industry and the ominous fate of so many exiting firms. Moreover, entry into the industry is risky because breweries have few uses other than producing beer. New entry involves considerable sunk costs. The 1980s and 1990s were decades in which the market mechanism wrung excess capacity out of the industry rather than inviting new firms and capacity in.

Import competition merits special mention in any discussion of new entry. Beer imports to the United States, which come mostly from Mexico, the Netherlands, Canada, and Germany, increased more than *32-fold* in the period from 1970 through 2006. In 2005, imports represented over 12.5 percent of domestic consumption, up from less than 1 percent in 1970. Imported beer no longer can be dismissed as an insignificant part of demand or supply. In 1998, for the first time, an imported beer (Corona Extra) became a top 10 brand. By 2005, this Mexican import was the number six brand in the country with 3.7 percent share of the total U.S. market.

Product Differentiation

When consumers find the product of one firm superior to other market alternatives, the favored firm can raise its price somewhat without losing these customers. Economists call this phenomenon "product differentiation" (marketing specialists call it "brand loyalty" or "brand equity"). The product differentiation of "premium beer" is important to understand. This phenomenon began years ago when a few brewers marketed their beer nationally and added a price premium to offset the additional transportation costs incurred by greater shipping distances. To secure the higher price, premium beer was promoted as superior in taste and quality, allegedly because of the brewing expertise found at their place of production (notably Milwaukee and St. Louis).

At one time, the premium price was offset by higher shipping costs. The construction of efficient, regionally dispersed breweries by firms like Anheuser-Busch and Miller, however, eliminated the transportation disadvantage. But the premium image remained. With transportation costs equalized, and production costs generally lower, these firms could wage vigorous advertising (and price-cutting) campaigns in areas where regional and local brewers were once the largest sellers.[17]

One indicator of an industry's advertising intensity is its ratio of advertising expenditures to sales. The average firm in the U.S. spends about 3 percent of its sales dollar on advertising. For some companies in the soap, cosmetic, and drug industries, the percentage is greater than 10 percent. For beer, this ratio is about 6 percent. In 2005, Anheuser Busch spent just over a half-billion dollars on media advertising compared to $230 million for Miller and $162 million for Coors. Because of its volume, Anheuser-Busch enjoys scale economies in advertising. In 2005, Anheuser-Busch spent about $5.00 per barrel on media advertising while Miller and Coors spent $6.00 and $7.70 per barrel respectively. Douglas F. Greer and others have argued that advertising, particularly television advertising, was a primary cause of increasing concentration in the industry. John Sutton offers a variation on this theme, suggesting that advertising is a

---

[17]The national brewers also have two other advertising advantages: (1) none of their advertising is "wasted," whereas regional brewers do not always find media markets (especially in television) that coincide with their selling territories; and (2) their advertising investment is less likely to be lost when a customer moves to another part of the country.

sunk cost that protects the leading firms from new competition. But the facts do not permit any tidy explanations or conclusions about the consequences of advertising because there is no hard-and-fast relationship between dollars spent on advertising and market share gained.

Miller has long been a heavy advertiser. In the period between 1967 and 1971, it generally spent twice as much per barrel as rival brewers. But Miller's market share did not expand then, nor did other firms feel compelled to emulate Miller's sizable promotional outlays. Miller was not able to secure more than a toehold in the superpremium segment of the market notwithstanding extraordinary per barrel advertising expenditures on Lowenbrau. In 1980 Miller High Life was the most heavily advertised brand of beer in the United States; that was the year its sales slowed down and began declining every year until the brand was repositioned at a lower price point. Schlitz spent more on advertising in 1975 and 1976 than either Anheuser-Busch or Miller, and yet sales of the Schlitz brand declined in that very time frame. Coors experienced expanding sales with very small advertising expenditures: from 1968 to 1974, during years of sizable growth, Coors spent only an average of 17 cents per barrel on media advertising. Coors's *growing* use of media occurred when its share position in many states was declining. Anheuser-Busch significantly increased its advertising expenditures on its Budweiser brand—total and per barrel—from 1991 to 1992 but Budweiser's total sales and share of market fell. On the other hand, Natural Light has been one of Anheuser-Busch's steadiest performers, even though the company often spends less than a nickel per barrel on its advertising.

To economists, beer is an example of an "experience good" because the product's characteristics can be evaluated primarily only after purchasing the good. With experience goods, advertisements laden with information are of little value to consumers because the validity of the information is largely verified post-purchase. Consequently, advertisements for experience goods tend to emphasize image and the identity of the seller's brand name. This characterizes much beer advertising. For example, SABMiller promotes Miller Lite with the catchphrase, "tastes great . . . less filling" while Coors emphasizes its slogan, "Rocky Mountain Refreshment."

Critics of these "noninformative" ads maintain that consumers are manipulated by them because they create artificial product differentiation for what are essentially homogeneous products. Some critics are particularly concerned that young people will become persuaded that their own identity depends upon emulating the images portrayed in the ads. Many economists, however, view consumers as rational agents capable of making self-interested decisions regarding the merits of experience goods. Although the content of beer advertisements may appear to be noninformative, "consumers are at least made aware of the existence of a product or service if they have observed an advertisement for it" and repetitive advertising increases the likelihood that a potential consumer will encounter such information and "alter his or her cache of knowledge."[18]

The total amount of resources devoted to beer advertising is large, but this is not surprising. A brewer wants to inform millions of actual and potential beer drinkers of the availability of its product. New beer customers come of age; old customers

---

[18]Robert B. Ekelund, Jr. and David Saurman (1988), 64.

may need reminding. The Supreme Court lent its support to this form of economic reasoning. In the context of another market, the Court opined ". . . advertising, however tasteless and excessive it sometimes may seem, is nonetheless dissemination of information."[19]

The three major domestic brewers of 1970s are, essentially, producers of premium brands. Premium beer is what economists call a normal good, with a positive income elasticity. Rising per capita income increased the demand for premium brands. Popular priced brands (now often called the "budget" segment) were once the leading sellers within their respective home states. No longer. Premium brands (regular and light) now hold about 65 percent of the market; imports, specialties, and superpremiums have about 17 percent. The loser in the past 3 decades has been popular-price beer, dropping from almost 60 percent in 1970 to 8.3 percent in 2005. Today, rising national income cuts against the demand for mainstream premium brands of beer and favors craft beers and imports. Specialty brands are not just the offspring of microbrewers. Several major brewers have had modest success with specialty brands, usually priced a notch below craft beers and import brands. Coors' Blue Moon brand is an example. Some beverage sector analysts speculate that the beer industry will someday have the same large array of specialty brands one now finds in coffee and wine.

Light beer, virtually nonexistent in 1970, has become the largest product segment in the beer industry, with about 50 percent of the market in 2005, almost all of this being brewed by the top three brewers, and much of it selling at premium prices. The decline of once-prominent brewers like Pabst, Schlitz, and Stroh is explained in part by their lack of success (compared to Anheuser-Busch, Miller, and Coors) in the light-beer segment of the market. Even import brands like Corona and Heineken are now available as light beers in the United States.

▬ III Conduct

Pricing

Judging from the early records of the preprohibition beer industry, competition in the industry was vigorous. Entry was easy; producers were many. Given these two charac-teristics, economic theory would predict a competitive industry, and the evidence bears this out. In fact, the early beer industry offers a classic example of the predictions of price theory. Because of the market's inelastic demand, brewers saw the obvious advantages of monopolizing the industry, raising prices, and gleaning high profits. Various types of loose and tightly knit cartels were seen as advantageous, but the diffi-culty of coordinating so many brewers and the lack of barriers to entry prevented these efforts from being successful, at least for long. The degree of competition is evidenced by this turn-of-the-century plea from Adolphus Busch to Captain Pabst:

> I hope also to be able to demonstrate to you that by the present way competi-tion is running we are only hurting each other in a real foolish way. The travel-ing agents . . . always endeavor to reduce prices and send such reports to their respective home offices as are generally not correct and only tend to bring

---

[19]See *Virginia State Board of Pharmacy v. Virginia Citizens Consumer Council*, 425 U.S. 748, 765 (1976).

forth competition that helps to ruin the profits . . . all large manufacturing interests are now working in harmony . . . and only the brewers are behind as usual; instead of combining their efforts and securing their own interest, they are fighting each other and running the profits down, so that the pleasures of managing a brewery have been diminished a good deal.

In a free enterprise economy, it is best that firms avoid any communications about prices. But if such letters are written, it is best if they decry vigorous market rivalry.

The beer industry also escaped the horizontal mergers that transformed the structure of so many industries such as steel, whiskey, petroleum, tobacco products, and farm equipment during the first great merger movement (1880 to 1904). Attempts were made, mostly by British businessmen, to combine the large brewers during this time. One sought the amalgamation of Pabst, Schlitz, Miller, Anheuser-Busch, and Lemp into one company, a feat that, had it been successful, would have altered the structure and degree of competition in the industry. But the attempt failed, and brewing entered prohibition with a competitive structure that responded with competitive pricing.

The Pricing Pattern

Beer is generally sold free on board (f.o.b.) the brewery, meaning that the brewer's costs end at the loading dock, and customers pay the freight. Some brewers sell on a uniform f.o.b. mill basis, but most vary their prices to different customers to reflect localized competitive conditions or to test perceived changes in the marketplace. The present pattern of prices dates back to the start of the twentieth century. For decades, premium beers generally were priced just above the level of popular-price beers, which in turn were above local (or "price" or "shelf") beer. Because of downward price pressure on premium beer, and the decline of independent brewers producing only popular-price beer, the marketing segments today are often broken down as premium (regular and light), near premium, and budget. Superpremium is beer selling at a price above premium. The major brewers market their own brand of superpremium, and most imported beers as well as the output of brewers in the craft segment fall in the superpremium price category.

The demarcation between local-popular-premium has become blurred in recent years, not only because of the introduction of the superpremium, but because the price differential between premium and popular-price brands has narrowed. At the same time, the distinction between local and popular beer on the basis of price has become murky because of pricing specials that regularly appear in either segment of the market and the repositioning of once premium brands, like Pabst Blue Ribbon, into a lower price tier. Some brands defy categories. Industry expert Robert S. Weinberg provides an example: "Life must be very confusing for a six-pack of Rolling Rock. It comes out of the brewery, and depending on the address it is sent to, it might be popular-priced beer, a premium, a super-premium, or a domestic specialty. Same beer, and an extraordinary marketing achievement."[20] Discounting also occurs in the beer industry, including the major premium brands. Much of the beer sold by Anheuser-Busch,

---

[20]Robert S. Weinberg, "Talking with Dr. Bob," *Modern Brewery Age*, Nov. 27, 2000, 12.

Miller, and Coors is on some form of deal: a direct price discount or an advertising or merchandising allowance.

Marketing

Although all industries are subject to various federal and state laws that affect the marketing of the industry's product, the beer industry faces an especially variegated pattern of laws and regulations concerning labeling, advertising, credit, container characteristics, alcohol content, tax rates, and litter assessments. For example, Michigan makes optional whether a beer label shows alcohol content, while Minnesota requires an accurate statement of alcohol content. In Indiana, advertising is strictly regulated; Louisiana has no such regulations. Some states require sales from the brewer to the wholesaler to the retailer to be only on a cash basis, whereas other states allow credit. Some states stipulate both the maximum and minimum size of containers. States also have varying requirements on the maximum and minimum permissible alcoholic content; in some, alcoholic content is different for different types of outlets.

In the 1970s, beer advertising was criticized because it allegedly could lead to monopoly problems. This turned out to be unfounded. More recently, beer advertising has been criticized from a public health perspective—that beer advertising increases alcohol abuse among specific populations, particularly underage consumers. The research of Jon Nelson suggests that advertising does not increase market demand but rather rearranges shares among brands. As a corollary, Nelson concludes that bans on advertising are not sound public policy because the evidence is weak that advertising increases total consumption (and therefore abuse). He does find that bans on *billboard* advertising of alcoholic beverages can reduce the demand for distilled spirits and wine but can increase the demand for beer. Nelson suggests that stricter enforcement of legal drinking age laws is a more effective way of restraining alcohol abuse by young people (Nelson, 2003). The research of Carol and Victor Tremblay (1995) offers a different perspective: that on balance there may be a social gain from restricting beer advertising. Economists do not always see eye to eye.

Government involvement in the beer industry also includes heavy taxation. The federal tax on a barrel of beer is $18.00 and, in 2005, the Treasury Department coffers gathered $3.65 billion in beer taxes. State taxes on beer vary substantially but in 2004 averaged $7.83 per barrel. In addition, brewers, wholesalers, and retail outlets pay federal, state, and sometimes local occupational taxes. Federal and state taxes paid by the beer industry exceeded $9.25 billion in 2004, making taxes the largest single cost item in a glass of beer.

Brewer-Distributor Relations

There is little forward integration by brewing firms into the marketing of beer. In the United States, brewers generally are prohibited by law from owning retail outlets, leaving wholesale distribution as the only legitimate forward vertical integration route.[21] Even wholesaling by brewers is prohibited in some states. The retailing of beer is done

---

[21]The exception—sometimes hard won—has been brewpubs, which represent vertical integration from brewing to retailing.

through two general types of independent outlets: on-premise consumption and off-premise consumption. On-premise sales are the leading retail channel followed by convenience stores and supermarkets. Brewers generally make higher margins with on-premise sales.

The political forces that finally ended prohibition hoped to temper the purported vices of alcohol by diminishing its sale in saloons and taverns. It was hoped that beer sold in grocery stores for in-home consumption would promote moderation. This meant that the channels of distribution cultivated preprohibition would fall out of favor. Instead of moving product to on-premise consumption, the postprohibition beer industry had to cater to off-premise consumption. Success in marketing meant getting beer to the retailer: originally the grocer and, later, the convenience store as well.

Most brewers rely on independent wholesalers to channel their product to retail outlets. Historically, most wholesalers have been family-run businesses. In recent years, the wholesaling of beer has been marked by numerous consolidations and mergers.[22] Some "family firms" are now big businesses with many wholesalers today concentrating their distribution on only one or two major brewers. Most Anheuser-Busch volume (62%) goes through exclusive distributors; those distributors who are not exclusive have less than 10 percent of their volume in rival brands. Anheuser-Busch estimates that only 5 percent of Miller's volume and 3 percent of Coors's volume travel through exclusive distributors. Miller and Coors often share the same beer wholesaler (in over 250 instances). Many localities now have only two beer distributors: one for Anheuser-Busch and one for all others. A typical Anheuser-Busch distributor markets less than 30 brands while a typical non-Anheuser-Busch distributor will handle over 100 brands from more than 2 dozen different brewers.

Every brewer has an economic interest in what happens to its beer once it leaves the brewery because consumers see the brewer's name on the container, not the name of the wholesaler (or retailer). Therefore, brewers negotiate contracts with wholesalers that specify the marketing obligations of each party. Even with the growth in the size of some beer wholesalers, brewers are increasingly involved in channel marketing. For example, large retail accounts often are called upon by the brewer, not wholesalers.

Major brewers generally support marketing their product through a three-tier distribution system. But some large retail customers, notably chain stores, prefer to purchase beer directly from brewers, bypassing the wholesale distributor. Some people worry that the "middleman" (the second tier of the beer industry's three-tier distribution channel) will be eliminated if large retailers are allowed to deal directly with brewers. But the middleman is not really eliminated if alcoholic beverages do not come to rest in some independent wholesaler's warehouse. From an economic perspective, what is happening is that the distribution function gets internalized within the parties to the direct-buy transaction.

The trend toward store brands and a closer integration between manufacturer and retailer, already common in food retailing, has not yet affected the beer industry. But the beer industry is not insulated from this prospect. In 2003, the convenience store chain 7-11 began selling its own private label beer, Santiago Cerveza De Oro, which it imports from El Salvador and prices below established import brands.

---

[22]Table 5-1 illustrates the decline in the number of independent beer wholesalers.

Just as some retailers may want to buy beer direct from the brewer, so may some consumers. The prospect of direct sales from brewer to consumer through e-commerce portends a further weakening of the three-tier system. In 2003, the Federal Trade Commission issued a report recommending an end to state bans on direct shipments of wine because e-commerce sales afford consumers lower prices, more choices, and increased convenience. The FTC dismissed as self-serving the argument of wine wholesalers that direct sales would encourage underage consumption. In 2005, the Supreme Court ruled that an individual state cannot stop its residents from buying *out-of-state* wine on the Internet (bypassing an *in-state* distributor) if that state allowed Internet sales to its citizens from wineries *in* the state.[23] When the FTC study became public, beer distribution expert Mark Rodman asked rhetorically, "Why is beer different than wine?"[24] The answer is, it is not different, and the prospect for direct sales of beer may be another step in undercutting traditional beer marketing channels.

Some retail accounts want to bargain with different distributors of the same brand of beer (possibly purchasing from a price-cutting wholesaler in another area). But many brewers have exclusive territories with wholesalers that prevent this. Exclusive territories enable brewers to offer incentives to distributors to cultivate a specific territory with less fear of free riding. An example of free riding would be a distributor who trans-ships dated beer to a territory that has been served by another distributor who, by careful stock rotation, had given that brand a reputation for freshness. Some critics, however, consider exclusive territorial restraints to be anticompetitive. In an important antitrust case against several major brewers, the New York Attorney General once challenged the use of exclusive territories. In 1993 the challenge ended when exclusive territories in beer distribution were found, on balance, to be procompetitive.

At one time beer wholesalers primarily distributed beer in kegs for on-premise draught consumption. In 1935, only 30 percent of beer sales were packaged—that is, in bottles or cans suitable for on- or off-premise consumption. Since that time there has been a major shift to packaged beer relative to draught; by 2005, 90 percent of beer sales were packaged in cans and one-way bottles. The trend to packaged beer once worked to the disadvantage of the small brewer. When beer sales were primarily for on-premise consumption, the small brewer could prosper by selling kegs to taverns in the immediate area; the local brewer offered freshness and transportation economies relative to larger, but more distant brewers. But packaged beer from the major brands increased the opportunity for national advertising campaigns, making on-premise customers more aware of the major brands, even if brewed miles away. The mass production of beer in bottles and cans also dovetailed with the desire for convenience that packaged sales offer to off-premise customers.[25]

Craft brewers compete against this trend by offering specialty beers that can be promoted in restaurants and bars as full-flavored alternatives to the major brands; some craft brewers are integrated vertically into brewpubs. Today, a visit to many

---

[23]*Granholm v. Heald*, 125 S.Ct. 1885 (2005)

[24]"FTC report supports internet sales and direct shipping for wine," *Modern Brewery Age*, July 14, 2003, p. 1.

[25]Kreuger Brewing in Newark, New Jersey, was a pioneer in this regard. It was the first company to market beer in a can convenient for off-premise consumption. Billions of "six-packs" (and now "suitcases") were to follow, becoming among the most ubiquitous packages for a product ever developed. Now even some imported beer is offered in cans (e.g., Heineken) and craft beer (Oskar Blues Brewery).

grocery and convenience stores will reveal the presence of numerous specialty brands (as well as imports) next to the products of the big three.

Beer and the Global Economy

The United States imports far more beer (25.7 million barrels in 2005) than it exports (3.9 million barrels in 2005). In some situations, the trade asymmetry is stark. For example, in 2005 the Dutch sold about 5.9 million barrels of beer to the U.S. and imported only 2,060 barrels of U.S. beer. Mexico, the Netherlands, Canada, and the United Kingdom are the main exporters of beer to the U.S. (in 2004 order of volume). Mexican and Canadian beers have a transportation cost advantage over their Dutch and U.K. rivals. When asked why Heineken did not build a brewery in the U.S. to reduce its transportation costs, the firm's U.S. president replied, "I like to have that small word 'imported' on the label . . . something would get lost if the bottle read brewed and bottled in the USA."[26]

The U.S. beer industry is a latecomer to the globalization of markets, but the process is underway. For example, in 1993, Anheuser-Busch purchased an 18 percent stake in the largest Mexican brewer (Cerveceria Modelo) and entered into a joint venture with the leading Japanese brewer (Kirin). In 2006, Anheuser-Busch acquired the rights to import the European brands of InBev. If a consumer imbibes a Bass, Stella Artois, or Beck's today in the United States, it was brought to her by Anheuser-Busch. As mentioned previously, Miller was acquired in 2002 by SAB, a London based, international brewer. In 1991, Coors entered into a joint venture with Jinro to build a large brewery in South Korea, and a license agreement with Scottish & Newcastle in Scotland to brew Coors beer for the European market. In 1992, Pabst dismantled its Fort Wayne, Indiana brewery and shipped it to China, where it once again produces Pabst Blue Ribbon beer.

While Anheuser-Busch is the largest brewer of beer in the world, it is not truly a global player. Heineken (Holland); Carlsberg (Denmark); Interbrew (Belgium); and Guinness (U.K./Ireland) better define a global brewer. Each has the majority of its volume produced outside of its home country. Among U.S. brewers with international aspirations, licensing production in foreign markets has been the favored mode of expansion. The actual export of product from the U.S. to foreign markets declined in the latter half of the 1990s.

▪▪▪ IV Performance

Externalities and Informational Asymmetries

Two kinds of "market failure" that economists recognize are externalities and information asymmetries. To the extent an industry is marked by externalities or information asymmetries, the economic performance of that industry is likely to be affected. The existence of market failure raises the question of whether government intervention might remedy the externality or information asymmetry in a policy-efficient manner.

A negative externality occurs when transactions between buyers and sellers reduce the economic welfare of individuals not party to the transaction. Air pollution is

---

[26]*Beer Marketer's Insights*, December 17, 2002, p. 4, quoting Frans van der Minne.

the textbook example of a negative externality. The beer industry is remarkably free of the negative externalities often associated with the *production* of products: air and water pollution. Brewing is a very "clean" industry (breweries must be more sanitary than hospitals, in fact) and brewing firms often are courted by localities seeking industry partly for this reason. The two important negative externality problems in brewing occur in the *consumption* of the product: litter and alcohol abuse. Most citizens are able to restrain their enthusiasm for the beer cans and bottles that end up as litter. And everyone in an automobile would like to avoid the negative externality of a drunk driver coming at them head-on.

To deal with litter, legislation banning or restricting the sale of beer containers has been proposed but only a few states and localities actually have passed such laws. The most restrictive of these laws was enacted in the college town of Oberlin, Ohio, which simply outlawed the sale or possession of beer in nonreturnable containers. The most well known of these laws is the Oregon bottle bill, passed in 1971, which banned all cans with detachable pull tabs and placed a compulsory 5-cent deposit on all beer and soft drink containers. Other states have followed with variations of the Oregon plan. The pull-tab can has disappeared as a result of this legislation, and the deposit cost has offered an inducement to the use of returnable containers or on-premise draught consumption. In Oregon and Vermont, mandatory deposit legislation apparently led to reductions of 60 and 80 percent, respectively, in roadside beverage container litter. However, the statewide (or local) approach cannot solve the problem (say, in Vermont) of customers going "over the line" (to New Hampshire) to avoid the deposit requirement and higher prices.

American brewers (with the exception of Coors) historically have opposed all litter taxes and bans on containers, stressing instead voluntary action and other litter-recovery programs. The latter, if generously financed, could solve the litter problem, but partially at the expense of nonproducers and nonconsumers.

The negative externality of driving while under the influence of alcohol was responsible for escalating the minimum drinking age in all states to 21 years of age. But this has had little impact upon young people driving under the influence of alcohol (DUI). Economic research suggests that young beer drinkers are sensitive to price increases. Indexing the federal tax on beer to the rate of inflation since 1951 would, by its impact on retail price, have discouraged enough drunk driving by young drivers to save an estimated 5000 lives in the period 1982 to 1988 (more than was saved by raising the minimum legal drinking age). But this would make beer more expensive to all those who do not abuse the product. As another strategy, the National Highway Safety Administration has endorsed a blood alcohol content (BAC) level of .08 (or above) as a per se driving violation. Most states currently define DUI at a BAC above .08, such as .10. The American Beverage Institute opposes lowering the BAC but supports stiffer penalties for those caught driving while intoxicated. The costs imposed upon third parties by alcohol abuse go beyond automobile accidents; and alcohol abuse, of course, is not limited to the consumption of malt beverages.

Asymmetric information occurs when one party to a transaction knows things about the product that the person on the other side does not know. Asymmetric information is present in the distribution of alcohol. Some consumers, often young ones, may not have as much information about the consequences of alcohol consumption as sellers have. And sellers may not have economic incentives to eliminate this asymmetry.

For example, beer advertisements rarely inform consumers of the negative consequences of excessive consumption. Regulations that offset the information asymmetry—as well as privately-funded campaigns such as Mothers Against Drunk Driving—may help remedy this market failure. Information that promotes temperance may reduce the market failure associated with beer (or other alcohol) consumption.

Competition

A third kind of market failure occurs when a market is monopolized, either by a single firm or a group of sellers who coordinate their price and output decisions. This is not an economic characteristic of the beer industry. There is no monopoly brewer who, insulated from competition, is able to enjoy the "quiet life."

In some industries, increasing concentration at the national level coupled with inelastic market demand might raise the specter of tacit or direct collusion. However, no evidence of price collusion is seen in the beer industry, nor is the prospect worrisome for the foreseeable future. Even during a period of increasing demand in the 1960s and 1970s, competition among brewers was so vigorous as to force the exit of marginal firms. Furthermore, competition along nonprice vectors is robust—such as new product introductions, promotional activities, packaging innovations, brand advertising, product freshness, and availability. As Gisser has argued, increasing concentration in brewing has enhanced consumer welfare as a handful of firms invested in new technologies that increased the efficiency of an initially unconcentrated market, resulting in lower prices to consumers.

One measure of an industry's rivalry is the extent of changes in market share or turnover in the ranking of its sellers.[27] The beer industry exhibits high mobility in this regard. Schlitz, the nation's second-ranking firm in 1976 and the "Beer That Made Milwaukee Famous," no longer is even brewed there. Pabst was the third leading seller as recently as 1975, ahead of Miller. It has become a shell of its former self. In 2002, for example, Pabst sold only 1 million barrels of its Pabst Blue Ribbon brand. As a consequence of market forces, the once prominent brewing trio of Heileman, Pabst, and Stroh lost over *22 million barrels* of sales from their brand portfolios during the decade 1988 to 1998.

Miller, the number eight brewer in 1968, bested a number of larger brewers in the marketplace and, by 1977, had become the number two brewer in the United States (a rank it has held since). But Miller, the darling of the industry in the 1970s, has experienced an absence of growth in the 1980s, the1990s, and into the twenty-first century. To offset stagnant sales on the Miller brand portfolio, in 2006 Miller acquired two trendy malt beverage brands (Sparks and Steel Reserve) from San Francisco virtual brewer, McKenzie River. Coors, the number three brewer, attained its current rank in part by moving from a regional to a national brewer (in 1976, Coors only marketed to 11 Western states). But Coors has been bested in a number of states where it was once the leading seller. For example, Coors once "owned" Oklahoma and California, with

---

[27]Robert S. Weinberg has the most extensive database on the rise and fall of U.S. brewers. I am indebted to him for his counsel and industry statistics. See "Tracking the Winners," *Modern Brewery Age*, Nov. 11, 2002, pp. 20–23.

54 percent and 40 percent of the sales in these states. By 2002, these percentages had slipped to 16 and 12 percent.

The one constant in all this has been Anheuser-Busch: number one since 1957. Alfred Marshall, the great Cambridge economist, believed that family-run firms could not long dominate a market because business skill would not be passed on generation to generation. The Busch family is an exception that proves this rule. Adolphus Busch, August A. Busch, Sr., August A. Busch, Jr., August A. Busch III, and now August A. Busch IV have led the firm and retained the firm's position as market leader.

Several factors contribute to Anheuser-Busch's strong leadership position. All of its breweries are large, low-cost facilities. Moreover, only two brands comprise much of the firm's output, and these are produced primarily in one package format (Budweiser and Bud Light in 12-ounce cans). This means Anheuser-Busch does not often incur the cost of changing brewing formulas or reconstituting packaging lines. In addition, because of its enormous volume, the company has per-barrel advertising costs significantly below many of its rivals. Thus, on the cost side of the competition ledger, Anheuser-Busch is favorably positioned.

On the revenue side of the competition ledger, Anheuser-Busch's pricing strategy builds on the firm's efficiencies in production. Most of its output is sold at premium and superpremium prices, which generate higher margins. The company's pricing strategy is to change its prices only in line with production-cost changes and to build overall profits through volume gains. TV ads for Anheuser-Busch products are acclaimed for their positive recall. On the other hand, the company has many chips on the Budweiser brand, whose domestic sales have declined in recent years. Should the bloom ever come off the Bud, Anheuser-Busch's position would become vulnerable.

The amount of beer imported into the U.S. has increased substantially in the past 2 decades and imports now provide an important source of rivalry to domestic premium brands. From 1996 to 2005, imports increased about 13 million barrels while domestic shipments increased less than 10 million barrels. In fact, the growth in beer consumption in recent years has been significantly import-driven. This leaves Anheuser-Busch, Miller, and Coors with a puzzle. The price elasticity for their major brands is sufficiently high that if these firms raise price, they lose volume. But if they lower price, they lose image. And image is important to many beer drinkers. The import and craft segments offer a huge array of brand styles (i.e., images). These segments are growing. In response, Anheuser-Busch has dramatically increased its brand portfolio, with offerings outside the Budweiser family. In 2007, the St. Louis brewer sold about 80 brands (up from 26 in 1997). Anheuser-Busch also has diversified into distilled spirits (Jekyll & Hyde) and markets European beers in the United States (InBev brands).[28]

Increases in concentration in brewing are neither the result nor the cause of market power. The reasons, rather, are benign: the exploitation of scale economies and the demise of suboptimal capacity; new or superior products; changes in packaging and marketing methods; poor management on the part of some firms; and the strategic use of product differentiation. As a consequence, Anheuser-Busch, Miller, and Coors no longer face an

---

[28]Anheuser-Busch also has a 50 percent interest in Grupo Modelo, the largest brewing company in Mexico, whose flagship brand is Corona. As a result, Anheuser-Busch has been the financial beneficiary of Corona's phenomenal success in the United States. However the growing demand for Corona Extra and Corona Light has come partially at the expense of Budweiser and Budweiser Light.

array of large-scale domestic brewers. Brands like Schlitz, Pabst, Old Style, Stroh, Ballantine, Schaefer, Falstaff, Olympia, Rheingold, Ruppert, Blatz, Lucky Lager, Hamm's, and the firms that produced them, are gone or are shadows of what they once were.

Today, in the U.S., 5 out of 10 times a consumer asks for a beer, it will be a Budweiser, a Budweiser Light, a Miller Lite, or a Coors Light. At retail, these brands sit on a shelf less than a week, compared to almost 12 days for imports and 2 weeks for craft beers (for wine, the average shelf life is 42 days and 33 for liquor). Retailers appreciate the quick inventory turn. But the big three domestic brewers now face significant import competition, in some cases from large brewers with operations in many countries, and significant competition from specialty or craft brewers. In the U.S., craft brewers have reached a critical mass where input suppliers now cater to them. Consequently, these brewers no longer need to cobble together their brewing operations. In addition, conferences now afford these firms access to information ranging from technical papers on yeast propagation to discussions about overseas distribution.[29]

In the 1970s, 1980s, and into the 1990s, the big three domestic brewers took market share from second-tier regional brewers. In the 1990s, the big three began to lose share to imports and craft brewers. This trend continues today. Such is the robustness of competition. The three major brewers also face increasing competition from other beverages, both alcoholic and nonalcoholic. For many consumers, wine, distilled spirits, and beer are interchangeable. But producers of wine and distilled spirits generally have been better at promoting their product as affordable luxuries. The beer industry, only recently, has begun to "romance the category" through on-premise marketing.[30]

CONCLUSION ▪▪▪▪▪▪▪

The structure of the beer industry and the conduct of its members mark it as a competitive industry. Consumers are pursued by price and nonprice marketing efforts. The changing fortunes of even major brewers indicate that the market for beer is not a stodgy oligopoly in which firms adopt a live-and-let-live posture toward each other. The number of exits from brewing indicates this is hardly an industry in which the inefficient producer is protected from the chilling winds of competition, while the arrival of many new firms reveals the absence of entry barriers.

SUGGESTIONS FOR FURTHER READING ▪▪▪▪▪▪▪

Publications

Ackoff, Russell L, and James R. Emshoff. 1975. "Advertising Research at Anheuser-Busch, Inc. (1963–1968)." *Sloan Management Review*, 16 (Winter).

———, 1975. "Advertising Research at Anheuser-Busch, Inc. (1968–74)." *Sloan Management Review*, 16 (Spring).

Adams, William James. 2006. "Markets: Beer in Germany and the United States." *Journal of Economic Perspectives*, 20 (Winter).

Baron, Stanley Wade. 1962. *Brewed in America*. Boston: Little, Brown and Company.

Baum, Dan. 2000. *Citizen Coors*. New York: Morrow.

---

[29]See, for example, the Brewers Association annual Craft Brewers Conference and any issue of the association's periodical, *The New Brewer*.

[30]Heineken now has advertisements that go head-to-head with distilled spirits, in recognition of the growing competition for "share of throat."

Beer Marketer's Insights. Published 23 times per year. West Nyack, NY.

Beer Marketer's Insights—Beer Industry Update. Annual. West Nyack, NY.

Clements, Kenneth W., and Lester W. Johnson. 1983. "The Demand for Beer, Wine and Spirits: A Systemwide Analysis." *Journal of Business*, 56 (July).

Chaloupka, F. J., M. Grossman, and H. Saffer. 1993. "Alcohol Control Policies and Motor Vehicle Fatalities." *Journal of Legal Studies*, 22 (January).

Consumer Reports. 2001. "Which Brew for You?" (August), 10–16.

Cornell, Martyn. 2003. *Beer: The Story of the Pint*. London: Headline.

Culbertson, W. Patton, and David Bradford. 1991. "The price of beer: Some evidence from interstate comparisons." *International Journal of Industrial Organization*, 9 (June).

Ekelund, Robert B. and David S. Saurman. 1988. *Advertising and the Market Process*. San Francisco: Pacific Research Institute.

Elzinga, Kenneth G. and Anthony M. Swisher. 2005. "The Supreme Court and Beer Mergers: From Pabst/Blatz to the DOJ-FTC Guidelines." *Review of Industrial Organization*, 26 (January).

Gisser, Mica. 1999. "Dynamic Gains and Static Losses in Oligopoly: Evidence from the Beer Industry," *Economic Inquiry*, 37 (July).

Greer, Douglas F. 1998. "Beer: Causes of Structural Change," in Larry L. Duetsch (ed.) *Industry Studies*. Armonk, NY: M. E. Sharpe.

Grossman, Michael, Jody L. Sindelar, John Mullahy and Richard Anderson. 1993. "Policy Watch: Alcohol and Cigarette Taxes," *Journal of Economic Perspectives* 7 (Fall).

Hernon, Peter and Ganey, Terry. 1991. *Under the Influence: The Unauthorized Story of the Anheuser-Busch Dynasty*. New York: Simon & Schuster.

Hogarty, Thomas F., and Kenneth G. Elzinga. 1972. "The Demand for Beer." *Review of Economics and Statistics*, 54 (May).

Horowitz, Ira, and Ann Horowitz. 1965. "Firms in a Declining Market: The Brewing Case," *Journal of Industrial Economics*, 13 (March).

Kerkvliet, Joe R., William Nebesky, Carol H. Tremblay, and Victor J. Tremblay. 1998. "Efficiency and Technological Change in the U.S. Brewing Industry." *Journal of Productivity Analysis*, 10 (November).

Lawler, Kevin and Kin-Pui Lee. 2003 "Brewing," in Peter Johnson (ed.), *Industries in Europe*. Cheltenham: Edward Elgar.

Lynk, William J. 1984. "Interpreting Rising Concentration: The Case Of Beer." *Journal of Business*, 57 (January).

_____. 1985. "The Price and Output of Beer Revisited." *Journal of Business*, 58 (October).

McConnell, J. Douglas. 1968. "An Experimental Examination of the Price-Quality Relationship." *Journal of Business*, 41 (October).

McGahan, A. M. 1991. "The Emergence of the National Brewing Oligopoly: Competition in the American Market, 1933–1958." *Business History Review*, 65 (Summer).

McNulty, Timothy J. 1986. "Image and Competition Keep Beer Industry Foaming," *Chicago Tribune*, (August 11), C1.

Modern Brewery Age: Blue Book. Annual. Stamford, CT: Modern Brewery Age Publishing Co.

Nelson, Jon P. 2001. "Alcohol Advertising and Advertising Bans: A Survey of Research Methods, Results, and Policy Implications," *Advances in Applied Microeconomics*, 10.

_____. 2003. "Advertising Bans, Monopoly, and Alcohol Demand: Testing for Substitution Effects using State Panel Data," *Review of Industrial Organization*, 22 (February).

The New Brewer. Bimonthly. Boulder, CO.

North American Brewers Resource Directory. Annual. Boulder, CO: Institute for Brewing Studies.

Ogle, Maureen. 2006. *Ambitious Brew*. New York: Harcourt, Inc.

Ornstein, Stanley I. 1981. "Antitrust Policy and Market Forces as Determinants of Industry Structure: Case Histories in Beer and Distilled Spirits." *Antitrust Bulletin*, 26 (Summer).

_____ and Dominique M. Hanssens. 1985. "Alcohol Control Laws and the Consumption of Distilled Spirits and Beer." *Journal of Consumer Research*, 12 (September).

Rehr, David K. 1997. *Political Economy of the Malt Beverage Industry*. PhD diss., George Mason University.

Robertson, James D. 1978. *The Great American Beer Book*. New York: Warner Books.

Rodman, Mark. 2000. "An Industry Caught in the Net," (Parts I and II), *Modern Brewery Age* (July 10) 32–40; (September 11), 22–36.

Sass, Tim R. and David S. Saurman. 1993. "Mandated Exclusive Territories and Economic Efficiency: An Empirical Analysis of the Malt Beverage Industry." *Journal of Law & Economics*, 36 (April).

Scherer, F. M., Alan Beckenstein, Erich Kaufer and R. Dennis Murphy. 1975. *The Economics of Multi-Plant Operations*. Cambridge: Harvard University Press.

Slosberg, Pete. 1998. *Beer for Pete's Sake*. Boulder, CO: Siris Books.

Sutton, John. 1991. *Sunk Costs and Market Structure*. Cambridge, MA: MIT Press.

Tremblay, Victor J. 1985. "A Reappraisal of Interpreting Rising Concentration: The Case of Beer." *Journal of Business*, 58 (October).

_____ and Carol Horton Tremblay. 1988. "The Determinants of Horizontal Acquisitions: Evidence from the U.S. Brewing Industry." *Journal of Industrial Economics*, 37 (September).

_____. 1995. "Advertising, Price, and Welfare: Evidence From the U.S. Brewing Industry." *Southern Economic Journal*, 62 (October).

Tremblay, Victor J., and Carol Horton Tremblay. 2005. *The U.S. Brewing Industry: Data and Economic Analysis*. Cambridge, MA: MIT Press.

Van Munching, Philip. 1997. *Beer Blast*. New York: Random House.

Wall Street Journal. 2005. "Can It," (August 26).

Weinberg, Robert S. 1999. "Watching the Market," *Modern Brewery Age* (March 22), 24–31.

_____. 2000. "Talking with Dr. Bob," *Modern Brewery Age* (Nov. 27), 10–15.

_____. 2001. "Taking the Long View," *Modern Brewery Age* (March 26), 16–23.

_____. 2002. "Tracking the winners," *Modern Brewery Age* (November 11), 20–23.

Wells, Ken. 2004. *Travels With Barley*. New York: Free Press.

Web sites

Brewers Almanac. Annual. Washington, DC: The Beer Institute. See http://www.beerinstitute.org/statistics.asp?bid=200

www.beerinstitute.org

www.beertown.org

www.coors.com

www.realbeer.com

CHAPTER 6

The Automobile Industry

JAMES W. BROCK

"The proverbial man from Mars," Douglas Dowd once mused, "would doubtless come to the conclusion that the automobile was the dominant fact in our producing, consuming, and perhaps our fantasy lives; he could plausibly conclude that the four-wheeled creatures run the society and that the two-legged creatures are its servants."[1]

Reports commissioned by the industry's trade association lend credence to this claim: They estimate that for every worker employed in automotive manufacturing, 10 additional workers are employed in the manufacture of steel, aluminum, copper, lead, plastics, textiles, vinyl, and computer components, and that overall, automobile manufacturing directly and indirectly generates 13 million jobs nationwide.[2] With Americans driving an estimated 3 trillion miles yearly, the Alliance of Automobile Manufacturers lauds "automobility" as "the core of individualism in America," affording Americans unparalleled access to more employment opportunities, more goods and services, and more learning opportunities (including concerts, museums, and natural parks).[3]

At the same time, however, automobiles account for approximately one-half of the 20 million barrels of petroleum consumed daily in the United States, much of it imported from geopolitically explosive foreign regions.[4] Cars and light trucks spew some 60 million tons of carbon monoxide into the nation's atmosphere each year, along with 7 million tons of nitrous oxides and volatile organic compounds.[5] And in what former Transportation Secretary Norman Mineta calls a "national tragedy," automobile

---

[1]Quoted in Stan Luger, *Corporate Power, American Democracy, and the Automobile Industry* (New York: Cambridge University Press, 2000), 1.
[2]Alliance of Automobile Manufacturers, "America's Automobile Industry is the Engine that Drives the Economy," www.autoalliance.org/economic
[3]Alliance of Automobile Manufacturers, "Contribution of the Automobile Industry to the U.S. Economy," Washington, D.C. (Winter 2001).
[4]U.S. Energy Information Administration, Annual Energy Review: 2004, Washington, D.C., Table 5.11; www.eia.dot.gov/emeu/aer/pdf/pages/sec5_25.pdf
[5]U.S. Census Bureau, *Statistical Abstract of the United States: 2006,* Washington, D.C., Table 361, "Air Pollutant Emissions by Pollutant and Source."

crashes kill 43,000 Americans annually, while injuring nearly 3 million others, at a cost exceeding $200 billion per year.[6]

Little wonder, then, that the American auto industry is considered so important that "[i]ts problems become national problems requiring national solutions."[7] An analysis of the structure of this industry, including the influence of that structure on the industry's conduct and performance, is essential in assessing these challenges and the public policy issues they pose.

░░░ I. History

The automobile as we know it first took shape in the 1890s, when early automotive pioneers experimented with gasoline engines, steam engines, and—particularly interesting in the light of the recent advent of hybrid vehicles—electric motors as sources of propulsion. By 1900, they had sold approximately 4,000 vehicles. Production expanded rapidly thereafter, reaching 187,000 automobiles by 1910. Entry into the industry was relatively easy, because the manufacturer of automobiles was primarily an assembler of parts produced by others. The new entrepreneur needed only to design a vehicle; contract with machine shops and independent producers for the engines, wheels, bodies, and other components; and promote to the public the car's availability.

The next decade marked the emergence of the Ford Motor Company as the dominant firm. Believing the demand for new cars to be price elastic, Henry Ford's goal was to provide an inexpensive car capable of reaching a large potential market. Standardization, specialization and mass production, he believed, were the keys to lowering manufacturing costs, and constant price reductions the way to tap successively larger layers of demand. "Every time I reduce the charge for our car by one dollar, I get a thousand new buyers," Ford said. His strategy was revolutionarily simple: Take lower profits on each vehicle and achieve a larger volume of sales and income. As Ford saw it, successive "price reductions meant new enlargements of the market, an acceleration of mass production's larger economies, and greater aggregate profits. The company's firm grasp of this principle . . . was its unique element of strength, just as failure to grasp it had been one of the weaknesses of rival car makers. As profits per car had gone down and down, net earnings had gone up and up."[8] By 1921, Ford's Model T, which remained essentially unchanged for 2 decades, accounted for more than half the market.

The 1920s witnessed a shift of pre-eminence from Ford to General Motors, the latter a combination of formerly independent firms (Chevrolet, Oldsmobile, Oakland, Cadillac, Buick, Fisher Body, Delco). GM adopted a two-pronged strategy: First, contrary to Ford's emphasis on a single model, GM offered a broad variety of models to blanket all market segments (its motto was "a car for every purse and purpose"). Second, again contrary to Ford's strategy, GM elected to modify its cars each year with a combination of engineering advances, convenience improvements, and cosmetic styling changes. GM believed that annual model changes, despite the expense, would stimulate replacement

---

[6]"Transportation Secretary Mineta Calls Highway Fatalities National Tragedy," news release, National Highway Traffic Safety Administration, Washington, D.C. (April 20, 2006).
[7]Donald A. Manzullo and Sheila R. Ronis, "U.S. Must Reclaim Its Industrial Base," *Automotive News* (September 26, 2005): 14.
[8]Ford Allen Nevins, Ford: *The Times, the Man, the Company* (New York: Scribner, 1954), 493.

demand and increase sales, and indeed, this strategy catapulted the company into unchallenged industry leadership for a half century. In this era, the groundwork was also laid for the high concentration that subsequently became the industry's hallmark.

Beginning in the mid-1950s, however, successive waves of imports increasingly challenged the domestic oligopoly. By the 1970s, imports had captured more than a quarter of the U.S. market and triggered repeated lobbying efforts by the Big Three — in collaboration with the United Auto Workers union — to demand government protection from foreign competition. In the 1980s, in response to the domestic industry's political campaigns, foreign firms began to construct new production facilities in the United States. The aggregate output of these "transplants" has now grown to nearly 4 million cars and light trucks per year — approximately half the combined production of GM, Ford, and DaimlerChrysler in the United States.

▪▪▪ II. Industry Structure

The most significant structural features of the U.S. automobile industry are buyer demand and the nature of the product; the number of rival manufacturers and their relative size (concentration); economies of scale; and barriers to the entry of new competitors.

Demand and the Product

The demand for automobiles is influenced by a variety of economic factors. First, the demand for new cars is predominantly a replacement demand, and because the purchase of a new car usually can be postponed, market demand can be quite volatile. Second, because the purchase of an automobile constitutes a major investment (at an average price of $22,000 in recent years), the demand for new cars is highly sensitive to macroeconomic conditions, including income, unemployment, and interest rates. Third, another key determinant of demand, of course, is price. Although the demand for new cars generally is slightly price elastic, the demand for particular makes and models is much more price sensitive owing to the availability of close substitutes. Finally, a revolution has transpired in the composition of new "car" demand in favor of light trucks, and sport utility vehicles in particular, and away from conventional cars (Figure 6-1). This composition, in turn, is importantly influenced by the price of gasoline, which became dramatically evident beginning in 2005 when record-high gas prices induced double-digit declines in the sales of the industry's largest, least fuel-efficient SUVs.[9]

Industry Concentration

The American auto industry has long been dominated by a triopoly of colossal firms. The advent of foreign transplants has eroded domestic concentration in production, while the growth of imports has lessened the Big Three's dominance at the retail level. Nonetheless, the Big Three firms remain dominant, while the impact of these procompetitive developments has been attenuated by the Big Three's political success in

---

[9]See Micheline Maynard, "The Summer of Detroit's Discontent," *New York Times* (July 28, 2006): C1, reporting consumer survey results indicating that in 2002, when gasoline was priced at $1.36 a gallon, 22 percent of potential car buyers cited fuel economy as an important consideration. But by mid-2006, when gasoline prices reached $3 or more per gallon, 60 percent of new car buyers surveyed identified fuel economy as an important factor in their decision to purchase a new vehicle.

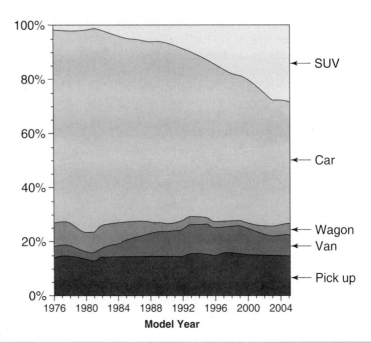

▪ ▪ ▪ **FIGURE 6-1** Sales Fraction by Vehicle Type (Three year Moving Average)

U.S. Environmental Protection Agency, "Light-Duty Automotive Technology and Fuel Economy Trends: 1975 Through 2006" (Washington, D.C.: July 2006). p. 18.

obtaining government restrictions on imports, by joint ventures and "alliances" linking the American oligopoly with its foreign rivals, and by mergers and acquisitions among the Big Three and foreign automotive firms.

Firm Size and Concentration.

General Motors remains the world's largest automobile manufacturer (Table 6-1). With assets of $475 billion, annual revenues of $193 billion, and an annual production volume of 8.3 million vehicles, GM ranks as the largest non-oil industrial corporation in the U.S. and the world. GM's annual revenues exceed the gross domestic product of all but a handful of nations. Measured by dollar revenues, DaimlerChrysler and Ford stand as the world's second and fourth largest non-oil industrial concerns; their production volume ranks them as the world's third and sixth largest automobile firms, respectively.

The Big Three's operations span the globe: Ranked either by sales or production, GM (including its Opel, Vauxhall, and Holden divisions) is the largest auto producer in Canada and Australia; second largest in the UK and Brazil; third largest in Germany; and fourth largest in Mexico. Ford ranks as the largest automobile manufacturer in the UK; third largest in Australia and Mexico; and third largest across Western Europe generally; while DaimlerChrysler ranks second largest in Germany and Canada.[10] The global reach of the Big Three has expanded in recent years as the result of a number of

---

[10]*Ward's Automotive Yearbook 2006* (Southfield, MI: Ward's Automotive Group 2006).

TABLE 6-1 World's Leading Automobile Producers, 2005

	Global Revenues (billions)	Global Vehicles Produced (thousands)
General Motors	$ 192.6	8,338
DaimlerChrysler	186.1	4,810
Toyota	185.8	8,232
Ford	177.2	6,632
Nissan-Renault	134.7	6,024
Volkswagen	118.4	5,219
Honda	87.5	3,410
Peugeot-Citroën	69.1	3,376
BMW	58.0	1,323
Fiat	57.8	2,057
Hyundai-Kia	57.4	3,393
Mitsubishi	42.6	1,363
Mazda	25.8	1,146
Suzuki	24.3	2,125

Source: "Global 500," *Fortune* (July 24, 2006) (revenues), and *Automotive News Global Market Data Book* (June 26, 2006) (production).

transnational mergers and acquisitions, including GM's purchase of Saab; Ford's acquisition of Jaguar, Volvo, and Land Rover; and the 1998 absorption of Chrysler by Daimler-Benz (an acquisition subsequently undone in 2007).

Concentration in U.S. automobile production is depicted in Table 6-2, where the Big Three's rise to dominance is evident, reaching a high-water mark of 88 to 98 percent over the period from 1946 to 1985. More recently, "transplant" facilities built by foreign

TABLE 6-2 Market Shares and Concentration: U.S. Automobile Production

Year	General Motors	Ford	Chrysler	Other U.S. Producers	Big Three
1913	12%	40%	*	48%	*
1923	20	46	2%	32	68%
1933	41	21	25	13	87
1946–1955	45	24	19	12	88
1956–1965	51	29	14	6	94
1966–1975	54	27	17	2	98
1976–1985	59	24	13	4	96
1992	42	24	9	25	75
2005**	27	23	15	35	65

*Chrysler not yet in existence.
**Passenger cars and light trucks combined.

Source: Lawrence J. White, *The Automobile Industry Since 1945* (Cambridge: Harvard University Press, 1971); *Automotive News, Market Data Book*, various years.

TABLE 6-3 Transplant Auto Assembly Facilities in U.S.

	Location(s)	Vehicle Production Capacity	Employment	Investment (millions)	Start
AutoAlliance[a]	Flat Rock, MI	240,000	3,766	$ 760	1997
BMW	Spartanburg, SC	120,000	3,000	2,000	1994
Honda	Lincoln, AL	300,000	4,300	1,100	2001
	East Liberty, OH	244,174	2,600	895	1989
	Marysville, OH	440,000	5,800	2,850	1982
	Greensburg, IN[b]	200,000	2,000	500	2008
Hyundai	Birmingham, AL	300,000[b]	2,700	1,100	2005
Mercedes	Vance, AL	100,016	1,900	300	1997
Mitsubishi	Normal, IL	240,000	3,150	1,378	1988
Nissan	Smyrna, TN	500,000	9,333	2,150	1983
	Canton, MS	400,000	5,537	1,430	2003
NUMMI[c]	Fremont, CA	361,486	5,630	1,700	1984
Subaru	Lafayette, IN	126,240	2,500	1,190	1989
Toyota	Georgetown, KY	500,000	7,000	5,152	1988
	Princeton, IN	149,986	2,400	1,500	1998
	Princeton, IN 2	150,000	2,200	1,000	2002
	San Antonio, TX[b]	200,000	2,000	850	2006
	Blue Spring, MS	150,000	na	na	2010

▪▪▪▪▪▪▪▪▪▪

[a]Joint venture between Mazda and Ford
[b]Projected
[c]Joint venture between GM and Toyota

Source: Center for Automotive Research, *Contribution of the International Auto Sector to the U.S. Economy: An Update* (March 2005): 4; Toyota website, toyota.com/about/operations/manufacturing/manu_location; Honda website, world.honda.com/news/2006

producers in the United States and detailed in Table 6-3, have eroded the Big Three's share of domestic production: Assembling nearly 4 million cars and light trucks, these transplants have come to represent approximately one-third of total U.S. production; collectively, they have invested an estimated $36 billion in building 43 U.S. plants that directly and indirectly employ 1.8 million workers,[11] while their combined output now exceeds the individual U.S. production volume of either GM, Ford, or DaimlerChrysler. (In addition to their American facilities, foreign firms operate assembly plants in Canada and Mexico.) It is important to recognize, however, that because a number of these transplants are cooperative ventures with the Big Three (Ford-Mazda, GM-Toyota, GM-Suzuki in Canada), they do not represent entirely independent competitors.

Concentration of sales within various vehicle segments is shown in Table 6-4, where it can be seen that the Big Three's dominance is greatest in the light truck

---

[11]"Contribution of the International Auto Sector to the U.S. Economy: Update," Center for Automotive Research (Ann Arbor, MI, March 2005), and Bernard Simon, "Detroit Displaced as 'Imports' Strive to Become Indigenous," *Financial Times* (April 19, 2006): 11.

TABLE 6-4 Market Share and Concentration of Sales by Vehicle Type, 2005

	General Motors	Ford	Daimler Chrysler Combined	Big Three
Cars				
Small	24%	16%	6%	46%
Mid-Range	27	11	13	51
Traditional and Upscale	16	24	12	52
Light Trucks				
Pickup	35	39	16	90
Van	23	20	28	71
SUV & Crossover	27	19	16	62
Large SUV	62	24	0	86

Source: Based on *Automotive News, Market Data Book,* 2006.

categories, particularly large SUVs—a dependence fraught with problematic consequences in a post–9/11 world of gyrating oil and gasoline prices.

Despite this variation across market segments, and although GM's share has declined over recent years, the Big Three continue to collectively dominate the American automobile market, together accounting for 60 percent of new vehicle sales and two-thirds of new vehicle production in the U.S.

Foreign Competition.

The import share of the American market rose from 0.4 percent in the immediate post–World War II decade, to 21 percent in the period from 1976 to 1983. Foreign producers—led first by Volkswagen (its original "Beetle" accounted for nearly half of all U.S. imports), then later by Japanese firms—provided a critical, if not the only source of significant competition for the Big Three in the post–World War II era. Initially, foreign firms focused their efforts on the low-priced, small-car segment of the market. Then, in the 1980s, after the Big Three succeeded in obtaining government limits on the number of Japanese imports into the country, Japanese firms moved into the midsize segments of the market—ironically, the mainstay of the domestic oligopoly. Japanese and European producers also began to achieve larger shares of the higher-priced luxury end of the market (including Toyota's Lexus and Nissan's Infiniti brands, in addition to BMW and Mercedes). To circumvent government trade restraints, foreign producers, led by the Japanese, also began building production facilities in the United States, where they employed American labor and management to replicate (and even exceed) their initial success from abroad. By 1992, imports had grown to comprise almost one-quarter of U.S. new-vehicle sales.

Since then the import share of U.S. sales has subsided to approximately 20 percent, as foreign firms have come to increasingly rely on U.S. sales of vehicles assembled in their American production facilities: Toyota's U.S. production, for example, now represents one-half of its total U.S. sales, while three-quarters of Honda's American sales are assembled in the U.S. (vehicles built by Japanese producers outside Japan exceeded their production within Japan for the first time in 2006). At the same time, the Big Three themselves *import* a substantial number of vehicles into the U.S. market from their assembly plants in Mexico and Canada: Ford's production in Canada and Mexico accounts for 40 percent of its sales in the U.S. market, while the figures for GM and Chrysler are 28 and 11 percent, respectively. Not all Big Three vehicles assembled in Canada and Mexico are sold in the U.S. market, of course, but clearly they are major importers—an irony given their political lobbying battles against vehicles imported into the American market by other firms. The Big Three also "re-badge" vehicles assembled abroad by foreign producers, and sell them as their own brands in the American market (including the Chevrolet Aveo, a vehicle produced in South Korea, and the Ford Festiva and Aspire models built by the Korean Kia firm in past years).

An emerging development is the advent of a nascent automobile industry in China, currently comprising some 15 firms, at least of one of which (Chery) has publicly entertained the prospect of importing a small car into the American market (another is contemplating producing vehicles under the legendary MG nameplate at a plant possibly to be constructed in Oklahoma). Because most of these firms are engaged in joint ventures with the world's major auto producers, including seven joint ventures with the American Big Three companies; because the Big Three may be less than enthusiastic about the prospect of exporting low-priced Chinese vehicles en masse into the American market; and because China's domestic demand for new cars may be virtually insatiable for the foreseeable future, the competitive significance of this development for the American market remains to be seen.[12] A related development occurred in late 2006, when an Indian automaker, Mahindi & Mahindi Ltd., was reportedly exploring the development of a network of American dealers as a precursor to its possible entry into the U.S. market.[13]

Needless to say, however, import quotas and the perennial threat of protectionism jeopardize the salutary effect that foreign competition has had in eroding concentration in the American market. In the 1990s, for example, the Big Three lobbied to persuade Congress to impose a numerical cap on Japanese auto sales, including a legislatively-enacted limit on the number of vehicles they would be allowed to produce in their U.S. transplant facilities. Transnational mergers between the Big Three and foreign producers may also undermine competition in the American market.

Joint Ventures and Alliances.

Another important feature of the industry's structure is the web of joint ventures and "alliances" among the Big Three and major foreign producers.

General Motors at various times has held partial ownership stakes in Suzuki, Fuji (Subaru), Isuzu, and Fiat, while GM and Suzuki have jointly acquired control of the Korean Daewoo automobile firm. (GM recently sold its ownership stakes in Isuzu and Fiat, while reducing its stake in Suzuki.) As indicated above, GM and Toyota jointly operate the NUMMI assembly plant in California; GM sold its stake in Subaru to Toyota, transferring Subaru's Lafayette, Indiana, assembly plant to Toyota. GM and Suzuki jointly operate the CAMI automobile assembly facility in Ontario, Canada. GM also has supply agreements with Honda for engines, and with Fiat and Isuzu for various powertrain components.[14] In mid-2006, a prospective joint venture arrangement

---

[12]See *Automotive News*, "2007 Guide to China's Auto Market" (May 14, 2007), for an in-depth survey.
[13]Lindsay Chappell, "Indian Automaker Targets U.S.," *Automotive News* (November 6, 2006), 1.
[14]"Guide to Global Automotive Partnerships," *Automotive News* (September 2005).

between GM and Nissan-Renault was also being explored, while GM is engaged in four joint ventures with emerging Chinese automotive firms.

Ford, in addition to purchasing Volvo, Jaguar, and Land Rover over the past decade, holds a one-third ownership stake in the Japanese firm Mazda; with Mazda, as indicated above, Ford jointly owns and operates the AutoAlliance transplant facility in Flat Rock, Michigan. Ford has formerly held substantial ownership stakes in the Korean Kia firm (which produced a number of vehicles for re-badging in the U.S. as Ford models), has entered into engine alliances with BMW and Peugeot,[15] and has formed alliances with two Chinese automotive firms.[16] Ford also has reportedly explored the prospect of an alliance with Toyota.[17]

Chrysler allied with Mitsubishi to jointly build and operate the "Diamond Star" transplant facility in Normal, Illinois. Although Chrysler subsequently sold its share of this plant, it retains a substantial ownership stake in Mitsubishi, and Mitsubishi continues to assemble some Chrysler models in its American production facility. DaimlerChrysler has engine supply agreements with BMW and VW, and has joined with GM to jointly develop hybrid automotive power systems.[18] Chrysler also is entertaining the prospect of a joint venture with an emerging Chinese firm, Chery, to produce a subcompact car for import into the U.S. market.

All told, global alliances involving the world's five largest producers have been estimated to encompass approximately three-quarters of the global automotive market.[19]

Reinforcing these ties among the leading auto companies are a number of cooperative research consortiums in the United States and abroad: The United States Council for Automotive Research (USCAR), for example, joins the Big Three in a variety of automotive areas, including materials and composites, electronics, manufacturing, recycling, and transmissions. The Clinton Administration's "Partnership for a New Generation of Vehicles" provided a government-financed umbrella of cooperation and support for the Big Three, as does its successor, the Bush Administration's "Freedom Cooperative Automotive Research" program. At the same time, the European Council for Automotive Research and Development (EUCAR) links European producers in a host of collective endeavors.[20]

Alliances and partnership pacts on this scale link the U.S. oligopolists with each other and with their major rivals around the globe. They foster, indeed, *require*, interfirm communication, coordination and cooperation. As such, they raise the question of whether they compromise the independence of decision making essential for effective competition. At a minimum, their existence suggests that the actual degree of concentration in the industry may be substantially higher than would be indicated by examining conventional market shares alone.

---

[15]Ibid.
[16]For a description of joint ventures involving emerging automotive firms in China, see "Guide To China's Auto Market."
[17]See Norihiko Shirouzu and Jeffrey McCracken, "Ford, Toyota See Alliance Potential," *Wall Street Journal* (January 22, 2007): A9.
[18]Ibid.
[19]"Extinction of the Predator," *Economist* (September 10, 2005): 63.
[20]See these consortiums' websites at www.uscar.org and www.eucar.org.

The Question of Economies of Scale

To what extent is high concentration in autos necessitated by economies of large-scale operation? The weight of the evidence suggests that, while substantial, economies of large size are not as extensive as might be assumed, and that they are becoming less so in some important ways.

First, scale economies in auto production have definite limits. The Big Three assemble their vehicles at numerous plants and locations, rather than concentrating their production in one or two gigantic plants. The capacity of their major assembly plants is 190,000 to 270,000 vehicles per year,[21] suggesting this range as a good indicator of what the firms consider the optimum-sized production facility to be.

Second, the Big Three in recent years have significantly *reduced* their size by divesting large portions of their parts- and components-making operations. General Motors, long the most vertically integrated of the Big Three, consolidated a number of its parts-making operations to form the "Delphi" division, which it spun off in 1999 in a move that reduced its workforce by one-third (200,000 employees), removed 208 manufacturing units from GM's administrative control, and created one of the world's largest auto parts producers in the process. "It is not an advantage to be vertically integrated," GM's chairman explained, "We are going to be a much faster company and focused on our core business of building cars and trucks."[22] Ford and Chrysler have taken similar steps to vertical dis-integrate themselves by spinning off their Visteon and Acustar parts-making operations. In a related vein, auto companies are increasingly outsourcing the production of entire modules (parts preassembled into complete units, such as prebuilt interiors with seats, instruments, trim, and electronic controls already installed) to outside suppliers. In fact, "modular assembly" is leading some auto makers to encourage suppliers to invest in and operate portions of the auto firms' final assembly lines, where their outsourced components are installed.[23] Industry experts estimate that such vertical dis-integration, and the corresponding reduction in corporate size it entails, may cut production costs and boost efficiency by as much as 30 percent.[24]

Third, operating fewer but more flexible assembly plants is increasingly seen as critical for achieving production efficiency in an industry where quicker changeovers between shorter runs of more niche-focused vehicles are increasingly important in responding to shifting consumer tastes and preferences.[25] Nissan, for example, claims that it can flexibly alter its three U.S. plants to produce any of the various models in its

---

[21]Harbour Report: 2006, 50–52.

[22]Rebecca Blumenstein and Fara Warner, "GM to Make Delphi Unit Independent," *Wall Street Journal* (August 4, 1998): A3.

[23]See James M. Rubenstein, *Making and Selling Cars: Innovation and Change in the U.S. Automotive Industry* (Baltimore: Johns Hopkins University Press, 2001):, 114–118; Robert Sherefkin, "GM Handing Off Interiors," *Automotive News* (January 29, 2001): 1; and Ralph Kisiel, "Supplier Park Partnership Works for DCX," *Automotive News* (August 7, 2006): 28F.

[24]Joann Muller, Kathleen Kerwin, and David Welch, "Autos: A New Industry," *Business Week* (July 15, 2002): 104; and David Welch, "How Nissan Laps Detroit," *Business Week* (December 22, 2003): 58–60.

[25]Neal E. Boudette, "Chrysler Gains Edge by Giving New Flexibility to Its Factories," *Wall Street Journal*, (April 11, 2006): 1; and David Barkholz, "BMW Subtracts to Add Flexibility in S.C.," *Automotive News*, (June 5, 2006): 16L.

product portfolio; Honda and Toyota can produce as many as six different models on some of their assembly lines, while BMW's Spartanburg, South Carolina, plant operates a flexible assembly line it claims is capable of building any of BMW's 35 various vehicle models in any sequence.[26]

Finally, the Big Three's own experience suggests that excessive organization size entails substantial *dis*economies of scale, and that gigantism is no guarantor of efficiency. For GM, the world's largest automotive concern, the classic symptoms of diseconomies of excessive scale have been bluntly described by the firm's former chairman, Jack Smith. According to Mr. Smith, GM by the 1990s "was a mess. We were the high-cost producer. We had unbelievable excess capacity. We had multiple vehicle and component divisions, all of them doing things differently. We had a huge central office. We had over 13,000 people with an elaborate maze of policy groups trying to coordinate the businesses, not to control them. . . . We were the tattered remnants of what (former president) Alfred Sloan had put together in the early 1920s."[27] GM's current chief executive, Rick Wagoner, corroborated this assessment in late-2005, when he bemoaned GM's inability to respond to changing market conditions and exclaimed, "We just couldn't react."[28]

The far-flung global empires that the Big Three amassed over the past 20 years, either through outright acquisitions or through cross-ownership alliances and joint ventures, seem also to have suffered under the burdens of the diseconomies of excessive organizational size: "Although the car industry has undergone much consolidation in the past decade," the London *Economist* observes, "most of it has been disastrous. Two unprofitable smaller firms, Jaguar and Saab, were swallowed by Ford and GM respectively only to cost billions in further losses. After Daimler-Benz snapped up Chrysler in a messy deal . . . it took six years to get the combined firm on an even keel." The magazine characterizes GM's experience with cross-company alliances as "nothing short of awful. . . . The idea was that GM would gain access to small-car know-how, while sharing in the success of its affiliates in their local markets. But it didn't work. GM has sold its stakes in Suzuki and Fuji Heavy Industries and had to fork out $2 billion to extricate itself from an obligation to buy the 90% of Fiat that it did not own."[29] The experiment, says another analyst, "cost GM dearly in time, management attention and money."[30] For this reason industry experts have been skeptical of an alliance between GM and Nissan-Renault, or a merger between GM and Ford (both of which were reportedly being considered in 2006), on the grounds that this would further

---

[26]See Ralph Kisiel, "Honda Plant Becomes A Model of Flexibility," *Automotive News* (May 14, 2007): 30F; idem, "Once-Rigid Assembly Plants Become Flexible," *Automotive News* (August 7, 2006): 28A; and Neal E. Boudette and Norihiko Shirouzu, "Amid Price War, Chrysler to Revamp Manufacturing," *Wall Street Journal* (August 2, 2005): A2.

[27]Quoted in "Just How Bad Was It, Jack?" *Automotive News* (May 6, 2002): 29.

[28]Jamie LaReau, "Wagoner: GM Couldn't React," *Automotive News* (December 12, 2005): 1.

[29]"Sayonara, General Moteurs," *Economist* (July 8, 2006): 53. For Chrysler's problems following its megamerger with Daimler-Benz, see Mark Landler and Micheline Maynard, "DaimlerChrysler Struggles to Turn the Corner," *New York Times* (September 10, 2003):C1; and Gail Edmondson and David Welch, "Dark Days at Daimler," *Business Week* (August 15, 2005): 31.

[30]Dave Guilford, "GM's Global Strategy was A Costly Flop," *Automotive News* (May 8, 2006): 14. See also Rob Golding, "Strategy of Growth by Conquest has Fallen Firmly Out of Favor," *Financial Times* "Special Report: Motor Industry" (February 28, 2006): 1.

compound the diseconomies of the firms' already-massive size.[31] The point was further corroborated in mid-2007, when Daimler divested itself of Chrysler, in a deal that some saw as effectively *paying* the buyer to take what Daimler had paid $36 billion to acquire 9 years earlier. "We obviously overestimated the potential of synergies," Daimler's chief executive tartly said of this radical reversal.[32]

Perhaps the problem of excessive organizational size in automobiles has best been summed up by James Schroer, former executive vice president of sales at Chrysler: "If there is one thing that has done the most harm to the Big Three, it is the word 'big' . . . you look around the industry and you see that the advantage is where companies are not big." Little wonder, then, that efficiency in auto production is seen in avoiding megamergers.[33]

Barriers to Entry

Barriers to the entry of new competition, another important element of market structure, are immense in this field.

First, the cost to construct production and assembly plants is daunting: Table 6-3, for example, indicates that Honda has invested nearly $3 billion in its Marysville, Ohio, assembly plant, while Toyota has invested $8 billion in its Georgetown, Kentucky, production facility, and forecasts investing upwards of $1 billion constructing a pickup truck assembly facility in San Antonio, Texas.

Second, a new entrant not only must assemble vehicles, it also must market and promote them to consumers—another substantial obstacle to new competition. GM perennially ranks as one of the nation's very largest advertisers, spending more than $4 billion yearly; Ford and Chrysler also rank among the top 10 leading national advertisers, with total advertising expenditures of $2.2 to $2.4 billion each in recent years.[34]

Finally, in addition to producing and marketing its cars, a new entrant would have to assemble a system of dealers to distribute and service its vehicles. This, too, is a substantial challenge, as GM, Ford, and Chrysler vehicles are retailed through some 15,000 dealerships nationally.[35]

It is not surprising, therefore, that over the post-World War II period, few new firms have commenced production in the U.S., or that those which have (the transplants) have been launched by established foreign firms.

---

[31]See "Rick's Place," *Economist* (July 8, 2006):13; and Neal Boudette, Norihiko Shirouzu, and Stephen Power, "GM-Renault-Nissan Wouldn't Be Easy," *Wall Street Journal* (July 3, 2006): B1.
Neither is the vaunted Toyota Company immune from the diseconomies of scale that are beginning to hamstring its American operations as the firm has grown into one of the world's very largest automakers. See Lindsay Chappell, "Stretched by Growth," *Automotive News* (May 14, 2007): 17–24.
[32]Quoted in Mark Landler, "A Corporate Divorce on the Cheap," *New York Times* (May 15, 2007): 6.
[33]See "Extinction of the Predator: How Merger Mania Has Been A Disaster for the World's Great Car Manufacturers," *Economist* (September 10, 2005): 63. Observes *Automotive News*: "BMW and Honda are medium-sized auto companies that succeed because of superb model lineups and superior brand value. . . . Let that be a lesson to others who hear the siren song of 'merge or die.' " "Chrysler's Lesson: Getting Bigger Isn't Always Better" (March 12, 2007): 12.
[34]*Advertising Age*, "100 Leading National Advertisers" (June 23, 2006).
[35]*Automotive News, Market Data Book 2006*, 44.

▐▌▌ III. Industry Conduct

Market behavior in the automobile industry validates what industrial organization theory predicts: Decades of high concentration fostered tacit collusion, uniformity of conduct and noncompetitive oligopolistic parallelism, while the advent of a more competitive, less concentrated industry structure has profoundly transformed company behavior in the field.

Pricing

As the largest seller, General Motors traditionally was the industry's price leader. GM initiated general rounds of annual price hikes in the late summer when the industry's new model lineups were being readied for the fall. Ford and Chrysler awaited GM's price disclosures, which they then matched, so that the Big Three's prices differed by just a few dollars across their range of models. The essence of this oligopoly pricing was conveyed by the *Wall Street Journal*: "Auto makers can maximize profits because in the oligopolistic domestic auto industry the three major producers tend to copy each other's price moves. One auto executive notes that if one company lowered prices, the others would follow immediately. . . . As a result, price cuts wouldn't increase anybody's market share, and 'everybody would be worse off,' he says." Sniffed another Big Three official, "we're not in the business of lowering prices; we're in the business of making money."[36]

The advent of foreign competition and transplants, however, and the erosion of domestic concentration, disrupted this noncompetitive pattern of pricing. In a sharp break from the past, prices now are continuously altered through the year. Prices also are more flexible—down as well as up—as a result of competition that compels the companies to constantly adjust the incentives they offer (rebates, lease terms, finance rates, "employee" prices). Thus, in the wake of 9/11, with the economy sliding into recession, GM launched its "Keep America Rolling" program of new-car rebates and interest-free loans, thereby effectively cutting prices (see Figure 6-2, where higher incentives suggest lower purchase prices). Ford and Chrysler were compelled to follow, with the result that new vehicle sales remained at near-record levels, rather than declining under the burden of rigidly maintained oligopoly prices as in the past.[37] By 2003, with the economy still in recession, the Big Three were offering average new-car incentives in excess of $4,000 per vehicle, which sustained their sales at near-record rates.[38] In 2005, in response to flagging sales, Ford and GM offered purchase incentives

---

[36]Amal Nag, "High New-Car Prices Keep Many Lookers Looking," *Wall Street Journal* (August 3, 1983): 1.
[37]Gregory L. White and Karen Lundegaard, "U.S. Auto Sales Accelerated 13%, Driven by Deals," *Wall Street Journal* (September 5, 2002): 1. The chief executive officer of GM, Rick Wagoner, has expertly conveyed the important cyclical difference between noncompetitive administered pricing under tight oligopoly, versus the pricing characteristic of more competitive structural conditions in the industry today: "Normally we took [the impact of] recessions in volume. Now, we did not take the volume down. We took prices down." Quoted in Joseph B. White, "GM Hints at Easing of Discounts," *Wall Street Journal* (September 10, 2003): D4. Thus, under competitive conditions, price reductions cushion output and employment declines during recessions, whereas recessionary output and employment declines were exacerbated under the rigid system of administered oligopoly prices in the past.
[38]Peter Brown, "Incentive Wars," *Automotive News* (January 20, 2003): 1; and Julie Cantwell, "Car Prices Fall, and an Industry Changes," *Automotive News* (November 25, 2002): 1.

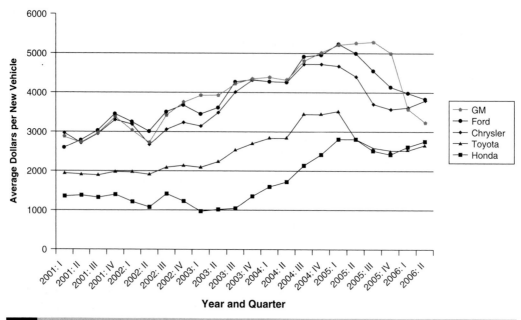

▪ ▪ ▪ **FIGURE 6-2** Value of New Vehicle Incentives

CNW Marketing Research, with permission.

exceeding $5,000 per vehicle; in the spring of 2007, GM and Chrysler set rebates of $7,500 to $8,000 for some slow-selling models.[39]

One consequence of this price competition is that new cars have become significantly more affordable, with the weeks of family income required to purchase a new car falling steadily from 31 in the mid-1990s to 24 to 25 by 2007 (an "affordability" increase of 23 percent over the period).[40] A second important consequence is that by keeping demand and production up, such competitive downward price flexibility cushions sales declines in the auto-industrial complex, and prevents them from exacerbating macroeconomic slowdowns in the economy at large as they had in the past.

Some auto makers complain bitterly about the advent of price competition. The chief executive officer of Chrysler, for example, has deplored it, charging that "All of these policies are just trashing the whole value chain and turning the product into a commodity."[41] Others have criticized competitive pricing as "an insidious, confusing carousel."[42] But GM's chief executive officer seems to have declared an end to interdependent oligopoly

[39]See Sholnn Freeman, "Car Buyers Get New Round of Discounts," *Wall Street Journal* (August 3, 2005): D1; Peter Brown, "Incentive Wars," *Automotive News* (January 20, 2003): 1; and John K. Teahen, "Detroit 3 Spend Big to Clear Out 2006s," *Automotive News* (April 9 , 2007): .

[40]This measure is calculated and published by Comerica Bank, and is available on the firm's website at www.comerica.com/Comerica_Content/Corporate_Communications/Docs/Auto_Affordability_Index_Q12007.pdf

[41]Mary Connelly, "DCX Embraces Rebates," *Automotive News* (April 7, 2003): 1.

[42]Micheline Maynard, "Nissan Chief Says Rebates Need to Stop," *New York Times* (April 13, 2006): C1.

pricing: "It's time to stop whining and just play the game," he recently said. "At GM, we're going to do what works for us. We fully expect our competitors to do what's best for them"—the epitome of a genuinely competitive marketplace mentality.[43]

Product Rivalry

A similar revolution has transformed product rivalry in the field. Here, too, decades of tight-knit oligopoly fostered a pattern of mutually interdependent behavior which, in turn, generated a bland homogeneity in the product offerings of the Big Three. Primary emphasis was on the superficial: two headlights versus four, recessed door handles versus nonrecessed, "fine Corinthian leathers," and so forth. Beginning in the 1990s, however, the advent of serious competition began to unleash a flood of new vehicles, designs and concepts. Spurred by competition, an industry habituated to a time scale more familiar to geologists began to operate at a much faster pace closer to that of fashion clothing. Two specific episodes highlight the magnitude of this sea change.

Oligopoly Restraint: The Case of Small Cars.[44]

At the conclusion of World War II, the small, lightweight, inexpensive automobile was seen as a prime means for expanding the postwar market in a manner analogous to Henry Ford's Model T decades before. In May 1945, General Motors and Ford disclosed they were considering the production of small cars; Chrysler announced similar plans the following year. But the Big Three did not seriously undertake to market such a vehicle until the 1970s, at least in the American market. (A small, economical car developed by GM was marketed in Australia in 1948 by a GM subsidiary; Ford's light car appeared the same year in France.) Attempts were made to meet increases in imports during the 1950s and 1960s, but these efforts seemed halfhearted and uninspired. The full impact of the industry's dilatory response hit with a vengeance in the 1970s, of course, when oil embargoes and skyrocketing gas prices unleashed a torrent of fuel-efficient Japanese imports into the American market that nearly bankrupted the Big Three.

Lawrence White explains the Big Three's lethargy in terms of classic oligopoly behavior: General Motors, Ford and Chrysler each seemed to recognize that vigorous entry into small cars by any one of them would compel entry into that segment by the others. Believing that the small-car segment was not large enough to profitably support all three firms and, further, believing that the availability of small cars would undermine higher prices and profits on sales of their large cars, the Big Three refrained from vigorously developing the small-car option. Foreign competitors, however, were not immobilized by such considerations because they had no established position to protect. The oil crises of the 1970s provided them entrée into the American market. They opportunistically broke through the logjam of tacit restraint and forced the domestic oligopoly to confront the challenge of building smaller, higher-quality and more fuel-efficient automobiles.

---

[43]Rick Wagoner, "Auto Boom is Ours to Lose," *Automotive News* (February 17, 2003): 14.
[44]This account is drawn from Lawrence J. White, "The American Automobile Industry and the Small Car, 1945–1970," *Journal of Industrial Economics* 20 (1972): 179; Paul Blumberg, "Snarling Cars," *New Republic* (January 24, 1983):12–14.

Oligopoly Restraint Dented: The Chrysler Minivan.[45]

Chrysler's minivan, introduced in 1983, quickly became one of the most successful automobile models ever built. By the mid-1990s, minivans accounted for more than a quarter of Chrysler's sales and perhaps as much as two-thirds of its profits.

But pioneering development work on the minivan concept had been done years before at both General Motors and Ford. By the late-1970s, in fact, GM designers had constructed a prototype of what has been described as a "dead ringer" for Chrysler's minivan. Ford designers, too, had developed the concept of a small, front-wheel-drive van. But Ford's top management dismissed the concept, while GM refrained from commercializing the minivan, partly for fear of cannibalizing its sales of conventional station wagons.

A renegade band of ex-Ford executives familiar with the minivan concept (led by Lee Iacocca) moved to Chrysler, however, where they faced disaster: Chrysler had narrowly escaped bankruptcy by virtue of a government bailout in 1979 and 1980, and desperately needed a new product success. The minivan concept was seized upon because, according to one Chrysler designer, "We didn't have much to lose." Their gamble paid off. Chrysler survived and prospered, largely because of the minivan's success and the risk taken in introducing it. Instead of viewing the market as fixed and comprising a few traditional product categories, Chrysler had opened an entirely new industry segment. Still, it took a near-fatal crisis to overcome the inertia and risk aversion bred by decades of oligopoly dominance.

Product Competition Unleashed.

The minivan marked a watershed in the onset of genuine product competition in the industry. The field ceased to be rigidly divided into a few fixed categories of cars and trucks. A more competitively structured industry triggered an explosion of vehicle types and segments: minivans, SUVs, crossovers, retros, and even crucks (car-truck combinations); as well as a flood of Azteks, Pacificas, Pathfinders, Escalades, and Tribecas that seemingly defy simple categorization. Consumers could now choose among hundreds of models across product segments unimaginable just a few years ago. In the process, product competition has transformed autos into a far more fashion-oriented field, in which a premium is put on creativity, flexibility, sensitivity to buyers' shifting tastes, smaller production runs, and entrepreneurial risk taking. In this competitive milieu, of course, bureaucratic size is a serious disadvantage, which may be an important reason why auto makers are concentrating more on design and assembly, while vertically dis-integrating themselves and outsourcing the production of more parts, components and modules to others.

A critical key in product competition, however, is offering a balanced portfolio of models: The Big Three's over-dependence on sales of larger, less fuel-efficient SUVs over the period from 1996 to 2003 rendered them precariously vulnerable to gasoline price movements, so that when gas prices rose to $3 per gallon in 2006, their sales and profits from these types of vehicles plunged. (Examples include sales drops over the first half of 2006 of 32 to 37 percent for Chrysler's Dodge Durango and Jeep Grand Cherokee SUV models; sales declines of 29 to 34 percent for Ford's Expedition and Explorer SUVs; and a sales drop of 22 to 44 percent for GM's Chevy Avalanche and

---

[45]This account is drawn from Alex Taylor, "Iacocca's Minivan," *Fortune* (May 30, 1994): 56–66.

Trailblazer SUV models).[46] Another key is perceived product quality and, as Figure 6-2 indicates, the Big Three continue to suffer from a perceived quality gap that requires them to offer greater incentives than their Japanese rivals in order to attract buyers.

▮▮▮ IV. Industry Performance

For decades, industry defenders insisted that the automobile field's highly concentrated structure was necessitated by the economies of large-scale production, the expense of modern innovation, and the dictates of modern industrial planning. John Kenneth Galbraith famously pronounced GM's massive size to be in the service of superior planning, and "for this planning—control of supply, control of demand, provision of capital, minimization of risk—there is no clear upper limit to the desirable size. It could be that the bigger the better."[47] Testifying before a congressional committee in 1974, GM officials agreed, asserting that the GM's massive size "has been determined by the product itself, the requirements of efficient manufacture, distribution and service, as well as market demand."[48]

In the light of the Big Three's subsequent performance, few today would have the temerity to make such claims. In fact, the advent of effective competition revealed just how badly the Big Three's performance had deteriorated during their decades of unchallenged oligopolistic supremacy—a decline they continue struggling to overcome.

Production Efficiency

One indication of the extent to which production inefficiency afflicted the Big Three is provided in Table 6-5, comparing labor productivity for U.S. and Japanese automotive firms in the early 1980s. These statistics show that massive size and market dominance are no guarantors of efficiency. They also reveal the degree to which the domestic oligopoly had fallen behind the state-of-the-art production practices being innovated by others: By the early 1980s, Nissan and Toyota were 3 to 4 times more productive than any of the Big Three.

Confronted with foreign competition, the Big Three have struggled over recent decades to improve their efficiency and shrink their bloated cost structures. They have been compelled to redesign their production operations, close antiquated plants, reorganize management structures, modernize facilities and purchasing practices, and cut billions of dollars from their costs. (Total employment at GM, for example, has dropped 61 percent, or by 520,000 employees, since 1979, with 35,000 additional job

---

[46]"U.S. Light-Vehicle Sales by Nameplate, June & 6 Months 2006," *Automotive News* (July 20, 2006): 39. As explained by GM, "High gasoline prices . . . have contributed to weaker demand for certain of our higher margin vehicles, especially our full-size sport utility vehicles, as consumer demand has shifted to more fuel-efficient, smaller and lower [profit] margin vehicles. Any future increases in the price of gasoline . . . could weaken further the demand for such vehicles. Such a result could lead to lower revenues and have a material adverse effect on our business." Form 10-K, filed with U.S. Securities & Exchange Commission, (March 28, 2006): I-17.

[47]John Kenneth Galbraith, *The New Industrial State* (Boston: Houghton Mifflin, 1971): 76. On this point some economists at the opposite end of the political spectrum agreed. See John S. McGee, "Economies of Size in Auto Body Manufacture," *Journal of Political Economy* 16 (October 1973): 239.

[48]U.S. Congress. Senate. Subcommittee on Antitrust and Monopoly, Hearings: The Industrial Reorganization Act, Part 4, Ground Transportation Industries, 93rd Cong., 2d sess., 1974, 2,468.

TABLE 6-5 Comparative Productivity: Early 1980s.

Firm	Vehicles Produced per Worker
General Motors	4.5
Ford	4.2
Chrysler	4.8
Nissan	11.6
Toyota	16.4

Note: *Average of data for years 1980 and 1983, adjusted to reflect differing degrees of vertical integration among producers.*
Source: © 1985 Harvard University Asia Center.

cuts coming as a result of an early retirement program begun from 2005 into 2006). And they have made substantial gains: Although the Big Three, as a group, continue to be at a productivity disadvantage compared to North American transplants operated by Honda, Nissan and Toyota, the magnitude of their relative disadvantage has declined, on average, from about 45 percent in 1995 to 14 percent by 2005 (measured by total labor hours per vehicle produced). In fact, some Big Three assembly plants now are among the most productive automotive facilities in North America.[49] The Big Three also are redesigning and re-equipping their plants to operate more efficiently by assembling different models on the same lines. But as Table 6-6 indicates, here, too, they continue to lag their transplant rivals.

The cost consequences of excessive size are long-lived in another important respect: As the Big Three shrink their size, increase their productivity, and reduce their employment, their ratio of retired to active workers has risen, so that they now face billions of dollars of "legacy costs" required to fund the retirement pension and health

TABLE 6-6 Proportion of North American Vehicles Produced on Flexible Assembly Lines

	2005	2007 (projected)
Nissan	88%	88%
Honda	69	69
Toyota	66	73
General Motors	46	66
DaimlerChrysler	32	78
Ford	22	41

Source: *Wall Street Journal* by Boudettem, Neal. Copyright 2006 by Dow Jones & Company, Inc.. Reproduced with permission of Dow Jones & Company, Inc. in the format Textbook via Copyright Clearance Center.

---

[49]Harbour Report: 1999, 175; Harbour Consulting, "Productivity Gap Among North American Automakers Narrows," news release, June 1, 2006; and Harbour Report: 2006, 31–32.

care programs the Big Three negotiated with organized labor in their less-competitive days.[50] GM, for example, estimates its pension liabilities at $124 billion over the years from 2006 to 2015, while Ford puts its pension liabilities at $83 billion[51]—billions of dollars of funds and liabilities that GM and Chrysler began divesting to the autoworkers' union in 2007. The oligopoly origin of this particular cost burden has been brilliantly captured by a former Ford labor relations executive, who says "We just focused on matching each other back then, not 'Hey, this will disadvantage us [relative] to the Asian auto makers.' "[52]

Dynamic Efficiency

Dynamic efficiency encompasses product innovation, a dimension in which the domestic industry's performance is distinguished by four features.

First, the rate, breadth, and depth of product innovation were great in the era before World War II, when the field was populated by numerous independents. Innovation competition was intense, and new people with new ideas could put their concepts (good and bad alike) into practice.

Second, with the consolidation of the field into a tight triopoly, the pace of technological innovation slackened. Innovations like front-wheel drive, disc brakes, fuel injection, fuel-efficient subcompacts, and utilitarian minivans languished in the hands of the Big Three. "Since competition within the industry was mild," David Halberstam writes, "there was no impulse to innovate; to the finance people, innovation not only was expensive but seemed unnecessary. . . . Why bother, after all? In America's rush to become a middle-class society, there was an almost insatiable demand for cars. It was impossible not to make money, and there was a conviction that no matter what the sales were this year, they would be even greater the next. So there was little stress on improving the cars. From 1949, when the automatic transmission was introduced, to the late seventies, the cars remained remarkably the same."[53]

Third, while the domestic oligopoly stagnated, foreign producers took the lead in advancing automotive technology and commercializing it. According to veteran industry writer Brock Yates, foreign firms forged ahead "with fuel injection, disc brakes, rack and pinion steering, radial tires, quartz headlights, ergonomically adjustable bucket seats, five-speed manual transmissions, high-efficiency overhead camshaft engines, independently sprung suspensions, advanced shock absorbers, and strict crash-worthiness standards."[54] By 1989, the contrast was striking: Reporting his impressions of the 1989 Tokyo Motor Show, the publisher of *Automotive News* gasped that "Japanese producers display more show cars, concept cars and new products than can be believed. . . . They continue to innovate, and their execution of new products is nearly flawless."[55] Of engine technology, another analyst opined that comparing the U.S. and Japanese

---

[50]See Dave Guilford, "Chief Juggling Officer," *Automotive News* (July 7, 2003): 1; and Lee Hawkins, "As GM Battles Surging Costs, Workers' Health Becomes Issue," *Wall Street Journal* (April 7, 2005): 1.
[51]Securities & Exchange Commission, Form 10-K for each firm.
[52]Quoted in Jeffrey McCracken, "Detroit's Symbol of Dysfunction," *Wall Street Journal* (March 1, 2006): A12.
[53]David Halberstam, *The Reckoning* (New York: Morrow, 1986), 244–45.
[54]Brock Yates, *The Decline and Fall of the American Automobile Industry* (New York: Vintage Books, 1984), 149.
[55]Keith Crane, "Tokyo: An Interesting Place for a Show," *Automotive News* (October 30, 1989): 12.

was like "comparing the Stone Age and today."[56] At the same time, Roger Smith, then chairman of GM, bemoaned his firm's glacial pace of new vehicle development, pointing out that GM's 60-month new-vehicle development cycle was "longer than it took for us to fight and win World War II."[57] Researchers laid bare the effect of the Big Three's decades of dominance and bureaucracy on their inability to innovate by the 1980s (see Table 6-7).

Fourth, the advent of competition from abroad has compelled the Big Three to become more innovative in every aspect of their products: from engines (multivalves, fuel injection) and brakes (computer controlled, antilock); to transmissions (five speed, six speed, continuously variable) and body styles (sport utility, crossover, and retro vehicles). Summarizing the broad sweep of events, GM vice-chairman Robert Lutz concedes, "We did bring it on ourselves, having built products 20-odd years ago which in many cases were well below best international standards in design, dynamics, craftsmanship and reliability."[58]

Here, too, however, years of lethargy opened a chasm that the Big Three constantly must struggle to overcome: The quality of their vehicles has significantly improved, but so too has the quality of the vehicles built by their Japanese rivals.[59] The Big Three have compressed their new-vehicle development time, but so too have Japanese producers. In the case of one of the most important technological breakthroughs in the industry in decades—hybrid vehicles employing a combination of conventional gasoline engines to charge electric motors powered by batteries—the Big Three once again have followed rather than led. After dismissing the Prius and Insight hybrids pioneered by Toyota and Honda in 1998 and 1999 as a public relations stunt lacking business justification, the Big Three soon found themselves scrambling to catch up and offer these vehicles at a time when gasoline prices had skyrocketed; sales of hybrids had jumped from 9,000 vehicles in 2000 to an annual rate exceeding 200,000 vehicles by mid-2006; and Toyota and Honda were into their third generation of hybrids and spreading this

TABLE 6-7 Automotive Product Development in the U.S. and Japan: Mid-1980s

	Japan	*United States*
Average Engineering Hours Per New Vehicle (millions)	1.7	3.1
Average Development Time Per New Vehicle (months)	46.2	60.4
Employees in Project Team	485.0	903.0
Die Development Time (months)	13.8	25.0

Source: James P. Womack, Daniel T. Jones, and Daniel Roos, *The Machine That Changed the World* (New York: Rawson Associates, 1990), 118.

---

[56]Jesse Snyder, "L.A. Show: Analyst Calls Japanese Leaner, Maybe Meaner," *Automotive News* (January 11, 1988): 6.
[57]Quoted in Albert Lee, *Call Me Roger* (New York: Contemporary Books, 1988), 96.
[58]Quoted in "Comment and Analysis: Motor Industry," *Financial Times* (February 17, 2006): 11.
[59]See the annual rankings for initial new-vehicle quality, as well as the longer-run rankings of dependability of vehicles a few years following purchase, by the J.D. Power firm at www.jdpower.com, and by *Consumer Reports* at www.consumerreports.org.

technology throughout their product lines.[60] In 2006, as in decades past, the Big Three once again had put themselves in the position of bringing to market what the market did not want; that is, the even bigger, even less fuel-efficient SUVs and pickups they had elected to develop instead.[61]

In what may be the next major technological breakthrough, independent American entrepreneurs skilled in electronics and computer engineering (not the Big Three) have begun launching all-electric sports cars. These vehicles are capable of breathtaking acceleration (zero to 60 in less than 4 seconds); they use lighter, more powerful batteries able to power the car for 250 miles and be fully recharged in 4 hours for less than $8 using a standard 220-volt outlet; and have motors only 15 inches long with only 3 moving parts. Working with development funds less than the sales revenues generated by GM every 2 hours, these independent innovators think the "time is right for electric vehicles, because of advances in batteries and electronics. Where's the skill set for that? In [Silicon] Valley, not Detroit."[62] Of the Big Three's past efforts in this area (such as GM's all-electric EV1 vehicles, which were leased in the 1990s and later repossessed by the firm and physically destroyed despite protestations and purchase offers by drivers[63]), these entrepreneurs challenge those who say electric cars have been tried and failed, insisting that "of course electric cars won't catch on if no one actually wants to drive them."[64]

Social Efficiency

Social efficiency concerns how well the industry has served the public interest in air pollution, automotive safety, and fuel consumption and the nation's dependence on foreign oil. The Big Three's performance in these areas has been distinguished for

---

[60]See Alex Taylor, "The Birth of the Prius," *Fortune* (March 6, 2006): 111; Don Sherman, "Hybrid History," *Automotive News* (June 12, 200): 34; "Hybrids: Toyota's Big Bet," *Automotive News* (March 21, 2005): 60; and Norihiku Shirouzu and Jathon Sapsford, "As Hybrid Cars Gain Traction, Industry Battles Over Designs," *Wall Street Journal* (October 19, 2005): 1. Taylor found that Toyota began developing its Prius hybrid in the early 1990s, long before the 2005 and 2006 spikes in gasoline prices, and at a development cost equivalent to that incurred in developing a conventional new vehicle.

For GM and Chrysler's battle against hybrid technology in California, see Jeffrey Ball, "How California Failed in Efforts to Curb Its Addiction to Oil," *Wall Street Journal* (August 2, 2006): 1. On the federal level, the Big Three successfully lobbied to cap the number of hybrid vehicles qualifying for federal tax credits, presumably to offset the "unfair advantage" achieved by their more innovative rivals. See Matt Vella, "Toyota Prius Tax Breaks Will Soon Be on Empty," *Wall Street Journal* (May 15, 2007): D5.

[61]See Rick Kranz and Amy Wilson, "Ford's Product Predicament," *Automotive News* (July 24, 2006): 3; Micheline Maynard, "The Summer of Detroit's Discontent," *New York Times* (July 28, 2006): C1; and Neal Boudette and Jeffrey C. McCracken, "Detroit's Cash Cow Stumbles," *Wall Street Journal* (August 1, 2006): B1.

[62]See Jennifer Saranow, "The Electric Car Gets Some Muscle," *Wall Street Journal* (July 27, 2006): D1; Michael Copeland, "Silicon Valley's New New Thing," CNNmoney.com (April 20, 2006); and Mark Rechtin, "Tesla Proving Electric Vehicles Can Burn Rubber," *Automotive News* (October 2, 2006): 26.

The leading innovator in this field, Tesla, has announced plans to open its first dealership in late 2007 in Southern California, with other dealerships projected to open thereafter in New York, Chicago, Miami, and San Francisco. The firm plans to sell 1,200 of its all-electric sports cars per year. The vehicle initially will be built by the British Lotus firm, with plans to construct an American assembly plant in New Mexico. See Mark Rechtin, "Factory Stores Will Sell Tesla EVs," *Automotive News* (May 14, 2007): 6.

[63]See "Dave Guilford, "EV1 Lessees to GM: Don't Take Our Cars," *Automotive News* (November 11, 2002): 4. These events inspired a movie in 2006, *EV Confidential: Who Killed the Electric Car?*

[64]"About Tesla Motors," www.teslamotors.com

decades by indifference and denial, followed by resistance and pleas of technological impossibility.

On automotive emissions, for example, the industry initially denied the problem: "[W]aste vapors are dissipated in the atmosphere quickly and do not present an air pollution problem," Ford Motor Company told government officials in smog-choked Los Angeles in the 1950s. "The fine automotive power plants which modern-day engineers design do not 'smoke.'"[65] Later, as automotive air pollution worsened and national concerns about the problem grew, the Big Three (in the guise of a research "joint venture") conspired to eliminate competition among themselves in researching and developing emissions control technology.[66] When government emission regulations were promulgated in the 1970s, the Big Three insisted that the regulations were impossible to meet, even though Japanese firms responded with innovative engines combining high performance with lower exhaust emissions (i.e., Honda's Compound Vortex Combustion Chamber, or CVCC, engine). In the 1990s, as a number of states began implementing tighter emission standards, the Big Three again attacked them as unattainable, even though foreign producers (led by Honda) were introducing newer engine designs able to meet the standards while offering *greater* power and acceleration. In the late 1990s, GM and Chrysler reportedly were outraged by Ford's declared goal of engineering its light trucks to be no more polluting than its cars; they were incensed that Ford betrayed what they considered a gentlemen's agreement to refrain from innovating reductions in light-truck emissions.[67] More recently, the Big Three have fought zero emissions vehicle standards in California, while foreign firms have introduced hybrids and hydrogen fuel cell vehicles able to meet those stricter regulations.

On the safety front, patents awarded to the Big Three in the 1920s and 1930s for such features as padded dashboards and collapsible steering wheel columns were shelved until their incorporation was mandated by government regulation. The industry insisted that safety should be optional, supplied only in response to consumer demand. Yet it refused to make available the product options and safety information essential for rational, free consumer decision making. It spent millions extolling horsepower while hiding behind its slogan that "Safety don't sell." Eventually, a decades-long battle between government and the industry produced results. The Big Three finally conceded the benefits of seat belts and, in the 1990s, after waging what the Supreme Court described as the "regulatory equivalent of war" against air bags,[68] the oligopoly discovered that "Safety really does sell," and began engineering air bags into its vehicles. More recently, as evidence concerning the safety hazards of sport utility vehicles began to accumulate,[69] the Big Three once again responded with protestations of ignorance, denial, and resistance. They were outraged when the Bush Administration's

---

[65]U.S. Congress. Senate. Subcommittee on Air and Water Pollution, Hearings: Air Pollution—1967, Part 1, 90th Cong., 1st sess., 1967, 158. Despite these public claims, the Big Three were sufficiently concerned about the problem to have begun privately researching it decades before. See "Smog Control Antitrust Case," *Congressional Record* (House ed.) (May 18, 1971), 15,626–27.

[66]See the documentation in "Smog Control Antitrust Case," especially at 15,627.

[67]Keith Bradsher, *High and Mighty* (New York: Public Affairs, 2002), 268–69.

[68]*Motor Vehicle Manufacturers Association v. State Farm*, 463 U.S. 29, 46 (1983).

[69]See Bradsher. For an opposing point of view, see Douglas Coates and James VanderHoff, "The Truth About Light Trucks," *Regulation* (Spring 2001).

chief of the National Highway Traffic Safety Administration (NHTSA), Dr. Jeffrey Runge, a veteran emergency room physician, warned of the higher rollover/fatality risk to occupants of SUVs (due to their higher center of gravity and greater propensity to flip), and cautioned consumers not to succumb to the illusion that these vehicles are safer than conventional cars.[70] (His warnings were validated by statistics indicating that U.S. traffic fatalities reached a 10-year high in 2002, driven upward by rollover crashes involving SUVs and pickups.[71]) The Big Three finally began engineering their SUVs to be safer, more stable and more resistant to lethal rollovers, but only after (according to the *Wall Street Journal*'s automotive expert) "a nasty scandal prompted by the loss of hundreds of lives, a storm of political outrage and the threat of unwelcome new federal regulation."[72]

In the area of fuel consumption, when asked in 1958 what steps his division was taking in fuel economy, the general manager of GM's Buick division quipped, "We're helping the gas companies, the same as our competitors."[73] The Big Three seemed to believe that gasoline would remain forever plentiful at 20 cents a gallon, as the fuel consumption of their fleets steadily worsened. Only months before the first OPEC oil embargo and gasoline crisis of 1973, when the Big Three's fleet averaged 13 miles per gallon, GM's chairman recommended faster licensing of nuclear electric power plants as a better way to respond to what he dismissively referred to as America's energy "problem."[74] In 1979, one month before the overthrow of the Shah of Iran and the nation's second energy crisis in 6 years, General Motors insisted that automotive "fuel economy standards are not necessary and they are not good for America."[75] In the early 1990s, in the wake of the Persian Gulf War, the Big Three unveiled what the *Wall Street Journal* called "some of the biggest and brawniest cars in years,"[76] while protesting that further gains in fuel economy were technologically impossible, even as Honda was unveiling lean-burning engines able to get 55 miles per gallon. Through the remainder of the decade, the Big Three successfully lobbied Congress to freeze mileage standards, and gorged themselves on sales of gas-guzzling light trucks and sport utility vehicles, while Toyota and Honda were developing fuel-efficient hybrid vehicles. From 2001 to 2003, in the face of political upheaval in Afghanistan, Iraq, Venezuela and Nigeria (each of which triggered spikes in gasoline prices) the Big Three were launching their biggest, heaviest, least fuel-efficient SUVs ever, including GM's Hummer, getting 12 miles a gallon. As a result, the fuel economy of the industry's new-vehicle fleet fell to a 22-year low, with most of the decline attributable to the growth of light trucks and SUVs (see Table 6-8). A similar scenario played out in 2005

---

[70]Karen Lundegaard, "Auto Safety Czar Warns Drivers of SUV Dangers," *Wall Street Journal* (January 15, 2003): 1. For an interesting exploration of the driver psychology involved, see Malcolm Gladwell, "Big and Bad," *New Yorker* (January 12, 2004): 28–33.

[71]National Highway Traffic Safety Administration, *2002 Annual Assessment of Motor Vehicle Crashes*, Washington, D.C. (July 2003).

[72]Joseph B. White, "Improved SUV Rollover Ratings Show Auto Industry Can Be Agile," *Wall Street Journal* (June 6, 2006): D5.

[73]Quoted in John Keats, *Insolent Chariots* (New York: Lippincott, 1958), 14.

[74]U.S. Congress. Senate, Committee on Commerce. Hearing: Automotive Research and Development and Fuel Economy, 93rd Cong., 1st sess., 1973, 564.

[75]Ed Cray, *Chrome Colossus* (New York: McGraw-Hill, 1980), 524.

[76]Joseph B. White and Neal Templin, "Gas Price Jump Finds Car Makers Backsliding on Fuel Efficiency," *Wall Street Journal* (September 14, 1990): 1.

TABLE 6-8 Characteristics of New U.S. Light-Duty Vehicles, 1975–2006

	1975	*1987*	*1997*	*2006*
Fuel Economy (miles per gallon)	13.1	22.1	20.9	21.0
Weight (pounds)	4060.0	3220.0	3727.0	4142.0
Horsepower	137.0	118.0	169.0	219.0
Acceleration (0 to 60 time in seconds)	14.1	13.1	11.0	9.7
Percent Light Truck Sales	19.0	28.0	42.0	50.0

Source: Robert M. Heavenrich, "Light-Duty Automotive Technology and Fuel Economy Trends: 1975 Through 2006," Office of Transportation and Air Quality, U.S. Environmental Protection Agency (July 2006).

and 2006, in the wake of the energy shortages and gasoline price spikes engendered by Hurricane Katrina.[77]

The nation's security, its foreign policy, and its military challenges clearly are involved when, as Senator John McCain has pointed out, modest improvements in automotive fuel efficiency could substantially reduce America's dependence on foreign oil by conserving as much petroleum as is currently imported from the Middle East.[78] President Bush, too, has deplored America's addiction to oil and urged Detroit to produce vehicles that are "relevant."

An important explanation for the Big Three's lackluster performance in all these areas once again may stem from the oligopolistic interdependence and mutual restraint bred by decades of dominance. As former GM president Alfred Sloan once confided, "I feel that General Motors should not adopt safety glass for its cars. I can only see competition being forced into the same position. Our gain would be purely a temporary one and the net results would be that both competition and ourselves would have reduced the return on our capital and the public would have obtained still more value per dollar expended."[79]

▮▮▮ V. Public Policy

Public policy toward the industry can be examined in four main areas: antitrust; protection from foreign competition; government regulation of automotive emissions, safety, and fuel consumption; and government/industry partnership programs.

---

[77]Congressman Sherwood Boehlert, Republican of New York, observes that Hurricane Katrina "swept away the illusion that a successful business strategy for automakers is to bet the farm on gas guzzlers and simply pray for eternally low gasoline prices." Quoted in *Automotive News* (September 19, 2005): 17. A GM official disagreed with this assessment, however, insisting that the adverse impact of higher gasoline prices on GM's sales of trucks "will decrease over time as people adjust to the thought of $3 a gallon, just as they did when it was $2 a gallon and just as they did when it was $1 a gallon." Quoted in Nick Bunkley, "G.M. Hopes a Line of Pickups Will Lead Back to Prosperity," *New York Times* (August 3, 2006): C3.
[78]Senator John McCain, Press Release, April 18, 2002.
[79]Quoted in U.S. Senate, Select Committee on Small Business, Hearings: Planning, Regulation, and Competition—Automobile Industry, 90th Cong., 2d sess., 1968, 967. For additional evidence of the adverse impact of this oligopolistic mentality in autos and other industries, see James W. Brock, "Antitrust Policy and the Oligopoly Problem," *Antitrust Bulletin* 51 (Summer 2006).

Antitrust Policy and Government Bailouts

Antitrust policy has never directly challenged the industry's concentrated structure, while the antitrust actions that have been taken have been tangential and peripheral. For example, in 1969, the government charged the Big Three with illegally conspiring to eliminate competition, but only in the smog-control field. In the early 1970s, the government charged GM and Ford with collusive pricing, but only in the fleet market for new cars sold to businesses and rental car agencies. In the 1990s, the antitrust agencies investigated anticompetitive practices in the industry, but only as they affected dealer efforts to impede vehicle sales on the internet. At the same time, the antitrust agencies have allowed a proliferation of joint ventures and alliances to link the domestic oligopoly with most of its major foreign rivals.

In what might be considered "failing company" antitrust policy, the government engineered the Chrysler bailout in 1979, in important part to prevent the industry from becoming even more concentrated. The bailout specter resurfaced from 2005 to 2007, with GM and Ford seeking government aid in the form of subsidies and tax breaks to improve the fuel efficiency of their vehicles, retool their factories, subsidize research and development of hybrid propulsion systems, and fund their health care costs.[80]

Protection from Foreign Competition

As we have seen, mutual oligopolistic interdependence solidified among the Big Three in the post-World War II era. This, together with the protection afforded by formidable entry barriers, insulated the Big Three from effective competition. Noncompetitive conduct, including vertical collusion between management and organized labor in generating a sustained escalation of wages and prices, flourished in this structural milieu.

Foreign competition eventually began to disturb this bonhomie, and induced the industry to seek government-imposed shelter from imports. Their efforts succeeded in 1981, when the Reagan administration forced "voluntary" quotas on Japanese producers. These "temporary" quotas, ostensibly intended to give the Big Three breathing space, were subsequently renewed throughout the remainder of the decade. Predictably, the quotas drove up the price of Japanese imports which, in turn, enabled the Big Three to push through sizable price boosts of their own. Yet in an ironic twist, these numerical restrictions impelled Japanese firms to take steps to circumvent them, first, by upgrading their offerings and moving into the larger, more profitable midsize and luxury segments of the market, and second, by constructing transplant assembly facilities in the United States.

Later, in the early 1990s, the Big Three resumed their import restriction fight, demanding that government re-impose quotas on Japanese cars as well as impose limits on the number of vehicles that Japanese firms could assemble in their American

---

[80]See Jeffrey H. Birnbaum and Sholm Freeman, "Just Don't Call It a Bailout," *Washington Post* (national weekly ed., December 12–19, 2005): 19; Laura Meckler and David Rogers, "GM, Ford Craft Plea for Limited Federal Assistance," *Wall Street Journal* (February 9, 2006): 1; and Neal E. Boudette and John D. Stoll, "Big Three Seek Battery Subsidies," *Wall Street Journal* (January 9, 2007): A14.

production facilities. They demanded that the government restrict imports of minivans, even though the Big Three accounted for 85 percent of U.S. minivan sales at the time, and even though Chrysler was the country's largest importer of minivans (assembled in its Canadian plants).

Since 2005 GM and Ford have been lobbying the Bush Administration to manipulate the value of the dollar relative to foreign currencies in order to force new-vehicle prices up in the American market. Their efforts reportedly succeeded in persuading Toyota to raise its prices in an attempt to aid GM and Ford, thereby heading off another outbreak of protective government policy in the U.S. market.[81]

Regulation: Safety, Pollution, Fuel Economy

Have government efforts to regulate automotive safety, emissions, and fuel consumption been too costly compared with the benefits obtained? Is it true, as the industry has long maintained, that "regulation adds unnecessary costs for consumers, lowers profits, diverts manpower from research and development programs, and reduces productivity — all at a time when our resources are desperately needed to meet the stiff competition from abroad?"[82] Or is it the case, as Henry Ford II once conceded, that "we wouldn't have had the kinds of safety built into automobiles that we have had unless there had been a Federal law. We wouldn't have had the fuel economy unless there had been a Federal law, and there wouldn't have been the emission control unless there had been a Federal law?"[83]

Is it true, as the industry contends, that government automobile regulations deny freedom of choice for consumers? Or do the Big Three exploit "free consumer choice" when it suits their purposes, but with no compunction about violating that principle when consumers might freely choose imported vehicles, or choose safer, less polluting, or more fuel efficient automobiles? Is it true, as the industry claims, that government regulations prevent it from obeying consumer sovereignty by supplying the vehicles that buyers desire? Or is it the case that if the industry had acted more responsibly, it might have lessened the need for direct government regulation? Do various government agencies, charged with regulating different aspects of automobile performance, subject the industry to contradictory requirements by pitting safety (larger, heavier vehicles) against fuel economy (smaller, lighter vehicles)? Or are the Big Three responsible for rendering such regulations contradictory by first lobbying for, and subsequently exploiting, the loopholes exempting sport utility vehicles from the safety, fuel economy, and emissions standards covering conventional cars?

Some economists contend that less coercive forms of regulation — for example, incentive-based measures involving fees imposed on the sale of unsafe, polluting,

---

[81]See "Toyota May Raise Car Prices," CNNMoney.com (June 10, 2005); and "Toyota Chief Fears GM, Ford Demise," CNNMoney.com (June 8, 2005).
[82]U.S. Congress. House. Committee on Government Operations, Hearings: The Administration's Proposals to Help the U.S. Auto Industry, 97th Cong., 1st sess., 1981, 129.
[83]U.S. Congress. Senate. Subcommittee for Consumers, Hearings: Costs of Government Regulations to the Consumer, 95th Cong., 2nd sess., 1978, 87.

gas-guzzling vehicles—would be more effective. But is it realistic to assume that the government would impose such fees if doing so would jeopardize the financial viability of a General Motors, a Ford, or a Chrysler? Would the government seriously consider shutting down GM, for example, if the firm refused to pay these fees? Conversely, given their size and political clout, would a threat by any of the Big Three to shut down almost inevitably force the government to grant regulatory delays, exceptions, and exemptions?[84]

Government-Industry Partnership

Finally, there is the issue of government/industry partnerships, such as the "Partnership for a New Generation of Vehicles" launched by the Clinton administration in the 1990s, and its successor, the "Freedom Cooperative Automotive Research" program commenced by the Bush administration in 2002. These programs bring the Big Three auto makers together, under government auspices and with government funding, to achieve breakthroughs in technology. A major goal of the Clinton administration's partnership program was to develop by 2003 "a vehicle that could achieve up to three times the fuel efficiency of today's comparable vehicle . . . while at the same costing no more to own and drive than today's automobile and while meeting the customer's needs for quality, performance and utility."[85] The Bush administration's "FreedomCAR" program has the goal of promoting the development of hydrogen as a primary automotive fuel in order to reduce American dependence on foreign oil, with the long-term objective of producing "cars and trucks that are more efficient, cheaper to operate, pollution-free and competitive in the showroom."[86]

These programs raise a host of nettlesome questions: First, are they boons or boondoggles? The Clinton program, for example, spent $1.6 billion, but the fuel efficiency of the Big Three's fleet worsened over the period from 1993 to 2002 when the program was in effect. It was Honda and Toyota, not the Big Three acting in concert with government, that introduced revolutionary hybrid-powered vehicles at affordable prices. Similarly, it is independent entrepreneurs working on limited budgets and without government support that today are pushing the frontiers of all-electric vehicular technology and attempting to commercialize it. Second, are these programs likely to achieve real breakthroughs? Or do they instead provide political cover for the Big Three, who can point to them as a way of deflecting more effective regulation?[87] And finally, do such industry-government partnerships promote innovation, or do they stifle it by providing the Big Three a forum in which to agree on what technological steps they will, and will not, undertake?[88]

---

[84]For an extensive analysis of how the Big Three can use their economic size and the threat of shutdowns to shape public policy, see Luger, op. cit. For recent examples of the capacity of the Big Three, acting in concert with organized labor, to influence regulatory policy, see Bradsher, 28, 68, 253, 394.

[85]Partnership for a New Generation of Vehicles, Program Plan, Washington, D.C., 1994.

[86]U.S. Department of Energy, "Energy Secretary Abraham Launches FreedomCAR," news release, January 9, 2002. The program's website is www.uscar.org/freedomcar

[87]See Harry Stoffer, "FreedomCAR: Real Solution or Tax Waste?" *Automotive New*, (June 10, 2002): 1, and Elizabeth Kolbert, "The Car of Tomorrow," *New Yorker* (August 8, 2003): 36–40.

[88]See Gregg Easterbrook, "Political Mileage," *New Republic* (October 9, 2000): 25–27.

CONCLUSION ▪▪▪▪▪▪▪

The Big Three's continuing travails (billions of financial losses in 2005 and 2006; layoffs of tens of thousands more workers; junk ratings accorded GM and Ford by the nation's credit-rating concerns; a plea by the nation's auto dealers that "For the good of everyone, [GM and Ford] must succeed and they need our help"[89]) attest to the power of competition and the consequences of decades of its atrophy. As such, these challenges underscore the decisive significance of an industry's structure in shaping its conduct and performance and, ultimately, the public policy challenges it presents.

SUGGESTIONS FOR FURTHER READING ▪▪▪▪▪▪▪

Publications

Automotive News, Market Data Book. Annual and weekly issues. Detroit, MI: Crane Publishing Co.

Bollier, David, and Joan Claybrook. 1986. *Freedom from Harm*. Washington, D.C.: Public Citizen.

Bradsher, Keith. 2002. *High and Mighty: SUV's—The World's Most Dangerous Vehicles and How They Got That Way*. New York: Public Affairs Press.

Ford, Henry. 1926. *My Life and Work*. New York: Doubleday.

Gertner, John. 2007. "From 0 to 60 to World Domination." *New York Times Sunday Magazine* (February 18), 34.

Halberstam, David. 1986. *The Reckoning*. New York: Morrow.

Harbour and Associates. Annual. *The Harbour Report on the North American Automobile Industry*. Troy, MI.

Iacocca, Lee. 1984. *Iacocca*. New York: Bantam.

Ingrassia, Paul, and Joseph B. White. 1994. *The Fall and Rise of the American Automobile Industry*. New York: Simon & Schuster.

Kwoka, John E. 2001. "Automobiles: The Old Economy Collides with the New," *Review of Industrial Organization* 19: 55.

Liker, Jeffrey K. 2004. *The Toyota Way*. New York: McGraw-Hill.

Luger, Stan. 2000. *Corporate Power, American Democracy, and the Automobile*. New York: Cambridge University Press.

Madsen, Axel. 1999. *The Deal Maker: How William C. Durant Made General Motors*. New York: John Wiley & Sons.

Maynard, Micheline. 2003. *The End of Detroit: How the Big Three Lost Their Grip on the American Car Market*. New York: Doubleday.

Parry, Ian W. H., Margaret Walls, and Winston Harrington. 2007. "Automobile Externalities and Policies," *Journal of Economic Literature* 65: 373.

Porter, Richard C. 1999. Economics at the Wheel: *The Costs of Cars and Drivers*. New York: Academic Press.

Rubenstein, James M. 2001. *Making and Selling Cars: Innovation and Change in the U.S. Automotive Industry*. Baltimore: Johns Hopkins Press.

U.S. Congress. Senate. Subcommittee on Antitrust and Monopoly. 1974. Hearings: The Industrial Reorganization Act, Parts 4 and 4A, Ground Transportation Industries, 93rd Cong., 2nd sess.

Ward's Automotive Yearbook. Annual. Detroit, MI: Ward's Communications.

White, Lawrence J. 1971. *The Automobile Industry Since 1945*. Cambridge: Harvard University Press.

Wright, J. Patrick. 1979. *On A Clear Day You Can See General Motors*. Grosse Pointe, MI: Wright Enterprises.

---

[89]*Wall Street Journal* (April 7, 2006): A14.

CHAPTER 7

The Music Recording Industry

PETER J. ALEXANDER*

The Recording Industry Association of America (RIAA), the trade association for the four large firms in the music recording industry, has issued thousands of subpoenas aimed at individual consumers whom they allege to be copyright violators. Most recently, in the spring of 2007, the RIAA sent pre-litigation letters to hundreds of college students at 13 different universities. According to the RIAA:

> The Recording Industry Association of America (RIAA), on behalf of the major record companies, today sent 400 pre-litigation settlement letters to 13 different universities. Each letter informs the school of a forthcoming copyright infringement lawsuit against one of its students or personnel. The RIAA will request that universities forward those letters to the appropriate network user. Under this new approach, a student (or other network user) can settle the record company claims against him or her at a discounted rate before a lawsuit is ever filed.[1]

According to Fred von Lohmann, senior intellectual property attorney at the Electronic Frontier Foundation:

> The RIAA is essentially asking universities to help them make it easier and cheaper to shake down more students. [Universities] need to ask themselves which side of this historical moment they want to be on—on the side of the four major record labels, or on the side of their students.[2]

Beyond the hyperbole, the music recording industry is a fascinating intersection of culture, technology, law, and economics. Without question, the ways in which music

---

*The views expressed here are those of the author and have not been approved or endorsed by the Federal Communications Commission.
[1]www.riaa.com/news/newsletter/022807.asp. Accessed April 7, 2007.
[2]insidehighered.com/news/2007/03/01/sharing. Accessed April 7, 2007.

is produced, distributed, sold, and consumed have changed substantially since the inception of the industry, just as types of popular music have changed over that time.

This economically small, yet culturally important, industry has been the center of controversy involving (1) alleged price fixing, (2) the widespread use of payola by the major firms in the industry, and (3) alleged copyright infringement by many consumers, in what amounts to a free-for-all over economic rents. The clash between the major firms and their consumers has erupted into legal open warfare. The Federal Trade Commission (FTC) and the courts have found the major firms guilty of overcharging consumers by nearly half a billion dollars in a scheme to artificially maintain high prices, the Federal Communications Commission has fined four major radio broadcast companies over 12 million dollars for complicity in accepting illegal payments from representatives of the major recording labels, and the industry has sued thousands of consumers for alleged copyright infringement.

In this chapter we first explore the history of the industry, with a particular focus on technological change. The focus on technology is helpful because the music recording industry's cost structure has evolved over the past 100 years from high fixed cost/high marginal cost to low fixed cost/low marginal cost. This differentiates the music recording business from other media and culture-based industries that currently have high fixed or first copy costs (e.g., motion pictures) and low marginal costs. In fact, this distinction in fixed cost structure might also suggest very different legal remedies and approaches to property rights and infringement because high upfront costs and uncertain profitability (possibly due to infringement) might actually diminish the flow of certain media and cultural products.

We then explore the structure, conduct, and performance of firms in the industry. As we noted, the industry is dominated by four large vertically integrated international firms and populated by a large number of much smaller, nonintegrated firms. Competition by small firms results from the extremely modest scale of efficient entry in production and digital distribution. Traditional physical distribution channels are dominated by the four large firms. Moreover, the large firms have apparently made extensive use of payola to have their products played on the radio, which is currently the most important mass marketing channel for the products of the industry. The dominance of the radio airwaves by the large firms is an important barrier to entry, which may significantly affect the rate of product innovation and the level of product variety consumers enjoy.

Finally, we explore some public policy issues related to the industry. In particular, we examine unauthorized peer-to-peer file sharing and discuss the implications of file sharing on industry revenues. Perhaps surprisingly, the most recent economic research suggests file sharing does *not* harm the industry—a finding implying that current legal and political approaches to property rights management and enforcement in the industry may be ill-advised and inefficient.

▪▪▪ I. History

The music recording industry is approximately a century old. For the first 50 years of its existence, the industry was largely dominated by a relatively small handful of firms that created and produced most of the industry's technology and consumer products. During this time, however, small independent firms often pioneered the new musical styles that became popular with consumers.

Intense, atomistic competition at the producer level in the industry emerged in the 1950s, in part because of a significant innovation in the technology of supply. During this period, concentration in the industry fell dramatically, and the number of new, small firms increased rapidly. Subsequent re-concentration of the industry, beginning in the 1960s, resulted from numerous mergers and acquisitions. Historical concentration levels in the industry from 1890 to 1988 (measured by the Herfindahl Hirschman Index) are charted in Figure 7-1.

In the industry's infancy (1890 to 1900), three firms—Victor, Columbia, Edison—produced most audio-related products, including playback devices (e.g., wax cylinder and record players) as well as the audio products themselves (e.g., wax cylinders and records). Patents held by these three firms were a substantial barrier to entry. This initial phase of high industry concentration was followed by a period of technological innovation (1900 to 1910) and the expiration of key patents (1914), both of which coincided with the entry of new firms and a modest dispersion of market share.

From a scale perspective, production (recording) and reproduction (manufacture) of the wax cylinders used for music playbacks was relatively costly, as each cylinder had to be individually produced. To make 10 copies of a recording, the performer either had to perform the song 10 times, or 10 recorders had to be recording simultaneously (or some combination of the two). After recording the performance, the recorded cylinders were replaced with new cylinders and the song was performed again. If a mistake were made during the performance, all 10 of the recording devices were stopped, the cylinders discarded and replaced, and the process began anew. Copyrights and scale economies limited the number of competitors and the quantity of new recordings produced. In 1892 for example, the total output of recorded music consisted of approximately 320 minutes. By 1894, that figure reached 1,000 minutes, or approximately 500 two-minute recordings.

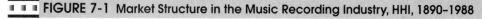

▪ ▪ ▪ **FIGURE 7-1 Market Structure in the Music Recording Industry, HHI, 1890–1988**

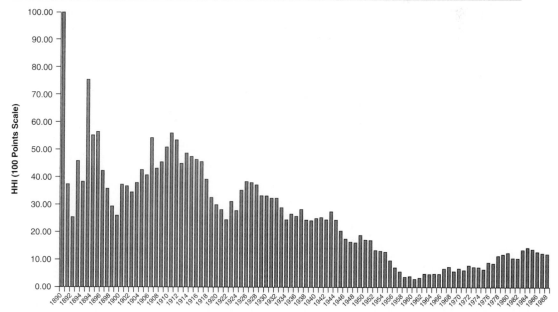

Less costly methods for mass-producing cylinders emerged by 1901. One new manufacturing method employed a pantographic technique in which a master recording was used to make copies by replaying the master as a cutting device for reproducing the same sound vibrations on new cylinders. Each original master could be copied approximately 25 times before it wore out. A session using 10 machines to record a single song could ultimately yield 250 cylinders, a 2,500 percent increase over the original technique. Another more efficient technique for mass producing cylinders used a reverse metal master stamper: Several thousands copies could be made from the original before the stamper wore down and had to be discarded. These techniques greatly reduced the cost of reproducing recorded products.

In the period from 1900 to 1920, the number of firms producing record players and records was increasing. In fact, over the 4-year period between 1914 and 1919, the number of establishments manufacturing phonographs and records grew at an average annual rate of 44 percent (Table 7-1). Unfortunately, these data are aggregated, and include the manufacture of both records and playback devices, and thus obscure the measurement of competition in the production of records at the producer level only. Consequently, these data represent a rough approximation of the extent of new competition in the music recording industry at the producer level.

However, the data may yield some clues. In 1914 and earlier, most manufacture and production was carried out by three large companies with over 1,000 employees each. Since the manufacture of playback devices was in general a large-scale endeavor, it is plausible that some of the new establishments present in 1919, especially those with four or fewer employees (a total of 30), were small independent firms focused on the more small-scale production of prerecorded music or music publishing. If all establishments with 100 or fewer employees are put in this category (no doubt a generous estimate) the total increases to 116.

Interpreted in this fashion, the data imply a relatively robust, if small-scale, competition at the producer level. This competition appears to have stimulated innovation in the products of the industry. Fink (1989) notes that "the expansion of

TABLE 7-1	Number of Establishments Producing Records and Phonographs, 1909–1929	
Year	*Number of Establishments*
1909	18
1914	18
1919	166
1921	154
1923	111
1925	68
1927	60
1929	59

recorded repertoire during the 1920s was significant. The first 'race' records began to appear. The commercial success [of some of these early recordings] was followed by the release of numerous other black recordings" (p. 7). Smaller new companies often pioneered these product innovations. Shaw (1987) observes that the first popular black female singer to be recorded was signed by Black Swan Records, a small independent company, in 1920.[3] Toll (1982) points out that "the innovators did things that were not generally accepted, and sometimes consciously challenged popular trends and tastes" (p.106).

From 1919 to 1925 the number of firms producing record players and/or records declined at an average annual rate of 14.8 percent.[4] While a handful of the independents grew in size and importance, in general the number of independent record companies decreased, in part as a result of mergers: Chapple (1977) finds that by 1929, "most of the smaller companies went out of business or were bought by the larger ones" (p. 92).

From 1930 to 1945, the music recording industry was essentially dormant when measured by industry revenues. This was a residual of the Depression of the 1930s and the hostilities of World War II, since shellac, the prime ingredient for record manufacture at that time, was extremely scarce during the war years.[5] This shortage increased both the cost of manufacturing records and their retail price. With the end of World War II, the shortage of shellac abated.

Perhaps more important for the music recording industry, however, was another innovation in the technology of supply: magnetic tape recorders. The pretape recording technology used for recording music was limiting in two ways: first, it was expensive to purchase, and second, it was "unforgiving" in production. By *unforgiving* we mean that if a mistake were made in the production process, the entire process was stopped, the master disk discarded and replaced by a new master, and the process begun again. According to Gelatt (1954), tape technology radically changed this situation.

> The economic attribute of tape recording transcended all others in its effect on phonographic history. Compared to the old method, tape was enticingly cheap. For an investment of a few thousand dollars one could buy a first-class tape recorder. Between 1949 and 1954 the number of companies in America publishing LP recordings increased from eleven to almost two hundred. (pp. 299–300)

In addition to reducing fixed costs, tape machines also provided an easy way to edit musical performances and thus reduced the marginal costs of recording music. Tape technology made it possible to correct mistakes by rerecording a flawed musical passage and then cutting the tape and replacing the flawed passage with the

---

[3]OKeh Records, a subsidiary of Columbia, followed Black Swan's release with *Crazy Blues*, a record that "sold so spectacularly that every record company quickly set about finding a female blues singer they could sign" (Shaw, p.69).

[4]In part, this may be due to the deepening of the new radio broadcast industry. Despite the obvious complementarities that exist between radio and music today, it is possible that the novelty of radio, its lower price, and its free content have displaced sales in the music industry.

[5]The industry transitioned to vinyl shortly thereafter.

correction. As Sanjek (1983) noted, "Magnetic ribbons were easy to edit, and corrections of flawed performances or misspoken lyrics, impossible on the earlier glass-based master recordings, were easy to make and effectively reduced production costs" (p. 38). Consequently,

> As tape equipment became more affordable, new recording studios sprang up around the nation. Many of the independents acquired tape machines themselves and learned recording techniques. As a result of these developments, the free-wheeling independents were now providing competition that could not be disregarded by Columbia, Decca, RCA Victor, and the new Capitol Label, which prior to 1948 accounted for three-fourths of all record sales. (p. 39)

By 1956, small, new, independent firms accounted for approximately 52 percent of the recording industry's total market share; by 1962, these firms accounted for 75 percent of the industry's total market sales. But in the period after 1962 and continuing to the present, major firms reacquired market share. Horizontal integration explains much of the current structure of the recording industry, as the mid-1960s marked the beginning of a long wave of mergers and a gradual reconsolidation of the field.

The development and refinement of digital production and reproduction in the 1980s embodies the most recent (and quite likely most provocative) technological change in the industry's history. Prior to the 1980s, the production and playback technologies of the music recording industry were analog-based, and music was produced and distributed using vinyl disks and magnetically encoded tape.[6] Compact disks, introduced to consumers in the 1980s, were the first important element in the music industry's shift to digital technology. The transition from analog to digital production and reproduction has had a potentially significant effect on supply-side costs within the industry: With digital products the marginal cost of producing, reproducing, and distributing perfect copies is functionally zero. Thus, unlike the case where the tape player made production cheaper but did not alter the costs of distribution, digital technology has significantly reduced costs throughout the entire process—production, reproduction, and distribution. It is significant to note, however, that to date, these innovations in supply technology have not triggered an expansion of new competition like that which corresponded to the introduction of magnetic tape recording in the 1950s.

▪ ▪ ▪ II. Market Structure

Currently, the music recording industry consists of four large international firms, and thousands of smaller (often single product) independent producers. The four large firms started out as single domestic labels and have acquired many independent labels

---

[6]The primary difference between analog and digital signals is that analog is a continuous form of encoding information, while digital is a discrete form. Thus, for analog technologies, information is encoded in a continuous stream while in digital technologies sound is encoded in discrete bits.

over time. They have grown to dominance via horizontal merger, control over physical distribution networks, and influence over the content of radio airplay.

Concentration

The Big Four—Vivendi Universal, Sony-BMG Corp. (a 50-50 joint venture between Sony and Bertelsmann), Time Warner Inc., and EMI Group—collectively account for approximately 82% of domestic music industry sales.[7] Market shares for these firms for recent years are shown in Table 7-2.

The Four Majors

The Big Four share a number of common features. For example, while firms in the industry have been bought and sold many times, each (excepting Time Warner, which was founded in 1958) can trace a long lineage in the music recording industry dating back to the turn of the twentieth century. In addition, each firm, except EMI, is a part of a much larger media conglomerate, with significant interests in motion pictures, television, cable and book publishing, among others. Finally, each of the four is vertically integrated into music publishing, production, manufacture, and distribution. Notably, with the exception of some mail-order interests and nascent online stores, the four majors do not have a significant retail presence.

Vivendi Universal Music (which ultimately emerged from the merger of two major firms, Polygram and MCA in 1998), is a subsidiary of a large French conglomerate, Vivendi Universal, and is currently the largest music company in terms of market share and recorded music revenues. Its operations encompass the production and distribution of recorded music (Polygram Distribution); the licensing of music copyrights; and music publishing. In fact, with over 1 million titles, Universal Music Group owns the

TABLE 7-2 Domestic Market Share of the Largest Recording Firms (in percent)

Year	Universal	Warner	Bertelsmann	Sony	EMI	HHI	CR
2007	32.3	20.2	—	24.7	10.0	2161	87.2
2006	31.2	19.2	—	26.8	10.1	2162	87.3
2005	31.7	15.0	—	25.6	9.6	1977	81.9
2004	29.6	14.7	15.2	13.3	9.9	1598	82.7
2003	27.5	17.3	13.8	13.9	10.1	1541	82.6
2002	28.9	15.9	14.8	15.7	8.4	1624	83.7
2001	26.4	15.9	14.7	15.6	10.7	1524	83.3
2000	28.0	15.4	19.4	13.5	8.7	1656	85.0
1999	26.4	15.8	16.1	16.3	9.5	1562	84.1

Note: *For the years 1999 to 2004, the CR refers to CR5. The CR data for 2005, after the joint venture of Sony and Bertelsmann (Sony-BMG), refers to CR4; market share for Sony includes Bertelsmann after 2004; 2007 data for first 9 months.*

Source: Nielsen SoundScan, various issues

---

[7]Sony and Bertelsmann joined their respective music operations in a 50-50 joint venture in 2004.

largest catalog of recorded music in the world: In 2002, one out of every four compact disks sold worldwide were Universal products. Some of Vivendi's other media holdings include Universal Studios (motion pictures), USA Networks (television), and Houghton Mifflin (book publishing). Vivendi's labels include A&M Records, Island Records, Universal Motown Records Group, Polygram, Interscope Records, Decca Records, and Def Jam recordings.

Sony BMG is a joint venture which is half-owned by Sony, and half-owned by Bertelsmann. Sony produces, manufactures (Sony Disk), and distributes (Sony Distribution) recorded music, in addition to holding a substantial interest in music publishing (Sony/ATV Music Publishing). Sony became a major presence in the music recording industry when it purchased CBS Records in 1988. Sony, of course, also produces a wide range of well-known consumer electronic products, including the Play Station, compact disk players, and televisions. Some of Sony's other media holdings include Columbia Pictures (motion pictures) and Tri-Star Pictures (motion pictures). Bertelsmann, a German conglomerate, is the second-largest global media conglomerate measured in terms of total revenue. Like Vivendi and Sony, the Bertelsmann music group produces, manufactures, distributes, and publishes recorded music. Bertelsmann's purchase of RCA in 1985 signaled its interest in becoming a major presence in the music industry. Bertelsmann's other media holdings encompass extensive book and magazine publishing interests, including Bantam, Doubleday, Random House, and Knopf. Bertelsmann also controls RTL, a major European television/radio broadcaster and content producer. Some of Sony-BMG's record labels include Arista, Rough Trade Records, Zomba Music Group, Windham Hill Records, Epic Records, and RCA Nashville.

Time Warner, a U.S.-based conglomerate, produces, manufactures (WEA), and distributes (WEA) recorded music, in addition to holding a substantial music publishing interest (Warner/Chappell Music). Warner-Chappell controls the publishing rights to over a million music titles. Time Warner's other significant media holdings include Warner Brothers (motion pictures), WB Network (television), HBO (television), Time Warner Cable (television), Time-Life (magazines), and Warner Books. Some of Time-Warner's record labels include Asylum Records, Atco Records, Atlantic Records, Elektra Records, Reprise Records, Sire Records, and Warner Brothers Records.

EMI, a British corporation, is the least diversified of the four major firms. Like the other four, EMI produces, manufactures, distributes, and publishes recorded music. The EMI group comprises over 100 record labels and is the second largest global publisher of music. Some of EMI's record labels include Blue Note Records, Capitol Records, Chrysalis Records, Caroline Records, Mute Records, and Virgin Records.

The Competitive Fringe

In addition to the four major firms, a host of small, independent labels produce music. During the 1950s and early 1960s, small, innovative companies introduced new products to consumers that became very popular, and these firms grew into formidable competitors. Among these were Mercury, Dot, Cadence, Atlantic, Roulette, Imperial, Chancellor, Cameo, and Vee-Jay. Most of these firms were eventually purchased by the more established, major competitors.

Currently, the collective market share of the fringe group is approximately 15 percent, and includes a vast array of smaller labels and independent artists that typically produce a handful of products each year.[8]

Distribution

The function of record distributors is to make the products of the music recording industry available to retailers who then sell the products to final consumers. Physical distribution has significant scale economies, is characterized by high entry barriers, and is dominated by the four vertically integrated music giants.

In the late 1950s and early 1960s, independent distributors were a significant alternative distribution channel for independent recording firms, as the rise in popularity of the products of new record companies induced new entry on the distributor side as well. However, merger activity in the 1960s and 1970s (and the acquisition of many of the formerly successful independent record companies) reduced the volume of many independent distributors, as the merged firms either internalized this function or used their own existing distribution networks. Since national distribution has significant scale features, independent firms did not have enough volume to compete.

Today, the four major producers are also the four major distributors. Thus, a competing company that wishes to create and sell new products must either independently distribute its product (which we have noted has significant scale features), or sign a "pressing and distribution" deal with one of the major labels, whereby the independent firm contracts with a major label for manufacture and distribution.[9]

Digital distribution has, and will continue to, displace physical distribution in the industry.

> Because the products of the music recording industry are produced using digital sequences, a digital distribution network [will] evolve as computer networks and digital information highways develop and deepen. The costs of distribution should decline dramatically, as physical distribution at a national or international level has significant scale features.[10]

However, industry-organized digital distribution has (at least on the part of the four large firms) lagged until recently, although independent digital distribution has become routine. The potential structural importance of the transition to digital technology is compelling, since digital distribution diminishes a significant barrier to entry.

New, industry-sanctioned, online services such as Apple Computer's "iTunes," which introduced its digital downloading service in 2003, have distributed over 1 billion individual songs to consumers at a price of $.99 each. In part, current industry efforts to put in place a profitable digital distribution network are driven by unsanctioned file sharing (that the industry claims is costing it billions of dollars in profits), as well as consumer demand for the convenience of downloading these products.

---

[8]A useful list of independent labels can be found at en.wikipedia.org/wiki/Category:Independent_record_labels

[9]Alternatively, the firm might distribute their products digitally via the Internet.

[10]Peter J. Alexander, "New Technology and Market Structure: Evidence from the Music Recording Industry," Journal of Cultural Economics 18 (June 1994): 121.

▮▮▮ III. Conduct

Pricing

Pricing in the music recording industry varies with the diversity of media formats such as vinyl records, cassette tapes, digital audio tapes, compact disks, and singles. Prices are generally higher on newly issued music products than on the nearly costless reissue of older music material on new formats (e.g., a product that was initially sold on a vinyl disk reissued on a compact disk). Table 7-3, using data generated by the RIAA, provides some recent nominal price averages, by various media formats.

It is useful to narrow the focus on pricing to compact disks because they currently comprise 85 percent of music sold, making them by far the most important component of the various product formats. Compact disks are a *bundle* of songs, as opposed to *singles*, which are individual songs. Much media content, besides compact disks, comes bundled (e.g., newspapers, news programs, cable and satellite broadcasting packages). As noted in the previous section, Apple's iTunes has sold over 1 billion individual songs; they effectively have unbundled the content, because the distribution platform they employ yields buyer flexibility (i.e., songs can be sold individually, and consumers can purchase any subset of the content they prefer). Consumers may resist bundling when they benefit from a relatively small subset of the content that is bundled. Thus, sales of compact disks may be sensitive to a desire on the part of consumers to avoid purchasing content from which they derive little or no pleasure.

In Table 7-4, the pricing analysis from Table 7-3 is extended by converting prices for compact disks from nominal to real values. Using these data, along with unit sales, the price elasticity of demand can be approximated. The average price elasticity of demand over the period from 1993 to 2005 is 3.8, which indicates that the demand for compact disks is highly elastic.

It is important to note that a wide range of prices exists depending on the product and the retailer. While the major record companies suggest list prices for their products, discounting is widespread, which makes discussion of list prices a tenuous

TABLE 7-3 Average (Nominal) Prices of Recorded Music by Format

Year	Vinyl Singles	LPs	CDs	Cassettes	Cassette Singles	CD Singles	Music Videos	DVDs
1997	$4.75	$12.33	$13.17	$8.82	$3.16	$4.09	$17.41	—
1998	4.76	10.00	13.48	8.96	3.58	3.81	18.68	—
1999	5.26	10.97	13.65	8.59	3.38	3.98	19.03	—
2000	5.48	12.59	14.02	8.24	3.54	4.17	15.49	$22.00
2001	5.71	11.91	14.64	8.08	—	4.59	18.60	20.00
2002	5.66	12.06	14.99	6.77	—	4.36	19.62	21.25
2003	5.66	14.47	15.06	6.32	—	4.34	20.11	21.12
2004	5.69	14.18	14.92	4.56	—	4.83	18.51	19.34
2005	5.74	13.92	14.91	5.24	—	3.89	17.82	19.41

Veronis Suhler Stevenson Bank, "Communications Industry Forecast and Report," various years.

TABLE 7-4 Real Compact Disk Prices and Quantity

Year	Average Price* (Real)	Quantity** (Units Shipped)
1993	$9.09	495.4
1994	8.62	662.1
1995	8.51	722.9
1996	8.13	778.9
1997	8.20	753.1
1998	8.27	847.0
1999	8.19	938.9
2000	8.14	942.5
2001	8.27	881.9
2002	8.33	803.3
2003	8.20	746.0
2004	7.87	767.0
2005	7.67	705.4
2006	7.39	614.9

*1982–1984 = 100; **In millions

Recording Industry Association of America, *Year-end Statistics*, various years.

endeavor at best.[11] In particular, electronics firms and nonspecialized chain stores, including Wal-Mart, have been among the biggest price discounters. In the mid-1990s, aggressive discounting by some of these nonspecialized retailers put significant financial pressure on some of the largest specialty music stores, and it appears that the major recording firms responded by trying lessen this price competition in order to raise prices and preserve distribution profit margins.

According to the FTC, the majors threatened to withdraw cooperative advertising expenditures from retailers if the retailer advertised a discounted price, even if the retailer used its own advertising funds for such advertisements. The FTC further held that this action stabilized retail prices at artificially high prices and eliminated price competition in the retail marketplace over the period from 1995 to 2000. Given that demand in the industry appears to be quite elastic, some of the decline in sales recently experienced by the industry may well be due to prices that were fixed at artificially high levels.

In the summer of 2003, Universal Music Group, the largest music company measured by market share, stunned the industry by announcing dramatic cuts of 24 percent in its wholesale prices. According to industry reports, UMG hoped these reductions would be passed along by retailers to consumers, and, assuming the standard inverse relationship between price and quantity demanded holds, that this would generate

---

[11]Typically, however, new compact disk releases are priced much higher than reissued older material.

greater demand and revenues for its products.[12] Others may have been compelled to follow suit because as Table 7-4 indicates, CD prices fell between 2003 and 2005.

Nonprice Rivalry and the Payola Issue

"When you hear a song played on the radio," the RIAA says, "that didn't just happen."[13] Unlike most produced goods, a prerecorded audio product's characteristics are not readily apparent to the consumer; that is, buyers in record stores cannot discern and evaluate a prerecorded audio product's attributes by touch, visual inspection, or any of the other means commonly used to evaluate products. Instead, a prerecorded audio product must be heard to be evaluated, and audio presentation is a prerequisite for the vast majority of purchases. Consequently, radio airplay tends to be one of the most important means for informing consumers of the existence and nature of new products.[14]

Some influence over the content of radio airplay results from "payola" expenditures.[15] Typically, payola involves firms or their representatives making payments to radio disc jockeys or station managers in return for airplay of the firm's products. According to Coase (1979), payola has been used routinely in the industry, frequently by new entrants attempting to gain market share. Coase concludes that in the 1950s,

> there can be no doubt that the new companies . . . relied on payola to obtain "exposure" for their records. These companies lacked the name-stars and the strong marketing organization of the major companies, and payola enabled them to expand their sales by making similar efforts in other markets. (pps. 315–316)

However, as a result of criminal prosecutions, congressional investigations, and increased penalties for engaging in providing payola, by the late 1970s payola appears to have become a significant barrier for small firms. By that time, Dannen (1990) suggests that the large firms used payola to obtain radio airplay and exclude small firms from obtaining airplay.

> The record companies understood on some level that if radio airplay were not free, it would mean a major competitive advantage. The big companies had budgets sufficient to outbid the small labels for airplay. After 1978, records put out by small labels began to vanish from the Top 40 airwaves. (pps.14, 15)

Table 7-5 lists the number of firms in the industry with only a single hit record over the period from 1976 to 1985. These data do not appear to contradict Dannen's assertion. According to Dannen, the large firms could outbid the small firms for airplay. Note that a radio station has a finite amount of airtime in any broadcast day, a fraction

---

[12]The stock price of EMI fell more than 10 percent on the day Universal announced the price cut, apparently on fears that the move by Universal signaled a possible price war in the industry. EMI's stock price is probably the best benchmark for estimating the effects of price cuts because of the big four companies EMI is, by far, the least diversified and most reliant on sales of recorded music.

[13]www.riaa.com/news/marketingdata/cost.asp. Accessed April 18, 2007.

[14]Online file sharing networks largely achieve the same end, although the means are different.

[15]Payola (supposedly a contraction of the words *payoff* and *Victrola*) refers to the practice of making illegal payments to radio stations in return for radio airplay. It is not illegal to pay for airplay, per se. It is, however, illegal to take payments for airplay and not reveal that the airtime had been paid for or sponsored.

TABLE 7-5 Number of Firms With One Hit Record

Year	Number of One-Hit Firms
1976	20
1977	21
1978	14
1979	15
1980	7
1981	9
1982	6
1983	7
1984	4
1985	4

Source: Peter J. Alexander, "New Technology and Market Structure: Evidence from the Music Recording Industry," Journal of Cultural Economics 18 (June 1994): 117.

of which is used for revenue generating advertising, while the remainder is used to attract customers for advertisers. Assuming that the station operator is indifferent between various musical inputs, the firm willing to pay the most for airtime, *ceteris paribus*, will purchase the airtime and presumably gain a competitive advantage with consumers.

Implicit in Dannen's argument is the idea that, in the 1970s, the major firms in the music recording industry recognized they might use payola as a barrier and instrument for raising rivals' costs, the rivals being small fringe firms or new entrants. Interestingly, Dannen notes that contact between the major firms and radio stations during the late 1970s had become indirect. The major labels could not allow their staff people to make payments to radio stations, given the increased penalties prescribed by the new Racketeer Influenced and Corrupt Organizations (RICO) statute. Instead, a small group of independent promoters, who referred to themselves as the "Network," were paid to represent the major firms' interests directly to radio station operators. According to Dannen,

> The term "Network" referred to the tendency of the promoters to work as a loosely knit team. Each member had a "territory," a group of stations over which he claimed influence. If a record company wanted national airplay for a new single, it could choose to hire one of the Network men, who would in turn subcontract the job to other members of the alliance. (pps. 11, 14)

Sidak and Kronemyer (1987) suggest that the rise of this Network enabled the major labels to exercise "precautionary ignorance":

> During the mid-1980s, a record company would retain independent promoters under contracts with incomplete and unspecified terms that reflected the record company's need to minimize its knowledge of the promoters' activities. The record company also might avoid inquiring whether the independent

promoter uses payola in conducting his business, and particularly whether he intends to use payola to promote the record for which the record company has retained him.

Given a higher penalty and assuming the probability of being detected making illegal payments did not fall, the expected cost of engaging in payola increased. In effect, contracting out promotion became the more efficient option given the change in the legal environment.

In sum, the amount of available airtime at any given radio station is extremely limited and expensive. Industry reports suggest that the number of new "adds" (i.e., songs added to the station's playlist) at major radio stations on a weekly basis is typically in the lower single digits. So, it is quite possible that relative scarcity of radio airtime, in conjunction with a lower per-unit cost of payola for the major firms, tends to foreclose radio access for smaller firms.[16] According to the *Wall Street Journal* (June 10, 2002), "To compete for a limited number of open slots on pop radio, labels say they typically pay independent promoters from $200,000 to $300,000 per song, and occasionally more than $1 million. These costs have escalated as the radio industry has consolidated, music companies say."

Several new developments in the music and radio industry might ameliorate or exacerbate this situation.

First, the Federal Communications Commission (FCC), the agency that regulates broadcasting, may issue a number of new low-power radio licenses. This increase in the supply of radio airtime may provide significant opportunities for small firms and new entrants in the music industry, as well as others. But these stations will likely be very low power and hence highly local, and thus the reach of any station will be very modest.

Second, "webcasting" or Internet radio, might become a more significant means of broadcasting music, which opens the possibility of a greater supply of airplay as well. However, some significant legal and political wrangling has recently occurred about the price per song webcasters must pay for using the products of the music recording industry in their webcasts,[17] and in the spring of 2007, the Copyright Royalty Board (CRB) dramatically raised Internet radio royalty rates.

Third, the structure of the radio industry itself has undergone a significant transformation, with concentration in the industry rapidly increasing in recent years. Moreover, the largest single radio station owner in the country, Clear Channel Communications with 1,233 stations owned nationwide (claiming over 26 percent of industry revenue), has entered the music promotion field. The increase in radio concentration and Clear Channel's move into promotion will be interesting developments to follow, as both may have significant implications for the music recording industry.

---

[16]This still leaves the question of why small firms couldn't simply pay more than the larger firms and obtain broadcast services. An explanation for this may be that, at the margin, it simply is not profitable for small firms to pay more than the price being paid by the large firms (i.e., the large firms are paying the monopoly price).

[17]On August 27, 2003, the Webcasters Alliance, a group with about 400 online music broadcasters, sued the recording industry in federal court, alleging that the major labels have unlawfully inflated webcasting royalty rates in an attempt to keep independent operators out of the market.

▪▪▪ IV. Performance

The concentrated, vertically integrated structure of recording has important consequences for industry profits, as well as for the quantity and types of products offered to
consumers.

Profitability

According to the RIAA, revenues in the industry have been falling for the past several
years, which the RIAA blames on unauthorized file sharing. But to calculate industry
profits, we also would need to know industry costs, and these data are not available. It
is entirely possible that industry revenues could decrease overall while industry profits
increase. In addition, data concerning the number of new releases in the industry are
not available. These data are important because aggregate annual revenues fall, all
other things being equal, if the number of new releases falls. Thus, we cannot determine
whether the reduction in industry revenue is induced, at least in part, by a reduction in
the number of new releases by the industry.

Product Diversity

Among the important performance values of a culture-based industry is product diversity. While production costs clearly place a constraint on the supply side of the market,
greater product diversity, all things being equal, is unambiguously welfare enhancing
for consumers because consumers can obtain products closer to their preferences.
Thus, an important related performance question is which type of market structure
(i.e., monopoly, oligopoly, or competition) best promotes product diversity?

Studies that simply count the number of hit songs and then relate them to market
structure have been employed to study this question. These studies, which are largely
impressionistic, suggest a negative linear link between structure and diversity: the
more atomistic the structure, the greater the diversity, and the more concentrated the
structure, the less the diversity.[18] In short, these studies suggest that competition is beneficial to diversity, and monopoly is detrimental.

On the other hand, research employing actual musical characteristics of hit songs,
rather than simply counting the number of songs, suggests that a moderately concentrated market structure may better promote actual diversity than either an atomistic or
a monopoly structure.[19] This analysis suggests that an atomistic market structure may
be characterized by a relatively high level of "me too" business, (i.e., excessive product
duplication). Thus, while a competitive structure may correlate with product innovation, it may not best promote product diversity. Importantly, this research also contra-
dicts the hypothesis that a monopoly market structure promotes maximum diversity.

---

[18]For example, see Bruce Anderson, Peter Hesbacher, K. Peter Etzkorn, and R. Serge Denisoff, "Hit
Record Trends, 1940–1977," *Journal of Communications* 30 (1980): 31–43; Richard Peterson and David
Berger, "Cycles in Symbol Reproduction: The Case of Popular Music," *American Sociological Review*
40(1975):158–73; and Eric Rothenbuhler and John Dimmick, "Popular Music: Concentration and Diversity
in the Industry, 1974–1980," *Journal of Communications* 32 (1982):143–49.
[19]Peter J. Alexander, "Product Variety and Market Structure: A New Measure and a Simple Test," *Journal
of Economic Behavior and Organization* 32 (1997): 207–214.

▪▪▪ V. Public Policy

Antitrust Policy

In 2000, the FTC charged that the four major recording companies "engaged in acts and practices that have unreasonably restrained competition in the market for prerecorded music in the United States through their adoption, implementation and enforcement of Minimum Advertised Price ('MAP') provisions of their Cooperative Advertising Programs."[20] The FTC found that the four major distributors punished retailers for lowering prices to consumers, and that as a result, consumers paid almost half a billion dollars in artificially inflated prices between 1998 and 2000. According to a joint statement issued by all four FTC Commissioners, the

> Commission has unanimously found reason to believe that the arrangements entered into by the four largest distributors of prerecorded music violate the antitrust laws in two respects. First, when considered together, the arrangements constitute practices that facilitate horizontal collusion among distributors, in violation of Section 5 of the Federal Trade Commission Act. Second, when viewed individually, each distributor's arrangement constitutes an unreasonable vertical restraint of trade under the rule of reason.[21]

The economic analysis offered by the FTC warrants quoting at length:

> The MAP (minimum advertised price) provisions were implemented with the anticompetitive intent to limit retail price competition and to stabilize the retail prices in the industry. Prior to the adoption of these policies, new retail entrants, especially consumer electronic chains, had sparked a retail "price war" that had resulted in significantly lower compact discs prices to consumers and lower margins for retailers.
>
> The complaints allege that the distributors were concerned that declining retail prices could cause a reduction in wholesale prices. Through these stricter MAP programs, the distributors hoped to stop retail competition, take pressure off their own margins, and eventually increase their own prices. The distributors' actions were effective. Retail prices were stabilized by these MAP programs. Thereafter, each distributor raised its wholesale prices.
>
> While some vertical restraints can benefit consumers (known as "efficiencies") by enhancing interbrand competition and expanding market output, plausible efficiency justifications are absent in this case.[22]

The Big Four denied the FTC's charges, but agreed in 2003 to settle without a trial and to refund $143 million in over-charges to customers.

More recently, in 2007, the Federal Communications Commission announced a preliminary framework for a consent decree involving four of the largest radio chain

---

[20]Federal Trade Commission, "Analysis to Aid Public Comment on the Proposed Consent Order," www.ftc.gov/os/2000/05/mapanalysis.htm

[21]Federal Trade Commission, "Record Companies Settle FTC Charges of Restraining Competition in CD Music Market," www.ftc.gov/opa/2000/05/cdpres.htm

[22]Federal Trade Commission, "Analysis to Aid Public Comment on the Proposed Consent Order," www.ftc.gov/os/2000/05/mapanalysis.htm

operators in the country.[23] Clear Channel Communications, CBS Radio, Entercom Communications, and Citadel Broadcasting have agreed to pay $12.5 million in fines for violating federal antipayola statutes. Specifically, the FCC found these major radio networks to have been taking money (or money equivalents) to play songs issued under the major recording firms' labels.

In addition to the fines, the four radio groups have agreed to dedicate 8,400 half-hour segments of airtime for independent record labels and local artists, although it is yet to be seen when these segments will take place during the broadcast day. While the FCC can only fine its licensees, the Department of Justice could bring criminal charges against the radio operators and the four large record companies, although this may be unlikely.

Digital File Sharing

The music recording industry is at the center of an explosive debate about digital file sharing, a debate that in some ways has shaped and is shaping the regulation of the internet. The music industry's trade association, the RIAA, asserts that digital file sharing is diminishing industry profits to the tune of billions of dollars of losses, and has issued pre-litigation letters and subpoenas to thousands of alleged music "pirates."[24]

The music industry has been very successful in its legal challenges against file-sharing firms such as Napster and MP3.com, but, until recently, unsuccessful in its attempts to copy protect its products or thwart peer-to-peer file sharing networks. The industry's frustration was evidenced by Senator Orrin Hatch (a major supporter of the industry and amateur singer), who suggested destroying users' machines if they refused to stop sharing files.[25]

While the music industry contemplated similar tactics, the industry's current strategy for reducing unauthorized file sharing appears to consist of three related tactics: (1) individualized legal actions (e.g., multitudes of threatening letters, subpoenas, and lawsuits) to increase the perceived cost to users of peer-to-peer networks; (2) price cuts; and (3) increased online digital distribution by industry-sanctioned distributors (e.g., Apple Computer's iTunes). Roughly, this works out to two carrots and one stick: It appears the industry is attempting to staunch unsanctioned sharing and increase legal purchases, while transitioning to large-scale digital distribution.

Technical Background

Given that a compact disk player uses a sequence of 0s and 1s to reproduce sound waves, consumers are able to use computers to play compact disks, as well as transfer songs (rip) from compact disks for storage and replay them on their computers. These

---

[23]Federal Communications Commission, Consent Decree, Adopted March 21, 2007, hraunfoss.fcc.gov/edocs_public/attachmatch/FCC-07-29A1.pdf
[24]In general, copyright law is designed to protect copyright holders from substantial unauthorized use of copy-protected objects. This legal protection, and the resulting capacity on the part of the copyright holder to exploit the benefits of innovation, is thought to provide appropriate incentives to create.
[25]It is interesting to note that Senator Hatch's suggested approach may violate 18 U.S.C.1030(a)(5), which prohibits knowingly causing "the transmission of a program, information, code, or command, and as a result of such conduct intentionally causing damage without authorization, to a protected computer," where damage is defined as "any impairment to the integrity or availability of data, a program, a system, or information."

types of files were, until recently, generally not shared with large numbers of other users, since, as late as 1997, the transfer of 3 minutes of music required 50 megabytes of hard-drive storage space and an enormous amount of time and bandwidth to move them across the Internet.

However, the development of the MP3 file format dramatically changed these storage and bandwidth requirements. MP3, created by engineers at the German company Fraunhofer Gesellshaft, is shorthand for Motion Picture Experts Group-Layer 3. It is an audio compression format that generates near compact disk–quality sound at approximately one-tenth to one-twentieth the size. For example, while each minute of music on a compact disk requires the equivalent of 10 megabytes of computer storage space, an MP3 format of the same piece could be stored on 1 megabyte or less. To give a practical example of the compression savings, consider that Elvis Presley's *Hound Dog* on compact disk requires 24 megabytes of hard disk space, but when converted to MP3 the storage requirement plunges to just 2 megabytes. On a 28.8-kilobit-per-second modem, the compact disk version of *Hound Dog* would take at least 1.5 hours to download from another computer; if the file were first converted to MP3, it would take approximately 8.5 minutes.

Clearly, MP3 technology has made digital file distribution more efficient. This increased efficiency is reinforced by the fact that more and more computers are connecting to the Internet via cable and fiber rather than modem, which significantly improves the speed at which files can be transferred.

Early Legal Action Against Central Servers

The music industry initially responded to nascent large-scale organized digital file sharing by taking legal action against the most prominent and sizable digital file distributors, MP3.com and Napster.com. These firms claimed protection citing "fair use" and "safe harbor," respectively.

However, in *UMG Recording, Inc. et. al. v. MP3.com*, Judge Jed S. Rakoff concluded that "defendant's infringement of plaintiffs' copyrights is clear" (92 F. Supp. 2d 349 [2000]). During the trial, MP3.com argued that its repository of legally purchased copyrighted material, which it distributed to registered users, was protected by "fair use." Judge Rakoff concluded that the "defendant's 'fair use' defense is indefensible and must be denied as a matter of law" (92 F. Supp. 2d 349 [2000]).

Moreover, in the Napster.com case, U.S. District Judge Marilyn Hall Patel refused a motion by Napster.com to dismiss the lawsuit against them, ruling that Napster.com was not entitled to "safe harbor" status as provided in the Digital Millennium Copyright Act (DMCA) of 1998. The safe harbor provisions of the DMCA were established to protect Internet service providers from liability and court-issued injunctions regardless of their knowledge, in the event that users of the service committed illegal actions. Judge Patel subsequently issued a preliminary injunction against Napster.com, ordering them to stop distributing copyrighted materials.

Note that MP3.com and Napster.com share common features, the most important of which may be that as distribution systems they rely on a series of central servers to guide the distribution of digital products. So, for example, if a user of either system sends out a request for a file, the request is routed through one of the firms' servers. Because requests for information relating to the location of MP3 files are routed through their servers, and because a federal judge has held such activity to violate existing copyright law, companies like MP3.com and Napster.com were obvious targets for legal remedy.

Peer-to-Peer File-Sharing Networks

The architecture of distribution systems such as MP3.com and Napster.com is organized around a series of centralized servers that direct electronic traffic and rout requests for files. In contrast, peer-to-peer file sharing systems like BitTorrent, Emule/Donkey, Gnutella, Tor, and Freenet are decentralized and do not use a central server. Rather, each individual computer that has the peer-to-peer software installed on it can become a server via a series of peer-to-peer connections. So if one machine has the required software and Internet connection, it can connect with another similar machine, which itself is connected to another similar machine, and so on.

The music industry's initial response to this kind of file sharing was to attempt to copy protect its products (including Sony's use of rootkits). Despite many efforts, however, these efforts have largely failed.[26] The industry's current response to peer-to-peer file sharing is to track down individuals who share files online, and issue pre-litigation letters and subpoenas to these users for alleged damages.

The RIAA tracks file sharing by hiring computer consulting firms who, in essence, monitor peer-to-peer networks for copy-protected works. These firms report the IP (Internet Protocol) address of the alleged infringing user to the RIAA. The RIAA then issues a subpoena to the user's ISP (Internet Service Provider), requesting that the ISP reveal the name and address of the alleged infringing user. The RIAA then uses this information to issue pre-litigation letters or subpoenas.

The consulting firms hired by the RIAA may try to lure peer users by putting out "honey pots," lists of files (e.g., popular songs) designed to entice requests from individuals, which then allow the firm to monitor the types of files shared by the user. The RIAA and their consulting firms also use a variety of other means to thwart peer networks, such as intentionally introducing malformed files (packets) into the network. Usually, however, the peer network is robust to such challenges. One effective counter-technique becoming common in peer networks is the use of *blocklists* (analogous to blacklists), which filter out IP addresses known to be used by the RIAA or their consultants to track users. In addition, peer software that employs encryption and proxy service (e.g., Tor, Mute, Waste) is becoming more common and user friendly. While not providing complete privacy (and generally operating at slower speeds), the architecture of this software is such that tracking online file sharing will become much more difficult and expensive, while peer users obtain greater levels of privacy.[27]

---

[26]In fact, in April, 2007, EMI announced that it would be selling its music online, without copy protection. This means that EMI's music will be playable on a variety of different devices, and not a single proprietary format, such as Apple's iPod. Whether the other major firms follow EMI's approach remains to be seen.
[27]Services that provide complete anonymity for users (e.g., Relakks) may also become more popular. These servers establish an encrypted connection between the server and user. The user sends the server an encrypted request for a file. The server seeks out and obtains the file, and transfers it, encrypted, to the user. Similar services have been available for some time, but ultimately, because the server must make a public request for a file, the file can be traced back to the server. Then, a subpoena can be issued requesting the IP address of the user who requested the file. However, if the server is located in a country that does not compel the ISP to keep records of users' IP addresses, or if the subpoena can only be issued for criminal and not civil offenses, these services may offer a high level of protection for the user.

Evidence and Estimates of Damages.

How economically damaging is digital file sharing activity to the music recording industry? A lot? A little? None at all? Until quite recently, all three of these answers appear plausible, given the paucity of evidence. The RIAA asked the court to enjoin Napster.com because "Napster is causing irreparable harm to plaintiffs and the entire music industry" and put the costs of piracy in the billions of dollars. Intuitively, it seems plausible that file sharing may displace some sales. However, the issue is subtle, and the margin for error potentially great. It is worth noting that, despite the industry's legal victory against MP3.com, Judge Rakoff, in establishing damages in the case, noted that "[P]laintiffs have not made any attempt at this trial to prove actual damages they may have suffered. The court views the absence of any proof of actual damages as a mitigating factor favorable to the defendant." (U.S. Dist. LEXIS 13293, CCH p28, 141 [September 6, 2000])

A recent study by two economists appears to have shed substantial light on the issue of potential damages. Felix Oberholzer-Gee and Koleman Strumpf, in what is likely the best empirical estimate given to date, find that file sharing has no significant negative effect on the sale of compact disks, and that most individuals who share files would not have purchased the music they downloaded. In fact, the authors find that peer-to-peer file sharing increases the sales of the most popular compact disks, and that every 150 peer-to-peer downloads of the most popular music increases compact disk sales by one unit. These results imply that current efforts by the RIAA to thwart file sharing may constitute a waste of social resources.

CONCLUSION ▪▪▪▪▪▪▪

The history of the music recording industry is one in which new technology has sparked entry, and many of these new entrants have been product innovators. However, as we noted, maximum product diversity (as distinct from product innovation) in the music industry may well be achieved when the four-firm concentration ratio is approximately 50 percent—not too high and not too low. Because radio airplay is a significant factor in exposing consumers to the industry's offerings, the structure and conduct of the radio industry is an additional important element conditioning structure, conduct, and performance in the music recording field. Payola has likely been an important impediment to new competition, especially considering the extraordinary reduction in technical scale economies that have been realized.

Perhaps most peculiarly, the costs of production, reproduction, and distribution in the industry are close to zero (from a physical standpoint), yet the industry structure in which four firms dominate the field has been essentially unchanged since the mid-1980s. One implication of this structure is that firms are able to more easily coordinate and carry out anticompetitive activities, such as price-fixing. Prices that are held artificially high generate social welfare losses (in the absence of perfect price discrimination), and may have accelerated and amplified the use of file sharing networks by consumers. The use of file sharing networks, and the subsequent litigation that has resulted from their use, may also induce welfare losses, and will likely influence public policy toward the internet in ways that may be unforeseen and undesirable.

SUGGESTIONS FOR FURTHER READING ▪▪▪▪▪▪▪

Journal Articles

Alexander, Peter, J. 2002. Peer-to-Peer File Sharing: The Case of the Music Recording Industry, *Review of Industrial Organization* 20: 151–161.[March]

Alexander, Peter J. 1997. "Product Variety and Market Structure: A New Measure and a Simple Test. *Journal of Economic Behavior and Organization* 32: 207–214. [February]

Black, M. and Greer, D. 1987. "Concentration and Non-Price Competition in the Recording Industry." *Review of Industrial Organization* 3: 13–37.

Coase, R. 1979. "Payola in Radio and Television Broadcasting." *The Journal of Law and Economics* 22: 269–328. [October]

Cunningham, Brendan M.; Peter J. Alexander, and Nodir Adilov. 2004. "Peer-to-Peer File Sharing Communities." *Information Economics and Policy* 16: 197–213. [June]

Oberholzer-Gee, Felix and Koleman Strumpf. 2007) "The Effect of File Sharing on Record Sales: An Empirical Analysis." *Journal of Political Economy* 115:1–42.

Peterson, R.A. and D.G. Berger. 1975. "Cycles in Symbol Production: The Case of Popular Music." *American Sociological Review* 40:158–173. [April]

Rothenbuhler, Eric and John Dimmick. 1982. "Popular Music: Concentration and Diversity in the Industry, 1974–1980." *Journal of Communications* 32:143–49.[Winter]

Sanjek, David. 1998. "Popular Music and the Synergy of Corporate Culture." In *Mapping the Beat: Popular Music and Contemporary Theory*. Thomas Swiss, John Sloop and Andrew Herman, (eds.). Malden, MA: Basil Blackwell.

Sidak J.G. and D. E. Kronemyer. 1987. "The 'New Payola' and the American Record Industry: Transactions Costs and Precautionary Ignorance in Contracts for Illegal Services." *Harvard Journal of Law and Public Policy* 10: 521–572.

Books

Burnett, R. 1996. *The Global Jukebox: The International Music Industry*. London: Routledge.

Cleveland, B. (ed.), 1999. *The Recording Industry Sourcebook*, 11th Edition. Emeryville, CA: Primedia Information Inc.

Chapple, S. and R. Garofulo. 1977. *Rock 'n' Roll is Here to Pay: The History and Politics of the Music Industry*. Chicago: Nelson-Hall.

Dannen, F. 1990. *Hit Men: Power Brokers and Fast Money Inside the Music Business*. New York: Times Books.

Lessig, L. 2002. *The Future of Ideas.* New York: Random House, Inc.

Fink, M. 1989. *Inside the Music Business*. New York: Schirmer Books.

Frith, S. and A. Goodwin, eds. 1990. *On Record.* New York: Pantheon Books.

Gelatt, R. 1977. *Fabulous Phonograph*. New York, Appleton-Century.

Sanjek, R. 1983. *From Print to Plastic: Publishing and Promoting America's Popular Music (1900–1980)*. Brooklyn, NY: Institute for Studies in American Music.

Taylor, Timothy D. 1997. *Global Pop*. New York: Routledge.

Toll, R. 1982. *The Entertainment Machine*. Oxford: Oxford University Press.

Industry Trade Publications and Other Resources

Billboard Magazine
Billboard Rock Monitor
Gavin Report
Music Yellow Pages
Radio and Records
Recording Industry Association of America
Variety

Links to Congressional Hearings, Court Decisions, and Related Resources

Federal Trade Commission Report, "Marketing Violent Entertainment to Children": www.ftc.gov/reports/violence/vioreport.pdf

Federal Trade Commission Press Release: "Record Companies Settle FTC Charges of Restraining Competition in CD Music

Market." Follow link on page to additional resources relating to the case: www.ftc.gov/opa/2000/05/cdpres.htm

Information Web site for the FTC/Music Industry Antitrust Litigation Settlement. Follow the various links on the page: www.musiccdsettlement.com/english/default.htm

Media Access Project—A nonprofit public interest law firm with a large number of useful links to media resources: www.mediaaccess.org/web/

Public Knowledge—general links to information relating to media, technology, and information: www.publicknowledge.org/

U.S. Representative Cannon introduces the Music Online Competition Act. Useful related links on page: www.house.gov/cannon/press2001/aug03.htm

8

The Telecommunications Industry

JAMES MCCONNAUGHEY[1]

At the dawn of the twenty-first century, telecommunications could lay reasonable claim as the most important U.S. sector. As one Federal Communications Committee (FCC) official recently testified, "Communications industries comprise one-sixth of our economy—and when you consider their social, cultural and political dimensions, there is no doubt in my mind that communications is the most formidable and influential enterprise in all the land."[2] Wireless, Internet Protocol (IP), and fiber technologies are feeding Americans' voracious demand for high-speed Internet—"broadband"—services. Globally, no other sovereign country has a telecom sector whose size exceeds that of the $923 billion market generated in the United States.[3]

Within the sector, bandwidth occupies a role of critical importance. Bandwidth measures communications carrying capacity to deliver voice, data, video, and text to the end user. Most basically, the United States finds itself in the throes of a bandwidth crosscurrent fueled by disruptive technologies. In one market, bandwidth is so plentiful that a capacity glut has led to a precipitous drop in transmission prices. In another market, a traditional bandwidth shortage persists though technological eddies and alternative

---

[1]The views expressed in this chapter are those of the author and do not necessarily represent the views of the Commerce Department. This writing has benefited immensely from the insights of my former collaborator, Manley R. Irwin, Emeritus Professor of Economics at the University of New Hampshire's Whittemore School of Business and student *extraordinaire* of the late Walter Adams.

[2]Testimony of FCC Commissioner Michael J. Copps, before the U.S. House Committee on Energy and Commerce, Subcommittee on Telecommunications and the Internet, Hearing on Oversight of the Federal Communications Commission, March 14, 2007.

[3]Telecommunications Industry Association, "TIA Report: Broadband Demand Drives Highest Telecom Industry Growth," Press Release, January 25, 2007. The European Union, a grouping of that continent's countries, boasts an estimated $1 trillion sector.

supply increasingly swirl nearby. The first market is the U.S. long-distance market; the second is the U.S. local telephone market.

The characteristics of each market differ markedly. The long-distance market is relatively open, invites market entry, and resides in an environment of de facto deregulation. Innovation in long-distance facilities and bandwidth proceeds at a furious pace. The local telephone market, by contrast, is still dominated by firms that are enjoying monopolist status. Historically, rivalry in this market has been at best stunted, entry has been episodic, and government regulation has stood as an institutional reality. The local exchange market of today still rests upon more than 100 million lines of the venerable twisted copper wire—the majority of all such "local loops"—that connect telephone central office switches to a customer's home or office. But the riptides of change are emerging.

It is the local telephone market—the copper wire pair—that has stood as a bandwidth bottleneck for over a century, and it is local telecommunications that has invited the attention of Congress, regulatory agencies, and Internet users. That the local telecom arena is now a top policy priority is illustrated by the following questions: How can the United States promote competition in a market that is concentrated? How can public policy modernize telephone investment to accommodate an apparently insatiable demand for information bandwidth? Which industry should be allowed to compete in local telephony: Line resellers? Equipment suppliers? Long-distance carriers? Cable television firms? Wireless operators? Electric power companies? Suppliers of aerospace hardware? Internet service providers?

Is the current clamor for alternatives to the copper wire based on a technological imperative, or does local telephony constitute the essence of a natural monopoly? If so, does local telephony call for more rather than less regulatory oversight? If the former, which government agency should exercise that oversight: a city, a county, a state, or the federal government? How can the public resolve an inevitable jurisdictional clash between state and federal agencies?

In the final analysis, bandwidth capacity is not merely a question of more or less, but rather it is an issue of economic incentives. Which institutional setting best delivers future electronic goods and services to the firm and consumer: a competitive market, a regulated market, or admixtures of both? Whatever choice is selected, that policy option will decisively configure a twenty-first century online economy.

▪ ▪ ▪ I. History

Telecommunications over the past 130 years has traversed four somewhat loosely defined stages: monopoly (1876–1894); competition/regulation (1894–1920), monopoly/regulation/antitrust (1920–1956), and antitrust/divestiture/deregulation (1956–present).

Monopoly

Consider the first stage—monopoly (1876–1894). The filing of two telephone patents on the same day of the same year presents an event that is unique in economic history.[4]

---

[4]The situation may be even more remarkable than we thought. Recent reports state that a German science teacher may have invented a crude but working "telephon" some 13 years before Dr. Bell in 1863. "Telephone's Real Inventor in Doubt," *Discovery News* (December 9, 2003). dsc.discovery.com/news/briefs/2003208/bell_print.html. Accessed May 7, 2004.

Suffice it to say that Alexander Graham Bell's patent prevailed over Elisha Gray's filing. The Boston Bell Patent Association, now in possession of a valuable property right, offered to sell the patent to the largest communication firm in the country, the Western Union Telegraph Company. Western Union management rejected the offer on the grounds that the $100,000 asking price was exorbitant. Today's students of corporate history generally agree that the Western Union Telegraph Company committed a commercial blunder of the first order.

To generate a return on its investment, the Boston Bell Patent Association was forced to offer telephone service to the public. Service commenced in Boston, Massachusetts, and the association assigned franchises in separate, exclusive geographic markets—especially heavily populated cities. In 1878, the Boston Bell Patent Association hired a young manager from the United States Postal Service, Theodore Vail, who took a 50 percent cut in salary and accepted the assignment to convert a telephone patent into a viable commercial venture.

Realizing its mistake, Western Union gave a research contract to the Thomas Edison laboratory to develop a rival telephone instrument. The Western Union Telegraph Company proceeded to establish a telephone subsidiary, the Home Telephone Company, but Vail was not intimidated by his $50 million rival. In fact, he took the offensive and charged Western Union with patent infringement. Vail not only threatened a patent suit, he pledged that Bell would enter the telegraph market. The mouse roared; the lion blinked. Western Union agreed to withdraw from the voice market and to sell its operating subsidiary to Bell. Vail, in turn, renounced any intention of offering telegraph service. Historians mark the 1879 cartel agreement as the "Magna Carta" of the telephone industry.

Within the next six years, Vail put in place the foundation of what was to become known as the Bell System by issuing exclusive franchises to prospective telephone companies. Although Bell assumed an equity stake in each operating company, each company raised its own capital. In 1881, Bell acquired Western Electric Company, a manufacturer that had supplied telegraph equipment to Western Union, and assigned it a license to manufacture telephone apparatus under the Bell patent. Then in 1885, Vail established a company that connected long-distance or toll lines to Bell's local telephone operations. The new American Bell Telephone Company provided local and long-distance service to customers or, in telephone parlance, its subscribers. For reasons that are not entirely clear, Vail left the company in the late 1880s. By then, the American Bell Company had gone public, the stock was performing well, and Vail was an individual of considerable wealth. However, he did not rest. He became a roving capitalist and started traction and electric power companies in Europe and South America. With his telephone holdings, Vail purchased a retirement farm in Vermont.

The basic Bell patent expired in 1894. Though market entry became the order of the day, the company's structure was positioned to deal with competition. The company was horizontally integrated, vertically tied between long-distance and local service, and vertically connected between telephone service and the manufacture of telephone equipment. In place, too, were the company's policies and practices. For one thing, the company did not sell Bell's telephone instrument; rather, the subscriber leased basic phone service. (At one time, Bell headquarters would not permit individual Bell affiliates to take ownership of the telephone handset.) Bell refused to make its long-distance lines available to competing telephone companies. The result of

American Bell's policies was that a non-Bell customer required two phones, one for local calls and one for toll or long-distance calls. To save money, a subscriber could lease a Bell instrument that permitted both local and toll calls. One by one, independent telephone companies found the logic of selling out to Bell compelling.

Competition/Regulation

Bell's patent expiration did foster the growth of independent, or non-Bell, phone companies, particularly in rural areas of the United States. The expiration also saw the rise of independent or non–Western Electric suppliers in the manufacturing market. Thus began an era of telephone competition. The results were predictable: Telephone rates dropped, usage increased, and productivity surged. By the turn of the century, Bell—now known as the American Telephone and Telegraph Company, or simply AT&T—saw its market share reduced to about half of the telephone service in the United States.

By the early 1900s, the financier J.P. Morgan acquired an equity stake in AT&T and prevailed upon Theodore Vail, at that point retired on his Vermont farm, to assume AT&T leadership. Once again, Vail's signature proved indelible. He instituted a personnel meritocracy, cut costs, improved service quality, pushed long-distance facilities to the West Coast, and acquired his old nemesis—the Western Union Telegraph Company. Under Vail, AT&T continued to buy independent telephone companies, denied toll access to local rivals, leased—did not sell—telephone instruments to subscribers, and purchased equipment almost exclusively from its Western Electric subsidiary for Bell operating companies.

Vail also possessed the gift of foresight. He was cognizant that telephone handsets, central office exchanges, and transmission lines had competitive substitutes. Marconi's vacuum tube radio in particular posed a threat to AT&T's investment in wire and cable. By 1910, Vail had centralized AT&T's research activities, laying the groundwork for what was to become a world-renowned private laboratory—Bell Telephone Laboratory.[5]

Vail was aware of public sentiment, if not hostility, toward big business "trusts" as they were called at the turn of the century. The government-driven breakup of the American Tobacco Company and the Standard Oil Companies loomed large on the corporate scene; when AT&T's Western Union purchase was challenged by the U.S. government, Vail deferred to the government and divested the Western Union Telegraph Company from Bell ownership. Vail nevertheless remained convinced that competition in telephony was unworkable. The telephone industry, he maintained, was a "natural" monopoly.

The European response to natural monopoly—nationalization—appeared straightforward enough, and Vail knew that the U.S. Postal Service under the Woodrow Wilson administration coveted AT&T ownership. Vail responded by observing that there was little difference between a private or a public monopoly. Both, in his opinion, remained unaccountable to the consumer. Vail's response to natural monopoly was regulation, government oversight, and a public watchdog—not unlike that of the Interstate Commerce Commission (ICC) in transportation.

Exhorted by the Bell telephone companies, Congress in 1910 amended the Interstate Commerce Commission Act to extend the ICC's jurisdiction over interstate

---

[5]John Brooks, *Telephone: The First Hundred Years* (New York: Harper and Row, 1975), 129.

telephone service. The Bell System supported legislation to extend state commission oversight to telephone services and facilities. Populists and monopolists found common cause in a mandate for "universal telephone service" to the public at large.

To solicit, indeed welcome, government regulation was regarded as corporate heresy in the early years of the 1900s. Nevertheless, Vail insisted that a government board, not unlike a jury, would monitor AT&T's service, rates, investments, and earnings. Vail said that his company must tell the truth about itself or someone else would.[6] However, regulatory due process carried a bonus; it immunized a telephone monopoly firm from antitrust assault. The result was that AT&T was to become the largest corporation in U.S. history.

Monopoly/Regulation/Antitrust

U.S. telephony grew and prospered over the next 40 years. In the 1920s, AT&T merged the research and development work of Western Electric and AT&T to form a single research entity, Bell Telephone Laboratories. AT&T also moved into broadcast radio, employing telephone lines to link the company's radio network as far west as Nebraska. Then the Bell System reversed itself and sold its broadcasting operations to RCA in the mid-1920s. Western Electric sold off its European operations to International Telephone and Telegraph (ITT) in order to concentrate on supplying the domestic equipment needs of the Bell operating companies. AT&T not only survived the Great Depression but continued its $9 dividend, a revenue flow so reliable that the company's stock was viewed as a bedrock investment for widows and orphans.

Franklin D. Roosevelt's New Deal inaugurated a series of alphabet agencies: the FPC, SEC, CAB, and FCC. The latter, the Federal Communications Commission, supplanted the ICC in 1934 and was assigned interstate telephone regulatory oversight. The commission's first major investigation probed AT&T's control of buyers and sellers of telephone equipment. Were such internal transactions, asked the commission, in the interest of the telephone consumer? AT&T obviously said yes, but the commission's staff wasn't so sure. A task force recommended that the FCC seek legislative authority over Western Electric's sales, prices, and earnings. Too radical even for the New Deal, the proposal was dropped in 1939. By then, foreign policy began to supersede U.S. domestic issues as the clouds of war descended over Europe.

Pearl Harbor brought World War II to the United States, and AT&T, the Bell Telephone Laboratories, and Western Electric made important contributions to the nation's defense effort. By 1946, the war was over and the FCC wrestled with a postwar development: to bring a new signal, television, to homes.

Then, in 1949, another antitrust shoe dropped. The Justice Department charged that AT&T's ownership of an unregulated supply affiliate (Western Electric) violated section 2 of the Sherman Antitrust law, which prohibits monopolization of trade. In 1956, the suit was settled by the Eisenhower administration through a consent decree between plaintiff and defendant. AT&T agreed to open its patent portfolio to all users and to confine its activities to regulated telephone service. Under the agreement, Western Electric was to remain part of the Bell System. The decree was not without controversy, however. The government claimed victory, but AT&T's response was

---

[6]Ibid., 143.

muted. From Bell's perspective, Vail's structure had been preserved; the institution of private monopoly and regulation was once again validated.

Antitrust/Divestiture/Deregulation

The next 28 years of the Bell System proved equally tumultuous. For one thing, regulators at the federal level began to question the underlying premise of AT&T's structure and policies. Worse, AT&T found itself caught in a crossfire between government antitrust and public utility regulation. Market entry into telephony clearly violated the premise of natural monopoly, and it came from none other than the FCC, often aided by the courts.

This was but a first step. By the 1970s, the FCC had ruled that subscribers could attach their own telephone sets to the Bell System's lines, that new firms could enter private interstate long-distance markets, that satellite communications companies could operate within the domestic United States, and that firms could lease and resell Bell's telephone circuits to end users.

Those decisions, a break from past practices, were opposed vigorously by AT&T and state public utility commissions (PUCs). AT&T protested that entry would thwart economies of scale, raise telephone rates, degrade service quality, and compromise the integrity of the best communications system in the world. AT&T took its case to Congress, where it sponsored the Consumer Communications Reform Act, legislation that, if enacted, would sanction telephone mergers, ban market entry, block competitive substitutes, and reverse the competitive policies of the FCC. AT&T's legislative effort failed.

AT&T's response to market entry also had an unintended effect: It elicited private antitrust action. Soon some dozen firms filed complaints in the courts. In November 1974, the Justice Department filed an antitrust complaint alleging that AT&T had blocked the entry of suppliers of telephone service, foreclosed telephone equipment manufacturers from selling to the Bell operating companies, stalled competitors' private branch exchanges (PBXs) from plugging into Bell's networks, and orchestrated a Bell System response to deny local circuits to AT&T's long-distance competitors. Nor was the department's proposed solution inconsequential: It sought horizontal and vertical divestiture of AT&T, which amounted to a dismemberment of the Bell System in the tradition of the Standard Oil breakup. Although the Bell System found an ally in the U.S. Department of Defense, President Reagan's attorney general insisted that AT&T had manipulated the regulatory process to perpetuate its telephone monopoly. Perhaps more distressing, the suit challenged AT&T's conviction that public utility regulation superseded the nation's antitrust laws. AT&T argued that the company was subject to oversight by 50 state commissions, and its practices and tariffs were sanctioned and approved by those regulatory bodies. Assistant Attorney General Baxter served notice that he would litigate the case to "his eye balls." The government presented its brief before a district court in Washington, D.C. After the plaintiff's case was concluded, AT&T asked that the suit be dropped. However, Judge Harold Greene wrote that the department's brief was not without merit and that AT&T indeed might have violated the nation's antitrust laws.

In January 1982, the parties reached a historic agreement. AT&T agreed to divest its 23 Bell operating companies and to reconstitute them as 7 independent Regional Bell Operating Companies (RBOCs): NYNEX, Bell Atlantic, BellSouth, Ameritech, Pacific

Telesis, Southwestern Bell, and US West. Restructured along geographical areas, the operating companies were to confine their activities to local, intrastate telephone services. AT&T retained Western Electric and Bell Laboratories and continued to provide interstate long-distance service to the public. The agreement took effect in January 1984.

AT&T would reimburse local telephone companies—the RBOCs—for the use of local telephone facilities (the "loop" in telephone parlance). Known as an access charge, this payment would ensure that local telephone service would remain affordable to the public at large. Put differently, a universal service support system required that business users subsidize residential subscribers, and that urban subscribers contribute to the telephone bills of rural users. In essence, users in competitive toll markets subsidized consumers in noncompetitive local markets.

The fourth stage of telecommunications experienced the rise of the online computer. A legacy of World War II, the computer was devised to enable the Army Corps of Engineers to calculate artillery tables. Unlike a voice or analog signal, the computer generated digital signals that were transmitted over telephone lines. By the 1950s, computers began to be used in commercial applications such as the generation of payrolls, accounts receivable, and sales data. Later, the intercontinental missile spurred the development of a U.S. early warning system across the North Pole. Radar dishes scanned the sky for intruders, fed information into computers, and relayed signals via telephone lines to the United States. The digital signal, modulated as an analog tone for line transmission, was then reconstituted at U.S. Air Force headquarters. National defense needs sired the modulation–demodulation unit, known as the modem, as a device to accommodate a digital signal. AT&T's tariffs, known as the Sage Network, were duly approved by the FCC.

Thermonuclear missiles raised the possibility of electromagnetic bursts capable of knocking out telephone circuits within the continental United States; the Department of Defense launched studies to address that potential threat. A Rand scientist, Dr. Paul Baran, proposed to assemble binary signals into packets routed through computers over many different telephone lines.[7] Reconstituted as a message at the receiver's terminal, packet switching was designed for digital transmission. In the 1960s, computers permitted remote users to access the arithmetic and memory of a mainframe computer. Sponsored by the Defense Department, computer terminal sharing suggested the possibility of distributed information processing not unlike that of an electricity utility—a computer utility.

In the mid-1960s, an FCC docket asked whether the U.S. analog telephone system could accommodate the impending needs of digital traffic. Did telephone rates and policies comport with growing use of online computers? Was telephone company investment responsive to the imperatives of a digital world?[8] The telephone industry's answer to the FCC's computer inquiry was reassuring: The computer required no fundamental change in the industry's regulation, investment, prices, or subscriber policies.[9] There was one

---

[7]Wilson Dizard, *MegaNet: How the Global Communications Network Will Connect Everyone on Earth* (Boulder, CO: Westview Press, 1997), 146.
[8]Before the Federal Communications Commission, Docket No. 16979, In the Matter of Regulatory and Policy Problems Presented by the Interdependence of Computer and Communication Services and Facilities, Notice of Inquiry, November 10, 1966.
[9]Stuart Matheson and Philip Walker, *Computers and Telecommunications: Issues in Public Policy* (Upper Saddle River, NJ: Prentice Hall, 1970), 153; Appendix C, 242–243.

exception: Subscribers could attach computers to phone lines via a modem provided by the telephone company.

The rapid pace of the advancement of technology since then has kept public policy makers busy. Technological change successively made obsolete the FCC's rulings in the original (1970) "Computer I" inquiry and "Computer II" inquiry (early 1980s). The "Computer III" inquiry (latter 1980s and the post–AT&T divestiture period generally) still stands but has been revised frequently to accommodate new technological, political, and legal realities. The attempts to draw a bright line between unregulated computers and regulated telephone service proved frustrating as commissions continually searched for an optimum mix of regulation and market forces.

In the 1980s, the personal computer (PC), born in a California garage, gained legitimacy when IBM and other suppliers entered the PC market. If the 1980s heralded the personal computer era, the 1990s were to become the era of the Internet. The Department of Defense's Advanced Research Products Agency network linked university computers over copper wire bandwidth. The introduction of a graphic user interface (icons and graphic signals) required larger bandwidth—more than the 56 kilobits per capacity of local telephone loops. [10] Copper wire was beginning to impose a limit on computer access speed.

The 1990s witnessed the computer and Internet Protocol (IP) as the driving force behind long-distance fiber networks. As Internet speed proved constrained by copper wire loop capacity, however, the local telephone line surfaced as a public policy issue of great moment. Congress passed the Telecommunications Act of 1996 in an attempt to address local loop congestion.[11] The act promised Regional Bell Operating Companies entry into the long-distance market if competition were introduced into the local telephone market.

The legislation represented a landmark effort to transform a monopoly into a competitive market. Prior to the act, some states had created leasing arrangements for entrants called competitive local exchange carriers (CLECs), affording interconnection with incumbent carrier networks at low wholesale rates. For its part, the FCC had introduced unbundling local network arrangements (comparably efficient interconnection and open network architecture) for unaffiliated data carriers on the same terms as information services affiliates of incumbent carriers. The Department of Justice and Regional Bell Ameritech reached a *quid pro quo* agreement whereby the latter would be let into long distance markets in return for making available parts of its network to competitors. While these measures proved meager in the short term, they laid the foundation for the local competition provisions of the new act.[12]

The ensuing years have seen an unfettered long distance market and a pirouette of policy actions aimed at the local telephone market, fundamentally altering the structure of the telecommunications sector.

---

[10]Comments of Philip J. Sirlin, Schroder & Co., in "Cable Industry," *Wall Street Transcript* (March 1, 1999): 8.
[11]Dick W. Olufs, *The Making of Telecommunications Policy* (Boulder, CO: Lynne Rienner, 1999), 135.
[12]For a good discussion of these public policy actions and others that have helped pave the way toward local competition, see Jonathan Nuechterlein and Philip Weiser, *Digital Crossroads: American Telecommunications Policy in the Internet Age* (Cambridge, MA: MIT Press, 2005), 66–68.

▪▪▪ # II. Market Structure

Market structure includes elements of demand, supply, and entry barriers in long-distance and local exchange markets.

Demand

As a derived demand, U.S. buyers consume about $293 billion worth of telecommunication services annually. Of that total, local service revenues account for $122 billion; long distance accounts for almost $64 billion.[13] Cellular and other wireless phone services, which represent a mix of local and long-distance minutes, add another $107 billion, having more than doubled in magnitude since the end of the 1990s—a veritable technological revolution.[14] The divide between voice and data traffic suggests another shift in buyers' tastes and preferences: Whereas voice traffic experiences single-digit growth, nonvoice or data traffic demand increases at some 200 percent per year. Internet demand, a subset of data traffic, is estimated to increase by 500 percent annually.[15] That the Internet ushers in a new era is seen by the following:

- Eighty percent of Internet traffic is driven by electronic commerce among business firms.
- The Intel Corporation states that its online microprocessor sales now total $1 billion per month.
- Cisco (Internet switches and routers) estimates that 80 percent of its sales are Internet driven.
- Dell computer (personal computers) observes that half of its PC sales originate on the Internet.
- GE's Internet has cut procurement cycles in half and processing costs by a third.
- Amazon (books, music, household goods) sales on the Web are growing at 33 percent per year, and now exceed $5 billion annually.
- In 1998, 13 percent of Internet users had banked or paid bills online; by 2005, the figure had risen to 41 percent.
- U.S. electronic commerce (e-commerce) retail sales revenues are booming, with the late-2006 total a quarter higher over the year before.

E-commerce is beginning to assume a generic pattern. First, a firm adopts the Internet to multiply customer access and to achieve cost economies. To secure a first-mover advantage, the firm reassesses its value chain and outsources high-cost activities. The firm's suppliers, no longer perceived as adversaries, tie their computers to their customer's database, quickening response time to consumer demand. Some e-commerce firms mandate that supplier operations be located within 15 minutes of final assembly lines. Greater transaction economies are passed forward to the customer in the form of lower prices.

The Internet, by direct access, permits a firm to circumvent traditional marketing or sales channels. Banks, for example, engage in online financial transactions and can

---

[13]FCC, Trends in Telephone Service, February 2007, Table 15.1, 2005 data (preliminary).
[14]Ibid.
[15]Reinhardt Krause, "Web Weaving Its Way through Telecom Industry," *Investor's Business Daily* (June 9, 1999): A4.

bypass a rival's investment in brick and mortar. Online brokerage services today challenge conventional investment houses; an online MBA program can reach students beyond a traditional university classroom. Geography no longer protects or insulates.

Web sites enable a firm to compress response time to buyers' shifting tastes. Ford Motor Company, for example, links 120 design engines worldwide, permitting a 24-hour design cycle.[16] Toyota claims it can deliver a customized car to a customer in 5 days. Once a firm enjoys an Internet-competitive advantage, rivals are sure to follow. Competitors have little choice. Failure to do so can prove traumatic. In an online environment, nouns become adverbs, such as *Googled or Yahooed.*[17]

That e-commerce occurs within an environment of accelerating change is seen in the observation of Jack Welch, former CEO of General Electric: The Internet, he said, represents "the greatest change in business in [his] lifetime."[18] The president of Intel commented that "all companies will be Internet companies or they won't be companies at all."[19] Market pressure fuels the adoption of e-commerce in the United States and throughout the world. It is estimated that in 2005 over 80 percent of the global demand for bandwidth came from Internet traffic.[20] Bandwidth now constitutes the new paradigm.

Supply

Long-Distance Market Shares The U.S. long-distance, or toll, market has undergone a sea change in recent years. Structurally, the industry features several firms with significant market shares, and many hundreds of providers share the rest of the field. The approximate market shares (based on 2005 long-distance carrier revenues) are depicted in Table 8-1.

The activity has been dizzying and transformative. Theodore Vail's progeny, AT&T, dominated the long distance market for decades, including the early period following the breakup of the former Bell System. As recently as 1995, the company could proudly boast of three-quarters of the toll market. But 10 years later, a dispirited AT&T possessed only an 18 percent market share.[21] MCI struggled for 6 years to enter the market, beginning in 1963. It prospered but was acquired by WorldCom in 1997 for $20 billion. Beset by accounting irregularities and other mismanagement, WorldCom spiraled into bankruptcy but then re-emerged as MCI, reorganized and with $35 billion of its debt eliminated. In 2005, Verizon acquired MCI for $8.5 billion.[22] Sprint, a Midwestern company, has famously pushed fiber optics transmission and historically

---

[16]Ira Brudsky, "The Case against Making Money the Old Fashioned Way," *Network World* (May 3, 1999): 47.
[17]"Internet Anxiety," *Business Week* (June 28, 1999): 86; Tim Burt, "Ford to Farm out Key Final Assembly Jobs to Contractor," *Financial Times* (August 4, 1999): 1.
[18]Matt Murray, "GE Now Views Internet as Crucial to New Growth," *Wall Street Journal* (June 23, 1999): 15.
[19]Matthew Benjamin, "Surf's Up: International Network Services Prepares to Ride Data Traffic Tidal Water," *Investor's Business Daily* (June 29, 1999): A9.
[20]See Sylvia Dennis, "Ovum Analyzes Global Telecoms and IP Markets," December 30, 1999, www .findarticles.com/p/articles/mi_m0NEW/is_1999_Dec_30/ai_58464673, Newsbytes News Network; and Thomas Bonnett, *Telewars in the States: Telecommunications Issues in a New Era of Competition* (Washington, D.C.: Council of Governors Policies Advisors, 1996), 19.
[21]FCC, Trends, Table 9.5.
[22]"MCI Ready for Post-WorldCom Life," *Washington Post* (November 1, 2003): E1; FCC, "FCC Approves SBC/AT&T and Verizon/MCI Mergers—Transactions Offer Significant Public Interest Benefits," October 31, 2005. SBC acquired AT&T for $16 billion and Verizon absorbed MCI for $8.5 billion.

TABLE 8-1 Long-Distance Market Shares

AT&T	18.1%
SBC	15.9%
BellSouth	5.9%
Verizon	16.2%
MCI	7.7%
Sprint	6.2%
Qwest	5.9%
Other (Wireline and Wireless)	24.1%
Total	100.0%

▪▪▪▪▪▪▪▪▪

Note: *AT&T, SBC and BellSouth have merged to form a new AT&T; Verizon has acquired MCI.*

Source: Federal Communications Commission, Trends in Telephone Service, February 2007, Table 9.5 (2005 data).

operated a long-distance service, but has now moved enthusiastically into wireless communications, spinning off its local wireline operations into a new firm named Embarq.[23] MCI WorldCom, outbidding BellSouth, announced its intent to acquire Sprint but was discouraged in 2000 by a skeptical Justice Department; later, a resilient BellSouth reportedly made serious overtures to an attentive AT&T.[24] Both did eventually merge, but as handmaidens to an aggressive SBC, who consummated the union by taking a "new" name: AT&T.[25] And Sprint found a new partner, a successful wireless carrier called Nextel.[26] Bursting onto the scene in recent years, wireless carriers as a group coupled with smaller wireline providers captured about one out of every four long-distance households in 2005.[27] Although no official statistics are yet available, the outlines of a new order in the long distance market can be gleaned by the merging carriers and their consolidated market shares set forth in Table 8-1. The new AT&T and the reconstituted Verizon appear to claim some 60 percent of this market, followed by a number of much smaller wireline and wireless providers.

Long-Distance Market Entry   Though classified as a loose oligopoly, the long-distance market has experienced a rash of startup firms, with corporations investing in high-speed data routers, fast switches, and optical fiber links.

Six companies (Qwest, Global Crossing, Frontier, Williams, IXC, and Level 3) entered the "backbone" toll market several years ago, although some have experienced

---

[23]"Sprint Prepares to Cut the Cord," *Washington Post* (June 6, 2005), D1.

[24]"Is BellSouth Just Window Shopping?" *Business Week* (November 5, 2001), 102; Shawn Young and Almar Latour, "BellSouth–AT&T Talks Face Hurdles," *Wall Street Journal* (October 27, 2003), www.online .wsj.com

[25]Ibid.; FCC, "FCC Approves Merger of AT&T Inc. and BellSouth Corporation," December 29, 2006; "SBC to Stick with the Storied AT&T Name," Associated Press, October 27, 2005.

[26]FCC, "FCC Approves Merger of AT&T Inc. and BellSouth Corporation," December 29, 2006. AT&T acquired Bellsouth for $87 billion.

[27]FCC, Trends, Table 9.5.

financial difficulties in recent years. Other firms on the market's edge include the aerospace industry. Even electric power companies are exploring the provision of broadband telecommunications services. In 2004, more than 2,800 firms identified themselves as toll carriers in the United States.

This entry pattern suggests that traditional market barriers might not be as formidable as they have been over past decades. Scale economies have traditionally been thought to pose a hurdle to long-distance entry. Apparently, that constraint has diminished as entrants perceive incumbent carrier investment as a handicap rather than an asset to bandwidth efficiency.

Certainly, one constraint that can give pause to any firm pondering market entry is the absolute size of the incumbent corporation. However, in U.S. long distance, neither market share nor corporate assets appears to have arrested the entry process. Government regulation for many years in the twentieth century constituted a barrier to market access. However, federal regulation of toll carriers today is largely benign.

A notable exception concerns the Regional Bell Operating Companies. Section 271 of the Telecommunications Act of 1996 permits RBOCs to supply "in-region" long-distance service, as long as a number of obligations are met. These requirements encompass the establishment of interconnection agreements that comply with a 14-point competitive checklist, such as nondiscriminatory access to RBOC network elements and unbundling of certain functions for use by competitors. The Act authorizes the FCC to judge whether the applicants have met these standards. RBOCs have now been permitted to offer long-distance services in all their respective home markets and could present significant rivalry to incumbent toll carriers.[28]

Moreover, the burgeoning use of e-mail by Americans and attractive offerings of "free" long-distance minutes as part of bundled-service wireless calling plans already have made inroads into long-distance revenues, thereby further reducing the primary base on which the national universal service system assesses contributions from carriers.[29]

Beyond labor, capital, and administrative expenses, long-distance firms incur other expenses, namely an access charge of 4 cents per minute for local loop facilities and a contribution to a universal service fund that includes an education, or e-rate, assessment used to support telecom purchases by public schools and libraries, as well as support for Internet access by rural health care providers. Such costs are currently borne by interstate carriers and their customers under the aegis of the FCC.

Competitive substitutes, such as Internet Protocol (IP) telephone services, pose a real alternative to switched voice service. Tied to the Internet, a PC in one location can send a packetized voice message to another PC. Internet service providers (ISPs) deliver "voice" as data transmission. The Telecommunications Act of 1996 exempted Internet traffic from local telephone access charges. Clearly, users are attracted to IP cost savings: One company reports that its telephone bill between its New Jersey and

---

[28]FCC, Trends, Table 9-7.
[29]Federal Communications Commission, "FCC Updates Approach for Assessing Contributions to the Federal Universal Service Fund," news release, June 21, 2006; and "Federal Communications Commission Adopts Interim Measures to Maintain Universal Service Fund," news release, December 13, 2002.

Dallas offices dropped from $2,500 per month to "pennies on the dollar."[30] The head of AT&T Labs compared IP to "Pac-Man—it will eventually eat everything in its way."[31]

Indeed, AT&T and several other firms launched "voice over IP" (VOIP) services at the end of 2003. The import of VOIP and other Internet-based services has not been lost on the FCC: The commission held a VOIP forum in December 2003 and then launched a landmark proceeding to examine this "challenge to established technological, market, and regulatory structures of our analog past."[32]

The RBOCs view IP telephony as a threat as well as an opportunity. Fearing financial bypass around their loop plant investment, BellSouth and QWEST (formerly US West) in the late 1990s imposed a local access charge on Internet service providers offering IP phone service—a charge that implies that thousands of ISPs may fall under the category of long-distance telephone companies.[33]

More recently, BellSouth announced its plan to deploy a form of IP telephone technology, initially to businesses in the Southeast.[34] In addition, QWEST's CEO, reacting to a 2003 court decision in Minnesota barring that state's PUC from regulating service provider Vonage's IP offering, declared that his firm would soon enter that market. His rationale was that it "might just be the opportunity to break up the massive regulatory logjam that exists today."[35] In the meantime, ISPs now solicit customers by giving away personal computers or rescinding monthly lease charges, or by offering alluringly low rates.

Local Telecommunications Unlike toll telecommunications, barriers to market entry in local telephone service remain formidable. The local loop plant traditionally has embodied the essence of a natural monopoly, and few communities or towns would let dozens of firms tear up streets in the name of consumer choice. State commissions, seemingly embracing the natural monopoly concept as equivalent to the public interest, have historically erected barriers to local market entry. A firm contemplating offering local telephone service typically must obtain a license of public convenience and necessity, and must receive the "eligible telecommunications carrier" designation before it can draw from the pool of universal service support monies. Entry in the local arena has not been for the faint of heart.

A second barrier to local competition hinges on matters of plant depreciation schedules. Regulatory officials reasoned that stretching plant economic life (i.e., outside wire) to 25 years would result in low annual depreciation expenses. Low expenses

---

[30]James DeTar, "Hearing a Pin Drop in Cyberspace, Phone Carriers Use Internet More," *Investor's Business Daily* (June 6, 1999): A6; "Telecommunications: Prognosis 1999," *Business Week* (January 11, 1999): 99.

[31]Peter Grant, and Almar Latour, "Battered Telecoms Face New Challenge: Internet Calling," *Wall Street Journal* (October 9, 2003). www.online.wsj.com. Accessed April 14, 2004.

[32]Federal Communications Commission, "FCC to Begin Internet Telephony Proceedings," news release, November 6, 2003.

[33]"Telecommunications: Prognosis 1999," *Business Week* (January 11, 1999): 99.

[34]"Battered Telecoms Face New Challenge: Internet Calling," Ibid.

[35]"QWEST to Pursue VOIP Services; CEO Cites Regulatory Vacuum," *TR Daily* (November 4, 2003). www.tr.com/newsletters/trd (available only with paid subscription). Accessed April 14, 2004. The Eighth Circuit Court of Appeals later upheld the FCC and the lower court in preempting the state regulators. Roy Mark, "VOIP Still on FCC's Open Road," March 21, 2007, www.internetnews.com/bus-news/print.php/ 3667111

translated into reduced monthly telephone bills to the consumer but also distorted price and investment signals for potential entrants.

A third entry barrier derived from a policy brokered between state and federal regulatory agencies. Over time, long-distance costs declined, but local telephone costs increased. State commissions solicited a revenue contribution from long-distance customers to subsidize local service. Prior to the breakup of the Bell System, this toll subsidy was subsumed within a complex cost-separations process. After the breakup, the toll subsidy was recycled as an access charge levied upon long-distance subscribers using a local carrier's wire. The result found local costs higher than local rates—a shortfall that was made up by a long-distance subsidy. Few firms would contemplate entering a local market where revenues did not cover costs.

In recent years, the FCC has adopted orders that make universal service assessments, such as those associated with access charges, more explicit and spread out more among service providers. The FCC, industry, and Congress fully grasp that much remains to be done in adapting the rapidly growing interstate support system to the new realities of competition and technological change.[36]

Today, the three Bell Operating Companies operate some 15,000 circuit switches and 119 million local access lines. With a plant investment of $175 billion, the RBOCs control about 85 percent of U.S. local lines.[37] Since the Bell System breakup, the RBOCs' aggregate local services market share (based on revenues) has remained relatively stable, but AT&T's long-distance share has plummeted. (See Figure 8.1.)

▪ ▪ ▪ **FIGURE 8-1** Share of U.S. Telephone Markets

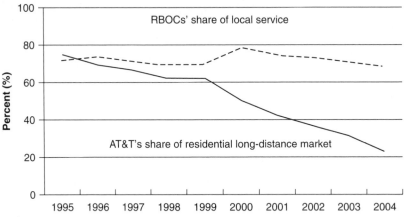

Author's estimates.

---

[36]See, for example, Written Statement on Universal Service by FCC Chairman Michael K. Powell before the Senate Committee on Commerce, Science, and Transportation, October 30, 2003; and FCC Commissioner Jonathan Adelstein, before the Senate Energy and Commerce Committee, March 14, 2006. See also "[House Telecom and Internet Subcommittee Chairman] Markey, Worried About USF Costs, Asks [FCC Chairman] Martin For Suggestions," *TR Daily*, April 2, 2007.
[37]Federal Communications Commission, Trends in Telephone Service, February 2007, Table 7.3; and FCC, Local Competition: Status as of June 30, 2006, Table 6; FCC, Statistics of Communications Common Carriers, November 7, 2005, Tables 1.1, 2.7.

The Telecommunications Act of 1996 embraced the concept of competitive local exchange carriers (CLECs) to compete with the RBOCs and independent local exchange carriers. However, competition thus far remains less than robust. RBOCs' market share reductions are modest though measurable as competitors' broadband offerings cause subscribers to jettison their second copper line into the house. The FCC has found that nationwide, local service competitors such as CLECs and resellers have managed to wrest only 15.8 percent of local service revenues from incumbent local exchange carriers. The trend has been encouraging, though: In 1998, local competitors accounted for 3.5 percent of local service revenues, meaning the total for 2004 jumped more than four-fold.[38] On the other hand, Dr. Robert Crandall of the Brookings Institution has concluded that local telephony remains concentrated because state regulators have succeeded in restricting entry into most intrastate markets.[39]

However uncertain the entry process is, CLECs and Internet service providers have had some influence on the local bandwidth market, particularly in the realm of high-speed Internet access known as broadband. CLECs have introduced digital subscriber line (DSL) equipment that multiplies bandwidth capacity to 30 times or more than a regular telephone dial-up modem; cable modems offered by cable TV companies provide bandwidth capacity that frequently exceeds that of copper wire by more than 70 times. Other loop alternatives include fixed wireless, satellite dishes, and third-generation (3G) wireless. Makers of high-altitude airships dream of creating floating platforms for delivery of voice, data, and video.[40] Most recently, a high-frequency wireless fidelity local area network (WiFi) has been catching on with consumers packing laptops at public "hot spots" such as hotels, airports, and restaurants, and with organizations that need wireless networks to augment their wire line capabilities. And an even more impressive—lower-cost, higher-speed—mobile wireless technology, WiMax, is being touted by Sprint and others as the harbinger of a 4G breakthrough.[41] Cable modems have captured almost 45 percent of the residential and business broadband market in the United States, though RBOCs have dropped DSL prices in response and made recent inroads.[42] Fiber to the home is emerging as a faster, higher-priced alternative. Still, competitive substitutes fall short of converting much of local telephony into a "contestable" market.

Today, as the nation moves to e-commerce, the local telephone line persists as a bandwidth bottleneck. While entry is occurring, the local market is becoming more concentrated. Horizontal merger is the culprit: Verizon, the RBOC formerly known as Bell Atlantic, for example, has acquired NYNEX and GTE. Southwestern Bell Communications (SBC) has purchased Pacific Telesis, Southern New England Telephone Company, Ameritech, and now BellSouth. (See Table 8-2.) And MCI's huge

---

[38]FCC, Trends in Telephone Service, 2007, Table 8.7.

[39]Robert W. Crandall, "Managed Competition in U.S. Telecommunications," working paper 99-1, AEI (Washington, D.C.: Brookings Joint Center for Regulatory Studies, March 1999), 15.

[40]See "About the Stratellite," accessed April 9, 2007, at www.sanswire.com/stratellitecomparisons.html

[41]"Sprint Embraces WiMax," Internetnews.com, August 8, 2006.

[42]FCC, High-Speed Services for Internet Access: Status as of June 30, 2006, January 2007, Chart 2; "SBC Yahoo DSL Cuts Prices Again," CNET News.com, September 30, 2003. www.news.com. Accessed April 14, 2004.

TABLE 8-2 Top Telecommunication Mergers

Announced	Target (country)	Acquiring Company (country)	Deal Value (billions)
12/29/06	BellSouth (U.S.)	AT&T (U.S.)	$86.00
05/11/98	Ameritech (U.S.)	SBC Comm. (U.S.)	72.36
07/28/98	GTE (U.S)	Bell Atlantic (U.S.)	71.32
01/18/99	AirTouch Comm. (U.S.)	Vodafone Group (U.K.)	65.90
06/14/99	US West (U.S.)	Qwest Comm. (U.S.)	48.48
10/01/97	MCI Comm. (U.S.)	WorldCom (U.S.)	43.65
02/17/04	AT&T Wireless (U.S.)	Cingular (U.S.)	41.00
02/20/99	Telecom Italia (Italy)	Olivetti (Italy)	34.76
12/15/04	Nextel (U.S.)	Sprint (U.S.)	35.0
04/22/96	NYNEX (U.S.)	Bell Atlantic (U.S.)	30.79
10/19/99	Orange (U.K.)	Mannesmann (Germany)	30.00
04/01/96	Pacific Telesis (U.S.)	SBC Comm. (U.S.)	22.42

Source: Wall Street Journal, 20 October 1999, A23. *New York Times,* 18 February 2004, C1; IDG News service, 02 January 2007, www.networkworld.com/news/2007/123006-fcc-att-bellsouth.html

$127 billion offer for Sprint almost came to fruition.[43] When asked about the fate of the remaining Bell company, Qwest (the former U.S. West), one analyst shrugged: "It's gone. It's just a matter of time till it gets taken out."[44]

Like Verizon, AT&T now controls some 30 percent of all local access lines in the United States. As one of its managers put it, "We love access lines."[45]

Cellular/Wireless Telecommunications At the same time, the burgeoning cellular telephone business has blossomed into an arena of take-no-prisoners marketing, stiff price competition, and technological gadgetry, which also is being fueled by recent federal rules permitting local phone number portability. Effective in late 2003, customers could for the first time keep their existing cell phone numbers as they switched to another wireless service provider, as well as transfer their traditional landline phone numbers to wireless systems. One pundit likened these actions to a "bloody mess, [like] throwing gasoline on a fire."[46] The current structure of this segment of the telecommunications market features rapid consolidation. In late 2003, six major mobile phone companies existed, accounting for more than 80 percent of the U.S. cell phone market. By late 2006, four carriers dominated the market (see Table 8-3). Many believe the number of leading firms in this field may fall further.[47]

---

[43]"Monopolies grow ever bigger: US telecom merger tops $100 billion mark," WSWS, October 7, 1999. www.wsws.org/articles/1999/oct1999/merg-o07_prn.shtml
[44]Peter Svensson, "Proposed Telecom Merger Causes Ripples," Associated Press, March 7, 2006.
[45]Gautam Naik et al., "Party Line: SBC and Ameritech Send Phone Industry Loud Wake-up Call," *Wall Street Journal* (April 12, 1998): 5.
[46]Matt Richtel, "Opening Pandora's Flip Phone: New Flexibility on Cell Numbers Creates Uncertainty," *New York Times* (November 24, 2003): C1.
[47]See, for example, "Rumor: Deutsch Telekom to sell T-Mobile USA," *T-Mobile Tracker*, July 3, 2005, www.mobiletracker.net/archives/2005/07/03/t-mobile-usa-for-sale. Accessed April 9, 2007.

TABLE 8-3 Largest U.S. Cell Phone Companies (Service Revenues as of 3Q)

	Revenues (billions)	*Market Share (%)*
Cingular Wireless*	$8.66	29.8
Verizon Wireless	8.47	29.1
Sprint Nextel	8.23	28.3
T Mobile	3.72	12.8

*Re-named AT&T on January 15, 2007.

Source: *Telebusillis* telebusillis.blogspot.com/2006/10/3q06-us-cellular-majors.html. Accessed April 6, 2007; stockholder reports.

Interestingly, incumbent local exchange carriers have major footholds in the market. For example, AT&T recently acquired top-ranked Cingular; Verizon is a 51-percent partner with European giant Vodafone in Verizon Wireless, which is ranked second; and Sprint Communications has spawned Sprint Nextel, rated number three. An incumbent local exchange carrier from Germany, Deutsch Telekom, controls fourth-ranked T-Mobile.

These companies find themselves in a world where cell phone revenues are booming while the local voice business erodes. In fact, telecom analysts believe that cumulative revenue growth for wireless services will total $108 billion in the United States from 2004 through 2008, while traditional wire line services are projected to decline by $80 billion over the same period.[48] It is a poignant fact that while landline telephone penetration plateaued at more than 90 percent two decades ago, wireless subscriber has skyrocketed to 76 percent today.[49] In fact, spending on wireless services exceeded long distance expenditures for the first time in 2003.[50] Broadband also is expected to yield positive returns during the span, perhaps less impressive in magnitude but a key to keeping wire line networks from being cannibalized by the wireless wave.[51] Moreover, many observers expect consolidation to occur among the existing wireless carriers as profit margins shrink, and a merger minuet already has begun.[52] A wild card in all of this is data; for example, wireless data revenues reached $8.7 billion for the latter 6 months of 2006, up 82 percent from $4.8 billion in the latter half of 2005.[53]

In sum, the market structure of U.S. telecommunications remains bifurcated. The long-distance market experiences vibrant entry; the local market retains market dominance in much of its business. Technological wild cards such as cellular and the Internet, and who plays them, though, will have a considerable effect on future outcomes.

---

[48]"Bells Urged to Hike Wireless Exposure," *TR Daily* (November 25, 2003). www.tr.com/newsletters/trd (available only with paid subscription). Accessed April 14, 2004.
[49]Federal Communications Commission, Trends in Telephone Service, Table 16.1; and CTIA, "Wireless Quick Facts,", www.ctia.org/advocacy/research/index.cfm/AID/10323. Accessed March 16, 2007.
[50]TIAonline press release, March 8, 2004. www.tiaonline.org/business/media/press
[51]Ibid.
[52]"Telecom Industry Abuzz on Merger Talks," *Atlanta Constitution-Journal* (January 15, 2004). www.ajc.com. Accessed April 14, 2004; "AT&T Wireless for Sale as Shakeout Starts," *New York Times* (January 21, 2004): C1.
[53]CTIA, previously cited.

▪▪▪ III. Market Conduct

Long Distance

Price and nonprice competition manifest themselves in the long-distance telecommunications market. To the extent that firms in the toll market are aware of rival pricing strategies, carrier prices tend to converge over time. A rate discount by one carrier is invariably countered by rivals. A firm, for example, may offer a discount on Sunday calls, but rivals might then trump the rate by extending discounts for calls to an entire weekend. Price competition is, in fact, so heated that carriers are not above employing "fighting brands" that require tapping digits to secure cheaper rates (e.g., "10-10-321"). Subscribers might be surprised to learn that some of those digit brands are affiliates of market leaders.[54] "Take No Prisoners" seems to be the only guiding rule. Who could have foreseen firms like PennyTalk bursting onto the scene with a penny rate for U.S. calls and 2 cents per minute for calls anywhere in the world?[55]

That price rivalry is standard operating procedure can be seen by rates offered by new long-distance suppliers, especially firms relying on fiber optics transmission. Here, rates are often not determined on the basis of time and distance, but instead reflect bandwidth quantity used by the customer. New pressures have emerged as wireless firms and local telephone companies offer unlimited or large blocks of minutes for long-distance calling. An upstart firm called Skype, already claiming 8 million "simultaneous" customers worldwide at peak periods in computer-to-computer calls, has announced it will offer in the United States and Canada unlimited Internet-based calling for $30 *per year* that will connect to landlines and mobile phones as well.[56] The increasing use of e-mail also has dampened demand and the price for long-distance offerings. Many believe that such calling has simply achieved commodity status.[57]

The long-distance market is characterized by nonprice competition, as well. Long-distance carriers encourage brand and customer loyalty, and proclaim circuit quality unmatched by rivals. Marketers increasingly tout bundled services as a standard offering to their subscribers, often obscuring once clear demarcations between local and long-distance traffic (as well as between telephony and cable television). The corporate market enables firms to generate Internet bandwidth for exclusive company use. Here, a firm leases bandwidth and purchases Internet routers or switches to secure a state-of-the art digital network. Such links, which enable the firm's Web site to link employees as well as customers and corporate suppliers, have emerged as a competitive strategy in markets where industry boundaries are now permeable.

---

[54]John J. Keller, "AT&T Prepares Campaign to Battle MCI's '10-321' Plan," *Wall Street Journal* (April 8, 1998): B7.

[55]A flat-rate 49 cents is charged as a call connection fee, with a 99-cent monthly service charge. www.pennytalk.com. Accessed March 21, 2007.

[56]Bruce Meyerson, "Phone, Cable Companies to Battle in 2007," Associated Press, December 15, 2006; "Show Me the Money," *CED Magazine*, December 15, 2006.

[57]See, for example, "AT&T buy shows how far voice calling has fallen," CNET News.com, February 2, 2005. Accessed at news.com.com/AT38T+buy+shows+how+far+voice+calling+has+fallen/2100-1037_3-5559540.html

Local Telecommunications

Local telephone companies control a critical piece of telecommunications real estate—the line between the end user and the company's central office switch. In the absence of competitive alternatives, local carriers enjoy pricing discretion at this last telecommunications mile—subject, of course, to regulatory approval. Every long-distance call ends or begins on the subscriber's local premises, and each toll user is assessed a fee of several cents per minute. From the perspective of a long-distance toll carrier, the access charge constitutes the carrier's largest expense. AT&T's access charge payments total $12 billion annually; since 1984, AT&T has paid the RBOCs more than $200 billion.

Whether the local access charge is reasonable or not is controversial. Long-distance carriers argue that RBOC fees far exceed cost and are exorbitant. RBOCs, on the other hand, insist that the charges must remain high to ensure telephone availability to all. Be that as it may, long-distance customers contribute $25 billion annually to local exchange users.

In addition to monthly service rates, local exchange carriers offer bandwidth options to corporate users. A local carrier, for example, will provide high-speed, broadband capacity T-1 leased lines that may vary from $1,000 to $3,000 per month. The Telecommunications Act of 1996 attempted to breathe competitive life into local telecommunications services. New entrants either resell RBOC circuits or place multiplex equipment in carrier central office locations. The former lease circuits wholesale at an 18 percent discount and attempt to compete with RBOC customers at the retail level. Lest one regard local competitors as fly-by-night operations, two major CLECs attempted to lease local circuits and compete in providing basic telephone service: AT&T and MCI.

AT&T invested $4 billion in an endeavor to enter the local lease service business, generating revenue of $86 million. However, AT&T's new CEO halted this strategy of market entry and labeled the leased route option a "fool's errand."[58] MCI spent $2 billion as a CLEC and then backed off lease circuits as a vehicle for local entry. Many CLECs allege that they are vulnerable to an RBOC wholesale/retail financial squeeze that, in effect, precludes them from effective customer access. Still, some competitors cling tenaciously, particularly where they are able to combine their own networks with facilities leased from the Bell companies at economical rates.[59]

Another type of CLEC provides broadband access at the local level by employing digital subscriber line (DSL) equipment in the RBOC's central office and then leasing RBOC lines to the customers' premises. Although DSL CLECs have penetrated the market somewhat, they, too, are beholden to RBOCs positioned in the dual role as supplier and rival. CLECs assert that RBOCs engage in dilatory tactics by claiming that the central office lacks DSL capacity, that CLEC equipment must be checked for safety, that CLEC filing papers are mislaid, and that contract penalties lock in telecommunications customers.[60] AT&T, in particular, alleged that 80 percent of RBOC lines were tardy or late in availability. Moreover, potential entrants allege that

---

[58]"New Boss, New Plan," *Business Week* (February 2, 1998): 124.
[59]AT&T news release, September 8, 2003.

RBOCs find central office capacity for their own DSL equipment often of the same make as that of their CLEC rivals. Some CLECs complain that when they approach RBOCs' customers, the RBOCs expedite DSL equipment as a way to foreclose competitive entry.

The FCC recently issued a landmark, and controversial, order that reaffirmed network unbundling requirements for RBOCs' voice telecommunications facilities but eliminated most requirements related to incumbent broadband networks. The latter action was heralded by the FCC's chairman as "taking vital steps across the desert . . . bold steps to promote broadband investment," but was castigated by another FCC commissioner as a "broadband policy blackout . . . simply the old system of local monopoly dressed up in a digital cloak."[61] An appellate court decision ensued that preempted state regulators while swapping leases for facilities-based competition; operating in a revamped local telephone market requires tenacity, deep pockets, and much patience.

Building on a broadband infrastructure, voice over the Internet is rapidly gaining momentum as the new technology of choice for providing voice services. A number of significant advantages are obtained: IP equipment is more efficient and costs substantially less than the traditional circuit-switched plant. An IP network also is not charged or assessed for universal service and wireless 911 emergency service. It can be adapted easily by cable companies seeking to offer voice services, and video calls and Web-based telephone messaging cost less under such architecture.

A new-generation technology, called IPv6, promises even more capabilities, better security, and lower operational expenses for Internet users.[62] Downsides can be found, though. Although the sound quality has improved dramatically, VOIP calls still are less reliable and the technology less proven than the traditional mode. IP still does not accommodate E911 connections well and often fails during a power blackout (unlike conventional phone service).

VOIP poses serious issues for policy makers: The absence of local access charges deals a significant blow to local carrier revenues. Law enforcement officials now able to tap phone lines for security reasons would not be able to undertake such measures with current versions of IP telephony. Because Internet phone service currently rides over traditional telephone or cable lines, it will not work unless the conventional phone network is intact. The FCC did recently vote to assess universal service charges against VOIP estimated interstate revenues for the first time.[63] But a recent adverse patent ruling against Vonage, the leading VOIP service provider, now threatens that firm's

---

[60]Henry Goldblatt, "The Real Target Is Your Dial Tone," *Fortune* (November 24, 1997): 116; David Rohde, "RBOC Termination Penalties Challenger," *Network World* (May 10, 1999): 39; Ronald Rosenberg, "AT&T's Armstrong Hits Bell Atlantic," *Boston Globe* (November 6, 1998): C2; Nick Wingfield, "No Mercy: Covad Communications Needs the Bell's Cooperation to Thrive. It Says It Isn't Getting Much," Wall Street Journal (September 21, 1998): R10.

[61]News releases of Chairman Michael K. Powell and Michael J. Copps, August 21, 2003, in the FCC's Triennial Review Order (CC Dockets 01-338, 96-98, 98-147). August 21, 2003.

[62]National Telecommunications & Information Administration, Technical And Economic Assessment of Internet Protocol (IPv6), January 2006. www.ntia.doc.gov/ntiahome/ntiageneral/ipv6/final/ipv6finalTOC.htm

[63]Federal Communications Commission, "FCC Updates Approach for Assessing Contributions to the Federal Universal Service Fund," press release, June 21, 2006.

viability going forward and may roil others in the market.[64] Given the huge stakes, it is no wonder that regulators debate among themselves about the right blend of market mechanism and government rules. [65]

▪▪▪ IV. Market Performance

Market performance parallels the dichotomy in long-distance and local service behavior and structure.

Long Distance

Although the toll telephone market approximates an oligopoly, the lowering of entry barriers has had a positive influence on carrier price, productivity, cost, and innovation. Rivalry is, in fact, so keen that toll service is in danger of becoming a commodity. In this market, price wars break out periodically.[66] Not so long ago, the average long-distance call was posted at the then astonishingly low price of 10 cents per minute. One carrier announced 5-cents-per-minute rates on one or more weekend days. AT&T countered with a 7-cents-anytime rate in response to a 5-cents offpeak plan by MCI and Sprint. Today a caller can pay as little as a penny a minute.[67] In real terms, toll telephone rates in the United States have dropped about two-thirds since 1984.[68] Falling rates stimulate telecom usage. In 1984, U.S. consumers completed 1.2 billion toll calls. By 2004, toll call usage had mushroomed to 71.9 billion calls per year.[69] Over that same period, AT&T saw its market share fall steadily. Long-distance rivalry also places a premium on cost efficiency. AT&T allocates 22 percent of its revenue to overhead cost, but MCI's smaller overhead has served as a benchmark for all carriers.[70] New optical fiber firms—traditional and nontraditional providers, such as cable TV companies—promise to make available further cost savings.

Competitive entry also forces modernization through capital spending in the toll market. In the 1980s, MCI and Sprint's adoption of fiber optics forced AT&T to write off $9 billion in investment and to inaugurate its own fiber investment program. Today, new fiber optic firms generate unrelenting pressure on toll costs and prices, with fiber costs approaching a penny per minute.

This trend suggests that the toll market has experienced immense productivity in transmission. In fact, productivity has been breathtaking: In 1975, a single optical fiber delivered 8,000 circuits; by 1995, a single fiber could accommodate 1.5 million

---

[64]"Patent Ruling Impact: The Internet Phone Upstart Could Lose a Technology and a Future," washingtonpost.com, April 6, 2007: D01.

[65]"Internet Telephone Challenges Social Contract," *New York Times* (January 5, 2004). www.nytimes.com. Accessed April, 14, 2004. See also "Telecommunications: Strong Signals the Bad Times Are Over," *Business Week* (January 12, 2004): 100–101.

[66]See, for example, Shawn Young, "A Price War Hits Internet Calling," *Wall Street Journal*, August 26, 2004: D1.

[67]www.Pennytalk.com

[68]FCC, Trends in Telephone Service, Table 12.3. Just since 1992, carriers' average revenue per minute of interstate toll service calls has dropped 60 percent, from 15 cents to 6 cents in 2004. FCC, Reference Book, 2006, Table 1.15.

[69]FCC, Statistics of Communications Common Carriers 2004/2005, Table 2.5.

[70]Seth Schiesel, "Long Distance Giants Report Solid Results for Quarter," *New York Times* (July 30, 1999): 14.

circuits.[71] More recently, new multiplexing techniques have lifted fiber capacity 16-fold. According to the Council of Economic Advisers, the cost of transmitting one bit of data over a kilometer of fiber optic cable fell by three orders of magnitude between the mid-1970s and the early 1990s. Productivity gains convert into falling costs and dropping prices and ultimately contribute to economic growth. [72]

Toll carriers are now providing IP equipment access in preference to conventional voice circuit switching technology. Here again, the telecommunications market reaps productivity gains from data routers and packet switching computers whose performance, in turn, follows Moore's Law (which holds that microprocessor productivity doubles every 18 months). The result is that IP equipment prices are falling 20 percent to 30 percent annually. One study finds that competition engendered by facilities-based VOIP service providers may have generated more than $100 billion in cost savings over a 5-year period.[73] This has not gone unnoticed: When Cisco recently announced that it had shipped its 2 millionth VOIP telephone, it noted that shipping the first million required more than 3 years, but reaching the second million took less than a year. [74]

Several U.S. toll carriers have a presence in wireless technology and service, and wireless rates are declining: From 1992 through 2006, the average local monthly bill decreased by more than 25 percent, with total annual minutes of use approaching two trillion in 2006.[75] The cell phone industry now targets the Internet market, permitting subscribers to "surf the net" while on the move. Many have wondered if Finland will serve as a prototype, where wireless has overtaken wire line facilities as the medium for voice communication. Indeed, the International Telecommunication Union (ITU), affiliated with the United Nations, estimates that worldwide there are 1.2 billion fixed telephone lines and 1.3 billion mobile phone subscribers.[76]

Meanwhile, CLECs and wireless carriers employ broadband access in an attempt to bypass RBOCs' local loop wire. Some cable TV companies now offer long-distance, local service, and Internet service packages, a prospect that raises the subversive notion that Internet telephony may well become a "free" good. Verizon (FiOS) and AT&T (U-verse) counter with fiber to the home or node, respectively, offering over 100 TV channels as part of the service bundle. The result: a rush to broadband, overtaking dial-up as the access mode of choice for households.[77]

[71]Michael King, "Too Much Long Distance," *Fortune* (March 15, 1995): 107.

[72]President's Council of Economic Advisors (CEA), Progress: and Competition in U.S. Telecommunications 1993–1998, February 8, 1999, 35. It is not unusual to find long-distance rates of 3 or 5 cents per minute. In addition, the Commerce Department has recently linked strong productivity growth of the telecommunications and information sector to recent growth in the U.S. economy more generally. Economics and Statistics Administration, Digital Economy 2003, Washington, D.C., December 2003.

[73]See NCTA, New economic study shows substantial economic benefits of facilities-based phone competition. September 21, 2006. www.ncta.com

[74]"Beyond the Bubble," *The Economist* (October 11, 2003): 18.

[75]CTIA semiannual wireless industry survey, Table 1, Chart 3. files.ctia.org/pdf/CTIA_Survey_Year_End_2006_Graphics.pdf

[76]"Beyond the Bubble," 1–2.

[77]A J.D. Power survey found in 2006 that 56 percent of residential customers subscribed to broadband access, which surpassed dial-up (44 percent) for the first time. "High-Speed Internet Overtakes Dial-Up in Market Share," *Broadband Access*, September 21, 2006, www.consumeraffairs.com/news04/2006/09/jd_power_high_speed.html

Local Telecommunications

In contrast, local telephone service prices have increased moderately since 1984. Local rates have not seen any dramatic price reductions, nor has the local telephone user benefited from price wars of the kind seen in the long-distance market. Indeed, from 1997 through 2005, the annual change in the Consumer Price Index (CPI) for local residential phone service ranged from +1.0 percent to +5.5 percent, while the interstate long distance rate for households dropped -0.7 to -11.2 percent over the same time span.[78]

The $25 billion in access fees paid by toll subscribers do stabilize local telephone rates. Still, the sunk investment of RBOCs conditions their performance. Huge embedded plant and facilities costs militate against a rapid conversion by RBOCs to new technologies such as IP; it is estimated that it will take years for a full conversion to IP by local incumbent carriers.[79]

Still, entry at the local level has had a therapeutic influence upon RBOC performance. As cable companies Comcast, Time Warner, Cox and others attract 27.7 million high-speed Internet customers—one-third higher than the DSL total—the RBOCs have undertaken competitive responses with some success: Verizon and AT&T have introduced price cuts for basic broadband access to $19.95 a month in hopes of wooing new subscribers.[80] The move to add DSL subscribers is a defense against cable companies that now offer broadband access bundled with video and phone services. Realizing they have no video offering to compete with cable, AT&T and Qwest Communications recently signed contracts with EchoStar's Dish Network to bundle video into their service package for phone and data services.[81] In addition, Verizon and to a lesser extent AT&T are seeking to "leapfrog" the cable companies by supplanting their copper wires with high-capacity fiber optic lines.[82]

RBOCs offer wireless capability across the nation and compete with affiliates of long-distance carriers. Although wireless rates have dropped in the United States, their 40-cents-per-minute cost stands in sharp contrast to an 8-cents-per-minute rate in Toronto, Canada.[83] Rate disparities once again suggest that an industry's economic performance is not unrelated to its structure.

In sum, the salutary effects of rivalry on carrier performance are striking: The U.S. long-distance market embraces the productivity gains of computers and telecommunications while coming to grips with commoditization and thin margins. In contrast, the U.S. local market has seemed comfortable with its technological lot and its large stream of access revenues. Is this quiet life about to become less quiet? Public policy will surely have a say.

---

[78]FCC, Trends in Telephone Service, Table 12.3.
[79]"Battered Telecoms Face New Challenge," 2.
[80]See www22.verizon.com/residential.com and www.usa.att.com/dsl
[81]"DSL Gaining at Cable's Expense?" CNET News.com, July 25, 2003. www.news.com.com. Accessed April, 14, 2004. See also "Price War Looms for High-Speed Net Access," *USA Today* (November 14, 2003): B1.
[82]"Internet Services Challenge Definition of 'Phone Company,' " *Washington Post* (October 23, 2003): E1; "AT&T Has 18,000 Video Subscribers," Associated Press, April 18, 2007. www.forbes.com/feeds/ap/2007/04/18/ap3627118.html?partner=alerts
[83]Peter J. Howe, "U.S. Cell Phone Costs Fall but Stay above Europe's," *International Herald Tribune* (June 24, 1999): 12.

▪▪▪ V. Public Policy

How should the United States address such questions as universal service subsidies, local competitive substitutes, and corporate mergers as multiple technologies and markets expand and converge? In answering these questions, the United States confronts three major policy options: maintain the status quo, enlarge regulatory oversight, or promote greater competition in local telecommunications. Each of these has advantages and drawbacks.

Status Quo: Pro

Those who defend a status quo policy marshal several arguments. First, the Telecommunications Act of 1996 introduced competition, CLECs, into the local telephone market. CLECs offer new transmission bandwidth that competes with RBOCs in the retail market. Cable firms now offer a broadband alternative to the copper wire pair and bundle Internet and local and long-distance as a service offering. Proponents of the status quo insist that local access charges are declining and that the annual billion-dollar subsidy ensures the universality of telephone service, particularly to the economically disadvantaged.

Proponents of the status quo also assert that competitive substitutes do intrude into the local market, whether DSL, fixed wireless, cable modems, or satellite relay. Some RBOCs are employing satellite dishes, terrestrial wireless, and super-fast fiber optics as means to confer fast Internet access to their customers. [84] The loop market, in short, is not a technological backwater.

A status quo policy insists that RBOC horizontal mergers are monitored to comply with a public interest standard. Adherents to the status quo challenge critics who contend that government oversight (state PUCs, the Federal Communications Commission, and the Department of Justice) is incapable of divining the merits of corporate consolidation. These regulatory bodies can and will determine whether horizontal affiliation generates scale efficiencies that position RBOCs to participate in a worldwide information market. If regulatory opponents disagree, they can pursue their case in the forum of legal due process. Regulatory institutions also possess the expertise and knowledge to monitor RBOC vertical diversification into the long-distance market. The FCC has examined the merits of the spate of recent RBOC and other mergers. Congress, in fact, empowered the FCC to assess whether sufficient competition exists in local telecommunications as a condition for RBOC entry into long distance.

The regulatory machinery, state and federal, can and will strike the right balance between competition and regulation. Indeed, the FCC has recently sought a rebalance in designating information service status on broadband technologies such as fiber, cable modems, broadband over power lines (BPL), and high-speed wireless.

Status Quo: Con

Critics of the status quo argue that the intent of the Telecommunications Act of 1996 to bring competition to local telecommunications has failed. RBOCs and a number of state utility commissions have opposed local competition at virtually every step,

---

[84]David Rohde, "Rivals Slam SBC/Ameritech Proposal," *Network World* (July 19, 1999): 29.

including filing briefs stating that the 1996 statute violates the U.S. Constitution. RBOCs, they say, will not tolerate competition in local facilities irrespective of subscriber demand for high-speed Internet access. Critics also remind status quo defenders that the market share of CLECs remains fragile and insignificant as a market force, particularly after the FCC deregulated various broadband services.

Second, critics of the status quo submit that universal service and the local access charge are nothing but an incumbent's ploy to protect its local telephone monopoly. RBOCs that demand that universal service be extended to the Internet are simply asking that their "natural" monopoly status be expanded in perpetuity. Intercarrier compensation for facilities use has been much studied and yet seemingly intractable for private and public resolution.

Third, critics observe that local competitive substitutes subsist at the sufferance of RBOC economic power. For one thing, the RBOCs manifest a conflict of interest. They engage in wholesale circuits and retail circuits. The result is that potential entrants are subject to a classic economic squeeze. Regulatory critics ask why AT&T withdrew from leasing RBOC lines after spending $4 billion. The answer, they say, is that RBOCs effectively choked off market entry. Those critical of the status quo remind Congress that not one RBOC merger has ever been enjoined by a state regulatory commission, the FCC, the Department of Justice, or the Federal Trade Commission. The nation's antitrust watchdogs, say critics, are not unlike Rip Van Winkle.

The result is more than disquieting: RBOCs are gathering more and more landlines into fewer and fewer hands. Certainly, RBOC horizontal acquisitions are not grounded on the premise of bringing high-speed bandwidth to the needs of electronic commerce. Rather, say critics, RBOC mergers are merely an accumulation of monopoly assets in an eternal search for guaranteed local subsidies.

Critics of a "steady as she goes" policy question the FCC's approval of SBC's $73 billion acquisition of Ameritech on the condition that SBC serve as a CLEC in 30 non-SBC markets. Presumably, FCC policy rests on the proposition that a marriage of two monopolies will somehow inspire "good" conduct and that FCC oversight will assure it. Critics of regulation insist that nothing in the past prevented SBC from establishing competitive services in Ameritech's territory or vice versa. Thus, under the guise of pursuing the public interest, the FCC has eliminated two competitors from the marketplace while touting the virtues of an Internet economy. Regulatory critics insist that the Internet was sired not by telephone monopoly but by telephone competition.

Finally, critics of regulation submit that a status quo policy is a case of institutional amnesia. Telecommunications policy today has forgotten why AT&T was broken apart in the first place: The courts approved the 1984 AT&T divestiture because of the obvious failure of government regulation. What, they say, has changed since then to inspire confidence in resurrecting the public utility principle?

Regulatory Option: Pro

Consider next the pros and cons of a second policy choice, more regulation. Those supporting more rather than less public oversight insist that competition at the local facilities level constitutes an elusive dream. The reality, they say, is that the copper loop will long remain embedded in the telephone plant. The loop is, has, and will remain a local monopoly. No market force will dissolve or remove that stubborn fact. In addition, incumbents can acquire or merge with LECs or CLECs, and markets thereby remain concentrated. Proponents of the regulatory option conclude that RBOC control of local facilities requires more rather than less public oversight.

Regulatory advocates note that the CLEC phenomenon was created by the Telecommunications Act of 1996. CLECs are a creature of Congress; their life can be sustained by artificial means only. Stated differently, promoting competition and regulation under our current policy is a prescription for chaos. Proponents of public oversight insist that state regulatory commissions should retain undiluted jurisdiction over local telephone plant. That policy has provided the United States with the best telecommunications system as measured by any standard. Federal intrusion into a local monopoly simply undermines the effectiveness of regulation at the state level.

Adherents to the regulatory option argue that not only has local telephone service been recognized as a universal subscriber right but also that universality can and must be extended to Internet users. The Internet market now reveals a digital divide that segregates those consumers who are financially endowed from those who are financially disadvantaged. Universal service has bridged a voice divide; universal service also can overcome an Internet divide. To ensure consumer equity, regulation must play an affirmative role. The FCC's e-rate makes available subsidies for K-12 schools and public libraries. Those constituencies must share the benefits of affirmative regulation. Moreover, as VOIP becomes more widespread in a world beset by unrest, law enforcement officials arguably will need the same wiretap access they now enjoy with respect to the public switched network in order to protect the public.

Advocates for regulation insist that competitive substitutes are often misconstrued by free-market advocates. New technology complements but does not replace existing telecommunications facilities and services. Regulation ensures a coordinated adaptation of assets by local telecommunications carriers. Moreover, few quarrel with the insistence that the Internet is endowed with important elements of "public convenience and necessity." If nothing else, widespread Internet access accords the United States a comparative advantage in a world of global competition; such supremacy has not occurred under current policies as the U.S. has of late failed to break into the top 10 country broadband ratings compiled by international organizations such as the Organization for Economic Cooperation and Development, and the United Nations.

According to some regulatory adherents, control over horizontal acquisitions by RBOCs must and should remain the province of state regulatory commissions. They, not the federal government, are ultimately responsible for local telephone performance. Nor do state commissions exercise that mandate alone. Some 30,000 local and county authorities are empowered to define and promulgate the interest of the consuming public. Certainly, no one can deny San Antonio or Detroit's right to judge whether cable modems are to be shared or will remain the exclusive property of cable TV firms.

Finally, regulatory advocates insist that RBOC vertical mergers do not occur in a vacuum. All acquisitions are studied and monitored for their public interest dimension. Only regulation can determine whether the public will benefit from local telephone competition or consolidation.

Regulatory Option: Con

Critics of the regulatory option insist that the cause of local bandwidth gridlock is none other than regulation itself. Any shortfall in RBOC economic performance rests ultimately upon government disincentives. RBOCs are utilities; not surprisingly, they behave as utilities. In addition, utilities institutionalize cost-plus. Critics suggest that regulation by state commissions masks and protects the poor performance of the RBOCs, and the goal of universal access is simply a front for monopoly privilege.

Regulatory critics contend that local access charges reinforce market power under a public interest fig leaf. RBOCs and state commissions may proclaim local technical diversity, but only because they have been unable to stifle new competitors. Regulatory critics contend that it is not the RBOC that is responsible for inadequate bandwidth or obsolete plant. Rather, responsibility rests with a public sector that aids and abets RBOC market power.

Local substitutes, say regulatory critics, have arisen in spite of, not because of, enlightened government oversight. State utility commissions might proclaim local technical diversity, but only because they have been unable to stop new entrants. After all, PUCs regard competitive substitutes as the antithesis of scale economies and a threat to the orderly premise of public oversight. Potential rivals are seen as cluttering up otherwise clean regulatory dockets.

Regulatory critics conclude that RBOC horizontal integration promotes market concentration. If nothing else, market concentration guarantees public sector job security. Critics suggest that Professor James Buchanan's well-known observations on the economics of public choice or Professor George Stigler's famous capture theory of regulation merit application in this context.

Doubters of regulatory efficacy point to lapses highlighted in the recent *Bell Atlantic vs. Twombly* court case. [85] In that case, the plaintiffs claim that (under the regulators' noses) the Bell companies illegally conspired to thwart competition by excluding new entrants from their territories and agreeing to stay out of each other's markets. Supporters retort that such "parallel conduct" is alleged but not yet proven and, besides, that is why there are antitrust laws.

Finally, skeptics warn of regulatory creep. "Net neutrality" advocates caution that Internet infrastructure firms such as the RBOCs and cable companies will establish toll roads on the information highway, discriminating against content providers like Yahoo, Google, eBay, and Microsoft, not to mention the average consumer. The critics reply that such talk promotes adoption of a solution where no problem currently exists, and that net neutrality prescriptions would discourage investment and retard innovation.

Competition Option: Pro

The competitive option concurs with the observation that the source of local bandwidth gridlock is regulation. Free-market advocates offer a simple policy remedy: Deregulate the local loop market. Canada has recently seen the light, why not us? In fact, do more. RBOCs manifest a conflict of interest to the extent they are wholesalers and retailers of local circuits. There should be little wonder that as a result CLECs

---

[85] *Bell Atlantic Corp. v. Twombly*, 127 S.Ct. 575 (2006).

subsist as bit players on the local telecom stage. RBOCs can throttle rivals through a time-honored vertical squeeze, accelerate new equipment, and then tie up rivals in regulatory due process where RBOCs hold a comparative advantage. That power was the thrust of the Justice Department's 1974 antitrust case against AT&T.

The remedy to the vertical squeeze, say procompetitive advocates, is restructuring (i.e., "divestiture II"). The RBOCs must spin off their retail operations from their wholesale operations.[86] The RBOCs' conflict-of-interest boil must be lanced in the tradition of the AT&T divestiture I. Then and only then will the public have any real opportunity to enjoy the benefits of price, cost, productivity, innovative performance, and, most important, adequate bandwidth capacity.

Free-market proponents insist that universal service is an anachronism. Market forces now ensure customer price, choice, and quality. Internet Protocol telephony holds the promise of making toll calls a "free" service. Under a policy of open markets, bandwidth access will no longer be reduced to a zero-sum game.

Open-market advocates contend that a thousand flowers can bloom in loop substitutes. Few in telecommunications, they argue, can predict which technology will prevail in the industry over the long term. Fewer still are regulatory bodies endowed with the gift of foresight. Rather, the give and take of market forces will yield undistorted signals for investment and pricing, and reveal technical options appropriate to tomorrow's consumer needs.

Finally, free-market proponents question whether RBOCs should be permitted to engage in horizontal acquisitions. Whatever the answer, market advocates suggest that regulatory authorities are the least qualified to make that determination. Rather, RBOC mergers must meet the test of the nation's antitrust laws.

Competition Option: Con

Skeptics of the competitive/antitrust option reply that the odds favoring RBOC structural reform are virtually nonexistent. For one thing, the RBOCs surely possess sufficient political power to block any move toward their own restructuring or divestiture. State regulatory commissions, they argue, accept their mandate to protect local RBOCs, posing a united front against libertarians convinced that a new era of deregulation is upon us.

Skeptics of open competition insist that universal service evokes images of equity and fairness, and reflects regulation at its best. Any proposal to deregulate local telephone service is tantamount to abandoning the telephone subscriber to the illusion of free choice. In any case, they insist, RBOCs and state commissions stand opposed to any move toward open local markets.

Opponents of competition note that local loop subsidies represent the classic economic dilemma of the commons. Someone must rise above narrow self-interest and determine the public good. To assault the local access subsidy is essentially to attack those citizens who are most vulnerable in our society. In exercising its mandate to impose an e-rate or Internet tax, the FCC is merely carrying out the wishes of Congress.

To ask the nation to desist from regulatory oversight is to dream about a fantasy world. Critics of competition insist that horizontal integration at the RBOC level is

---

[86]Peter Howe, "Breakup, Then Buildup," *Boston Globe* (June 6, 1999): F7.

now U.S. telecommunications policy. The FCC has conditioned and approved a number of mergers: Bell Atlantic with NYNEX, and then with GTE; SBC with PacTel, SNET, Ameritech, and BellSouth; US West with Qwest. In a world of global competition, bipartisan agreement now demonstrates that the nation's antitrust laws are a legacy of a bygone era.

Critics of competition insist that RBOC and cable company entry into each other's market is increasingly a fact of life. However, if public policy is adamant that RBOCs must share telephone lines, cable firms will be under enormous pressure to do the same. Critics of local competition conclude that any policy must accept the fact that RBOCs exhibit market preeminence, that divestiture is not a serious proposal on any public agenda, and that market entry in loop bandwidth will remain impervious to genuine competition as RBOCs dominate fiber and high-speed wireless options. Public utility regulation, in short, must not be consigned to the ash heap of public policy history.

CONCLUSION ▪▪▪▪▪▪▪

Two decades after the Bell System breakup, the drift of the American economy toward electronic commerce continues to accelerate. Technological convergence and Schumpeterian-style "creative destruction" are redrawing market boundaries and reconfiguring traditional corporate alignments.[87] Services are bundled, telcos and cable companies fight over wireless spectrum and TV fare, and fiber optics deployment accelerates.[88] RBOCs are consolidating, long distance carriers are being subsumed, iPODs are vanquishing CDs and record stores, YouTube and Internet television run roughshod over the DVD market, and Bell Labs now flies a French flag.[89] The long-distance telecom market today experiences quantum jumps in bandwidth growth and productivity. Juxtaposed against that dynamism stands the quiescent but awakening local exchange market. Can these two markets—so distinct in tradition, technology, regulation, and access—be bridged? Thus far, no consensus has emerged. Ultimately, the public must decide which policy options are appropriate. The process is likely to include an admixture of technology, economics, and political maneuvering.[90] To that extent, the issues generated by an e-commerce economy are sure to remain a front-burner controversy on the public policy agenda for the foreseeable future.

---

[87]See, for example, "Cable vs. Fiber," *Business Week*, November 1, 2004: 36; "Comcast Aims to Become the Google of Television," *Chicago Tribune*, October 20, 2005; "Your Television is Ringing," *The Economist*, October 12, 2006.

[88]For example, pundits are watching intently the competing fiber deployment strategies of AT&T (shorter-term, fiber-to-the-node) and Verizon (longer view, fiber-to-the-home).

[89]In November 2006, the United States approved French telecom equipment manufacturer Alcatel's $11.8 billion acquisition of Lucent Technologies, the former Bell System's Western Electric, including the renowned Bell telephone Laboratories. "Lucent-Alcatel Merger Gets Final Thumb's Up," Reuters, November 20, 2006. As another sign of the times, in January 2006, Western Union quietly stopped sending telegrams for the first time in 145 years, and by that fall had been invited to join the S&P 500. www .businessweek.com/ap/finacialnews/D8KC5P2O0.htm

[90]To give an indication how complex this process will be, consider that scientists are hard at work determining how to re-design the current Internet for the future. As one of its members passionately argues, "Let's invent the car instead of giving the same horse better hay." See, e.g., "A broad-based team of Stanford researchers aims to overhaul the Internet," Stanford Report, March 14, 2007. http://news-service.stanfrod .edu/news/2007/march14/clean-031407.html

SUGGESTIONS FOR FURTHER READING ▪▪▪▪▪▪▪

Publications

Brock, Gerald W. 2003. *The Second Information Revolution*. (Cambridge, MA: Harvard University Press).

Cairncross, Frances. 1997. *The Death of Distance*. (Cambridge, MA: Harvard Business School Press).

Computer Science and Telecommunications Board of the National Research Council. 2001. *The Internet's Coming of Age*. (Washington, D.C.: National Academy Press).

Thomas L. Friedman. 2005. *The World is Flat*. (New York: Farrar, Strauss, and Giroux).

Nuechterlein, Jonathan and Philip J. Weiser. 2005. *Digital Crossroads: American Telecommunications Policy in the Internet Age* (Cambridge, MA: MIT Press).

CHAPTER 9

The Airline Industry

WILLIAM G. SHEPHERD AND JAMES W. BROCK

For three decades "Deregulation" has been a potent rallying cry: Get government off the back of business! Rein in the "nanny state"! Liberate consumers and producers in a free marketplace to allocate resources and determine the prices, quality, and methods of providing goods and services.

But what does effective deregulation require? Does it mean *no* government policy whatsoever? Does it require merely an absence of government intervention in the marketplace? In a laissez-faire environment, will competition automatically flourish as an effective mechanism for regulating society's economic decision making? Or can privately contrived mergers, monopolies, and anticompetitive practices subvert competition and thwart the ultimate goals of deregulation?

These are the core questions that continue to animate an analysis of the nation's airline industry—a field that was comprehensively regulated by the federal government for forty years before deregulation commenced in the late-1970s. These questions are of more than idle academic interest: According to the Air Transport Association, commercial aviation in the U.S. directly and indirectly contributes $1.2 trillion to the nation's gross domestic product, $380 billion to earnings, and supports over 11 million jobs. Airline officials portray the industry as critically important to the nation's well-being, "a vital infrastructure for U.S. commerce, carrying 620 million passengers and 22 billion ton miles of cargo each year," as well as "an essential social and business link between America's cities and its smaller communities."[1]

At the same time, however, the industry is the subject of scathing indictments in the media and Congress. Feature articles in prominent publications, as well as witnesses testifying before congressional committees, level charges of "airline hell," plead for an air passenger bill of rights (including the provision of adequate water for those trapped for hours on delayed planes), and decry the depredations inflicted on a flying public portrayed as verging on outright revolt.

---

[1]Campbell-Hill Aviation Group, "Commercial Aviation and the American Economy," study prepared for the Air Transport Association of America, March 2006, i; Leo F. Mullin, Chairman and Chief Executive Officer, Delta Airlines, prepared testimony before the U.S. Congress. Senate. Committee on Commerce, Science, and Transportation, October 2, 2002.

Clearly, airline deregulation continues to be hotly debated, especially in the wake of the 9/11 terrorist attacks in 2001, and the multibillion dollar airline losses, the bankruptcies of four major carriers, and the billions of dollars of government financial support that followed thereafter.

▮▮▮ I. History

Every school child learns that the aviation age was launched in 1903, when the Wright Brothers piloted their motor-driven contraption through the air for 12 seconds over Kitty Hawk, North Carolina, covering a distance shorter than the wingspan of a modern commercial jetliner.

A decade later, the first scheduled air service commenced on the St. Petersburg–Tampa Air Boat Line, carrying a manifest of a single passenger twice a day across Tampa Bay for a fee of $5. Intrepid travelers soon could fly from Long Island to Detroit (an air trip of 4 days), or from Chicago to Seattle (5 days), usually with rail tickets included in the fare "just in case." Seated in canvas yacht chairs, refreshed by windows that could be opened, and braced with "burp bags," passengers tipped pilots for safe landings and asked them to sign official "certificate of flight" stubs attached to their tickets. Early air passengers could thrill to the roar of hand-cranked aircraft engines and grass landing fields, while braving the loss of body heat (and sometimes consciousness) in unpressurized aircraft climbing over mountain ranges. They could fly the "Route of the Conquistadors" or contemplate the consequences of patronizing the "Fireball Air Express."[2]

To stimulate the fledgling field, the federal government began awarding contracts in the 1920s to carry the nation's mail through the air. Initially, these contracts were limited in scope and competitively bid for by carriers. Subsequently, however, government air mail contracts became instruments of privilege, providing a handful of carriers with permanent operating rights over major routes and cities, monopoly rights that were officially grandfathered in place by the Civil Aeronautics Act of 1938.[3] The 1938 Act created the Civil Aeronautics Board (CAB) and charged it with regulating interstate air travel in order to promote a high degree of safety, sound economic conditions, and proper adaptation of air transportation to the country's commercial, postal, and defense needs. To carry out its mandate, the CAB was given four key powers: (1) The entry power to grant or deny the "certificates of public convenience and necessity" an airline was required to hold before being allowed to fly interstate routes; (2) the rate power to approve or reject the fares charged by carriers; (3) the power to approve or deny mergers involving certificated carriers, with approval conferring immunity from the antitrust laws; and (4) the power to approve or disapprove collusive agreements among carriers, again with approval conferring immunity from the antitrust laws.

Unlike the regulation of such "natural monopolies" as telephone service and electricity, however, competition was initially supposed to play an important role in achieving

---

[2]Carl Solberg, *Conquest of the Skies: A History of Commercial Aviation in America* (Boston: Little, Brown and Co., 1979); and R.E.G. Davies, *Rebels and Reformers of the Airways* (Washington, D.C.: Smithsonian Institution Press, 1987).

[3]For details see Horace M. Gray, "Air Transportation," in *The Structure of American Industry*, rev. ed., Walter Adams ed. (New York: Macmillan, 1954), 466–469.

the goals set forth for the CAB. Thus, the commission whose recommendations shaped the 1938 legislation urged that there "must be enough competition to serve as a spur to the eager search for progress," and that there "must be no arbitrary denial of the right of entry of newcomers into the field where they can make an adequate showing of their readiness to render a better public service than could otherwise be obtained. There must be no policy of a permanent freezing of the present air map, with respect either to the location of its routes or the identity of their operators. The present operators of airlines have no inherent right to a monopoly of the routes that they serve."[4] The 1938 Act emphasized that "no certificate shall confer any proprietary, property or exclusive right in the use of any air space, civil airway, landing area or air navigation facility."

Air travel grew spectacularly, as Table 9-1 records, from 6,000 passengers in 1926, to 400,000 in 1930, reaching 3 million by 1940. A cynic might say the modern age of air travel had arrived by 1946, when *Fortune* magazine published a feature article asking "What's Wrong with the Airlines?" and reported that to "travel by plane, a passenger must now sacrifice his comfort, his sleep, and often his baggage. He must endure inconveniences that rise to the level of punishment" with only his sins to "drearily contemplate."[5]

Perhaps this was because the CAB had come to conceive its primary mission to be protecting the field—including the dominant grandfathered carriers American, United, Eastern, and TWA—from competition. Thus by 1975, despite an exponential explosion in air traffic over the preceding decades, the CAB had refused to authorize a single major new trunk carrier to compete. Nonscheduled carriers attempting to

TABLE 9-1 U.S. Scheduled Airline Travel, 1926–2005

Year	Domestic Passengers Emplaned (thousands)
1926	6
1930	385
1940	2,803
1950	17,468
1960	56,351
1960	56,351
1970	153,662
1980	272,829
1990	423,565
2000	610,600
2005	670,360

Source: Air Transport Association, U.S. Airlines: Annual Operations, Traffic, and Capacity, available at www.airlines.org/econ

---

[4]Quoted in U.S. Congress. Senate. Subcommittee on Administrative Practice and Procedure. Report: Civil Aeronautics Board: Practices and Procedures, 94th Cong., 1st sess., 1975, 213.
[5]*Fortune* (August 1946): 73–201.

enter the industry after World War II by combining post-war surplus military aircraft with droves of decommissioned pilots, and offering deeply discounted fares to promote traffic, were harassed and tightly circumscribed by the CAB. Carriers other than the incumbent majors were rigidly compartmentalized within regional geographic areas and relegated to subsidiary "feeder" status. At the same time, the CAB restricted the number of major carriers allowed to compete on routes. The board seemed to abhor the prospect of price competition: It rejected proposed fares when they were below the fares of other carriers, especially when they threatened to reduce the profits of incumbent airlines. Over time the board effectively came to function as a cartel forum where carriers could discuss and agree on the fares that the CAB subsequently would validate and enforce. It permitted anticompetitive mergers and, at times, encouraged them, while steadily expanding the range of airline practices exempted from the antitrust laws.[6]

By the 1970s, the consequences of 40 years of government regulation seemed clear: The industry was artificially concentrated in the hands of a few major airlines, despite the fact that the growth in traffic could support far more carriers. Routes were inefficiently gerrymandered among carriers to placate incumbent operators. Airfares on regulated interstate routes were as much as double the fares charged on comparable but unregulated *intra*state routes within large states, particularly Texas and California, where price competition was allowed by state aviation agencies. The CAB seemed congenitally compelled to regulate each and every area in which carriers might attempt to compete, including carry-on luggage and free drinks, while planes wastefully flew half empty.[7]

The case for deregulating the industry reached critical mass. Bolstered by economic studies demonstrating that CAB regulation stifled competition, institutionalized inefficiency and inflated fares, the appeal of airline deregulation spread across the political spectrum. By 1975, free-market Republicans and consumer-oriented Democrats alike supported deregulation and its promise to lower airfares, expand consumer choice, and promote efficiency.

In 1978, the Airline Deregulation Act was passed, calling for free entry by 1980 (subject to safety and technical operating requirements), free pricing by 1983, and the abolition of the CAB by 1985. The Act declared that, henceforth, the paramount goal of public policy would be the "encouragement, development, and maintenance of an air transportation system relying on actual and potential competition to provide efficiency, innovation, and low prices, and to determine the variety, quality, and price of air transportation services."[8] Highlighting the emphasis on competition, the Act underscored the importance of the "prevention of unfair, deceptive, predatory, or anticompetitive practices in air transportation," including "the avoidance . . . of unreasonable industry concentration, excessive market domination, and monopoly power."[9]

---

[6]See Walter Adams and James W. Brock, *The Bigness Complex*, 2nd ed., chapter 17 and the sources cited therein (Palo Alto, CA: Stanford University Press, 2004).
[7]Ibid.
[8]Airline Deregulation Act of 1978, Public Law 95-504, 92 Stat. 1706, 1707 (October 24, 1978).
[9]Ibid.

Thus liberated, the major carriers quickly began adjusting their routes and schedules, while a number of smaller regional airlines (US Airways, Piedmont, Delta) vigorously expanded the geographic scope of their operations. By 1983 more than 60 new carriers had commenced interstate service, including People Express, Southwest, New York Air, and World Airways. They cut fares by 20 to 40 percent and offered "few frills" service, with the result that air travel grew at a rate significantly above the historical trend.

Subsequently, however, a number of developments decisively shaped the industry.

First, a rapid-fire series of mergers and acquisitions in the mid-1980s enabled the majors to strengthen their positions by absorbing promising new competitors: Northwest acquired Republic Airlines, one of its major regional rivals in the upper-Midwest. TWA acquired Ozark Airlines, an expanding regional carrier in the lower-Midwest region. Delta acquired Western Air Lines, another formidable regional carrier in the Rocky Mountain West, while US Airways acquired Piedmont and Pacific Southwest, two more expanding regional carriers. At the same time, Texas Air acquired control of Continental, Eastern, and People Express.

Second, the major carriers bolstered their collective dominance by gaining control (either directly or indirectly via operating agreements) of many of the nation's leading commuter airlines—small carriers which, had they remained independent, might have expanded their operations and become more competitive regionally or even nationally.

Third, the majors implemented hub-and-spoke route systems for funneling passengers into central hub airports where they were transferred between planes and dispatched again to their final destinations. The result, as we will see in the next section, was to divide the country into a patchwork of powerful hub monopolies.

Finally, 9/11 triggered a total shutdown of the nation's air space and the grounding of all aircraft. Its aftermath, including an economic recession followed by soaring fuel prices, jarred the industry, especially the largest carriers. Commercial air traffic dropped in 2001 and 2002, but began rising again after 2002, and by 2004 had reached record levels. Yet this interruption in growth, while not unprecedented, exacerbated trends already underway in the industry, including the relatively higher costs of the major carriers' operations, leading, in turn, to the bankruptcy of United, US Airways, Delta and Northwest during the period from 2002 to 2005.

▪▪▪ II. Structure

The most important elements of the industry's structure are the nature of demand, the relative size and concentration of carriers, the proliferation of alliances and cooperative agreements among airlines, and barriers to effective competition.

The Nature of Demand

For distances of 300 miles or more, no close substitutes exist for the speed of air travel. Another important characteristic of demand is the urgency of the trip and the flexibility of the flyer's schedule: Leisure travelers have considerable leeway in planning their trips; they can travel near or far away, at one time of year or another, and they can do so by car, train, or bus instead of by air. As a result, this group is quite sensitive to price;

in economic parlance, its price elasticity of demand is high. In contrast, passengers flying for professional purposes (such as business) typically do not have such flexibility in their scheduling: They must travel long distances, frequently on short notice, so their price elasticity of demand for air travel is low. These differing passenger groups and elasticities of demand create an incentive for carriers to engage in price discrimination by charging higher fares to professional travelers and lower fares to leisure passengers—contingent, of course, on the carriers' ability to limit competition for the high-fare, low-elasticity passengers.

Relative Firm Size and Concentration

Approximately 120 certificated air passenger carriers operate in the U.S., classified into three main categories: The majors are the largest carriers, operating extensive national and international routes (sometimes also referred to as legacy or network carriers). National carriers are smaller lines operating route systems that are less extensive and more focused (for example, Delta, a major carrier, serves 457 destinations in 97 countries with 1,500 flights daily, while JetBlue, a national carrier, serves 50 destinations); these lines typically are referred to as low-cost carriers, owing to their low cost, low fare policies. Regional/commuter carriers are the most numerous category, encompassing some 80 operators; these firms fly smaller aircraft on thinly traveled routes to and from smaller communities, primarily feeding passengers into the larger carriers' national and international systems.

The majors represent the lion's share of traffic, accounting for 84 percent of U.S. commercial air passenger traffic, while national and regional/commuter carriers account for 13 percent and 3 percent of the remainder, respectively. The economic physiognomy of these various carriers is depicted in Table 9-2, where the disproportionate relative size of the major airlines is apparent.

Concentration in the industry can be analyzed in a number of dimensions. Table 9-3 depicts trends in airline concentration at the national level, where it can be seen that the initial effect following deregulation in 1978 was to lower the level of national concentration as new carriers entered the field and as existing carriers expanded their operations. The rash of mergers during the mid-1980s, however, reversed this trend, and raised concentration, with the top eight carriers coming to account for 91 percent of the nation's air passenger traffic by 1992. Since then, concentration at the national level has subsided, with the combined share of carriers other than the Big Eight growing from 9 percent in 1992 to 17 percent more recently. This decline in concentration has been induced by successful upstarts like Southwest Airlines (whose operations have grown from three Boeing 737s serving three cities within Texas in 1971, to 445 aircraft and 31,000 employees today), with a national market share that has grown from 2 percent in 1987 to 12 percent; JetBlue, whose operations have grown since it commenced operating in 2000 from 21 aircraft to 93 aircraft; and AirTran, whose operations have expanded from 53 planes and operating revenues of $211 million in 1997, to 108 aircraft and revenues of $1.8 billion today. Still, the eight largest carriers continue to collectively account for 83 percent of all passenger traffic, bolstered by the acquisition of TWA by American Airlines in 2001 (providing American a dominant position at St. Louis), and the merger between USAirways and

TABLE 9-2 U.S. Airlines 2006

	Operating Revenues (millions)	Passengers Carried (thousands)	Number of Aircraft Operated	Number of Employees
Major Carriers				
American	$ 22,269	76,922	672	75,972
United	19,112	57,367	458	54,877
Delta	17,110	63,838	480	52,229
Continental	12,701	35,645	356	32,478
Northwest	12,504	44,900	380	35,735
US Airways[a]	11,611	51,781	374	21,894
Southwest	8,798	95,663	445	31,291
Other Carriers				
Alaska Airlines	3,273	21,050	110	9,045
SkyWest[b]	3,068	29,986	416	14,485
JetBlue	2,176	17,807	93	7,560
American Eagle	1,917	17,977	300	12,000
AirTran	1,841	19,709	108	8,000
ExpessJet[c]	1,655	15,976	274	6,700
Comair	1,249	10,233	168	6,500
Mesa	1,162	12,979	198	5,000
Frontier	1,111	8,517	55	5,000
Pinnacle[d]	833	8,608	139	3,700
ATA	803	2,559	32	4,534
Air Wisconsin	579	5,356	70	2,300

[a] includes America West, merged in 2005.

[b] includes Atlantic Southeast Airlines, merged in 2005.

[c] doing business as Continental Express.

[d] doing business as NWA Airlink.

Source: Bureau of Transportation Statistics, U.S. Department of Transportation, www.transtats.bts.gov/carriers.asp, and company web sites.

America West in 2005 (providing USAirways a dominant position at America West's Phoenix hub). And as we shall see subsequently, few nonmajor carriers are genuinely independent competitors, but instead frequently operate as close affiliates of the major airlines.

On the largest, most heavily traveled routes, Table 9-4 shows that concentration remains high, with the two largest carriers typically accounting for two-thirds or more of passenger traffic. Although smaller low-cost carriers have expanded their presence in recent years, from operating in 1,594 domestic city-pair markets in 1998 to 2,304 city-pair markets by 2003, the General Accountability Office finds that nearly 3,500 of the nation's top 5,000 city-pair air markets continue to be dominated by a single carrier

TABLE 9-3 Industry Concentration: Nationwide

Year	Top Four Airline Share	Top Eight Airline Share
1978	51%	78%
1983	45	73
1992	66	91
2000	61	86
2006[a]	53	83

Note: Calculated on basis of revenue passenger miles flown.

[a] Twelve months ending November 2006. American Airlines includes American Eagle; Delta includes Comair; Northwest includes Mesaba and Pinnacle; Continental includes ExpressJet; US Airways includes America West.

Source: Air Transport Association, Economic Reports 1978–2000 (Washington, D.C.) (for individual carrier data); Bureau of Transportation Statistics, Department of Transportation, Schedule T-1 (www.transtats.bts.gov/homepage.asp) for industry totals for each year, and for 2006 data.

TABLE 9-4 Industry Concentration: Major U.S. Air Routes, May 2005–April 2006

Route	Largest Carrier and Share	Second Largest Carrier and Share	Top Two Carriers Combined
Chicago-New York	American 36%	United 28%	64%
Chicago-Los Angeles	American 39	United 35	74
Atlanta-New York	Delta 59	AirTran 21	80
Chicago-Washington	United 53	American 24	77
Atlanta-Washington	Delta 63	AirTran 24	87
Chicago-Denver	United 49	American 18	67
Los Angeles-New York	JetBlue 31	American 28	59

Note: Chicago includes Midway and O'Hare airports. New York includes LaGuardia, Kennedy, Long Island, and Newark, NJ, airports. Los Angeles includes Burbank, Ontario, and Santa Ana airports. Washington includes National and Dulles airports. American Airlines includes affiliate American Eagle. Delta Airlines includes affiliates Atlantic Southeast, Chautauqua, and Comair. United Airlines includes affiliate Air Wisconsin.

Source: Bureau of Transportation Statistics data collated by Steven C. Martin, Assistant Director, U.S. Government Accountability Office.

controlling half or more of all passenger traffic, with 85 percent of these markets dominated by a major legacy airline.[10]

At the regional and metropolitan level, the monopolizing impact of the hub-and-spoke route systems instituted by the majors following deregulation is evident in

---

[10]U.S. General Accountability Office, "Airline Deregulation: Reregulating the Airline Industry Would Likely Reverse Consumer Benefits and Not Save Airline Pensions," Washington, D.C. (June 2006): 17; and idem, "Commercial Aviation: Legacy Airlines Must Further Reduce Costs to Restore Profitability," Washington, D.C. (August 2004): 45–47.

TABLE 9-5 Industry Concentration: Major Hub Airports

Airport	2006 Top Two Carriers and Market Shares (%)		1980 Top Carrier and Market Share (%)	
Atlanta	Delta	74[a]	Delta	52
	AirTran	17		
Chicago O'Hare	United	39[b]	United	32
	American	39		
Cincinnati	Delta	94[c]	Delta	38
	American Eagle	2		
Cleveland	Continental	60[d]	United	41
	Southwest	10		
Dallas/Ft. Worth	American	85[e]	Braniff	36
	Delta	3		
Denver	United	53[f]	United	27
	Frontier	18		
Detroit	Northwest	77[g]	Republic	21
	Southwest	3		
Houston	Continental	86[d]	Texas	
	American	3	International	18
Minneapolis/St. Paul	Northwest	79[g]	Northwest	42
	United	3		
Philadelphia	USAir	48[h]	Eastern	21
	Southwest	11		
Salt Lake City	Delta	75[i]	Western	28
	Southwest	12		

[a] includes affiliate Atlantic Southeast.
[b] includes affiliate Air Wisconsin.
[c] includes affiliates Atlantic Southeast, Comair, Chautauqua.
[d] includes affiliate ExpressJet.
[e] includes affiliate American Eagle.
[f] includes affiliate SkyWest.
[g] includes affiliates Pinnacle and Mesaba.
[h] includes affiliate Air Wisconsin.
[i] includes affiliates SkyWest and Atlantic Southeast.
Source: Bureau of Transportation Statistics, Department of Transportation, www. transtats.bts.gov/homepage.asp; and Julius Maldutis, "Airline Competition at the 50 Largest U.S. Airports—Update," Salomon Brothers, May 6, 1993.

Table 9-5, where the magnitude of single-firm dominance increased dramatically at many of the nation's major airports. The recent financial problems of a number of major carriers, however, have created opportunities for smaller carriers to establish or expand significant footholds at some major airports. With United embroiled in bankruptcy, for example, Frontier has been able to expand its presence at United's Denver hub from 9 to 18 percent of air passenger traffic over the past 5 years. Similarly, Delta's bankruptcy has enabled independent AirTran to expand its presence at Delta's Atlanta Hartsfield hub from 10 to 17 percent of the traffic. Likewise, US Airways' bankruptcy and elimination of Pittsburgh as one of its hubs enabled Southwest to commence service to that city in 2005 and to obtain a 9 percent share of traffic (as USAirways' share dropped from 76 percent to 37 percent). Whether these positions can be sustained as the major carriers emerge from bankruptcy and financial reorganization remains to be seen.

Operating Agreements and Alliances

Interwoven through these overlapping layers of concentration is a dense web of operating agreements, affiliations and alliances among carriers. First, operating agreements link the nation's leading regional airline operators with the major carriers and, through them, link the major carriers to each other. Delta, for example, has operating agreements for feeder service with SkyWest, Chautauqua Airlines, Shuttle America, and Freedom Airlines, in addition to operating its own Comair regional subsidiary that it acquired in 2001. Air Wisconsin works in partnership with United Airlines and US Airways in providing regional feeder service. SkyWest operates United Express as a feeder for United Airlines; SkyWest also operates Delta Connection as a feeder for Delta; and the bulk of SkyWest's pricing, scheduling, ticketing and seat inventory decisions are determined primarily by United or Delta. Pinnacle Airlines operates as Northwest Airlink in feeding passengers to Northwest Airlines, as does Mesaba Airlines, while ExpressJet operates as Continental Express, a regional feeder for Continental Airlines. Chautauqua Airlines and Mesa Air each operate as American Connection for American Airlines; Delta Connection for Delta; United Express for United Airlines; and US Airways Express for US Airways.[11] In addition to these affiliations, American operates its own American Eagle feeder subsidiary. Because of these cooperative agreements, the number of genuinely independent carriers in the industry is significantly fewer than the listing in Table 9-2 might otherwise suggest.

Second, the majors have forged cooperative scheduling, ticketing, and marketing partnerships with each other in their U.S. operations in recent years: United and US Airways—the second- and sixth- largest carriers in revenues—implemented an agreement in 2003 to reciprocally issue tickets on each other's flights, to cross list each other's flights as their own, and to honor frequent flyer miles accumulated by passengers traveling on either airline. Delta, Northwest and Continental—the third-, fourth- and fifth- largest carriers—have joined to create similar marketing partnership agreements among themselves, as have American and Delta with Alaska Airlines and Hawaiian Airlines. In addition, the largest stockholder in the merged US Airways/America West corporation is also the largest stockholder in Northwest and Continental, and the second-largest stockholder in American Airlines.[12]

Third, on a global scale, the majors have formed alliances with leading foreign airlines that have evolved into the three major international groupings depicted in Table 9-6. Clearly these are significant cooperative arrangements combining as partners the dominant U.S. airlines with virtually all the leading carriers throughout the world.

---

[11]Company web sites.
[12]Micheline Maynard, "Outside Investors to Control Merged Airline," *New York Times* (June 29, 2005): C3.

TABLE 9-6 Global Airline Alliances

Alliance	U.S. Partners	Foreign Partners
OneWorld	American	Aer Lingus
		British Airways
		Cathay Pacific
		Finnair
		Iberia
		LAN Airlines
		Qantas
SkyTeam	Delta	Aeroflot
	Continental	AeroMexico
	Northwest	Air France
		Alitalia
		CSA Czech Airlines
		KLM Royal Dutch Airlines
		Korean Air
Star Alliance	United	Air Canada
	US Airways	Air New Zealand
		ANA
		Asiana Airlines
		Austrian
		BMI
		LOT
		Lufthansa
		Scandinavian Airlines
		Singapore Airlines
		South African Airways
		Spanair
		Swiss Air
		TAP Portugal
		Thai Airlines
		Varig

Source: Company web sites.

These affiliations require an extensive degree of cooperation among major actual and potential rivals, both domestically and internationally. As such, they suggest that the effective degree of concentration of decision-making in the industry is greater than firms' individual market shares alone might otherwise indicate. Adding the domestic market shares of the regional affiliates of the major carriers to the 2006 national concentration data in Table 9-3, for example, raises the four-firm concentration ratio from 53 to 58 percent, and the eight-firm concentration ratio from 83 to 88 percent, indicating that the recent decline in concentration at the national level may be less than meets the eye. Internationally, as we will see subsequently, these alliances also raise questions about the competitive benefits likely to follow from "Open Skies" negotiations currently being conducted between the United States and the European Union to lower national barriers and promote greater competition among American and European air carriers, when those carriers are cooperating as partners.

Barriers to Entry

At the time deregulation commenced, some economists hailed the airline industry as a "contestable" market in which market shares, mergers, and concentration levels would be irrelevant owing to the high mobility of resources in the field: Existing carriers, they said, could quickly move planes and alter schedules to compete on different routes; by the same token, new carriers could quickly put new aircraft into operation on selected routes. Monopoly and oligopoly market power, they concluded, would be fleeting and inconsequential.[13] Alas, the emergence of a host of daunting barriers subsequently refuted this contestability theory.

First, the nation's largest, most congested airports (Chicago O'Hare, Washington National, New York's LaGuardia and Kennedy) are accessible only to carriers holding government slots, or permits to land and depart aircraft at particular time periods throughout the day. The bulk of these slots were originally allocated to the dominant carriers already operating at these airports, and they have maintained or even increased their share of them. In 2001, for example, American and United were found to control together 90 percent of the landing and takeoff slots available at Chicago's O'Hare airport; at Washington National, 98 percent of the available slots were found to be held by American, Delta, Northwest, United, and US Airways. By hoarding slots (or charging exorbitant fees to sell or lease them), dominant carriers can prevent new competitors from serving these major airports.[14]

Second, the dominant carriers exert an additional measure of control over access to these and other airports through agreements negotiated with local airport authorities concerning the use of gates, terminals, ticket counters, and baggage and ground-handling facilities. In one indepth analysis, the General Accounting Office found the major carriers to control 94 percent of all gates leased at the nation's largest airports, with 86 percent of these leased on an exclusive-use basis. As a result, dominant carriers can limit competition either by refusing to lease their gates to other carriers (even when they are underutilized), or by leasing them only at onerous rates. In addition, majority-in-interest contracts enable dominant carriers to veto airport expansions that could provide the additional terminals

---

[13]See William J. Baumol, John C. Panzer, and Robert D. Willig, *Contestable Markets and the Theory of Industrial Structure* (San Diego: Harcourt Brace Jovanovich, 1982); Elizabeth E. Bailey, "Contestability and the Design of Regulatory and Antitrust Policy," *American Economic Review* 71 (May 1981): 178–183; and Elizabeth E. Bailey and John C. Panzar, "The Contestability of Airline Markets During the Transition to Deregulation," *Law & Contemporary Problems 44* (Winter 1981): 125–145. For a criticism of this theory, see William G. Shepherd, "'Contestability' versus Competition," *American Economic Review* 74 (September 1984): 572–587.

[14]U.S. Congress. Senate. Subcommittee on Antitrust, Business Rights, and Competition. Hearing: Airline Competition: Clear Skies or Turbulence Ahead? 106th Cong., 2d sess., 2001, 67; John H. Anderson, U.S. General Accounting Office, "Domestic Aviation: Service Problems and Limited Competition Continue in Some Markets," statement before the U.S. Congress. House. Subcommittee on Aviation, April 23, 1998; and U.S. General Accounting Office, "Airline Deregulation: Barriers to Entry Continue to Limit Competition in Several Key Domestic Markets," report to the Chairman. U.S. Congress. Senate. Committee on Commerce, Science, and Transportation, October 1996.

and gates needed by new competitors.[15] In other cases dominant carriers have lobbied airport authorities to destroy old gates and concourses, thereby preventing them from becoming available to potential competitors.[16]

Third, the majors have leveraged ticketing and reservation systems into yet another barrier to competition. During the 1980s and 1990s, computer reservation systems operated by American and United came to be utilized by most travel agents and corporate travel departments; by manipulating the onscreen presentation of flights, these carriers could disadvantage other airlines, while compelling other carriers to pay high fees to have their flights included in these computer displays. More recently, similar charges of manipulation have been leveled against the Orbitz online ticket system jointly launched by the country's largest carriers in 2000 (divested to outside owners in 2004), as well as in the case of major carriers paying Internet travel sites to preferentially list their flights over those of competitors.[17] Bonus payments and commission overrides paid to travel agents and corporate travel departments for booking high percentages of their flights on major carriers create another obstacle to competition, as do frequent flyer programs that effectively reward travelers for refusing to patronize other carriers, including new entrants.[18]

Fourth, incumbent carriers can lobby in the political arena to create additional barriers to competition, such as lobbying against the certification to operate for an otherwise qualified new competitor (as in the case of Richard Branson's effort to launch Virgin America, a new airline in the U.S.[19]), or imposing onerous route restrictions on potential competitors (as has been the case for 3 decades with government regulations sharply limiting Southwest and other carriers' interstate flights from Dallas Love Field, and which only recently have begun to be slightly relaxed), or exploiting regulatory efforts to combat air traffic congestion to limit access by low-far carriers to major airports.[20]

---

[15]The classic study of the gate barrier is U.S. General Accounting Office, "Airline Competition: Industry Operating and Marketing Practices Limit Market Entry," Washington, D.C., August 1990, 36, 42, 47–54. For additional studies, see U.S. General Accounting Office, "Airline Deregulation: Barriers to Entry Continue to Limit Competition in Several Key Domestic Markets," 1996; and Transportation Research Board, *Entry and Competition in the U.S. Airline Industry* (Washington, D.C.: National Academy Press, 1999).

For specific recent examples of the impact of this barrier to competition, see Bruce Ingersoll, "Gateless in Detroit," *Wall Street Journal* (July 12, 1999): 1; Edward Wong, "Denver's Idle Gates Draw Covetous Eyes," *New York Times* (August 5, 2003): C1; and Scott McCartney, "For United's Rivals, Gates of Hell Are Found at LAX," *Wall Street Journal* (June 7, 2005):D4. One indicator of the importance of the role of gates at airports is provided by Southwest Airlines' recently reported purchase of access to six gates at Chicago's Midway airport for $87 million. "Judge Backs Southwest's Deal to Buy ATA's Gates at Midway," *New York Times* (December 22, 2004): C7.

The same access problem seems to be emerging in Europe, prompting the *Economist* to point out it "is not much use having open skies without open airports." "Turbulent Skies," *Economist* (July 10, 2004):61.

[16]*Spirit Airlines v. Northwest Airlines*, 431 F.3d 917 (6th Cir. 2005), 3.

[17]See "Southwest Air's Suit Says Travel Web Site Misleads Consumers," *Wall Street Journal* (May 7, 2001): A10, and Scott McCartney, "Paid Placements Hit Travel Booking Sites," *Wall Street Journal* (November 9, 2004): D1.

[18]On the impact of bonuses and discounts, see General Accounting Office, "Airline Deregulation," and Scott McCartney, "Continental Air Loses Some Accounts After Data-Disclosure Demand," *Wall Street Journal* (February 6, 2001):B1.

[19]For example, see U.S. Congress. Senate. Committee on Commerce, Science, and Transportation. Hearing: Foreign Investment in U.S. Carriers, 109th Cong., 2d sess., 2006.

[20]For details and analysis, see www.setlovefree.com. See also Melanie Trottman, "Southwest Boosts Dallas Service," *Wall Street Journal* (October 18, 2006):D13, and Christopher Conkey, "Plan to Unclog New York Airports Is a Mixed Bag," *New York Times* (December 20, 2007): D8.

Finally, as we shall see in the following discussion, the ability of major carriers to inflict lethal predatory price cuts on new competitors has served as yet another powerful barrier to entry in air transportation.

The Question of Economies of Scale

Little evidence indicates that high levels of concentration in airlines are dictated by economies of scale or scope of operations. In fact, to the contrary, the evidence suggests that the largest carriers suffer higher costs and lower productivity, and that these diseconomies of excessive size have grown more pronounced over the post-9/11 period.

Figure 9-1 records the substantial cost inefficiency of the major legacy carriers relative to smaller, low-cost airlines over the period from 1998 to 2004, while Figure 9-2 shows the higher productivity of smaller carriers compared to the majors.

One important factor in the majors' higher costs is the fact that they have been in operation longer, and employ a more senior and, thus, more highly paid workforce. Reinforcing this factor are the munificent contracts and pensions negotiated by the carriers with their unionized workforce, in a process best characterized as a coalescence of power among firms dominating the output market and labor organizations dominating the input market.[21]

ⁱⁱⁱ FIGURE 9-1 Airline Operating Cost Differentials 1998–2004

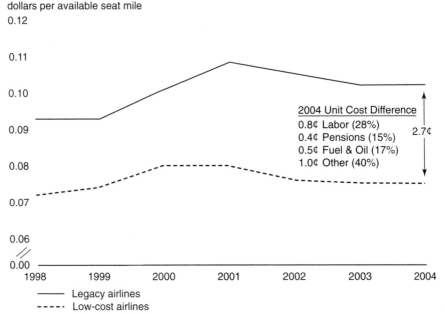

Source: U.S. General Accountability Office, "Commercial Aviation: Bankruptcy and Pension Problems are Symptoms of Underlying Structural Issues" (Washington, D.C., September 2005), p. 8.

---

[21]See Bigness Complex, cited previously, Part VI, and Steven Greenhouse, "Unions Are a Victim of Their Own Success at the Nation's Airlines," *New York Times* (April 26, 2003):B3.

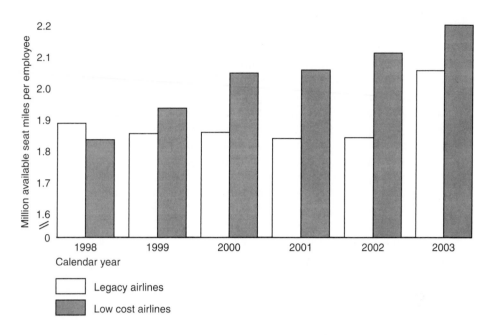

▪ ▪ ▪ ▪ **FIGURE 9-2** Comparative Labor Productivity in Airlines 1998–2003

Source: U.S. General Accountability Office, "Commercial Aviation: Legacy Airlines Must Further Reduce Costs to Restore Profitability" (Washington, D.C., August 2004), p. 28.

Yet as Figure 9-1 indicates, the inefficiency of the majors stems from more than labor costs alone. In fact, Southwest, the industry benchmark for efficiency, pays its pilots and flight attendants as much, if not more, than the majors pay their employees,[22] yet its overall average operating cost is 33 to 44 percent lower than that of American, United, Delta, Northwest or Continental.

Experts estimate that possibly as much as two-thirds of the cost advantage of smaller, low-cost carriers is attributable to a variety of more efficient business practices.[23] First, smaller, low-cost carriers operate simpler aircraft fleets, typically employing only one or two types of aircraft on all their routes (Southwest, for example, flies only Boeing 737s; JetBlue flies only Airbus A320 and Embraer 190 aircraft). These more uniform fleets simplify maintenance and parts operations, and enhance the flexibility of crews and crew assignments, thereby enabling smaller carriers to hold down their costs and operate more productively than the major carriers, which operate fleets that are a hodge-podge of various aircraft, with each type of craft requiring its own parts, maintenance, and crews.

Second, perhaps because smaller carriers lack the luxury of dominant positions and are compelled to be more attuned to their competitiveness, they have kept their fuel costs lower than the majors in recent years by engaging to a greater extent in the use of hedging techniques in commodities markets.

---

[22]See Jeff Bailey, "On Some Flights, Millionaires Serve the Drinks," *New York Times* (May 15, 2006):1.
[23]"Special Report: Airlines Under Siege," *Economist* (March 27, 2004):68.

Third, the monopoly hubs erected by the majors have significantly inflated their costs. Because these hubs require large numbers of flights to be scheduled to arrive and depart at hub airports within a few narrow time periods, the majors have gates, ground facilities, and airport crews that sit idle much of the day, which raises their operating costs.[24] In contrast, smaller carriers operating point-to-point route systems are able to better utilize their fleets by limiting the time their planes spend on the ground, as well as by making more efficient use of their airport gates by spreading their flights through the day—an important efficiency the majors are now attempting to emulate.[25] The costs of monopoly hubs for the majors are further inflated when they operate unneeded or underutilized gates and ground facilities in order to prevent potential competitors from obtaining access to them.

Finally, the organizational turmoil wrought by mergers and acquisitions have compounded the diseconomies of excessive scale, including US Airway's merger with America West in 2005, and American Airline's acquisition of TWA in 2001.[26]

As a result of these factors, the majors' average operating costs are consistently and substantially higher for flights of all lengths.[27] In fact, it is telling that the largest carriers in recent years have responded to their cost disadvantages by significantly reducing their scale and downsizing their workforces, fleets, and route and hub operations. (Cutbacks include 66,000 fewer people employed by American, United, Delta, Northwest, and Continental; 243 fewer planes flown by United and American; abandonment of hubs by Delta at Dallas-Ft. Worth, by US Airways at Pittsburgh, and by American at Nashville; and capacity reductions of 36 to 49 percent [measured by available seat-miles flown] at American, United, and Delta since 2001). Delta, for example, emerged from bankruptcy in the spring of 2007 with 35 percent fewer employees and 28 percent fewer aircraft in its fleet compared to 7 years before.

▪▪▪ III. Conduct

Pricing in the industry is characterized by mutual interdependence and noncompetitive parallelism among an oligopoly of majors, buttressed by monopoly pricing at dominated hubs and routes, and sustained by predatory price cuts to contain or eliminate new competitors. The expansion of independents in recent years has injected more

---

[24]See U.S. General Accountability Office, "Commercial Aviation: Legacy Airlines Must Further Reduce Costs to Restore Profitability" Washington, D.C. (August 2004), 28–29.

[25]See Micheline Maynard, "In Airline Shift, More Nonstops Make Schedule," *New York Times* (May 4, 2005):1; Ariel Hart and Micheline Maynard, "Another Clock Is Ticking at Delta Air Lines," *New York Times* (January 29, 2005):B2; and Micheline Maynard, "USAirways Plans a Major Overhaul of Where It Does and Does Not Fly," *New York Times* (July 28, 2004):C1. According to one analysis, USAirways, American Airlines, and Delta have increased their number of point-to-point flights by 64 percent, 46 percent, and 56 percent, respectively, over the period from 2003 to 2005. Regional Airline Association, *Regional Horizons*, January/February 2006, available at www.raa.org

Interestingly, the inefficiency of the hub-and-spoke method is being recognized in the European airline industry. See Kevin Done, "A Business Model Going Places?" *Financial Times* (October 14, 2005):13.

[26]See Melanie Trottman, "US Air, After Merger, Wrestles With Frequent Ire," *Wall Street Journal* (June 7, 2006):D4, and Edward Wong, "American Airlines to Cut Jobs, Planes and Flights," *New York Times* (August 14, 2002):C1.

[27]See JayEtta Z. Hecker, U.S. General Accounting Office, "Commercial Aviation: Despite Turmoil, Low-Cost Airlines are Growing and Profitable." Testimony before U.S. Congress. House. Subcommittee on Aviation, June 3, 2004, 8.

competitive pricing into the field, but only on the routes where independents have been able to evade the majors' predatory moves.

Oligopoly Pricing Nationally

Mutually interdependent behavior emerged as concentration solidified in the field following deregulation. As the industry became more concentrated, the major carriers began to recognize that a significant pricing move by any one of them would elicit a quick response from the others and, especially, that a price cut by any one of them would be quickly matched by the others, reducing profits for them all.

Thus, when the former chairman of American Airlines, Robert Crandall, was asked in 1989 why his carrier did not offer lower fares to attract major corporate customers, he replied, "Because it would be dumb. The reality is that you will go to Detroit because you have to go to Detroit whether the fare is $175, $275 or $375." A US Airways vice president responded similarly when asked why his airline did not try to gain more traffic by pricing below the identical fares charged by major carriers on their Denver to Dallas routes: "If I know that if I cut my fare $20 today, you're going to cut yours $20 tomorrow, then it's stupid for me to do it." As a Delta official observed about airline pricing during the years immediately following deregulation, "We went through a period of bashing each other's heads in over fares. It took us a while to learn how to compete."[28]

Learning how to compete meant learning how to set the general structure of fares through a tacitly collusive process of price leadership and price followership: One major carrier takes the lead in communicating its intentions concerning a change in airfares, and the others either follow the leader and adopt similar fare changes themselves, or, alternatively, refuse to follow the leader, thereby compelling the initiator to scale back or abandon its pricing change. In either event, fares tend to be uniform across the major carriers, and to move in lockstep.

Recognition of this mutual interdependence enables the majors to fly in remarkably tight pricing formation. In the spring of 2005, for example, Northwest led two general fare boosts quickly matched by the other majors. When Continental led with a third price hike, the other majors initially followed once again. However, Northwest subsequently rescinded its fare hike on some routes where it faced competition from independent carriers—a move that was misinterpreted by Delta as a general reduction in all Northwest's fares, so that Delta and the other majors cut all their fares. Once the misunderstanding was recognized, the majors quickly re-raised their fares in line with Continental's original increase.[29]

The computer systems into which airfare information is fed facilitate communication and signaling among the majors through the way they elect to file their fare plans (start date; stop date; price change; specific routes, airports and passenger classes

---

[28]Quoted in Christopher Winans and Jonathan Dahl, "Airlines Skid on Bad Moves, Bad News," *Wall Street Journal* (September 29, 1989):B4; and "Flying the Unfriendly Skies," special edition, *Philadelphia Inquirer* (December 1989):4.

[29]See Melanie Trottman, "Continental Reverses Course on Airfare Increase," *Wall Street Journal* (March 22, 2005):A5, and idem, "Major Airlines Reinstate Increase of $10 Round-Trip for U.S. Fares," *Wall Street Journal* (March 23, 2005):D3. For earlier examples, see "Northwest Changing Its Mind Again," *Wall Street Journal* (August 24, 1998):C19; and Susan Carey, "All in a Day's Flying: Fares Rise, Fall, Rise 5% Again in 24 Hours," *Wall Street Journal* (September 9, 1997):A6.

affected). By the specific nature of the fare information they feed into these systems the majors are able to closely monitor each other, and, at times, to communicate their dismay with one another (including the infamous *FU* letter code attached to fares filed to signal displeasure about a rival's competitive pricing). The majors can enforce pricing discipline among themselves by, for example, selectively focusing fare cuts on a rival carrier's most lucrative routes in order to compel it to refrain from competitive pricing on other routes and regions.[30] Tacitly collusive pricing is reinforced at times by threats among the majors to reduce their fares if the group's pricing solidarity is breeched, as occurred in 2005, when one carrier issued a news release responding to reports that another major was considering substantial fare reductions, and ominously warned that such price reductions would "immediately adversely and significantly affect industry revenues."[31] Major carriers also may punish independent pricing by revoking marketing agreements with the perpetrator.[32]

Monopoly Pricing Regionally

At the regional level, the majors are able to price monopolistically at their hub airports and on the routes they dominate. One estimate of the extent to which fares at dominated hubs exceeded airfares at more competitively served airports, prepared in 2001, is depicted in Table 9-7. It shows, for example, that passengers flying from Cincinnati (a hub dominated by Delta) pay fares 35 to 78 percent greater than comparable fares at more competitively structured airports, while passengers at Minneapolis (Northwest dominated) pay a monopoly premium of 46 to 63 percent. Overall, passengers at dominated hubs were estimated to pay 54 percent higher fares for short-haul flights, 31 percent higher fares for long-haul flights, and an overall average 41 percent higher fares for flights of all lengths combined.[33]

Another manifestation of monopoly pricing is the dramatic impact the entry of a low-fare carrier has on a dominant airline's fares. When Southwest began serving US Airways' hub at Philadelphia, for example, US Airways dropped its one-way walk-up fares to Phoenix from $1,180 to $299, to Las Vegas from $921 to $299, and to Chicago from $700 to $99.[34] With a monopoly on nonstop service from Atlanta to

---

[30]For informative reports on this tacit collusion and disciplining process in action, see Scott McCartney, "Airfare Skirmish Shows Why Deals Come and Go," *Wall Street Journal* (March 19, 2002):B1; Melanie Trottman, "America West is Pressed by Rivals," *Wall Street Journal* (April 22, 2002):A3; Asra Q. Nomani, "Fare Warning: How Airlines Trade Price Plans," *Wall Street Journal* (October 9, 1990):B1; and Asra Q. Nomani, "Dispatches from the Air-Fare Front," *Wall Street Journal* (July 11, 1989):B1.

[31]Northwest Airlines, "Northwest Responds to Media Inquiries Concerning Reported Delta Fare Initiative," news release, January 4, 2005. Marketing alliances among the majors may reinforce this tacitly collusive pricing discipline. "When you have 20 percent of the market [Continental and Northwest combined]," says the CEO of Continental about that airline's affiliation with Northwest, "United will say . . . 'Screwing with one might be the same as screwing with the other.' Now, as a joined-at-the-hip partner with Northwest, you better watch out if we do get upset. We have a lot of different ways that we can pay you back." Quoted in U.S. Congress. Senate. Subcommittee on Antitrust, Business Rights, and Competition. Hearing: Airline Competition: Clear Skies or Turbulence Ahead? 106th Cong., 2d sess., 2001, 62.

[32]See Melanie Trottman, "America West Is Pressed by Rivals," *Wall Street Journal* (April 22, 2002):A6.

[33]For corroborating evidence developed from an indepth analysis of Delta's Atlanta hub, see Thorsten Fischer and David R. Kamerschen, "Price-Cost Margins in the US Airline Industry using a Conjectural Variations Approach," *Journal of Transport Economics and Policy* 37 (May 2003): 227.

[34]Micheline Maynard, "Southwest Comes Calling, and a Race Begins," *New York Times* (May 10, 2004):C1.

TABLE 9-7 Fare Differentials: Dominated vs. Nondominated Airports 2001

	Fare Differential for:		
Dominated Hub	*Short-Haul Routes*	*Long-Haul Routes*	*All Routes*
Cincinnati	+ 78%	+ 35%	+ 57%
Pittsburgh	+ 86	+ 18	+ 57
Minneapolis	+ 46	+ 63	+ 55
Charlotte	+ 75	+ 23	+ 54
St. Louis	+ 38	+ 61	+ 49
Memphis	+ 57	+ 29	+ 43
Atlanta	+ 49	+ 28	+ 41
Detroit	+ 51	+ 21	+ 40
Denver	+ 37	+ 28	+ 29
All	+ 54	+ 31	+ 41

Note: *Dominated hubs* defined as hub airports where no low-fare carrier operates. Fare differences controlled for route distance and traffic density differences.

Source: JayEtta Z. Hecker, U.S. General Accounting Office. Testimony before the U.S. Congress. Senate. Committee on Commerce, Science, and Transportation, March 13, 2001.

Los Angeles, Delta's fare was $1,151 for a one-way walk-up ticket; when AirTran and JetBlue began competing on the route, Delta cut its fare 80 percent, to $249.[35] In another study, the Department of Transportation found that on routes from Atlanta (Delta dominated) where independent carrier AirTran entered, airfares fell 43 percent, but when AirTran exited those routes, Delta subsequently raised its fares by 55 percent.[36]

Finally, the ability of the majors to charge on the same flight high fares to passengers with less price-elastic demand (i.e., business, professional, last-minute travelers), and lower fares to passengers with more price-elastic demand (i.e., leisure, vacation travelers), further attests to monopoly pricing power. Given that there is no comparable difference in the cost of carrying each class of passenger, effective competition for the patronage of each group would prevent carriers from engaging in such price discrimination. And, in fact, evidence suggests that the difference between full and discount fares is greatest at the most monopolized hubs, while the entry of competition narrows the full-to-discount price differential.[37]

---

[35]Edward Wong, "Delta Gets Some Stiff Competition on a Key Route," *New York Times* (May 28, 2003):C1; and Martha Brannigan, "Discount Carrier Lands Partners in Ill-Served Cities," *Wall Street Journal* (July 16, 2002):1. For recent efforts by communities to attract low-cost carriers in order to exert downward competitive pressure on airfares, see Scott McCartney, "Airports Battle Carriers' High Fares," *Wall Street Journal* (November 14, 2006):D6.

[36]U.S. Department of Transportation, "Domestic Airline Fares: Fourth Quarter 1998 Passenger and Fare Information," Washington, D.C., July 1999, 40.

[37]Melanie Trottman, "Equalizing Air Fares," *Wall Street Journal* (August 17, 2004):B1; and U.S. Department of Transportation, Office of the Assistant Secretary for Aviation and International Affairs, "Dominated Hub Fares," Washington, D.C., January 2001.

Competition versus Predatory Pricing

When and where competition does break out, the impact on airfares is significant. When AirTran and JetBlue began service in 2003 from the Delta-dominated Atlanta hub to Los Angeles, for example, Delta's one-way fare on the route dropped 88 percent, from $1,031 to $119. When Southwest Airlines began service at US Airways' Philadelphia hub in 2004, US Airways' fares dropped 46 to 90 percent on various routes (including a reduction of the fare on flights to Los Angeles from $1,259 to $299). Likewise, JetBlue's inauguration in 2001 of transcontinental service from New York's JFK to the west coast triggered a decline in airfares on those routes by some 40 percent generally. An earlier study by the Department of Transportation found that entry by independent low-cost carriers led to fare decreases of 35 to 40 percent on average nationwide.[38]

Sharp price cuts by incumbent majors that are limited in duration and narrowly focused on particular routes entered by new carriers may predatorily eliminate competition rather than sustain it, however. Examples abound: When Frontier initiated service from Denver (a United-dominated hub) to Billings, Montana, it offered an average fare of $100, half the prevailing fare charged by United. United slashed its fare to match Frontier; when Frontier then exited the route, United raised its fare above the original level.[39] When start-up Spirit Airlines attempted to enter Northwest's Detroit hub with airfares of $49 to $109 on flights from Detroit to Boston and Philadelphia (compared to Northwest fares of $250 to $411 on these routes), Northwest slashed its fares, added planes and seat capacity and temporarily incurred financial losses on those particular routes. When Spirit subsequently abandoned those routes, Northwest raised its fares back up to their original levels and reduced its seat capacity.[40] Likewise, when start-up Western Pacific Airlines entered the Dallas-Colorado Springs route, American cut its average fare on the route by half and more than doubled the number of seats flown; Western Pacific's subsequent exit enabled American to boost its fare back up to the level set prior to Western Pacific's entry.[41]

A general analysis of the response of incumbent carriers to new competition prepared for the Department of Transportation found that in 10 of 12 cases examined, the new entrant's fare was at least 50 percent below the average fare charged by incumbent carriers prior to entry, and that in three-fourths of the cases, the average fare of the incumbents fell by one-third or more within 6 months following competitive entry. Within 2 years, however, the new entrant had abandoned the routes, enabling the

---

[38]U.S. Department of Transportation, "The Low-Cost Airline Service Revolution," Washington, D.C., April 1996, 9.

[39]U.S. Congress. Senate. Committee on Commerce, Science, and Transportation. Hearing: Aviation Competition, 105th Cong., 2d sess., 2000, 29.

[40]See *Spirit Airlines v. Northwest Airlines*, 431 F.3d 917 (6th Cir. 2005). For additional examples, see U.S. Congress. Senate. Committee on the Judiciary. Hearing: Airline Hubs: Fair Competition or Predatory Pricing? 105th Cong., 2d sess., 1998; and U.S. Department of Transportation, Office of the Secretary, "Enforcement Policy Regarding Unfair Exclusionary Conduct in the Air Transportation Industry," Findings and Conclusions, January 17, 2001.

[41]*United States v. AMR Corp.*, 140 F. Supp. 2d 1141 (D.C. Kansas, 2001). Judge Marten considered neither this, nor sharp declines in American's profitability on these routes, evidence of a violation of the antitrust laws.

incumbents to raise their fares.[42] The study found dominant carriers employing a variety of practices to reinforce this pricing pressure on competitors, including sandwiching flight times closely around those scheduled by a new entrant; boosting frequent flyer awards to passengers flying on those particular routes; and raising the commissions (overrides) paid to travel agents for scheduling passengers on the dominant carrier's flights.

The financial losses and bankruptcies suffered by major carriers in recent years have curbed their capacity to engage in these tactics and, as we have seen, new entrants and independent carriers have been able to expand their market presence and downward pressure on prices as a result. Whether this is a permanent development or only temporary remains to be seen, however, as the major carriers emerge from bankruptcy and financial reorganization.[43]

▮▮▮ IV. Performance

In *The Wealth of Nations*, Adam Smith delineated the adverse performance consequences of monopoly power: The price of the monopolized item is "the highest which can be squeezed out of the buyers." Potential competitors are excluded from a business "which it might be both convenient and profitable for many of them to carry on." Inefficiency bred by an absence of effective competition "seldom allows the dividend of the company to exceed the ordinary rate of profit in trades which are altogether free," while the monopolist is constantly contriving what Smith called "absurd and oppressive" schemes. In the case of the airline industry, Smith's assessment of two centuries ago seems prescient.

First, as indicated in the preceding section, fares on dominated routes and hubs are greatly inflated compared to the fares charged on routes and at airports where competition is effective.

Second, these high fares cause a misallocation of resources by inducing an underconsumption of service (what Smith called "understocking the market"). The extent of this allocative inefficiency is revealed when a new carrier enters a dominated route, with the immediate effect of a drop in price and a substantial increase in air travel. According to one study, competitive entry and the corresponding decline in airfares typically trigger air travel increases of 61 to 86 percent—a measure of the degree to which service is artificially understocked in the absence of competition.[44] Another indicator is the fact that metropolitan areas are finding they benefit by losing a monopoly hub, because the subsequent decline in airfares serves as an advantage in promoting regional economic development.[45] Considerable resources are also wasted when passengers drive to board flights at nondominated hubs (frequently flying back to the

---

[42]Clinton V. Oster and John S. Strong, "Predatory Practices in the U.S. Airline Industry," study prepared for the U.S. Department of Transportation, January 15, 2001.

[43]See Evan Perez and Nicole Harris, "Despite Early Signs of Victory, Discount Airlines Get Squeezed," *Wall Street Journal* (January 17, 2005):1.

[44]U.S. Department of Transportation, Office of the Assistant Secretary for Aviation and International Affairs, "Dominated Hub Fares," Washington, D.C., January 2001.

[45]See Scott McCartney, "Why Travelers Benefit When an Airline Hub Closes," *Wall Street Journal* (November 1, 2005):D1; and Melanie Trottman, "How a City Can Win by Losing Its Airport Hub Status," *Wall Street Journal* (April 28, 2004):B1.

dominated-hub city they drove away from), and rent cars and hotel rooms for overnight and weekend stays, all in an effort to escape the high fares charged by dominant carriers—a phenomenon that negates the inherent advantages of air travel in terms of speed and convenience.

Third, the monopolistic hub systems implemented by the majors have inflated costs and undermined operating efficiency. As we have seen, it is the largest carriers that have the highest operating costs and the least efficient systems.

Fourth, post-9/11 the industry suffered cumulative financial losses of $35 billion between 2001 and 2005. But the decline in industry profitability began in 1998 and, as Figure 9-3 shows, the major carriers have incurred the bulk of these losses, while smaller airlines have continued to operate profitably. And although a dozen small carriers also declared bankruptcy over the post-9/11 period, the mega-bankruptcies of United, US Airways, Delta, and Northwest indicate that large organizational size is certainly no guarantor of superior performance or enhanced ability to withstand economic shocks.[46]

Finally, on the innovation front the record is mixed. On the one hand, the major carriers have been quick to incorporate newer, quieter, more fuel-efficient aircraft into their fleets. They also have been quick to computerize their operations and capitalize on the Internet. On the other hand, however, these new technologies often have been twisted into instruments of market power by manipulating computer reservation

▪ ▫ ▫ ▫ **FIGURE 9-3** Airline Operating Profits and Losses 1998–2004

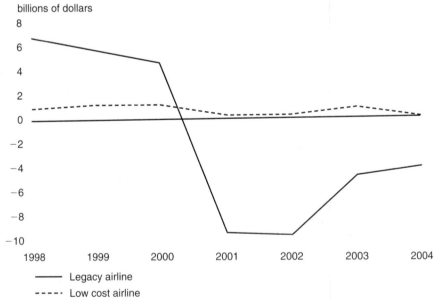

Source: U.S. General Accountability Office, "Commercial Aviation: Legacy Airlines Must Further Reduce Costs to Restore Profitability" (Washington, D.C., August 2004), p. 35.

---

[46]The Air Transport Association maintains detailed databases of airline bankruptcies and industry profitability, accessible via links at www.airlines.org/econ

systems to favor the operators' airlines, by exploiting computer systems to better communicate and collude on airfares, and by manipulating the Internet to potentially lessen competition from other airlines and alternative channels for distributing tickets. Smaller carriers, including Southwest, have been more innovative in designing and managing their routes and ground operations for maximum efficiency.

V. Public Policy

Major public policy issues in the industry include reregulation, antitrust policy, air traffic control, direct government aid to airlines in the wake of 9/11 and heightened security concerns, and "Open Skies" efforts to deregulate international air travel.

Reregulation?

Was deregulating the airlines a mistake? Do technology and cost structures render competition inherently unworkable in this field, and should the industry be reregulated?

The answer is *no* on all three counts. No credible evidence demonstrates that airlines are subject to such overwhelming economies of scale as to render monopoly and tight-knit oligopoly technologically inevitable or economically desirable. To the contrary, it is the largest carriers and the most monopolized hubs that suffer the highest costs, not the lowest. In fact, experience during the initial years following deregulation demonstrated that competition was feasible and desirable as new carriers flocked into the field, as existing carriers rearranged their routes and fares in accordance with consumer preferences, as competition spread throughout the air transportation system, and as airfares declined and air travel expanded.

Antitrust Policy

The public policy failure was not in deregulating the field, but in failing to recognize that enforcement of the antitrust laws would be paramount in nurturing competition and combating private efforts to subvert it. The failure was not one of deregulation but, instead, the mistake of assuming that an absence of government intervention, in and of itself, would guarantee that effective competition would prevail. As the Antitrust Modernization Commission recently emphasizes, "Antitrust enforcement is an important counterpart to deregulation."[47]

First, as we have seen, a spate of acquisitions was permitted in the mid-1980s, which enabled the dominant trunk carriers to absorb rapidly expanding, potentially competitive regional carriers. The 1978 deregulation statute gave the Department of Transportation authority to block anticompetitive mergers, but the department approved these and other acquisitions, a number of which were opposed by the Reagan administration's antitrust division. Congress subsequently transferred antitrust authority over airline mergers to the Antitrust Division of the Justice Department. The Justice Department finally did block a merger between United and US Airways proposed in 2000. At the same time, however, it allowed American to acquire TWA and its St. Louis hub monopoly, apparently without encouraging the acquisition of financially troubled TWA by a smaller, low-cost carrier which could have

---

[47]Antitrust Modernization Commission, "Report and Recommendations," Washington, D.C., 2007, ix.

significantly enhanced competition in the field. Later, in 2005, US Airways was allowed to absorb America West; US Airways' effort to acquire Delta in 2006 (which threatened to trigger a spate of mergers between other majors) died of its own accord without any discernible resistance by the antitrust authorities.

Second, the antitrust agencies and the Transportation Department have allowed a proliferation of operating agreements, alliances, and partnership pacts concentrating the majors' control over most of the nation's leading regional and commuter carriers—smaller carriers whose independence could have enabled them to develop into a source of new competition (as one of them, Atlantic Coast Airlines, a feeder carrier for Delta, attempted to do in 2004 and 2005 by becoming Independence Air). The agencies also have permitted the majors to steadily concentrate control over international air travel in the hands of a triopoly of global alliances (typically with an accompanying exemption from America's antitrust laws), acting only recently to block American's effort to tighten its affiliation with British Airways in an arrangement that would have monopolized air travel between a number of major American cities and London's Heathrow airport.[48] In recent years the agencies have allowed the majors to affiliate among themselves by integrating their routes and ticketing, including an affiliation between United and US Airways, as well as a code-sharing agreement among Delta, Northwest, and Continental.

Third, government agencies have done little to prevent the majors from constructing formidable barriers to competition (slots, gates, ground facilities), or to dissolve these obstacles once they have been erected. An exception is the majors' manipulation of computer reservation systems, where the Transportation Department promulgated rules regulating the nondiscriminatory presentation of flight information on screens and displays.

Fourth, the Justice Department prosecuted collusive behavior among the majors in the early 1990s by challenging their methods of communicating with each other through their computerized fare-filing practices.[49] But Justice has not challenged the highly concentrated industry structure that renders such collusion virtually inevitable in a field dominated by oligopolists who rationally recognize the fact of their mutual interdependence.

Fifth, the Justice Department belatedly moved to prosecute predatory pricing in the field in 1999 by filing an antitrust suit against American Airlines, charging the carrier with illegally driving new competitors from its Dallas hub. Despite evidence that American slashed its fares on these targeted routes, deliberately chose to suffer temporary losses in profitability, had higher costs than new entrants, and raised fares after the new competitors had been eliminated, the court dismissed the government's charges without allowing the case to proceed to trial. American, the court held, had "engaged only in bare, but not brass, knuckle competition."[50] (The court apparently was unwilling to distinguish pricing that reflects the competitive process from predatory pricing that

---

[48]See, for example, U.S. Department of Justice, Public Comments before the Department of Transportation, U.S.-U.K. Alliance, Docket OST-2001-1029, December 17, 2001.
[49]*United States v. Airline Tariff Publishing Co., et al.*, Complaint, Civ. Action No. 92-2854, filed December 21, 1992. The carriers subsequently settled with the Justice Department without contesting these charges.
[50]*United States v. AMR Corp.*, 140 F. Supp. 2d 1141 (D. Kan. 2001), affirmed by the Tenth Circuit Court of Appeals, 2003-2 Trade Cas. (CCH) P74,078 (July 3, 2003).

destroys the competitive process.) However, in late 2005, the Sixth Circuit Court of Appeals reinstated a predatory pricing lawsuit filed by Spirit Airlines against Northwest, directing that this antitrust action proceed to trial. A reasonable trier of fact, the court held, "could find that at the time of predation, the market . . . was highly concentrated, Northwest possessed overwhelming market share, and the barriers to entry were high. Accordingly, [the court could conclude] that Northwest engaged in predatory pricing . . . in order to force Spirit out of the market."[51]

Incredibly, in the light of this minimalist record of government antitrust enforcement, some industry officials recently have urged that antitrust policy be abandoned even further so as to enable the major carriers to merge with each other,[52] a recommendation the evidence strongly suggests would exacerbate the majors' high costs while strengthening their market power.

Air Traffic Control

The Federal Aviation Administration (FAA) operates the nation's air traffic and air navigation system, including airport towers, air route traffic control, flight stations, radar facilities, communications and computer systems, and air traffic rules and regulations. It presides over 20,000 landing fields and guides 46 million aircraft a year. Its annual budget of $14 billion is expended on these operations and on airport construction grants, as well as compensating 40,000 air traffic controllers and aviation safety inspectors.[53]

The major public policy issues here concern the efficiency with which the FAA operates, whether it is modernizing its operations in line with technological advances and the growth of air travel (including the growth of private and corporate aircraft), and the methods for generating its funding.

Airlines complain that the deficiencies of an antiquated air traffic control system cost them billions of dollars each year in flight delays and cancellations, wasted fuel, missed connections, and lost baggage, and that the problem is getting worse as the number of aircraft, passengers, and flights grows within the confines of an air traffic control system designed a half-century ago.[54] However, the airlines themselves may have compounded these problems with their personnel cutbacks and employee pay cuts of recent years.[55] FAA funding, some contend, is inequitable and inefficient because, they say, it disproportionately burdens airlines by relying primarily on passenger ticket taxes, while subsidizing hundreds of thousands of small, personal, general aviation aircraft that pay little of their cost of using the air system and, thus, have little economic incentive to use the nation's scarce airspace efficiently[56] (a claim hotly

---

[51]*Spirit Airlines v. Northwest Airlines*, 431 F.3d 917 (2005).
[52]"UAL CEO: US Skies Need Deregulation," CNNMoney.com, September 25, 2005.
[53]Federal Aviation Administration, Administrator's Fact Book, April 2007.
[54]See the testimony of James C. May, President, Air Transport Association of America, before the U.S. Congress. House. Subcommittee on Aviation, March 21, 2007, available at transportation.house.gov/hearings/hearingdetail.aspx?NewsID=78.
[55]Melanie Trottman and Susan Carey, "As Pay Falls, Airlines Struggle to Fill Jobs," *Wall Street Journal* (May 16, 2007):1.
[56]See the testimony of Calvin L. Scovel, Inspector General of the Department of Transportation, before the U.S. Congress. House. Subcommittee on Aviation, March 21, 2007.

disputed by the nation's 400,000 private aircraft owners and pilots[57]). Others report that the FAA's multibillion dollar next generation traffic control modernization effort is suffering a number of serious problems.[58] Some have expressed interest in the prospect of privatizing the nation's air traffic control system, either in whole or in part, as has been done in the United Kingdom, Germany, Australia, and Canada.[59] But this option might only exacerbate market power problems, particularly if primary influence over a privatized air traffic control agency were assigned to the major airlines as the largest stakeholders in the operation of the system. Others suggest airport landing fees that vary and are higher at heavily-congested times in order to encourage carriers to spread their flights more evenly through the day, thereby reducing delays.

9/11 and Government Aid

In the wake of the 9/11 terrorist attacks, and in response to the industry's plea for government help in a time of crisis, legislation was enacted providing government subsidies to air carriers. The Air Transportation Safety and System Stabilization Act provided up to $5 billion in cash grants payable to airlines in direct proportion to their size. The act established an additional fund of up to $10 billion in government-backed loan guarantees for carriers deemed financially meritorious by a newly created Air Transportation Stabilization Board (ATSB) composed of the Secretary of Transportation, Secretary of the Treasury, Comptroller General, and the Chairman of the Federal Reserve. In 2003, Congress provided an additional $2.4 billion in security-related subsidies to the industry, while major pension legislation enacted in 2006 accords preferential treatment to the major airlines in their financial accounting for pensions.

According to the Department of Transportation, $4.6 billion in emergency direct payments was disbursed to air carriers, with $3.2 billion of this total (70 percent) going to American, United, Delta, Continental, Northwest, and US Airways. In addition, 16 carriers applied for government loan guarantees: Six of these were approved by the ATSB, while the rest were rejected. The largest applications approved were US Airways ($900 million) and America West ($380 million); the largest submission rejected by the ATSB was United's original application for over $1 billion in government loan guarantees, an application that the carrier unsuccessfully resubmitted for re-approval in 2003.[60] In addition, the government Pension Benefit Guarantee Corporation since 2001 has assumed the pension obligations of United, TWA, USAir and Delta, at a cost exceeding $10 billion.[61]

---

[57]See the testimony of Phil Boyer, President, Aircraft Owners and Pilots Association, before the U.S. Congress. House. Subcommittee on Aviation, March 21, 2007.

[58]See U.S. General Accountability Office, "National Airspace System: Transformation will Require Cultural Change, Balanced Funding Priorities, and Use of All Available Management Tools," Washington, D.C. (October 2005).

[59]See U.S. General Accountability Office, "Air Traffic Control: Characteristics and Performance of Selected International Air Navigation Service Providers and Lessons Learned from Their Commercialization," Washington, D.C. (July 2005).

[60]The government cash grants are detailed by the Department of Transportation at www.dot.gov/affairs/carrierpayments.htm; details of the government loan guarantees have been compiled by the Air Transport Association at www.airlines.org/files/z110.htm

[61]U.S. General Accountability Office, "Commercial Aviation: Bankruptcy and Pension Problems," 54.

Such direct government aid raises some important public policy questions. First, does this aid represent an essential response to a national crisis tragically focused on air transportation, including the shutdown of the nation's air system and greatly increased security concerns? Or did 9/11 and its aftermath exacerbate trends already underway in the industry prior to that event, especially among the major carriers, who already were experiencing declining profitability caused by high fares, high costs, expensive mergers, and lavish executive and labor union compensation?

Second, was the creation of the ATSB to provide government loan guarantees an admirably pragmatic response to a catastrophic event? Or did it invest a small board with the power to pick winners and losers, thereby subjecting its determinations to suspicions of political lobbying, favoritism, and "rent seeking"? Will future government regulatory actions in the field be influenced by considerations of their consequences for the particular carriers whose multimillion dollar debts the federal government has guaranteed?

Third, was a unique opportunity to promote competition squandered by not making billions in government grants, loan guarantees and pension supports contingent on dominant carriers taking steps to relinquish their stranglehold on slots, gates, ground facilities, and routes to and from their hub monopolies? Would that not also have promoted the public interest? Conversely, does disbursing billions in government aid to carriers in proportion to their size reward monopoly and oligopoly rather than combat them?

Aviation Security

Programs and procedures to enhance aviation security have escalated sharply since 9/11. They include more thorough preflight screening of passengers, improved measures for detecting explosives, more thorough baggage screening, more air marshals on more flights, strengthened airfield and airport security, and the installation of hardened flight deck doors and cargo containers on aircraft. The costs of aviation security have increased sharply in line with these expanded measures, from an estimated $1 billion annually prior to 9/11, to approximately $5 billion per year since then.

The key economic issues here are two-fold. First, what is the economically optimal level of aviation security that should be provided? This, of course, is a matter of weighing the benefits of security against the costs of providing it, and is no simple matter when hundreds or thousands of lives hang in the balance and air routes are increasingly international in scope. A related policy question is whether security efforts should encompass a variety of procedures across a wide range, or whether instead they should be focused primarily on the specific procedures that provide the most security per dollar spent.[62]

Second, who should pay these costs? The airlines' trade association contends that aviation terrorism is a threat to the entire nation; that defending against aviation terrorism thus is an integral element of national defense; and that as such, the cost of aviation security should be paid for in the same way that national defense is financed, that is, by general government revenues collected from U.S. taxpayers at

---

[62]For an economic analysis of these and other security issues, see Walter Enders and Todd Sandler, *The Political Economy of Terrorism* (New York: Cambridge University Press, 2006).

large.[63] In fact, the Aviation and Transportation Act of 2001 shifted much of the responsibility for aviation security to the newly created Transportation Security Administration (an agency that in 2002 was absorbed into the new Department of Homeland Security). Annual taxes and fees charged airlines and passengers have paid for one-third of aviation security costs since then, with general revenue tax dollars covering the rest.[64] Yet it is a maxim of economics that resources are allocated most efficiently when producers and consumers are faced with the full costs of their activities. If the bulk of the costs of aviation security are paid for by others, then airline service will be underpriced and overconsumed. Indeed, if air travel is as vital to the nation as the carriers' trade association claims, should the nation's taxpayers pay for other costs of the airlines' operations as well, including wages, fuel, and aircraft? Put differently, aren't restaurants responsible for the safety of their food, and pharmaceutical firms responsible for the safety and efficacy of their medicines? If so, why should airlines be treated differently? But with a number of the nation's major carriers only now emerging from bankruptcy, is assigning them responsibility for more of the costs of aviation security unlikely because it might jeopardize their fragile financial condition? If so, has the government, and the public, effectively become a hostage to the bigness complexes that the major carriers constitute?

Open Skies and International Aviation

Finally, we address the issue of international competition. Since the 1940s, the ability of airlines to fly between nations has been tightly regulated by bilateral treaties negotiated on an individual, country-by-country basis.[65] These treaties typically specify the particular carriers allowed to fly between the two nations, the specific cities and airports these carriers are permitted to serve, and the specific number of flights they are permitted to operate, traditionally with a heavy emphasis on protecting and advantaging each nation's main domestic carriers. Over the past two decades, however, efforts have been building to liberalize international air travel between nations through so-called Open Skies agreements.[66] These negotiations assumed a measure of urgency following the European Court of Justice's ruling in 2002 that narrow, bilateral aviation agreements negotiated between the United States and individual member states of the EU violated EU commercial policy by discriminating against the carriers of all EU member-nations not party to each of these treaties. Negotiations on this front culminated in a possibly watershed agreement between the European Union and the U.S., ratified by the EU in the spring of 2007, ostensibly allowing any EU carrier to fly to any U.S. city, and any American carrier to fly to any city in the EU member states.

---

[63]Testimony of Mr. Jim May, President, Air Transport Association, U.S. Congress. Senate. Committee on Commerce, Science, and Transportation, June 22, 2004.

[64]See Bartholomew Elias, "Aviation Security: Issues Before Congress Since September 11, 2001," Congressional Research Service, Report for Congress, February 6, 2004; and Kenneth M. Mead, U.S. Department of Transportation, "Aviation Security Costs, Transportation Security Administration," testimony before the U.S. Congress. Senate. Subcommittee on Aviation, February 5, 2003.

[65]For a comprehensive history, see Brian F. Havel, *In Search of Open Skies* (Boston: Kluwer, 1997).

[66]For an analysis of recent developments in this area, see U.S. General Accounting Office, "Transatlantic Aviation: Effects of Easing Restrictions on U.S.-European Markets" (Washington, D.C.), July 2004.

The European Commission claims that reduced government barriers and freer competition between U.S. and EU carriers potentially can increase passenger traffic by as much as 50 percent, generate $20 billion in consumer benefits, and create 80,000 new jobs.[67] But the outcome of this latest agreement is unclear, in part because the incumbent carriers whose dominant positions are most threatened are strenuously resisting it.[68] The question also remains of how much competitive benefit such an Open Skies arrangement will actually generate, given that most major American and foreign carriers are already operating together as alliance partners. The consumer benefits will be even less if, as was the case in the U.S., deregulation succeeds at the international level, only to be followed by anticompetitive mergers, consolidation, and global monopoly hubs.

CONCLUSION

Alfred Kahn, economist and erstwhile industry regulator dubbed the father of airline deregulation, once famously quipped that for him, commercial jets were just marginal costs with wings. Armed with an understanding of the industry's structure, conduct and performance, students of industrial economics may see this and more as events—and lessons—unfold in this remarkable field over the years to come. Students, analysts, and aficionados will continue to ponder whether what the editors of the *Wall Street Journal* hail as the freedom to "book with someone else"[69] really does serve as an effective regulator of economic decision making and promoter of the public interest in this field.

SUGGESTIONS FOR FURTHER READING

Books

Bailey, Elizabeth E., David R. Graham, and Daniel P. Kaplan. 1985. *Deregulating the Airlines.* Cambridge, MA: MIT Press.

Caves, Richard E. 1962. *Air Transport and Its Regulators: An Industry Study.* Cambridge, MA: Harvard University Press.

Dempsey, Paul S., and Andrew R. Goetz. 1992. *Airline Deregulation and Laissez-Faire Mythology.* Westport, CT: Quorum Books.

Gittell, Judy Hoffer. 2005. *The Southwest Airlines Way.* New York: McGraw-Hill.

Kahn, Alfred E. 2004. *Lessons From Deregulation: Telecommunications and Airlines After the Crunch.* Washington, D.C.: AEI-Brookings Joint Center for Regulatory Studies.

Morrison, Steven A., and Clifford Winston. 1995. *The Evolution of the Airline Industry.* Washington, D.C.: Brookings Institution.

Peterson, Barbara S. 2004. *Blue Streak: Inside JetBlue.* New York: Penguin Group.

Petzinger, Thomas. 1995. *Hard Landing.* New York: Random House.

Government Reports and Other Sources

Air Carrier Association of America (www.acaa1.com), an association of low-fare air carriers.

Air Transport Association (www.air-transport.org) for economic statistics and data, including ATA annual economic report on the industry.

---

[67]European Commission, Directorate-General for Energy and Transport, Information Note: Air Transport Agreement between the EU and US, March 6, 2007.

[68]See Kevin Done, "BA and Virgin Launch Last-Minute Effort to Halt EU-US Aviation Deal," *Financial Times* (March 6, 2007):4.

[69]"The Politics of JetBlue," editorial, *Wall Street Journal* (February 24, 2007):A8.

Aviation & Aerospace Almanac, Washington, D.C.: Aviation Week (discontinued after 2003).

Bureau of Transportation Statistics, U.S. Department of Transportation (www.transtats.bts.gov) for extensive databases on the airline industry.

Hecker, JayEtta Z. 2001. U.S. General Accounting Office. "Aviation Competition: Challenges in Enhancing Competition in Dominated Markets." Testimony before the U.S. Congress. Senate. Committee on Commerce, Science, and Transportation, March 13.

———. 2001. "Airline Competition: Issues Raised by Consolidation Proposals." Testimony before the U.S. Congress. Senate. Subcommittee on Antitrust, Business Rights, and Competition, February 7.

Transportation Research Board, National Research Council. 1999. *Entry and Competition in the U.S. Airline Industry.* Washington, D.C.: National Academy Press.

U.S. Congress. House. Subcommittee on Aviation. Hearing: U.S.-E.U. Open Skies Agreement, 109th Cong., 2d sess., 2006.

———, Senate. Committee on Commerce, Science, and Transportation. Hearing: State of the Airline Industry: Potential Impact of Airline Mergers and Industry Consolidation, 110th Cong., 1st sess., 2007.

———, Senate. Committee on Commerce, Science, and Transportation. Hearing: Foreign Investment in U.S. Carriers, 109th Cong., 2nd sess., 2006.

———, Senate. Committee on the Judiciary. Hearing: Airline Consolidation: Has It Gone Too Far? 107th Cong., 1st sess., 2002.

———, Senate. Subcommittee on Antitrust, Business Rights, and Competition. Hearing:

Aviation Competition and Concentration at High-Density Airports, 107th Cong., 1st sess., 2002.

———, Senate. Committee on the Judiciary. Hearing: International Aviation Alliances, 107th Cong., 1st sess., 2001.

———, Senate. Committee on Commerce, Science, and Transportation. Hearing: Airline Passenger Fairness Act, 106th Cong., 1st sess., 2000.

———, Senate. Committee on the Judiciary. Report: Civil Aeronautics Board Practices and Procedures, 94th Cong., 1st sess., 1975.

U.S. Department of Transportation. 1996. The Low Cost Airline Service Revolution. Washington, D.C.: April.

U.S. General Accountability Office. 2006. "Airline Deregulation: Reregulating the Airline Industry Would Likely Reverse Consumer Benefits and Not Save Airline Pensions." Washington, D.C.: June.

———. 2005. "Commercial Aviation: Bankruptcy and Pension Problems are Symptoms of Underlying Structural Issues." Washington, D.C.: September.

———. 2004. "Commercial Aviation: Legacy Airlines Must Further Reduce Costs to Restore Profitability." Washington, D.C.: August.

———. 1999. "Aviation Competition: Effects on Consumers from Domestic Airline Alliances Vary," Washington, D.C.: January.

Wayne, Leslie, and Michael Moss. "Bailout for Airlines Showed the Weight of a Mighty Lobby," *New York Times* (October 10, 2001): 1.

10

C H A P T E R

The Banking Industry

Steven Pilloff

The commercial banking industry provides financial services to a substantial portion of firms and households in the United States and is one of the largest, most important sectors of the nation's economy. Banks provide a wide range of financial products and services, but their traditional activities fall largely into two basic areas: They offer customers safe, liquid, and convenient deposit products; and they lend deposited funds to consumers, governments, and businesses that need to borrow money. Typically, banks pay interest to depositors and collect interest from borrowers. A large portion of their profits comes from the difference in interest received from loans and interest paid on deposits. Therefore, high loan rates and low deposit rates are associated with high profitability. Banks also generate income by charging fees on deposit, loan, and other financial products and services.

The industry is made up of commercial banking institutions chartered either by the national bank regulator (the Office of the Comptroller of the Currency) or by the state bank regulator in the bank's home state. Some institutions operate as independent banks and are the only entity in their organization; others operate as part of a bank holding company that owns one or more banking institutions and may also own nonbank subsidiaries such as data processing, specialty lending, investment banking, and venture capital firms. Excluded from this definition of the commercial banking industry are nonbank depository institutions (e.g., savings banks, savings and loan associations, and credit unions) and nonbank, nondepository firms (e.g., mortgage companies, consumer finance firms, and mutual fund organizations). Also excluded are any nonbank subsidiaries of bank holding companies.

Throughout this chapter, the terms *bank* and *banking organization* are used to refer to an independent bank or to the aggregate of all bank subsidiaries owned by the same bank holding company. The term *banking institution* refers to an entity that has its own bank charter, an independent bank, or an individual bank subsidiary of a bank holding company.

The description of bank activities as collecting deposits and extending loans overly simplifies commercial banking. For one thing, banks also provide financial services in numerous other areas—trust, investment advisory services, and cash management, for example. Moreover, the deposit and loan options available to customers are numerous and varied. Banks typically offer many types of deposit accounts: savings, demand deposit (checking), money market deposit, and certificates of deposit, each with different features such as rate and fee schedules, minimum balance requirements, and withdrawal restrictions. A key feature of bank deposits is that they are federally insured, typically up to $100,000, and provide a level of safety that cannot be matched by nondepository firms.[1] The credit products provided by banks also are varied and include, for example, automobile, residential mortgage, and consumer loans and commercial and home equity lines of credit.

Each product or service offered by banks could potentially be analyzed as a separate market. Each has unique characteristics, is offered by a different (though often overlapping) set of firms, and is demanded by a different (though again often overlapping) set of customers. For example, mortgage loans, automobile loans, checking accounts, and cash management services could all potentially be considered distinct product markets. Nonetheless, commercial banks are the only firms that provide the broad range of financial services that are commonly considered commercial banking.[2] As a result, banks may have the unique ability to form long-term customer relationships that have a special economic importance beyond the actual products and services being obtained. Customers of financial services frequently view a commercial bank as their primary financial services provider and typically obtain multiple financial services from that institution.[3]

In this chapter, commercial banking is considered to involve two distinct markets, retail banking and corporate banking, each of which consists of the set of traditional deposit, loan, and other financial services that are provided by banks to a particular type of customer. The retail segment of commercial banking consists of financial services offered to households and small businesses. Not only does nearly every bank engage in retail banking, but most banks engage exclusively in retail banking.

Evidence suggests that the relevant geographic market for retail banking is local. On the demand side, retail customers strongly prefer to bank locally, so they typically

---

[1]Federal deposit protection is provided by the Federal Deposit Insurance Corporation (FDIC). Federal law provides up to $250,000 in deposit insurance coverage for self-directed retirement accounts, and up to $100,000 in coverage for all other types of accounts. These limits apply to each separate account registration at a given institution. Therefore, a household or company can fully protect nonretirement deposits above $100,000 by maintaining several accounts, each with less than $100,000, at an institution under different account holders or by maintaining multiple accounts, each with less than $100,000, under the same account holder at different institutions. Deposits held at savings banks and savings and loan associations are protected by the same insurance; deposits held at credit unions receive similar protection.

[2]The notion that various banking products and services are part of the same product is firmly established. For example, the Supreme Court has recognized that the appropriate product market for evaluating the competitive effects of bank mergers is the cluster of bank products and services offered by banking institutions. One of the most well-known cases establishing this principle is *United States v. Philadelphia National Bank*, 374 U.S. 321, 357 (1963).

[3]These and other findings from the Federal Reserve Board's 1993 Survey of Small Business Finances and 1992 Survey of Consumer Finances are discussed in Myron L. Kwast, Martha Starr-McCluer, and John D. Wolken, "Market Definition and the Analysis of Antitrust in Banking," *The Antitrust Bulletin* (Winter 1997): 973–995. More recent data from the Survey of Consumer Finances are reported in Dean F. Amel and Martha Starr-McCluer, "Market Definition in Banking: Recent Evidence," *The Antitrust Bulletin* (Spring 2002): 63–89. More recent data from the Survey of Small Business Finances are reported in Traci L. Mach and John D. Wolken, "Financial Services Used by Small Businesses: Evidence from the 2003 Survey of Small Business Finances," *Federal Reserve Bulletin* (October 2006): A167–A195.

obtain their financial services from a bank near their home or office. On the supply side, it is relatively costly for banks to provide retail services to customers not living or working close to a bank office, because retail accounts typically involve small amounts of money. In addition, the number of bank offices is large and growing, which is consistent with banks continuing to maintain a strong local presence to most effectively deliver services.

Corporate banking involves providing financial services to large businesses—commercial deposit and loan products, as well as sophisticated financial services such as foreign exchange. A relatively small number of large banks are involved in corporate banking. The accepted relevant geographic market for corporate banking is regional, national, or even international. Because corporate accounts typically involve large sums of money, large firms have a sizable financial incentive to search across a wide range for their best alternative; they are also likely to have the resources and expertise to engage in such a search. And because the potential profits associated with large businesses are substantial, making bank search costs relatively less important, banks are also likely to not be locally limited in their pursuit of corporate banking business.

Although both retail and corporate banking are important components of the commercial banking industry, this chapter focuses on retail banking, which is much better suited for an analysis within the structure-conduct-performance framework. Retail banking has received substantial attention from antitrust authorities because retail customers are more geographically limited and retail markets are smaller. As a result, extensive research has been done on the proper definition of retail markets and the relationship between market structure, bank performance, and to a lesser extent bank conduct. Corporate banking raises competitive concerns much less frequently, and few studies have been directed at this segment of the industry.[4]

▪▪▪ I. History

For much of its history, the U.S. commercial banking industry has mainly comprised a large number of small, local organizations. Federal and state legal restrictions on bank activities were major reasons for the development of this structure. Restrictions on branching and interstate banking, which limited the ability of both state-chartered and federally chartered banks to grow large and operate over sizable geographic areas, were particularly influential.

Essentially all banks operate a head office where deposits are accepted and loans are originated.[5] Most banks also maintain branch offices. For many years, state-chartered banks were prohibited from operating branches outside their home state. In fact, in many states, state-chartered banks were permitted to operate branches only in a limited portion of the state, such as the bank's home county or its home and contiguous counties; in other states, branching was completely prohibited. A bank that wanted to operate in an area of the state in which it was prohibited from branching needed to

---

[4]Throughout the remainder of this chapter, the term *commercial banking* refers to retail banking unless explicitly specified otherwise.

[5]Exceptions include a small number of Internet banks, which conduct all business without any physical offices and constitute an extremely small segment of the industry.

form a bank holding company and establish (or purchase) a separate bank subsidiary, with its own charter and head office.

Before 1927, federally chartered banks were prohibited from branching. The McFadden Act of 1927 gave national banks some expanded branching rights, but still limited them to the same branching restrictions imposed on state-chartered institutions. Therefore, national banks were essentially prohibited from interstate branching, and in many cases were limited in the extent of intrastate branching they could engage in.

Although no banks could branch across state lines, a loophole in the McFadden Act nevertheless made it possible for a bank holding company to conduct interstate banking by purchasing a banking institution operating in a state different from the acquiring holding company's home state. However, the Douglas Amendment to the Bank Holding Company Act of 1956 prohibited such interstate acquisitions unless the state legislature of the target institution's home state expressly permitted such acquisitions. For many years, no states had laws permitting interstate acquisitions.

The banking industry also faced other restrictions, most notably the Glass-Steagall Act of 1933, which mandated that commercial banking (gathering deposits and making loans) and investment banking (underwriting stocks, bonds, and other securities) remain separate activities.[6] Although various restrictions greatly affected the structure of the banking industry, restrictions on branching and interstate banking had the greatest influence.[7]

In recent years, many restrictions on interstate banking have been lifted. In 1975, Maine's state legislature passed a law allowing bank holding companies headquartered in other states to make acquisitions in Maine. Other states followed, so that by year-end 1984, eight states had enacted enabling legislation, and by year-end 1995, every state had passed legislation allowing some interstate banking. Restrictions on branching also have been relaxed. Many states have liberalized their branching rules, so it has become easier for banks to expand their operations within their home state. Most states currently allow statewide branching, with the remaining few permitting limited intrastate branching.

In 1985, the Office of the Comptroller of the Currency also began to facilitate interstate branching for national banks under an existing rule referred to as the Thirty-mile Rule. This rule allowed a national bank to relocate its head office anywhere within 30 miles, even if it meant moving the office into a different state. Following the move, the original head office could be operated as a branch. Banks used this type of expansion to enter new states, and many bank holding companies used it to consolidate subsidiaries.

The Riegle-Neal Interstate Banking and Branching Efficiency Act, enacted in 1994, removed many of the remaining limitations on interstate banking and branching. Interstate banking was facilitated as bank holding companies could purchase banking institutions in any state. Riegle-Neal also removed restrictions on interstate branching: A banking

---

[6]The Gramm-Leach-Bliley Financial Services Modernization Act (GLBA) was passed in 1999 and removed many of the restrictions on firms engaging in banking and other financial activities. Of particular importance, it repealed restrictions on banks affiliating with securities firms contained in the Glass-Steagall Act.
[7]Although the Glass-Steagall Act legally separated commercial and investment banking prior to passage of GLBA in 1999, regulatory decisions had already blurred the line before the Act was passed. For example, the Federal Reserve Board determined that, under section 20 of the Bank Holding Company Act, bank holding companies could form subsidiaries that engaged in a limited number of certain underwriting activities.

institution in one state could merge with an institution in another state, creating a single institution with branches in multiple states. Such mergers could take place among affiliated banks (owned by the same holding company) or unaffiliated banks. States were given the opportunity to opt out of interstate branching by merger by June 1, 1997, but only two, Texas and Montana, elected to do so. The prohibition on interstate branching expired in Texas in 1999 and in Montana in 2001. Although merger is the primary way that banks enter new states, banks may also establish new interstate branches in those states that explicitly authorize such entry.

▬▬▬ II. Structure

The structure of the commercial banking industry has changed markedly since 1990, largely as a result of extensive consolidation. The number of banks has declined and concentration at the national level has risen; interestingly, average concentration at the local level has not changed nearly as much. The number and size of very large banks has also increased, a development with potentially important consequences for the industry.

Mergers

Historically, the banking industry has consisted mainly of a large number of small, locally oriented organizations. Although the industry continues to exhibit this basic structure, it has changed dramatically in recent years. Much of the change is attributable to the extensive merger and acquisition activity that has taken place.[8]

Merger Activity

From 1990 to 2005, nearly 3,800 bank mergers involving $3.6 trillion in acquired assets were completed in the United States (Table 10-1). The pace of merger activity generally increased in the early 1990s, remained high through the mid- and late-1990s, and then generally declined to lower levels after peaking in 1998.

A small proportion of the deals have accounted for a large share of the total acquired assets. These large mergers, involving a target with substantial assets, generally became more common over time. Mergers in which the target had total assets of at least $1 billion accounted for about 7 percent of all deals, but more than 85 percent of all acquired assets. The 59 deals with a target that had total assets of at least $10 billion involved nearly 70 percent of all acquired assets, while the 13 acquisitions of banking organizations with total assets of at least $50 billion accounted for roughly 39 percent of acquired assets.

In 1998, merger activity reached an unprecedented level, when several of the largest bank combinations in history took place (NationsBank-BankAmerica, Banc One-First Chicago NBD, and Norwest-Wells Fargo). Several other sizable and many smaller deals also took place. Almost 13 percent of industry assets were acquired. In addition, The Travelers Group, a large, diversified nonbank financial services firm with extensive insurance and securities activities, and Citicorp, a large banking organization, merged to form the largest banking organization in the United States.

---

[8]The terms *merger* and *acquisition* are used interchangeably throughout this chapter.

TABLE 10-1 Bank Mergers and Acquisitions (1990–2005)

Year	Number	Bank assets acquired (in billions of dollars)	Percent of total industry assets[a]	Mergers with Acquired Assets Greater Than $1 billion	$10 billion	$50 billion
1990	118	68.8	2.0	10	1	0
1991	147	126.8	3.7	11	2	0
1992	240	157.8	4.5	23	3	1
1993	303	106.4	2.9	16	2	0
1994	360	117.5	3.0	16	2	0
1995	357	183.1	4.3	17	4	0
1996	313	322.1	7.1	22	7	2
1997	311	179.5	3.6	17	4	0
1998	379	677.3	12.6	32	8	3
1999	250	243.0	4.3	18	5	1
2000	183	177.0	2.9	16	2	1
2001	179	316.1	4.9	22	7	2
2002	148	55.2	0.8	11	1	0
2003	148	56.7	0.8	6	2	0
2004	196	734.0	9.0	27	7	3
2005	159	110.8	1.3	10	2	0
Total	3,791	3,632.1	—	274	59	13

[a] Total industry assets measured as of December 31.
Sources: SNL Securities, Federal Reserve Board, and Reports of Condition and Income (Call Reports).

Merger Motivations

The gradual removal of geographic restrictions on branching and interstate banking made consolidation possible in the commercial banking industry but does not explain why the merger wave took place. The extensive acquisition activity has been driven by the belief of bankers that substantial gains can be achieved by acquiring other organizations.

A key and commonly cited source of anticipated gains is reduced costs resulting from economies of scale.[9] Economies of scale exist when average costs decline as firm size increases. If scale economies exist in the banking industry, then larger banks would have lower average costs than smaller banks. As a result, they would be able to earn greater profits, either by lowering their prices (raising deposit rates, lowering loan rates, or lowering fees) to attract more customers or by increasing their profit margins (by maintaining prices and enjoying a greater spread between income and expenses) or through some combination of the two.

---

[9]A somewhat related, although less relevant, concept in a discussion of retail commercial banking is economies of scope. Scope economies occur when it is less expensive to jointly produce multiple outputs than to produce them separately. Scope economies are more relevant in the context of combining commercial banking with other financial service activities such as investment banking or insurance.

In the commercial banking industry, economies of scale may derive from several sources. Technology is a particularly important potential factor. Banks rely heavily on extensive computer systems, which involve substantial fixed costs and relatively smaller variable costs. Because their total computing and maintenance costs increase relatively little as transaction volume increases, banks may benefit from operations that generate a large number of transactions. Greater size also enables banks to increase employee specialization, possibly resulting in more effective and efficient operations. Another source of economies of scale is advertising. It may be efficient for large banks, which operate over wide geographic regions, to advertise through radio, television, and large newspapers, which reach broad areas. In contrast, advertising by small banks through those media may reach many individuals who, being well outside the bank's service area, are not potential customers. Mergers may also eliminate redundancies: Many back-office functions that are performed separately by two independent banks may possibly be conducted at lower cost by one consolidated bank. For example, following a merger it may be possible to eliminate one bank's check processing facility or payroll department. Likewise, when both the acquiring and target banks operate branches in the same neighborhood, some of those branches can often be closed following a merger without greatly inconveniencing customers.

However, consolidation may also result in greater market power; that is, a greater ability to sustain prices (interest rates, fees) above competitive levels without being forced by market pressures to lower them. If two banks competing in the same market merge to create a high market share, then (assuming that the postmerger market is sufficiently concentrated) the resulting banking organization may be able to exercise market power. Customers of the consolidated bank may be more willing to accept higher prices because no alternatives may be more attractive than maintaining their existing banking relationship, even with higher prices. If smaller banks in the market recognize that higher prices do not necessarily result in numerous customer defections, they may follow the market leader by raising their own prices. In the premerger, less concentrated market, neither merging party may have been able to sustain high prices because many customers of each partner may have viewed the other partner as a convenient alternative and would have transferred their business if prices were raised or service quality deteriorated.

The merger of two banks that are not direct competitors could also result in greater market power because the consolidated bank may benefit from certain aspects of size that may be associated with greater market power. Large banks generally have substantial resources, or "deep pockets," from which to draw, allowing them more flexibility in pricing strategies. For example, a large bank may decide to set its prices above the competitive level in a market. Smaller banks in that market might try to undercut those prices to attract customers. In turn, the large bank could retaliate by drastically lowering prices, even to the point at which it would incur losses. Because of its greater financial resources, the large bank likely would be able to sustain losses for a longer time than the small banks. Knowledge that this sequence of events might take place could then dissuade small banks from undercutting the prices charged by the large bank. They may elect to be price followers because failure to do so could invite this kind of pricing discipline. Hence, extensive financial resources may enable large banks to exercise market power by exerting price leadership.[10] A large bank also may increase its market power after a merger if it is able to strengthen its brand identity. Because large banks may advertise more frequently, maintain more offices, and have a more prominent profile as a result of involvement in public activities such as sponsoring local sporting events, customers may develop a stronger familiarity with their brand. This familiarity may lead customers to have greater trust in a recognized bank and be willing to pay higher prices for that bank's products and services.

Finally, mergers may benefit banks by reducing risk through diversification. With limited exposure to any particular geographic region, industry, or product type, a large and diversified bank is less vulnerable to economic problems in any single area. Greater diversification may also make large banks better equipped to take advantage of emerging profit opportunities. In particular, geographically diverse organizations are likely to be better suited to allocating resources to new opportunities, because they can easily transfer resources from less profitable to more profitable regions. Smaller, more locally oriented banks do not have similar outside resources to draw on to take advantage of such opportunities.

Failures and New Bank Formations

Although mergers and acquisitions have been the dominant force driving changes in the structure of the banking industry since 1990, the failure and formation of banking institutions have also played a role. There were 466 banking institutions with total assets of $81.5 billion that failed between 1990 and 2006 (Table 10-2).[11] Most of these failures took place in the first few years of this period. Failures have been fairly rare since 1994, largely as a result of the economic recovery in the southwestern United States and the strong overall expansion of the U.S. economy during most of the period. In recent years, failure rates have continued to remain low. In fact, there were no bank failures in either 2005 or 2006. The decline in failures after the early 1990s is also attributable to generally falling interest rates: Banks have typically not faced the difficult situation in which their fixed-rate assets are not generating sufficient funds to meet obligations on deposits, for which rates adjust frequently.

During the period when 466 banking institutions failed, more than four times as many new banking institutions were formed (See Table 10-2). However, the large number of new formations may overstate their importance to the industry. New institutions generally start out small and remain that way for many years. Also, some of the 2,126 institutions classified as new were formed by established bank holding companies, so they are actually expansions of existing firms.

The number of start-ups undoubtedly has been limited by various barriers to entry into the industry. One barrier has been legal restrictions that severely limit the potential pool of parties allowed to open a banking institution. For example, securities firms, which are already prominent financial services providers, were prohibited from operating

---

[10]Large banks may benefit from economies of scale, if they exist, in a similar manner as from deep pockets. Moreover, as discussed subsequently, some raise concerns that the very largest banks may be considered by regulators as too big to be allowed to fail—a status that might afford such banks more freedom to exert an anticompetitive influence in markets in which they operate.
[11]In addition, about 500 thrift institutions (savings banks and savings and loan associations) failed over the period.

TABLE 10-2 Bank Failures and Formations (1990–2006)

Year	Failures		Formations
	Number	*Assets (in billions of dollars)*	*Number*
1990	159	10.7	165
1991	108	44.0	106
1992	100	15.6	72
1993	42	2.9	61
1994	11	0.9	50
1995	6	0.8	102
1996	5	0.2	145
1997	1	0.0	188
1998	3	0.3	194
1999	7	1.5	232
2000	6	0.4	192
2001	3	0.1	129
2002	10	2.9	91
2003	2	1.1	111
2004	3	0.2	122
2005	0	0.0	166
2006	0	0.0	N/A
Total	466	81.5	2,126

Source: Federal Deposit Insurance Corporation web site (www2.fdic.gov).

commercial banks until the Gramm-Leach-Bliley Financial-Services Modernization Act (GLBA) was passed in 1999 and repealed restrictions on banks affiliating with securities firms. This relaxation of restrictions on the type of firm that can own and operate a commercial bank has broadened the pool of potential commercial banking firms. Nonfinancial firms, however, continue to be prohibited from owning commercial banks, so many companies that may want to start a new bank are legally prohibited from doing so.[12]

Even as legal barriers to entry erode, others not attributable to legal restrictions will continue to exist —barriers that discourage not only the formation of start-up banks but also the opening of branches in new markets by existing banks. A lack of accurate and comprehensive information gives rise to one of these nonstatutory barriers. Operating a bank, particularly extending credit, requires extensive knowledge of market conditions. Although profitable banking opportunities may exist in a given community, a party unfamiliar with local businesses and residents may be unable to exploit those opportunities. Evaluating credit risks can involve a great deal of uncertainty, and making bad loans can result in large losses and possibly failure. Therefore,

---

[12]See the following related discussion of industrial loan companies. For example, Wal-Mart filed an application with the FDIC in 2005 to open a special type of bank called an industrial loan company. Opposition from politicians, bankers, and consumers was intense, however, and the FDIC delayed its decision on whether or not to approve the application. Finally, in response to the opposition, Wal-Mart withdrew its request in early 2007.

prospective bankers may be hesitant to begin operating in a market they are unfamiliar with, even if the market offers potentially profitable opportunities.

Another entry barrier not related to legal restrictions is that motivating customers to change banks may be difficult. Customers face substantial switching costs when they change from one bank to another. Such tasks as opening and closing accounts and arranging for direct deposits and automatic bill payments to be processed differently can be aggravating and time-consuming. As a result, many customers are likely to stay with their current bank, even if another bank offers better prices or service.

Number and Absolute Size of Banks

A key development in the U.S. commercial banking industry has been a large decline in the total number of firms: Between 1990 and 2006, the number fell more than 30 percent from 9,221 to 6,271 (See Table 10-3). The decline is expected to continue, with additional firms leaving the industry mainly through merger. However, the common view is that the industry will continue to have a relatively large total number of organizations.

A major consequence of the consolidation-driven decrease in the number of organizations has been a rise in the number of very large banks, particularly since the late 1990s. At year-end 2006, 20 banks had at least $100 billion in total consolidated assets, including 7 with assets of more than $250 billion and 3 with assets greater than $1 trillion. In contrast, only a handful of banks had assets exceeding $100 million as recently as the mid-1990s.

The size of the very largest banks may continue to increase in the near future, but at some point, their growth is likely to level off. The Riegle-Neal Act of 1994 placed a cap

TABLE 10-3 Banking Organizations (1990–2006)

Year	Total
1990	9,221
1991	9,007
1992	8,730
1993	8,318
1994	7,896
1995	7,571
1996	7,313
1997	7,122
1998	6,839
1999	6,742
2000	6,676
2001	6,570
2002	6,491
2003	6,415
2004	6,334
2005	6,312
2006	6,271

Source: Federal Reserve Board. Data for 2006 are as of June 30, and all other data are as of December 31.

of 10 percent on the share of deposits that a banking organization can control as a result of an interstate acquisition. Therefore, the largest banks will reach a point where extensive additional growth will be legally constrained. In fact, at last one bank has approached the limit: Based on data from year-end 2006, Bank of America Corporation controls just under 10 percent of all U.S. deposits. Merger-related growth may not ultimately be limited to 10 percent, however, because Congress might raise the cap.

Industry and Market Concentration

As consolidation has progressed and the number of moderately large and very large banking organizations has risen, the banking industry has become increasingly concentrated; that is, fewer banks have come to account for a greater proportion of industry deposits (See Table 10-4).

Coinciding with the relaxation of branching and interstate banking laws, deals through which large banks moved into new territory became more common in the 1990s, increasing the prominence of leading banks. Between 1990 and 2006, the share of deposits under the control of the 10 largest banks more than doubled, growing from 20.0 percent to 44.5 percent. The 25, 50, and 100 largest banks also increased the share of deposits under their control. However, increases among these broader groups of banks are all driven by increased deposit shares for the largest banks. For example, the share controlled by banks ranked 11 through 25 showed little change, and that of banks ranked 26 through 100 dropped by 11 percentage points.

TABLE 10-4 Concentration of the U.S. Banking Industry (1990–2006)

| | *Percentage of Total Domestic Deposits Held by the* | | | |
Year	*10 largest banks*	*25 largest banks*	*50 largest banks*	*100 largest banks*
1990	20.0	34.9	48.9	61.4
1991	22.7	37.5	49.6	61.3
1992	24.1	39.2	51.7	62.6
1993	25.0	41.0	53.8	64.6
1994	25.2	41.5	54.6	65.9
1995	25.6	43.0	55.8	66.9
1996	29.8	46.8	59.0	68.6
1997	29.9	47.0	59.6	69.1
1998	36.7	51.2	62.6	70.9
1999	36.5	51.6	62.3	70.6
2000	36.1	51.4	62.7	71.3
2001	40.6	54.9	64.4	72.0
2002	40.3	54.5	64.5	72.2
2003	40.6	54.7	64.5	72.3
2004	45.0	58.5	66.9	73.7
2005	44.2	58.2	67.3	73.9
2006	44.5	58.8	67.7	74.2

Source: Reports of Condition and Income (Call Reports). Data for 2006 are as of June 30, and all other data are as of December 31.

Although concentration at the national level provides information about the relative roles of large and small firms in the banking industry, that measure does not provide information on the structure of the local markets that are most relevant for conduct and performance in retail banking. Concentration at the local level provides this information because banking markets for retail services tend to be local. Urban (defined as metropolitan statistical areas, or MSAs, based on 1999 definitions) and rural (non-MSA counties) local areas are analyzed separately because the two types of markets differ in some key ways, particularly physical size and density of population and commercial activity, that may influence competitive interactions among banks.

Concentration at the local level can be measured in several ways. The number of banks provides a simple measure of the number of choices customers have. In markets with fewer banks, customers are likely to have fewer convenient choices, and banks are more likely to be able to exercise market power. The three-firm concentration ratio (CR3)—the aggregate share of deposits controlled by the three banks with the greatest individual market shares—provides a measure of the prominence of the leading firms. The Herfindahl-Hirschman Index (HHI) is a widely used measure that takes into account the market shares of all banks in the market, but it gives larger banks a disproportionate influence. The HHI is computed as the sum of the squared market shares of every bank in the market; it ranges in value from 10,000 for a monopoly to nearly zero for a market with numerous competitors, each with a small market share. In markets having a high HHI, the leading bank or banks have a substantial market share, while in markets having a low HHI, no single bank has a sizable market share. Therefore, the ability to exercise market power should be positively related to the HHI.

Concentration, as measured by both CR3 and HHI, declined between 1990 and 2006 in both urban and rural markets (Table 10-5). During this period, concentration in rural markets was, not surprisingly, much higher than in urban markets. Because they are smaller than urban markets, rural markets can profitably support fewer banks than urban markets. Many banks cannot operate in a rural market with a small market share because they cannot generate sufficient revenues to cover their costs. In contrast, a small share of an urban market involves a greater level of activity, so it is easier to earn sufficient revenue to cover costs.

Using the Department of Justice's definition of a highly concentrated market as one with an HHI above 1,800, rural markets clearly qualify as being highly concentrated. The level of concentration in urban markets is more ambiguous. Although the average urban market can be considered highly concentrated throughout most of the period, the average HHI dipped below 1,800 in 2006. However, it is not clear that the change in the average HHI reflects a meaningful change in the level of competition, as the average urban HHI was in the lower end of the highly concentrated range in 1990 and the higher end of the moderately concentrated range in 2006.[13]

---

[13]Measures of local concentration cited in the text and tables only include commercial banks. When analyzing proposed bank mergers, antitrust authorities often include, on at least a partial basis, savings banks and savings and loan associations. When measures are computed with thrift institutions receiving at least partial weight, a somewhat different picture of local concentration emerges. For example, computing the HHI with the deposits of thrift institutions included at 50 percent, as is typically done by the Federal Reserve Board in its competitive analysis, yields lower average levels than when thrifts are completely excluded (HHI below 1,600 in urban markets and below 3,700 in rural markets). In urban areas, those levels increased over the full period from 1990 to 2006, although declines between 1998 and 2006 offset some of that increase. In rural areas, the average HHI with thrift deposits weighted at 50 percent remained stable over the full period, but it also showed variation, increasing from 1990 to 1993, before declining from 1994 to 2006.

TABLE 10-5 Average Concentration of Urban and Rural U.S. Banking Markets (1990–2006)

Year	Urban Banking Markets (MSAs)		Rural Banking Markets (non-MSA counties)	
	CR3	HHI	CR3	HHI
1990	67.5	2,010	89.6	4,291
1991	66.7	1,977	89.3	4,257
1992	67.5	2,023	89.2	4,222
1993	66.9	1,994	89.3	4,234
1994	66.6	1,976	89.1	4,208
1995	66.3	1,963	88.8	4,171
1996	66.9	1,991	88.7	4,145
1997	66.0	1,973	88.4	4,119
1998	65.8	1,975	88.0	4,088
1999	65.1	1,935	87.6	4,064
2000	64.5	1,921	87.2	4,019
2001	63.9	1,889	86.8	3,978
2002	63.5	1,860	86.6	3,951
2003	62.8	1,846	86.4	3,946
2004	62.1	1,820	86.2	3,934
2005	62.1	1,825	85.9	3,904
2006	61.2	1,785	85.5	3,847

Source: Summary of Deposits. Data are as of June 30. CR3 is the three-firm concentration ratio and HHI is the Herfindahl-Hirschman Index. MSAs are defined with 1999 definitions.

Although average concentration in rural and urban banking markets has decreased over time, levels have varied considerably from market to market. For example, Table 10-6 indicates that in 2006, half of urban markets had an HHI between 1,267 and 1,986; the level of the HHI for the other half of the urban markets was outside this range. Rural markets showed even more dispersion in HHI levels, as the middle half had HHIs in the broad range between approximately 2,300 and 4,900.

The substantial increases in concentration in the commercial banking industry during the 1990s at the national level and the declines at the local level reflect the influence of consolidation. Mergers have enabled banks to become increasingly larger by enhancing their presence within states and across large regions of the country. However, mergers have not resulted in banks substantially increasing their presence in local markets. These patterns are consistent with the anticipated effects of antitrust policy in banking. Mergers between banks that do not compete with each other in local markets do not raise serious antitrust concerns, and few limits other than interstate banking restrictions have been placed on these so-called "market-extension" mergers. In contrast, mergers between banks that operate in the same local markets do raise antitrust concerns, especially when one or both have a large local presence. Antitrust authorities seek to limit the amount of change in the HHI, the postmerger level of the HHI, and the level of the consolidated bank's postmerger market share resulting from

TABLE 10-6 Variation in Concentration of Urban and Rural
U.S. Banking Markets (2006)

	Urban Banking Markets (MSAs)	Rural Banking Markets (non-MSA counties)
	HHI	*HHI*
Minimum	522	975
25th percentile	1,267	2,292
Median	1,614	3,221
75th percentile	1,986	4,852
Maximum	8,411	10,000

Source: Summary of Deposits. Data are as of June 30. HHI is the Herfindahl-Hirschman Index. MSAs are defined with 1999 definitions.

these "in-market" mergers. Therefore, banking antitrust policy has, to a large extent, restricted in-market mergers, and most of the substantial consolidation activity in the industry has involved market-extension deals.

Relevant Market Definition

A key issue in applying the structure-conduct-performance framework to an analysis of the commercial banking industry is determining the relevant market, a task that involves defining both the product and geographic markets. As previously discussed, the relevant product market is ambiguous, as commercial banking encompasses numerous financial services, many of which might be considered a unique product. For this analysis, the relevant product market is assumed to be the group of financial products and services constituting retail banking.

The relevant geographic market in retail banking is the area within which banks can reasonably turn for customers, and customers can reasonably turn for banks. Surveys show that most retail customers establish relationships with banking organizations that have a physical presence close to where they live or work (in the case of households) or close to where they are located (in the case of small businesses). Therefore, for the analysis in this chapter the relevant geographic market is assumed to be local. Such an approach is consistent with most research and is the approach taken by antitrust authorities.

In the future, however, expansion of the area considered the relevant geographic market may be warranted. Technologies such as telephone banking, ATMs, personal computers, and the Internet may enable banks lacking a physical presence in a geographic region to provide convenient financial services to customers in that region. These technology-based delivery systems allow customers to make deposits, apply for loans, discuss financial needs, and obtain updated account information without having to visit a traditional "brick and mortar" bank office or, in some cases, even interact with a live person. Although many nontraditional delivery systems are already available, consumer and small business surveys suggest that they are not yet widely accepted. Most customers still appear to prefer that their bank have a local physical presence. Nonetheless, the increasing influence of technological advances on the retail banking industry suggests that the relevant geographic size of retail banking markets should be reassessed regularly. In addition, several recent studies have found that certain state-level measures may be becoming increasingly related to prices and profits, which highlights the current relevance of the issue of market size.[14]

Role of Nonbank Firms

Commercial banks are the largest, most prevalent, most diversified group of depository institutions operating in the United States. However, they are not the only depository institutions in the country. Thrift institutions (savings banks and savings and loan associations) and credit unions are also relatively important providers of depository services, including insured deposit accounts. Thrifts held total assets of $1.7 trillion and credit unions had $710 billion at the end of 2006, respectively, compared with domestic assets of $10.0 trillion for commercial banks. In addition, nonbank, nondepository firms provide some of the same financial services as commercial banks.

Thrift Institutions

Thrift institutions raise funds primarily by collecting consumer deposits and invest funds principally in mortgage and other consumer loans. Thrift deposits are protected up to $100,000 (outside of self-directed retirement accounts) or $250,000 (in self-directed retirement accounts) by the same federal deposit insurance that covers bank deposits. For many years, thrifts provided a limited set of consumer-oriented financial services because they were restricted in the types of accounts they could offer and loans they could make. Of particular importance, they were restricted from originating commercial loans. Beginning in the early 1980s, restrictions on their activities, including commercial lending, were relaxed, but few thrifts have taken full advantage of these expanded powers.

Although many thrift institutions engage in some commercial lending, relatively few do so in more than a limited way.[15] In contrast, nearly all commercial banks make some commercial loans, and a large majority has a nontrivial share of their assets in commercial loans. Because a large proportion of commercial loans are extended to small businesses, the limited involvement of thrifts in commercial lending suggests that they do not provide much competition to banks in at least one important retail banking product, small business lending.

The lack of full competition from thrifts in retail banking is recognized by antitrust authorities. In the competitive analysis of proposed bank mergers, thrifts are typically regarded as market competitors, but their role is generally viewed as limited. However, antitrust authorities often treat those thrifts that provide a full set of bank products and services, including more than a modest amount of commercial lending, as full members of the commercial banking industry. In this chapter, thrifts are not included

---

[14]For example, Lawrence J. Radecki, "The Expanding Geographic Reach of Retail Banking Markets," *Federal Reserve Bank of New York Economic Policy Review* (June 1998): 15–34; Steven J. Pilloff and Stephen A. Rhoades, "Structure and Profitability in Banking Markets," *Review of Industrial Organization* (February 2002): 81–98; Erik Heitfield and Robin A. Prager, "The Geographic Scope of Retail Deposit Markets," *Journal of Financial Services Research* (February 2004).

[15]Steven J. Pilloff and Robin A. Prager, "Thrift Involvement in Commercial and Industrial Lending," *Federal Reserve Bulletin* (December 1998): 1025–1037. This article discusses the involvement of thrifts in commercial lending and shows that the large majority are much less active in such lending than commercial banks.

in the analysis; as a result, measures of concentration may be somewhat overstated, especially in some markets having a large thrift presence.

Credit Unions

Credit unions are nonprofit, cooperative financial institutions that collect deposits from and make loans to members. Deposits at credit unions outside of self-directed retirement accounts are protected up to $100,000, while deposits at credit unions in self-directed retirement accounts are protected up to $250,000 by federal insurance administered by the National Credit Union Administration. For each credit union, members must share a "common bond," such as belonging to the same organization or being employed by the same company. Membership requirements greatly limit the competitive importance of credit unions because they are unable to gather deposits from or make loans to many potential customers. However, in recent years, the importance of credit unions that are open to all individuals that live, work, pray, or attend school in a geographic area such as a county or cluster of counties has increased. Credit unions such as these tend to offer more competition to banks.

Another characteristic of credit unions that impairs their competitive importance is their tendency to offer a relatively narrow set of products. Not only are they limited by regulation in the range of products and services they may offer, but many credit unions are also very small, so they cannot efficiently provide more than basic deposit and loan products.

Industrial Loan Companies and Industrial Banks

In recent years, industrial loan companies and industrial banks (often collectively referred to as ILCs) have been the focus of a substantial amount of concern and attention, especially because Wal-Mart filed an application in 2005 (which has since been withdrawn) to open and operate an ILC. According to the Federal Deposit Insurance Corporation (FDIC), an ILC is an FDIC-supervised financial institution that can be owned by a commercial firm that is not regulated by a federal banking agency. Target Corporation and Harley-Davidson are two examples of commercial firms that own an ILC.

Regulators are concerned that owners of ILCs receive less oversight than owners of commercial banks and other depository institutions. A key fear is that by operating with less supervision, owners of ILCs may be more likely to experience severe financial difficulties than highly regulated parents like bank holding companies. Moreover, financial problems may spread more easily from a commercial firm to a subsidiary ILC and then possibly throughout the financial system and economy than they would in the case of a more regulated financial parent like a bank holding company. The more regulated bank parents are also concerned about ILCs: Being subject to less rigorous regulatory standards may provide an unfair competitive advantage in banking for the commercial parents of ILCs. Legislators and regulators are analyzing the potential problems of ILC ownership by commercial firms not subject to banking regulations, and are considering possible ways to address any relevant concerns.

Other Nonbank Firms

The financial services industry has many specialized firms that compete in certain respects with commercial banks. This competition is limited, however, because specialized firms do not offer as full a complement of financial services as banks provide. For example, nonbank (and nonthrift) mortgage originators compete with banks for residential mortgages but not for other loan products, and certainly not for federally insured deposit products. Likewise, many consumer finance companies specialize in lending to consumers but offer no credit services to businesses and no deposit products to anyone. On the deposit side, money market mutual funds, which are not federally insured, offer some competition to bank deposit products, but none to loan products. Because nonbank institutions offer a limited set of products and services, they are less likely to form the special type of customer relationships that banks form.

▪▪▪ III. Conduct

According to the structure-conduct-performance model, market structure affects bank performance by influencing bank conduct; that is, the ways in which banks compete with each other and the intensity of that competition. Like firms in other industries, banks engage in price competition. Unlike prices in many other industries, however, bank prices can be ambiguous, making price comparisons difficult for customers. Banks also compete with each other in several ways unrelated to price.

Price Competition

Banks engage in price competition. But this competition is not nearly as straightforward as in many other industries, because the price of bank products may not be immediately obvious to customers. First, the price of many financial services involves both an interest rate and fees. In some cases, interest rates will vary depending on the customer's account balance, typically increasing with account size. Moreover, because banks tend to charge a variety of fees payable under widely varying circumstances, fees may also be difficult for customers to determine as they evaluate a product's price. Some fees, such as monthly account fees, are assessed regularly; others are assessed only when a specific service, such as an ATM, is used; still others are charged only when some condition, such as a minimum balance requirement, is not satisfied. Therefore, two customers having the same type of account at the same institution could pay very different prices if their banking practices differed greatly. Prices would differ even more if the size of their account balances tended to differ greatly.

Adding to customers' difficulty in evaluating the price of bank products is the nature of the business. Commercial banking is marked by customers maintaining a multiproduct relationship with a primary organization, and the most meaningful price for retail banking services is likely to be a composite price of a set of products and services. Such a composite price may be difficult for customers to calculate. Moreover, the products and services included in the set (as well as the weight assigned to each) likely differ from customer to customer depending on individual banking needs. Despite these problems, price competition among banks may be driven by a desire by banks to establish and maintain customer relationships. As such, banks may establish pricing schedules designed to attract and retain a particular customer base.

Nonprice Competition

Banks also compete in several ways unrelated to price. The location of branch offices and ATMs is an important form of nonprice competition. Another important area of nonprice competition is customer service: Length of operating hours, length of waiting times for tellers, loan officers, customer service representatives, and access to senior personnel are just a few of the elements banks can control that determine the level of service they provide. Banks also compete in providing services through alternative delivery channels, such as the Internet and the telephone, that may be more convenient than traditional brick and mortar offices for some customers.

The set of products offered is another dimension along which banks compete. Product variety directly influences a bank's ability to meet customer needs because the types of products it offers affect its attractiveness to various classes of customers. Some banks offer many different products to appeal to a broad cross-section of customers; others may offer a small set of highly specialized products.

Brand recognition is also an important component of competition among banks. Through advertising and involvement in community activities such as sponsorship of local events, banks attempt to establish an institutional image such as "integral part of the community," "trustworthy," or "knowledgeable." Much of the brand imaging in the retail banking industry revolves around the fundamental differences between small and large banks: Small banks tend to emphasize their local ownership and management and their ability to provide personalized service; large banks tend to emphasize their wide product offerings, extensive experience, and vast resources as tools to help customers succeed in a complex financial world. Both types of banks often try to convey their contributions to the local communities in which they operate.

Relationship Competition

Banks compete in developing customer relationships to enhance their prospects for cross selling. Cross selling—selling additional products and services to existing bank customers—can be a lucrative and efficient means of expanding business. For example, a bank may encourage its checking account customers to take out a home equity loan, or a bank holding company may try to sell the products of its nonbank subsidiaries, such as an insurance policy or investments, to its banking clientele.

In attempting to sell additional products, a customer's existing bank or bank holding company has several advantages over other banks. First, because it regularly interacts with customers when they conduct business at a bank office or ATM, over the telephone, or over the Internet, it has many opportunities to cross sell. Customers may be more responsive to these approaches than to more impersonal or intrusive methods such as media advertising, direct mail, and telephone solicitations that other banks must rely on. Another advantage for an existing bank holding company is the information it possesses about its customers. Such information may enable a bank to identify those products most likely to be desired by particular segments of its customer base, allowing it to better focus its marketing and cross selling efforts. For example, a customer who applies for a home mortgage loan may be in the market for homeowners insurance as well. A third advantage is the trust that an established relationship may engender between a customer and a bank; customers may be more likely to place their confidence in a bank they already do business with.

Cross selling, or the potential for cross selling, is viewed by some banks as such an important aspect of competition that they actively seek to increase their opportunities to engage in it. For example, the potential synergy of cross selling was a primary motivation for the 1998 merger of Citicorp and Travelers, which created Citigroup, an extremely large and diversified financial firm. The enactment of the Gramm-Leach-Blilely Act in 1999 enabled banks to expand their range of financial service offerings. It facilitated continued bank efforts to cross sell to customers, because it expanded the amount of non-bank products and services that may be provided by firms engaged in banking. Although there is and has been great enthusiasm for cross selling, it is not clear that cross selling basic banking services and such diverse products as insurance and investments can yield large synergies. For example, the combination of financial activities at Citigroup does not appear to have been successful, as the company sold its insurance operations only a few years after the merger.

Influence of Entry Barriers on Competition

Bank conduct, or competition, may be influenced by the numerous barriers that make it difficult for both new and existing organizations to enter markets. These barriers—including customer switching costs, lack of clear information about market conditions, and legal restrictions on who is allowed to operate a bank and where they are allowed to operate—give incumbent firms advantages that may affect their conduct and facilitate the exercise of market power. If entry barriers are sufficiently high, a bank (or potential banker) may still be deterred from entry, even if existing firms in the market are charging high prices and earning high profits.

Special Issues Related to Large Banks

An important development that may influence conduct in the banking industry is the increased prominence of large banks, which may behave differently than smaller banks and may exert a unique effect on competition. In fact, the mere presence of a large bank in a market may affect competition indirectly by influencing the behavior of smaller rivals.

As discussed earlier, large banks having access to considerable resources may be able to sustain market prices above competitive levels. If large banks benefit from economies of scale, they may also be able to charge lower prices or offer superior service relative to smaller banks. Moreover, if large banks are diversified, they may be able to reallocate their resources to profitable opportunities more easily than smaller, more locally concentrated banks.

Large banks may also have a negative influence on competition as a result of multimarket contact. In banking, multimarket contact occurs when two or more banks compete with each other in several geographic areas, or markets. Consolidation has resulted in increased contact of this nature. Specifically, a bank may be less inclined to act aggressively in an individual market where the bank faces rivals from other markets, because those rivals could retaliate in those other markets. On the other hand, if a bank faces other banks that it does not encounter elsewhere, it may be more willing to exploit competitive advantages without such fear of retaliation.

Large banks, particularly those with a small share of a local market, may increase competition because they can easily draw on out-of-market resources to exploit profitable opportunities. This ability may restrain other banks with large shares of the market from exercising market power. If locally dominant banks attempt to raise prices, the large bank may bring in resources from elsewhere to exploit the opportunity. Such a response would eventually drive prices down toward their competitive level.

Anticipation that large banks might respond to high prices in this way would discourage locally dominant banks from trying to sustain high prices in the first place.[16]

Finally, very large banks may also benefit from being considered too big to fail.[17] Although bank regulators do not assert that an explicit too-big-to-fail policy exists, many market participants and observers believe that regulators would not allow a very large bank to fail because a failure of such magnitude could be severely damaging to other financial institutions and to the financial system as a whole. Therefore, it is believed that regulators would bail out a troubled large bank and not allow depositors and other customers to suffer meaningful losses. If customers believe that very large banks would not be allowed to fail, however, such banks may be perceived as being less risky than similar, but smaller, rivals. This difference in perceived risk, in turn, could give such banks an important competitive advantage, as customers may be more likely to use (or pay a higher premium to use) their services rather than those provided by smaller competitors.

▪▪▪ IV. Performance

The structure-conduct-performance paradigm asserts that market structure influences bank conduct, which in turn affects performance. Because direct observation and measurement of bank conduct is difficult, empirical research generally focuses on the relationship between structure and performance.

Influence of Market Structure on Performance

Prices

In unconcentrated banking markets, consumers are likely to have numerous convenient banking alternatives. If any one bank attempts to charge excessively high prices, many of its customers can presumably switch to another bank. For this reason high prices are generally less sustainable in unconcentrated markets. In more concentrated markets, however, higher prices may be easier to sustain. Fewer banks operate and market shares are larger, so customers have fewer convenient alternatives. They may accept higher prices or poorer service if transferring to a rival bank that charges lower prices or offers better service is too inconvenient. If all banks in the market know that high prices can be sustained, they all are likely to charge high prices.

Empirical research has generally found that market structure is related to bank prices in a way that suggests that the exercise of market power increases with concentration. Many studies have found that loan interest rates rise and interest rates paid on deposits fall as local market concentration increases.[18] No significant relationship

---

[16]See William M. Landes and Richard A. Posner, "Market Power in Antitrust Cases," *Harvard Law Review* 94 (March 1981): 937–996, for a thorough discussion of this hypothesis.

[17]See Gary H. Stern and Ron J. Feldman, *Too Big To Fail: The Hazards of Bank Bailouts* (Washington, D.C.: Brookings Institution Press, 2004) for a thorough discussion of these issues.

[18]For example, Timothy H. Hannan, "Market Share Inequality, the Number of Competitors, and the HHI: An Examination of Bank Pricing," *Review of Industrial Organization* (February 1997): 25–35; Anthony W. Cyrnak and Timothy H. Hannan, "Is the Cluster Still Valid in Defining Banking Markets? Evidence from a New Data Source," *The Antitrust Bulletin* (Summer 1999): 313–331. Erik Heitfield and Robin A. Prager, "The Geographic Scope of Retail Deposit Markets," *Journal of Financial Services Research* (February 2004).

between market concentration and bank fees has been identified in the limited research that has been conducted on that subject.[19]

Efficiency

The market structure in which a bank operates may influence bank incentives for and managerial dedication to cost savings. In less concentrated, more competitive markets, market forces exert pressure on managers to work hard to maximize profits, making efficient operations a top priority. If managers are unable to maximize profits, returns are low and they may be relieved of their duties or forced to sell the bank to a more efficient and profitable rival. In the worst case, an inefficient bank could become insolvent and fail.

In more concentrated markets, however, competition is less intense, so banks have the ability to sustain prices at levels that generate sizable profits. That ability may lead managers to operate inefficiently either for their own personal benefit or for that of the bank. For instance, a manager may direct costly resources toward preserving the existing market structure or pursuing additional market share so that large profits continue or are increased. Or a manager may prefer to sacrifice some firm profits in order to live a "quiet life" or to enjoy costly perks such as a large staff or luxurious offices. The additional profit generated by greater efficiency may not, in the manager's opinion, be worth the additional effort. Even if they operate their banks at inefficient levels, above-competitive pricing may make it possible for managers to earn returns for shareholders that compare favorably with other investment alternatives. Finally, managers may operate less efficiently in more concentrated markets because they lack ability and yet are not forced to exit banking; high profits generated from above-competitive prices may mask a lack of managerial skill.

Empirical analysis indicates that bank efficiency is negatively related to concentration.[20] Managers of banks in markets that are less concentrated and governed more strictly by competitive pressures are more effective at operating efficiently than managers of banks in more concentrated, less competitive markets.

Profitability

Because greater market concentration is associated with higher prices—higher loan rates and lower deposit rates—greater concentration might be expected to lead to a greater net interest margin (the difference between interest income and expenses) and a corresponding rise in bank profitability. However, research findings indicate that as concentration increases, efficiency drops, in which case greater concentration might be expected to lead to a decline in bank profitability. Studies of bank profits and market structure indicate that the concentration-pricing relationship is stronger than, and is

---

[19]Timothy H. Hannan, "Bank Fees and Their Variation across Banks and Locations," Working paper, Board of Governors of the Federal Reserve System, December 1996.
[20]For example, Allen N. Berger and Timothy H. Hannan, "Using Efficiency Measures to Distinguish Among Alternative Explanations of the Structure-Performance Relationship in Banking," *Managerial Finance* (1991): 6–31; Allen N. Berger and Timothy H. Hannan, "The Efficiency Cost of Market Power in the Banking Industry: A Test of the 'Quiet Life' and Related Hypotheses," *Review of Economics and Statistics* (August 1998): 454–465.

only partially offset by, the concentration-efficiency relationship.[21] Banks operating in more concentrated markets earn higher profits than banks operating in less concentrated markets.

Influence of Size on Performance

Greater size may enable large banks to operate more efficiently and more profitably than their smaller rivals and to exert a unique influence on market competition. If so, the trend of ever-larger banks controlling ever-larger shares of the industry may be affecting the performance of both large banks and their smaller rivals.

Performance of Large Banks

Data for commercial banks of various sizes indicate that small banks are, on average, generally less profitable and less efficient than larger banks (Table 10-7). In 2006, three of the four smallest groups of banks (assets of $1 billion or less) were less profitable, as measured by average return on assets (net income divided by end-of-year assets), than the two groups of larger banks (assets between $1 billion and $10 billion, and assets over $10 billion). One group of smaller banks was equally as profitable as the larger banks, however.

Evidence on the relationship between bank pricing and bank size is mixed. Strong evidence suggests that larger banks charge higher fees than smaller banks.[22] For example,

TABLE 10-7 Profitability and Efficiency of U.S. Banks by Size Class (2006)

Asset size ($ millions)	Mean return on assets (as a percentage)	Mean efficiency ratio (as a percentage)
less than 100	0.92	71.6
101–300	1.12	65.6
301–500	1.29	62.6
501–1,000	1.19	62.4
1,001–10,000	1.28	57.0
more than 10,000	1.29	56.8

Source: Federal Deposit Insurance Corporation web site (www2.fdic.gov).

Return on assets is computed as net income divided by year-end assets. Efficiency ratio is computed as noninterest expense divided by the sum of noninterest income and net interest income.

---

[21]For example, Elizabeth S. Laderman and Steven J. Pilloff, "Using County-Based Markets to Support and Federal Reserve Markets to Implement Bank Merger Policy," *Journal of Competition Law and Economics* (2007); Steven J. Pilloff and Stephen A. Rhoades, "Structure and Profitability in Banking Markets," *Review of Industrial Organization* (February 2002): 81–98; Steven J. Pilloff, "Multimarket Contact in Banking," *Review of Industrial Organization* (March 1999): 163–182; Stephen A. Rhoades, "Market Share Inequality, the HHI, and Other Risk Measures of the Firm-Composition of a Market," *Review of Industrial Organization* (December 1995): 657–674.

[22]Summary statistics of survey data on bank fees are reported in Board of Governors of the Federal Reserve System, Annual Report to the Congress on Retail Fees and Services of Depository Institutions, yearly.

one study found that in 2002, banks with assets of more than $1 billion charged an average fee of more than $23 for a stop payment order compared with $17 for institutions with assets of less than $100 million; similarly, large banks charged $26 on average for a bounced check while small banks charged about $20. Because the study summarized fee data for all large banks with assets of more than $1 billion, it is unclear how fees charged by the very largest banks differ from those charged by other large banks.

Studies of the relationship between bank size and loan rates provides evidence suggesting that large banks charge lower prices than their smaller rivals. For example, research has found a significant negative relationship between bank size and the rates charged on similar types of commercial loans.[23] However, because loan rates are frequently set to reflect the expected risk of a loan, differences in rates between large and small banks may reflect differences in the types of loans made and the types of businesses served, rather than a difference in prices for a similar product.

In sum, large banks clearly charge higher fees but, because they charge lower loan rates, it is not clear if they charge higher overall prices. Moreover, it is unclear whether the fees charged by the very largest banks differ from those charged by other large institutions.

Although economies of scale have been found for smaller banks, little evidence demonstrates that large-scale economies extend to the very largest banks. The precise point at which scale economies disappear is unclear; studies have found benefits from increased size for banks with assets up to somewhere in the range of $100 million to approximately $10 billion or $25 billion.[24] Regardless of where economies of scale actually cease to exist, the evidence suggests that efficiency gains from economies of scale are more likely and larger for smaller banks than for the larger ones. Therefore, banks that have been most active in the merger movement and have used acquisitions to grow substantially are unlikely to derive substantial benefits from scale economies.

Average efficiency ratios calculated from 2006 commercial bank data indicate that bank size is positively related to efficiency (See Table 10-7). The efficiency ratio, a measure commonly used by bankers and financial analysts, is calculated as total noninterest expense divided by the sum of net interest income (interest revenue less interest expense) and noninterest revenue. A lower ratio corresponds to greater efficiency. The smallest banks are the least efficient and could benefit the most from increasing their size: The average ratio for that group (total banking assets of $100 million or less) was 71.6 percent, compared with 65.6 percent for banks in the next-larger size group (assets of $100 million to $300 million). Average efficiency ratios decrease over subsequent size ranges, with the two largest size groups having average ratios of about 57 percent.

Finally, large banks appear to be no better than, and possibly inferior to, smaller banks in attracting and retaining customers. One study found that, from 1990 to 1996,

[23]See Anthony W. Cyrnak and Timothy H. Hannan, "Is the Cluster Still Valid in Defining Banking Markets? Evidence from a New Data Source," *The Antitrust Bulletin* (Summer 1999): 313–331; and David A. Carter, James E. McNulty, and James A. Verbrugge, "Do Small Banks Have an Advantage in Lending? An Examination of Risk-Adjusted Yields on Business Loans at Large and Small Banks," *Journal of Financial Services Research* (October 2004): 233–252.

[24]For example, Allen N. Berger and Loretta J. Mester, "Inside the Black Box: What Explains Differences in the Efficiencies of Financial Institutions?" *Journal of Banking and Finance* (1997): 895–947; David B. Humphrey, "Why Do Estimates of Bank Scale Economies Differ?" *Federal Reserve Bank of Richmond Economic Review* (September-October 1990): 38–50.

the average market share of the approximately 50 largest banks in the industry declined somewhat in markets in which they had engaged in no mergers or acquisitions during the study period.[25] The pattern of declining market share was particularly pronounced in rural areas, but even in urban areas, where large banks maintained constant market shares, large banks demonstrated no special ability to attract customers. These results are consistent with those of other studies, which have shown that large banks are not especially successful at obtaining and holding onto market share.[26]

In summary, large banks appear to perform better than their smaller rivals, as large banks are more profitable and efficient. The evidence on pricing is mixed: Large banks charge higher fees, but they also charge lower rates on loans; moreover, it is unclear whether the fees charged by the very largest banks in fact differ from those charged by banks of other sizes. Finally, the inability of large banks to grow their share of deposits in local markets is consistent with large banks not having sizable competitive advantages over smaller rivals that enable them to attract and retain customers.

Performance of Other Banks Facing Large Banks

The presence of a large bank may influence the performance of other banks in the market. In particular, if large banks have some unique influence on competition, the presence of a large bank in a market may affect the performance of smaller, more locally oriented banks that also operate in the market. In fact, several studies suggest that large banks may lower the level of competition in markets in which they operate.

One study found that the profitability (as measured by return on assets) of small banks that operate in a single rural market in which a large bank also operates are higher than that for comparable small banks that do not compete with a large bank.[27] This finding is consistent with the idea that large banks exert a special anticompetitive influence on the market, such as disciplinary pricing. However, it does not support the idea that large banks with small or moderate market shares competitively prevent the exercise of market power by smaller banks with large market shares.

Finally, one study has found that multimarket contact—the extent to which banks in a given market also compete with each other in other markets—is positively related to the profitability of all banks in the market.[28] This result suggests that when banks compete with each other in several markets, they may be more willing or able to act cooperatively or, alternatively, less willing to compete aggressively in any particular market for fear of retaliation in the other common markets. This lack of vigorous competition appears to influence all the banks in a market, large and small alike. However, large banks are more likely to be strongly influenced by multimarket contact because

---

[25]Steven J. Pilloff and Stephen A. Rhoades, "Do Large, Diversified Banking Organizations Have Competitive Advantages?" *Review of Industrial Organization* (May 2000): 287–302.

[26]For example, John T. Rose and John D. Wolken, "Geographic Diversification in Banking, Market Share Changes, and the Viability of Small, Independent Banks," *Journal of Financial Services Research* (March 1990): 5–20.

[27]Steven J. Pilloff, "Does the Presence of Big Banks Influence Competition in Local Markets?" *Journal of Financial Services Research* (1999): 159–177. Also, see John D. Wolken and John T. Rose, "Dominant Banks, Market Power, and Out-of-Market Productive Capacity," *Journal of Economics and Business* (August 1991): 214–229.

[28]Steven J. Pilloff, "Multimarket Contact in Banking," *Review of Industrial Organization* (March 1999): 163–182. Also, see Gary W. Whalen, "Nonlocal Concentration, Multimarket Linkages, and Interstate Banking," *The Antitrust Bulletin* (Summer 1996): 365–397.

they have extensive operations in many markets and are more likely to encounter each other frequently. Therefore, competition in markets in which large banks operate is most likely to be strongly affected by multimarket contact.

▪▪▪ V. Public Policy

Bank Expansion Policy and Broader Economic Performance

A well-functioning banking system can potentially increase economic performance if it helps improve the allocation of resources to those who can use the resources most productively.[29] Evidence supports the view that the relatively recent relaxation and elimination of restrictions on the ability of banks to expand geographically has helped to improve the functioning of the banking industry, which in turn has helped to improve the performance of the broader economy.

After geographic deregulation took place, many banks were legally able to acquire less efficient and less profitable banks that had been protected before deregulation from being taken over by a stronger performer. As a result, many mergers took place where a more efficient and more profitable bank bought a less efficient and less profitable one. Deals of this type enabled an increasing share of the banking industry to be held by banks that operated with greater efficiency and profitability.

Another potential benefit for the broader economy from the rapid consolidation that followed deregulation stems from large banks, particularly those with operations in many geographic areas, being generally more diversified and therefore less risky than smaller rivals. Large, diversified banks may be able to maintain credit flows during difficult times to affected geographic areas because they can draw on resources from other areas. Moreover, because the overall performance and condition of diversified banks are not dependent on any single community, a large bank may not be severely harmed by a local or regional downturn and may be more able and willing to maintain the flow of credit to an economically suffering area. In contrast, a smaller, more local bank may be unable or unwilling to extend credit to a troubled area. The continued flow of credit that a large bank may provide can potentially promote economic stability in an area undergoing a downturn, thereby reducing the duration and severity of any downturn. Empirical research confirms that measures of economic stability increased following deregulation.

The results of other empirical analyses of state-level economies also support the assertion that a more efficient banking system with large, well-diversified banks can benefit the performance of the real economy. Several studies find that various measures of state-level economic performance, including growth and the rate of new business formations, improved after geographic restrictions on banking in the state were eased. In sum, the results of past research are consistent with relatively efficient banks buying less efficient ones, improving performance and reducing risk through diversification, and then helping the local or regional economy to grow, strengthen, and become more stable.

---

[29]The discussion of the economic benefits of deregulation and the importance of the banking industry to economic growth are based on remarks by Randall S. Kroszner, Board of Governors of the Federal Reserve System, at the Conference on the Future of Financial Regulation, London School of Economics, London, England, April 6, 2006.

Bank Merger Policy

Currently, antitrust policy toward the U.S. commercial banking industry is concerned primarily with mergers, particularly with whether proposed transactions violate antitrust standards. The goal is to limit concentration in retail banking markets that are defined as being local in scope. The discussion in this chapter suggests that this approach is appropriate: High local levels of concentration are associated with higher prices, higher profits, and lower efficiency. Prohibiting transactions that would result in high levels of concentration appears to be an effective way of maintaining markets that are sufficiently competitive that customers have adequate choices and banks cannot sustain extremely high prices.

One issue that merits scrutiny, but which is not incorporated in current policy, or is only minimally incorporated, is whether very large banks have a unique effect on competition independent of their presence (i.e., market share) in a local banking market. Key differences may exist among banks of different sizes in their behavior, performance, and effect on rivals. The issue is important because the dichotomy between the largest organizations in the industry and the many community banks is increasing. Not only are mergers creating larger and larger banking firms that have substantial resources and operate over extensive geographic areas, but also developments in information technology, regulation, and financial markets are enabling large banks to provide increasingly complex and varied financial products that smaller rivals cannot provide. Understanding issues such as whether large banks have unique sources of market power, and whether banks of different sizes differ substantially in their ability to operate efficiently and meet customer needs, is critical in designing and implementing an effective antitrust policy.

Another issue that warrants continued examination is the size of the relevant banking market that should be used when assessing concentration. The relevant geographic market, at least for retail banking, is considered to be local. Expanding the geographic scope of the relevant market might be increasingly appropriate, because with growing use of the Internet and other advanced technologies, banks may be able to serve customers without having a nearby physical presence. If customers can complete all banking transactions through alternative delivery channels and are comfortable doing so, then retail banking markets may not be limited to local areas. However, until customers feel more comfortable about establishing and maintaining a relationship with a bank that does not have a nearby physical presence, technological advances will not effectively extend the borders of retail banking markets. Determining the appropriate size of banking markets is an important issue that could have a substantial effect on antitrust policy, because if markets were to be enlarged, fewer mergers would likely raise serious competitive concerns.

Lending to Risky Borrowers

Substantial media, consumer, regulatory, and legislative attention has been paid recently to the issue of subprime lending, which has been defined by Edward Gramlich of the Board of Governors of the Federal Reserve System as "the extension of credit to higher-risk borrowers who do not qualify for traditional, prime credit."[30] Accompanying their acceptance of substantial risk, lenders charge especially high loan rates and fees.

---

[30]Remarks by Governor Edward M. Gramlich at the Texas Association of Bank Counsel 27th Annual Convention, October 9, 2003.

While the potential benefits from subprime lending are great, so are the risks and the potential downside. In fact, in 2007, the downside associated with substantial risk had clearly become a reality: Defaults on subprime mortgage loans, which occur when borrowers do not make promised payments, were occurring much more frequently than in recent periods. For example, the number of defaults in the first quarter of 2007 was 35 percent higher than in the first quarter of 2006.[31] High default rates resulted in many subprime lenders and other investors experiencing severe financial problems, including some that were forced to cease operations and declare bankruptcy.

A key question often asked is whether the high rates and fees charged to subprime borrowers reflect fair compensation for substantial risk or, instead, constitute unfair and predatory practices. For example, so-called payday loans, a popular form of subprime lending, are often defended by supporters as providing credit to a segment of the population that would otherwise have no access to credit, but criticized by detractors as being predatory. Payday lending derives its name from the practice of many borrowers, often without much savings and employed in low-wage jobs or receiving other regular benefits like social security, to seek access to funds for a short period of time. These borrowers then frequently use their wages or government checks to quickly pay off the loan on payday or shortly thereafter. Payday loans are typically made for a week to a month with the large majority equaling less than a few hundred dollars.[32]

Critics contend that subprime credit, such as payday lending, is often predatory. The accusation is that loans are made to inappropriate borrowers, who frequently (some would say predictably) become unable to make scheduled payments. The borrowers subsequently are subject to hefty penalties that can be so onerous that they must pay back substantially more than the amount originally borrowed. An even more severe consequence is that some high-risk borrowers who experience credit problems ultimately lose their home, car, or other personal property.

A great deal of government resources has been allocated to protecting those borrowers most vulnerable to victimization at the hands of unscrupulous subprime lenders. For example, the Truth in Lending Act requires banks engaged in consumer lending to make accurate and full disclosures to customers. Other local, state, and federal laws such as the Fair Credit Reporting Act, the Truth in Savings Act, and the Community Reinvestment Act have been enacted to protect potential borrowers as well.

Tying Arrangements

Illegal tying is an issue that has increased in importance since the enactment in 1999 of the Gramm-Leach-Bliley Act enabling banks to expand their range of financial service offerings. Although the removal of many restrictions on the activities of firms engaged in banking has increased opportunities for firms to provide multiple products to customers, it has also increased opportunities for banks to strong-arm customers into buying unwanted products in order to obtain necessary ones. The potential problem is most severe when banks possess substantial market power in a particular product market.

---

[31]Christopher Conky, "Predatory Lending: Hard to Tame," *Wall Street Journal* (May 7, 2007): A5.
[32]An excellent discussion of payday lending can be found in Michael A. Stegman, "Payday Lending," *Journal of Economic Perspectives* (Winter 2007): 169–190.

With certain exceptions, banks are prohibited by federal law from making the purchase of one product or service that is not a traditional bank product or service a requirement for the purchase of another product or service. For example, a bank cannot require a customer to obtain insurance from another subsidiary of the bank's holding company in order to receive a loan from the bank. In contrast, a bank may condition a traditional banking product and service on another traditional product or service.[33] In recent years, the Federal Reserve Board has worked to clarify the difference between illegal tying and acceptable efforts by banks to develop relationships.

ATM Surcharge Fees

One source of bank revenue that many bank customers particularly dislike is the ATM surcharge fee, which is imposed when a customer of a bank uses an ATM not owned by that bank. The fee is levied by the ATM owner and is charged directly to the ATM user in addition to any other fees imposed by the ATM user's bank. Paying this fee often leads many consumers to feel that they are being gouged by ATM operators and unfairly forced to pay to access their own money. Banks contend that they are simply charging a fair price for providing consumers with the ability to conveniently access their deposits. Moreover, the banks assert that consumers who do not want to pay a surcharge fee can avoid the fee by accessing their accounts through a different channel.

Surcharge fees were first allowed in 1996 as a result of a change in the rules imposed by the networks that oversee ATMs. Public response was vehement. In fact, some areas went so far as to attempt to ban banks from imposing ATM surcharges. However, over the past decade, much of the initial outrage has subsided, and although customers may resent and would certainly prefer not to pay surcharge fees, the fee has become widespread and is generally accepted.

In addition to consumer issues, the ATM surcharge fee also raises antitrust issues. In particular, large banks, which tend to own numerous ATMs located over an extensive area, may be able to use surcharge fees to encourage customers of small banks to switch to larger banks. One way that small bank customers can avoid surcharges is to switch to a larger bank with more widely distributed ATMs. In this manner, customers can increase the likelihood that an ATM owned by their bank will be conveniently located whenever they need or want cash.

Conclusion ▮▮▮▮▮▮▮

Commercial banking is one of the largest and most important industries in the United States. A substantial portion of businesses and households rely on commercial banks as their primary source of credit and as a safe and convenient place to keep cash.

Since 1990, the banking industry has been affected by a number of developments — mainly mergers and acquisitions but, to a lesser extent, failures and new formations. These events have transformed the industry but have not substantially affected

---

[33]The discussion of tying arrangements and the example are based on remarks by Susan Schmidt Bies, Board of Governors of the Federal Reserve System, at the Securities Industry Association Annual Meeting, Boca Raton, Florida, November 5, 2004.

competition, which, for retail banking, takes place at the local level. Although the industry has experienced a large decline in the number of banks and an associated emergence of larger banks that control more of the industry, the evidence is mixed regarding whether substantial size enables large banks to influence competition. Moreover, although competition may be affected by increased market concentration at the local level, changes in (and levels of) average concentration since 1990 do not indicate that mergers have resulted in substantially less competition during this period.

In future years, banks should continue to be the primary providers of financial services to many American households and businesses. Moreover, the industry is likely to experience further structural change as consolidation, regulatory reforms, and technological developments take place at a rapid pace. Therefore, identifying relevant markets and understanding the key factors that influence competition in those markets will continue to be an important element of effective public policy.

Suggestions for Further Reading ▪▪▪▪▪▪▪

Adams, Robert M. 2002. "Retail Commercial Banking: An Industry in Transition." In *Industry Studies*, edited by Larry L. Duetsch, 3rd edition, Armonk, NY: M.E. Sharpe, 170–193.

Berger, Allen N., Rebecca S. Demsetz, and Philip E. Strahan. 1999. "The Consolidation of the Financial Services Industry: Causes, Consequences, and Implications for the Future." *Journal of Banking and Finance* (February): 135–194. This paper is in a special edition of the journal in which many other interesting articles on the consolidation of the financial services industry appear.

Edwards, Corwin D. 1955. "Conglomerate Bigness as a Source of Market Power." In *Business Concentration and Price Policy,* Princeton, NJ: Princeton University Press, 331–359.

Group of Ten. 2001. *Report on Consolidation in the Financial Sector.*

Pilloff, Steven J. 2004. "Bank Merger Activity in the United States, 1994–2003." Staff Study 176, Board of Governors of the Federal Reserve System, Washington, D.C. (May).

Rhoades, Stephen A. 1993. "Commercial Banking: Two Industries, a Laboratory for Research." In *Industry Studies*, edited by Larry L. Deutsch, Englewood Cliffs, NJ: Prentice Hall, 271–305.

Shull, Bernard and Gerald A. Hanweck. 2001. *Bank Mergers in a Deregulated Environment: Promise and Peril.* Westport, CT: Quorum Books.

CHAPTER 11

The Health Care Industry

JOHN GODDEERIS

No U.S. industry is larger or more important than health care. National health expenditures now account for 16 percent of gross domestic product. In other words, more than $1 in every $7 spent on final goods and services produced in the United States is devoted to health. Collectively in 2005, we spent $2 trillion, or in per capita terms, $6,700 for every man, woman, and child in America.

The health care industry encompasses an immense variety of goods and services: An expectant mother's visit to her doctor for a prenatal checkup; a pair of contact lenses; a surgical operation to replace a failing hip; or the drug cocktail that keeps a potential AIDS patient symptom-free are all among the outputs of the health care sector. Figure 11-1 shows the major components of national health expenditures, as defined by the U.S. Centers for Medicare & Medicaid Services (CMS). The largest categories, in order, are hospital care, physician and clinical services, prescription drugs, and nursing home care. The "other" category includes a wide range of goods and services, such as dental care; home health care; the services of other professionals such as chiropractors and optometrists; over-the-counter medications; durable medical equipment such as eyeglasses, hearing aids, and wheelchairs; the costs of administering government health programs and private health insurance; and government-funded public health services and medical research.

The sheer size of the health care sector makes it a key component of the U.S. economy. In addition, some of our most intense policy debates revolve around health care issues. In the early 1990s, continuing rapid increases in health care spending along with growth in the number of uninsured led to calls for a major overhaul of our health care system. President Clinton proposed a sweeping reform in 1993, which was hotly debated in Congress and the national media. That effort ultimately stalled. For a time, the emergence of managed care health insurance seemed to slow the growth of spending, and general economic prosperity made health care reform a less pressing need. Restrictions on choice imposed by managed care led to protests from doctors and patients, and then a return to less-intrusive forms of insurance. In the

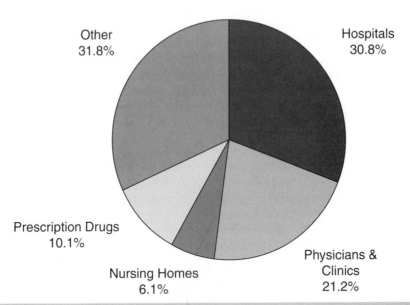

Other
31.8%

Hospitals
30.8%

Prescription Drugs
10.1%

Nursing Homes
6.1%

Physicians &
Clinics
21.2%

▮▮▮ **FIGURE 11-1** National Health Expenditure 2005, by Type of Service

Source: Centers for Medicare & Medicaid Services, National Health Accounts http://www.cms.hhs.gov/
nationalhealthexpenddata/.

early twenty-first century, health care spending surged again and the number of uninsured grew, focusing renewed attention on the health care economy. Massachusetts
and some other states have taken major steps aimed at increasing coverage, but the
specter of rising spending looms over these efforts and clouds their long-run
prospects.

Even aside from its size and policy importance, the health care industry is a fascinating field for students of industrial organization to examine. Traditional relationships between patients, doctors, health insurers, hospitals, and other suppliers of
care have undergone much change in the last 20 years, with no equilibrium yet in
sight.

▮▮▮ I. History

Today, we take it for granted that medical care is not only expensive but also very powerful. A typical day in the hospital cost about $1,500 in 2005 and several times as much
for intensive care. Modern hospital care, however, can often save the lives of heart
attack victims or those suffering from severe burns or trauma from an automobile acci-
dent. People need a mechanism, either private insurance or support through public
programs, to enable them to obtain care without the risk of staggering financial losses.
The fact that nearly 47 million Americans (15.9 percent of the population) are uninsured and lack such a formal mechanism is widely viewed as a serious public policy
problem.

Things were not always this way. A century ago, medical care was not very expensive, and medical insurance was virtually nonexistent in the United States. The workers' compensation system was developing in the early twentieth century, making employers responsible for the costs of work-related injuries, but workers were much more concerned about income losses from lost work time than about the costs of medical care.

In 1929, the first year for which we have reasonably good data on national health expenditures, health spending was only about 3.5 percent of GDP. One important reason that the health care industry was much smaller is that the capabilities of medicine at the time were quite limited. In 1976, the President's Biomedical Research Panel wrote:

> Fifty years ago the term *technology*, and for that matter *science*, would have seemed incongruous in a discussion of medical practice. The highly skilled practitioner was a master of diagnostic medicine, but the ultimate intentions of his skill were limited to the identification of the particular illness, the prediction of the likely outcome, and then the guidance of the patient and his family while the illness ran its full, natural course.[1]

That situation gradually changed. As technology improved, hospitals began to evolve from charitable institutions used only by the poor to facilities for the treatment of serious illness or injury. In 1929, the first prototype for a Blue Cross health insurance plan was developed at Baylor University, enabling subscribers to pay a little each month to avoid large bills when hospital care was needed. The idea spread, backed by groups of hospitals that saw it as a way to increase revenue during the Great Depression. Blue Shield plans, organized by doctors as a mechanism for prepaying for physician care, began to emerge a decade later.

Still, by 1940 only 9 percent of the American public had any private health insurance, and national health expenditures stood at about 4.1 percent of GDP. A remarkable transformation was beginning, however. During World War II, a time of tight labor markets at home, employee fringe benefits were exempted from wage-price controls and became an important tool for attracting and retaining workers. The fact that the cost of health insurance to the employer was not counted as part of the employee's taxable income made insurance a preferred form of compensation even after the war ended. At the same time, advances in surgery and increases in the cost of hospital care increased the financial risks associated with not having insurance coverage.

This combination of circumstances led to a rapid spread of health insurance. By 1950, over half the population had some private coverage. The numbers continued to grow, reaching 82 percent of the population by 1975.[2] Private insurance has remained closely tied to employment: In 2005, 88 percent of those with private insurance got it through their own job or that of a family member (usually a parent or spouse).[3] For a variety of reasons, health insurance is less expensive if purchased by large groups than if purchased by individuals, and place of employment is one natural basis for grouping.

---

[1]President's Biomedical Research Panel, Report of the President's Biomedical Research Panel (Washington, D.C.: Government Printing Office, 1976).
[2]Health Insurance Association of America, *Source Book of Health Insurance Data, 1990* (Washington, D.C.: Health Insurance Association of America, 1990).
[3]Carmen DeNavas-Walt, Bernadette D. Proctor, and Cheryl Hill Lee, *Income, Poverty, and Health Insurance Coverage in the United States: 2005* (Washington, D.C.: U.S. Census Bureau, 2006). www.census.gov/prod/2006pubs/p60-231.pdf

The favorable tax treatment of employer-provided health insurance also encouraged the link between health insurance and jobs.

In the era of the War on Poverty and President Johnson's Great Society, new government programs extended coverage to groups that had difficulty obtaining it. Medicare and Medicaid were enacted in 1965 and grew rapidly. Medicare is a federal program that provides substantial, though incomplete, health insurance coverage to nearly all of those aged 65 and over and to some disabled individuals less than age 65. Medicaid is a federal-state matching program aimed at providing coverage for the poor. In practice it reaches far from all of the poor, and coverage varies considerably across states. Both programs made significant contributions to reducing the residual number of Americans with no source of insurance.

Although the overall trend in the last 60 years has been toward expanding insurance coverage, private coverage has eroded in recent years. The share of the population without either public or private coverage has increased. The most widely accepted estimates show that 86.1 percent of the population had health insurance in 1990, with 73.2 percent having some private coverage, but that the shares had fallen to 84.1 and 67.7 percent respectively in 2005.[4]

Even more striking than the spread of public and private insurance has been the growth of health care spending. Between 1950 and 2005, health care spending per capita went from $460 (in 2005 dollars, using the GDP deflator to adjust for changes in the price level) to $6,300, an increase of 1,270 percent over and above the general increase in prices.[5] By comparison, real GDP per capita grew by about 210 percent over the same period. Figure 11-2 displays the growth of health care spending since 1960 in a slightly different way. It shows for each year the percentage increase over the previous year in per capita spending on health care, after adjusting for general inflation. Over the entire period, health care spending per capita grew faster than the general price level in every year, and in all but 5 years it increased at least 3 percentage points faster. The average of the net annual changes over the period is 4.9 percent. Interestingly, the 4 years of slowest growth all occurred in the mid-1990s, though rapid increases returned, with some slowing apparent in the most recent data.

What can account for such dramatic growth of spending, sustained over such a long period? Surely several factors have contributed, but most economic experts stress that the growth of insurance and spending are closely entwined, each feeding on the other, along with a third factor, the advance of knowledge. New knowledge creates new capabilities for diagnoses and treatments, often at high cost.[6] The health care financing system in place for most of the second half of the twentieth century, increasingly dominated by third-party payment as time went on, imposed little restraint on the adoption and application of innovations in health care that, however costly, offered some hope of medical benefit.

---

[4]DeNavas-Walt, Proctor, and Lee. *Income, Poverty, and Health Insurance Coverage in the United States: 2005.*

[5]Health care spending is measured here by health services and supplies, which is national health expenditures minus spending on research and construction of new facilities.

[6]Joseph Newhouse, "An Iconoclastic View of Health Cost Containment," *Health Affairs* 12 (Supplement 1993): 152–171; and Burton A. Weisbrod, "The Health Care Quadrilemma: An Essay on Technological Change, Insurance, Quality of Care, and Cost Containment," *Journal of Economic Literature* 29 (June 1991): 523–552.

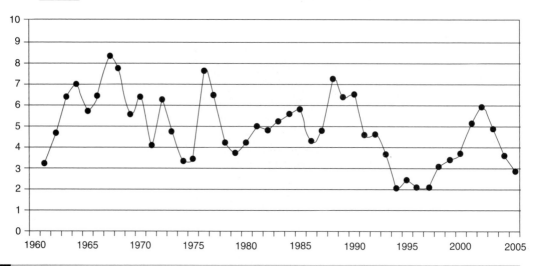

FIGURE 11-2 Annual Percentage Increases in Real Health Spending per Capita

Sources: Author's calculations using data from Centers for Medicaid Services (health services and supplies), U.S. Census Bureau (resident population) and U.S. Bureau of Economic Analysis (GDP deflator).

▪▪▪ II. Industry Structure

We focus on three key components of the health care industry: health insurance, physicians, and hospitals.[7] Before we turn to these components of the supply side of the industry, a brief look at its current sources of revenue will provide helpful background. Figure 11-3 breaks down national health expenditures by source of funds. It shows that nearly half (45.4 percent) of all spending on health is publicly funded, and that Medicare and Medicaid each individually account for a substantial fraction of the total. The "other public" category includes spending on a number of things, the largest of which are public health activities, programs of the Veterans Administration and the Department of Defense (including health care coverage for the dependents of armed services personnel), direct appropriations to state and local government hospitals, and medical research. On the private side, payments by way of private insurance are nearly three times those that come directly from consumers' pockets.

The breakdown in Figure 11-3 is true on average, but as Table 11-1 shows, sources of revenue vary a good deal by type of service. For hospital care, for example, the out-of-pocket share is much smaller than the overall average, at about 3 percent, while Medicare alone accounts for 30 percent of revenues. Medicaid is especially

---

[7]The most significant omission is any special consideration of prescription drugs. Drugs are increasingly important both to health and as a share of health care expenditures. The pharmaceutical industry is an important area of study in its own right (F. M. Scherer, "The Pharmaceutical Industry—Prices and Progress," *New England Journal of Medicine* 351 (August 26, 2004): 927–932.

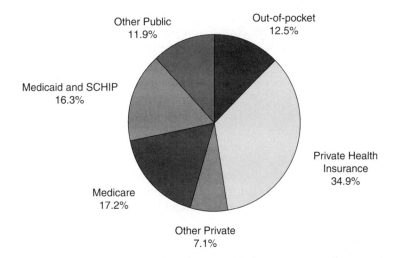

Out-of-pocket
12.5%

Other Public
11.9%

Medicaid and SCHIP
16.3%

Private Health
Insurance
34.9%

Medicare
17.2%

Other Private
7.1%

▪ ▪ ▪ ▪ **FIGURE 11-3** National Health Expenditures in 2005 by Source of Funds

Source: Centers for Medicare & Medicaid Services, National Health Accounts http://www.cms.hhs.gov/
nationlhealthexpenddata/
SCHIP refers to State Children's Health Insurance Program.

TABLE 11-1 Sources of Revenue by Type of Service: 2005

	Hospital Care	*Physicians Services*	*Prescription Drugs*	*Nursing Homes*
Out-of-Pocket	3.3%	10.1%	25.4%	26.5%
Private Insurance	35.5	48.3	47.4	7.5
Other Private	4.5	6.4	0.0	3.7
Total Public	56.8	35.3	27.2	62.3
Medicare	29.5	21.2	2.0	15.7
Medicaid and SCHIP (State Children's Health Insurance Program)	18.0	7.6	20.8	44.1

Source: Centers for Medicare & Medicaid Services, National Health Accounts, www.cms.hhs.gov/
nationalhealthexpenddata

important for nursing homes, accounting for 44 percent of their revenues, while private insurance accounts for less than 8 percent. The absence of an outpatient prescription drug benefit in Medicare and incomplete private insurance coverage for drugs left a relatively high share of those expenses paid directly out-of-pocket (prescription drug coverage was added to Medicare in late 2003, becoming effective in 2006).

Health Insurance

Health insurance facilitates access to most health care services for most of the population, and is a good place to begin examining the structure of the health care industry. Most health insurers in the United States prior to the mid-1980s played a passive role in the provision of health care. The insurance contract defined the financial terms of the policy, including the premium, scope of services covered, and cost-sharing arrangements for the enrollee. Decisions about what services to provide were left to the patient and his or her doctor. Choice of doctor was also unrestricted.

Health insurance was at first dominated by Blue Cross and Blue Shield plans, nonprofit organizations established by hospital and doctors' associations. Later, companies operating in other lines of insurance, so-called commercial insurers such as Aetna, Travelers, New York Life, and Prudential, entered the market. By the early 1950s, they had as a group surpassed Blue Cross-Blue Shield in total number of people covered.

For policies written by commercial insurers, sometimes called indemnity policies, the doctors, hospitals, and other providers of covered services would bill the enrollee, who would pay the bill and then recover the insured amount from the insurer. In the case of policies written by Blue Cross and Blue Shield, as well as for individuals covered by Medicare and Medicaid, coverage was more commonly in the form of service benefits. The insurer agreed to cover a specified set of services when needed, with perhaps some cost-sharing on the part of the enrollee. Providers would be paid (or "reimbursed") directly by the insurer. For doctors, this meant they were paid according to what they charged for services, with some screens applied to assure that a doctor's charge was not out of line with customary fees in the community or with the doctor's own usual charge. Hospitals and other providers were usually reimbursed for costs incurred. Regardless of whether the indemnity or service benefit approach was used, the insurer took little active role in treatment decisions.

In the last 20 years the health insurer's role changed dramatically. Managed care emerged and largely swept the marketplace, though its more intrusive forms have lately declined. While the concept of managed care encompasses a broad range of organizational forms and management tools, its various manifestations have in common an attempt to go beyond consumer cost-sharing and benefit package design to influence the nature of the care an enrollee receives as well as the choice of provider.

At one end of the managed care spectrum is the staff model health maintenance organization (HMO). In a staff model HMO the doctors caring for the enrollees are employees, or part owners, of the organization providing health insurance. Because the HMO agrees to provide care to its enrollees for a fixed premium, the organization has an incentive to minimize the cost of providing that care. Given that additional services do not generate additional revenue (except consumer cost-sharing payments, if any are used), each additional dollar of cost reduces the organization's net profits. If the organization's incentive to minimize cost can be translated to its medical staff, the staff may be expected to manage the care of enrollees in a cost-conscious way.

The staff model HMO has been in practice for many years. The term *health maintenance organization* was coined in the early 1970s, but the most successful example of the staff model, the Kaiser Health Plan, dates back to the collaborative efforts of medical entrepreneur Dr. Sydney Garfield and industrialist Henry Kaiser in the 1930s.[8] The Kaiser Plan grew to over 1 million enrollees by 1962, and over 2.5 million by 1972. Another early example of this model, which used to be called prepaid group practice, is the Group Health Cooperative of Puget Sound, founded in 1947, and today serving more than 500,000 enrollees in the northwest.

Other types of HMOs contract nonexclusively with groups of doctors or Independent Practice Associations (IPAs) of individual doctors. This form integrates the insurance plan less tightly with physicians than the staff model, as the same doctors might contract with several other HMOs and also see patients not affiliated with any HMO. The insurer, however, can still attempt to influence the provision of care by a variety of methods, including monitoring the use of services (e.g., requiring preapproval of nonemergency hospital admissions, reviewing length of hospital stay), requiring that enrollees be approved for specialty care by a "gatekeeper" primary care physician, selectively contracting with doctors and hospitals rather than allowing enrollees unrestricted choice, or using payment methods other than straight fee-for-service to influence provider incentives. For prescription drug coverage, the set of drugs covered and the manner in which they can be obtained may also be limited.

Other forms of managed care use some or all of these tools, in various forms and combinations. The lines between different types of organizations are increasingly blurry. In a preferred provider organization (PPO), the insurer contracts selectively with a preferred set of providers at discounted rates and creates incentives in the form of reduced cost-sharing for enrollees to use those providers. Typically, PPOs also use some forms of utilization management. Many HMOs now also include a point-of-service (POS) option, which allows enrollees to see providers outside the regular network, usually with considerably higher cost-sharing by the enrollee.

Figure 11-4 shows the rapid evolution of health insurance markets. In 1980, managed care meant only HMOs, which had less than 10 percent of the group insurance market nationally. By 1988, PPOs had emerged, but conventional insurance still accounted for 73 percent of enrollment. From that point the market share of conventional health insurance declined rapidly in favor of the various forms of managed care, falling to 3 percent by the year 2006.

In addition to the decline of conventional insurance, Figure 11-4 displays another important trend. In the late 1990s insurance premium increases had moderated, and the economy was growing at a good pace. Doctors and patients began to rebel against the intrusion of insurers into medical decisions, and the market turned away from the more aggressive forms of managed care. The total market share of HMOs, including POS plans, declined a good deal in favor of PPOs, which now account for more than 60 percent of the group insurance market. The source for Figure 11-4 also introduced a new category in 2006, the high deductible health plan with savings option, a form of insurance discussed near the end of this chapter.

The use of managed care also increased in the 1990s in the publicly funded Medicare and Medicaid programs. Since 1985, Medicare has contracted with HMOs on

---

[8]Paul Starr, *The Social Transformation of American Medicine* (New York: Basic Books, 1982). The Kaiser Plan is technically a group model rather than a staff model HMO. Rather than employing its doctors, the health plan contracts in each region where it operates with a single medical group, which serves only Kaiser patients.

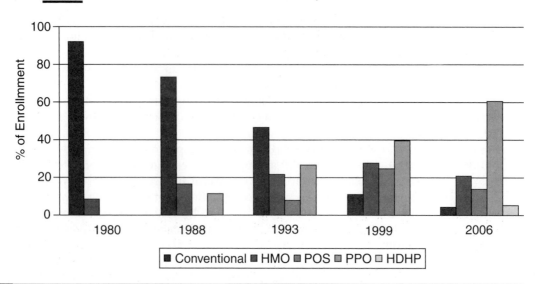

▪▪▪ **FIGURE 11-4** The Changing Employee Health Insurance Market

HDHP means high deductible health plan with savings option.

Sources: Kaiser Family Foundation, Employer Health Benefits 2006 Annual Survery, Exhibit 5.1, http://www
.kff.org/insurance/7527/sections/ehbs06-5-1.cfm; 1980 numbers from D. M. Cutler and R. J. Zechhauser, "The
Anatomy of Health Insurance," in *Handbook of Health Economics,* Figure 4.

a risk-contract basis, paying a fixed amount per enrollee, often referred to as a capitation (per head) payment. The HMO then bore the risk that the enrollee's expenditures
might be higher or lower than the capitation amount. Medicare paid HMOs 95 percent
of the average of what it expected to spend on fee-for-service Medicare enrollees in the
same geographic area. The number of enrollees participating in risk contracts grew
slowly. About 1 million participated in 1987, at that time about 3 percent of Medicare
enrollees. By the end of 1995, the number was 3.1 million, and by the end of 1999 about
6.9 million, or 18 percent of enrollees. By 2003, however, a number of HMOs had
stopped participating, due largely to changes in Medicare's payment methods, and
enrollment fell to 13 percent of the Medicare population. The program has now been
rechristened Medicare Advantage and opened to other types of private plans. In
response to more attractive payment policies, participation has increased again. About
19 percent of Medicare enrollees participated in Medicare Advantage in early 2007.[9]

While Medicare has thus far made managed care participation a matter of enrollee
choice, many states require that their Medicaid beneficiaries enroll with a managed
care plan. Initially, federal law prohibited states from restricting the choice of medical
providers for Medicaid beneficiaries (though the low payment rates characteristic of
Medicaid often made it difficult for beneficiaries to find doctors willing to see them).
The law changed in 1981, allowing states to experiment with managed care and other
innovative approaches. Managed care participation was still low going into the 1990s,

[9]Kaiser Family Foundation, Medicare Advantage Fact Sheet, March 2007, www.kff.org/medicare/upload/
2052-09.pdf

but has expanded very rapidly since then.[10] In 1991, less than 10 percent of Medicaid beneficiaries were in managed care. By 1995, the number had grown to 32 percent, and by 2005 to 63 percent, almost 29 million enrollees. Some of this enrollment is in a mild form of managed care called primary care case management, in which a primary care doctor agrees to manage the care of a set of enrollees but is not at risk for the cost of hospital and specialty care. However, this model has been shrinking relative to capitated models, in which the managed care organization is at risk for the costs of all covered services.

A notable trend among HMOs and health insurers is a movement away from nonprofit organizational forms toward entities organized as for-profit businesses. Early HMOs were predominantly organized as nonprofits, the only type eligible for federal subsidies under the HMO Act of 1973. When direct federal subsidies ended in the early 1980s, market share began to swing heavily toward for-profits, partly as a result of entry of new for-profit HMOs and their growth, but also from conversion of nonprofit HMOs to the for-profit form. Between 1981 and 1997, the percentage of HMO enrollees in nonprofit plans plummeted from 88 percent to 37 percent, where it has roughly stabilized.[11] In 1994, the national Blue Cross and Blue Shield Association decided for the first time that for-profit firms could affiliate with the organization, paving the way for a number of regional Blue Cross plans to convert to for-profits.

Before leaving the subject of the structure of health insurance markets, some mention should be made of the phenomenon of self-insurance. Insurance is fundamentally a way of transferring risk from an individual or group to an insurer, who, by virtue of pooling together large numbers of enrollees with largely independent risks, is better able to accept it. For large employers, those with 500 employees or more, pooling within the firm accomplishes much of what an insurer could provide in this regard. Many large employers find it attractive to self-insure—that is, bear the risks associated with random year-to-year fluctuations in health care utilization—to escape some state and federal regulations associated with purchased health insurance, and perhaps to gain more control over the insurance they provide and how it is administered. In 2001, half of all covered workers were in self-insured plans, with higher percentages for workers employed by larger firms.[12]

Physicians

In his influential 1974 book on health care and economics, *Who Shall Live?*, Victor Fuchs called the physician the "captain of the team" in health care. While managed care challenged the physician's preeminent position, Fuchs's characterization remains largely accurate. In addition to the medical and surgical services they provide directly, physicians admit and discharge patients from hospitals, order diagnostic tests, and prescribe drugs, although these tasks are now frequently scrutinized by insurance providers. About 700,000 medical doctors were active in patient care in 2004, according to American Medical Association data. Fuchs notes that a century ago, two out of three

---

[10]Data come from the CMS web site: www.cms.hhs.gov/MedicaidDataSourcesGenInfo/04_MdManCrEnrllRep.asp.
[11]Kaiser Family Foundation, Trends and Indicators in the Changing Health Care Marketplace, www.kff.org/insurance/7031/print-sec5.cfm
[12]Jon R. Gabel, Gail A. Jensen, and Samantha Hawkins, "Self-Insurance In Times Of Growing And Retreating Managed Care," *Health Affairs* 22 (March/April 2003): 202–210.

persons employed in health care were doctors. As the health care system developed, with the rise of the modern hospital and the nursing home industry, and the introduction of a broad variety of other types of specialized services such as physical therapy and respiratory therapy, employment opportunities vastly expanded for other workers without the breadth and depth of training of an M.D. The number of nonphysician health care workers has risen much faster than the number of doctors, to the point where the ratio is now about 11 to 1.[13]

Doctors spend more years in training than almost any other workers. Medical school generally requires 4 additional years after a bachelor's degree, and is usually followed by at least 3 additional years in a hospital-based residency program to obtain board certification as a specialist or as a generalist family practitioner. The need to be accepted by a medical school and then complete this long training period is clearly an important barrier to entry into the medical profession. Some economists have argued that the control exerted by the American Medical Association (AMA) over the number of medical school slots available and the length of the training period has helped keep doctors' incomes artificially high. The counter argument in favor of supply restrictions and extensive training has been that they promote quality of care, which consumers would find difficult to evaluate in the absence of professional certification.

Medicine continues to be a very highly paid profession. Average physician income in 2003 was $203,000.[14] An important question for public policy is whether this level is artificially high given the amount of time invested in training, the ability required, and the work effort exerted by the typical doctor (mean hours in medically related activities are about 53 per week). Several older studies (1985 or earlier) addressed this question by examining whether the rate of return on the investment in a medical education is unusually high.[15] An important component of the investment costs are the opportunity costs of foregone earnings during the long training period. The weight of the evidence suggests that a medical degree has been an economically attractive investment, with rates of return usually estimated at 13 percent or higher, even after accounting for the high costs of acquiring one. A recent study also finds high rates of return to medical education, but even higher ones for some alternative professional fields.[16]

Table 11-2 shows the number of medical doctors involved in patient care from 1975 to 2004, and the breakdown by type of practice. Between 1975 and 2004, the number of doctors in patient care increased by nearly 80 percent on a per capita basis, resulting primarily from a buildup in medical school capacity that began in the late 1960s, and also from an inflow of foreign-trained doctors. For most physicians, the base of practice is in an office rather than in a hospital, and the fraction of doctors who are office-based has increased since 1975. Nearly 15 percent of doctors are in residency or other training programs, usually hospital-based, and another smaller fraction are employed as full-time hospital staff.

---

[13]National Center for Health Statistics, Health United States 2006, Table 108, www.cdc.gov/nchs/hus.htm for total health care workers.

[14]Ha T. Tu and Paul B. Ginsburg, "Losing Ground: Physician Income, 1995–2003," Center for Studying Health System Change, June 2006, www.hschange.com/CONTENT/851/

[15]See Paul Feldstein, *Health Care Economics*, 6th ed. (Clifton Park, NY: Thomson Delmar, 2005), 340–342 for a summary and references.

[16]W.B. Weeks and A.E. Wallace, "The More Things Change: Revisiting a Comparison of Educational Costs and Incomes of Physicians and Other Professionals," *Academic Medicine* 77 (April 2002): 312–319.

TABLE 11-2 Doctors in Patient Care by Type of Practice

	1975		1985		1995		2000		2004	
	(in thousands)	*%*	*(in thousands)*	*%*	*(in thousands)*	*%*	*(in thousands)*	*%*	*(in thousands)*	*%*
Total	311.9		448.8		582.1		647.4		700.3	
Office-based	215.4	69	330.2	74	427.3	73	490.4	76	538.5	77
Training	57.8	19	75.4	17	96.4	17	95.7	15	102.3	15
Hospital staff	38.7	12	43.2	10	58.5	10	61.3	9	59.2	8

Source: American Medical Association, Physician Characteristics and Distribution in the U.S., 2006 edition.

Traditionally, most doctors have been self-employed or partners in small groups. Table 11-3 summarizes data on changes over time in the distribution of office-based physicians by style and size of group. In 1969, the majority of office-based physicians, 78 percent, were in individual practice, which the AMA defined to include offices with one or two physicians. By 1995, those in individual practice were still in the majority, but barely so. By 2001, about 56 percent of doctors were in practices of 3 or more physicians.[17] Both single-specialty and multispecialty group practices have grown considerably as a share of all physicians, and, within each type, the average group size has increased. Within physicians' offices the trend has been toward larger numbers of aides per physician. The number of aides per physician in office-based practice was 1.54 in 1970 and had grown to 2.45 by 2001.[18]

TABLE 11-3 Trends in Distribution of Office-Based Physicians, by Group Affiliation

	% Distribution of Physicians			*Average Size of Group*		
	1969	*1980*	*1995*	*1969*	*1980*	*1995*
Individual Practice	78.3	67.2	51.9			
Group Practice	21.7	32.8	48.1	6.2	8.2	10.5
Single-specialty	7.1	10.9	20.1	4.1	4.8	6.2
Multispecialty	13.2	20.1	25.8	10.1	15.2	25.4
Family or General Practice	1.5	1.8	2.1	3.5	4.5	5.6

Source: Adapted from Paul J. Feldstein, *Health Care Economics*, 5th ed. (1999), Table 10.2, 247. Albany, NY: Delmar Publishers.

---

[17]John D. Wassenaar and Sara L. Thran, *Physician Socioeconomic Statistics*, 2003 edition (Chicago, IL: American Medical Association Press).
[18]Feldstein, *Health Care Economics*, 221.

The trend toward larger groups suggests that economic advantages to group practice have increased over time. Some economies of scale exist in production, particularly in the way physicians delegate tasks to allied health workers and use other inputs to production. A group of physicians may be able to fully utilize a certain type of aide or piece of equipment where a solo practitioner could not. Consumers may also prefer to deal with groups for convenience in getting appointments, and because a group can develop a kind of "brand-name" image for quality which the consumer would have more difficulty in assessing at the individual doctor level. Several physicians who share a practice are also likely to experience less variability in workload and income at the individual level than would a solo practitioner, and this risk-spreading feature of groups is valuable. Still, increasing group size also has its disadvantages. For example, if a group of doctors shares the costs of a set of inputs, individual incentives to economize in the use of those inputs are blunted. The distribution of physician group size thus reflects a balancing at the margin of those forces that push in the direction of larger and smaller size, as well as differences in size of market (a small town cannot accommodate a large multispecialty group) and in preferences of doctors and consumers concerning style of practice.

Another reason for doctors to form into larger groups could be to position themselves to be responsible for managing all health care needs—or some well-defined subset of it—for a defined population of enrollees, and to accept payment on a capitation basis. Accepting capitation payments is, in effect, acting like a health insurer. The advantage of capitation from the group's point of view is that it has a greater incentive to manage the total costs of care and can profit from doing so effectively. Capitation is risky for an individual doctor or a small group, however, because the patient population the group can handle may be too small to predict accurately the level of costs that will be incurred, even if care is managed efficiently. Increasing group size can reduce that risk. In some parts of the country, large groups, sometimes numbering in the hundreds of doctors, contract with managed care plans and sometimes directly with employers on a capitation basis.[19]

The growth of managed care spurred more affiliations of physician practices with hospitals, insurers, or physician practice management companies (PPMCs), although some of those affiliations proved to be short-lived. Doctors or groups that had been in independent practice sometimes sold the physical assets of their practices to a hospital or managed care organization and accepted salaried compensation. Frequently, however, the buyers became dissatisfied with the performance of salaried physicians and found it more advantageous to contract with independent groups. PPMCs, a phenomenon of the 1990s, sometimes bought the assets of groups of doctors, negotiated contracts with managed care organizations, and provided certain management services to the groups, in return for a share of net revenues after practice expenses had been paid. A few publicly traded PPMCs grew very rapidly in the mid-1990s, but seemed to overemphasize expansion at the expense of good management, and just as quickly went into decline. MedPartners, FPA Medical, and PhyCor are three PPMCs that grew quickly but have exited the market or gone into bankruptcy.

---

[19]J. C. Robinson and L. P. Casalino, "The Growth of Medical Groups Paid Through Capitation in California." *New England Journal of Medicine* 333, no.25: 1684–1687.

Despite the development of a variety of business models under which physician practice is organized, most physicians practice as independent professionals, not as employees, and some form of fee-for-service is the predominant method by which they are paid. In the AMA survey of physicians for 2001, 65 percent of nonfederal, nonresident physicians identified themselves as self-employed or as independent contractors, with only 35 percent calling themselves employees.[20] Capitation payments at the level of the individual physician continue to account for only a small share of total physician revenues. While 88 percent of doctors in 2001 reported at least some managed care contracts (with the percentage varying between 82 and 93 across the nine census regions), only 7 percent of a doctor's practice revenues, on average, came from capitated contracts. Interest in forming large multi-specialty groups also appears to have waned, in part because of difficulties in coordinating the activities of such groups. Medium-sized (5 to 20 doctors) single-specialty groups are increasingly common.[21]

Hospitals

Hospitals are unusual economic entities. Most are organized as nonprofit firms. In 2005, about 70 percent of community hospital beds were in private nonprofit entities, another 16 percent in hospitals run by state or local governments, and 14 percent in for-profit firms. Like any such firm, the nonprofit hospital is not owned by individuals, so no one has a claim to any profits that might accrue to it. While the administrators are responsible to the hospital's board of trustees, the trustees do not represent ownership in the same way that a private corporation's board of directors does. In addition, decisions about use of a hospital's resources—its beds, employed staff, and equipment—are made to a large extent by its medical staff—doctors who practice in the hospital but generally are not its employees.

Table 11-4 provides data on the evolution of community hospitals since 1946, the year of the passage of the Hill-Burton Act, subsidizing the construction and expansion of hospitals. "Community hospitals" is a broad classification used by the American Hospital Association (AHA). It includes 85 percent of all hospital beds, excluding only 5 percent that are in federal hospitals and 10 percent in long-term hospitals of various types. Table 11-4 shows strong expansion in the number of hospitals that continued until about 1970, and even stronger growth in the number of beds, continuing into the 1980s. Hospital admissions grew much faster than the population from 1946 to about 1980, but began to decline thereafter. Since 1995 admissions have again increased, a bit faster than the population. Average length of hospital stay began to decline earlier than admissions, as can be inferred from the fact that admissions per bed grew in the 1970s, but occupancy levels declined. The average patient stayed nearly 8 days in 1975 but less than 6 in 2005. Optimal occupancy levels for hospitals are a good deal less than 100 percent, as the need for beds fluctuates and it is important to hold some reserve capacity to accommodate periods of peak demand. However, nationwide occupancy levels of under 70 percent, as have existed since the mid-1980s, are surely indicative of excess bed capacity in the industry, though not in every market.

---

[20]Wassenaar and Thran, *Physician Socioeconomic Statistics.*
[21]L.P. Casalino et al., "Benefits of and Barriers to Large Medical Group Practice in the United States," *Archives of Internal Medicine* 163, no. 16 (September 8, 2003): 1958–1964.

TABLE 11-4 Selected Statistics for Community Hospitals

Year	Hospitals	Beds (in thousands)	Admissions (in thousands)	Occupancy	Outpatient Visits (in thousands)
1946	4,444	473	13,655	0.72	
1950	5,031	505	16,663	0.74	
1960	5,407	639	22,970	0.75	
1970	5,859	848	29,252	0.78	133,545
1980	5,830	988	36,143	0.76	202,310
1990	5,384	927	31,181	0.67	301,329
1995	5,194	873	30,945	0.63	414,345
2000	4,915	824	33,089	0.64	521,404
2005	4,936	802	35,239	0.67	584,429

Source: American Hospital Association, *Hospital Statistics* (Chicago: Health Forum LLC, 2003).

Table 11-4 also shows very rapid growth in the number of outpatient hospital visits. The movement toward shorter hospital stays and substitution of outpatient for inpatient care is driven by technological changes, such as the development of less invasive laser-assisted surgical techniques, and by changing attitudes about the benefits of prolonged hospitalization. It has also been spurred by cost-containment efforts by managed care organizations, and earlier by Medicare, which focused heavily on the reduction of inpatient care. Inpatient care was undoubtedly overused in the 1960s and 1970s, as there was little incentive for doctors or their well-insured patients to weigh costs against potential benefits. The pendulum probably swung too far, however, in the direction of shorter stays, at least for a time. In the quest to reduce hospital usage because the average cost per patient day is high, the fact that marginal cost near the end of a stay may be much lower is often insufficiently appreciated.[22] If a bed would otherwise be unoccupied, the incremental cost of extending the stay of a patient needing relatively little care is modest.

Hospitals are multiproduct firms. For inpatient care alone, the Medicare program now recognizes for payment purposes over 500 diagnosis-related groups (DRGs), classifications of patients based on their medical problems. Even this large number of categories lumps together patients with widely varying severity of illness and needs for care. Differences across hospitals in average cost per admission are strongly related to differences in the mix of diagnoses among the patients that they treat. Holding patient mix constant, research studies do not indicate substantial economies of scale beyond very small-sized hospitals, and any economies are probably exhausted at a size between 200 and 300 beds. In 2005, about 72 percent of community hospitals had fewer than 200 beds. The 28 percent of hospitals that were larger, however, accounted for about 70 percent of admissions.

---

[22]Uwe E. Reinhardt, "Our Obsessive Quest to Gut the Hospital," *Health Affairs* 15 (Summer 1996): 145–154.

An Integrated Delivery System (IDS) is a vertically integrated organization that combines some or all of the inputs needed to provide the full range of medical services an individual might require: hospitals, physicians, outpatient clinics, home health care agencies, nursing homes, and so forth. A group or staff model HMO with its own hospitals (Kaiser is the outstanding example) is one form of IDS. An IDS may also be organized around a group of physicians. In the 1990s, many hospitals and groups of hospitals sought to create IDSs with themselves at the center. They affiliated with physician groups—sometimes hiring doctors on a salaried basis—and with other elements of the continuum of care. Some hospital-based IDSs met the necessary legal requirements to become HMOs. IDSs can also contract with HMOs, or directly with purchasers of care.

From an economic viewpoint, the concept of a hospital-based IDS has a certain appeal. Such an organization seems positioned to take on capitation contracts for the full package of care, potentially cutting out a layer of administrative cost by bypassing insurance middlemen. At least at its top level, the organization has incentives to be conscious of the costs of the resources it uses—substituting, for example, outpatient for inpatient care, or preventive for acute care where appropriate. But it may be difficult to transmit those top-level incentives to decision makers in other parts of the organization. The success of such an organization depends heavily on the behavior of its affiliated physicians, but if a large part of their compensation is in guaranteed salary, for example, their incentives to work hard and direct the use of other inputs optimally are attenuated. It is not clear from economic theory that a vertically integrated health care organization will out-compete one that purchases most of its inputs through market transactions (e.g., an IPA-model HMO, or PPO) and creates incentives through contracts. As the market share of tightly managed care has declined, so also has hospitals' interest in vertical integration. The AHA surveys show a rather sharp recent decline in the share of community hospitals reporting an ownership interest in an HMO, from a peak of 23 percent in 1997, to 15 percent in 2001.

Horizontal integration—affiliating with other hospitals, either in the same market or across markets—is another matter. Hospital markets have become more concentrated since 1980, both through reductions in the number of hospitals (evident in Table 11-4 through 2000), and through the combination of hospitals into systems under a common management. If system hospitals operating in the same market are counted as a single hospital, the average number of hospitals per market dropped by about 25 percent between 1981 and 1994, according to one study.[23] In the peak years of the mid-1990s, more than 100 hospital mergers took place per year. Public attention focused heavily on acquisition of nonprofit hospitals by for-profit chains, especially by Columbia/HCA (now HCA), the largest and most aggressive chain. HCA acquired or negotiated joint venture agreements to manage 35 formerly nonprofit hospitals in 1995 alone. But for-profit chains became less aggressive about expansion in the wake of a federal government investigation of HCA, which began in 1997. In any case, most hospital mergers occur within the nonprofit sector. Consolidation has slowed but

---

[23]David Dranove, Carol. J. Simon, and William D. White, "Is Managed Care Leading to Consolidation in Health-Care Markets?" *Health Services Research* 37, no. 3 (2002): 573–594.

continues. A study of 12 nationally representative communities showed that hospital market concentration increased in all 12 markets from 1996 to 2000.[24]

Service Lines and New Provider Structures

Interest in integrated delivery systems for providing comprehensive health care has recently declined. An emerging trend is for providers to organize themselves around particular lines of service. Frequently, service lines represent care for particular diseases or organ systems (cancer care, heart care, or orthopedics), but they may also be more or less narrow groupings of medical services (imaging or ambulatory surgery).

A focus on service lines often means taking services traditionally performed in full-service hospitals and moving them to other environments. One way is through small hospitals specializing in one type of care, usually owned at least in part by the doctors who practice in them. The number of specialty hospitals grew from 31 in 1997 to 113 in 2003.[25] The service line challenge to hospitals can also come, however, from groups of doctors operating out of ambulatory facilities. The number of ambulatory surgery centers is growing quite rapidly, from 2,462 in 1997 to 3,735 in 2003. Hospitals are also aggressively marketing their own service lines: creating heart centers, cancer centers, and other focused units within their own walls, often in partnerships with doctors.[26]

▪▪▪ III. Conduct

Before Managed Care

Physicians

In the postwar, pre-managed care period, markets for physician and hospital care were not characterized by overt price competition. The large majority of doctors practiced on a fee-for-service basis. In the early 1960s, before the introduction of Medicare and Medicaid, about 60 percent of payments for physicians' services still came directly from consumer pockets. Doctors were, to some degree, subject to the usual restraint of consumer demand when setting fees. But obtaining relevant information was difficult for consumers because of the complexity of the set of services that doctors provide and the difficulty of judging quality. It was made more difficult by prohibitions against advertising, which were supported by the AMA and often legally enforced (but not since 1982, when the Supreme Court ruled against such prohibitions). Thus, even though a large number of doctors practiced in a typical metropolitan area, each individual enjoyed some degree of local monopoly power.

By 1975, the share of physician revenues coming directly from consumers was down to 37 percent, with 35 percent coming from private insurers and 28 percent from public programs. Payments for services were, by then, heavily influenced by the policies of insurers and government payers. Medicare and most insurers adopted the

---

[24]Kelly J. Devers, et al., "Hospitals' Negotiating Leverage with Health Plans: How and Why Has It Changed?" *Health Services Research* 38, no. 1, part 2 (2003): 419–446.

[25]John K. Iglehart, "The Emergence of Physician-Owned Specialty Hospitals," *New England Journal of Medicine* 352, no. 1 (2005): 78–84.

[26]Robert A. Berenson, Thomas Bodenheimer, and Hoangmai H. Pham, "Specialty-Service Lines: Salvos in the New Medical Arms Race," *Health Affairs* 25 (Web Exclusive, July 2006): w337–w343.

"usual, customary, and reasonable" approach to reimbursement, which paid what the doctor charged unless it was out of line with what that doctor usually charged for the same service, or what was customary for other doctors in the same community. (The "customary" screen was often set at the 75th or 80th percentile of charges in the community.) Such an approach is sensible for an insurer who is a small part of the market and is simply trying to match market rates. As the market becomes dominated by insurers paying in this way, however, this approach tends to freeze in place existing differences in fees across doctors, locations, and types of services, and to encourage continued upward drift of charges.

Health economists have devoted a great deal of attention to the question of how much control physicians have over the demand for their own services.[27] This question has important implications for the effect of an increase in physician supply, such as the one the United States has experienced since the late 1960s (see Table 11-2). Standard economic analysis says that an increase in physician supply leads to lower fees and doctors' incomes, as the supply curve shifts out against a downward-sloping demand curve. But because patients rely so heavily on them for advice, might not doctors who find themselves less busy when the number of competitors rises simply recommend more services, in effect shifting the demand curve outward to match the increase in supply?

While it strikes most people (especially noneconomists!) as plausible that doctors can influence demand for their services, the importance of the demand-inducement phenomenon eludes precise quantification. Evidence suggesting that inducement exists, such as the common finding that doctors' fees are higher in places where physicians are more densely located, may have alternative explanations. Perhaps, for example, consumers are willing to pay more when physicians are more numerous because of greater convenience, shorter waits for services or more attention from the doctor. The extent of doctors' power to induce demand thus remains an unsettled area of research. Under tightly managed care, physicians often have financial incentives to recommend fewer rather than more services. As managed care has become less restrictive, the issue of induced demand has gained renewed policy relevance.

Hospitals

In the early 1960s only about 20 percent of hospital revenues came directly from consumers. By 1969, that share had fallen to under 10 percent, with 56 percent accounted for by public sources and 20 percent by Medicare alone. Medicare and most private insurers also gave consumers little or no financial incentive to choose less costly over more costly hospitals. If the consumer paid anything out-of-pocket for a hospital stay, the amount was usually the same regardless of the hospital chosen.

A number of theories of the behavior of nonprofit hospitals have been proposed. Some depict the hospital's administration as seeking to maximize a combination of quantity and quality of care. Another model views the hospital as being run in the interest of its staff physicians. Both types of models are broadly consistent with the behavior of hospitals during this period. Hospitals needed physicians to bring in

---

[27]The Feldstein, Phelps, and Folland, Goodman, and Stano textbooks cited in the suggested readings all have extensive discussions of this issue with references to the literature.

patients, so they made the work environment attractive to the doctors by providing support staff, including interns and residents, and by adding the latest facilities and services. In addition to satisfying the medical staff, these actions signaled that the administrators were running a high-quality institution in which the trustees and the community could take pride. The accommodating payment system of the time, along with advancing technology, provided the other ingredients for increases in expenditures. Spending growth was even faster for hospitals than for the health care industry as a whole. On average, over the entire period from 1960 to 1979, expenditures in community hospitals rose more than 7 percentage points per year in excess of general inflation.

Such increases could hardly go unnoticed. The states, the federal government, and, to some extent, Blue Cross plans explored a number of regulatory approaches to restraining expenditure growth in hospitals. Certificate-of-Need (CON) regulation is an attempt to control capital investment by requiring that a hospital (or other entity) demonstrate that a need exists in the area before investing in new beds or expensive equipment. This approach was tried in most states, with the earliest adopting it in the 1960s, and it was supported for a time by federal law. But economic studies of CON generally conclude that it is ineffective in reducing the growth of total hospital spending: Any expenditure-reducing effects it may have through reductions in the number of beds appear to be offset by higher spending in other areas. Some economists have argued that a regulatory process of this kind is likely to be captured by existing hospitals, which have advantages in political clout and control of information, and may be a barrier to potentially valuable innovation.

A number of states also experimented with regulation of the rates at which hospitals were paid for services. The weight of the evidence on rate regulation, from studies that compare hospital spending increases in states that adopted regulation with states that did not, suggests that in some cases it was at least modestly effective in slowing spending growth. Nonetheless, hospital rate regulation was largely abandoned as managed care spread.

A development of great importance to hospitals was Medicare's change in its method of paying for inpatient care, beginning in 1983. At that time, Medicare accounted for 28 percent of all hospital revenues, and an even higher share in the typical community hospital. The program shifted from reimbursing hospitals on an actual cost basis to paying predetermined rates based on the patient's diagnosis. The new system creates a clear incentive to reduce lengths of stay, as additional days of care add costs but generate no additional revenue. Hospitals responded strongly to this incentive. Lengths of stay for Medicare patients, which had been already been falling slowly, dropped rapidly in the first few years of the Prospective Payment System (PPS). Average length of stay had dropped from 11.2 days in 1975 to 10.3 in 1982, a little less than a day over 7 years, but it then fell an additional 1.7 days over the next 3 years as PPS took effect.

The response to the new system showed that an incentive directed at hospitals could affect their resource use, despite the fact that doctors make the decisions about discharging patients. Medicare remains very important for hospitals, accounting for 30 percent of all hospital revenues in 2005. Hospitals respond to the incentives Medicare creates, which, however well intentioned, are sometimes perverse. For example, after the PPS began paying hospitals for inpatient care at a fixed rate per case, reimbursement for care provided after discharge in other settings was still done on a cost basis. This created incentives for hospitals to provide skilled nursing care and home care, to discharge patients as early as feasible (sometimes to a different bed in the same facility), and to collect additional revenue from the provision of post-acute care, thereby shifting costs as much as possible to the cost-reimbursed sector. Medicare expenses on skilled nursing care and home care soared and Congress attempted to address the problem in the Balanced Budget Act of 1997, but getting the incentives right while protecting the access of seniors to important medical services is no easy matter.

Medicare payment policy has been implicated in the recent rise of service line competition discussed earlier and the accompanying migration (sometimes) of services from general hospitals. One factor contributing to these trends is technological change that has made it possible to deliver sophisticated services in smaller settings, often more conveniently for the doctor and patient. But another is imperfections in the current system of payment to providers, with Medicare an important contributor. Some types of services are much more profitable than others under current payment policies, and providers respond to these incentives by competing intensely for the profitable ones.[28]

Health Insurers

As discussed earlier, health insurers in the pre–managed care era largely left the organization and delivery of care to the providers. Commercial insurers did compete with Blue Cross and Blue Shield to sell plans to employers. They made significant inroads, surpassing the Blue plans in total enrollees from the early 1950s onward, despite certain advantages held by the Blues. The Blues were organized as nonprofits and, as such, enjoyed some federal and state tax advantages over for-profit plans. As plans originally organized by hospital associations and medical societies, they also had some advantages in dealing with providers. For example, in some states, Blue Cross received significant discounts on hospital care compared to what was charged to commercial insurers.

Commercial insurers competed by offering an insurance package different from that of the Blues, and pricing it differently. The Blues emphasized service benefits and first dollar coverage for hospital care (so individuals faced no copayments or deductibles for inpatient care), but placed limits on the total number of days covered. These limits left the individual facing large risks in the case of long stays. In contrast, commercial insurers offered major medical insurance, covering a wide range of services, with deductibles, copayments, and better coverage for extremely high-cost events. The philosophy of the Blues was also to practice community rating, to set premiums equally across a community to spread risks broadly. The problem with community rating in a competitive market for insurance is that groups that expect their health care costs to be lower than the community-wide average have an incentive to split themselves off. Large employers who believed that they had relatively healthy workers turned to commercial insurers (or to self-insurance) to get premiums based on their own experience rather than community rates. As time went on, the Blues responded to

[28]Paul B. Ginsburg and Joy M. Grossman , "When the Price Isn't Right: How Inadvertent Payment Incentives Drive Medical Care," *Health Affairs* 24 (Supp. Web Exclusive, August 9, 2005): w5.376.

competition by behaving more like the commercial insurers, adopting experience rating for large groups.

Managed Care and Conduct

An important contributing factor in the transformation of the health insurance market to managed care in the 1980s and 1990s was the growing concern on the part of employers, especially large ones, with the costs of the insurance. The HMO Act of 1973 promoted HMO growth to some degree, and enrollment grew rapidly from a small base in the 1970s. By the 1980s, the idea of managed care was becoming more familiar, and employers began to look to insurers for ways to gain control over rising premiums, even if it meant placing some restrictions on enrollees' choice of medical providers and access to services. The PPO concept also emerged in the early 1980s as a less restrictive form of managed care, and a more palatable one to many employees. Pressured by employers, health insurers began to compete in new ways, including selectively contracting with hospitals and doctors, negotiating with them for lower payment rates, and implementing other tools of utilization management.

As Figure 11-4 suggests, most health insurance in most parts of the country now incorporates managed care techniques in at least their milder forms. Market areas vary widely in the degree of penetration of managed care plans, the aggressiveness of price competition among plans, and the extent to which plans have put pressure on providers. Especially in those places where managed care became most aggressive, providers felt pressured to change their behavior or risk being left out of preferred networks, which could considerably reduce demand for their services. Some of their responses involved banding together to become actively engaged in managing care. As discussed earlier, some large physician groups—especially in California—accepted capitation payments and took responsibility for all, or a defined subset, of their enrollees' health care.

More frequently, however, managed-care organizations purchase services from providers using some form of fee-for-service, seeking the lowest rates they can get. Rather than being reimbursed for what they consider reasonable costs or charges, as they were in the past, hospitals and doctors now often find that payment is determined by what the market will bear. They thus find themselves in price competition with their peers to a degree not previously experienced.

Research findings suggest that managed care changed the way hospitals compete. Formerly, hospital competition focused on quality to attract doctors and patients. Markets with more hospitals might therefore experience a "medical arms race," resulting in greater duplication of services and higher unit costs. Evidence from the 1980s and 1990s, however, indicates that when managed care dominates insurance markets, prices of hospital services are lower where competition is more intense, as traditional industrial organization theory predicts.[29]

Predictably, both hospitals and doctors have shown more interest in horizontal combinations (mergers of hospitals, or affiliation with larger physician groups by doctors) to gain bargaining leverage with insurers.

---

[29]Reviewed in David Dranove and Mark Satterthwaite, "The Industrial Organization of Health Care," in *Handbook of Health Economics*. See also Daniel Kessler and Mark McClellan, "Is Hospital Competition Socially Wasteful?" *Quarterly Journal of Economics* (May 2000): 115, 577–615.

▪▪▪ IV. Performance

How are we to assess the performance of the U.S. health care industry? Rising expenditures, as summarized in Figure 11-2, have certainly been a cause for concern and a driving force behind recent structural changes in the industry. By increasing labor costs, higher health insurance premiums surely spurred employers' interest in managed care. Cost growth in Medicaid and the pressure it placed on government budgets drove state and federal governments in the same direction.

It is important to recognize that rising expenditure on a group of products does not necessarily imply that the industry is performing poorly. For example, if prices fall because of cost-reducing innovations, as with personal computers, an increase in spending will follow naturally if demand is elastic. Total spending could also rise if new, higher quality but more costly products replace older ones—a more likely scenario for health care. A study analyzing the treatment of heart attacks between 1983 and 1994 found that while spending per case was rising, the quality-adjusted price was actually falling about 1 percent per year if improvements in survival were accounted for in a reasonable way.[30]

Still, suspicion is strong that prior to the managed-care era, health spending was too high and rose too rapidly. The suspicion stemmed partly from beliefs about the financing system in place at the time: Providers of care and well-insured consumers had incentives to expand services as long as the expected benefits were positive, with little regard for costs. Managed care seemed to change that for a time in the mid-1990s, but rapid spending growth has returned.

American health care may also need improvement in areas other than spending growth. Comparisons of health data across countries, for example, are not particularly flattering to the U.S. system. The United States ranks first by a wide margin in amount spent, but is much further down the list in most indicators of population health. Table 11-5 provides comparative data on a few countries, along with median values for a set of 30 (mostly high-income) countries surveyed by the Organization for Economic Cooperation and Development (OECD). On a per capita basis, with due allowance for differences in national currencies, the United States spent more than twice as much as the median OECD country, and 47 percent more than the second-highest country, Switzerland. While the positive correlation is strong between health care spending and income across countries, our spending is high even relative to our incomes. If we compare health spending as a share of GDP, the United States, at 15.2 percent in 2003, leads all other developed countries by a large margin (Switzerland is next at 11.5 percent, with no other country above 11 percent). Yet despite our high spending, we fare poorly in comparisons of the most common measures of population health, such as infant mortality and life expectancy. The United States ranks 25th in the OECD in infant mortality, and 23rd in female life expectancy.

We should be cautious, however, about condemning the U.S. health care industry based on the data in Table 11-5. Aggregate measures of population health are influenced in important ways by factors over which the health care system has no direct control. For example, greater income inequality and relatively high poverty rates in the

---

[30]David M. Cutler et al., "Are Medical Prices Declining?" *Quarterly Journal of Economics* (November 1998): 991–1024.

TABLE 11-5 Health Care Spending and Health in Selected Countries: 2003

	Per Capita	*Percent of GDP*	*Female Life Expectancy (in years)*	*Infant[a] Mortality*
United States	$4,933	15.2	80.1	6.9
Canada	2,998	9.9	82.4	5.3
Germany	3,005	10.9	81.4	4.2
Japan	2,249	8.0	85.3	3.0
United Kingdom	2,347	8.3	80.7	5.3
OECD Median	2,401	8.6	81.3	4.4

[a]Deaths per 1,000 live births

Source: Organisation for Economic Co-operation and Development, OECD Health Data 2006, www.oecd.org

United States, as compared with other developed countries, likely contribute to high infant mortality. Lower mortality, though relatively easy to measure, is also not the only health system output of importance. Alleviation of pain and anxiety and improvements in physical and mental functioning are among other outputs that should count. Perhaps if we could reliably measure these forms of value-added, the relative standing of the United States would improve. Still, it is natural to look at the Table 11-5 data and wonder whether the incremental spending in the United States, as compared to other countries, brings with it commensurate benefits.

Another phenomenon indicating room for improvement in the American health industry (and probably elsewhere in the world) is the existence of substantial variation across geographic areas in the use of particular types of medical procedures, from relatively simple ones like hernia repair to very expensive surgeries such as coronary bypass and hip replacement.[31] Variations in use rates are too large to explain by chance or by variation in illness across areas. While these variations are not well understood, they seem to indicate that different standards of appropriate treatment somehow get established in different communities, which reflects considerable uncertainty among doctors about the effectiveness of care in many circumstances. The social payoff to getting better information about what really works and reducing medical practice variations might be very large. One estimate of deadweight losses from practice variations puts them, conservatively, at about $11 billion annually in the late 1990s.[32] A good case can be made for a greater government role in expanding knowledge about the effectiveness of medical procedures. While a large insurer might gain competitive advantage from investing in research on effectiveness and putting it into practice, the potential social gains are much larger than what any one firm could expect to capture.

---

[31]Study of variations in medical practice was pioneered by John Wennberg and his collaborators. See for example, information about their work in the Dartmouth Atlas of Health Care, at www .dartmouthatlas.org

[32]Charles S. Phelps, "Information Diffusion and Best Practice Adoption," in A.J. Culyer and J.P. Newhouse, eds., *Handbook of Health Economics* (Amsterdam: North-Holland, 2000).

The Institute of Medicine's (IOM) Quality of Health Care in America Committee has recently drawn attention to the related issue of preventable medical errors. The IOM's 2001 report spoke of a "quality chasm" between what our health care is and what it could be, noting that "tens of thousands of Americans die each year from errors in their care, and hundreds of thousands suffer or barely escape from nonfatal injuries that a truly high-quality system would largely prevent."[33]

One other common indictment of American health care points to the significant share of the population with neither private nor public health insurance coverage, 15.9 percent in 2005. In nearly every other OECD country, virtually 100 percent of the population has insurance coverage. The high uninsured rate in the United States cannot reasonably be blamed on the poor performance of the health care industry, nor can the industry be expected to rectify the situation on its own. If a solution is to be found, collective action through government policy changes will certainly be required.

Effects of Managed Care

Did managed care make a difference in health system performance, and, if so, in what ways? Despite the considerable attention focused on managed care by the media, policy makers, health care interest groups, researchers, and the general public, these questions are surprisingly difficult to answer with confidence. The mid-1990s slowdown of growth in real per capita health spending (Figure 11-2) closely followed the shift in health insurance to managed-care techniques (Figure 11-4), and the more recent acceleration of spending growth follows the movement toward less restrictive forms of insurance. While it is tempting to infer that managed care was effective in restraining spending growth, this simple correlation does not necessarily imply a causal link. Researchers have tried to identify the effects of managed care by looking for natural experiments, exploiting the fact that managed care was embraced at different times and to different degrees in different parts of the country. A few studies have shown that health care spending grew less rapidly in places where managed care market penetration was greater, but the evidence is not overwhelming.[34]

A great deal of research has also explored whether and how managed care organizations use resources differently than do traditional insurance providers. Such comparisons must be interpreted carefully: Individuals still exercise some choice in the type of insurance plan they enter; differences observed across types of insurance might reflect differences among the kinds of people who enroll as much as differences in how the plans perform. If on average managed care enrollees are younger and healthier, for example, failure to account for this will bias comparisons of plan performance. Secondly, there is so much variation across managed care plans that it may be difficult to generalize across studies. As Figure 11-4 indicates, unmanaged, conventional health insurance has nearly vanished, at least in the private insurance sector. The blurring of the lines between different forms of health insurance increases the difficulty of doing comparative studies of performance.

---

[33]*Crossing the Quality Chasm: A New Health System for the 21st Century* (Washington: National Academy Press 2001): 2.
[34]Evidence on this issue and other aspects of managed care performance is summarized in Sherry Glied, "Managed Care," in A.J. Culyer and J.P. Newhouse, eds., *Handbook of Health Economics* (Amsterdam: North-Holland, 2000).

Notwithstanding these caveats, most of the evidence points in the direction of lower resource use for HMOs as compared to traditional fee-for-service medicine (much less evidence is available on the use of resources in PPOs).[35] Studies show fairly consistently that HMOs reduce the use of inpatient hospital care. Evidence is more mixed for physician care outside the hospital, which is not surprising given the conflicting incentives at work. HMOs would be expected to scrutinize the use of all types of services more closely, but they might also provide more preventive care to deter future hospitalizations and substitute less expensive outpatient services for more expensive inpatient ones. Some studies show more use of physician care in HMOs as compared to fee-for-service, but the difference is usually not large enough to offset the reduced use of hospital care. Studies that compare HMOs with fee-for-service in the use of particularly expensive services where there is some discretion about use (such as cesarean section in childbirth) indicate that HMOs use them less frequently.

Effects on quality of care are of at least as much interest as those that relate to cost. Here, the evidence is very mixed. Robert Miller and Harold Luft find equal numbers of statistically significant results showing higher or lower quality in HMOs.[36] This mix of findings is not so surprising, and does not imply that any of the studies were incorrect or poorly executed. A more plausible interpretation is that quality of care really is sometimes better, sometimes worse in HMOs, depending on the particular organization, type of disease, and other circumstances. One well-conducted study of chronically ill elderly people, for example, found that HMOs provided lower quality care for physical health but better quality for mental health.[37]

An optimistic view of the evidence is that the incentives faced by managed care organizations, at least in the HMO forms, lead them to provide health care at lower cost than traditional fee-for-service arrangements, without systematically adverse effects on quality. Even such a guarded conclusion should be regarded tentatively, and we must be careful not to overgeneralize across the extremely diverse landscape of managed care. If the optimistic view is correct, however, it prompts one to ask why the less restrictive forms of managed care have been gaining ascendancy. Perhaps consumers misperceive quality differences among plans, or perhaps researchers are not capturing all of the aspects of quality that consumers care about. The incentives that consumers typically face when making a choice among plans may also come into play, a subject that we will discuss when we turn to public policy issues.

Managed Care and Provider Compensation

Some observers believe that to the extent that managed care reduced the cost of health insurance, it did so primarily at the expense of providers, by exercising market power to force them to accept lower payments. One study found that average physician real income declined by 7.1 percent between 1995 and 2003, while it increased 6.9 percent

---

[35]Robert H. Miller and Harold S. Luft, "Managed Care Performance Since 1980," *Journal of American Medical Association* 271 (May 18, 1994):1512–1519, and "Does Managed Care Lead to Better or Worse Quality of Care?" *Health Affairs* 16 (September/October 1997): 7–25.
[36]"Does Managed Care Lead to Better or Worse Quality of Care?"
[37]John E. Ware, Jr., et al., "Differences in 4-Year Health Outcomes for Elderly and Poor, Chronically Ill Patients Treated in HMO and Fee-for-Service Systems," *Journal of the American Medical Association* 276 (1996): 1039–1047.

for other skilled professionals.[38] The reasons for this slow growth are not entirely clear. However, a study looking at earlier data from the period from 1985 to 1993 found that incomes of primary care doctors grew most rapidly and of hospital-based specialists most slowly in states where managed care market share was growing fastest.[39] Because managed care plans often emphasized (especially during this period) primary care gatekeeping and reductions in inpatient hospital utilization, these findings suggest that demand from managed care plans influenced physician income in ways that health insurers traditionally did not. Over the period from 1995 to 2003 however, primary care doctors fared even worse than specialists in income growth.

A study in Massachusetts, although limited in scope, provides some fascinating information about the effect of managed care on provider payments. David Cutler and his colleagues looked at detailed information on treatment of heart attack patients who had insurance coverage through one large employer (which covered over 250,000 individuals), during the period between 1993 and 1995.[40] The employees could choose relatively unmanaged indemnity coverage or one of several HMOs. Heart attack care is an interesting case to study: While enrollees chose their insurance plans, they would have done so before the attack occurred, and it is unlikely that the healthiness of heart attack patients would differ systematically across insurers. Heart attack survivors also receive different types of procedures of varying cost, and it is frequently claimed that the most expensive procedures, such as coronary bypass surgery, are overutilized in the United States. HMOs might be expected to be more selective in approving such expensive procedures than indemnity insurers.

Cutler and colleagues found that payments per heart attack treated were only about 61 percent as high in the HMOs ($23,600 as compared to $38,500). However, when they placed patients into categories by the type of treatment they received, the costs for HMO patients were lower by a similar ratio in each of the categories, suggesting that the overall difference in cost is not primarily a result of substituting less expensive forms of treatment. At least in this case, it appeared that a large share of the reduction in cost must have come from lower payments to providers. Interestingly, the authors could also find no difference in quality between the HMOs and indemnity insurers as measured by deaths or rates of hospital readmissions due to complications.

Effects of Consolidation

As noted earlier, one type of provider reaction to pressure from managed care has been to consolidate into larger entities. Much of this activity has been horizontal—physicians forming into groups and hospitals affiliating with other hospitals. Such consolidation could lower costs of production if important economies of scale are achieved. However, actions that increase market concentration always raise questions about effects on prices. It is not hard to believe that a primary aim of many hospital mergers is to gain bargaining power relative to managed care insurers, by reducing the

[38]Ha T. Hu and Paul B. Ginsburg, Losing Ground: Physician Income, 1995–99, Tracking Report No. 15, June 2006, Center for Studying Health System Change, www.hschange.com/CONTENT/851/
[39]Carol J. Simon, David Dranove, and William D. White, "The Impact of Managed Care on the Physician Marketplace," *Public Health Reports* 112 (May-June 1997): 222–230.
[40]David Cutler, Mark McClellan, and Joseph P. Newhouse, "How Does Managed Care Do It?" *Rand Journal of Economics* 31, no. 3 (Autumn 2000): 526–548.

insurer's ability to play off one hospital against the other. These issues have not escaped the notice of U.S. antitrust authorities. The Federal Trade Commission and the Department of Justice held a series of hearings on competition in health care in 2003.[41]

Hospitals have increasingly chosen to affiliate in multihospital systems, frequently with other hospitals in the same local market, but also with hospitals that had not been direct competitors in other geographic areas. Some of these affiliations are rather weak, with the individual hospitals remaining largely autonomous, but joining forces to achieve some economies in activities such as the purchasing of supplies. Others are formal mergers or acquisitions. One reason for affiliating with a larger hospital system that extends beyond one's market area is to get access to greater management expertise for coping with rapidly changing market conditions. Other reasons include better access to capital for modernization or expansion, or to gain some benefits (probably small) from shared activities such as joint purchasing. The direct effect on a hospital's local market power from affiliating with hospitals elsewhere is likely to be small.[42]

Mergers with hospitals in the same market could be a different story. We should not expect the merger of two hospitals—unless they were very small—to produce significant economies through such avenues as the sharing of overhead functions. However, in a market with underutilized bed capacity or excessive duplication of services—a common state of affairs for U.S. hospitals in recent decades—a merger might facilitate reductions in capacity and more rational planning as new services are added, thereby reducing costs of care. On the other hand, mergers that increase market concentration raise concerns about market power and control over prices.

As with many aspects of the changing health care marketplace, a consensus view has not emerged about the effects of mergers on hospital prices. A reasonable inference to draw from recent research on hospital mergers is that the opposing effects on prices are present: an efficiency-enhancing or cost-reducing effect that tends to depress prices, and a market power effect that increases them. One study using a large national data set from 1986 to 1994 found that the price-reducing effect tended to be stronger.[43] However, the market power effect, which seems to exist for nonprofit hospitals as well as for-profits, may be getting stronger over time.[44]

Concentration has also been increasing in markets for health insurance, but we know even less about its effects. Many recent mergers have involved insurers operating in different locations. For example, through a series of mergers, all 14 Blue Cross Blue Shield plans that converted to for-profit firms have combined in a single entity, WellPoint Inc., with some 34 million covered lives in 2006. A larger total enrollment base offers more data that can be used to analyze and improve the effectiveness of techniques for managing care. Although care must be delivered locally, for the most

[41]A wealth of information from these hearings is posted on the Internet at www.ftc.gov/ogc/healthcarehearings/

[42]A recent study of California hospitals found some contrary evidence. Affiliating in a system with hospitals outside its local market seemed to allow a hospital to increase its prices more quickly, perhaps because the system's leverage was helpful in bargaining with insurers. See Glenn Melnick and Emmett Keeler, "The Effects of Multi-Hospital Systems on Hospital Prices," *Journal of Health Economics* 26 (2007): 400–413.

[43]Robert A. Connor et al., "Which Types of Hospital Mergers Save Consumers Money?" *Health Affairs* 16 (November/December 1997): 62–74.

[44]E. B. Keeler, G. Melnick, and J. Zwanziger, "The Changing Effects of Competition on Non-Profit and For-Profit Hospital Pricing Behavior" *Journal of Health Economics* 18 (1999): 69–86.

part, if an organization succeeds in developing a wide knowledge base and effective tools for managing care, gains could be made from exploiting this competitive edge in many markets simultaneously. Large multi-location employers might also find some advantages in dealing with managed care organizations that are similarly far-flung.

Evidence suggests, not surprisingly, that HMO premiums and profits are lower in markets with more HMOs.[45] Mergers of managed care organizations that formerly operated in different areas are not particularly troubling, as they do not increase market power in relevant market areas. Roger Feldman and colleagues found that between 1994 and 1997, concentration in the HMO industry increased at the national level, but fell in most local markets.[46] They note that some of the larger mergers in this time period, such as Aetna with U.S. Healthcare, FHP with Pacificare in 1996, and Aetna and Prudential in 1999, merged plans that were in many cases already operating in the same markets. The concentration-increasing effect was nonetheless often offset by entry of new HMOs at the same time.

By some measures, most local markets for health insurance are now quite concentrated. Product market definition is always a key issue in measuring concentration, and how closely HMOs compete with PPOs is an important question for antitrust policy that is receiving some attention.[47] Even if HMOs and PPOs are viewed as one market, however, a recent study of 294 metropolitan areas by the AMA concluded that 95 percent would be considered highly concentrated according to government merger guidelines.[48]

▬▬▬ Public Policy Issues

The most basic public policy question about the economics of health care concerns market versus nonmarket allocation: Is it best to harness the power of the market for allocating resources as effectively as possible, recognizing and adjusting for the peculiarities of the product and the industry? Or is health care so special that it is better to rely on nonmarket mechanisms, as in the United Kingdom, Canada, and many other countries? Compared with other parts of the U.S. economy, the role of government as regulator and purchaser of health care is unusually extensive. Looking across countries, however, our health care system is easily the most market driven. The comparative data in Table 11-5 lead one to wonder whether we have the right idea.

In a 1963 article generally considered the seminal paper in health care economics, Nobel laureate Kenneth Arrow argued that uncertainty in the incidence of disease and the effectiveness of treatment, and the institutional adaptations to that uncertainty, largely account for the peculiarities of health care as an economic industry.[49]

---

[45]Douglas Wholey, Roger Feldman, and Jon B. Christianson, "The Effect of Market Structure on HMO Premiums," *Journal of Health Economics* 14 (1995): 81–105; and M. V. Pauly et al., "Competitive Behavior in the HMO Marketplace," *Health Affairs* 21, no. 1 (2002): 194–202.

[46]R. D. Feldman, D. R. Wholey, and J. B. Christianson, "HMO Consolidations: How National Mergers Affect Local Markets" *Health Affairs* 18, no. 4 (July/August 1999): 96–104.

[47]See the materials from the April 23, 2003, session of the FTC-DOJ hearings referenced above.

[48]"Competition in Health Insurance: A Comprehensive Study of U.S. Markets. 2005 Update" 2006. www.ama-assn.org/ama1/pub/upload/mm/368/compstudy_52006.pdf

[49]Kenneth J. Arrow, "Uncertainty and the Welfare Economics of Medical Care," *American Economic Review* 53 (1963): 941–969.

Uncertainty about illness and the demand for care create a demand for insurance, which may be satisfied through private arrangements or through social insurance programs such as Medicare and Medicaid. Individuals do not want to have to worry about the cost of health care at a time of serious need, and they are willing to pay for insurance to protect them against that eventuality. As taxpayers, we also are willing to provide assistance for the poor to help them in meeting unpredictable medical needs. Arrow also emphasized the patient's uncertainty about the effectiveness of health care and the imbalance of information between doctor and patient. When a health problem presents itself, the doctor is expected to be much better informed than the patient about the consequences of alternative courses of action, and the patient will rely heavily on the doctor's advice.

In the light of these features of health care, it is reasonable to be skeptical that unfettered market forces are the answer to resource allocation problems. The usual argument that markets will allocate resources efficiently relies on the discipline imposed by well-informed buyers spending their limited budgets shrewdly, which ensures that only sellers who can deliver the best value per dollar will survive. Because of the asymmetry of information, however, patients are poorly equipped to play this role. And while health insurance is surely, on balance, a good thing, it brings with it reduced price sensitivity at the time that care is received.

We have long had social institutions, such as licensure and the code of ethics under which physicians practice, to help guard against under-provision of services or inferior quality. As insurance coverage grew and technological progress expanded the potential to spend money on health care, we found ourselves with a system that promoted spending growth while creating few incentives to weigh cost against benefit at the margin. *Moral hazard,* which in this context means the tendency of the insured to overuse services, inevitably driving up premiums, became a serious and persistent problem.

Managed care seemed to change that picture. It swept into the marketplace as purchasers sought new ways to deal with moral hazard. It provided a countervailing force to other features of the system that push in the direction of insufficient attention to cost. But backlash from consumers and doctors led managed care organizations to expand their networks and scale back their intrusion into clinical decisions. Rapid increases in premiums returned, renewing concerns about the costs of health care.[50] Have market forces been given their best shot, only to fail the test?

Advocates of a regulated, single-payer system for the U.S. would say yes, but those with a stronger faith in markets believe that better institutional arrangements may yet evolve. One hope for the market is managed competition, a concept pioneered and tirelessly advocated by Alain Enthoven, among others.[51] The key idea is that consumers should exercise informed and cost-conscious choice primarily at the point of choosing a health insurance plan, rather than by shopping for health care services.

---

[50]In addition to increases in health spending per capita (See Figure 11-2), increases in insurance premiums are another indicator of rising spending. Following several years of relatively slow growth, average premiums for employer-provided health insurance grew by more that 10 percent each year from 2001 through 2004. The average increase was 7.7 percent in 2006. See information from the Kaiser Family Foundation Annual Employer Health Benefits Survey, www.kff.org/insurance

[51]A recent example of his thinking is Alain C. Enthoven and Laura A. Tollen, "Competition in Health Care: It Takes Systems to Pursue Quality and Efficiency" *Health Affairs* Web Exclusive (September 7, 2005). content.healthaffairs.org/cgi/reprint/hlthaff.w5.420v1.pdf

Insurers then compete for the consumer dollar, ideally by offering packages that are attractive in terms of both cost and quality of care. The insurers play the role of selecting providers and developing effective mechanisms for managing care. Differences in consumer preferences can be accommodated, as long as individuals bear the additional cost of choosing a more expensive plan. Some may be willing to pay more for free choice of doctor and comprehensive coverage, while others will accept greater restrictions on choice and benefits in exchange for lower premiums.

To make an analogy, most purchasers of personal computers do not pay great attention to the makers of the component parts, and most would find it difficult to assess the reliability of one hard drive or wireless network card relative to another. They rely more on the incentives of the manufacturer assembling the package, be it a major corporation like Dell or Hewlett-Packard or a local retailer, to make good judgments about quality and cost in selecting components. Performance in this market seems very satisfactory.

But choosing a health insurance plan is, of course, far different from choosing a personal computer. To begin with, the adverse consequences of a bad choice are potentially much more severe. The proponents of managed competition have always recognized, as the name itself implies, that the environment in which insurance plans compete must be managed or regulated to achieve the best results. We next examine some major public policy issues relating to how competition could be managed and what we can reasonably expect from this strategy.

Cost-Conscious Consumer Choice

Despite the managed care backlash, Enthoven still envisions that in a well-structured system, most consumers would choose a managed care plan organized as an integrated delivery system (IDS), accepting some restrictions on the providers they can see. It has not happened yet, he argues, because few consumers are given the right incentives. Managed competition advocates believe that consumers should select from a variety of health insurance plans, facing the incremental cost of more expensive plans, and reaping the financial benefit of choosing less expensive ones. But for most workers with job-related coverage, this is not the current reality. Most employers who provide coverage offer only a single carrier. In 1997, according to a large national survey of employers, only 43 percent of enrollees in job-related insurance plans were offered a choice of plans, and only 23 percent had a choice of insurance carriers. Of those employers who offered a choice of plans, only 28 percent made equal dollar premium contributions regardless of which plan was chosen (as managed competition principles dictate).[52] By all accounts, choice in employer-provided plans has declined further since that survey was conducted.

Greater consumer choice could be promoted through policies that encourage purchasing cooperatives, which are insurance brokers who pool workers from many firms and offer individuals a wider choice of plans. The Massachusetts health care reform creates a mechanism called the "connector" designed to do this. Federal tax policy might also be changed to encourage more cost-conscious choice. The open-ended

---

[52]M. Susan Marquis and Stephen E. Long, "Trends in Managed Care and Managed Competition, 1993–1997," *Health Affairs* 18 (November-December 1999): 75–88.

nature of the current tax preference for employer-provided health benefits favors more expensive plans. Instead of excluding all employer payments for health insurance from taxable income, the size of the exemption an employer or individual receives could be capped, so that high-cost plans are not subsidized at the margin. President Bush has proposed doing just that, by converting the open-ended exclusion to a fixed standard deduction available to anyone with qualifying health coverage.

Can Consumers Assess Quality?

Many consumers demonstrate a willingness to pay more for higher quality in all kinds of products from coffee to cars, so it would be surprising if they would not do the same for something as important as health care. But do employers and consumers have, or can they get, the information necessary to make reasonable judgments about the quality of health care plans? If those who choose among plans are unable to assess quality, the entire premise of the managed competition strategy is called into question.

Measuring health care plan and health care provider quality is a rapidly evolving field. The National Committee for Quality Assurance (www.ncqa.org) has been reporting on HMO quality since the early 1990s, and continues to refine its measures. The Agency for Healthcare Research and Quality has a compendium of health care report cards, listing over 200, sponsored by a variety of governmental agencies, insurers, purchasing groups, and other organizations (www.talkingquality.gov/compendium/).

But measuring the quality of such a complex product is difficult. Ideally, we would like to measure a health plan or provider's performance by its impact on the health of the relevant population. However, it is difficult to separate the plan or provider's contribution from other factors that influence health. Hospitals that do poorly in mortality-based measures of quality, for example, consistently object that such measures do not adequately account for how severely ill their patients are. Because quality measures are always imperfect, their use may distort provider behavior. A cautionary recent finding is that after New York and Pennsylvania began publishing hospital and surgeon mortality rates for coronary bypass surgery, surgeons were more reluctant to operate on the sickest patients.[53]

Current measures of health plan performance often focus on structural measures such as the qualifications of network doctors, intermediate outcomes such as the percentage of pregnant enrollees who get prenatal care in the first trimester, and measures of patient satisfaction. Additional research to develop more reliable ways to measure performance in the dimensions that most matter to consumers warrants public support.

Is Competition Workable?

Aside from demand-side policies to give consumers the incentive to choose in a cost-conscious way among health plans and the information needed to do so wisely, managed competition relies on a sufficient supply of health plans to offer consumers a real choice and make collusion difficult. To consider the potential for competition on the supply side, we should examine the minimum efficient scale of an integrated

---

[53]David Dranove et al., "Is More Information Better? The Effects of 'Report Cards' on Health Care Providers," *Journal of Political Economy* 111, no. 3 (2003): 555–588.

delivery system, the size required to operate at minimum average cost per enrollee in relation to the size of relevant markets. One study did so by looking at the staffing patterns and use of hospital services in relation to enrollees in large staff model HMOs.[54] The authors found that a community of 360,000 could support three independent networks of physicians and three hospitals of about 240 beds each, but some types of acute services would not need to be available in all hospitals. A smaller community of 180,000 could still support three independent physician networks but would need to share all hospital inpatient facilities to achieve productive efficiency. The authors noted that 37 percent of the American population lives in health care market areas smaller than 360,000 in population, and 29 percent in markets smaller than 180,000. At the other extreme, 42 percent are in markets with population greater than 1.2 million.

We may conclude that in major metropolitan areas market size is not a serious obstacle to competition among health care plans, but that a significant share of the population lives in areas where several fully independent delivery systems cannot compete and be efficient. Even in areas with a fairly large population base, market power exercised by health plans with substantial market share, combinations of providers, or providers of highly specialized services may still lead to less than optimal results. Vigilant antitrust enforcement will likely be a key component of any market-based approach to health policy, but we are still learning what appropriate antitrust policy entails in practice.

High-Risk Populations and the Uninsured

In any year, the use of health care resources is highly concentrated among a small part of the population, with 1 percent of the heaviest users accounting for 30 percent of all expenditures, and the top 10 percent accounting for 70 percent of spending. To the extent that high usage is predictable on the basis of such factors as age or pre-existing conditions, a competitive market in insurance will tend to segregate, with higher-risk groups paying higher premiums. If legal restrictions are made on premium differences or they are not practical for other reasons, health plans will have incentives to attract healthy enrollees and avoid the sick.

This has been a particular concern for the Medicare program when contracting with managed care plans on a capitation basis. Originally, Medicare paid managed care plans a capitation rate equal to 95 percent of what it would expect to pay for fee-for-service enrollees in the same geographic area. If those who join managed care plans were typical Medicare beneficiaries, the program could expect to save 5 percent, on average, on each one. But it appears that managed care plans attracted relatively healthy Medicare enrollees, who would have spent less than 95 percent of the average had they stayed in the fee-for-service system, so the program actually spent more while paying at a discounted rate. Medicare has since improved its methods for risk adjustment. The effectiveness of these improvements for reducing plans' incentives for

---

[54]Richard Kronick et al., "The Marketplace in Health Care Reform," *New England Journal of Medicine* 328 (January 14, 1993): 148–152.

focusing on the healthy are difficult to determine as yet, in light of major changes in the overall level of payments to private plans.[55]

Any resources devoted to competition for a preferred set of enrollees are wasted from a social perspective—one group or plan's gain comes almost entirely from costs imposed on other groups, plans, or individuals. It also seems unfair that those unlucky enough to be struck with a serious and chronic illness should be burdened further with higher insurance premiums or difficulty in obtaining coverage. The conceptually appropriate solution is clear: Do not vary premiums by risk status (at least for those elements of risk outside the individual's control), but adjust payments to insurers to reflect differences in expected cost. If risk-adjusted payments are made accurately, such a system would be fair to insurance plans and consumers, and would remove incentives for insurers to compete for preferred risks.

Two obstacles stand in the way of widespread adoption of risk-adjustment schemes. One is that despite considerable ongoing research, we are in the early stages of learning how to do risk adjustment properly. The second is that to apply risk adjustment widely in the private sector, a mechanism would be needed for pooling premium payments very broadly across insured groups, and then redistributing them to insurance plans on a risk-adjusted basis. Such a pooling would be possible if most insurance were obtained through purchasing cooperatives, but it is not in the current system.

A large uninsured population, as exists in the United States today, is also not compatible with effective managed competition. Two related problems can be cited. First, the uninsured receive care in emergency situations that often costs more to provide than the recipients are able to pay. Providers must recover the unreimbursed costs of such care in some way, and, to the extent possible, will try to shift the costs into premiums paid by the insured. Because various providers and health plans will not bear the costs of uncompensated care equally, due to differences in location and other factors, these extra costs will distort competition among providers and among plans. Second, in order to survive in the competitive process, providers and plans have incentives to avoid bearing the costs of uncompensated care. The uninsured are likely to find it more difficult to get needed care in a market-driven system than in the earlier world of more passive insurers and employers. For these reasons, advocates of managed competition argue that it will work best if accompanied by government action to assure universal health care coverage.

Consumer-Directed Health Care

For now managed competition is not a concept in great favor among employers who sponsor health coverage. The more fashionable idea for market advocates is *consumer-directed health care*.[56] This term means different things to different people, but in contrast to managed competition it directs its incentives at the point of service rather than at the point of insurance plan choice. Usually it involves a health plan with a large deductible—$1,000 or more—and other cost-sharing. Public policy has encouraged

---

[55]Medicare Payment Advisory Commission, The Medicare Advantage Program and MedPAC Recommendations, March 21, 2007, www.medpac.gov/publications/congressional_testimony/ 032107_W_M_testimony_MA_CZ.pdf
[56]Melinda B. Buntin, et al., "Consumer-Directed Health Care: Early Evidence about Effects on Cost and Quality," *Health Affairs* 25 (Web Exclusive, October 2006): w516–w530.

linking high deductible plans with tax-favored savings accounts that can be used to cover out-of-pocket expenses. Advocates of the consumer-directed model argue that until the deductible is spent, individuals have strong incentives to economize on health care use, as it is clear that they are spending their own money. While high deductible plans account for only a small share of the health insurance market (four percent of covered employees were in high deductible plans with a savings option in 2006, according to the Kaiser Family Foundation), they are making inroads.

Consumer financial incentives have an important role to play in promoting more efficient use of health resources. That role will be enhanced if and when more useful measures of comparative quality and cost at the level of individual hospitals and physician groups are developed to help consumers make better choices. However, even apart from the issue of whether consumers are capable of making knowledgeable choices about service use and among providers, extensive cost-sharing at the point of service inevitably conflicts with the risk-spreading role of insurance. For that reason, consumer-directed plans include stop-loss features, setting a limit on out-of-pocket spending, beyond which the enrollee is fully covered.

In light of the concentration of health care consumption among a small percentage of users, a large share of total health spending is accounted for by individuals who would exceed their out-of-pocket limits. These individuals (undergoing major surgeries or requiring lengthy hospital stays, for example) would be given no incentive to economize at the margin. Consumer cost-sharing is one tool, but it may be best regarded as a complement rather than a substitute for other tools available to insurers (such as provider payment mechanisms and selective contracting).

Technology and Spending Growth

A final question about market mechanisms in health care is whether they can provide the right incentives for new technology and spending growth over time. Managed care creates greater incentives than traditional insurance to adopt innovations that reduce cost and to eliminate those that add cost with no benefit. But what about innovations for which the expected benefits exceed the risks, but at high cost? Most health economists believe that the long-term growth of health care spending has been most associated with the adoption of new technologies and treatment techniques offering at least some medical benefit, so this question has important implications for spending growth and consumer welfare. Recent research that attempts to assess the benefits and costs of technological innovations in some important classes of illness concludes that although costs have been large, benefits have been much greater.[57] We should therefore guard against constructing a system that creates too little incentive for costly but beneficial innovation.

Yet should we be willing to pay any price for small gains in longevity or quality of life? New research finds that an expensive and common procedure called angioplasty provides no gain in longevity for patients with stable heart disease, as compared with treatment with drugs and lifestyle changes, though it provides somewhat better relief of chest pain.[58]

---

[57]David M. Cutler, *Your Money or Your Life: Strong Medicine for America's Health Care System* (New York: Oxford University Press, 2004).
[58]William E. Boden et al., "Optimal Medical Therapy with or without PCI for Stable Coronary Disease," *New England Journal of Medicine* (March 26, 2007). www.nejm.org

Should patients have access to either form of treatment, with no consideration of the difference in cost? Some new cancer drugs have been priced as high as $100,000 per year of treatment. How an insurance plan makes coverage decisions in these situations may depend on its liability for a lawsuit, and on how the legal system defines *necessary care.* One can imagine a system in which, if the legal environment allows it, some insurance plans are liberal in their coverage of technologies, while others offer lower premiums but are much stricter, and consumers choose among them. As a result, individuals with greater ability to pay would gain access to some forms of treatment that others would not. We may or may not be willing to live with the consequences of such a system, which, to some degree, already exists, but the issues are important for public policy to consider.

CONCLUSION ▪▪▪▪▪▪▪

Dissatisfaction with rising health care spending led to the managed care revolution of the 1990s. That revolution has been rolled back, though by no means entirely reversed. A return to rapid spending increases has created a new clamor for change. Enthoven's vision is of a more rationalized market, with consumers choosing among competing, largely self-contained, integrated health care delivery systems, accountable for quality. This runs counter to recent trends toward broader networks—a trend that seems to indicate that consumers place a high value on free choice of providers at the point of service. Rising costs may yet generate more interest in managed competition ideas and more restricted networks. But if we do not embrace managed competition, what are the alternatives? One possibility is the eventual adoption of a highly regulated, single-payer system, though such an outcome hardly appears imminent.[59] Consumer-directed care has drawn some attention but does not appear to be a complete solution.

Whatever the future holds, interest in controlling the growth of health care spending will not fade away, nor will interest in choice, quality, and equitable access to beneficial care. If we rely heavily on market forces to guide resource allocation, as seems likely for the foreseeable future, getting the incentives created by the legal and regulatory environment right, and supplementing private with public resources where appropriate, will continue to challenge policymakers.

SUGGESTIONS FOR FURTHER READING ▪▪▪▪▪▪▪

Arrow, Kenneth J. 1963. "Uncertainty and the Welfare Economics of Medical Care." *American Economic Review* 53: 941–969.

Cohen, Jonathan. 2007. *Sick: The Untold Story of America's Health Care Crisis.* New York: Harper Collins.

Cutler, David M. 2004. *Your Money or Your Life: Strong Medicine for America's Health Care System.* New York: Oxford University Press.

Dranove, David. 2002. *The Economic Evolution of American Health Care: From Marcus Welby to Managed Care.* Princeton, NJ: Princeton University Press.

---

[59]High-profile advocates include Physicians for a National Health Program www.pnhp.org, and film-maker Michael Moore in his recent movie *Sicko.*

Enthoven, Alain C. 1980. *Health Plan*. Reading, MA: Addison-Wesley.

Fuchs, Victor R. 1974. *Who Shall Live?* New York: Basic Books.

Joskow, Paul L. 1984. *Controlling Hospital Costs*. Cambridge: MIT Press.

Newhouse, Joseph P. 2002. *Pricing the Priceless: A Health Care Conundrum*. Cambridge, MA: MIT Press.

Starr, Paul. 1982. *The Social Transformation of American Medicine*. New York: Basic Books.

Textbooks

Feldstein, Paul J. 2005. *Health Care Economics*, 6th ed. Clifton Park, NY: Thomson Delmar.

Folland, Sherman, Allen C. Goodman, and Miron Stano. 2007. *The Economics of Health and Health Care*, 5th ed. Upper Saddle River, NJ: Pearson Prentice Hall.

Getzen, Thomas E. 2007. *Health Economics and Financing*, 3rd ed. New York: John Wiley and Sons.

Phelps, Charles E. 2003. *Health Economics*, 3rd ed. Boston: Addison-Wesley.

Technical Paper Collection

Culyer, A.J., and J.P. Newhouse, eds., 2000. *Handbook of Health Economics*, Vols. 1A and 1B. Amsterdam: North-Holland.

CHAPTER

The Public Accounting Industry

PHILIP G. COTTELL, JR.

The scene was striking: A well-dressed man at the pinnacle of his career standing with grave face and raised hand, about to testify before an enraged committee of Congress. Who was this? A crime boss? A furtive financier of terrorists? An illegal drug kingpin? No. He was an accountant and a leading member of a profession that hitherto had been held in the highest regard.

In the fall of 2001, Enron, the seventh-largest corporation in the United States, collapsed after it came to light that it had massive liabilities that were not disclosed on its financial statements. Shortly thereafter, other large firms, notably Worldcom and Tyco, were found to have improper and perhaps fraudulent accounting records. Amidst the maelstrom of scandal surrounding these colossal failures stood an "industry" whose duty is supposed to be protecting the public from these financial disasters. But the person testifying was Joseph Berardino, chief executive of Arthur Andersen, one of the largest public accounting firms in the world and Enron's auditor. His firm, along with four large companies of similar size, stood atop the accounting profession, whose role is to ensure the fidelity of the accounting information, records, and reports essential to the functioning of the nation's financial markets.

Just how important is the accounting profession to the economy? One measure is suggested by the increase in ownership of equity securities by the American public. In 1952, when the accounting profession was at or near its high water mark, approximately 4.1 percent of the population owned equity securities. In 1981, just before consolidation and price competition erupted in the accounting field, ownership of equities had expanded to 14.1 percent of the public. Today, ownership of equities, either directly or through mutual funds, is far more widespread. According to the Investment Company Institute, half of the population now owns equity securities, many through investments in mutual funds. In addition many participate in pension plans and retirement programs, the returns on which depend on their investments in the stocks and bonds of publicly traded firms. Equity ownership increased from 54.1 million households in 2002 to 56.9 million households in 2005. Ownership of publicly traded companies, either directly or indirectly, and the efficiency with which the nation's financial capital is allocated among alternative uses, hinges on confidence and faith in the veracity of the firms' financial reports.[1]

I. History

While evidence of accounting records reaches back to biblical times, the earliest record of a public accounting engagement in the United States occurred before the American Revolution. In 1766 Benjamin Franklin asked James Parker to act as his representative in accounting for the final settlement of the sale of a printing business.[2] In 1866 public accounting took the form in which it chiefly operates today when the first accounting partnership, Veysey and Veysey, was established in New York. Two decades later the predecessors to two of today's Big Four accounting firms emerged when Deloitte, Dever, Griffiths and Company (forerunner of Deloitte), and Price Waterhouse and Company (forerunner of PricewaterhouseCoopers), certified corporate security offerings in 1890.[3]

At the outset the profession was accorded a special legal status which enabled it to thrive. In 1896 the state of New York granted certified public accounting its first legal recognition. During the period from 1896 to 1913 this recognition subsequently spread to 31 states. In the latter year the sixteenth amendment to the Constitution, which established the income tax, was ratified—a singular event that gave a great boost to the accounting profession owing to the need to define, calculate, and track business and personal income. By 1921 all 48 states had enacted laws giving special recognition to certified public accountants; all the states had recognized the status of public accountants and granted them a special legal "franchise."[4]

The stock market crash in 1929, the financial scandals that subsequently were exposed, and the ensuing depression triggered new growth in the demand for the services of public accounting firms. In instituting reforms for financial reporting, President Franklin Roosevelt signed into law two important new statutes, the Securities Act of 1933, and the Securities Act of 1934. The 1934 Act created a new government agency charged with regulating the nation's financial markets, the Securities and Exchange Commission (SEC). Using the authority given it by these acts, the SEC required all new and continuing registrants of publicly traded securities to have their financial statements audited by independent certified public accountants. During the public hearings on these acts, Col. Arthur H. Carter, senior partner of Haskins and Sells (forerunner of Deloitte) and president of the New York State Society of Certified Public Accountants, averted a complete government takeover of the task of auditing publicly traded companies by persuading the Senate Committee on Banking and Currency not to assign the auditing function to a government agency. Instead, audits were to be performed by firms in the private sector, a development that not only highlighted the importance of the accounting profession but also triggered another quantum leap in the demand for the profession's services.

---

[1] Investment Company Institute, "Equity Ownership in America," available at www.ici.org/statements/res/rpt_05_equity_owners.pdf
[2] J. D. Edwards, *History of Public Accounting in the United States* (East Lansing, MI: Michigan State University Press, 1960), 43–44.
[3] Ibid., 48–49.
[4] J. P. Previts, *The Scope of CPA Services* (New York: John Wiley & Sons, 1985), 34–35.

The accounting field reached the peak of its standing and reputation in the United States beginning in the 1940s and continuing through the mid-1960s. During this era the public accounting business was practiced as a profession rather than as an "industry." Strong codes of professional ethics among accounting firms discouraged price competition. Partners at accounting firms were rewarded and recognized for the high quality of the audit services they provided to their clients rather than for securing new business. The term *Big Eight*, referring to the eight largest public accounting firms, was coined in the 1960s.[5]

As the decade of the 1960s closed, however, new economic forces began to impinge upon public accounting, gradually transforming the biggest firms from organizations strongly imbued with professional values to firms that pursued the profit-making goals associated with conventional business success. Until 1972, the partners of the Big Eight firms had kept themselves at the forefront of the process of setting accounting principles, the ways and means by which companies assemble, compute, and report financial information to the public. In 1972, however, the Financial Accounting Standards Board (FASB) was created and has been the predominant standard setter ever since. This development removed Big Eight partners from center stage in shaping and setting accounting standards; by the 1980s the Big Eight partners had completely withdrawn from active public dialog about accounting principles.[6]

Another key event occurred in 1977, when the Supreme Court ruled in *Bates vs. State Bar of Arizona* that lawyers could advertise, and that professional codes of ethics prohibiting advertising by lawyers constituted an illegal restraint of trade in violation of the antitrust laws.[7] The American Institute of Certified Public Accountants (AICPA), which published and enforced the accounting profession's code of ethics, was pressed by the Department of Justice and the Federal Trade Commission (FTC), which charged that parts of the accounting field's ethics codes were in restraint of trade. The AICPA succumbed to these pressures and abolished its professional ban on competitive bidding. Then during the 1970s the FTC compelled the institute to drop rules prohibiting advertising, as well as codes proscribing uninvited solicitation of other accounting firms' clients. In the 1980s the FTC further pressured the AICPA to eliminate its professional ban on commissions and contingency fees in a change that profoundly altered the climate in which audit firms conducted their affairs. As a result of these developments, accounting firms began actively competing with each other in aggressively pursuing profits, a development that put great strains on traditional professional values,[8] and that completed the transformation of accounting from a profession into a profit-driven business.

▪▪▪ II. Industry Structure

From the 1960s to the mid-1980s the accounting industry was dominated by the Big Eight accounting firms: Arthur Andersen, Arthur Young, Coopers and Lybrand, Ernst and Whinney, Deloitte Haskins and Sells, Peat Marwick Mitchell, Price Waterhouse,

[5]S. A. Zeff, "How the U.S. Accounting Profession Got Where It Is Today: Part I." *Accounting Horizons* 17 (September 2003): 191–195.
[6]Ibid., 195–200.
[7]Philip G. Cottell and Terry M. Perlin, *Accounting Ethics: A Practical Guide for Professionals* (Westport, CT: Quorum Books, 1990), 33.
[8]Zeff, "U.S. Accounting Profession, Part I," 202.

and Touche Ross. During the 1980s the pressures unleashed by competition compelled these firms to look for new ways to expand their size and profitability. Because large accounting firms found internal growth difficult due to the obstacles associated with the formation of capital in this field, mergers became the prime means by which they expanded.

Mergers and Consolidation

The first major merger occurred in 1986 when Peat Marwick Mitchell merged with KMG Main Hurdman to create KPMG Peat Marwick. (The resulting firm has since shortened its name to KPMG.) KMG Main Hurdman had been a U.S. affiliate of Klynveld Main Goerdeler, a large European accounting firm. Because of the extensive network that Klynveld Main Goerdeler had in Europe and elsewhere abroad, the merged firm became the largest accounting firm internationally, and the second-largest accounting concern in the United States. The competitive advantages stemming from its extensive European presence induced other accounting firms to seek new growth opportunities.

Thus, in 1989 a blockbuster merger occurred when Ernst and Whinney combined with Arthur Young to form Ernst and Young (Figure 12-1). This was the first joining together of two Big Eight firms; the resulting organization became the largest accounting firm both nationally and internationally. Later that year, the two smallest of the Big Eight firms—Deloitte Haskins and Sells, and Touche Ross— merged to become Deloitte and Touche. This combination created the third-largest firm both nationally and internationally; the merged firm subsequently shortened its name to Deloitte.

A third megamerger, between Arthur Andersen and Price Waterhouse, was announced in 1989 but later called off. Over the next 9 years several other mergers were proposed but failed to come to fruition. As a result the industry operated for a decade with six dominant firms, known as the Big Six.

Then in 1998, sixth-ranked Price Waterhouse merged with fifth-ranked Coopers and Lybrand to create the field's second-largest firm, PricewaterhouseCoopers. At this juncture the industry temporarily stabilized with five major firms. Finally, in 2002 the industry consolidated to the Big Four. Andersen, the fourth-ranked firm, was indicted for obstruction of justice by the Justice Department because of its role as auditor of the collapsed Enron Corporation. This, in turn, triggered a mass exodus of Andersen partners and staff as well as clients. As a result, Andersen ceased to exist after 2002. These mergers, which collapsed the Big Eight into the Big Four (sometimes cynically referred to as the "Final Four"), are depicted in Figure 12-1.[9]

A Three-Tiered Structure

Thousands of public accounting firms provide auditing services in the United States. However, these firms operate in what is generally recognized as a three-tiered, segmented structure. At the top of this tiered structure sit the Big Four (Table 12-1). These firms are widely recognized as having the capability to audit large, multinational corporations, and they are substantially larger than other accounting firms. They have

---

[9]General Accounting Office, "Public Accounting Firms: Mandated Study on Consolidation and Competition" (July 2003): 11.

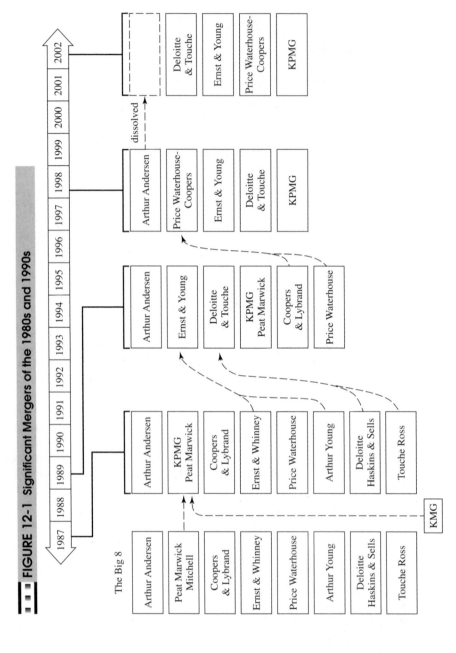

FIGURE 12-1 Significant Mergers of the 1980s and 1990s

Source: General Accounting Office, Public Accounting Firms: Mandated Study on Consolidation and Competition, July 2003, p. 11.

TABLE 12-1 Firm Size

| Firm | Fiscal Year Ending | Most Recent FYE U.S. Net Revenue (in millions) | Number of Partners | Number of Nonpartner Professionals | Number of Offices | Number of SEC Clients | Revenue Split as a Percentage | | | |
							Audit	Tax	Consulting	Other
Deloitte	May-05	$ 7,814	2,560	23,841	103	1,454	44%	30%	22%	4%
Ernst & Young	Jun-05	6,331	2,130	15,900	97	1,897	72	27	0	1
Pricewaterhouse Coopers	Jun-05	6,167	2,019	20,056	91	1,778	63	26	0	11
KPMG	Jul-05	4,359	1,607	13,184	93	1,254	77	23	0	0
Second Tier										
RSM McGladrey	Apr-06	1,281	775	4,567	125	103	46	33	18	3
Grant Thornton	Jul-06	898	444	3,575	48	411	64	25	11	0
BDO Seidman	Jun-06	558	240	1,803	34	301	62	23	15	0

thousands of partners, tens of thousands of employees, and billions of dollars in annual revenues.

Below the Big Four are the medium-sized accounting firms. The number of firms in this second tier is not universally agreed upon, but most lists would include at least three: RSM McGladrey, Grant Thornton, and BDO Seidman. Firms in this second tier have the capability to audit public companies but, as we will see, they operate at a significant competitive disadvantage because of their smaller scale.

The third tier of firms is simply all the rest. This tier contains accounting firms as small as a single practitioner, whose business consists chiefly in tax and write-up work for small businesses, up to larger regional firms that may provide audit services to non-SEC clients or to an occasional SEC client. Their ability to compete for SEC client work is severely inhibited, however.[10]

Concentration

Concentration among accounting firms is high and has increased significantly over recent years. Figure 12-2 shows that in 1988 the top four firms (Price Waterhouse, Arthur Andersen, Coopers & Lybrand, and KPMG) audited 63 percent of total public company sales. The next four firms (Ernst and Whinney, Arthur Young, Deloitte Haskins and Sells, and Touche Ross) were significant competitors, auditing 35 percent of total public company sales. By 1997, the top four firms audited 71 percent of public company sales, with two major competitors (Coopers & Lybrand and KPMG) auditing an additional 28 percent. By 2002, the top four firms audited 99 percent of public company sales with no significant competitors,[11] a situation which has remained relatively unchanged: In 2004 the Big Four had 99 of the 100 largest publicly traded Fortune companies and more than 99% of the revenue generated from the audits of those companies.[12]

Further analysis of the four-firm concentration ratio based on the total number of clients (rather than clients' sales) yields similar results. This measure of concentration increased from 51 percent in 1988, to 65 percent in 1997, reaching 78 percent in 2002. Not surprisingly, the large public segment of the client market is even more concentrated: The Big Four audit approximately 97 percent of all public companies with sales between $250 million and $5 billion, and virtually all public firms with sales greater than $5 billion.[13]

Internationally, the Big Four generate over $47 billion in global net revenue, with research by foreign regulators suggesting that the markets for audit services for large public companies in other countries are as highly concentrated as in the United States. In recent years the Big Four audited over 80 percent of all public companies in Japan, at least 90 percent of all listed companies in the Netherlands, virtually all major listed companies in the United Kingdom, and over 80 percent of listed companies in Italy.

Another method for measuring concentration is the Hirschman-Herfindahl Index (HHI), obtained by summing the squares of the market shares of individual firms. As a

---

[10]Public Accounting Report, "Annual Survey of National Accounting Firms—2003" (February 28, 2003): 3–6.
[11]General Accounting Office, "Public Accounting Firms," 21.
[12]Public Accounting Report, "PwC Is Tops in Fortune Audits" (April 15, 2004): 1.
[13]General Accounting Office, "Public Accounting Firms," 16–22.

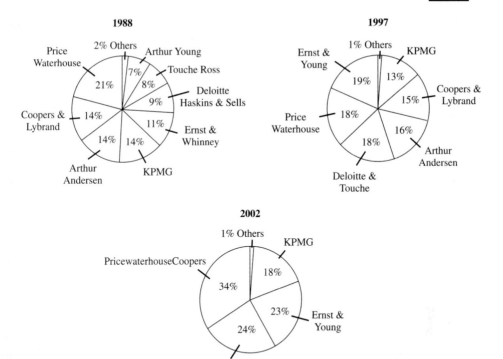

■ ■ ■ ■ **FIGURE 12-2** **Percentage of Public Company Audit Market by Total Sales Audited, 1988, 1997, and 2002.**

Source: General Accounting Office, Public Accounting Firms: Mandated Study on Consolidation and Competition, July 2003, p. 21.

general rule, an HHI below 1,000 is considered indicative of an unconcentrated market predisposed to behave competitively, whereas an HHI above 1,800 indicates a highly concentrated market in which the firms have the potential for significant market power—the ability to profitably maintain prices above competitive levels for a significant period of time (or lessen competition in other ways, such as product quality, service, or innovation). Figure 12-3 shows that following the merger of Price Waterhouse and Coopers & Lybrand, and the dissolution of Andersen, the market consists of just a handful of major firms with the potential for significant market power.[14]

Evaluated by client size, Figure 12-4 shows that HHIs (based on number of clients) for firms auditing public companies with total sales between $1 million and $100 million are all below the 1,800 threshold. However, HHIs for companies with sales over $100 million are consistently above the 1,800 threshold, again indicating the potential for significant market power in the auditing of larger companies' accounts.[15]

---

[14]Ibid., 19.
[15]Ibid., 20.

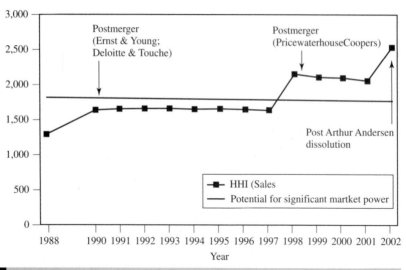

▪ ▪ ▪ **FIGURE 12-3** Hirschman-Herfindahl Indexes, 1988–2002

Source: General Accounting Office, Public Accounting Firms: Mandated Study on and Consolidation Competition, July 2003, p. 19.

The most dramatic impact of consolidation among accounting firms appears to be the limited number of auditor choices for most large national and multinational public companies should they choose to change auditors. Of the firms responding to recent surveys, 88 percent indicated they would not consider using a non–Big Four firm for their audit and attest needs. Additional evidence of reluctance to use non–Big Four firms is provided by data concerning the 1,085 former Andersen clients that changed auditors between October 2001 and December 2002. Only one large public company with assets over $5 billion that previously had been audited by Andersen switched to a non–Big Four firm. Thus for most large public firms, the maximum number of available choices of audit and attest services has declined from eight in 1988 to four today.

Client choices can be even further limited as a result of potential conflicts of interest, new independence rules (discussed in the public policy section in this chapter), and industry specialization by accounting firms, all of which may reduce even more the number of viable auditing alternatives. A hypothetical example illustrates this point: Suppose a large multinational company that used one Big Four firm for its audit and attest services and another Big Four firm for its outsourced internal audit function seeks to hire a new accounting firm because its board of directors has decided that the company should change auditors every seven years. In this case, the company would appear to have only two remaining alternatives if it believed that only Big Four firms had the resources needed to audit its operations. However, one of the remaining two Big Four firms might not enter a bid because its market niche in this particular industry encompasses only smaller companies. Consequently the large multinational firm would be left with only one alternative. Conceivably, other circumstances might arise in which a company could have *no* viable alternatives for global audit and attest needs.[16]

---

[16]Ibid., 25–30.

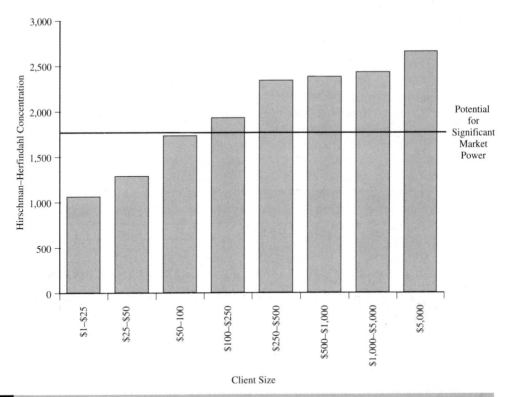

▪▪▪▪ **FIGURE 12-4** Hirschman-Herfindahl Indexes (Based on Number of Clients), 2002

Source: General Accounting Office, "Public Accounting Firms: Mandated Study on Consilidation and Competition", July 2003, p. 20.

In fact, Dennis Nally, the CEO of PricewaterhouseCoopers, goes so far as to claim that if one of the remaining Big Four firms were to fail, the audit industry as we know it today would simply cease to exist.[17]

Barriers to Expansion

In a recent in-depth study, the General Accounting Office (GAO) identified five significant barriers to entry and expansion of smaller accounting firms attempting to compete for the audit work of large corporate clients. First, smaller firms generally lack the staff, technical expertise, and global reach to audit the far-flung operations of major multinational companies. Large corporations that responded to a survey affirmed this finding. Of the large companies that stated they would not consider using a non–Big Four auditor, 91 percent said that the capacity of smaller firms was of great or very great importance in their unwillingness to do so. This problem is particularly daunting with respect to professional staff. As Table 12-1 above shows, the smallest of the Big Four has more than twice as many partners, and three times as many nonpartner professionals, as the largest second-tier firm. Because of the complexity of large national

---

[17]Dennis Nally, address delivered at Miami University, Oxford, Ohio, March 22, 2007.

and multinational firms, it is not uncommon for an audit engagement to require hundreds of staff personnel, which most smaller accounting firms cannot afford to commit to any single client. This obviously limits their ability to compete with the Big Four for large audit clients. Yet, without having large clients, it is difficult to build the capacity needed to attract large clients. In fact, as Table 12-2 shows, the gap between the first and second tier of public accounting firms widened considerably between 1988 and 2002. However, since that time the gap has narrowed a bit in some dimensions. This disparity has resulted in a dual market structure—one market where the Big Four compete with several smaller accounting firms for the accounts of medium and small public companies, and another where essentially only the Big Four compete to audit the largest corporate clients.

A second barrier is reputation. Smaller accounting firms face a challenge in establishing recognition and credibility among large national and multinational public companies, on the one hand, and among capital market participants on the other. Some large corporations surveyed by the GAO reported that although some smaller accounting firms have the capability to provide audit services to large multinational companies, the boards of directors of those concerns might not consider retaining the services of smaller auditing firms as an option. Other respondents stated that despite recent accounting scandals involving the Big Four, many capital market participants and investors continue to expect audit opinions to come from one of the Big Four. Thus, firms seeking to establish or maintain their credibility in the capital markets may continue to engage one of the Big Four.

TABLE 12-2 Gap Between First- and Second-Tier Firms

Accounting Firm	Average Real Revenue (in millions)	Average Number of Partners	Average Number of Nonpartner Professional Staff	Average Number of Offices	Average Number of SEC Clients
			1988		
Big Eight	$1,566	1,126	10,991	105	1,359
Next Tier	$ 288	364	2,118	57	234
Gap	**$1,278**	**762**	**8,874**	**48**	**1,125**
			2002		
Big Four	$4,468	2,029	15,664	101	2,046
Next Tier	$ 290	292	1,532	47	245
Gap	**$4,178**	**1,736**	**14,132**	**54**	**1,801**
			2005		
Big Four	$6,168	2,079	18,245	96	1,596
Next Tier	$912	486	3,315	69	272
Gap	**$5,256**	**1,593**	**14,930**	**27**	**1,324**

Source: General Accounting Office, Public Accounting Firms: Mandated Study on Consolidation and Competition, Washington, D.C., July 2003. The GAO added an additional firm, Crowe, Chizek and Company to the second tier. The 1988 second-tier firms include Laventhol & Horwath. Crowe Chizek and Company replaced this now nonexistent firm in the 2002 data. Gap figures may not sum due to rounding.

A third barrier to auditing the very largest clients' financial accounts is risk and liability. Many second-tier firms consider the litigation risks and insurance costs associated with auditing the largest companies to make expansion into that segment less attractive. Even if smaller firms were able to purchase additional insurance to manage the increased risk associated with auditing large public firms, they would still lack the size to achieve economies of scale by spreading their litigation risk and insurance costs over a larger base. As a result, many second-tier accounting firms believe they have more attractive opportunities for growth in the mid-sized segment of the public company audit market and in the private company audit area, where risk-return prospects are more attractive.

A fourth barrier is capital formation. Large amounts of capital would have to be raised to build the organizational infrastructure required to compete with the Big Four in the large public company audit market. Public accounting firms are effectively prohibited by law from operating under a corporate structure. Thus the ability to raise outside capital is severely limited because under the partnership structure in which accounting firms must operate, access to equity markets by selling stock is unavailable. To expand their operations, smaller accounting firms thus must look to other options, such as borrowing, merging with other accounting firms, or tapping the personal resources of their partners and employees. But raising capital through borrowing is difficult because accounting firms are professional service organizations whose primary asset is the expertise of their employees, and they thus lack the collateral required to secure loans. Mergers, internal growth, and the personal resources of partners also do not seem to afford viable options for raising the large amounts of capital needed to compete to audit the accounts of large clients.

Finally, state laws and regulations—primarily those dealing with licensing requirements—represent a fifth significant barrier. Firms wishing to expand nationally face the burden and expense of obtaining licenses for staff members in individual states across the country. All 50 states, the District of Columbia, Guam, Puerto Rico, and the U.S. Virgin Islands have varying laws governing the licensing of certified public accountants, including varying requirements for education, examinations, and expertise. Moreover, potential state and federal duplication of regulatory oversight pose a proportionately greater burden for smaller firms than for the Big Four. This barrier may have been compounded by passage of the Sarbanes-Oxley Act, discussed subsequently, which calls for greater regulatory oversight of accounting firms' compliance with auditing standards and rules.[18]

■■■ III. Industry Conduct

In the heyday of public accounting, the Big Eight refrained from using price as a basis for competition. Instead, the field prided itself on being a profession where hard competition was considered unseemly and discouraged. The Big Eight openly charged higher prices than their smaller rivals, justifying their higher fees by insisting that the client was paying for a quality audit. Throughout the 1970s, accounting firms, abstaining from advertising, gained their reputations by taking tough stands in interpreting

---

[18]General Accounting Office, "Public Accounting Firms," 45–52.

and enforcing accounting standards without regard to the consequences for retaining, or losing, their clients. The guiding presumption was that clients wanted their auditors to keep them out of trouble and, therefore, wanted their auditors to object if an accounting practice might lead to problems in the future. In effect, the policy of being tough on accounting standards was the core of what today would be considered an accounting firm's competitive strategy.[19]

The Advent of Price Competition

Several developments induced the profession to abandon the "profession" paradigm and begin to behave more like a conventional, profit-driven industry. We have seen that antitrust actions by the Federal Trade Commission and the Department of Justice forced the profession to repeal its ethics codes discouraging competitive bidding and direct solicitation of clients. With the fetters of ethics removed, firms began to more vigorously compete with one another. S. A. Zeff relates an anecdote exemplifying the sea change in attitude that occurred among the top managers of large accounting firms:

> The arrival of a profoundly altered competitive climate in the practice of public accounting was underscored in a remark attributed to Michael Cook [partner-in-charge of Deloitte and Touche, now Deloitte] in 1985: "Five years ago if a client of another firm came to me and complained about the service, I'd immediately warn the other firm's chief executive. . . . Today I try to take away his client."[20]

At the same time the large accounting firms began to aggressively compete with each other, opportunities for growth in the market for audit services began to diminish. As a result, the top managements of the large accounting firms began to emphasize other services, particularly tax and consulting services, as more lucrative ways to expand. These service lines not only were more profitable, they offered greater growth opportunities as well.

Merger activity among their corporate clients reinforced these commercial pressures on accounting firms. First came pressure from merging clients to show healthy earnings to demonstrate the success of the mergers and acquisitions they had undertaken. Second, mergers caused accounting firms to lose accounts as two clients merged to form one. Third, merged corporations put further downward price pressure on audit fees. As a result of these factors, by the 1990s the audit market was saturated, and accounting firms competed by looking to other areas for growth and profitability including, most notably, the provision of management consulting services.

As their consulting practices grew, the Big Eight eventually dropped requirements that members of the firms' management qualify as CPAs, the credential that had long been the hallmark of the profession. Because consultants were able to generate higher-margin work, they put pressure on their colleagues in the other two main branches of the industry, audit and tax services. Gradually the emphasis of those members of the firms, too, shifted toward profitability. Since audit and tax work did not produce high

---

[19]A. R. Wyatt, "Accounting Professionalism—They Just Don't Get It!" Address at the annual meeting of the American Accounting Association, Honolulu, Hawaii, August 4, 2003.
[20]S. A. Zeff, "How the U.S. Accounting Profession Got Where It Is Today: Part II," *Accounting Horizons* 17 (December 2003): 272.

and growing profits, audit partners were encouraged to bring in consulting work. Cross-selling a range of consulting services to clients became an important criterion in evaluating the job performance of audit partners. Those with technical accounting and auditing skills previously considered vital to internal firm advancement found themselves increasingly relegated to marginal roles.

As Wyatt sees it, these attitudinal changes in the auditing field paralleled some less desirable changes in American business more generally:

> Just as greed appears to have been the driving force at many of the companies that have failed or had significant restructurings, greed became a force to contend with in the accounting firms. In essence, the cultures of the firms had gradually changed from a central emphasis on delivering professional services in a professional manner to an emphasis on growing revenue and profitability. The gradual change resulted in the firm culture being drastically altered over the forty years leading up to the end of the century. The historical focus of accounting firms was on quality of service to clients in order to provide assurance to investors and creditors on the fairness of the clients' financial statements. The credibility added to a client's financial statements by the clean audit opinion was the central reason for a CPA firm's existence. This focus gave way to a focus on an ever expanding range of services offered to a client pool fighting to achieve the short term earnings per share growth expected of them in the marketplace.[21]

In an era when competition among accounting firms increasingly focused on consulting services, profits on audit fees became razor thin. Indeed, in many cases they came to be, in effect, loss leaders: Accounting firms were willing to accept lower audit fees because they believed the audit process allowed them to get a foot in the door to do more lucrative consulting work. As a result, in some cases auditors found themselves auditing the very services that their colleagues in the firm had sold to the client—a conflict of interest rife with opportunities for abuse.

Following the collapse of Arthur Andersen, however, the behavior of the remaining Big Four has significantly changed. Due to pressure from regulatory authorities as well as from market forces, three of the Big Four have divested themselves of their consulting practices. (Deloitte is the exception.) This, in turn, has ushered in a new era in which firms are expected to engage even more fiercely in price competition in providing their auditing services.

The Behavior of Fees

Audit fees generally remained flat or decreased slightly from the late 1980s through the mid-1990s, but since then have been rising on an inflation-adjusted basis. It is not possible to isolate the effects of consolidation and competition from several other changes in the economy that have affected the accounting field and how the firms conduct their business. These changes include evolving changes in audit scope (the magnitude of effort firms employ during an audit engagement); technological developments;

---

[21]Wyatt, "Accounting Professionalism."

the growth of management consulting services; evolving audit standards; and legal reforms that have altered audit firms' legal liabilities.[22]

One difficulty in studying price competition in the auditing industry is the paucity of data concerning changes in audit fees over time. One study used a proxy measure—audit revenues for the accounting firm divided by the dollar value of client assets audited—as a surrogate for the audit fee. The results indicated that this price measure fell for merging and nonmerging accounting firms alike.[23] Another study used audit fees charged to a small sample of companies. This analysis found that the average audit fee per client declined from $3.4 million in 1989 to $2.8 million in 1997 on an inflation-adjusted basis. Although the results were limited because of the small sample size, the study found no evidence that Big Six mergers had produced a permanent increase in audit fees.[24]

In addition, the Manufacturers Alliance conducts a periodic survey of the audit fees paid by 130 firms. This survey indicates a downward trend in audit fees per $100 of public company revenues from 1989 through 1995. (The latter year is important because of enactment of the Private Securities Litigation Reform Act, which limited the legal liability exposure of accounting firms.) The survey found a slight increase in audit fees from 1995 through 1999 for U.S. and foreign companies; it also revealed that American companies paid lower audit fees than their foreign counterparts over the survey period.

The General Accounting Office has used its own proxy—net average audit revenues for top-tier firms as a percentage of total sales audited—to analyze the behavior of audit fees. They also have found that audit fees declined slightly from 1989 through 1995, but rose from 1995 through 2001. However, no determination could be made as to whether mergers and consolidation had negatively or positively impacted audit fees in either period.

Although audit fees constitute only a tiny fraction of the expenses of a public company being audited, some evidence suggests that these fees have increased most recently, with indications that they may rise further in the years ahead. As we have seen, some experts contend that during the 1980s and 1990s audit services became loss leaders for accounting firms to gain entry into more lucrative professional service markets, primarily management consulting services. Once the new client had been secured, the firm would develop a relationship with the client and use it as a basis for selling additional services. While a low audit fee might not cover the cost of the audit, high-margin fees generated from the additional consulting services could conceivably more than cover shortfalls from audit work. With accounting firms now cutting back on some of these other lines of service, however, they may have to raise their audit fees to make up for these lost profits. For this reason, evidence of flat and low audit fees since 1989 may reveal little about the potential for exercising pricing power in the future.

After the passage of Sarbanes-Oxley, market participants, experts, and academics agreed that prices were likely to rise further as a result of new regulatory requirements

---

[22]General Accounting Office, "Public Accounting Firms," 31.
[23]S. Ivancevich and A. Zardkoohi, "An Exploratory Analysis of the 1989 Accounting Megamergers," *Accounting Horizons* 14 (2000): 136–155.
[24]K. Menon and D. Williams, "Long-Term Trends in Audit Fees," *Auditing: A Journal of Practice and Theory* 20 (2001): 115–136.

and related changes in the scope of audit services. Moreover, auditing standards themselves will likely increase the amount of audit work required in an engagement. According to the Public Accounting Report, research shows that audit fees rose a whopping 30.1 percent for Fortune 100 firms in 2001, followed by a 17.8 percent increase in 2002. The *Washington Post* reported that audit fees for the Fortune 1000 increased by an average of $2.3 million, or 66% percent between 2003 and 2004. The audit bills of 12 of the 648 companies responding to another survey rose more than $10 million.[25] During this period *Accountancy Age* reported that PricewaterhouseCoopers was able to increase its audit revenue by a massive 134% due largely to Section 404 of the Sarbanes-Oxley Act; KPMG experienced 109% growth, Ernst & Young 96% growth and Deloitte brought up the rear with a still whooping 78% growth.[26] Experts expect double-digit audit fee growth rates to continue for the foreseeable future. According to Mark Cheffers, a consultant on auditor liability, more thorough oversight of auditing and greater scrutiny of consulting fees will drive these increases. In addition, firms will find themselves in the position of having to raise rates to compensate for the additional liability risks they face in a post-Enron environment.[27] Because of these complexities, no overall conclusion can yet be reached regarding the influence of market power, high concentration, or anticompetitive behavior on the fees charged by large accounting firms.[28]

Competition in Labor Markets

In addition to competing for clients, the Big Four aggressively compete in the labor market for talented people. Evidence of this abounds on college campuses each fall, where Big Four recruiting efforts take on the tenor of fraternity and sorority rush, including expansive tents where food and clothing with the firms' logos are freely distributed. Nor is competition in the labor market restricted to college campuses. Firms constantly mine their clients and their competitors for qualified people as well. This is in marked contrast to earlier years when the accounting profession was more stable. In the "good old days," an employee either stayed with the firm for an entire career or, if he or she chose to leave, would not expect to be rehired by the same firm. Contrast that environment with the recent one at Andersen shortly before its collapse, where the firm had a "boomerang award" for professionals who were returning, a not uncommon event.

Concern does exist, however, about the accounting profession's ability to continue to attract the best and the brightest. One former national partner has opined that when accounting firms no longer operate in the glamorous consulting business, they will be less able to attract the best and the brightest talent for the more mundane auditing function,[29] a development which, should it come to pass, could adversely affect the quality of audits generally.

---

[25]C. Johnson, "Higher Audit Fees, More Accountability: Sarbanes-Oxley, Three Years Later," *Washington Post* (July 30, 2005): D1.

[26]*Accountancy Age*, available at www.accountancyage.com/accountancyage/news/2036847/audit-fees-double

[27]Public Accounting Report, "Fortune 100 Audit Fees Expected to Increase in 2003 and Beyond" (May 31, 2003): 2.

[28]General Accounting Office, "Public Accounting Firms," 32–35.

[29]Personal interview with David Phillips, October 31, 2003.

IV. Industry Performance

Performance involves an assessment of how efficiently and effectively an industry discharges its economic role. Accounting, however, differs from other industries in an important and unique way. Firms in other industries meet buyer demand by providing a service or producing a product efficiently and profitably. The auditing industry, however, furnishes something that goes far beyond this. Its role is one of ensuring the integrity and accuracy of the financial information on which the financial functioning of the entire economy depends. Moreover, those who depend on the services provided by auditors—the public and investors—do not pay for this service. Because of this, the issue of independence is of paramount importance in assessing the performance of this field.

Concentration and Competition

Despite the high degree of concentration among accounting firms, no evidence to date indicates that competition in the field has been impaired. The GAO conducted one set of economic tests to ascertain whether consolidation in the auditing industry has had any discernible anticompetitive effects. They employed a simple model of pure price competition to determine whether the high degree of concentration in the market for audit services was inconsistent with a price-competitive process. (The model is designed to simulate a market driven by pure price competition, in which clients choose auditors solely on the basis of price; neither quality nor reputation, for example, are incorporated in the model.) The GAO's simulation results suggest that a market driven solely by price competition could result in a high degree of market concentration in accountancy: The model generated simulated market shares that were close to the actual market shares of the Big Four. Specifically, the model predicted that in a purely price-competitive world the Big Four would audit 64 percent of companies in the sampled market, which is very close to the actual market share of 62.2 percent for the companies included in the simulation. Moreover, the GAO's model predicted that the Big Four would audit 96.3 percent of companies in the sample with assets greater than $250 million, compared to the 97 percent of these companies actually audited by the Big Four in 2002.

While the evidence to date does not appear to indicate that competition in the market for audit services has been undermined, the increased level of concentration, coupled with recently imposed restrictions on the provision of nonaudit services by auditors to their clients, could increase the potential for collusive behavior or the exercise of market power in the future.

The Quality of Auditing

A host of theories have been expounded as to how competition among accounting firms, auditor tenure, and accounting firm size might impact audit quality. Restatements of financial statements due to accounting improprieties provide one proxy for measuring audit quality. Several recent studies have found financial restatements as a result of accounting irregularities to have increased over recent years, especially for larger corporations. This evidence suggests that audit quality may have been deteriorating. Because larger companies typically employ larger accounting firms that traditionally have been perceived as providing higher quality audits, the trend toward larger company financial restatements further heightens concerns about audit quality. During the years leading up to the passage of Sarbanes-Oxley, the GAO found it especially disturbing that in some high-profile restatement cases it appeared that auditors identified problems but failed to ensure that clients appropriately addressed their concerns, thus raising questions about auditor independence and audit quality.[30]

A recent report by the SEC lends credence to these concerns (see Table 12-3): The SEC determined that financial reporting and disclosure violations rose nearly 64 percent over the 5-year period it examined.[31] Moreover, the trend of increasing restatements accelerated: The number of revisions of financial reports by publicly traded companies surged to a record 1,295 in 2005, nearly double the previous year's mark of 650. The total number of 2005 restatements works out to one restatement for every 12 public companies compared with one for every 23 public companies in 2004.[32]

The upward trend in restatements continued in 2006. According to research by Glass Lewis, companies with U.S.-listed securities filed 1,538 financial restatements in 2006, up 13% from 2005.[33] Some company officials and other observers blame the complexity and overreaching requirements of the Sarbanes-Oxley Act for the rise in restatements. Others disagree, maintaining that investors are getting better information because of the act.

Smaller firms were more likely to have restatements but smaller firms are where financial reporting problems have historically existed. In fact, Glass Lewis reported that 2006 saw a 14 percent decrease in the number of restatements from companies that were mandated to comply with the controversial Section 404 of the Sarbanes Oxley Act. Glass Lewis concluded this was evidence the larger companies were making progress on "cleaning up their books." On the other hand, the smaller

---

TABLE 12-3 Financial Reporting and Disclosure Violations

Year End July 31	Violations	Increase	Percent Increase	Cumulative Increase	Cumulative Percent
1998	91				
1999	61	(31)	(34.1%)	(31)	(34.1%)
2000	110	50	83.3	19	20.9
2001	105	(5)	4.5	14	15.4
2002	149	44	41.9	58	63.7

Source: Securities and Exchange Commission, Report Pursuant to Section 704 of the Sarbanes-Oxley Act of 2002, Washington, D.C., 2003. Available at www.sec.gov/news/studies/sox704report.pdf

---

[30]General Accounting Office, "Public Accounting Firms," 36–37.
[31]Securities and Exchange Commission, "Report Pursuant to Section 704 of the Sarbanes-Oxley Act of 2002," (Washington, D.C., 2003), 1–2. Available at www.sec.gov/news/studies/sox704report.pdf
[32]Government Accountability Office, "Financial Restatements: Update of Public Company Trends, Market Impacts, and Regulatory Enforcement Activities," March 5, 2007.
[33]S. Taub, "Study: Restatements Up, but SarBox Works" CFO.com, February 28, 2007. Available at www.cfo.com/article.cfm/8769763?f=search

companies—those not yet required to comply with Section 404—had a 40 percent increase in restatements.[34]

Interestingly, companies audited by the smallest audit firms were six times more likely to restate than those audited by the Big Four. The auditor with the highest restatement rate (12 percent) was Grant Thornton; the Big Four auditor with the highest restatement rate (7.1 percent) was KPMG.[35] When this fact is coupled with the fact that the Big Four are abandoning their more risky audit clients, the problem of quality audits compounds.

The Importance of Independence

Auditor independence and audit quality are inextricably linked. In fact, most would consider auditor independence itself to be an integral component of the quality of the audit performed. To make intelligent investment decisions, investors must rely on financial statements published by publicly held corporations. It is the auditor's opinion that furnishes investors with assurance that the client firm's financial statements have been subjected to a rigorous examination by an objective, impartial, and skilled professional, and that investors, therefore, can rely on their accuracy.[36] To effectively perform its function, an auditor thus must take an unbiased viewpoint when conducting audit tests, when evaluating the results of those tests, and when issuing reports and opinions concerning the client's financial statements.

Independence exists at three distinct levels. At the first, and highest, level is the honesty, objectivity, and responsibility that enables the auditor to take an unbiased stance. The second level of independence refers to the relationship of the auditor to the client. Here independence means avoiding any relationship that would be likely, even subconsciously, to impair the auditor's ability to take an unbiased viewpoint. Thus, the public accountant must avoid personal and business relationships with clients that could cause even the most well-meaning person to compromise his or her professional judgment. On the third level, independence means the auditor should avoid any relationship with a client that might suggest to a reasonable observer that a conflict of interest exists. The common terminology used in the auditing field to describe these concepts are *independence in fact* and *independence in appearance*.

Independence is one of the most elusive characteristics of professional conduct in the accounting profession. We have little basis to doubt independence in fact in a particular circumstance until the most dramatic of events, an audit failure, comes to light. An audit failure occurs when an independent auditor opines to third parties that a client's financial statements are fairly presented in accordance with generally accepted accounting principles when, in fact, they are not. Investigations following these failures often reveal a lack of independence in fact as a primary contributing factor.[37] A lack of independence in fact on the part of Anderson conceivably contributed to the most

---

[34]Ibid.

[35]S. Taub, "Restatements Surged in 2005, Says Study," CFO.Com, March 6, 2006. Available at www.cfo.com/article.cfm/5591688/1/c_5591729.

[36]Securities and Exchange Commission, "Final Rule: Revision of the Commission's Auditor Independence Requirements" (Washington, D.C., 2003). Available at www.sec.gov/rules/final/33-7919.htm

[37]Cottell and Perlin, *Accounting Ethics*, 29–32.

dramatic audit failure in history, that of Enron.[38] In the case of other recent high-profile audit failures such as Sunbeam Corporation, Xerox, WorldCom, Waste Management, and Adelphia Communications, speculation and charges have swirled around independence of fact issues and questions.

Independence in appearance refers to the perception of others about an auditor's independence. Most of the value of the audit report stems from the belief by investors that an objective, unbiased review has been conducted concerning the financial reports being published. Therefore, if auditors are independent in fact, but readers of financial statements or members of the public believe them to be advocates for the client, most of the value of the audit function is lost. Users of financial information can have faith in an auditor's representations only when they are confident that the auditor has acted as an impartial judge. The very credibility of the public accounting profession thus ultimately depends on this perception of independence (rather than the fact of independence).[39]

Despite the high profile of failures in the auditing and financial world, these matters should be kept in perspective. When one considers the sheer number of audits conducted by large public accounting firms each year, as well as the immense complexity of the audits of large multinational corporations, the miracle is that so few audit failures occur. The reason financial failures of large companies attract headline news, in other words, is because they are so rare.

The Issue of the Scope of Services Provided

The importance of independence leads to another unique dimension of the performance of this field. This is the "scope of services" issue: Whether nonaudit practice is appropriate for a public accounting firm, and whether there is a point at which nonaudit practice, particularly consulting, begins to overwhelm independence on the audit side, thereby jeopardizing audit quality and putting at risk the accounting firm's duty to the public.

As we have seen, the growth of consulting services by the Big Eight began to accelerate rapidly from the mid-1970s onward. Table 12-4 shows the percentage of fees earned by the largest public accounting firms in their three primary lines of business: accounting and auditing, tax services, and management consulting. Note that in 1975 all of the Big Eight generated over 60 percent of their gross revenues from accounting and auditing practice. By 2000, however, none of the Big Five generated even half of their gross revenues from accounting and auditing. The most dramatic change occurred at PricewaterhouseCoopers. Its predecessor, Price Waterhouse & Co., was known as the firm that shunned management consulting work prior to the mid-1970s, but its percentage of gross revenue from consulting grew from 8 percent at that time to nearly 50 percent by 2000.[40]

---

[38]In pleading guilty in early 2004 to federal charges, Enron's former chief financial officer, Andrew Fastow, said that he "and other members of Enron's senior management fraudulently manipulated Enron's publicly reported financial results. Our purpose was to mislead investors and others about the true financial position of Enron and, consequently, to inflate artificially the price of Enron's stock and maintain fraudulently Enron's credit rating." John R. Emschwiller and Thaddeus Herrick, "Fastow Plea Deal May Boost Cases Against Enron's Ex-CEOs," *Wall Street Journal* (January 15, 2004): A3.

[39]Cottell and Perlin, *Accounting Ethics*, 33.

[40]Zeff, "Accounting Profession, Part II," 270.

TABLE 12-4 Percentage of Gross Fees Derived from Accounting and Auditing/Tax/Management Consulting Work

	1975	1990	2000	
Arthur Andersen & Co.	66/18/16	35/21/44		Arthur Andersen & Co./Andersen Consulting
		48/38/14	43/31/26	Arthur Andersen & Co.
Price Waterhouse & Co.	76/16/8	51/26/23	33/18/49	Pricewaterhouse-Coopers
Coopers & Lybrand	69/19/12	56/19/25		
Peat Marwick Mitchell	68/21/11	53/27/20	45/38/17	KPMG
Ernst & Ernst	73/17/10	53/25/22	44/30/26	Ernst & Young
Arthur Young & Company	69/17/14			
Haskins & Sells	74/15/11	57/23/20	31/20/49	Deloitte & Touche
Touche Ross & Co.	62/24/14			

Sources: 1975: *The Accounting Establishment* (1976, 30).

1990: *International Accounting Bulletin*, Issue No. 84 (March 1991), p. 13, and the firms' annual reports for 1990 to the SEC Practice Section of the AICPA's Division for CPA Firms.

2000: The firms' annual reports for 2000 to the SEC Practice Section of the AICPA's Division for CPA Firms.

By 1994, the SEC grew increasingly alarmed about this trend toward consulting and away from traditional auditing. One SEC concern was the threat this development posed to auditor independence and objectivity; another concern was the expanding role of nonaudit personnel, who are not bound by the accounting profession's code of ethics, at the top management levels of accounting firms. These concerns grew as the decade of the 1990s progressed. At the same time, concern was growing about a phenomenon known as the "intimidation factor"—the inability of an individual auditor to withstand pressure from an aggressive client.[41]

Following the collapse of Andersen, and in response to public outcry, the Big Four took steps to address these concerns. Three of the Big Four have spun off their consulting wings; today, only Deloitte remains a large accounting firm with a significant consulting business. (Three of the leading second-tier firms continue to maintain consulting practices.) As Figure 12-5 shows, among the 100 largest public accounting firms the percentage of revenue from consulting has steadily decreased since 2000, while the percentage from auditing has steadily increased. In addition, developments also indicate that large public accounting firms are taking steps to disassociate themselves from clients they suspect might cause potential problems. As Table 12-5 shows, 23 percent of the audit changes experienced by the Big Four and the second tier are attributable to voluntary resignation by the auditing firm, rather than to dismissal by the client.

---

[41]Ibid., 269–280.

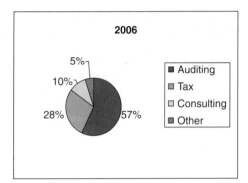

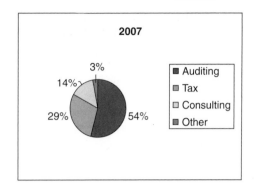

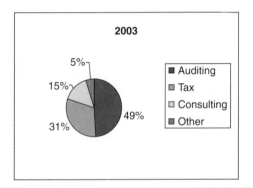

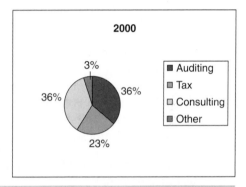

▪ ▪ ▪ ▪ **FIGURE 12-5** Breakdown of Accounting Firm Revenue

Source: Public Accounting Report, August 31, 2006.

TABLE 12-5 Dismissals and Resignations: 2006

Auditor	*Audit Client Changes*	*Dismissals*	*Voluntary Resignations*	*Percent Change Due to Resignation*
Deloitte	68	52	16	23.5%
Ernst & Young	85	70	15	17.6
KPMG	72	56	16	22.2
PricewaterhouseCoopers	125	101	24	19.2
BDO Seidman	36	21	15	41.7
Crowe	4	3	1	25.0
Grant Thornton	30	20	10	33.3
McGladrey & Pullen	7	6	1	14.3
Totals	427	329	98	23.0

Source: Public Accounting Report, September 30, 2006.

The trend toward a rising resignation rate began in the late 1990s and has jumped substantially since 2001. Accounting firms also have become focused on the risk profiles of their clients. They increasingly scrutinize the strength of the client's audit committees, the independence of its board of directors, and its practices concerning financial reporting generally. This trend peaked in 2003 when the change due to resignation was 30.4 percent.[42] The Big Four resignation rate dropped significantly in the fourth quarter of 2005, the biggest drop since the year 2001. Because the resignation rate has fallen steadily since 2003, the rate may be beginning to stabilize, although it is too early to tell conclusively. However, local and regional auditor resignations ticked up during the period, leaving the overall resignation rate a shade higher.[43]

From a performance perspective, the accounting firms' decision to abandon high-risk clients has important but conflicting implications. On the one hand, it has the desirable effect of motivating client companies to clean up their operations and procedures. The inability to retain an auditor is expensive both in terms of finding a new auditor and, more importantly, in the capital markets where it may raise the firm's cost of obtaining capital. On the other hand, abandoned clients may obtain audits of lesser quality, thereby potentially depriving the investing public of better financial information.

The majority of SEC registrants who were dropped by Big Four audit firms were absorbed by non–Big Four firms with local and regional firms gaining the most audit clients.[44] This has had a dual effect: On the one hand competition has been enhanced because opportunities have been provided for smaller audit firms to become more active in the market for audit services. On the other hand, from a public policy standpoint, those firms that pose the most risk to the investing public may be receiving a lower quality audit.

▪▪▪ V. Public Policy

Over the 40 years following enactment of the Securities Acts of 1933 and 1934, the public accounting profession thrived as a self-regulated institution. The SEC, which had the authority to regulate the industry, took a hands-off approach. This arrangement worked well, chiefly because accountants took great pride in their professionalism. Although they lived comfortably, the temptation to amass great wealth was seemingly lacking. Moreover, the profession held market forces at bay with a code of ethics which, as we have seen, discouraged aggressive competition.

By law, accounting standards—the rules that guide the preparation of corporate financial statements—are the province of the SEC, which has, however, traditionally delegated this responsibility to accounting practitioners. Until 1972 the profession performed the function of setting accounting standards through the American Institute of Certified Public Accountants (AICPA). However, in the early 1970s controversy arose about the AICPA's standard-setting body, the Accounting Principles Board (APB). Critics claimed that the APB was too dominated by the Big Eight, who, in turn, were

---

[42]Public Accounting Report, "Largest Firms Taking Proactive Stance to Dumping Clients" (November 15, 2003): 1, 7.
[43]Public Accounting Report, "Big Four SEC Resignation Rate Plummets" (January 15, 2007): 5.
[44]D. V. Rama and W. J. Reas, "Resignation by the Big 4 and the Market for Audit Services," *Accounting Horizons* 20 (June 2006): 97–109.

believed to be susceptible to influence by their clients in setting accounting standards. As a result of these concerns, the AICPA was compelled to yield that function to a newly created body, the Financial Accounting Standards Board (FASB) in 1972. Since then, accounting standards described as Generally Accepted Accounting Principles (GAAP) have been established by the FASB through its Statements on Financial Accounting Standards and historically have been supported by the SEC. Although the AICPA lost its influence in setting financial accounting standards, it retained its authority to establish standards and guidelines governing the conduct of audits, a role it retained until the recent eruption of corporate financial scandals. Since then the role of the AICPA in this area, too, has begun to erode with greater public and government scrutiny of the functions and duties of external auditors.

Winds of change are blowing in the profession with respect to standard setting. Accounting standards for U. S. reporting companies presently are governed under GAAP. For the rest of the world, standards are found in International Financial Reporting Standards (IFRS). With the world shrinking and an increasingly global economy, two sets of accounting standards make less and less sense. In fact, Dennis Nally, CEO of PricewaterhouseCoopers flatly predicts that IFRS will become the single worldwide accounting standard in the near future.[45] However, because that would require the powerful FASB and SEC to abdicate significant authority and influence, this result is hardly assured.[46]

Meanwhile, the SEC is taking an increasingly active role with respect to the FASB and, thus, ultimately in the setting of accounting standards. In March, 2007, the foundation that oversees the FASB agreed to give the SEC more involvement in the process governing appointments to the FASB. One member calls this "a big step on a slippery slope toward the SEC becoming the parent of the FASB." Arthur Levitt, former SEC chairman, acknowledges that this changed appointment process raises the specter of political influence. However, he contends that the risk of undue political pressure is offset by the danger in the current system whereby special interests in the business and accounting community exert undue influence over the setting of accounting standards.[47]

The SEC and Independence

During the 1990s the SEC became increasingly concerned about the independence question. With criticism of the auditing industry growing, the AICPA appointed an Advisory Panel on Auditor Independence to examine the issue. This panel expressed dissatisfaction with the practice of the Big Five in expressing their clients' views before the FASB in its standard-setting deliberations because it seemed to violate the principle of independence in appearance. In 1996, SEC Chairman Arthur Levitt issued a stern warning to the profession:

> I'm deeply concerned that "independence" and "objectivity" are increasingly regarded by some [in the accounting profession] as quaint notions. . . . I caution

---

[45]D. Nally, address at Miami University, Oxford, Ohio, March 22, 2007.
[46]See "Speaking in Tongues," *Economist* (May 19, 2007): 77–78.
[47]D. Reilly and K. Scannell, "SEC Is to Get More Sway Over FASB," *Wall Street Journal* (March 28, 2007): C1–C2.

the [accounting] industry, if I may borrow a Biblical phrase, not to "gain the whole world, and lose [its] own soul."[48]

In its role of providing regulatory oversight to the public accounting industry, the SEC has issued rules governing the independence of auditors. In 2003 the SEC issued a significant modification of these rules entitled "Final Rule: Revision of the Commission's Auditor Independence Requirements."[49] These new rules encompass four key principles for identifying relationships that impermissibly render an accountant not independent of an audit client in the eyes of the SEC.

The first principle involves financial and employment relationships. Prior to modification, the rule attributed to an entire auditing firm the ownership of stock shares held by every partner in the firm, including managerial employees and their families. Interpretation of this rule tended to be quite captious. For example, suppose the spouse of a partner in a national accounting firm living in Des Moines owned a hundred shares of the Cyclops Corporation, headquartered in Buffalo. Before the Buffalo office of the accounting firm could acquire Cyclops as an audit client, the spouse in Iowa would have had to divest those shares. The rule was extremely unpopular with partners in the Big Four because it severely restricted investment opportunities. The latest revision narrowed the application of this rule by constricting the circle of firm personnel whose investments are imputed to the auditor. The SEC stated its belief that independence will be protected and the rule made more workable by focusing only on those persons who can actually influence an audit, rather than encompassing all the partners in the accounting firm.

The second principle deals with the provision of nonaudit services. Here the SEC adopted a policy that for the first time identifies specific nonaudit services as rendering the auditor not independent of the client. In so doing the SEC has effectively banned nine kinds of consulting services from being provided by accounting firms to their audit clients: (1) bookkeeping or other services related to the audit client's accounting records or financial statements; (2) financial information systems design and implementation; (3) appraisal or valuation services and fairness opinions; (4) actuarial services; (5) internal audit services; (6) management functions; (7) human resources services; (8) broker-dealer services; and (9) legal services. In each of these nonaudit service lines, the SEC concluded that there is a potential impermissible influence of nonaudit relationships on audit objectivity, or that investor confidence would be adversely affected by reasonable concerns about nonaudit services compromising audit objectivity.[50]

The third principle addresses quality controls, and requires accounting firms to have policies and systems in place to ensure that the rules on independence are not violated. The accounting firm must also provide means to promptly remedy independence violations upon discovery.

The final principle requires public disclosure of nonaudit services. The amendments require registrants to disclose in their proxy statements their audit fees, fees for financial information systems design and implementation, and fees for other nonaudit

---

[48]Zeff, "Accounting Profession, Part II," 278.
[49]Securities and Exchange Commission, "Final Rule."
[50]Ibid.

services rendered by the principal accountant to a company. In addition, the SEC requires companies to disclose whether their audit committees have considered if the provision of financial information systems and other nonaudit services by the company's principal accountant is compatible with maintaining the principal accountant's independence.

Within the purview of these principles, the SEC has issued a number of rules that specifically pertain to audit partners and accounting firms, and are intended to prevent abuses uncovered following the collapse of Enron, Worldcom, and others. Thus, an audit partner cannot be compensated on the basis of how much nonauditing services he or she sells to a client; the top two accounting partners on a client's audit are required to rotate off every 5 years and must wait a minimum of 5 years before returning to that client's work; audit professionals must wait a year before accepting employment with a client and overseeing the auditing firm's work; and audit firms must disclose how much revenue they obtain from their nonauditing operations.[51]

The Sarbanes-Oxley Act

The Sarbanes-Oxley Act (SOA), passed in 2002, is perhaps the single most important piece of legislation affecting corporate governance, financial disclosure, and the practice of public accounting since U.S. securities laws were first enacted in the 1930s. The act establishes a Public Company Accounting Oversight Board (PCAOB), a private sector, nonprofit corporation created to oversee the auditors of public companies to protect the interests of investors and promote the public interest in the preparation of informative, fair, and independent audit reports. With the establishment of the PCAOB several major responsibilities, formerly resting with the profession, are moved closer to the governmental sector. Section 103 provides that the PCAOB shall (1) register public accounting firms; (2) establish, or adopt, by rule, "auditing, quality control, ethics, independence, and other standards relating to the preparation of audit reports for issuers"; (3) conduct inspections of accounting firms; (4) conduct investigations and disciplinary proceedings, and impose appropriate sanctions; (5) perform such other duties or functions as necessary or appropriate; (6) enforce compliance with the act, with the rules of the Board, professional standards, and with the securities laws relating to the preparation and issuance of audit reports, including the obligations and liabilities of accountants with respect thereto; and (7) set the budget and manage the operations of the Board and the staff of the Board.[52]

The PCAOB must cooperate on an ongoing basis with designated professional groups of accountants and any advisory groups convened in connection with standard-setting for auditing. Although the board can "to the extent that it determines appropriate" adopt auditing standards proposed by those groups, the board will have authority to amend, modify, repeal, and reject any auditing standards suggested by the groups. The board must also report on its standard-setting activity to the SEC on an annual basis, a provision that removes from the accounting profession the authority to establish standards governing the ways and means by which audits of publicly held firms are conducted.

---

[51]Public Accounting Report, "SEC Passes New Rules" (January 31, 2003): 1, 4.
[52]American Institute of Certified Public Accountants, "Summary of Sarbanes-Oxley Act of 2002" (2003), available at www.aicpa.org/info/sarbanes_oxley_summary.htm.

The Sarbanes-Oxley Act also requires the PCAOB to adopt an audit standard to implement the internal control review required by Section 404(b) of the act. (Internal control refers to the means by which companies ensure the integrity of their accounting and financial records.) The required internal control standard must oblige the auditor to evaluate whether the internal control structure and procedures include records that accurately and fairly reflect the transactions of the issuer, provide reasonable assurance that transactions are recorded in a manner that will permit the preparation of financial statements in accordance with Generally Accepted Accounting Principles, and provide a description of any material weaknesses in the client's internal controls.

Sarbanes-Oxley further requires accounting firms to be regularly inspected. Section 104 calls for annual quality reviews to be conducted for firms that audit more than 100 client companies; firms that audit fewer companies must be reviewed every 3 years. This section also gives PCAOB the authority to discipline wayward auditors. The Board can impose sanctions on an accounting firm that has failed to reasonably supervise any associated person with regard to auditing or quality control standards, or that has violated any other approved audit standards. The Board's findings and sanctions are subject to review by the SEC. Moreover, the act gives the SEC broad oversight of the PCAOB. The SEC may assign it additional responsibilities, review its actions, and discipline the board itself if it does not fulfill its responsibilities.

Sarbanes-Oxley requires the accounting profession to pay for the board created to oversee it. Thus, to audit a public company, a public accounting firm must register with the PCAOB. The Board shall collect a registration fee and an annual fee from each registered public accounting firm, in amounts sufficient to recover the costs of processing and reviewing applications and annual reports. The PCAOB shall also establish by rule a reasonable "annual accounting support fee" as necessary to maintain the Board.[53]

Finally, Title II of Sarbanes-Oxley addresses auditor independence. Among its various provisions are requirements for auditor rotation, definitions of conflict of interest, and codification of services prohibited by auditors. (The SEC was assigned broad authority to issue rules to ensure auditor independence. These rules, discussed in the previous section, were issued in 2003.)

The PCAOB opened its doors in 2003, effectively ending decades of self regulation of the public accounting profession. It has taken the task of writing auditing standards for the AICPA. To date four auditing standards have been written. The most controversial of these is the second standard, which requires an extensive audit of internal controls in conjunction with the audit of financial statements. In 2007 the PCAOB approved a series of changes to Auditing Standard Number 2 designed to remove some of the provisions of the standard that critics found objectionable.

Clearly, an outcropping of new regulatory rules and laws have been proliferated in responding to the recent rash of accounting and financial scandals. (A similar regulatory reaction appears to be commencing in the European Community in response to the scandalous collapse in 2003 of the huge Parmalat firm, in what has been labeled one of the great frauds in European financial history.)[54] Ultimately, however, the high level of concentration in the accounting field may pose an insuperable challenge to

---

[53]Ibid.

[54]"Special Report: Europe's Corporate Governance," *Economist* (January 17, 2004): 59–61.

tougher regulation: Any severe sanction could put one of the Big Four firms out of business, thereby strengthening the dominance of the remaining majors and concentrating the field to even higher levels. Already, the dominance of the Big Four threatens to render unworkable a concept the SEC has been considering to enhance independence by requiring companies to rotate audit firms every 5 years. More generally, this raises the question whether the Big Four have reached a point where they are too big, too important, and too few for any one of them to be allowed to fail. If so, this would effectively place them beyond the reach of effective regulation.[55]

Because of the Sarbanes-Oxley act and other regulations, auditing expenses have increased tremendously. At the same time, many clients have expressed the view that they receive less overall advice and support from their auditors, who may feel caught in a no-win situation between the demands of regulators, law enforcement, the plaintiff's bar, and their clients. Legal risks in the profession have become quite uncertain since the demise of Andersen. In fact, the profession is close to becoming effectively uninsurable. Because auditing firms are prohibited from seeking outside equity funding, they remain voluntary organizations funded by individual partners. They cannot be successful if the risks are perceived to greatly exceed the rewards. High quality personnel are likely to take their time and money elsewhere in this high-risk environment.[56]

Controversy has increased concerning the requirements of the Sarbanes-Oxley Act in general and Section 404 in particular, which deals with internal control. At a conference sponsored by the Treasury Department to discuss financial market competitiveness in the winter of 2007, Alan Greenspan, former chairman of the Federal Reserve, said he saw no need for most of the provisions of the Sarbanes-Oxley Act. He contended that the business scandals that prompted the law did not suggest any massive breakdown of corporate governance in America. Jeffrey Immelt, CEO of General Electric Co., said the regulatory system is "just too gosh-darn complex." Meanwhile, the Committee on Capital Markets Regulation, a voluntary group comprising members drawn from financial firms, law, and academia, issued a report in late 2006 raising alarms that the global share of corporate stocks issued in the U.S. has dropped substantially over the period from 2000 to 2005.[57] Among other recommendations, the committee called for new laws limiting the liability of audit firms from legal damages, and exempting small firms from the more onerous burdens imposed by the Sarbanes-Oxley Act. In May 2007, Treasury Secretary Henry Paulson announced plans to create an advisory committee to recommend adjustments in the accounting process, with committee members to include representatives from investor advocates, as well as from accounting firms and corporations.

On the other side of the controversy stands former SEC Chairman Arthur Levitt, who calls these concerns "specious." Warren Buffett, the famous investor and chair of Berkshire Hathaway, posed the rhetorical question: If things are so bad, why are U.S. corporate profits so good? They and others contend that the increased regulation under Sarbanes-Oxley is essential to insure investor confidence and sustain the functioning of the nation's financial markets, and that the critics' case is empirically

[55]Paula Dwyer, "The Big Four: Too Few to Fail?" *Business Week* (September 1, 2003): 34.
[56]U.S. Chamber of Commerce, "Auditing: A Profession at Risk" (January 2006), 4–8.
[57]Available at www.capmktsreg.org

unfounded.[58] Ann Yerger, executive director of the Council of Institutional Investors agrees, and warns against forgetting the recent catastrophic failures of boards and auditors to protect investor interests.[59] Her position is that the sharp rise in the number of restatements of corporate financial accounts demonstrates that Sarbanes-Oxley is working, not that it is failing.[60]

It is generally accepted that the intense consolidation in the public accounting profession has left many clients unhappy and capital markets vulnerable to shock in the event of further consolidation. In the end competition is usually the best way to ensure good customer service and, in turn, provide good service to the investing public.[61] Only time will tell whether effective competition can be maintained given the current structure and governance of the auditing industry. This is especially the case as the U.S. and EU begin striving to harmonize their differing accounting and auditing regulations, with the goal of achieving a single trans-Atlantic standard by 2009.[62]

CONCLUSION ▪▪▪▪▪▪▪

Public accounting firms perform a vital function in a capitalist economy in which financial markets depend upon accurate financial information to allocate trillions of dollars of funds. While external auditors cannot ensure perfect information, they can provide assurance to others that the financial statements they audit are fairly and accurately representative of the financial position of the reporting entity. This "attest" function is one on which the financial markets place immense weight; as recent events show, the consequences can be catastrophic when auditing firms fail to perform it effectively.

In its first 4 decades, the practice of accounting was conducted in a relatively sheltered profession. Once the profession was opened to market forces, however, dysfunctional behavior began to appear as profit maximization led the industry to seek profits and growth beyond its traditional auditing base. Ironically, actions by the antitrust agencies to promote competition in the field may in the long run have paved the way to an industry with greater concentration and less competition. While forcing the profession to abandon its ethics codes had the short-run effect of stimulating competition, those competitive forces, in turn, may ultimately have generated a tight oligopoly with significant barriers to entry.

With the passage of the Sarbanes-Oxley Act the accounting profession stood at a crossroads: Either the practice of accounting would accept far-reaching reform, or it would cease to exist in its present form. The only other alternative, it seems, would be for the profession to cede its auditing functions to a government agency, a development that could render accounting even more politicized. More recently, in the wake of the collapse of the subprime mortgage and credit markets in 2007, the auditing profession seems to have more resolutely stood its

---

[58]See Greg Ip, "Maybe U.S. Markets Are Still Supreme," *Wall Street Journal* (April 27, 2007): C1; and Alan Murray, "Wall Street's Capital 'Crisis' Moves to Back Burner," *Wall Street Journal* (May 23, 2007): A2.
[59]Quoted in D. Solomon, "A Summit on U.S. Rules: Too Gosh-Darn Complex." *Wall Street Journal* (March 14, 2007): C4.
[60]See Deborah Solomon, "Treasury Targets Restatements," *Wall Street Journal* (May 18, 2007): A2.
[61]U.S. Chamber of Commerce, "Auditing: A Profession at Risk," 16–19.
[62]Office of the White House, "Framework for Advancing Transatlantic Economic Integration Between the United States of America and the European Union," Annex 6: Financial Markets (April 30, 2007). Available at www.whitehouse.gov/news/releases/2007/04/20070430-4.html

ground and refused to buckle under pressures by clients to soften the accounting for their financial losses.[63] The profession, it seems, has stabilized, but it is not out of the woods yet. In *The Fellowship of the Ring*, Galadriel tells the fellowship, "But this I will say to you: Your Quest stands upon the edge of a knife. Stray but a little and it will fail, to the ruin of us all. Yet hope remains while the company is true." The Big Four accounting firms would do well to take these words to heart.

SUGGESTIONS FOR FURTHER READING ▬▬▬▬▬▬▬

American Institute of Certified Public Accountants. 2003. "Summary of Sarbanes-Oxley Act of 2002." Available at www.aicpa.org/info/sarbanes_oxley_summary.htm

Cottell, P. G. and T. M. Perlin. 1990. *Accounting Ethics: A Practical Guide for Professionals.* Westport, CT: Quorum Books.

Edwards, J. D. 1960. *History of Public Accounting in the United States.* East Lansing, MI: Michigan State University.

Emerson's Professional Services Review. Published bimonthly. Bellevue, WA: Emerson Company.

Levitt, Arthur. 2002. *Take on the Street.* New York: Pantheon.

Public Accounting Report. Published semimonthly. Atlanta, GA: Aspen Publishers, Inc.

Rama, A. V. and W. J. Read. 2006. "Resignations by the Big 4 and the Market for Audit Services" *Accounting Horizons* 20 (June): 97–109.

United States General Accounting Office 2003. "Public Accounting Firms: Mandated Study on Consolidation and Competition." July.

Securities and Exchange Commission 2003a. "Final Rule: Revision of the Commission's Auditor Independence Requirements." Available at www.sec.gov/rules/final/33-7919.htm.

Securities and Exchange Commission 2003b. "Report Pursuant to Section 704 of the Sarbanes-Oxley Act of 2002." Available at www.sec.gov/news/studies/sox704report.pdf

Zeff, S. A. 2003. "How the U.S. Accounting Profession Got Where It Is Today: Part I." *Accounting Horizons* 17 (September): 189–205.

_____. 2003. "How the U.S. Accounting Profession Got Where It Is Today: Part II." *Accounting Horizons* 17 (December): 267–286.

---

[63]David Reilly, "In Current Crunch, Auditors Stand Firm on Accounting Practices," *Wall Street Journal* (October 17, 2007): C1. Their resolve may have been bolstered by the fact that the Public Company Accounting Oversight Board created by the Sarbanes-Oxley Act brought its first major enforcement action against a Big Four accounting firm in 2007. See Judith Burns, "Deloitte Receives $1 Million Fine," *Wall Street Journal* (December 11, 2007): C8.

CHAPTER 13

The College Sports Industry

JOHN L. FIZEL AND RANDALL W. BENNETT

Sports are big business in the United States. Nike, Inc., the maker of athletic footwear, apparel, and equipment, reported revenue of $15 billion in 2006. The Washington Redskins National Football League team was sold in 1999 for $800 million, while the Boston Red Sox baseball club was sold in 2002 for $700 million. Alex Rodriguez signed a $252 million 10-year contract to play baseball for the Texas Rangers from 2001 to 2010—a value exceeding the $250 million owner Tom Hicks paid to buy the team franchise in 1998.

Big business is not confined to athletic companies or professional sports. The big-time programs (Division I-A) of the National Collegiate Athletic Association (NCAA) produced over $4 billion in revenue in the 2004–05 academic year, or four times the $1.07 billion generated in the academic year 1988–89. Major college football coaches, such as Bob Stoops of the University of Oklahoma, Mack Brown of the University of Texas, and Kirk Ferentz of the University of Iowa, have compensation packages that exceed $2 million annually, ranking them above college presidents and state governors as the highest paid university and state employees. These salaries are likely to rise substantially in the wake of Nick Saban's January 2007 move from the Miami Dolphins of the National Football League (NFL) to coach the University of Alabama, with a $32 million contract over 8 years. Coaches often earn additional income through sports camps, media shows, and endorsement contracts with athletic apparel companies. CBS paid $6 billion for television rights to the NCAA Division I basketball tournament from 2003 through 2013.

College sports are a lucrative and growing business, but not without turmoil. Reports of athletes obtaining cash payments, cars, and falsified academic credentials are widespread. Between 1977 and 1985, football players at Texas Christian University were paid between $35,000 and $40,000 apiece to attend the school. In 1998, a former office manager at the University of Minnesota admitted to completing more than 400 pieces of course work for 20 basketball players over the years from 1993 through 1998. A booster of the University of Michigan basketball program gave over $600,000 to at least four members of the team in the 1990s. The president of St. Bonaventure University admitted a junior college basketball player from a nonacademic program in welding over the objection of the school's compliance director; the resulting scandal over the ineligible player cost the president his job. An indication of relative power within some universities occurred during the 2003 football season: The president and athletic director of Auburn University held a secret meeting with the football coach of the University of Louisville to discuss replacing Tommy Tuberville as coach at Auburn. When the meeting became public both the president and athletic director resigned while Coach Tuberville received a contract extension.

Why the controversy in collegiate sports? The NCAA depicts itself as a beleaguered organization waging a noble fight against dishonest coaches, lax administrators, and greedy athletes who violate the rules against under-the-table payments and other special favors. However, the situation is better analyzed by examining the economic incentives associated with a cartel: The universities operating college athletic programs are cartel members, and the NCAA is the cartel manager. A cartel is a group of rivals that suppresses economic competition by agreeing to coordinate their individual behavior and to follow rules and practices that maximize their economic benefits. No less an authority than Walter Byers, executive director of the NCAA from 1951 to 1987, has described the NCAA as a cartel "operated by not-for-profit institutions contracting together to achieve maximum financial returns."[1] The success of the NCAA cartel is such that Harvard University economist Robert Barro has called the NCAA the most effective monopoly in America.[2] Although cooperation among cartel members increases group profits, each member has an incentive to circumvent the group rules to increase its individual share of the collective profits. For example, if one university paid signing bonuses to the best high school athletes, it might be able to win more games, increase attendance at games, enhance private donations from excited fans, and reap the dollar rewards from appearing in a postseason tournament or bowl game. Yet, if many members cheat, the increased competition will cause an escalation in bonus payments, fewer profits, and less certain and surely more limited benefits for all. Thus, the successful cartel must limit autonomous behavior by enforcing and monitoring its rules. However, the rules themselves are political, and no matter what policies the cartel promulgates, they reflect a compromise among divergent interests. As with any compromise, some cartel members will be more satisfied than others. Therefore, churning will occur as members constantly weigh the benefits of joint versus individual action.

▬▬▬ I. History

The original incentive for forming the NCAA, as well as the impetus for its early growth, was not based on financial goals related to cartel behavior. Instead, the catalyst for the development of the NCAA was the violence and lack of standard playing rules in college football. In the late 1880s, football was a cross between rugby and soccer, retaining some rules from each of its ancestors as well as developing additional rules of

---

[1]Walter Byers, *Unsportsmanlike Conduct: Exploiting College Athletes* (Ann Arbor: University of Michigan Press, 1995), 374.
[2]"The Best Little Monopoly in America," *Business Week* (December 9, 2002): 22.

its own. College teams constantly looked for new tactics to win in this evolving sport, with many the successful strategies involving increasingly violent player behavior. In 1905 alone, the college football season resulted in 18 player deaths and 159 serious injuries.

As injuries and deaths grew, fan appeal fell. Some colleges attempted to limit violent tactics only to lose on the field to the universities that continued to employ them. The industry was facing the classic "prisoner's dilemma": All colleges had much to gain from cooperatively banning violent play, but each had an individual incentive to use unilaterally successful tactics. Little could be done without some formal agreement or means to punish aberrant behavior.

President Theodore Roosevelt reacted to the carnage by calling on colleges to reform athletics. He organized a meeting with representatives of several schools hoping to create a cooperative plan to limit brutal and destructive play. No agreement could be reached. Shortly thereafter, a number of colleges dropped football as a sanctioned sport. A new sense of urgency developed, and a second meeting was called. From this latter meeting came the Intercollegiate Athletic Association of the United States, changing its name to the NCAA in 1910.

Implementation of standardized rules and prohibition of violence in football quickly reduced the rate of injury. At the same time, the popularity of the game increased. NCAA membership grew rapidly as more schools sought the benefits of cooperation, while growing acceptance of the NCAA allowed the organization to standardize rules for other college sports. But the NCAA and its membership soon recognized that cooperation in the area of rules of play could be expanded to other areas of competition, and the attention of the NCAA turned from standardizing these rules to instituting the foundations for cartel control of college sports.

Input Controls

Cartel development began with the effort to limit competition for athletic talent. Contending that colleges should be limited to amateur athletics, the NCAA worked to remove professionals from collegiate sports. Many teams at the time were packed with "hired guns," players who were not students, often had no link to the college, and participated for a paycheck. The NCAA declared that eligible athletes must be full-time students. In addition, eligibility was limited to 3 years. (Freshmen were ineligible to play.) The NCAA also declared that "no student shall represent a college or university in any intercollegiate game or contest . . . who has at any time received, either directly or indirectly, money, or any other consideration."[3] To facilitate implementation of the rules, the NCAA recommended in 1919 that members should schedule games only with opponents who abided by NCAA rules.

Predictably, the result was widespread cheating because no enforcement mechanism was in place to police adherence to the amateurism and athletic compensation rules. Colleges that disregarded the rules and offered lucrative contracts to talented athletes gained the financial rewards of a winning program. With lax enforcement and great incentives for noncooperative behavior, the labor restraint rules were largely ineffective.

---

[3]Byers, 40.

These shortcomings were addressed in the Sanity Code of 1948, which established standards for financial aid to student athletes and created an enforcement apparatus to deal with rules violations. In pursuit of amateurism, the NCAA enacted rules that athletes and nonathletes were to be treated identically. Aid could be based upon need or academic merit, but not on athletic ability; need-based grants were to make no distinction between athletes and other students. Student athletes in the top 25 percent of their high school class, or who had a grade point average (GPA) of B or better in college, were eligible to receive merit aid, even if they had no demonstrated need.

The Sanity Code also established the NCAA Compliance Committee to handle allegations of rules violations. This first attempt to crack down on schools that violated the rules was hindered, however, because the only penalty available was to revoke membership. The rule breaker would be tossed out of the NCAA if two-thirds of NCAA members voted for expulsion. In fact, in 1950 the Compliance Committee voted to expel seven schools, the so-called "Seven Sinners," for rules violations (Villanova, Boston College, Virginia, Maryland, Virginia Military Institute, The Citadel, and Virginia Polytechnic Institute). But the two-thirds vote of all NCAA members needed to confirm the expulsions was not obtained, indicating the reluctance of the NCAA membership to punish rule violators, at least when faced with the imposition of such a drastic penalty. This lack of will led to the abolition of the Sanity Code in 1951, and the Compliance Committee died the following year. In 1953, the NCAA enacted a range of penalties less severe than termination of membership in an attempt to improve enforcement and in 1954 established the Committee on Infractions to deal with rules violations. For the first time, the NCAA had the means and the ability to enforce athletic labor market restraints.

Output Controls

Having restrained competition for athletic talent, the NCAA began to control industry output by asserting jurisdiction over all aspects of contract negotiations for college football telecasts. The NCAA Television Plan consisted of exclusive contracts with the television networks that limited the number of telecasts and the number of appearances by individual college members over a specified period of time, and also stipulated the times at which games could be televised. The financial gains from restricting output quickly became apparent: The initial television contract (1952) generated $1.15 million; by 1962, the contract went for $5.1 million; in 1972, $12 million; and in 1992, $59 million.

This spectacular growth in broadcast revenues, combined with the NCAA's process for distributing these fees, created tensions within the organization. The few members that had football teams with sufficient fan interest to generate substantial broadcasting fees were sharing those fees with the large number of member schools whose teams enjoyed far more limited fan support. The revenue-generating members became disgruntled with the cartel's allocation mechanism. To save the cartel, the NCAA would have to address the diverse interests of its members.

In 1973, the NCAA responded by creating three subgroups with the organization: Divisions I, II, and III. By having a common commitment to athletics and common revenue-generating capacity within divisions, more of the broadcasting fees earned within a given division could be distributed among the members of that division. But several of the elite schools were not placated. They threatened to leave the cartel unless they were provided even greater sovereignty within the organization. The response was more restructuring. Division I was further subdivided according to the size of football programs: I-A, I-AA, and I-AAA. Division I basketball remained unchanged. This divisional split brought stability to the cartel, at least temporarily.

The NCAA thus began as an organization dedicated to creating uniformity in playing rules and reining in brutal play. Once members began cooperating on these issues, however, there was little additional cost to determining how to control competition for inputs and outputs within the college sports industry. In short, the evolution of the NCAA provides a classic example of the genesis of a cartel.

▪▪▪ II. Structure

Colleges in the United States can belong to one of two organizations that oversee male and female intercollegiate athletics: the NCAA, and the National Association of Intercollegiate Athletics (NAIA). While all big-time college athletic programs belong to the NCAA, the size diversity of NCAA membership is illustrated by the football attendance figures in Table 13-1. The major football programs of Division I-A, recently renamed the Football Bowl Subdivision, play before tens of thousands of fans, led by the University of Michigan with a 2005 average home game attendance of 110,915. The next level, Division I-AA, recently renamed the Championship Subdivision, has fewer athletic scholarships available and generally includes smaller schools. The average attendance is 10,000 or less, with the University of Montana leading the way with a 2005 average of 22,479 per home football game. NCAA Division II schools are allowed even fewer scholarships and average 5,000 or fewer in attendance per game, led by West Texas A&M with 13,089 fans per 2005 home game. NCAA Division III schools are not allowed to give athletic scholarships and average about 2,000 fans per game, with St. John's of Minnesota averaging a division-leading 7,925 spectators per football game in 2005. The NAIA comprises a homogeneous group of smaller schools that do not place great emphasis on intercollegiate sports or have large fan bases, and so are similar to NCAA Division III schools.

In sum, as noted by Fleisher, Goff, and Tollison, "[f]or all practical purposes, the NCAA today directs and controls all major revenue-producing collegiate athletic events."[4]

Entry and Entry Barriers

Unfortunately for the NCAA, its success at restricting competition and increasing profits results in a clamor for admittance to membership by outsiders eager to share in the cartel's profits. Rapid entry has resulted in divergent interests and potential rule breaking, a situation exacerbated by heterogeneity in revenue-generating capability. Also, monitoring and enforcing rules for member behavior has become more difficult. In short, the stability of the cartel is jeopardized.

The NCAA had 1,027 active members in 2005. Multiply this by the number of coaches, players, potential recruits, alumni, and fans at each institution and it quickly

---

[4]A. Fleisher, B. Goff, and R. Tollison, *The National Collegiate Athletic Association: A Study in Cartel Behavior* (Chicago: University of Chicago Press, 1992), 55.

TABLE 13-1 Attendance at NCAA Football Games

Division I-A

Year	No. of Teams	Total Attendance	Per-Game Attendance
1982	97	24,771,855	43,689
1987	104	25,471,744	41,963
1993	106	25,305,438	41,281
1999	114	29,032,973	43,593
2005	117	32,641,526	46,039

Division I-AA

Year	No. of Teams	Total Attendance	Per-Game Attendance
1982	92	5,655,519	11,709
1987	87	5,129,250	11,151
1993	115	5,356,873	8,599
1999	122	5,949,345	9,001
2005	116	5,436,122	8,521

Division II

Year	No. of Teams	Total Attendance	Per-Game Attendance
1982	126	2,745,964	4,443
1987	107	2,424,041	4,481
1993	142	2,572,053	3,582
1999	147	2,504,118	3,343
2005	147	2,989,274	3,842

Division III

Year	No. of Teams	Total Attendance	Per-Game Attendance
1982	195	2,002,857	2,223
1987	209	1,982,506	2,021
1993	197	1,636,270	1,752
1999	218	1,996,221	1,881
2005	227	2,088,019	1,840

Source: National Collegiate Athletic Association, *NCAA Football*, various issues, and NCAA web site, www.ncaa.org

becomes apparent that monitoring all potential rule-breaking activities would be prohibitively expensive, if not impossible. If monitoring is impossible, then cheating should be rampant. Although the NCAA cannot closely monitor each rule-related activity, it can use probabilistic evidence to infer when a member's behavior may deviate from the rules.[5] This process compares current performance with the historic performance of its members: If current performance improves significantly, suspicion increases that the college has cheated. Resources can be allocated to launch a more intense investigation to determine whether cheating has actually occurred.

---

[5]For examples, see ibid.

If cheating cannot be controlled, the cartel will disintegrate. The NCAA, however, can apply sanctions to punish cheaters who are caught, and these sanctions have become increasingly severe in recent years. For instance, the NCAA can reduce the number of athletic scholarships a college can grant. The NCAA can also limit television appearances and prohibit a college from appearing in lucrative postseason tournaments. When an appearance in a Bowl Championship Series (BCS) game such as the Rose, Sugar, Orange, or Fiesta Bowl is worth over $17 million per team, the NCAA clearly has powerful means to enforce adherence to its rules.

Although violations of NCAA rules are often cast in terms of legality or illegality, these rules are not public law. The NCAA is a private organization governed by rules that have been adopted by representatives of its member institutions. Although it is not illegal for a college athlete to sign a product endorsement contract, it may be a NCAA violation to accept a job linked to his fame as a collegiate athlete. The perception that NCAA rules are law does, however, aid in enforcement. The "legal" ramifications of their actions may deter potential perpetrators of rule violations. Recently, however, NCAA rules have begun to seep into the legal system. In addition to the NCAA punishing an athlete and a college if an agent pays an athlete, many states now consider it a felony for an agent to offer something of value to anyone as a means of inducing a student-athlete to sign with an agent. To provide uniformity across states the NCAA has been promoting the Uniform Athlete Agent Act (UAAA) to state legislatures. This legislation has been enacted into law in 35 states as of June, 2006, with one more state currently considering adoption. Only ten states had no regulation of sports agents as of June, 2006. In addition to criminal sanctions, the UAAA allows the athlete and the school to sue the sports agent for civil damages if violations of the act cause harm to either party. Various proposals at the federal level have also addressed sports agent behavior. Although other students on campus and workers in general are allowed to seek legal advice and representation as they see fit, athletes are not. The NCAA's influence seems to be creeping beyond the narrow confines of college sports.

Entry considerations have traditionally focused on keeping peace within the ranks. With so many member colleges in the NCAA, the concern has always been that a disgruntled group of members could form a new, separate league of their own. (We will discuss later the rise and fall of the College Football Association as an example of this course of action.) To be effective, the number of seceding teams must be sufficient to form an alternative league with a full slate of games and potential postseason play. But as indicated previously, the creation of subgroups within the NCAA increases the homogeneity of colleges within each division and reduces incentives for cheating. Thus, Division I-A football colleges can enact rules that apply only to them; they need not be impeded by the legislative dictates of smaller, less sports-oriented colleges.

The entry barriers that do exist consist primarily of limiting admission to various NCAA divisions, especially Division I-A football. A Division I-A football entrant must offer at least 16 varsity sports (male and female); play at least 5 home games against other Division I-A members; average 15,000 or more in attendance per home game once in every 2-year period; grant an average of 90 percent or more of the maximum allowable football scholarships for each 2-year period; and award at least 200 total athletic scholarships or spend at least $4,000,000 on athletic scholarships for all sports each year. The NCAA also requires Division I-A conferences to have at least eight members. A quick glance back at Table 13-1 shows just how restrictive these rules are.

Until August 2, 2003, a college could meet these minimum standards and be accepted for 3 years as provisional member of Division I-A. While provisional entrants comply with division rules, they do not receive division benefits. Currently, change of division membership requires an exploratory year plus 4 more provisional years. The number of provisional entrants was 96 in 1995, 67 in 1998, 59 in 2001, 28 in 2002, and 17 in 2004. The NCAA has clearly slowed migration between divisions in an attempt to retain divisional homogeneity.[6]

▪▪▪ III. Conduct

Although the market share of the NCAA is nearly 100 percent, the threat of disharmony among the large number of members and the growing threat of new entrants put severe strains on the cartel. The stresses are so serious that much of the output control once held by the NCAA is being eroded. The NCAA today is better viewed as an input cartel, but even its labor controls are being tested.

Output Control

Control of broadcasting rights to college football telecasts is one key dimension of output control. As noted earlier, this control initially generated large, rapidly rising broadcasting fees. Increased dissension about the distribution of these fees, however, fueled a restructuring of the NCAA. The resulting split into divisions in 1973 was only a temporary solution to the growing disparity in revenue generation across the membership, and dissatisfaction soon returned.

The College Football Association (CFA), founded in 1977, was an outgrowth of this dissension. The CFA included most of the Division I-A schools except those from the Big Ten and PAC Ten conferences. (Originally the CFA members threatened complete secession from the NCAA but stopped short when they did not have the support of the Big Ten and PAC Ten schools.) Instead, the CFA focused solely on gaining control of football telecast revenues. The CFA also planned to garner more television appearances and generate more television revenue for its member schools. In 1981, the CFA signed an agreement with NBC that fulfilled these goals. The NCAA immediately threatened penalties. Later that year, the University of Oklahoma and University of Georgia filed suit against the NCAA, alleging that the NCAA Television Plan, by limiting television exposure by any one team, was an illegal restraint of trade in violation of the antitrust laws.

The 1983 Television Plan allowed two networks, ABC and CBS, each to air 14 telecasts annually. These telecasts could be a mixture of national and regional games, but each network was required to telecast at least 82 different teams over a 2-year period. ABC and CBS together had to show at least 115 different teams over the 2-year life of the Plan. The NCAA also mandated that teams be limited to four national appearances and six total appearances during this period. Finally, all teams involved in a telecast received equal remuneration, regardless of the attractiveness of the game to viewers

---

[6]The slowing of entry into Division I programs despite profit incentives prompts R. Sandy and P. Sloan to ask, "Why don't all colleges that can possibly beg or borrow the money start Division I-A programs?" See "Why do U.S. Colleges have Sports Programs?" in *Economics of College Sports*, ed. John Fizel and Rod Fort (Westport, CT: Praeger, 2004).

and fans or the number of stations that broadcast the game. In some years, for example, Oklahoma, University of Southern California (USC), Appalachian State, and the Citadel each received the same compensation, even though the Oklahoma-USC game was broadcast over 200 stations while the Appalachian State–Citadel game was broadcast on only four.

The NCAA acknowledged that its Television Plan restrained trade but pointed out that professional sports had often been granted exemptions from prosecution when restrictive business practices were necessary to promote competitive balance. The NCAA asserted that if colleges were given the right to negotiate their own contracts, a proliferation of telecasts would ensue with most appearances being awarded to traditional football powers. Because television appearances are a key aid in recruiting top athletes, the NCAA feared that a distribution of appearances skewed toward the traditional powers would accentuate inequality among football programs; existing powers would prosper, while nonpowers would suffer.

Nevertheless, in 1984, the Supreme Court held that the NCAA Television Plan restricted output and fixed prices in violation of the Sherman Antitrust Act.[7] The ruling granted individual colleges the property right to their college football telecasts—a right the schools had an option to sell or assign at their discretion.

The demise of NCAA television control had three significant outcomes. Soon after the Court's ruling, colleges, conferences, and select organizations of colleges frenetically pursued local, regional, national, and cable outlets to televise their games. The number of network games doubled shortly after the ruling, while the price per network game dropped from $2.3 million to $0.6 million. Also, Bennett and Fizel, and Fort and Quirk, find that competitive balance on the field has been enhanced by the Court's decision.[8] Contrary to the NCAA's argument, NCAA control over television was not necessary to generate more equality of playing strength among Division I football teams. Finally, the case initially was a coup for the CFA and its partial secession from the NCAA. However, over time, the CFA began to face internal pressures similar to those experienced by the NCAA. Eventually, several prominent members left the CFA and, in 1997 it ceased operations.

In response to the development of the CFA and the future threat of similar alliances by major Division I programs, the NCAA changed its Division I structure of governance in 1997 from one school/one vote to a representative system based upon conference votes. The Division I-A conferences now have a majority of votes on both the Division I Board of Directors and the Division I Management Council, even though Divisions I-AA and I-AAA have more schools. The votes of the former members of the CFA now have a larger impact on NCAA policy, with the less than surprising result that the NCAA is now allocating a higher percentage of revenues to those institutions.[9]

---

[7]See *The National Collegiate Athletic Association v. Board of Regents of the University of Oklahoma and University of Georgia Athletic Association*, 468 U.S. 85 (1984).

[8]Randall W. Bennett and John L. Fizel, "Telecast Deregulation and Competitive Balance," *American Journal of Economics and Sociology*, 54 (1995): 183–200; R. Fort and J. Quirk, "Introducing A Competitive Economic Environment into Professional Sports," in *Advances in the Economics of Sports*, ed. W. Hendricks (Greenwich, CT: JAI Press, 1997), 11–26.

[9]For a detailed analysis of the restructuring, see Joel Maxcy, "The 1997 Restructuring of the NCAA: A Transaction Cost Explanation" in *Economics of College Sports*, ed. John Fizel and Rod Fort, (Westport, CT: Praeger, 2004).

Another area that escapes NCAA control is postseason play in Division I-A football. Currently, 119 Division I-A football schools participate in the only sport for which the NCAA does not sponsor a national championship. Why would the NCAA ignore championship play in the sport that generates the largest revenue for the typical Division I-A school? The answer lies in the historical development of the postseason bowl system. Since the University of Michigan defeated Stanford University 49–0 in the 1902 Rose Bowl, a system of postseason bowls has developed as a reward for a successful football season. The Rose Bowl was first played in 1902, the Orange and Sugar Bowls in 1935, the Sun Bowl in 1936, the Cotton Bowl in 1937, the Gator Bowl in 1946, the Liberty Bowl in 1959, and the Fiesta Bowl in 1971. By 2006, the number of Division I-A postseason bowl games had grown to 32.

The mythical national champion of Division I-A football historically has been determined by polls of sportswriters or coaches, not by performance on the playing field as is done for Divisions I-AA, II, and III football. Dissatisfied with this arrangement, the major football programs began tinkering with the bowl system in 1991 in an attempt to arrange for the Number 1 and Number 2 teams in the coaches' and press polls each year to play in a national championship game at an existing bowl. This initial bowl coalition became the bowl alliance for the 1995 season, in a system where the Orange Bowl, Sugar Bowl, and Fiesta Bowl would trade off as hosts for this national championship game. This game was not, however, a true national championship, because the finalists were determined through the polls and not by a playoff system, and two major conferences, the Big Ten and PAC Ten, were not initially involved. These conferences were not ready to sever the lucrative arrangement that tied their conference champions to the Rose Bowl—the bowl with the biggest payout—for the chance to play for the national championship. The Big Ten, PAC Ten, and the Rose Bowl did join the bowl alliance for the 1998 season, however, forming the Bowl Championship Series (BCS). The championship game would rotate among the Orange, Sugar, Fiesta, and Rose Bowls. The compromise that brought the Big Ten and PAC Ten into the BCS allows their champions to still meet in the Rose Bowl when they are not involved in the championship game.

The BCS added another bowl, the National Championship Game, to be played the week following the four BCS bowls just mentioned, starting in January 2007 and pitting the top two teams in the BCS standings against each other. This was in part a reaction to rumblings from the non-BCS schools about being shut out of the lucrative BCS bowls. Adding a fifth BCS bowl would make it somewhat easier for non-BCS teams to be included. Until 2007 the University of Utah, in the 2005 Fiesta Bowl, was the only non-BCS team to be chosen for a BCS bowl. This was due to a requirement that any non-BCS school had to be ranked sixth or better in the BCS standings to be eligible. This has been changed so that now a non-BCS team is eligible if it is ranked in the top 12 of the BCS standings, or the top 16 and ranked higher than the champion of an automatically qualifying conference. Boise State University became the second non-BCS team to qualify, and played in the Fiesta Bowl in 2007 (both Utah and Boise State won their games against BCS opponents).

Bowl directors and major conference commissioners—not the NCAA—administer the BCS. The administrators have reduced the emphasis on polls to determine the championship game participants by relying on a combination of (1) team record, (2) Associated Press and ESPN/USA Today poll rankings, (3) computer rankings, and (4) a measure of strength of schedule based on opponent performance. Because team record and strength of schedule are accounted for in the computer rankings, the BCS currently combines an average of computer rankings with the *USA Today* coaches' poll and the Harris Interactive College Football Poll to determine its rankings. The 1999 Fiesta Bowl hosted the first BCS game, in which the University of Tennessee was crowned national champion after defeating Florida State 23–16. Other BCS champions include LSU in 2004, USC in 2005, Texas in 2006, and Florida in 2007.

A true playoff system would likely be much more lucrative than the current bowl system. One proposal from the late 1990s was for a 16-team Division I-A football play-off tournament to pay the NCAA about $380 million per year for 8 years—much larger than the $168 million the bowls paid out following the 2002 season. DeLoss Dodds, the athletic director of the University of Texas at the time, said that colleges are "leaving $2-million a year, per school, on the table" by not going to a playoff system.[10]

For comparison, consider the returns from the collegiate basketball postseason play-offs controlled by the NCAA. CBS has paid the NCAA $6 billion for the rights to telecast the NCAA basketball tournament from 2003 through 2013. The 2007 basketball tournament alone is expected to rake in an additional $500 million in television advertising. On a per-game basis, the advertising income for basketball playoffs is nearly twice that of football playoffs. The advertising bonanza for the basketball playoffs represents 75 percent of the total annual advertising revenue for college basketball, whereas the advertising revenue for the football playoffs is only 22 percent of its total annual advertising.[11]

Although many argue that college revenues would be enhanced if the NCAA could gain control of postseason play in football, others offer counter arguments. One weakness of the argument for playoffs is that they would lengthen the college football season. The 16-team playoff tournament proposal would have scheduled the championship game the week before the Super Bowl in mid-January. Graham B. Spanier, Penn State president and chairman of the NCAA Division I Board of Directors at the time, said, "There is a great concern about commercialization, professionalism, and extending the season, and I can tell you that most of the presidents I've spoken with are not persuaded by the money that's potentially on the table."[12] The existing bowls oppose a postseason tournament because they fear they would lose autonomy or even be eliminated entirely by a playoff system. Conference commissioners argue against playoffs stating that they would reduce the importance of the regular season for most teams, hurt or destroy existing bowls, and possibly eliminate the opportunity for postseason bowl play for many teams. Over half of the 119 teams that played Division I-A football in 2006 participated in a bowl game. If a 16-team playoff destroys the minor bowl games, many fewer teams will earn postseason play. Walter Byers, former executive director of the NCAA, argues that major college football programs do not want a playoff system because they do not want the money generated from postseason play to be funneled through the NCAA, where it is likely that funds will flow to nonparticipating schools and to the NCAA itself. Currently, as

---

[10]Welch Suggs, "Can $3-billion Persuade Colleges to Create a Playoff for Football?" *Chronicle of Higher Education* 6 (August 1999): 2.
[11]"TNS Media Intelligence Releases March Madness Advertising Trends Report" (March 6, 2007). Available at www.tns-mi.com/news/03062007.htm.
[12]Suggs, 3.

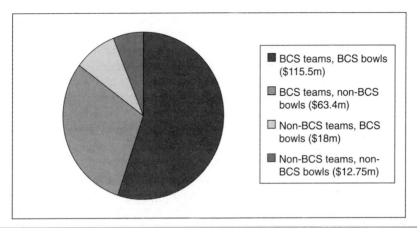

FIGURE 13-1 Distribution of College Football Bowl Revenues, 2006 and January 2007.

BCS includes six major conferences: ACC, Big East, Big Ten, Big 12, Pac 10, SEC, and Notre Dame. BCS Bowls are the Rose, Fiesta, Orange, and Sugar Bowls plus the National Championship game.
Source: Thomas O'Toole, "$17 Million BCS Payouts Sound Great, But . . ." *USA Today online,* December 6, 2006.

Figure 13-1 shows, the power football conferences (BCS teams) receive more than 85% of the revenue from bowl games, even with non-BSC Boise State University being selected for a BCS bowl. For the 2006 season the BCS bowls paid $17 million to the conference champion of the six BCS conferences, and $4.5 million to a second team from that conference to make a BCS bowl. Florida and Ohio State equally racked up a (BCS) national championship game jackpot worth about $36 million, even though they will share the windfall with schools from their respective conferences.[13] Although conference members share the payouts with the rest of the conference, Notre Dame is an independent in football, so the BCS paid Notre Dame an unshared $4.5 million to play in the Sugar Bowl. The BCS has agreed to pay the 5 non-BCS conferences 9 percent of expected BCS net revenue, or $9 million for the 2007 bowl games. These schools received another 9 percent, or $18 million, because Boise State University participated in the 2007 Fiesta Bowl.

There is no doubt that the NCAA will work diligently to develop a proposal for a postseason football tournament/playoff. But can the NCAA design a proposal that overcomes the academic concerns of college presidents, the distribution concerns of institutional football powers, and the lobbying that will inevitably come from bowl administrators?

Input Control

An output cartel increases profits by enabling members to collectively limit output and increase prices. Conversely, an input cartel increases profits by enabling members to collectively *lower* the price paid for the input. The NCAA has created a voluminous

---

[13]Jon Saraceno, "Saying the System Exploits Collegians Stretches the Point," *USA Today* (January 5, 2007). Available at www.usatoday.com/sports/columnist/saraceno/2007-01-05-saraceno_x.htm.

system of rules aimed at controlling the cost of inputs in collegiate sports, with most of the regulations directed at the recruitment and compensation of athletes.

The NCAA contends that the proliferation of its recruiting controls enhances competitive balance by standardizing rules within the organization. Yet an examination of some of the rules shows they are effective monopsonistic ploys to reduce recruiting expenditures. Potential recruits are limited in the number of on- and off-campus contacts they may have with representatives of a college's athletic program. Direct contact is also limited to certain months of the year. Each of these stipulations reduces the per-recruit cost of recruiting. The total costs of recruiting are further reduced because colleges are limited in the number of athletic scholarships they can award. A Division I-A college can grant in any year a maximum of 85 scholarships in football and 13 in basketball; scholarship limits apply to other sports as well. Freshman eligibility also reduces the total costs of recruiting by giving colleges 4 rather than 3 years of service by the athlete, and by reducing the number of costly ventures into the recruiting fray. Recruits sign a National Letter of Intent to indicate their chosen college. Once signed, the recruit cannot enroll in another institution without forfeiting 2 years of athletic eligibility. Once signed, the chosen college and all other colleges can immediately terminate expenditures for wooing this particular athlete. Moreover, the scholarship is guaranteed for only 1 year and may be revoked in the future at the whim of the university. If the scholarship is terminated, the athlete will typically have to forgo a year of competitive play should he or she transfer to another athletic program.[14]

Despite the importance of recruiting rules, the predominant feature of the NCAA cartel is the compensation package paid to athletes. Under the guise of "amateurism" the NCAA has severely limited athletes' compensation relative to their value to the institution, while coupling the ability to receive compensation with a variety of changing academic standards.

In 1956, the NCAA initiated athletic scholarships independent of need or academic merit. The scholarships were limited to tuition, room, board, and incidentals, "not to exceed the cost of attendance at the school." In almost 50 years, these compensation limits have changed little. If anything, compensation has decreased over time. The NCAA now allows athletes to hold limited jobs to cover the difference between the full cost of attending college and the value of the athletic scholarship. NCAA President Myles Brand has even said he approves of the idea of giving athletes an additional $2000 to $3000 per year to meet the scholarship-cost differential. State legislators also find athletic scholarships limiting and have initiated legislation to have schools pay athlete expenses beyond tuition, room, board, and book fees.[15]

The NCAA strictly enforces the existing compensation limits. Departures from the rules, no matter how slight, can bring severe penalties. For example, UCLA's basketball team was prohibited from playing in the postseason tournament because recruits were given free UCLA shirts and the team received a free Thanksgiving dinner from an athletic booster. These perks were violations because they were available to basketball players but not to students on the campus at large.

---

[14]Dan Wetzel, "Letter of Intent Benefits Schools, Not Athletes," *CBS SportsLine* (November 12, 2001).
[15]Doug Tucker, "Many Big 12 Coaches Favor Paying Players," *Kansas City Star Telegram* (September 22, 2003); and "Extra Money for Athletes Gaining Steam," *USA Today* (September 19, 2003): 1C.

The shrinking compensation paid to athletes occurs as the revenues of the NCAA are skyrocketing. College athletic programs are generating annual revenues greater than $1 billion in ticket sales and television. The bowls following the 2006 football season alone paid out $210 million, while the men's basketball tournament brought in more that $500 million in television revenue. A winning basketball or football team can provide enough revenue to finance a college's entire athletic program. Clearly, monopsonistic exploitation is profitable.

A number of methods exist for assessing the extent to which athletes are underpaid relative to the revenue stream they generate. What if competition for athletic services were introduced across the entire NCAA? When this happened in Major League Baseball, player salaries increased to 50 to 60 percent of total team revenues. If 50 percent of the Division I-A football revenue were allocated among the football players in this Division, each player would receive $35,000 to 40,000 per year. What if compensation followed the revenue sharing rules of the National Basketball Association (NBA)? Charlie Bell played in three NCAA Final Fours and won a national basketball championship during his Michigan State University basketball career (1998 to 2001). His annual scholarship and aid package was worth an estimated $10,000. If the NCAA used the NBA formula, Bell would have made $1.3 million in his 4-year career, or $345,666 per season, according to calculations made by ESPN.com. Or, what if athletes were paid an amount equal to their economic value to an athletic program? Marginal revenue product analysis suggests that the appropriate average compensation of athletes is similar to the estimates provided above, and indicates that monopsonistic exploitation is even greater for star players. Brown and Jewell conclude that the annual marginal revenue product of individual college football and basketball stars is at least $400,000 and $1,000,000, respectively.[16]

The NCAA argues that amateurism is an essential part of the product it sells, and that its compensation prohibitions are necessary to minimize commercialization of collegiate sports. Nevertheless, the NCAA does not prohibit other competitive and commercial activities: Athletes are courted with lavish stadiums, training facilities, locker rooms and specially outfitted athletic dormitories. Customers are wooed with college brand apparel, videos, logos, and advertisements. Business interests are exploited for stadium billboards, electronic ads on scoreboards, sponsorship of bowl games, logos on team uniforms, and exclusive apparel and equipment contracts. Only the athletes seem to be barred from the financial benefits of big-time college sports.

In 1965, the NCAA began developing academic eligibility standards in response to the accusation that colleges were accepting ill-prepared student athletes who had little chance of academic success. These standards also reinforced the NCAA claim that amateur sports required educational objectives to supersede profit-making objectives. The success of academic standards, however, has been limited both legally and practically.

The initial academic standard was the 1.6 rule, which restricted freshman athletic scholarships to those who could expect a freshman GPA of 1.6, or above, based upon high school academic performance and standardized SAT or ACT scores. The 1.6 rule continued through the 1960s and early 1970s, when campus upheaval led many colleges

---

[16]R. Brown and R. T. Jewell, "Measuring Marginal Revenue Product in College Athletics: Updated Estimates," in *Economics of College Sports*, ed. John Fizel and Rod Fort (Westport, CT: Praeger, 2004).

to relax admission standards for all students. In 1973, the NCAA voted to rescind the 1.6 rule and to let colleges set their own admission standards for athletes. This led to a period of declining graduation rates, followed by college presidents leading a fight to reinstate academic requirements for incoming student athletes. The result was enactment of Proposition 48 in 1983. Freshman eligibility under Proposition 48 required that a student be a high school graduate, obtain at least 700 on the SAT or 15 on the ACT, and earn at least a 2.0 GPA in 11 core high school courses. Students who did not meet these standards were not eligible to practice or play during their freshman year of college and had only 3 years of eligibility left.

Proposition 16 was passed by the NCAA in 1996, replacing Proposition 48. It required college freshman to have a high school diploma, and a minimum GPA in 13 core high school courses, with this GPA linked to standardized test scores by a sliding scale: The higher the high school GPA, the lower the allowable standardized test score. For instance, a student with a 2.0 GPA in these core courses needed to score 1,010 or higher on the SAT to achieve freshman eligibility; an SAT score of less than 820 rendered the student ineligible for his or her freshman year regardless of high school GPA.

The standards were revised in 2002 for all students entering college after August 1, 2003. The number of core high school courses was raised to 14, and the sliding scale relating the GPA in these courses to the standardized test score was extended to eliminate the minimum SAT score. Now, a potential athlete can score a 400, the lowest possible score on the SAT, and still be eligible as long as he or she has a core GPA of at least 3.55. The number of core high school courses required for students entering college after August 1, 2008, has since been raised to 16, while the sliding SAT scale remains unchanged. The NCAA combined this easing of entrance standards for poor standardized test takers with new rules that will make it more difficult for athletes to retain eligibility throughout their college years. Athletes must now complete at least 24 semester hours of course work prior to their second year of college, then complete at least 18 semester hours each academic year, and complete at least 6 semester hours each term. The new standards also require that athletes attain at least 90 percent of the minimum cumulative GPA needed to graduate by the beginning of their second year, at least 95 percent by the start of their third year, and 100 percent by the start of each succeeding year. The standards governing the percent of degree requirements completed each year were also strengthened. Students will need to finish 40 percent rather than 25 percent of their degree requirements prior to the beginning of their junior year; 60 percent rather than 50 percent prior to their fourth year; and 80 percent rather than 75 percent by the beginning of their fifth year. Failure to meet these standards will make the athlete ineligible to play.

Despite the SAT and high school course requirements, athletes continue to have average SAT scores below those of other students.[17] While the initiation of these propositions may have reduced differences between the academic backgrounds of athletes and nonathletes, measurable differences continue to exist. These data are consistent with admission policies that pave the way to recruit excellent athletes who are marginal students but also create a situation where the student athlete will often be at a

---

[17]J. Fizel and T. Smaby, "Participation in Collegiate Athletics and Student Grade Point Averages," in *Economics of College Sports*, ed. John Fizel and Rod Fort (Westport, CT: Praeger, 2004).

disadvantage in competing with his or her peers in the classroom. Athletes also appear to opt for less rigorous curricula and are significantly slower in advancing to an academic degree. The NCAA's latest graduation numbers show that 62 percent of all Division I athletes who entered college in 1998 and 1999 graduated within 6 years, compared to 60 percent of all students. But these aggregate figures are misleading: Men's basketball is the lowest of all sports with a graduation rate of 43 percent, with black players graduating at a 38 percent rate. Baseball shows a graduation rate of 45 percent, while 54 percent of football players graduate within 6 years. Female athletes graduate at a higher 71 percent rate, compared to 63 percent for all female undergrads; male athletes graduate at a rate lower than all male students, 55 percent versus 57 percent.[18]

In addition to the rules for initial eligibility and progress toward a degree just discussed, the NCAA has instituted a program to penalize teams that do not exhibit adequate academic performance. The NCAA uses the Academic Progress Rate (APR) to identify teams with inadequate academics. Teams with APRs that predict less than a 50 percent graduation rate can be penalized with a loss of scholarships. In 2006 the NCAA identified 99 teams from 65 colleges that would lose scholarships due to poor academic performance. Not surprisingly men's basketball, baseball, and football make up 61 of the 99 teams. The NCAA also reported that 40 percent of the teams in these sports are in danger of losing scholarships in the future.[19] Critics contend that while penalties for inadequate academic performance are needed in college sports, loss of scholarships does not go far enough. The Knight Commission argues that teams with graduation rates below 50 percent should be ineligible for bowl games or championship tournaments.[20] If a ban on bowl games had occurred for those with graduation rates less than 50 percent and a 15 percent disparity in racial graduate rates, then none of the top five Bowl Championship Series games could have been played. (Ohio State, the top-ranked team for most of the year, was the worst offender, graduating only 32 percent of its black football players, an incredible 53 percentage points below the 85 percent graduation rate for its white players.[21])

The market for coaches provides a sharp contrast to the market for athletes because head coaches operate in a market close to the textbook competitive ideal. They are free to accept whatever salary and fringe benefits they are offered in the open competition for their services by colleges. The existence of potential National Football League or National Basketball Association assistant and head coaching positions intensifies the college-level competition over coaches. Many star basketball and football coaches are earning annual salaries exceeding $1 million.

In 1991, however, the NCAA instituted a restricted-earnings rule that limited the income of assistant coaches. Restricted-earning coaches could be paid a maximum of $16,000 per year and faced other limitations. For example, the third assistant coach for a Division I men's basketball team could receive only $12,000 in salary with up to $4,000

[18]Brad Wolverton, "Graduation Rates Remain at Record High," *Chronicle of Higher Education* (January 27, 2006): A41.

[19]Brad Wolverton, "NCAA Rescinds Scholarships at 65 College," *Chronicle of Higher Education* (March 10, 2006):A35.

[20]Brad Wolverton, "Under New Formula, Graduation Rates Rise," *Chronicle of Higher Education* (January 6, 2006): A49.

[21]Derrick Z. Jackson, "Graduating to a New Standard," *Boston Globe* (December 4, 2006). Available at www.boston.com/sports/colleges/extras/12_04_06_graduation_rates

additional summer earnings, but was prohibited from off-campus recruiting and could hold this job for a maximum of 5 years. The NCAA's stated intentions were to provide low-cost, entry-level positions for young and inexperienced coaches, and to prevent a bidding war for assistant coaches that would result in competitive imbalance as the sports powerhouses outbid others for the best assistants. A group of restricted-earnings coaches disagreed, however, and sued the NCAA, alleging that the rule limiting their pay was an illegal restraint of trade in violation of antitrust law. The NCAA argued that the restricted-earnings rule was a reasonable restraint of trade, similar to other restraints the courts have allowed. For instance, the NCAA is allowed to limit the size of coaching staffs, the number of games played per season, and financial aid to athletes in order to foster competitive balance. The NCAA also argued that the rule was enacted as an alternative to completely eliminating these coaching positions to reduce costs.

In 1995, a U.S. district court found that the restricted-earnings rule did indeed violate antitrust law and ordered the NCAA to cease and desist from setting assistant coaches' pay. After the appellate court upheld the verdict in 1998, a jury awarded damages of $11.2 million for restricted-earnings basketball coaches and $11.1 million for coaches in other sports affected by the restricted-earnings rule. These damages of $22.3 million were then tripled under antitrust law to nearly $67 million. After an appeal that ended in March 1999, the NCAA settled the case for $54 million.

This decision once again prompts the nagging question: Why are restricted earnings illegal when applied to coaches, but not when applied to the players themselves?

▪▪▪ IV. Performance

Most college sports lose money. This assertion is commonly made by representatives of collegiate athletic departments and the NCAA, and increasingly believed by the media.[22] For example, officials at Michigan and UCLA have regularly claimed financial shortfalls in their athletic budgets, yet these schools play football in stadiums seating more than 100,000, traditionally have strong basketball teams, compete regularly in NCAA postseason competitions, do well in minor sports as well as in football and basketball, and are located in heavily populated metropolitan areas. They typically report revenue near $100 million annually. These schools are also supported by the NCAA's power to control pricing of output and payments to inputs. How is it that these schools operate in the red? And, if these goliaths struggle to be profitable, what is the financial health of other, smaller institutions and their athletic departments? The information in Table 13-2 indicates average real losses exist throughout the NCAA membership lending support to the sports-lose-money assertion.

Despite these deficits, schools race to build new, ever more palatial stadiums and arenas. In the 7 years prior to 2001, capital expenditures at Division I-A institutions increased by 250 percent. The increasing prevalence of reported deficits have even caused athletic departments to ask for financial support from the general fund, capital fund, or other general revenue resources of the university. In 1989, Table 13-3 reports no institutional support was diverted from educational needs to athletic departments

---

[22]See *USA Today* (August 15, 2003): 1C, 11C, 16C; *USA Today* (July 15, 1999):16C; and J. Schulman and W. Bowen, *The Game of Life: College Sports and Educational Values* (Princeton, NJ: Princeton University Press 2001).

TABLE 13-2 Average Real Profit per Institution (Thousands of 2005 Dollars)

Division	1995	1997	1999	2001	2003
I-A	−$243	−$936	$0	−$654	−$633
I-AA	−2,066	−2,340	−2,510	−3,707	−3,903
I-AAA	−1,702	−2,106	−2,852	−3,053	−3,692
II with football	−1,094	−1,053	−1,369	−1,417	−1,688
II without football	−729	−936	−1,027	−1,199	−1,371

Source: Daniel L. Fulks, *Revenues and Expenses of Divisions I and II Intercollegiate Athletic Programs 2002–2003* (Indianapolis, IN: NCAA Publications, 2005).

TABLE 13-3 Athletic Department Budget Deficits: Division I-A

Year	No. of Teams	Percentage of Programs with Deficit When Institutional Support Excluded	Percentage of Programs with Deficit When Institutional Support Included
2003	117	60	25
2001	114	65	32
1999	104	54	29
1997	98	56	31
1995	87	52	14
1993	85	49	24
1989	87	40	40

Source: Daniel L. Fulks, *Revenues and Expenses of Divisions I and II Intercollegiate Athletic Programs, 2001* (Indianapolis, IN: NCAA Publications, 2005).

with deficits in Division I-A; today institutional support defrays, on average, the financial shortages of over 50 percent of the athletics departments.

These data, however, misrepresent the true profitability of college athletics because they are derived using accounting practices that cause reported profits to understate true economic profits. The two most important of these practices are overestimating the cost of athletes, and omitting the positive promotional effects sports teams have on admissions and financial contributions to colleges.

Consider first the data reported by the NCAA for the major revenue sports—Division I-A football and Division I basketball (see Table 13-4). These profit statistics differ dramatically from media reports implying athletic department losses. The revenue growth from 1989 to 2003 was approximately 199 percent for football and 159 percent for basketball. During the same period, expenses for football and basketball grew by only 127 percent and 135 percent, respectively. The result of this disparity in growth rates is a tripling or quadrupling of profits per team.

Also, the reported expenses overstate the true economic expenses of each athlete. This report indicates costs of approximately $70,000 per football player and $185,000 per basketball player. However, the NCAA sets the maximum allowable payment to

TABLE 13-4 Revenues and Expenses of Division I-A Football and Basketball

Division I-A Football

Year	Average Revenue per School	Average Expenses per School	Average Expenses per Player
2003	$12,970,000	$7,050,000	$70,050
2001	10,920,000	6,170,000	61,700
1999	9,040,000	5,260,000	52,600
1997	7,630,000	4,425,000	44,250
1995	6,440,000	4,099,000	40,099
1993	6,300,000	4,013,000	40,130
1989	4,340,000	3,112,000	31,120

Division I-A Basketball

Year	Average Revenue per School	Average Expenses per School	Average Expenses per Player
2003	$4,250,000	$2,230,000	$185,833
2001	3,640,000	1,970,000	164,166
1999	3,160,000	1,580,000	131,666
1997	2,850,000	1,298,000	108,166
1995	2,500,000	1,219,000	101,583
1993	2,120,000	1,091,000	90,917
1989	1,640,000	948,000	79,000

▪▪▪▪▪▪▪▪▪

Source: Daniel L. Fulks, *Revenues and Expenses of Divisions I and II Intercollegiate Athletic Programs, 2001* (Indianapolis, IN: NCAA Publications, 2005).

athletes to cover all in-kind and direct payments for the "cost of attending school." Brown claims that the ceiling for such payments is $20,000.[23] If correct, the total expenses for football players are about one-third, and the total expenses for basketball players about one-eighth of what the NCAA claims. Granted, travel expenses and capital allocations must be added to this per-player expense.

But the story concerning the expenses allocated per athlete is still incomplete. Thus far we have considered only the potential average cost of the athletes rather than the marginal cost to the college of enrolling these students. Given that few colleges operate at full capacity, the marginal cost of admitting an additional student is near zero: The colleges will not hire new faculty or build new classrooms to educate the athlete. Booster contributions, rather than college resources, finance many of the scholarships. When scholarship payments are based on marginal costs, athletic department profits increase substantially.

Sheehan and Goff each estimated the impact on athletic budgets if appropriate economic costs for employment of athletes were used (see Table 13-5). Sheehan finds

---

[23]R. Brown, "Measuring Cartel Rents in the College Basketball Recruitment Market," *Applied Economics* 26 (1994): 27–34; and R. Brown, "An Estimate of the Rent Generated by a Premium College Football Player," *Economic Inquiry* 31 (1993): 671–684.

TABLE 13-5 Adjusted Profits for Top 109 Athletic Departments

Profits/Losses *(millions of dollars)*	*Percent of Athletic Programs*	
	Sheehan	*Goff*
Unprofitable Programs < –1.0	7%	0%
–1.0 to –0.1	9	10
Profitable Programs 0.0 to 0.9	13	11
1.0 to 1.9	13	7
2.0 to 3.9	20	24
4.0 to 6.9	17	22
7.0 to 9.9	7	11
> 9.9	14	15
Median Program Profits	$2.5	$3.9

Source: Adapted from R. Sheehan, *Keeping Score* (South Bend, IN: Diamond Communications 1996); B. Goff, "Effects of University Athletics on the University," in *Economics of College Sports,* ed. John Fizel and Rod Fort (Westport, CT: Praeger, 2004).

16 percent, and Goff 10 percent, of athletic programs in deficit, a far cry from the 60 percent indicated by the NCAA data in Table 13-3.

Athletic department accounting practices also underestimate the revenue attributable to the signing of athletes. In addition to providing games for consumption, athletic departments can also be construed as a public relations branch of the college. Athletic events provide a large amount of advertising for the colleges. Such promotions can increase student applications as well as enhance endowments and gifts from boosters. Each can be a significant source of income for the institution.

In short, collegiate sports are profitable. Appropriate cost and revenue adjustments turn apparent deficits into million-dollar profits. Skousen and Condie demonstrate that Utah State athletics that publicly reported a loss of $700,000 actually turned a $360,000 profit.[24] Borland, Goff, and Pulsinelli show that the alleged loss of $1.5 million in the athletic department at Western Kentucky is actually a $700,000 net gain to the college.[25] Noll provides evidence that a $3 million deficit at the University of Michigan should more accurately be interpreted as a $5 million profit.[26] Obviously, institutions may wish to mask these surpluses as they pump boosters or college presidents for funds to support the sports "arms race" and to continue financing bigger stadiums, more elaborate training facilities, and amenities such as chartered jets to attract athletes.

Even NCAA President Myles Brand cautions that the rate of budget growth for athletic departments needs to be moderated; as athletic departments dip deeper into their school's general funds to cover such costs, he warns that the academic mission

[24]C. Skousen and F. Condie, "Evaluating a Sports Program: Goalposts v. Test Tubes," *Managerial Accounting* 60: 43–49.
[25]M. Borland, B. Goff, and R. Pulsinelli, "College Athletics: Financial Burden or Boon?" in *Advances in the Economics of Sports*, ed. G. Scully (JAI Press: Greenwich CT, 1992).
[26]R. Noll, "The Economics of Intercollegiate Sports," in *Rethinking College Athletics,*" ed. J. Andre and D. James (Philadelphia: Temple University Press, 1991).

could be increasingly pressured. No doubt his comments are made in part to stave off suggestions that the tax exempt status of the NCAA should be revoked. As the former Chair of the U.S. House Ways and Means Committee recently has pointedly asked, "Why should the Federal government subsidize educational institutions when the subsidy is being used to help pay for escalating coaches' salaries, costly chartered travel, and state of the art athletic facilities? What about the NCAA reports that public universities spend as much as $60,000 per men's basketball player—how does that further the educational mission of universities?" In the context of these subsidies, he wonders, "Why are there such low graduation rates among athletes—only 55% for football players at Division I-A schools and 38% for basketball, compared with 64% for all students." With graduation rates for black athletes even lower, his questions (and those of Senator Charles Grassley more recently) suggest these students are victims of schools that want their touchdowns and baskets without providing them an education.[27]

▪▪▪ V. Public Policy

College athletics has clashed with a number of public policies legislated by Congress, and the courts have become increasingly embroiled in determining violations of these laws and appropriate remedies. Recent cases have held that NCAA rules have violated antitrust laws enacted to promote competition and prevent anticompetitive practices. Recent judicial decisions also have held that NCAA rules have violated antiracial discrimination laws. Battles concerning gender equity, athlete compensation, and the possible revocation of the NCAA's federal tax exemption are apt to be the next major legal challenges faced by collegiate athletics. How these challenges are resolved will have a significant impact on the structure and functioning of the college sports cartel.

Title IX

Perhaps no issue has caused more controversy for athletics departments and the NCAA than gender equity or Title IX compliance. As Cedric Dempsey, the past president of the NCAA, has said, "I do not know of any topic in college athletics that brings emotions to the surface more quickly than Title IX. People from all perspectives on this issue have assailed me. It is absolutely impossible to engage this topic without frustrating or even angering somebody."[28]

Title IX of the Education Amendments of 1972 states that "no person in the United States shall, on the basis of sex, be excluded from participation in, be denied the benefits of, or be subjected to discrimination under any education program or activity receiving federal funds."[29] Uncertainty about what Title IX meant was clarified by the U.S. Supreme Court in 1984, when it ruled that violations of Title IX only affected federal

---

[27]See Jack Carey, "It's Up to Schools to Control Sports Spending," *USA Today* (October 31, 2006): 5C; "Who Profits from College Sports?" *Wall Street Journal* editorial (October 13, 2006): W13; and Paul Fain, "Senator Wants Review of Tax Breaks for College-Issued Bonds and Sports," *Chronicle of Higher Education* (April 4, 2007). For the NCAA's position, see Brad Wolverton, "NCAA Defends Tax-Exempt Status as Congressional Scrutiny of Colleges Increases," *Chronicle of Higher Education* (November 16, 2006).
[28]"NCAA's Commitment to Title IX Still Strong," *NCAA News* (March 15, 1999): 2. Also available at www.ncaa.org/news
[29]20 U.S.C. section 1681(a).

money going to areas directly involved in the violation.[30] Since college athletics receive few federal funds, movement toward Title IX compliance was slowed due to the lack of effective penalties. This changed dramatically, however, with the 1988 enactment of the Civil Rights Restoration Act, which barred institutions that violate civil rights laws from receiving any federal money in *any* area of their entire operations. The particular activity need not receive federal funds; it is enough that the institution receives federal funds for any of its activities to be covered under Title IX.

The impact of Title IX on women's athletics has been immense: The number of women's sports offered and the number of female athletes participating in sports has exploded. At the high school level, female participation in athletics has grown from less than 300,000 before the passage of Title IX to more than 2.8 million today, an increase of over 800 percent. Prior to Title IX fewer than 32,000 women participated in intercollegiate athletics, a number that has risen by 500 percent to more than 200,000 women who participate today.[31] The NCAA had no interest in women's athletics prior to Title IX. The Association of Intercollegiate Athletics for Women (AIAW) was the primary organization for women's athletics at the time. Title IX forced the NCAA to take more interest in women's sports. The AIAW was in trouble once the NCAA started sponsoring intercollegiate championships for women's sports in the early 1980s because the NCAA funds most of the expenses associated with participating in its championships. This was something the poorer AIAW could not afford, and the organization folded in 1983.

The conflicts arising from Title IX are mainly due to disputes about how compliance with the law should be determined. The Civil Rights Office of the Department of Education, which enforces Title IX, has promulgated three criteria for determining compliance with the law. If at least one of these three criteria is fulfilled, compliance is met.

The first is the "proportionality" test. This test requires that the participation of women and men in intercollegiate sports should reflect the gender proportions of the full-time undergraduate student body at the institution. A school with 60 percent women and 40 percent men should have women comprise approximately 60 percent of the school's intercollegiate athletes. Athletic scholarships and other forms of support should also reflect the gender proportion of students. The second compliance test is to show a continuing expansion of programs for the under-represented sex that is "responsive to developing interests and abilities of that sex."[32] If programs for the under-represented sex are expanding fast enough to satisfy the student body, then the school is complying with Title IX. The third test for compliance is to demonstrate that existing programs have satisfied the under-represented group's "interests and abilities" in intercollegiate sports.

A recent court case illustrates these tests in action. In 1991, Brown University sponsored 16 men's sports and 16 women's sports. Brown decided to cut university funding for four sports—men's golf and men's water polo, and women's gymnastics

[30]See *Grove City College v. Bell,* 465 U.S. 555, 573–74 (1984).

[31]Donna de Varona and Julie Foudy, Minority Views on the Report of the Commission on Opportunity in Athletics, (February 2003): 2, also available at www.savetitleix.com/minorityreport.pdf; and Welch Suggs, "Gender Quotas? Not in College Sports," *Chronicle of Higher Education* (July 1, 2005): A24.

[32]"Comment: Use of Proportionality Test is Out of Control," *NCAA News* (April 12, 1999): 4; also available at www.ncaa.org/news.

and women's volleyball. Members of the women's teams sued the University for violating Title IX. The 1990–1991 school year's athletic participation was 63 percent men and 37 percent women, while the student body was 51 percent women. Brown argued that the disparity was due to a lower level of interest by women in athletics, and that the school was complying with Title IX by matching offerings with interests. A survey of potential students found that 50 percent of the men and 30 percent of the women had an interest in playing intercollegiate sports. It was also noted that eight times as many men as women participated in intramural sports at Brown.[33]

In 1995, the district court ruled that Brown had violated Title IX. The court said that Brown did not meet any of the three criteria set by the Office for Civil Rights. The participation relative to enrollment numbers violated the proportionality standard, the demotion of two women's programs did not correspond to expanding opportunities, and the two demoted programs had the necessary interest of women students because Brown was able to field teams in them.

Brown appealed this decision to the U.S. Court of Appeals, which upheld the lower court's finding. The court said:

> [T]o assert that Title IX permits institutions to provide fewer athletics participation opportunities for women than for men, based upon the premise that women are less interested in sports than are men, is (among other things) to ignore the fact that Title IX was enacted in order to remedy discrimination that results from stereotyped notions of women's interests and abilities. . . . Interest and ability rarely develop in a vacuum; they evolve as a function of opportunity and experience. . . . [W]omen's lower rate of participation in athletics reflects women's historical lack of opportunities to participate in sports.[34]

This ruling makes it difficult to demonstrate Title IX compliance on any basis other than proportionality.

The U.S. Supreme Court declined to review this decision in 1997, and Brown settled the case the following year. It agreed to maintain women's sports participation within 3 percentage points of the women's undergraduate student body percentage. The focus on proportionality is typical. In 1996 the Office of Civil Rights in the Department of Education declared that proportionality was a *safe harbor*, meaning that a school is presumed to be in compliance with Title IX if proportionality is met. This primacy of proportionality led to a lawsuit by the National Wrestling Coaches Association, which was later joined by organizations representing other so-called minor sports, alleging that proportionality is in reality an illegal quota that has resulted in the elimination of many men's college sports teams.

Adding women's sports and cutting men's sports has been common in the era of Title IX. This, in turn, has provoked heated protest by those involved with men's non-revenue sports: They charge that athletic departments facing limited budgets and the Title IX proportionality standard expand women's programs by eliminating nonrevenue men's sports. Statistics offer some support. The 1984–1985 season was the peak

---

[33]Walter Olson, "Title IX from Outer Space," *Reason* (February 1998): 50–51.
[34]"Brown Title IX Decision Upheld on Appeal," *NCAA News* (December 2, 1996): 2; also available at www.ncaa.org/news

for male athletic participation, with NCAA members averaging 254 per school, and Division I schools averaging 318 each. For the 2001–2002 season NCAA members averaged 205 male athletes, almost a 20 percent decrease from 1984 to 1985. Division I schools averaged 264 male athletes from 2001 to 2002, a reduction of almost 17 percent from 1984 to 1985. Over the same period the number of female athletes has increased from an average of 98 to 150 per school for the NCAA as a whole, and from 115 to 205 for members of Division I—a 53 percent increase for all schools and a 78 percent increase for Division I members.[35]

The numbers indicate that proportionality has not yet been attained. Women now make up 43 percent of all NCAA athletes, which is up substantially from the participation rate of about 28 percent for 1984 to 1985. But this percentage still falls far short of proportionality because the majority of undergraduate students are women. The preceding numbers also make clear that the movement toward proportionality has been achieved by increasing opportunities for women and decreasing opportunities for men.

In 2002 the U. S. Department of Education established the Secretary of Education's Commission on Opportunity in Athletics to study Title IX. The commission's recommendations were issued in the following year, accompanied by a separate minority report submitted by two commissioners and advocates of women's athletics. Recommendations of the Commission included a request that the Department of Education clearly explain that each of the three criteria for meeting Title IX are independent methods of compliance; that reducing men's teams to attain compliance is a disfavored practice; that the Department of Education should establish standards regarding private funding of particular teams facing elimination of university funding; that walk-ons be excluded from proportionality calculations; that schools could conduct interest surveys to help demonstrate compliance; and that proportionality would no longer be a safe harbor.

Mike Moyer, executive director of the National Wrestling Coaches Association, especially welcomed the recommendations that would give flexibility in meeting Title IX, and the elimination of safe harbor status for the proportionality test.[36] The two dissenting commissioners, Donna de Varona and Julie Foudy, argued in their minority report that the majority recommendations would result in a weakening of Title IX and reduce opportunities for women athletes. Rod Paige, Secretary of Education, initially declared that the department would only consider implementing the recommendations that were passed by consensus. In July 2003 the Education Department announced no changes would be made in the way Title IX will be enforced. Women's rights groups lauded the announcement, while those who attacked the use of proportionality predicted that reductions in men's sports will continue as schools attempt to conform to Title IX.

In 2005 the Department of Education explicitly laid out what schools needed to do to satisfy the third test of meeting the interests and abilities of the underrepresented group. An e-mail survey designed to get a high response rate could provide sufficient evidence that the needs of women athletes are being met. Advocates of women in sports have protested this interpretation, arguing that much more than a single survey

---

[35]Welch Suggs, "Cutting the Field: As Colleges Eliminate Teams, the Lessons Athletes Learn are Losing Out to Commercial Interests," *Chronicle of Higher Education* (June 6, 2003): A37.
[36]Kay Hawes, "Title IX Report Shares Center Stage With Dissenting View," *NCAA News* (March 3, 2003): 4, available at www.ncaa.org/news/2003/20030303/active/4005n01.html

is needed to show compliance with Title IX. Perhaps more important to the schools considering using this method, the NCAA has called this Department of Education policy disappointing and unsatisfactory.[37]

A 2006 decision by James Madison University to cut 7 men's teams and 3 women's teams to comply with Title IX demonstrates that proportionality is still in force: Prior to these cuts, over half the athletes on campus (50.7%) were women, but 61 percent of the undergraduate student body is female. After cuts affecting 144 students, the participation rate of women athletes increased to 61 percent. The university explicitly stated that the teams were eliminated to come into compliance with Title IX, rather than as a cost-cutting move.[38]

The attack on proportionality was primarily aimed at reducing the elimination of nonrevenue men's sports. The argument seems logical: Facing a need to allocate funds to satisfy Title IX proportionality, the athletic director has little alternative but to add nonrevenue women's sports at the expense of nonrevenue men's sports. Compelling as the argument may be, the facts tell a different tale. If Title IX requirements place an undue burden on athletic budgets, one would expect the axe to fall disproportionately on Division III men's nonrevenue sports because at this level neither men's football nor basketball generate profits to subsidize their continued existence. In contrast, profits from football and basketball in Division I-A can be used to spare the demise of nonrevenue men's sports.

However, a profitable football program is no guarantee that men's or women's sports will receive adequate funding. Table 13-6 presents data compiled by the Women's Sports Foundation on the change in the number of men's sports between 1978 and 1996. In contrast to expectations, the data show that the offerings of men's sports declined in Divisions I-A and I-AA, but actually *increased* in Divisions I-AAA, II and III, with the largest net decrease in Division I-A. Similarly, Leeds, et al. found

TABLE 13-6 Changes in Men's Sports (1978–1996)

NCAA Division	Number of Sports Added	Number of Sports Deleted	Net Change
I-A	22	113	−91
I-AA	68	129	−61
I-AAA	93	56	+37
II	344	286	+58
III	400	269	+131
Total	927	853	+74

Source: Adapted from D. Marburger and N. Hogshead-Makar, "Is Title IX Really to Blame for the Decline in Intercollegiate Men's Non-Revenue Sports?" *Marquette Sports Law Review* 14, no. 1 (2003); 65–93.

[37]Brad Wolverton, "Education Dept. Affirms Use of E-Mail Surveys in Title IX Compliance," *Chronicle of Higher Education* (March 31, 2006): A42.

[38]Allison Kasic, "Untilting the Playing Field: Title IX, On the Way Out?" *National Review Online* (October 18, 2006).

that Division I-A football programs have an almost uniformly negative impact on offerings for women. They predict that, on average, premier football programs will drain approximately $184,000 per year from women's sports.[39]

Although this behavior may appear counterintuitive, such action is consistent with budget allocations in accordance with profit maximization. Athletic directors in Division I have an incentive to dedicate a greater portion of their budgets to football and basketball because the marginal benefit of a dollar spent on these programs exceeds the marginal benefit of a dollar spent on the football and basketball in Division II or III or on nonrevenue sports. In practice, the athletic director cannot eliminate all nonrevenue sports because the NCAA requires a minimum number of varsity sports for membership in Division I, and Title IX insulates women's nonrevenue sports from budgetary cuts. Thus, the athletic director slows the growth of nonrevenue women's programs and cuts nonrevenue men's programs. As a result we can expect the continuation of reverse gender discrimination lawsuits against universities in addition to the gender discrimination lawsuits filed by female athletes.

Eliminate the Monopsony

Current NCAA policies governing athletic compensation violate the spirit of antitrust laws, but the NCAA claims these policies are needed to protect the competitive balance and amateur status of collegiate sports. These defenses may no longer be valid, if they ever were.

The NCAA has used the competitive balance argument in previous cases involving restrictive practices. This argument failed in the NCAA's attempt to maintain control over college football telecasts. Without control of telecasts, the NCAA claimed that broadcasts would be skewed to the traditional football powers, allowing them to recruit more successfully and thereby increasing the onfield disparity between the traditional powers and their lesser rivals. The Supreme Court rejected this claim and assigned control of telecasts to the individual schools. Empirical evidence suggests that competitive balance has increased, not declined, since the telecast restrictions have been lifted.

The competitive balance argument also failed when the NCAA imposed a salary cap on assistant coaches. Without the salary cap, the NCAA claimed that the best coaches would all be drawn to just a few schools, which would destroy competitive balance. But the fact is that with or without a salary cap, the coaches already had an incentive to go to the best sports schools because these programs provide better training and exposure. A change in the compensation structure does not affect competitive balance, but it does alter the allocation of resources: A salary cap transfers monies from coaches to the colleges. The same is true for college athletes—compensation restrictions transfer monies from the players to the colleges without affecting competitive balance.

The NCAA's second line of defense is that it provides amateur sports contests. If athletes were paid and collegiate sports commercialized, the NCAA claims, demand for college sports would decline. This argument is commonly and uncritically accepted, but for most colleges that engage in big-time sports, the game is not now broadly viewed as amateur. Audiences do not view the players as student athletes; they accept

---

[39]M. Leeds, Y. Suris, and J. Durkin, "College Football and Title IX," in *Economics of College Sports*, ed. John Fizel and Rod Fort (Westport, CT: Praeger, 2004).

the commercialization of college sports. Billions of dollars in NCAA revenues indicates that acceptance, too. We agree with Noll, who stated:

> College sports are already professionalized at universities that house their athletes separately, that advertise themselves as preparatory schools for a career in professional sports, and that fail to graduate nearly all of their players. America wants big-time sports, professional and collegiate, and as long as they do, colleges will supply it . . . the damage of professionalism has been done, and is probably irreversible even if one wanted to undertake the task of changing the system.[40]

It is also doubtful that colleges would lose a significant portion of their audience and revenue if the athletes were paid. Fan support has been steadily growing even as the sport has become commercialized. Boosters—the biggest supporters of college sports—are typically the ones attempting to pay athletes to recruit them. Perhaps popularity and demand would even accelerate if the hypocrisy tainting the amateur status of collegiate sports were removed. Certainly, the Olympics has lost none of its appeal and has generated increased revenues since it abandoned the requirement that its participants be amateurs.

Occasionally, supporters of the NCAA monopsony will argue that underpayment is a temporary phenomenon, and that athletes soon will make millions as professionals. The soon-to-be-rich athletes are subsidizing the less fortunate. This claim is invalid on three counts. First, counteracting the ability to become professionals, the NBA and its union have recently (2005) limited American players' ability to enter the league early by setting a minimum age of 19 and a minimum of 1 year past high school graduation. In addition, in 2004, Maurice Clarett, a college sophomore, unsuccessfully challenged under the antitrust laws the NFL's rule preventing players from entering the league until at least 3 years following high school graduation. Both the NBA's new rule and the NFL's rule on underclassmen increase the potential for exploitation of stars. Second, less than 1 percent of all collegiate athletes actually make it to the professional ranks. Finally, collegiate athletes typically come from poorer households than the average college student; often they come from quite disadvantaged backgrounds. Thus, the NCAA not only blocks the functioning of this labor market, it does so in a regressive way that hurts poorer, less-advantaged students the most.

The question remains, how should athletes be paid? Several alternatives have been suggested. The players could unionize. A fundamental factor in the NCAA's current power is that colleges do not recognize athletes as employees. But if athletes were viewed as employees, they would be eligible to unionize and bargain for pay. They would also be eligible for workers' compensation for injuries sustained in practice and play. (Athletic department concern over worker's compensation is a major deterrent to recognizing athletes as employees.) This arrangement would be similar to that in professional sports, where an alliance of teams bargains with a union of players to establish rules and compensation packages. An athlete compensation fund could be set up for each college, and colleges could distribute the funds among the players as they saw

---

[40]Noll, "The Economics of Intercollegiate Sports," 208.

fit. They could pay athletes a signing bonus to enroll, pay rewards for competitive performance, or establish trust funds. To emphasize the concept of student athlete, compensation could be linked to graduation: If athletes do not graduate, they forego a portion of their agreed-upon remuneration.

Player compensation does have its side effects. If a college currently uses profits from its basketball and football programs to subsidize nonrevenue sports, the nonrevenue programs may suffer unless they can obtain financial support from the college or other sources. Many colleges might drop some sports due to the diminished profits. The basic issue is whether athletes in profitable sports should bear the cost of supporting less profitable programs. An increase in the cost of athletic talent might also precipitate a significant decline in the salaries of coaches. However, fans might get to view higher-quality collegiate sporting contests as the top athletes continued to play college sports longer rather than jumping early to professional leagues. Most important, collegiate athletes would earn a competitive salary in exchange for the value of their services.

CONCLUSION ▪▪▪▪▪▪▪

The NCAA and its member schools have created a vast college sports cartel that pays its most important resources, the athletes, far below what they would earn in a competitive market. The NCAA operates behind a veil of amateurism as its members generate revenues comparable to professional sports, practice and play in facilities that rival those found in professional sports, and pay their top coaches salaries comparable to those paid to coaches of professional teams. Only the student athletes are bound to amateur status and prevented from sharing in the bounty generated by their play.

Yet ironically, as the wealth of the cartel increases, its strength may be eroding. A recent string of losing court battles is stripping away the veil of amateurism. Gender equity requirements are causing serious profit allocation difficulties. The specter of competing leagues portends the possible necessity of bidding competitively for human resources. Employee rights may soon be granted to athletes. Federal education subsidies may be limited to general educational funds only. Meanwhile, points of conflict multiply with the growing size and diversity of NCAA membership.

The NCAA has responded to threats in the past by expanding its reach—in membership as well as in its rules and regulations. Yet NCAA regulations have done little to promote amateurism and little to improve on-the-field competitiveness. Depken and Wilson report that regime changes such as the Sanity Code, the minimum GPA, the dividing of the NCAA into multiple divisions, and the BCS have had a negative influence on the competitive environment of NCAA sports. Likewise, NCAA rule-enforcement policies often harm competitive balance.[41]

Clearly, the NCAA is facing legal and political challenges from outside the organization. Its rules and enforcement policies are exacerbating internal tensions. Once again the college sports cartel is beginning to crack, and only the future will reveal how it will respond to these latest challenges.

---

[41]C. Depken and D. Wilson, "Institutional Change in the NCAA and Competitive Balance in Intercollegiate Football," and "The Impact of Cartel Enforcement in Division I-A Football," both in *Economics of College Sports*, ed. John Fizel and Rod Fort (Westport, CT: Praeger, 2004).

SUGGESTIONS FOR FURTHER READING ▪▪▪▪▪▪▪▪

Byers, W. 1985. *Unsportsmanlike Conduct: Exploiting College Athletes.* Ann Arbor: University of Michigan Press.

Fizel, J. and R. Fort, eds. 2004. *The Economics of College Sports.* Westport, CT: Praeger.

Fleisher, A., B. Goff, and R. Tollison. 1992. *The National Collegiate Athletic Association: A Study in Cartel Behavior.* Chicago: University of Chicago Press.

Fort, R., and J. Quirk. 1999. "The College Football Industry." In *Sports Economics: Current Research.* Ed. J. Fizel, E. Gustafson, and L. Hadley, 11–26. Westport, CT: Praeger Publishers.

Knight Foundation Commission on Intercollegiate Athletics, Ten Years Later. 2001. (Miami: Knight Foundation).

Koch, J. 1982. "The Intercollegiate Athletics Industry." In *The Structure of American Industry,* ed. Walter Adams, 325–346. New York: Macmillan Publishing Co.

Noll, R. 1991. "The Economics of Intercollegiate Sports." In *Rethinking College Athletics.* Ed. J. Andre and D. James, 197–209. Philadelphia: Temple University Press.

Schulman, J. and W. Bowen. 2001. *The Game of Life: College Sports and Educational Values.* Princeton, NJ: Princeton University Press.

Sperber, M. 1990. *College Sports, Inc..* New York: Henry Holt.

_____. 2000. *Beer and Circus: How Big Time College Sports is Crippling Undergraduate Education.* New York: Henry Holt.

U.S. Department of Education, Commission on Opportunity in Athletics. 2003. "Open to All: Title IX at Thirty." Washington, D.C., February 28, 2003.

CHAPTER 14

Public Policy In A Free-Enterprise Economy

JAMES W. BROCK

Controlling power in a free society and guarding against its abuse is the crux of the American political-economic experience. Indeed, the American nation was forged from the colonists' protest against the arbitrary power of the British Crown.

Once liberated, the nation's founders understood that in creating a governance structure for a free society, they must provide for a government strong enough to restrain individuals from infringing on the liberties of one another. At the same time, they recognized that additional safeguards were required to prevent government itself from being transmuted into an instrument of oppression. Throughout their deliberations, the founders displayed a profoundly dyspeptic view of human nature. They understood (as Thomas Burke put it in 1777) that "power of all kinds has an irresistible propensity to increase a desire for itself"; that "power will sometime or other be abused unless men are well watched, and checked by something they cannot remove when they please"; and that the "root of the evil is deep in human nature."

Their solution for resolving this dilemma was incorporated in the Constitution and predicated on two transcending principles. First, it is the *structure* of government, not the personal predilections of those who govern, that is paramount; and, second, in Jefferson's words, "it is not by the consolidation or concentration of powers, but by their distribution, that good government is effected." Their master plan was to construct a system of checks and balances—a Newtonian mechanism of countervailing powers—operating harmoniously in mutual frustration. The goal was to prevent what the founders considered the ultimate threat to a free society: the concentration of power and the abuses that flow from it. In Federalist Paper 51 James Madison observed:

> It may be a reflection on human nature that such devices should be necessary to control the abuses of government, but what is government itself, but the greatest of all reflections on human nature? If men were angels, no government

389

would be necessary. If angels were to govern men, neither external nor internal controls on government would be necessary. In framing a government which is to be administered by men over men, the great difficulty lies in this: you must first enable the government to control the governed; and in the next place oblige it to control itself. A dependence on the people is, no doubt, the primary control on the government; but experience has taught mankind the necessity of auxiliary precautions.

The American Antitrust Tradition

Subsequent events demonstrated that in a free society the problem of power is not confined to the political realm alone. A century after the Constitution was ratified, during the post–Civil War era, an explosion of pools, trusts, cartels, and monopolies demonstrated the need to address economic power as well. To guard against excessive private, as well as governmental, concentrations of power, Americans recognized the necessity of preventing "autocrats of trade" from ensnaring them in a new kind of industrial feudalism. "If we will not endure a king as a political power," Ohio Republican Senator John Sherman warned, "we should not endure a king over the production, transportation, and sale of any of the necessaries of life." Unless Congress addressed the problem of private economic power, he urged, there would "be a trust for every production and a master to fix the price for every necessity of life."[1]

In theory, Adam Smith showed how the competitive marketplace regulated and neutralized economic power—how it dispersed economic decision-making power in the hands of a multitude of rivals and compelled each to perform well in the public interest, thereby transforming the private vice of self-interest into a public virtue. In theory, Smith showed how a competitive market system harnessed private economic decision making and channeled it along socially beneficial lines by compelling innovation, progress, and efficiency in allocating resources in accordance with society's preferences. In theory, he showed how a competitive market system provided economic freedom and opportunity, while rendering private economic decision making accountable to the citizenry.

In reality, however, the corporate combination and trust movement of late nineteenth-century America showed that as an effective system of economic governance, the competitive market is neither self-perpetuating nor an immutable artifact of nature. Events demonstrated that without strictly enforced rules of the game, the competitive market could be eroded and subverted through cartel agreements not to compete, as well as through mergers and monopolization by dominant firms.

Maintaining competition as the primary regulator of America's economic affairs is the central goal of the antitrust laws. Like the Constitution, American antitrust laws provide for a structure of governance—a social blueprint for organizing economic decision making and for guarding against its abuse. Like the Constitution, the antitrust laws seek to disperse power into many hands rather than allowing it to be concentrated in the hands of a few. Just as the purpose of the Constitution is to prevent any political faction from monopolizing the coercive power of the state, so the basic objective of the antitrust laws is to prevent private organizations from monopolizing society's economic decision making.

---

[1] Hans B. Thorelli, *The Federal Antitrust Policy: Origination of an American Tradition* (Baltimore: Johns Hopkins University Press, 1955), 180.

The Sherman Act, the nation's first antitrust statute, enacted in 1890, prohibits two major types of interference with competitive free enterprise: cartels and monopolization. Section 1 of the Sherman Act, dealing with cartels, states, "Every contract, combination . . . or conspiracy in restraint of trade of commerce among the several States, or with foreign nations, is hereby declared illegal." As interpreted by the courts, this makes it unlawful for businesses to agree to fix prices, restrict output or productive capacity, divide markets or allocate customers, or exclude competitors by systematic resort to oppressive tactics and predatory practices. In short, it enjoins collective actions by competitors aimed at controlling the market and short-circuiting its regulatory discipline.

Section 2 of the Sherman Act, which addresses structural concentrations of economic power, provides that "every person who shall monopolize or attempt to monopolize, or combine or conspire to monopolize any part of the trade or commerce among the several States, or with foreign nations, shall be deemed guilty . . . and . . . punished." Section 2 makes it unlawful for firms to obtain a stranglehold on the market, either by forcing rivals out of business or by absorbing or controlling them. It prohibits a single firm (or group of firms acting jointly) from dominating an industry or market. Positively stated, Section 2 promotes a decentralized economic structure in which a sufficient number of independent rivals ensure effective competition.

The Sherman Act's proscriptions are general, perhaps even vague, and essentially negative. Directed primarily against *existing* dominant firms and *existing* trade restraints, the Sherman Act proved incapable of addressing specific practices that could be used to achieve the proscribed results. Armed with the power to dissolve existing monopolies, the enforcement authorities could not, under the Sherman Act, attack the growth of monopoly in advance and prior to its realization. For this reason, Congress enacted supplementary legislation in 1914 "to arrest the creation of trusts, conspiracies and monopolies in their incipiency and before consummation." In the Federal Trade Commission Act of 1914, Congress established an independent commission to police the economic field against "all unfair methods of competition," as well as to conduct expert studies of competition and monopoly in the economy.

With the Clayton Act of the same year, Congress targeted four specific practices that experience had shown to be potent methods for creating monopoly positions: (1) price discrimination (that is, cutthroat competition and predatory price cutting); (2) tying contracts and exclusive dealership agreements; (3) mergers and acquisitions; and (4) interlocking boards of directors among rival firms. Emphasizing their preventative purpose, the act generally declared these practices unlawful, not in and of themselves, but where their effect "*might* be to substantially lessen competition or *tend* to create a monopoly." Price discrimination, for example, would be illegal only if used systematically as an instrument for destroying competition, as it was in the hands of the Standard Oil and American Tobacco trusts. Similarly, the Clayton Act's merger provisions (as amended by the Celler-Kevauver Act in 1950) prohibit any business merger or acquisition whose effect may be to substantially lessen competition or to tend to create a monopoly in any line of commerce in any region of the country. The emphasis in the Clayton Act is on preventing anticompetitive problems from arising in the first place, rather than struggling with how to remedy them after they have become entrenched.

Economics of a Free Market

Producers   Consumer

Economics of Security

Producers   Consumer

▪▪▪ **FIGURE 14-1** The Antritrust Challenge

Source: Thurman W. Arnold, Cartels or Free Enterprise? Public Affairs Pamphlet 103, 1945. Reproduced by courtesy of Public Affairs Commission, Inc.

The philosophy of American antitrust policy perhaps has been best articulated by Judge Charles Wyzanski:

> Concentrations of power no matter how beneficently they appear to have acted, nor what advantages they seem to possess, are inherently dangerous. Their good behavior in the past may not be continued; and if their strength were hereafter grasped by presumptuous hands, there would be no automatic check and balance from equal forces in the industrial market. And in the absence of this protective mechanism, the demand for public regulation, public ownership, or other drastic measures would become irresistible in time of crisis.
>
> Dispersal of private economic power is thus one of the ways to preserve the system of private enterprise. . . . [Moreover,] well as a monopoly may have behaved in the moral sense, its economic performance is inevitably suspect. The very absence of strong competitors implies that there cannot be an objective measuring rod of the monopolist's excellence. . . . What appears to the

outsider to be a sensible, prudent, nay even a progressive policy of the monopolist, may in fact reflect a lower scale of adventurousness and less intelligent risk-taking than would be the case if the enterprise were forced to respond to a stronger industrial challenge.

Industrial progress, he wrote, "may indeed be in inverse proportion to economic power; for creativity in business as in other areas, is best nourished by multiple centers of activity, each following its unique pattern and developing its own esprit de corps to respond to the challenge of competition."[2]

Antitrust Under Fire

Over the years, these traditional precepts have been attacked from both ends of the political-economic spectrum.

The Challenge from the Left

On the left, an antitrust policy of competition enforced by law has long been dismissed as a savage, counterproductive anachronism. Instead, concentration and market dominance are believed to be the inevitable products of industrial advance, with more direct social control (comprising negotiation and compromise among organized blocs of industry, labor and government) considered a superior approach.

This was true of the epic consolidation and trust wave at the turn of the twentieth century. Pioneer labor leader Samuel Gompers, for example, at the time rejected antitrust policy (the early enforcement of which had been directed against labor unions): "We have seen those who know little of statecraft and less of economics urge the adoption of laws to 'regulate' interstate commerce, 'prevent' combinations and trusts," he charged, but government "is not capable of preventing the legitimate development or natural concentration of industry."[3] Strong labor unions, he believed, would neutralize the power of the trusts, while enabling workers to bargain for a larger share of the fruits of industrial gigantism and market concentration. Herbert Croly, a leading progressive of the time, was sure that monopolistic trusts marked "an important step in the direction of the better organization of industry and commerce"; he advocated scrapping the antitrust laws in favor of a national policy aimed at fostering "a more positive mode of action and more edifying habit of thought" among business and labor leaders.[4] Socialists of the day asserted with biblical certitude that we "have left the Egypt of competition . . . and are now wandering in the desert of monopoly, which we must pass through to reach the promised land of universal co-operation."[5]

This criticism of antitrust from the left re-emerged during the Great Depression of the 1930s, and became the touchstone for the National Industrial Recovery Act of 1933 (NIRA). The NIRA was enacted to launch a new economic regime of "constructive

---

[2]*United States v. United Shoe Machinery Corp.*, 110 F. Supp. 295 (1953), affirmed per curiam, 347 U.S. 521 (1954).

[3]Quoted in Joseph Dorfman, *The Economic Mind in American Civilization*, vol. 3 (New York: Viking Press, 1949), 217.

[4]Herbert Croly, *The Promise of American Life*, Harvard Library edition (Cambridge, MA: Harvard University Press, 1965), 358–59, 397.

[5]Quoted in Jack Blicksilver, *Defenders and Defense of Big Business in the United States, 1880–1900* (New York: Garland, 1985), 68.

cooperation," which, it was believed, would lift the country from the depths of depression: Business would get self-government, relief from destructive competition, and immunity from the antitrust laws. Labor leaders saw the NIRA as ushering in the kind of social planning and industrial self-government they had long advocated, including the rights of workers to organize and bargain collectively with business. Progressive government leaders like Rexford Tugwell held the NIRA would demonstrate that "cooperation not conflict" was the superior principle for restoring confidence and getting the economy moving again.[6] These goals, New Dealers believed, could be achieved only by replacing competition with a system of national planning along individual industry lines—sector-by-sector planning cooperatively undertaken by business and labor, and overseen by government in the public interest.

In the 1980s, the anemic performance of the U.S. economy, coupled with the specter of a world-triumphant "Japan Inc.," sparked another resurgence of cooperation and coalition advocacy from the left (under the rubric of industrial policy) as an alternative to America's antitrust tradition. Pointing to a flood of foreign imports into American markets, lagging U.S. productivity, and stubbornly high unemployment, industrial policy advocates charged, "What used to work won't work. For the world has changed."[7] The only viable course, they insisted, lay in a consciously constructed national industrial policy comprising tripartite planning, and negotiation and compromise among management, labor, and government. These advocates pointed to postwar economic miracles in Japan and other East Asian nations for what they considered proof of the superior results such cooperation could achieve. And they derided traditional antitrust concerns about disproportionate economic size and power as antiquated and destructive in a new global age. Even if General Motors were the only auto company in the country, these advocates claimed, it would still be "in a competitive fight for its life with the Japanese and Germans. And it doesn't make sense to hamstring General Motors or anybody else with antitrust laws since they must operate in an international competitive environment."[8]

As a guidepost for economic policy, however, the left's infatuation with "cooperationism" and organizational gigantism suffers from a number of fatal flaws. The first fundamental defect is the problem of the coalescence of power among organized groups, which are predisposed to protect their parochial private interests rather than promote the public wellbeing. Advocates of "coalition capitalism" assume that powerful private groups will act in ways, and toward ends, that will promote good economic performance. But such power blocs instead may recognize their mutual interest in preserving the status quo, and aggrandizing their power and influence at the public's expense.

This is not idle conjecture. The consequences of the National Recovery Administration (NRA) in the 1930s, for example, were hardly what its proponents promised. The NRA enabled business groups to cartelize industries, and labor groups

---

[6]See Ellis W. Hawley, *The New Deal and the Problem of Monopoly* (Princeton, NJ: Princeton University Press, 1966), 19–33.

[7]U.S. Congress. House. Subcommittee on Economic Stabilization, Hearing: Industrial Policy, Part 1, 98th Cong., 1st sess., 1983, 173.

[8]Lester C. Thurow, "Abolish the Antitrust Laws," *Dun's Review* (February 1981): 72. See also Thurow, *The Zero-Sum Solution* (New York: Simon & Schuster, 1985).

to raise wages, while government rubber-stamped their self-serving schemes. Yet in 1934, at the close of congressional hearings on the NRA, Senator Gerald Nye was

> forced to the conclusion that the power of monopoly has been greatly increased during the stay of the NRA; that invitation to monopoly in the United States is greater than ever before. In view of what amounts to suspension of the antitrust laws, the small independent producers, the small business man generally, whether buyer from, competitor of, or seller to large monopolized industries, and the great mass of ultimate consumers, are seemingly without protection other than that given by the NRA. And the NRA is not giving this protection. On the contrary, it has strengthened, not weakened, the power of monopoly.[9]

In the steel industry, corporate giants and organized labor honed cooperative industry control into a fine art form. For decades, Big Steel and the United Steelworkers union coalesced to engineer a steady record of sustained price-wage-price inflation in a key industrial commodity. When foreign competition threatened to disrupt their collaboration, they have cooperated to lobby government for restraints on imports. These import restraints have served the narrow interests of steel management and labor. But by inflating steel prices, they have jeopardized the competitiveness of the vastly larger constellation of American steel-using firms and the far greater number of workers those firms employ (12.8 million steel-using jobs versus 226,000 steel-making jobs, according to one recent estimate).[10] At the same time, steel management and labor collectively negotiated billions of dollars of pensions, retirement programs, and other legacy costs the companies could not afford, and which the industrial-labor complex in steel has dumped on society by forcing the federal government to assume financial responsibility for them (at the cost of $7 billion as a result of the bankruptcies of such steel giants as LTV, Bethlehem, and National).[11]

In airlines, collective bargaining between the dominant carriers and organized labor (especially the powerful pilots union) has driven the giants' costs sky high, while pushing them to the brink of bankruptcy and beyond (including employee-owned United, which collapsed in bankruptcy in 2002, and Delta, USAirways, and Northwest Airlines, which each declared bankruptcy over the period from 2002 through 2005). The management-labor complex in airlines, like that in steel, is also dumping its collectively bargained legacy costs of pension and retirement programs on society via the federal government's pension insurance fund. The airline industry, too, has preferred to privatize its gains while socializing its costs.

---

[9]Quoted in Leverett S. Lyon et al., *The National Recovery Administration: An Analysis and Appraisal* (Washington, D.C.: Brookings Institution, 1935), 709. See also Barbara Alexander, "The Impact of the National Recovery Act on Cartel Formation and Maintenance Costs," *Review of Economics and Statistics* 76 (May 1994): 245–54.

[10]Gary Clyde Hufbauer and Ben Goodrich, "Steel Policy: The Good, the Bad, and the Ugly," International Economics Policy Brief 03-1, Institute for International Economics, January 2003, and Consuming Industries Trade Action Coalition, "Steel-Consuming Jobs vs. Steel-Producing Jobs, 1999," available at www.citac-trade.org

[11]On the steel industry generally, see Walter Adams and James W. Brock, *The Bigness Complex: Industry, Labor, and Government in the American Economy*, 2nd ed. (Palo Alto: Stanford University Press, 2004), chapters 19 and 21.

In professional sports, mutual accommodation between players and owners has empowered the "sports-industrial complex" to blackmail communities by threatening to relocate teams unless they are accorded a bounty of public subsidies. Billions of dollars of professional sports welfare provides profits for owners, astronomical salaries for players, and palatial stadiums for both, while depriving local communities of desperately needed funds for education, transportation, and genuine job development.[12] And in defense weapons procurement, cooperation between the government as a buyer of weapons, and the defense contractors that produce them—including the notorious revolving door by which the same officials occupy influential positions in organizations on *both* sides of the market—is scarcely a model of economic rectitude. It has tainted billions of dollars of reconstruction contracts in post-Saddam Iraq. It is evident in the scandal surrounding the Pentagon's recent procurement of aerial refueling aircraft from Boeing (where a purchasing official for the Pentagon was negotiating for the Air Force on the buyer side, while at the same time negotiating for an executive position with Boeing on the supplier side) This situation led Senator John McCain to conclude that "the Air Force appeared not so much to negotiate with Boeing as to advocate for it, to the point of appearing to allow the company too much control not only over pricing and the terms and conditions of the contract, but perhaps also over the aircraft's capabilities."[13] The deleterious consequences of cooperationism in military procurement is further evident in the Coast Guard's effort to bolster the nation's homeland security by allowing two defense weapons giants to collectively control all major aspects of a $17 billion modernization program—a cooperative endeavor that has generated billions of dollars in cost overruns for ships that break in half.[14]

Antitrust critics on the left also harbor a misplaced faith in the virtues of corporate gigantism. General Motors has long stood as the world's largest automotive concern, with annual revenues exceeding the gross national product of all but a few nations. Yet GM has perennially suffered from the bureaucratic sclerosis endemic to its mammoth size. It strains credulity to suggest that GM's afflictions are somehow due to its being too small, when the firm has only been able to improve its economic performance in recent years by substantially paring its size, and when the megamerger of Chrysler and Daimler (as well as Ford's acquisitions of Land Rover, Jaguar, and Volvo) have generated disastrous results.

In steel, a century of merger-induced corporate gigantism failed to produce paragons of efficiency or technological innovativeness. Instead, America's steel giants became backward bureaucracies that lost sales, market share, and hundreds of thousands of jobs when confronted, first, by competition from abroad, and later, by more

---

[12]See *Bigness Complex*, Chapter 22.

[13]On Boeing's tanker program, see Senator McCain's opening statement before the U.S. Congress. Senate. Committee on Commerce, Science and Transportation, Hearing: Lease of Boeing Tankers to U.S. Air Force, September 3, 2003; U.S. Congressional Budget Office, Assessment of the Air Force's Plan to Acquire 100 Boeing Tanker Aircraft, Washington D.C., August 2003; and Anne Marie Squeo and J. Lynn Lunsford, "How Two Officials Got Caught by Pentagon's Revolving Door," *Wall Street Journal* (December 18, 2003): 1.

[14]See Eric Lipton, "Billions Later, Plan to Remake the Coast Guard Fleet Stumbles," *New York Times* (December 9, 2006): 1; and Office of Inspector General, Department of Homeland Security, "Improvements Needed in the U.S. Coast Guard's Acquisition and Implementation of Deepwater Information Technology Systems," Washington, D.C., August 2006.

efficient U.S. mini-mills at home. These small state-of-the-art producers revolutionized the field while winning markets from such supposedly invincible suppliers as Japan and South Korea.

In pharmaceutical drugs, megamergers over the past decade that have consolidated the field into a few massive firms have been justified in the name of promoting the research and development of new life-saving medicines. Yet the new-product pipelines of the merged giants have become steadily drier, compelling them to turn increasingly to smaller, more innovative firms for their new breakthrough medicines, while raising questions of whether massive size is antithetical to technological progress in pharmaceuticals.[15] And in airlines, the biggest carriers suffered the greatest losses during the period leading up to and following the 9/11 attacks, while smaller carriers (Southwest, Jet Blue, and AirTran) managed to operate more profitably.

Nor are these infirmities and failures of corporate bigness unique to the United States. Abroad, merger-induced gigantism failed to provide economic salvation for Western European nations (especially Britain and France), which became enthralled by the corporate bigness mystique during the 1950s and 1960s. The putative "national champions" industry and government leaders urged to merge to dominate their national industries (including British Leyland in automobiles, British Steel, and Bull in French computers) subsequently came to be known as lame ducks in the 1970s and 1980s. Suffering chronic losses, these merged firms became dependent on economic life support from their home governments. According to Paul Geroski and Alexis Jacquemin, these "new super firms did not give rise to a new competitive efficiency in Europe. Indeed, by creating a group of firms with sufficient market power to be considerably sheltered from the forces of market selection, the policy may have left Europe with a population of sleepy industrial giants who were ill-equipped to meet the challenges of the 1970s and 1980s."[16]

As for East Asia, advocates of coalition capitalism have ignored a key strength of Japan's postwar economic miracle, while celebrating what events in Japan and South Korea have revealed to be a serious infirmity of incestuous industry-banking-government relationships.

The strength of Japan's postwar performance is attributable in important part to a competitive domestic market structure put in place by American occupation authorities during the years immediately following World War II. Under the direction of General Douglas MacArthur, a massive deconcentration program was implemented. Sixteen of Japan's largest holding companies were dissolved outright, 26 were dissolved and reorganized, and another 19 firms with "excessive concentration" were dismembered. The two largest Japanese holding companies, Mitsui and Mitsubishi, were divided into hundreds of successor firms, while an accompanying divestiture program forced the sale of perhaps as much as one-half the value of all Japanese corporate securities.[17] Later, during the 1950s and 1960s, industrial concentration trends in Japan and

---

[15]See Adams and Brock, *Bigness Complex*, Chapter 4; John Simmons, "When Big Pharma Gets Too Big, CNNMoney.com, December 4, 2006; idem, "Is Outsourcing the Prescription for Pfizer?" CNNMoney.com, December 6, 2006.

[16]Paul A. Geroski and Alexis Jacquemin, "Industrial Change, Barriers to Mobility, and European Industrial Policy," *Economic Policy* (November 1985): 175.

[17]Walter Adams and James W. Brock, "The Bigness Mystique and the Merger Policy Debate: An International Perspective," *Northwestern Journal of International Law & Business* (Spring 1988): 36–43.

the United States diverged, with average market concentration declining in Japan while rising in the U.S. In fact, Japanese industrialists strenuously resisted government efforts to promote oligopoly gigantism by limiting major industries to a few national champions. In automobiles, Honda, Subaru, and Mazda overcame government efforts to limit the field to the two incumbent firms, while in electronics, Sony overcame Ministry of International Trade and Industry (MITI) efforts to stifle it by impeding the then-unknown firm's efforts to procure electronics production rights in the U.S.[18] Conversely, Japan's decade-long slump during the 1990s was exacerbated by corporate gigantism and the debilitating consequences of coalescing power, including the collapse of banks as weak as they were big, and intimate relationships between bank giants and government regulators.[19]

Keiretsu arrangements of cross-corporate stock holdings among industrial firms and banks were revealed to be a trap during the 1990s. In Japan, families of cross-connected industrial and financial firms grew dependent on each other for subsidies and financial bailouts, while their dependence on easy sales to corporate family members rendered them complacent and vulnerable to competition from abroad.[20]

In South Korea, large conglomerates (*chaebol*) came to be perceived as too big to be allowed to fail; allocated the lion's share of financial capital in an effort to forestall their collapse, they hamstrung banks and starved the Korean economy of investment capital. The Asian meltdown of the latter 1990s compelled the Korean government to begin to free itself from the *chaebol* by forcing these giants to cut their size, focus their operations, and improve their performance, while liberating banks to redirect their lending toward smaller, more vibrant firms.[21]

At bottom, the Achilles heel of the kind of cooperative capitalism advocated on the left is the problem of power and interest-group politics. As Henry C. Simons pointed out long ago, "Bargaining organizations will contest over the division of the swag, but we commonly overlook the fact that they have large common interests as against the community and that every increase of monopoly power on one side serves to strengthen and implement it on the other." To promote such coalescing power, Simons warned, would be to "drift rapidly into political organization along functional, occupational lines—into a miscellany of specialized collectivisms, organized to take income away from one another [but] incapable of acting in their own common interest or in a manner compatible with general prosperity."[22]

---

[18]See Christopher Wood, *The End of Japan Inc.* (New York: Simon & Schuster, 1994), 77, and Michael E. Porter and Mariko Sakakibara, "Competition in Japan," *Journal of Economic Perspectives* 18 (Winter 2004): 27–50.

[19]See James Brooke and Ken Belson, "Japanese Plan to Overhaul Banks Hits A Stone Wall," *New York Times* (October 23, 2002): C1; Sheryl Wu Dunn, "A New Acid Test for Tokyo as It Tackles Banking Crisis," *New York Times* (September 1, 1998): C4; Jathon Sapsford and Robert Steiner, "Japan's Banks Struggle with Many Problems," *Wall Street Journal* (January 22, 1997): 1; and Michael Williams, "Many Japanese Banks Ran Amok While Led by Former Regulators," *Wall Street Journal* (January 19, 1996): 1.

[20]"Fall of A Keiretsu: How Giant Mitsubishi Group Lost Its Way," *Business Week* (March 15, 1999): 90.

[21]See Michael Schuman and Namju Cho, "Troubles of Korean Conglomerates Intensify, Signaling End of an Era," *Wall Street Journal* (March 25, 1997): A11; "The Giants Stumble," *Economist* (October 18, 1997): 67; Meredith Woo-Cumings, "How Industrial Policy Caused South Korea's Collapse," *Wall Street Journal* (December 8, 1997); and *Economic Crisis and Corporate Restructuring in Korea*, ed. Stephan Haggard, Wonhyuk Lim and Euysung Kim (New York: Cambridge University Press, 2003).

[22]Henry C. Simons, *Economic Policy For A Free Society* (Chicago: University of Chicago Press, 1948), 119, 219.

The Challenge from the Right

On the right, economic Darwinists have long criticized America's traditional antitrust philosophy, urging that it be supplanted by a simple policy of laissez faire. This, they contend, would promote good economic performance by unleashing the benefits of natural selection among the economically fittest firms.

Concentration of power in the trusts, William Graham Sumner claimed a century ago, "is indispensable to the successful execution of the tasks which devolve upon society in our time . . . . The concentration of power (wealth), more dominant control, intenser discipline, and stricter methods are but modes of securing more perfect integration. When we perceive this we see that the concentration of wealth is but one feature of a grand step in societal evolution." Monopolists, he said, are "the naturally selected agents of society for certain work. They get high wages and live in luxury, but the bargain is a good one for society."[23] John D. Rockefeller, father of the Standard Oil trust, put the point in botanical terms: "The growth of a large business is merely a survival of the fittest. The American Beauty rose can be produced in the splendor and fragrance which bring cheer to its beholder only by sacrificing the early buds which grow up around it. This is not an evil tendency in business. It is merely the working-out of a law of nature and a law of God."[24]

A modern exponent of this view, Robert Bork, sees a striking analogy between a free market system and Darwinian evolution:

> The familiarity of that parallel, and the overbroad inferences sometimes drawn from it, should not blind us to its important truths. The environment to which the business firm must adapt is defined, ultimately, by social wants and the social costs of meeting them. The firm that adapts to the environment better than its rivals tends to expand. The less successful firms tend to contract — perhaps, eventually, to become extinct.

There is no valid justification, Bork says, to interfere with the natural operation of a free market system. Laissez faire, he contends, will produce optimal results, and private monopoly and market power should be of no concern because both lack durability: "A market position that creates output restriction and higher prices will always be eroded if it is not based upon superior efficiency."[25] As the neo-Darwinists see it, "[t]he only important source of long-lasting monopoly is the government," especially today, when global competition and technological change "are making market competition a more potent force for prosperity and progress and undermining any justification there ever was for government to pursue an active antitrust policy."[26]

---

[23]William Graham Sumner, "The Concentration of Wealth: Its Economic Justification," in *On Liberty, Society, and Politics: The Essential Essays of William Graham Sumner* (Indianapolis: Liberty Fund, 1992), 149–50, 155.

[24]Quoted in Richard Hofstadter, *Social Darwinism in American Thought*, rev. ed. (Boston: Beacon Press, 1955), 45.

[25]Robert H. Bork, *The Antitrust Paradox*, rev. ed. (New York: Free Press, 1993), 118, 133. In fairness, Judge Bork found Microsoft's monopoly of computer operating software to be an exception to his general laissez-faire rule. See Robert H. Bork, "There's No Choice: Dismember Microsoft," *Wall Street Journal* (May 1, 2000): A34.

[26]Harold Demsetz, "The Trust Behind Antitrust," in *Industrial Concentration and the Market System*, ed. Eleanor M. Fox and James T. Halverson (Chicago: American Bar Association, 1979), 51, and Dwight R. Lee and Richard B. McKenzie, "Technology, Market Changes, and Antitrust Enforcement," Center for the Study of American Business, Policy Study No. 155, February 2000, 16.

Alas, this doctrine, too, suffers from a number of fatal congenital defects. First, it is based on a *post hoc ergo propter hoc* fallacy: The mere existence of a monopolist, oligopolist, or corporate giant is assumed to prove that it must have achieved its position solely because of its superior performance. This is no more than an assertion, devoid, more often than not, of empirical substantiation. In fact, while economic Darwinism makes superior economic performance the centerpiece of its policy position, its advocates concede that such economic performance is difficult, if not impossible, to measure scientifically. Judge Bork, for example, admits that "the real objection to performance tests and efficiency defenses in antitrust law is that they are spurious. They cannot measure the factors relevant to consumer welfare, so that after the economic extravaganza was completed we should know no more than before it began."[27] Likewise, Judge Easterbrook urges us "to avoid econometric [empirical] answers when we can," because "[t]hey are expensive as well as potentially indeterminate."[28] These modern-day Darwinists despair the prospect of evaluating economic performance, even though they posit it as the transcending goal of public policy.

Second, economic Darwinism is concerned primarily with static managerial efficiency rather than dynamic social efficiency. It thus falls victim to the sin of suboptimization: The relevant question is not whether GM or Ford produces gas-guzzling sport utility behemoths at the lowest average total cost, but whether they should be producing such gas guzzlers at all. The relevant question is not whether Microsoft writes operating software at lowest unit cost, but whether other, fundamentally different operating systems would be preferred if software producers and users were free from Microsoft's monopoly hold.[29]

Third, economic Darwinism assumes that any firm that no longer delivers superior performance will be displaced by newcomers, yet it ignores the capacity of powerful incumbent firms to build private storm shelters—or to lobby government to build public storm shelters for them—to shield themselves from Schumpeterian gales of creative destruction. It ignores the difference between the legal freedom of entry and the economic realities deterring the entry of newcomers into concentrated industries. The airline industry provides one case in point. After deregulating the field in the 1980s to enable competition to better regulate economic decision making, a laissez faire policy subsequently permitted mergers to consolidate the industry into a tightly knit oligopoly of giants controlling formidable fortress hub monopolies across the country. Oil provides another example of a small group of powerful firms recognizing that their collectively dominant position affords them (in the words of BP officials) "significant opportunities to influence the crude supply/demand balance"; enables them (according to ExxonMobil officials) to force an unruly independent competitor "to either give up or change its street pricing policy"; and empowers them to manipulate supplies to implement what they call "price uplift scenarios."[30]

---

[27]Bork, *Antitrust Paradox*, 124.
[28]Frank H. Easterbrook, "On Identifying Exclusionary Conduct," *Notre Dame Law Review* (1986): 979; and idem, "Ignorance and Antitrust," in *Antitrust, Innovation, and Competitiveness*, ed. Thomas M. Jorde and David J. Teece (New York: Oxford University Press, 1992), 119.
[29]This was Judge Jackson's conclusion when, after considering voluminous evidence, he found "Microsoft mounted a deliberate assault upon entrepreneurial efforts that, left to rise or fall on their own merits, could well have enabled the introduction of competition into the market for Intel-compatible PC operating systems." Conclusions of Law, *United States v. Microsoft Corp.*, 97 F. Supp. 2d 59 (DDC 2000).
[30]See James W. Brock, "Antitrust Policy and the Oligopoly Problem," *Antitrust Bulletin* 51 (Summer 2006): 238–40, and the sources cited therein.

Fourth, proponents of laissez faire emphasize the disciplining influence of international competition in a new global age. But they ignore the capacity of powerful domestic firms, once they become dominant, to subvert foreign competition at home and abroad. In recent years, for example, the Justice Department has uncovered and prosecuted a host of global cartels, collecting more in fines over the past decade than during the Department's entire 100-year history. Recent antitrust prosecutions of the world's largest producers of food preservatives, animal feed additives, and vitamins have vividly revealed the ability of global rivals to fix world prices, rig global market shares, and eliminate international competition. (In the case of the global citric acid cartel, the president of the Archer Daniels Midland Company assured his foreign conspirators that "[o]ur competitors are our friends and our customers are our enemies."[31]) Transnational alliances and mergers, like those conjoining the world's major airlines and allying the world's automotive giants, can also short-circuit the discipline of the global marketplace. They provide contemporary support for what Sir Alfred Mond, the organizer of Imperial Chemical Industries, the giant British chemical combine, pointed out long ago: "The old idea of the heads of great businesses meeting each other with scowls and shaking each other's fists in each other's faces and . . . trying to destroy each other's business may be very good on the films, but it does not accord with any given facts."[32]

Fifth, economic Darwinists decry economically foolish government policies which, they say, are the prime evil to be combatted. Yet they ignore the fact that in a representative democracy, government does not operate in a vacuum, so the anticompetitive government policies they condemn are the product of political lobbying by powerful economic groups bent on manipulating the state. They ignore the fact that in a representative democracy, disproportionate economic size entails disproportionate influence in the political arena, as corporate giants mobilize the considerable political resources at their command—executives and labor unions, suppliers and subcontractors, governors and mayors, senators and representatives, Democrats and Republicans—in their efforts to twist public policy to their anti-social ends.

Thus, corporate bigness complexes can lobby for government import restraints to immunize them from foreign competition, at great expense to the economy (as the steel industry has done repeatedly). They can obtain billions of dollars in government subsidies by whipsawing states and communities against one another in bidding to attract or retain their plants and facilities. They can violate their defense contracts with government, immune from the "death sentence" disbarment penalty meted out to smaller firms for committing similar transgressions.[33] They can fail to innovate, while lobbying government for legislation to penalize the innovativeness of others (as GM has done in the case of hybrid automobiles pioneered by Toyota and Honda).[34] They can placate labor by negotiating munificent retirement programs, then dump them on the government when they decide the pensions they negotiated are too burdensome (as recently

---

[31]For in-depth analyses of these global cartels, see Kurt Eichenwald, *The Informant* (New York: Broadway Books, 2000); and John M. Connor, *Global Price Fixing* (Boston: Kluwer Academic Publishing, 2001).
[32]Quoted in George Stocking and Myron Watkins, *Cartels in Action* (New York: Twentieth Century Fund, 1946), 429.
[33]Anne Marie Squeo, "Are Firms Too Big to Debar?" *Wall Street Journal* (June 10, 2003): A4.
[34]Harry Stoffer, "Toyota, Honda Lose Out on Hybrid Credits," *Automotive News* (December 1, 2003): 1.

Security Through
Government Control

Free
Enterprise

Security Through
Monopoly

𝕀 𝕀 𝕀 𝕀 **FIGURE 14-2** The Public Policy Choice

Source: Thurman W. Arnold, Cartels or Free Enterprise? Public Affairs Pamphlet 103, 1945. Reproduced by courtesy of Public Affairs Commission, Inc.

has been the case with steel and airline giants).[35] They are accorded privileged treatment in these ways and others because, as Federal Reserve Chairman Alan Greenspan has insightfully said of merged megabanks, they "are entities that create the potential for unusually large system risks in the national and international economy should they fail."[36] As evidenced by government bailouts of Lockheed, Chrysler, Long Term Capital Management, big banks with souring loans in Mexico and East Asia, and major airlines in the post-9/11 period, large firms can survive, not because they are better, but because they are bigger—not because they are fitter, but because they are fatter.[37] Because economic Darwinists permit economic size and power while ignoring its larger political ramifications, they are like Henry David Thoreau's neighbors who, he observed, "invite the devil in at every angle and then prate about the garden of Eden and the fall of man."

[35]U.S. General Accounting Office, "Pension Benefit Guaranty Corporation's Single-Employer Insurance Program: Long-Term Vulnerabilities Warrant 'High Risk' Designation," Washington D.C., July 23, 2003.
[36]"The Evolution of Bank Supervision," remarks by Alan Greenspan, American Bankers Association, Phoenix, AZ, October 11, 1999.
[37]In the case of banking, for example, see Gary H. Stern and Ron J. Feldman, *Too Big To Fail: The Hazards of Bank Bailouts* (Washington, D.C.: Brookings Institution, 2004).

Finally, economic Darwinians fail to make the crucial distinction between individual freedom, on the one hand, and a free economic *system* on the other. As Jeremy Bentham recognized long ago, it is not enough to shout "laissez faire" and oppose all government intervention because "[t]o say that a law is contrary to natural liberty is simply to say that it is a law: for every law is established at the expense of liberty—the liberty of Peter at the expense of the liberty of Paul."[38] If individual rights were absolute and unlimited, they would (as Thomas Hobbes recognized 400 years ago) provide license to commit the grossest abuses against society, including destroying the freedoms of others. Considered in this light, the Darwinian admonition not to penalize the winner of the race is irrelevant for public policy purposes. Instead, the meaningful challenge is how to reward the winner without including in its trophy the right to impose disabling handicaps on putative competitors, or the power to dictate the rules by which future races shall be run—or the discretion to eliminate the institution of racing altogether.

CONCLUSION ▪▪▪▪▪▪▪

The purpose of American antitrust policy is to maintain the structural prerequisites for effective competition. The goal is to protect the decentralized decision-making system of the competitive marketplace from encroachment by central planning, whether by the state, or by private monopolists, oligopolists, and cartels. The objective is to maintain regulatory control by the invisible hand of the competitively structured market, and to guard it from the depredations of private economic power blocs operating as despotic governments, free from competitive checks and balances and accountability, but with no assurance that their private decision making will promote the public good.

Recent events, at home and abroad, in the economy and elsewhere, have diminished neither the importance of these goals nor the validity of these concerns.

SUGGESTIONS FOR FURTHER READING ▪▪▪▪▪▪▪

Acs, Zolton J. 1999. *Are Small Firms Important?* (Boston: Kluwer Academic Publishers).

Adams, Walter, and James W. Brock. 2004. *The Bigness Complex*, 2nd ed. (Palo Alto, CA: Stanford University Press).

_____. 1991. *Antitrust Economics on Trial: A Dialogue on the New Laissez-Faire* (Princeton, NJ: Princeton University Press).

Blair, John M. 1972. *Economic Concentration: Structure, Behavior and Public Policy* (New York: Harcourt Brace Jovanovich).

Bork, Robert H. 1993. *The Antitrust Paradox*, rev. ed. (New York: Free Press).

Brandeis, Louis B. 1934. *The Curse of Bigness* (New York: Viking).

Brock, James W., and Kenneth G. Elzinga. 1991. *Antitrust, the Market, and the State: The Contributions of Walter Adams* (Armonk, NY: M.E. Sharpe).

De Jong, Henry W., and William G. Shepherd. 2007. *Pioneers of Industrial Organization* (Northampton, MA: Edward Elgar Publishing).

Dewey, Donald. 1990. *The Antitrust Experiment in America* (New York: Columbia University Press).

Edwards, Corwin D. 1949. *Maintaining Competition* (New York: McGraw Hill).

Fetter, Frank A. 1931. *The Masquerade of Monopoly* (New York: Harcourt, Brace and Co.).

---

[38]J. Bowring ed., *The Works of Jeremy Bentham*, vol. 3 (Edinburgh: W. Tait, 1843), 185.

Fox, Eleanor M. 2002. *The Competition Law of the European Union* (Eagan, MN: West Group).

Friedman, David. 1988. *The Misunderstood Miracle: Industrial Development and Political Change in Japan* (Ithaca, NY: Cornell University Press).

Galbraith, John Kenneth. 1978. *The New Industrial State*, 3rd ed. (Boston: Houghton Mifflin).

Graham, Otis L. 1992. *Losing Time: The Industrial Policy Debate* (Cambridge: Harvard University Press).

Hadley, Eleanor M. 1970. *Antitrust in Japan* (Princeton, NJ: Princeton University Press).

Hawley, Ellis. 1966. *The New Deal and the Problem of Monopoly* (Princeton, NJ: Princeton University Press).

Hofstadter, Richard. 1944. *Social Darwinism in American Thought* (Boston: Beacon Press).

Johnson, Peter. 2003. *Industries in Europe: Competition, Trends and Policy Issues* (Northampton, MA: Edward Elgar).

Katz, Richard. 1998. *Japan: The System that Soured* (Armonk, NY: M.E. Sharpe).

Liebhafsky, H.H. 1971. *American Government and Business* (New York: Wiley).

Lippman, Walter. 1937. *The Good Society* (Boston: Little, Brown).

Lowi, Theodore. 1979. *The End of Liberalism*, 2nd ed. (New York: Norton).

Machlup, Fritz. 1952. *The Political Economy of Monopoly* (Baltimore: Johns Hopkins University Press).

Martin, Stephen. 2007. "The Goals of Antitrust and Competition Policy," forthcoming in *Issues in Competition Law and Economics*, ed. Wayne Dale Collins (Chicago: American Bar Association).

May, James. 1989. "Antitrust in the Formative Era: Political and Economic Theory in Constitutional and Antitrust Analysis, 1880–1918." *Ohio State Law Journal* 50: 257–395.

Olson, Mancur. 1982. *The Rise and Decline of Nations* (New Haven, CT: Yale University Press).

Peterson, Wallace C., ed. 1988. *Market Power and the Economy* (Boston: Kluwer Academic Publishers).

Peritz, Rudolph J.R. 1996. *Competition Policy in America, 1888–1992* (New York: Oxford University Press).

Porter, Michael E. 1990. *The Competitive Advantage of Nations* (New York: Free Press).

Reich, Robert B. 1991. *The Work of Nations* (New York: Knopf).

Rosenbaum, David I. 1998. *Market Dominance* (Westport, CT: Praeger).

Seager, Henry R., and Charles A. Gulick, Jr. 1929. *Trust and Corporation Problems* (New York: Harper).

Simons, Henry C. 1948. *Economic Policy for a Free Society* (Chicago: University of Chicago Press).

Spencer, Herbert. 1982. *The Man versus the State* (Indianapolis: Liberty Fund).

Stiglitz, Joseph E. 2003. *The Roaring Nineties* (New York: W.W. Norton).

Stocking, George W., and Myron W. Watkins. 1946. *Cartels in Action* (New York: Twentieth Century Fund).

_____. 1948. *Cartels or Competition?* (New York: Twentieth Century Fund).

_____. 1951. *Monopoly and Free Enterprise* (New York: Twentieth Century Fund).

Sullivan, Lawrence A., and Warren S. Grimes. 2006. *The Law of Antitrust* (St. Paul, MN: Thomson/West).

Sumner, William Graham. 1992. *On Liberty, Society, and Politics: The Essential Essays of William Graham Sumner*, ed. Robert C. Bannister. (Indianapolis: Liberty Fund).

Thorelli, Hans B. 1955. *The Federal Antitrust Policy: Origination of an American Tradition* (Baltimore: Johns Hopkins University Press).

Thurow, Lester C. 1985. *The Zero-Sum Solution* (New York: Simon & Schuster).

Waller, Spencer W. 2005. *Thurman Arnold: A Biography* (New York: New York University Press).

Whittaker, D.H. 1997. *Small Firms in the Japanese Economy* (Cambridge: Cambridge University Press).

Name Index

A

Ackoff, Russell L., 152
Adams, Walter, 86, 127, 238, 397
Adams, William James, 152
Adelman, M.A., 33, 46, 57
Alexander, Peter J., 183, 191
Anderson, Bruce, 197
Anderson, Richard, 153
Apt, Jay, 94
Areeda, Phillip, 116
Arrow, Kenneth J., 321
Audretsch, David B., 86

B

Bailey, Elizabeth, 246
Bailey, Jeff, 249
Baldick, Ross, 67
Bank, Veronis Suhler
         Stevenson, 192
Baran, Paul, 211
Barkholz, David, 164
Baron, Stanley Wade, 152
Baum, Dan, 128, 152
Baumol, William J., 246
Beckenstein, Alan, 154
Bell, Alexander
         Graham, 207
Belson, Ken, 398
Benjamin, Matthew, 214
Bennett, Randall W., 368
Berenson, Robert A., 310
Berger, Allen N., 285
Berger, David, 197
Birnbaum, Jeffrey H., 179
Blair, John M., 57
Blumberg, Paul, 169
Blumenstein, Rebecca, 164
Blumsack, Seth A., 94
Boden, William E., 327
Bohi, Douglas R., 54
Bonbright, James C., 60
Bonnett, Thomas, 214
Bonsack, James, 100
Borenstein, Severin, 85
Bork, Robert H., 399

Borland, M., 379
Boudette, Neal E., 164, 165, 175, 179
Boue, Juan Carlos Venezuela, 57
Bowen, W., 376
Bradford, David, 153
Bradsher, Keith, 176
Brand, Myles, 379
Brannigan, Martha, 253
Bringhurst, Bruce, 52
Brock, James W., 58, 86, 127, 155,
         235, 238, 397, 400
Brooke, James, 398
Brooks, John, 208
Brown, Peter, 167, 168
Brown, R., 372, 378
Brudsky, Ira, 214
Buchanan, James, 231
Bulow, Jeremy, 127
Buntin, Melinda B., 326
Busch, Adolphus, 143, 144, 151
Bush, President George,
         96, 178, 181
Bushnell, James B., 85
Butler, Steven, 44
Byers, Walter, 361, 362, 370

C

Capehart, Thomas C., 106
Carey, John, 119, 380
Carey, Susan, 259
Carter, Col. Arthur H., 331
Carter, David A., 287
Casalino, L.P., 306, 307
Casazza, Jack, 60, 89, 98
Chaloupka, F.J., 153
Chappell, Lindsay, 162, 166
Chernow, Ron, 57
Chichilnisky, Graciela, 57
Christianson, Jon B., 321
Cicchetti, Charles J., 93
Clements, Kenneth W., 153
Clinton, President William, 163, 294
Coase, R., 194
Coates, Douglas, 176
Colpier, Ulrika Claeson, 87
Condie, F., 379

Conky, Christopher, 290
Connelly, Mary, 168
Connor, Robert A., 320
Copps, Michael J., 205, 224
Cornell, Martyn, 128, 153
Cornland, Deborah, 87
Cottell, Philip G., 332
Crandall, Robert W., 219
Crane, Kenneth, 173
Craver, Richard, 123
Cray, Ed, 177
Croly, Herbert, 393
Culbertson, W. Patton, 153
Culyer, A.J., 317
Cutler, David M., 315, 319, 327
Cyrnak, Anthony W., 287

D

Dahl, Jonathan, 251
Dannen, F., 194, 195
de Varona, Donna, 381, 383
Delea, Frank, 89, 98
Delmas, Magali, 87
Demsetz, Harold, 399
DeNavas-Walt, Carmen,
         296, 297
Denisoff, R. Serge, 197
Dennis, Sylvia, 214
Depken, C., 387
DeTar, James, 217
Devers, Kelly J., 310
Dimmick, John, 197
Dizard, Wilson, 211
Done, Kevin, 250, 264
Dorfman, Joseph, 393
Dowd, Douglas, 155
Dranove, David, 309, 314, 324
Dubin, Jeffrey A., 93
Duke, James B., 100
Durkin, J., 385
Dwyer, Paula, 357

E

Easterbrook, Gregg, 181, 400
Eckel, Edwin C., 57

Edison, Thomas, 58, 59, 207
Ekelund, Jr., Robert B., 142, 153
Elias, Bartholomew, 262
Elzinga, Kenneth, 153
Emshoff, James R., 152
Enders, Walter, 261
Enthoven, Alain C., 322
Etzkorn, Peter, 197

F

Fairclough, Gordon, 106
Feldman, R.D., 321
Feldman, Roger, 321
Feldman, Ron J., 284
Feldstein, Paul, 304
Fink, M., 186
Finon, Dominique, 97
Fisher, Thornsten, 252
Fizel, John L., 368, 374
Fleisher, A., 364
Ford, Henry, 156
Fort, Rod, 368
Foudy, Julie, 381
Fox, Eleanor M., 399
Franklin, Ben, 58, 331
Freeman, Sholm, 179
Freeman, Sholnn, 168

G

Gabel, Jon R., 303
Galant, Jean-Michel, 97
Galbraith, John Kenneth, 171
Ganey, Terry, 153
Gardner, Bruce L., 29
Garfield, Dr. Sydney, 301
Gaskins, Darius, 48
Gelatt, 187
German, Kira, 99
Geroski, Paul A., 397
Gibson, George R., 52
Ginsburg, Paul B., 313, 319
Gisser, 150
Gisser, Mica, 153
Gladwell, Malcolm, 177
Goff, B., 379
Goldblatt, Henry, 224
Golding, Rob, 165
Gollop, Frank M., 85
Gompers, Samuel, 393
Goodrich, Ben, 395
Gramlich, Edward, 290
Grant, Peter, 217
Gray, Horace, 236
Greenspan, Alan, 402
Greer, Douglas F., 141–143,
    153
Griffen, James M., 48, 86, 98
Grossack, Irvin M., 53
Grossman, Joy M., 313–314
Grossman, M., 153
Guilford, Dave, 165, 173, 175

H

Halberstein, David, 173
Halverson, James T., 399
Hannan, Timothy, 284,
    285, 287
Harris, Jeffrey, 109
Hartshorn, J.E., 33, 57
Hatch, Senator Orrin, 199
Hawes, Kay, 383
Hawkins, Samantha, 303
Hawley, Ellis W., 394
Heal, Geoffrey, 57
Heitfeld, Erik, 284
Henderson, David R., 54
Hendricks, W., 368
Hernon, Peter, 128, 153
Hesbacher, Peter, 197
Hirsch, Richard F., 87,
    88, 98
Hitfeld, Erik, 279
Hofstader, Richard, 399
Hogarty, Thomas F., 153
Horowitz, A., 133, 153
Horowitz, I., 13, 153
Horsnell, Paul, 43, 57
Horwich, George, 54
Howe, Peter, 232
Hu, Ha T., 319
Hufbauer, Gary
    Clyde, 395
Hurst, Eric, 90

I

Ibrahim, Youssef M., 36
Iglehart, John K., 310
Irwin, Manley R., 205
Islas, Jorge, 87
Ivancevich, S., 344

J

Jackson, Derrick Z., 375
Jacquemin, Alexis, 397
Jaffe, Adam, 99
James, D., 379
Jensen, Gail A., 303
Jesse, Edward V., 18
Jewell, R.T., 373
Johnson, C., 345
Johnson, Lester W., 153
Johnston, David Cay, 85
Jorgenson, Dale W., 85
Joskow, Paul L., 61, 62, 69, 70,
    84, 85, 86, 87, 93

K

Kahn, Alfred, 263
Kahn, Edward, 85
Kaiser, Henry, 301
Kamerschen, David R., 252

Kammen, Daniel M., 88
Kasic, Allison, 384
Kaufer, Erich, 154
Kaufman, B.I., 53
Keeler, E.B., 320
Keller, John J., 222
Kendrick, John W., 85
Kerkvliet, Joe R., 139, 153
Kerwin, Kathleen, 164
King, Michael, 226
Kisiel, Ralph, 165
Klein, J. Douglass, 86
Kleit, Andrew N., 86, 98
Klemperer, Paul, 127
Kluger, Richard, 127
Kolbert, Elizabeth, 181
Kranz, Rick, 175
Kronemyer, 195
Kronick, Richard, 324
Kroszner, Randall S., 289
Kulick, Jonathan, 96
Kwoka, John E., 59, 75, 87

L

Lander, Mark, 165
Landes, William M., 284
Landler, Mark, 166
LaReau, Jamie, 165
Latour, Almar, 215, 217
Lave, Lester B., 94
Lawler, Kevin, 153
Lee, Albert, 174
Lee, Cheryl Hill, 296, 297
Lee, Kin-Pui, 153
Leeds, M., 385
Lenin, 58
Levitt, Arthur, 353
Long, Colin M., 93
Long, Stephen E., 323
Loughran, David S., 96
Luft, Harold, 318
Luger, Stan, 155
Lundegaard, Karen, 167, 177
Lynk, William J., 153

M

Mabro, Robert, 34, 43, 57
Manzullo, Donald A., 156
Marion, Bruce W., 29
Marquis, M. Susan, 323
Martin, Andrew, 119
Martin, Steve, 41
Matheson, Stuart, 211
Mattei, Enrico, 35
Maynard, Micheline, 157, 165, 168,
    175, 244, 250
McCain, Senator John, 178
McCartney, Scott, 247, 252
McClellan, Mark, 319
McConnaughey, James, 205
McConnell, J. Douglass, 153

McCracken, Jeffrey, 163, 173
McCraw, Thomas K., 98
McGahan, A.M., 153
McNulty, Timothy, 153, 287
Means, Gardiner C., 60
Meckler, Laura, 179
Meeusen, Karl, 81, 85
Melnick. G., 320
Menon, K., 344
Meyerson, Bruce, 222
Miller, Robert, 318
Mineta, Norman, 155
Morgan, J.P., 208
Moss, Diana L., 57, 106
Mouawad, Jad, 41
Moyer, Mike, 382
Mullahy, John, 153
Muller, Joann, 164
Munson, Richard, 98
Murray, Matt, 214

N

Nag, Amal, 167
Naik, Gautam, 220
Nally, Dennis, 339, 353
Nebesky, William, 139, 153
Nelson, Jon, 145, 153
Nemet, Gregory F., 88
Neuechterlein, Jonathan, 212
Newhouse, J.P., 317, 319
Niu, Jui, 67
Noll, R., 379, 386
Nomani, Asra Q., 252

O

O'Connell, Vanessa, 119
Oberholzer-Gee, Felix, 202
Ogle, Maureen, 128, 153
Olson, Walter, 382
Olufs, Dick W., 212
Ornstein, Stanley, 153

P

Paige, Rod, 383
Panzer, John C., 246
Parker, James, 331
Patel, Judge Marilyn Hall, 200
Paulson, Henry, 357
Perlin, Terry M., 332
Peterson, Richard, 197
Pham, Hoangmai, 310
Phelps, Charles S., 315
Phillips, Charles F., 58, 98
Pilloff, Steven J., 279, 286
Pollitt, Michael, 75, 87
Porter, Michael E., 398
Posner, Richard, 284
Powell, Michael K., 224
Prager, Robin A., 279, 284
Previts, J.P., 331

Price, Michael, 25
Proctor, Bernadette, 296, 297
Puller, Steven L., 86, 98
Pulsinelli, R., 379

R

Radecki, Lawrence J., 279
Rakoff, Judge Jed S., 200
Rama, D.V., 352
Ramos-Real, Francisco Javier, 69
Ray, Dennis, 60
Reas, W.J., 352
Rehr, David, 153
Reilly, D., 353
Reinhardt, Uwe E., 308
Rhoades, Stephen A.,
     279, 286, 288
Richtel, Matt, 220
Robertson, James D., 153
Robinson, J.C., 306
Rockefeller, John D., 399
Rodman, Mark, 147, 154
Rogers, David, 179
Rogers, Richard T., 18
Ronis, Sheila R., 156
Roosevelt, President
     Franklin, 209
Roosevelt, President Theodore,
     59, 362
Rose, Kenneth, 81, 85, 87
Rose, Nancy L., 69
Rosenberg, Ronald, 224
Rothenbuhler, Eric, 197
Rubenstein, James M., 164

S

Saffer, H., 153
Sakakibara, Mariko, 398
Sampson, Anthony, 32, 35, 57
Sandler, Todd, 261
Sanjek, R., 188
Sapsford, Jathon, 175
Saraceno, Jon, 371
Saranow, Jennifer, 175
Sass, Tim R., 154
Satterthwaite, Mark, 314
Saurman, David, 142, 153, 154
Scannell, K., 353
Scherer, F.M., 140, 154
Schiffman, Roger, 60
Schmalensee, Richard, 86
Schmidt, Shelton, 86
Schneider, S.A., 34, 57
Schroer, James, 166
Schulman, J., 376
Shepherd, William G., 235
Shirouzou, Norihiko, 163,
     165, 175
Sidak, J.G., 195
Siegfried, John J., 86
Simon, Bernard, 160

Simon, Carol J., 309, 319
Sindelar, Jody, 153
Sirlin, Philip J., 212
Skousen, C., 379
Sloan, Frank, 126
Slosberg, Pete, 128, 154
Smaby, T., 374
Smith, Adam, 390
Smith, Bruce A., 87
Smith, Rebecca, 84, 85, 96
Snyder, Jesse, 174
Solberg, Carl, 236
Spanier, Graham B., 370
Squeo, Anne Marie, 401
Starr, Paul, 301
Stern, Gary H., 284
Steven Greenhouse, 248
Stevenson, Rodney, 60
Stigler, George, 231
Stoffer, Harry, 181, 401
Stoll, John D., 179
Strumpf, Koleman, 202
Suggs, Welch, 370, 383
Sumner, Willian Graham, 399
Suris, Y., 385
Sutton, John, 154
Svensson, Peter, 220
Swisher, Anthony M., 153

T

Tarbell, Ida M., 57
Taub, S., 347, 348
Taylor, Alex, 175
Taylor, Jerry, 62
Templin, Neal, 177
Tenant, Richard, 127
Terrell, Dek, 86
Thompson, Howard, 60
Thorelli, Hans B., 390
Thran, 307
Thurow, Lester C., 394
Tirole, Jean, 84
Tokat, Yesim, 87
Toll, R., 187
Tollen, Laura A., 322
Tollison, R., 364
Toman, Michael A., 54
Tremblay, Carol H., 128, 139, 145,
     153, 154
Tremblay, Victor J., 128, 139, 145,
     153, 154
Trottman, Melanie, 247, 250, 251,
     252, 253, 259
Tucker, Doug, 372
Turner, Donald, 116
Turner, Louis, 39, 57

V

Vail, Theodore, 208, 209, 214
van der Minne, Frans, 148

Van Doren, Peter, 62
Van Munching, Philip, 128, 154
Vanderhoff, James, 176
Verbrugge, James A., 287
von Lohmann, Fred, 183

W

Wagoner, Rick, 169
Wald, Matthew L., 96
Walker, Philip, 211
Wallace, A.E., 304
Walters, Greg, 43
Ware, Jr., John E., 318
Warkentin-Glenn, Denise, 70
Warner, Fara, 164
Warwick, M.W., 64
Wassenaar, 307
Weeks, W.B., 304
Weimer, David Leo, 54
Weinberg, Robert S., 134,
    144, 150

Weiser, Philip, 212
Welch, David, 164
Welch, Jack, 214
Wells, Jim, 46, 128
Wells, Ken, 154
Westcott, Paul, 25
Westinghouse, George,
    58, 59
Wetzel, Dan, 372
White, Gregory L., 167
White, Joseph B., 177
White, Lawrence J., 159
White, William D., 309
Wholey, Douglas, 321
Wilcox, Clair, 60
Williams, D., 344
Willig, Robert D., 246
Wilson, Amy, 175
Wilson, D., 387
Winans, Christopher, 251
Wingfield, Nick, 224
Winston, Mark L., 29

Wolak, Frank A., 85
Wolfram, Catherine, 86, 93
Wolverton, Brad, 375, 384
Wong, Edward, 247, 253
Wood, Christopher, 398
Wyatt, A.R., 342
Wyzanski, Judge Charles, 392

Y

Yaisawarng, Suthathip, 86
Yates, Brock, 173
Yergin, Daniel, 57
Young, Edwin, 25
Young, Shawn, 215, 225

Z

Zardkoohi, A., 344
Zeff, S.A., 332, 342,
    349, 354
Zwanziger, J., 320

Subject Index

A

agriculture industry
  asymmetric information, 11
  Capper-Volstead Act, 17
  commodity markets, 10–11
  commodity programs, 24, 25–26,
    26–27
  competition, role of, 22
  conduct, 14–19
  countercylical payments, 24–25
  direct payments, 24
  enterprise size, 7
  farm payments, 28–29
  farmers and risk, 2
  innovations, 21
  market power dilemma, 16–19
  marketing loans, 25
  niche markets, 9–10
  organic farming, 10
  overview, 1–2
  performance, 19–23
  structure, 2–14
  thin market, 15
  transport costs, 11
  vertical linkages, 11–14
airline industry
  alliances, 244–246
  antitrust policy, 257–259
  barriers to entry, 246–250
  competition, 254–255
  conduct, 250–255
  demand, and, 239–240
  firm size and concentration,
    240–244
  history, 236–239
  monopoly, 252–253
  oligopoly, 251–252
  public policy, 257–263
  structure, 239–250
alliances
  airline industry, 244–246
  automobile industry, 162–163
antitrust policy, 390–393
  airline industry, 257–259
  automobile industry, 179
  cigarettes, 116–118

petroleum industry, 52–53
telecommunications industry,
    210–212
asymmetric information, 11
automobile industry
  antitrust policy, 179
  barriers to entry, 166
  demand and the product, 157
  dynamic efficiency, 173–174
  economies of scale, 164–166
  firm size and concentration,
    158–161
  foreign competition, 161–162,
    179–180
  government-industry partnership,
    181–182
  history, 156–157
  industry concentration, 157
  industry conduct, 167–171
  industry performance, 171–178
  industry structure, 157–166
  joint ventures and alliances,
    162–163
  oligopoly restraint, 169–170
  overview, 155
  pricing, 167–169
  product competition, 170–171
  product rivalry, 169
  production efficiency, 171–173
  public policy, 178–182
  regulation, 180–181
  social efficiency, 175–176

B

banking industry
  barriers to entry, 283
  conduct, 281–284
  credit unions, 280
  efficiency, 285
  failures, 272–273
  history, 267–269
  industrial loan companies and
    industrial banks, 280
  market concentration, 275–278
  mergers, 269–272, 290
  nonbank firms, 279

nonprice competition, 281
overview, 265–267
performance, 284–289
price competition, 281
profitability, 285–286
public policy, 289–292
relationship competition,
    282–283
structure, 269–281
thrift institutions, 279–280
barriers to entry
  airline industry, 246–250
  automobile industry, 166
  banking industry, 283
  cigarettes, 105–106
barriers to expansion, 339–341
beer industry
  18th Amendment, 130
  brewer-distributor relations,
    145–148
  competition, 150–151
  concentration, 131–132
  craft brewers, 131–132
  decline, 132–134
  demand, 131
  economies of scale, 138–140
  entry into the market,
    140–141
  global economy, and
    the, 148
  history, 129–131
  market growth, 130
  marketing, 145
  mergers, 135–138
  performance, 148–152
  pricing, 143–145
  product differentiation,
    141–143
  size of market, 134–135
  structure, 131–143
  widening of markets, 134
brownouts, 63

C

Capper-Volstead Act, 17
cartel dynamics, 49–52

cigarettes
  advertising and promotion,
      108–109
  antitrust action, 116–118
  barriers to entry, 105–106
  cancer era, 102–103
  concentration, 104–105
  conduct, 108–112
  history, 100–103
  individual market shares,
      106–108
  industry structure, 104–108
  litigation, 119–121
  "low-delivery" products,
      development of, 115–116
  MSA, challenges to, 123–125
  overview, 99–100
  performance, industry, 112–116
  pricing, 109–110
  product development, 114–115
  profits, 113
  public policy, 116–126
  regulation, 118–119
  settlement-induced price
      increased, 121–123
  shelf space, battle for,
      111–112
Clayton Act, 391
college sports industry
  conduct, 367–376
  entry and entry barriers,
      364–367
  history, 361–364
  monopsony, 385–386
  overview, 360–361
  performance, 376–380
  public policy, 380–387
  structure, 364–367
  Title IX, 380
commodity markets, 10–11
commodity programs, 24, 25–26,
      26–27
competition
  agriculture industry, 22
  airline industry, 254–255
  automobile industry,
      170–171
  beer industry, 150–151
  public accounting industry, 345
  telecommunications industry,
      231–232
competitive fringe, 190–191
cooperatives, 71
countercylical payments, 24–25

D

demand
  airline industry, 239–240
  automobile industry, 157
  beer industry, 131
  electricity industry, 77–78
dynamic efficiency, 173–174

E

economies of scale
  automobile industry, 164–166
  beer industry, 138–140
  electricity industry, 69–70
electricity industry
  alternative energy, promoting, 97
  brownouts, 63
  conduct, 78–85
  cooperatives, 71
  coordination function, 63–67
  demand characteristics,
      77–78
  economies of scale and natural
      monopoly, 69–70
  electric reliability councils, 65
  environmental policy, 94–96
  environmental pollution,
      90–91
  Federal power organizations, 71
  generating plants, 67–69
  generation, 76–77
  history, 58–62
  investor-owned utilities, 71–72
  local retail distribution, 75–76, 78
  market concentration, 75
  market power and market
      manipulation, 84–85
  mergers and acquisitions, 74–75
  municipality owned
      organizations, 71
  nonutilities, 73–74
  performance, 85–91
  pricing: local distribution, 79–81
  pricing: transmission and
      congestion, 82–84
  pricing: wholesale distribution,
      81–82
  productivity and efficiency, 85–87
  public policy, 91–97
  regulation and restructuring,
      91–94
  reliability and congestion,
      88–90
  structure, 62–78
  technological innovation, 87–88
  transmission, 76
  vertical industry structure, 63
entry into the market
  beer industry, 140–141
  college sports industry, 364–367
environmental policy
  electricity industry, 94–96
environmental pollution
  electricity industry, 90–91

F

farm payments, 28–29
foreign competition
  automobile industry, 161–162,
      179–180

G

government-industry partnership,
      181–182

H

health care industry
  conduct, 310–314
  health maintenance organization,
      300–301
  history, 295–298
  hospitals, 307–310
  overview, 294–295
  performance, 315–321
  physicians, 303–307
  preferred provider organization,
      300–301
  public policy, 321–328
  structure, 298–310

J

joint ventures and alliances
  airline industry, 244–246
  automobile industry, 162–163

L

laissez faire, 401

M

mergers
  banking industry, 269–272, 290
  beer industry, 135–138
  electricity industry, 74–75
  public accounting industry,
      333–336
monopoly
  airline industry, 252–253
  telecommunications industry,
      209–210
monopsony, 385–386
music recording industry
  competitive fringe,
      190–191
  conduct, 192–196
  digital distribution, 191
  history, 184–188
  overview, 183–184
  payola, 194–196
  performance, 197
  pricing, 192–193
  profitability, 197
  public policy, 198–202
  structure, 188–191

O

oligopoly
  airline industry, 251–252
oligopoly restraint
  automobile industry, 169–170

P

petroleum industry
  antitrust policy, 52–53
  cartel dynamics, 49–52
  conduct, 48–52
  consolidation and integration,
    44–48
  crude oil, market for, 30–31
  cultivation of crude supplies
    outside OPEC, 40–43
  domination by major oil
    companies, 32–34
  fringe supply and cartel
    output, 38
  government policy responses
    to OPEC, 53–55
  International Energy
    Agency, 54
  National Security, and, 55–56
  North Sea oil markets, 43–44
  OPEC, role of, 36–40
  overview, 30–31
  public policy, 52–56
  rise of independent oil
    companies, 34–36
  Strategic Petroleum Reserve
    (SPR), 54
  structure and structural change,
    31–48
  U.S. demand for, 37
pricing
  automobile industry, 167–169
  beer industry, 143–145
  cigarettes, 109–110
  music recording industry, 192–193
product rivalry, 169
production efficiency, 171–173
public accounting industry
  barriers to expansion, 339–341
  competition, 345

  concentration, 336–341, 346
  conduct, 341–345
  Hirschman-Herfindahl indexes,
    338
  history, 331–332
  mergers and consolidations,
    333–336
  overview, 330–331
  performance, 346–352
  price competition, 342–343
  public policy, 352–358
  Sarbanes-Oxley Act, 355–358
  structure, 332–341
public policy
  agriculture industry, 23–28
  airline industry, 257–263
  automobile industry, 178–182
  banking industry, 289–292
  cigarettes, 116–126
  college sports industry, 380–387
  electricity industry, 91–97
  health care industry, 321–328
  music recording industry, 198–202
  petroleum industry, 52–56
  public accounting industry,
    352–358
  telecommunications industry,
    228–233

R

regulation
  automobile industry, 180–181
  cigarettes, 118–119
  telecommunications industry,
    229–231

S

Sarbanes-Oxley Act, 355–358
Sherman Act, 390–391

social efficiency, 175–176
structure
  agriculture industry, 2–14
  airline industry, 239–250
  banking industry, 269–281
  college sports industry,
    364–367
  electricity industry, 62–78
  health care industry, 298–310
  music recording industry,
    188–191
  public accounting industry,
    332–341

T

telecommunications industry
  antitrust, 210–212
  cellular/wireless communications,
    220–222
  competition, 231–232
  competition/regulation, 208–209
  history, 206–212
  market conduct, 222–225
  monopoly/regulation/antitrust,
    209–210
  overview, 205–206
  performance, 225–227
  public policy, 228–233
  regulation, 229–231

V

vertical industry structure, 63
vertical linkages
  agriculture industry, 11–14